Praise for *Arc o* W9-CZR-821

"A cracking good yarn of murder, mayhem and courtroom drama ... A model of literary nonfiction that holds the reader like a fast-paced detective novel. Stories that matter should be told as though they mattered. This Boyle has done with uncommon success." —*The Washington Post*

"Kevin Boyle's *Arc of Justice* is by far the most cogent and thorough account yet of the Sweet trial and its aftermath. . . . Boyle vividly recreates the energy and menace of Detroit in 1925." —*The New York Times Book Review*

"*Arc of Justice* does justice both to its complex protagonists and the issues they embraced. Masterfully weaving crime reporting and social history, Boyle has produced a fine and moving work." —*Los Angeles Times*

"*Arc of Justice* is one of the most engrossing books I have ever read. It is, at once, a poignant biography, a tour-de-force of historical detective work, a gripping courtroom drama, and a powerful reflection on race relations in America. Better than any historian to date, Kevin Boyle captures the tensions of the Jazz Age. . . . *Arc of Justice* is a masterpiece."
—Thomas J. Sugrue, professor of history, University of Pennsylvania, and author of the Bancroft Prize-winning *Origins of the Urban Crisis*

"Boyle has written a book that ought to become a standard text and might just become a classic of historical literature. . . . He is masterful at placing every nuance of the Sweet case within a larger context."
—*Houston Chronicle*

"What a powerful and beautiful book. Kevin Boyle has done a great service to history with *Arc of Justice*. With deep research and graceful prose, he has taken a single moment, the hot September day in 1925 when Ossian and Gladys Sweet moved into a bungalow on Garland Avenue in Detroit, and from that woven an amazing and unforgettable story of prejudice and justice at the dawn of America's racial awakening."
—David Maraniss, winner of the Pulitzer Prize and author of *They Marched into Sunlight* and *When Pride Still Mattered*

"A clear, precise snapshot of an incident that belongs in our collective memory . . . This is a tale worth listening to." —*Salon.com*

"Writing with the immediacy of a journalist and the flair of a novelist, [Boyle has] produced a history that's at once an intense courtroom drama, a moving biography, and an engrossing look at race in America in the early 20th century." —*The Christian Science Monitor*

Also by Kevin Boyle

The UAW and the Heyday of American Liberalism, 1945–1968

Muddy Boots and Ragged Aprons:
Images of Working-Class Detroit, 1900–1930 (coauthor)

Organized Labor and American Politics:
The Labor-Liberal Alliance, 1894–1994 (editor)

ARC OF JUSTICE

ARC OF JUSTICE

A SAGA OF RACE,

CIVIL RIGHTS, AND MURDER

IN THE JAZZ AGE

❖

KEVIN BOYLE

PICADOR

HOLT AND COMPANY
NEW YORK

www.picadorusa.com
www.twitter.com/picadorusa • www.facebook.com/picadorusa

Picador® is a U.S. registered trademark and is used by Henry Holt and Company under license from Pan Books Limited.

For book club information, please visit www.facebook.com/picadorbookclub or e-mail marketing@picadorusa.com.

Designed by Victoria Hartman

The Library of Congress has cataloged the Henry Holt edition as follows:

Boyle, Kevin, 1960–
    Arc of justice : a saga of race, civil rights, and murder in the Jazz Age / Kevin Boyle.—1st ed.
      p. cm.
    ISBN 978-0-8050-7933-3
    1. Sweet, Ossian, 1895–1960—Trials, litigation, etc. 2. Darrow, Clarence, 1857–1938. 3. Trials (Murder)—Michigan—Detroit. 4. African Americans—Civil rights—Michigan—Detroit—History—20th century. 5. African Americans—Civil rights—History—20th century. 6. Detroit (Mich.)—Race relations. 7. United States—Race relations. I. Title.
  KF224.S8B69 2004
  345.73'02523'0977434—dc22

                                 2004047352

Michigan Humanities Council Edition ISBN 978-1-250-01084-1

First published in the United States by Henry Holt and Company

First Picador Edition: September 2011

10 9 8 7 6 5 4 3 2

For Vicky, Abby, and Nan

with all my love

❖

The arc of the moral universe is long,
But it bends toward justice.

—*Abolitionist Theodore Parker, c. 1850s*

That Justice is a blind goddess
Is a thing to which we blacks are wise.
Her bandage hides two festering sores
That once perhaps were eyes.

—*Langston Hughes, 1923*

CONTENTS

AUTHOR'S NOTE

Throughout the *Arc of Justice*, I refer to African Americans by the now antiquated terms "Negro" and "colored" as well as the still common "black." I do so for dramatic purposes: readers of early drafts told me that seeing "African American" in the text jarred them out of the story, so I substituted terms common in the 1920s. By that choice, I mean no disrespect to the subjects of the book or to present-day readers.

ARC OF JUSTICE

AMERICA: 1925

The migrants filled the train stations of the South every day in the summer of 1925, waiting on ramshackle wooden platforms of crossroads towns such as Opelousas, Louisiana, and Andalusia, Alabama, and in cantilevered caverns such as Atlanta's Union Station. When the northbound trains pulled in, hissing and steaming, the travelers picked up cardboard suitcases bought at five-and-dimes or battered trunks carried since freedom came. Summoning up their courage, they strode past the Pullman porters—race men like themselves—making their way down the platforms to the grimy Jim Crow cars, settling into their seats for long rides north.[1]

The landscapes rolling past the tense faces looked familiar: the seas of cotton fields that flowed from the Mississippi River to the Georgia coast; the tobacco plantations that ran from North Carolina to the outskirts of Washington, D.C.; the squalid lumber camps of East Texas; the blackened coal towns of Appalachia; and the rough mill villages of the Carolina Piedmont. Every place they passed bore the brand of segregation and the Jim Crow laws. Every station had its "whites" and "coloreds" signs hanging above separate waiting rooms. Every view had its hidden terrors.

Eight men had been lynched by white mobs in the first half of 1925, a quiet year by previous standards. Black newspapers like the *Chicago Defender* and the *Pittsburgh Courier* had given the atrocities front-page coverage. Porters had tucked the papers into their bags and carried them home to the South, to the barbershops and the roadhouses, the churches and the cafés. So the travelers had to wonder. Was that collection of sharecroppers' shacks slipping by as the train passed Greenwood, Mississippi, the place where a few months ago a posse murdered Hal Winters because he dared defend his daughter from the landlord's advances? Was that gnarled tree on the horizon just beyond Scarboro, Georgia, the site where a mob doused Robert Smith in gasoline and set him ablaze in March?[2]

Gradually, the world outside the filthy windows became less and less familiar. At some point, the cotton fields gave way to wheat and corn; the rolling hills of Appalachia sloped into the flatlands of the Midwest. Mining camps gave way to factory towns, where the trains slowed to crawls as they passed mammoth warehouses and crossed street after nameless street. When the trains pulled into stations here, the migrants saw no signs for whites or coloreds.

In the early days of the migration, during the Great War, travelers sometimes celebrated crossing into the North by breaking into song or prayer, but so many migrants had made the trip north now—almost a million southern-born blacks since 1917—that the joy was tempered. They knew now that northern whites were as capable of brutality and murder as southern men. Rampaging whites had killed twenty-three blacks during a week of rioting in Chicago in the bitter summer of 1919.[3]

Yet it was still hard to remain calm as the trains reached the outskirts of one of the great cities, where the industrial districts alone dwarfed anything the South could claim. Gary's vast steelworks, one of the wonders of the modern world, sprawled across the prairie south of Chicago. The streets of Trenton and Hoboken were warrens of tool shops and warehouses. On the banks of the listless Rouge River just outside Detroit, Henry Ford was building an automobile factory large enough to employ all of Nashville or Norfolk.

The migrants grew increasingly excited as the distant, hazy outlines of the downtown skylines appeared. Pillars of steel and glass gradually filled the cars' windows. Even the smallest skyscrapers—the twenty-one story Flatiron Building in lower Manhattan or the imposing Book-Cadillac Hotel in downtown Detroit—would have been landmarks almost anywhere in the South. Here they faded into the shadows of buildings that seemed to soar upward forever. Chicago's newly opened Wrigley Building stood majestically above the Loop, its brilliantly illuminated clock tower drawing all eyes, day or night. In New York, the

Woolworth Building's elegant terra-cotta façade reached almost eight hundred feet into the sky, higher than any other building in the world. Behind those structures rose the skeletons of the next generation of skyscrapers, sure to be even taller, even more stunning.[4]

◆

The nation's cities sparkled in the summer of 1925. New York and Chicago, with more than two million residents each, were among the largest cities in the Western world, while Detroit, home to the fabulous new auto industry, was America's great boomtown, an industrial juggernaut of unprecedented power. Europe's cultural hegemony had died in the course of the Great War, its lifeblood drained away in the mud of Flanders's fields. Urban America filled the void, drowning out the ancien régime's death knell with the pounding of the jackhammer and the riotous joy of the jazz band.[5]

New York, Chicago, and Detroit coursed with cash in the mid-1920s. The war had made the United States the world's banker. The great American investment houses—J. P. Morgan, Goldman Sachs, Lehman Brothers—managed staggering sums, pouring international wealth into the soaring stock market and swelling corporate coffers. Manufacturers pushed their companies to new heights. Backed by the investment houses, many consolidated their operations. By the summer of 1925, the economy was awash in mergers, each larger and more spectacular than the last. Sprawling factories, marvels of machinery, poured out wonderful new products as merchants battled to build the grand stores befitting them. In 1924, Macy's completed additions that brought its floor space to two million square feet. The next spring, Detroit's leading retailer, J. L. Hudson, launched construction of a store twenty-one stories high, the world's tallest, and as lavish as anything Macy's or Marshall Field's could muster. The cities literally glowed with salesmanship, the new science of the 1920s. In the spring of 1925, a giant Moses towered over Times Square, advertising Cecil B. DeMille's epic *The Ten Commandments*. Every few minutes, a flash of electric light struck the tablets he held over his head.[6]

The cities' sparkle wasn't simply financial. It was also cultural. Massive immigration in the late nineteenth century had made the major urban centers strikingly polyglot places. By the turn of the century, the foreign-born and their children far outnumbered the native-born in almost every large city. The war slowed the mass migration from Europe, but it launched the Great Migration of Negroes from the

South. There were fifty-seven hundred blacks living in Detroit in 1910, ninety-one thousand in New York. Fifteen years later, Detroit had eighty-one thousand colored citizens, New York almost three hundred thousand.[7]

The flood of people—foreign-born and native-born, white and black—fit no single profile. Some of the newcomers were learned; others couldn't read or write. Some had spent their lives in cities; others had never been beyond the boundaries of their villages. A minority were professionals: businessmen and teachers, doctors and lawyers, priests, ministers, and rabbis. Most were working people who filled the factories, built the homes, scrubbed the floors, and nursed the babies of the well-to-do. These new residents brought more than brawn to the cities, though. They brought their religions, their politics, their institutions, and their art. They jammed the streets on the feast days of their village saints and they emptied them on the Day of Atonement. They talked of revolution in the cafés of Greenwich Village and of patronage politics in the saloons of working-class Chicago. They opened tiny storefront churches and substantial fraternal lodges. They rushed to the vaudeville theaters, where Jewish entertainers honed their craft, and to the ghetto dancehalls, where ragtime bands pushed the boundaries of American music. And they elbowed their way into the cities' public life. By the early 1900s, ethnic politicians filled city council seats and mayors' offices in city after city.

At first, native-born Americans were almost universally appalled by the world that the black and white migrants were building on the Lower East Side of New York or Chicago's Back of the Yards. In the early days of the twentieth century, though, a tiny number of sophisticates embraced immigrant working-class life as an antidote to the poisonous constraints of Victorian bourgeois culture. The first wave were artists enthralled by the color, the noise, the sheer vitality of the immigrant wards and determined to weave that life into an art that defined the modern and a politics that fostered liberation. In the 1920s, "slumming" became a mania, as urban elites sought out the exotic, the "real," wherever they could find it. They packed into the speakeasies that filled the cities after the imposition of Prohibition, where they could rub shoulders with Italian, Irish, or Jewish gangsters. They filled theaters to see ethnic entertainers such as Ragtime Jimmy Durante, late of Coney Island, or the anarchic Marx brothers. And in the most startling turn of them all, they discovered the Negroes living in their midst.[8]

In the early 1920s, sophisticates scrambled to grab a share of the black life that the southern migration was bringing into the cities. White producers mounted all-black musicals. White couples fumbled with the Charleston. And white patrons poured into Chicago's South Side jazz joints and Harlem's nightclubs. If they were lucky, they squeezed into the Vendome, where Louis Armstrong held the floor, or Edmond's Cellar, where Ethel Waters sang the blues. The frenzy was shot through with condescension. White slummers thought black life exciting because it was "primitive" and vital. Visiting the ghetto's haunts became the era's way to snub mainstream society, to be in the avant-garde. "Jazz, the blues, Negro spirituals, all stimulate me enormously," novelist Carl Van Vechten wrote H. L. Mencken in the summer of 1924. "Doubtless, I shall discard them too in time."[9]

◆

When the trains pulled into their terminals, the migrants jostled against one another as they began to gather up their belongings. Finally, they filed onto platforms already mobbed with passengers and porters. Many must have paused, unsure of what to do and where to go, then simply decided to follow the flow of people up the stairs to the stations' grand concourses. There they faced for the first time the grandeur of the city. Detroit's Michigan Central Station was a Beaux Arts masterpiece, a four-story colonnade dominated by a sequence of ornate arches and glittering chandeliers. The rotunda of the Illinois Central Station, built to awe visitors to Chicago's legendary World's Fair of 1893, was swathed in a marble wainscoting fourteen feet high. But nothing surpassed the great terminals of Gotham: Penn Station, with its main concourse sheathed in soaring steel and glass, and Grand Central Station, its great hall flooded with light from three monumental arched windows, its vaulted ceiling decorated by massive murals of the constellations. "You can identify the boys and girls [from the country] if you stand in Grand Central . . . and watch their behavior as they step from the train," *National Geographic* reported. "They hesitate a moment, oblivious to the crowds, looking upward, gripping their bags and bundles, hearing New York, sensing it."[10]

If they were lucky, the newcomers had friends or relatives waiting; they'd scour the crowds for familiar faces or hope to hear some voice calling their name, some voice they prayed they still might recognize. There would be the moments of reunion, hands outstretched in greeting, the sudden comforts of warm embraces. Others had no one to meet them. How terrifying it must have been to work through the waves of people alone, to step through the terminal's doors and onto the street without a guide. The Illinois Central stood at the southern end of Chicago's Grant Park, just outside the Loop. Detroit's station faced a large park ringed by hotels and boarding houses and beyond that, Michigan Avenue, the busiest thoroughfare on the city's west side. Penn Station fronted bustling Seventh Avenue, while Grand Central stood just twelve blocks away, facing elegant Park Avenue. All the streets pulsed with energy. Pedestrians, newsboys, shoeshine men, and redcaps crowded the sidewalks. Cabbies jockeyed for fares. Automobile horns blasted as drivers battled for places at the curb. Streetcars clanged by, jammed with riders. In the clamor, no one paid attention to a colored man or woman standing alone, wondering where to go and how to make his way in a new America.

•

American cities didn't simply sparkle in the summer of 1925. They simmered with hatred, deeply divided as always. Native-born Americans had been denouncing foreigners since the first wave of immigrants—the ragged refugees of blighted Ireland—poured into the cities in the desperate days of the 1840s. Time and again in the late nineteenth and early twentieth centuries, urban whites proved themselves capable of savagery toward their black neighbors.[11] But no matter how deep their divisions, the cities never developed the formal systems of segregation perfected in the South. Then came the Jazz Age. And suddenly the very changes that made the cities glitter triggered a backlash so bitter that the nation's great metropolises skidded toward their own version of Jim Crow.

The backlash was fueled by a fear of moral decay. Many native-born whites were appalled by the cities' celebration of immigrant and black cultures, with its implicit condemnation of traditional standards and its unmistakable whiff of amalgamation. Political conflict and economic strain made the backlash even more incendiary. For the better part of a generation, native-born politicians had been trying to check ethnic influence in city governments. Their efforts were driven partly by self-interest, partly by their belief that politicians of immigrant stock simply weren't capable of providing disinterested public service. Calvin Coolidge, a dour Yankee from the tiny hamlet of Plymouth Notch, Vermont, had been propelled to national prominence in 1919, when as governor of Massachusetts he had broken a strike by the overwhelmingly Irish Catholic Boston police. Four years later, he became president of the United States. But his confrontation with the Boston cops still haunted him. "The unassimilated alien child menaces our children," he told the readers of *Good Housekeeping*, "as the alien industrial worker, who has destruction rather than production in mind, menaces our industry."[12] Politicians weren't alone in sounding the alarm. From his opulent estate just outside Detroit, Henry Ford raged against Jewish bankers and their Bolshevik allies, who were conspiring to destroy all that Anglo-Saxon businessmen had built, his fury tinged with longing for those halcyon days when immigrants and Negroes knew their place.

At least Ford had his millions to console him. Many native-born whites didn't have wealth or power to buffer them from the changes sweeping over the cities. They were solid citizens—schoolteachers and shopkeepers, office workers and factory foremen, tradesmen and housewives—and they'd worked hard to build a secure and respectable life for their families. Many resented the foreigners who intruded on their world. Now the cities were filling with Negroes as well, a race many native-born whites considered even more degraded than the wretched refuse of Europe's teeming shores. Everyone knew that Negroes were a breed apart, they said, charming in their simplicity but also frightening in their volatility, their carnality, their utter incapacity to learn the lessons of civilized society. It hadn't been so bad when only a few blacks lived in the cities. But now they were everywhere, walking the streets, riding the streetcars, looking for jobs and houses that put them alongside decent white people.

In the early 1920s, native-born whites braced themselves against the threats the city posed. Shopkeepers' associations mounted boycotts against foreign-born competitors. Church groups campaigned against lewd entertainment and demanded that Prohibition be enforced. Veterans' organizations tried to purge public schools of textbooks that didn't celebrate Anglo-Saxon culture with sufficient fervor. Foremen and tradesmen used their lodge halls to prevent immigrants and Negroes from gaining access to the better-paying factory jobs. And thousands of people poured into the newest and most exciting of the cities' many fraternal clubs, the Ku Klux Klan, which had been revived by D. W. Griffith's 1915 film, *Birth of a Nation*, a paean to the Reconstruction-era KKK. The founders of the new Klan were businessmen, pure and simple, who stood for "One Hundred Percent Americanism." They protected traditional morality: they defended the virtue of white womanhood, assailed bootleggers and their besotted clients, celebrated sobriety and the triumph of a Protestant God. They made sure that all those who threatened the nation—blacks, of course, but also Catholics, Jews, and the foreign-born—were kept in their place. It was a brilliant sales job. In the early 1920s, the Klan broke out of its southern base, racing through the small towns of the Midwest and West. And it absolutely exploded in the big cities. By 1924, Detroit's Klan had thirty-five thousand members, Chicago's fifty thousand. The money rolled in, for memberships, robes, rulebooks. And the hatred spewed out from the Klan rallies and marches, protests and political campaigns that spread across urban America.[13]

The anger seething up from the streets blended with the fears of the well-heeled to create a fierce political movement. But the combination wasn't stable. Powerful men like Coolidge and Ford weren't always comfortable with the hoi polloi of white America; when fifty thousand Klansmen in full regalia paraded past the White House in August 1925, Coolidge snubbed them.[14] But Anglo-Saxon politicians and businessmen also found plenty of common ground with their robed brethren.

The nativists' campaign reached high tide in 1924. Anti-immigrant groups had been demanding for years that Congress restrict entry into the United States. The pressure became intense in the early 1920s. Veterans groups lobbied their representatives, the Klan launched a massive letter-writing campaign, businessmen endorsed restriction, and nativist scientists and authors appeared before congressional committees to explain the growing threat to the American racial stock. Congress finally surrendered in the spring of 1924. The National Origins Act imposed such strict limits on the number of immigrants allowed into the country that, for all intents and purposes, it ended the great era of immigration, now eight decades old. Ethnic spokesmen pleaded with the president to veto the bill. But Coolidge remained silent, as was his habit.[15]

The nativists followed up their triumph in Congress with a raw display of political power. It was a presidential election year in 1924. When the Republicans met at their convention, a few delegates proposed that the GOP condemn Klan intolerance. But the Invisible Empire's influence was so strong that the proposal went down in flames. The Democrats' convention, held at Madison Square Garden, took an even more bitter turn. For some time, the governor of New York, Al Smith, had been positioning himself to run for the presidency.

Smith was a first-rate politician. But he was also an Irish Catholic, the son of working-class parents, born in a third-floor walk-up on the Lower East Side, educated in the Fulton Street Fish Market and the smoke-filled rooms of Tammany Hall. The party's nativists were apoplectic at the thought of such a man in the White House. So they deadlocked the convention. Ballot after ballot, Smith's supporters and opponents battled over the nomination. At one point in the proceedings, William Jennings Bryan, the ancient populist turned champion of traditional values, stood up to address the convention. The Smith supporters in the gallery, New York's aspiring ethnics, showered him with catcalls. He raised his leonine head to them. "You," he shouted in the voice that had thrilled generations, "do not represent the future of our country." So it seemed. After 103 ballots, Smith—and his immigrant world—went down to defeat.[16]

The cities' white supremacists never had such signal victories. Their campaigns were more local, their initiatives more piecemeal. But they were in their own way even more sweeping than those of the nativists. No one outside the South suggested that the flow of blacks into the cities be prohibited. Bit by bit, however, urban whites carved a color line through the city. When the migration northward began during the war, blacks had been able to find a range of factory jobs. The opportunities shrank in the early 1920s, as many employers decided that all but the most menial and dangerous work should be reserved for whites. More and more white shopkeepers banned black customers from their stores and restaurants. And, most ominously, whites decided that blacks couldn't live wherever they wanted. They were to be hidden away in a handful of neighborhoods, walled into ghettos. Businessmen infused the real estate market with racist rules and regulations. White landlords wouldn't show black tenants apartments outside the ghetto. White real estate agents wouldn't show them houses in white neighborhoods. Bankers wouldn't offer them mortgages. Insurance agents wouldn't provide them with coverage. Developers wrote legal restrictions into their deeds, barring blacks from new housing tracts.

As the structures of segregation hardened, white homeowners became more and more determined to protect their neighborhoods' racial purity. Those whites who could afford to do so left the ghetto. Those who had no black neighbors organized to keep their areas lily-white. They formed legal organizations—protective associations, they called them—to write clauses into their deeds prohibiting the sale of their homes to blacks. They monitored real estate sales to make sure no one broke the color line. And if a black family somehow managed to breech the defenses, they could always drive them out, quietly if possible, violently if necessary.

The cities weren't segregated in one quick rush. White real estate agents, bankers, and homeowners had begun shaping Chicago's ghetto in the first decade of the twentieth century; white Detroiters didn't follow their example until the late 1910s and early 1920s. What's more, no one coordinated the businessmen's practices and the homeowners' actions. They spread by quiet agreement, sealed by a handshake in the boardroom, a directive from the home office, a conversation over coffee in the neighbor's kitchen. But the forces of the marketplace have a way of imposing discipline on disparate behaviors. By the summer of 1925, racial restrictions were assuming the power of convention across the urban North. As they did, the glittering cities of the Jazz Age were inexorably being divided in two.

◆

The migrants knew about the ghettos. Sometimes they just knew a name—Harlem, Chicago's Black Belt, Detroit's Black Bottom—sometimes even less: a direction from the train station, a stop on the streetcar line, an address committed to memory. So they set out for the subway line that ran uptown, the State Street el to South Side Chicago, or the Michigan Avenue streetcar to Detroit's east side, hoping that this was the correct place to go, that these trains were the last trains of a journey that seemed to be stretching on and on.

Racial etiquette heightened the tension. Southern whites expected blacks to be obsequious. Would northern whites expect the same? What would happen if they accidentally brushed against a white woman in the crush to board the subway train? Could they take the empty seat toward the front of the car, as they had been told they could? Or would it be better to sit in the back and avoid even the possibility of a confrontation? There was only a split second to make a decision that, if wrong, might have catastrophic consequences.

The ride across town must have seemed terribly long. The subway trains rumbled in and out of darkness; the streetcars clattered through the crowded streets. Finally, the migrants saw the stop they'd been waiting for, at 125th Street, on the rim of Harlem; at South State and 26th Street; on St. Antoine Street, in the heart of Black Bottom. As the trains rumbled away without them, the migrants turned toward the dazzling lights. The main thoroughfares were magical places. New-comers were amazed by the sweep of black-owned businesses: "restaurants, barbershops, pool halls, cabarets, blind pigs, gamblin' joints camouflaged as 'Recreation Clubs,'" a migrant to Detroit remembered. They were awed by the street life, by the pushcart vendors hawking fresh fruits and vegetables; by the street-corner orators selling socialism, separatism, or salvation; by the jazz and blues clubs pitching their performers to the locals and the slummers. "What a city! What a world!" thrilled poet Arna Bontemps upon his arrival in Harlem in 1924.[17]

But the migrants couldn't live in the stores and the nightclubs. No matter how entranced they might be, they eventually had to leave the gaudy brilliance of the business strips and head down the side streets in search of housing. There were a handful of attractive streets, like Harlem's 138th and 139th: Strivers' Row.[18] For the most part, though, the glamour of the main streets gave way to poverty. Knowing that the migrants had nowhere else to go, landlords had carved Harlem's brownstones and the workmen's cottages of Black Bottom and the Black Belt into tiny apartments, which they rented at exorbitant rates. The profits rarely found their way back into the buildings. Paint peeled from the clapboards. Broken windows remained unmended, leaky roofs unrepaired. As they took in the sights, many migrants sagged with disappointment, but they knew they had few alternatives. So they simply trudged on, looking for the address they'd been given, for a rooming house where they could spend the night, for a flat they could make their own, trying to find a home better than the one they'd left behind.

ONE

WHERE DEATH WAITS

The streets of Detroit shimmered with heat. Most years, autumn arrived the first week of September. Not in 1925. Two days past Labor Day and the sun blazed like July. Heat curled up from the asphalt, wrapped around telephone poles and streetlight stanchions, drifted past the unmarked doors of darkened speakeasies, seeped through windows thrown open to catch a breeze, and settled into the city's flats and houses where it lay, thick and oppressive, as afternoon edged into evening.[1]

Detroit had been an attractive place in the nineteenth century, a medium-size midwestern city made graceful by its founders' French design. Five broad boulevards radiated outward like the spokes of a wheel—one each running east, northeast, north, northwest, and west—from the compact downtown. Detroit's grand promenades, these boulevards were lined with the mansions of the well-to-do, mammoth stone churches, imposing businesses, and exclusive clubs. Between the boulevards lay Detroit's neighborhoods, row after row of modest single-family homes interspersed with empty lots, waiting for the development that boosters continually claimed was coming but never seemed to arrive.[2]

The auto boom changed everything. Plenty of cities had automakers in the early days, but Detroit had the young industry's geniuses, practical men seduced by the beauty of well-ordered mechanical systems and fascinated by the challenge of efficiency. German and French manufacturers had invented automobiles in the 1870s. It was Detroit's brilliance to reinvent them. In the early days of the twentieth century, the city's aspiring automakers had disassembled the European-made horseless carriages, studying every part, tinkering with the designs, searching for ways to make them work more smoothly and to manufacture them more cheaply. By 1914, when Henry Ford unveiled his restructured Highland Park plant north of downtown, the process was complete. Ford had created a factory as complex as the automobile itself, floor after floor full of machines intricately designed and artfully arranged to make and assemble auto parts faster than anyone thought possible. Three hundred thousand Model T's rolled out of the factory that year, inexpensive, elegantly simple, utterly dependable cars for ordinary folk like Ford himself.[3]

Ford's triumph triggered the industrial version of a gold rush. Other manufacturers grabbed great parcels of land for factories. The Dodge Brothers, John and Horace, started work on a complex large enough to rival Ford's on the northeast side; Walter Chrysler built a sprawling plant on the far reaches of the east side, near the Detroit River; Walter O. Briggs scattered a series of factories across the city. Aspiring entrepreneurs filled the side streets with tiny machine shops and parts plants that they hoped would earn them a cut of seemingly unending profits. The frenzy transformed Detroit itself into a great machine. By 1925, its grand boulevards were shadowed by stark factory walls and canopied by tangles of telephone lines and streetcar cables. Once fine buildings were now enveloped in a perpetual haze from dozens of coal-fired furnaces.[4]

More than a decade had passed since Henry Ford, desperate to keep his workers on the line, doubled their wages to an unprecedented five dollars a day. Word of Detroit's high-paying jobs had shot through Pennsylvania mining camps, British shipyards, Mississippi farmhouses, and peasant villages from Sonora to Abruzzi. Tens of thousands of working people poured into the city, lining up at the factory gates, looking for their share of the machinists' dream. Eleven years on, they were still coming. In 1900, when Ford was first organizing his company, Detroit had 285,000 people living within its city limits. By 1925, it had 1.25 million. Only New York, Chicago, and Philadelphia were bigger, and Detroit was rapidly closing the gap. "Detroit is Eldorado," wrote an awed magazine reporter. "It is staccato American. It is shockingly dynamic."[5]

And it was completely overwhelming. While the auto magnates retreated to the serenity of their sparkling new suburban estates, working people struggled to hold on to a sliver of space somewhere in Detroit's vast grid of smoke gray side streets. In the center city, where Negroes and the poorest immigrants lived, two, three, or more families shared tiny workmen's cottages built generations before. Single men jammed into desperately overcrowded rooming houses, sleeping in shifts so that landlords could double the fees they collected for the privilege of eight hours' rest on flea-infested mattresses. Beyond the inner ring, a mile or so from downtown, the nineteenth-century city gradually gave way to a sprawl of new neighborhoods. First came vast tracts of flats and jerry-rigged houses for those members of the working class lucky enough to find five-dollar-a-day jobs. Immigrants clustered on the east side of the city, the native-born on the west side, all of them paying premium prices for homes slapped up amid factories, warehouses, and railroad yards or along barren streetscapes. Workers' neighborhoods blended almost imperceptibly into areas dominated by craftsmen and clerks, Detroit's solid middle strata, who struggled mightily to afford the tiny touches that set them apart from the masses: a bit of distance from the factory gates, a patch of grass front and back. Finally, out near the sub-urbs' borders lay pockets of comfortable middle-class houses, minia-ture versions of the mock Tudors and colonial revivals favored by the upper crust, so beyond the means of most Detroiters it wasn't even worth the effort of dreaming about them.[6]

Garland Avenue sat squarely in the middle range, four miles east of downtown, halfway between the squalor of the inner city and the splendor of suburban Grosse Pointe. Despite its name, it wasn't an av-enue at all. It was just a side street, two miles of pavement running straight north from Jefferson Avenue, Detroit's southeastern boule-vard, to Gratiot Avenue, the northeastern boulevard.

In 1900, Garland was nothing more than a plan on a plat book, but developers had raced to fill it in. To squeeze out every bit of space, they cut the street into long blocks, broken by cross streets that could serve as business strips. Then they sliced each block into twenty or thirty thin lots 35 feet wide and 125 feet deep. A few plots were sold to families who wanted to build their own homes, the way working people always used to do. On the remaining lots, developers built utilitarian houses for the middling sort: long, narrow wood-frame, two-family flats, one apart-ment up, another down, each with its own entrance off a porch that ran the length of the front. Behind each house was a small yard, barely big enough for a garden, leading out to the alleyway; in front was a postage-stamp lawn running from the porch to the spindly elms planted at curb-side. Only a few feet of open space separated one building from another, a space so small that, from the right angle, the houses seemed to fade one into another, much as one machine seemed to fade into another along an assembly line.[7]

The people who lived up and down the street didn't have the education, the credentials, or the polish of the lawyers, accountants, and college professors who lived in the city's outer reaches. But they had all the attributes necessary to keep themselves out of the inner city, and that's what mattered most. Of course, they were white, each and every one. The vast majority of them were American born, and the few foreigners living on the street came from respectable stock; they were Germans, Englishmen, Irishmen, and Scotsmen, not the Poles or Russians or Greeks who filled so much of the east side. Some of them were native Detroiters, and virtually all the rest had come to the city from other northern states, so they knew how to make their way in the big city: they understood how to work their way into the trades, how to use a membership in the Masons or the Odd Fellows to pry open employment-office doors, how to flash a bit of fast talk to sway a reluctant buyer.[8]

Such advantages helped the people of Garland find solid jobs, a blessing in a city that burned through workingmen, then tossed them aside. A minority of the men worked as salesmen, teachers, and shop clerks, the sort of jobs that didn't pay particularly well but kept the hands clean. A few more were craftsmen, the elite of the working class, trained in metal work or carpentry or machine repair and fiercely proud of the knowledge they carried under their cloth caps. Many more had clawed their way to the top rung of factory labor. They were foremen, inspectors, supervisors, men who spent their days in the noise and dirt of the shop floor making sure that others did the backbreaking, mind-numbing work required to keep shiny new cars flowing out of the factories.[9]

Most of the women worked at home. They rose early to make husbands and boarders breakfasts sufficient to steel them for a day of work, then bustled children off to school—the youngest to Julia Ward Howe Elementary, a brooding two-story brick building at the intersection of Garland and Charlevoix, three blocks north of Jefferson; the older ones to Foch Middle School and Southeastern High. Mornings and afternoons were spent shopping and sweeping and washing clothes streaked with machine oil and alley dirt. Their evenings were devoted to cooking and cleaning dishes while their husbands relaxed with the newspaper or puttered out in the garage.

No matter how many advantages the families along Garland Avenue enjoyed, though, it was always a struggle to hold on. Housing prices had spiraled upward so fearfully the only way a lot of folks could buy a flat or a house was to take on a crippling burden of debt. The massive weight of double mortgages or usurious land contracts threatened to crack family budgets. Men feared the unexpected assault on incomes that at their best barely covered monthly payments: the commission that failed to come through; the rebellious work crew that cost a foreman his job; the sudden recession that shuttered factories for a few weeks. And now they faced this terrible turn of events: Negroes were moving onto the street, breaking into white man's territory. News of their arrival meant so many things. A man felt his pride knotted and twisted. Parents feared for the safety of their daughters, who had to walk the same streets as colored men. And everyone knew that when the color line was breeched, housing values would collapse, spinning downward until Garland Avenue was swallowed into the ghetto and everything was lost.[10]

•

Word that a colored family had bought the bungalow on the northwest corner of Garland and Charlevoix had first spread up and down the street in the early days of summer. The place was kitty-corner to the elementary school and directly across Garland from the Morning Star Market, the cramped neighborhood grocery where many of the women did their daily shopping. The rumors had caused a lot of consternation, much tough talk, and some serious threats. But most people were still surprised when, the day after Labor Day, policemen took up positions around the house.[11]

The Negroes had arrived in the morning, half a dozen of them. Since they didn't have much furniture, they'd finished the move in no time at all. But the police had stayed all day and into the night. They returned first thing the next morning. A couple of patrolmen wandered listlessly back and forth along the blistering sidewalk as school let out at 3:15. An even larger official presence was in position—eight officers stationed around the intersection—when the men came home from the factories a few hours later.[12]

Garland wasn't a friendly street. Neighbors might nod as they went to work, chat in line at the market. Kids might play together. But there were a few too many transients—a young couple renting out a flat, a single man boarding in a back bedroom—for folks to really feel connected to one another. Even longtime residents generally kept to themselves.

On the evening of September 9, 1925, though, neighbors couldn't wait to get outside. Partly, it was the soaring temperatures that drew them down to the street. But it was the pulsing energy, the surging excitement that really tugged at them. The Negroes were nowhere to be seen; there were no lights burning in the bungalow, no sign of movement anywhere on the property. But everyone knew they were in there. And everyone knew that the police were stationed out front because there might be trouble.[13]

So people finished up their suppers and, one by one, drifted out to Garland. It was close to seven when Ray and Kathleen Dove brought their baby daughter onto the porch of their flat, almost directly across from the colored family's house. Ray had spent the day in the Murray Body plant, up near the Ford factory, where he worked as a metal finisher. It was a sweaty, dangerous job, grinding down the imperfections in steel auto bodies, making them as smooth as customers expected them to be. As usual, Ray came home anxious for an evening of relaxation. Kathleen sat in the chair she brought outside and Ray leaned against the railing, watching the baby play at his feet. Their two boarders, George Strauser and Bill Arthur, soon joined them. Strauser kept himself occupied by writing a letter. Arthur, only three days in the neighborhood, was content to sit with his landlords and pass the time while the sun slowly set.[14]

As they chatted, the sidewalk in front of the Doves' house began to fill up with excited neighborhood children. Thirteen-year-old George Suppus dragged his little brother down the street as soon as they had finished their after-dinner chores. He met his best friend, Ulric Arthur, in front of the market. The three boys stood around for a while, watching the corner house, until a cop told them to move on. Then they wandered over to the Doves' front lawn, where no one seemed to care how long they loitered.[15]

Most adults wouldn't admit to sharing the kids' curiosity, so those anxious to be outside fished for excuses. Leon Breiner, a foreman at the Continental Motors plant, lived a dozen houses north of the Doves, in a frame cottage much more modest than the bungalow the Negroes had bought. He had good reason to stay at home: his wife, Leona, suffered from a heart condition and the heat left her drained and often cross. But Breiner grew restless sitting alongside her in the rockers they had on their small front porch, and he volunteered to pick up a few items from the Morning Star Market down at the corner. Puffing on his pipe, he headed down toward the police.[16]

Otto Lemhagen arrived at the corner shortly after seven to spend some time with his brother-in-law, Norton Schuknecht, a man of stature, an inspector in the Detroit Police Department, commander of the McClellan Avenue Station. This was all very impressive to Lemhagen, who in his career had risen all the way to investigator at the telephone company. Garland lay within Schuknecht's precinct, so Lemhagen knew his brother-in-law would be spending the evening out at the coloreds' house, making sure nothing untoward happened. Lemhagen sidled up to him while he stood kitty-corner from the bungalow, chatting with his lieutenant.

While the two men passed the time, Garland took on the feel of a carnival. Traffic was growing heavier, and there were knots of people in the school yard—maybe twenty, thirty people, or more—mostly women and children. Some sat on the lawn. A few tossed a baseball around on the gravel playground. More neighbors meandered up and down Garland or Charlevoix, sometimes alone, other times in small groups, although Schuknecht's patrolmen weren't allowing any of them onto the sidewalk directly in front of the Negroes' house. There was an air of good humor on the corner, an easy sociability that Garland Avenue rarely experienced. People talked about mundane matters: the weather, their summer vacations, the new school year. But Lemhagen also caught snatches of bitterness seething through the growing crowd. "Damn funny thing," he heard someone on the school yard say, "that the police wouldn't go in there and drag those niggers out."[17]

Eric Houghberg felt that same mix of bonhomie and anger as he made his way home from work a few minutes later. The twenty-two-year-old plumber—an angular young man, with ears too large for his long, thin face—rented a room in the upstairs flat next door to the Doves. He knew that the Negroes' presence riled people. Hadn't his landlady greeted him at the door yesterday afternoon with the taunt, "You got new neighbors over there. That's the nigger people. That's the people trying to move in over there." Houghberg wasn't the sort of man who went looking for trouble. But he couldn't resist the pull of the street, the chance to break his routine, to share the warm night air with people like himself. So he rushed upstairs to grab a bite to eat and to clean up: a quick wash, a shave, a new set of clothes. It was a bit of vanity, that's all. He wanted to wipe away the grime of the day, to look his best.[18] Who knew what might happen on a night like this?

•

By 5:30, the late summer sun was already starting to sink toward the row of tightly packed houses. The light that had been filtering through the drawn curtains began to fade. But the gathering darkness did nothing to dissipate the heat that had built up over the course of the day. With the windows barely cracked open and the doors shut fast, the bungalow on the corner was enveloped in a suffocating stillness.

Dr. Ossian Sweet sat at the card table he'd set up in the dining room. He was a handsome man, short, dark, and powerfully built. A month short of thirty, he looked ten years older: his hairline was receding, his waistline was expanding, his face was taking on the roundness of middle age. Other men might have hated to see their youth slipping from them. Sweet cultivated the illusion of maturity. Where he came from, black men were permanently "boys," never worthy of white men's respect, never their equals. Dr. Sweet was no boy. He was a professional man, better educated, wealthier, more accomplished than most of the whites he encountered. He wanted others to know it the moment they saw him. So he favored tailored suits, well cut and subdued. He bought crisp white shirts and tasteful ties. He wore the round, tortoise-shell glasses popular with college men. He kept his mustache neatly trimmed, his hair stylishly short.[19]

Sweet attempted to project the casual confidence, the instinctual authority that set doctors apart from the ordinary run of men. It didn't come to him naturally. As a child, he had shared in the backbreaking work of his parents' Central Florida farm, tending the fields his father rented, hauling water from the stream so that his mother could do the laundry, caring for the ever-growing brood of brothers and sisters who filled every cranny of the tiny farmhouse his parents had built by hand. His mother and father had taught him what they could, immersing him in the religious traditions that had sustained the family through generations of struggle, making him want to succeed. Then, when he was thirteen years old, they had sent Ossian away, not because they wanted one less mouth to feed, though lifting that burden was a blessing, but because they loved him. Get away while you're young, they told him. Go north. Get an education.

And he did, though he left Florida with only as much as he could glean from six years in a one-room schoolhouse that shut down when harvest time came. It took him twelve more years to fulfill his parents' instructions, a dozen long, hard years of schooling to master the material that would make him an educated man and earn the pride that was expected of the race's best men, all the while working as a serving boy for white people—washing dirty dishes, waiting tables, carting luggage up hotel stairs—just to pay tuition and buy the books his professors required him to read. Ossian never excelled, but he got an education, as fine an education as almost any man in America, colored or white, could claim. By age twenty-five, he had earned his bachelor of science degree from Wilberforce University in Ohio and his medical degree from Washington, D.C.'s Howard University, the jewel in the crown of Negro colleges.

He'd come to Detroit in 1921 with virtually nothing, but in the four years since then he'd built a thriving practice down in Black Bottom, the city's largest ghetto; he'd earned the respect of his colleagues at Dunbar Memorial, the city's best colored hospital; he'd helped his brother Otis launch his professional career. Best of all, Ossian had found in his wife, Gladys, a young woman of grace, charm, and social standing, a wonderfully suitable doctor's wife. As a gift to them both—and a balm for their pain—Ossian had taken his bride on the sort of adventure one reads about in novels: a year-long stay in Vienna and Paris, where he completed postgraduate studies on the cutting edge of medical science.[20]

Yet, despite all those victories, Ossian remained, deep down, the frightened Florida farm boy trying to carry his family's expectations on his narrow shoulders. He didn't doubt his abilities; he knew he was a fine physician, better than most. But he often tried too hard to impress—to find just the right phrase, to strike just the right pose, to keep just the right distance—to reassure himself. Now, as the darkness slowly descended around him, his carefully constructed veneer crumbled away. He didn't feel sure of himself. He felt terribly, terribly afraid.[21]

This house was supposed to have been one more grand accomplishment. Ossian and Gladys had first seen the bungalow in late May 1925. She loved it from the start. A city girl, born in Pittsburgh, raised in a small but comfortable house in Detroit only a few miles north of Garland, Gladys knew quality when she saw it. She'd desperately wanted a home with a yard, where Iva, their fourteen-month-old daughter, could play. This house had much more to offer as well. The first-floor brick still had the sharply defined edges of new construction; the shingles above were newly painted. The front porch, shaded by the sloping roof, looked so cool and inviting, Gladys could imagine long evenings there, sitting on the swing, talking and reading.[22]

The interior was, if anything, even more attractive. The original owner, a Belgian-born contractor by the name of Decrudyt, had built it for his family, and he obviously had wanted the best. The first floor had the cool elegance of the arts and crafts style. Polished oak trim framed the long living room and the dining room behind it. Solid squared pillars stood on either side of the archway that divided the two rooms.

A built-in hutch—glass-fronted doors above, generous drawers below—dominated the dining room's far wall; on the opposite side of the room, small built-in bookcases, nestled into the base of the pillars, echoed the effect of compact craftsmanship that the hutch created. Gladys reveled in the small touches: the flower pattern on the decorative tiles surrounding the gas fireplace in the living room, the leaded-glass windows on the south side, the stylish chandelier hanging low in the dining room, the small alcove that extended from the same room. This would be the place to put the piano she envisioned them having, the place where she could re-create the music that had always filled her parents' home.[23]

Gladys had been thrilled by the spaciousness, so welcome after months of making do at her mother's house. Truth be told, she was pleased that her home had one more room than her mother's; she was moving up, ever so slightly, the way the next generation was supposed to do. Iva could have her own room. She and Ossian would take the front bedroom, overlooking Garland, for themselves. It was small, barely big enough for a bed and a dresser. But they'd get the morning sun streaming in through the three dormers and they'd avoid the late-night noise on Charlevoix, where the streetcar ran.[24]

Ossian also liked the house, maybe not for the stylish touches—though he was a stylish man—but for the message the house delivered. Most Negroes lived in Black Bottom on the eastern end of downtown Detroit. When he first came to the city, Ossian had lived there himself. But established physicians—doctors with solid practices and families to raise—almost always lived in better neighborhoods, and Ossian wanted nothing less for his young family. He deserved a home such as this, the newest, most impressive house on the block.[25]

But Ossian also saw the dangers he would be facing if they moved here. He had already seen what white men could do, and sometimes the memories grabbed hold of him. He could see himself as a small boy again, listening to the terrifying stories of colored men mutilated and murdered at the phosphate pits just outside his hometown. With terrifying clarity he could still see the mob of whites, hundreds and hundreds of them, gathered around that black boy, Fred Rochelle, the one who lived a few blocks from the Sweet family, who had been accused of raping a white girl. He could pick out individuals amid the throng, ordinary people from the white side of town—the jeweler, the livery owner, the butcher—their faces alight with anticipation as they waited for the moment when the torch met the pyre and the flames began to lick at Rochelle's battered body. Then the memories flashed to another time, another place, so far from Florida and yet so similar. Ossian could see the gangs of white soldiers and sailors roaming the streets of Washington, D.C., the summer after the war, looking for Negroes to maim and kill, marching up Seventh Street toward Howard University, toward the medical school, toward Ossian himself. He could see them coming for him.[26]

Ossian's status wouldn't protect him; he knew that. He read the atrocities that the race papers reported. He knew that social standing hadn't protected the four Johnson brothers—one a doctor like Ossian, another a dentist like Otis—riddled with bullets while sitting handcuffed in the backseat of a sheriff's automobile in the woods of Arkansas in 1919. It hadn't saved A. C. Jackson, the colored doctor shot down like a dog, his chest ripped open by a shotgun blast during the Tulsa riot in 1921. It hadn't saved the prosperous little town of Rosewood, Florida, a couple hours north of Ossian's hometown, when a rumor of rape triggered a white pogrom in January 1923. No one could say how many colored people died that day—a dozen, two dozen bodies had been dumped in unmarked graves—but Rosewood was gone, burned to the ground, its survivors scattered to the winds. No, Ossian's hard-won status wouldn't shield him at all, if the white people on Garland Avenue decided that they didn't want him as a neighbor.[27]

Still, it was hard to resist, to walk away, to just give up. Gladys had been so pleased with the bungalow, he didn't want to disappoint her or let her see just how terrified he was by the thought of moving in. Others encouraged him as well. His friend and colleague, Dr. Edward Carter, insisted that the purchase was a straightforward business proposition. Real estate was a good investment in a city like Detroit, he said, and a man of Ossian's age, health, and earning power shouldn't be afraid of debt. Ossian knew that he'd have to stretch to make the purchase. He had to pay far more than the neighborhood standard—the owner, Mrs. Smith, was asking $18,500—as whites always charged black home buyers a premium. But he could rent out two of the bedrooms: his brother, Otis, needed a place to stay, and there were plenty of other colored men who'd be happy to pay for a room in such a house. So he set his fears aside. On the fifth of June, he handed over $3,500 as a down payment.[28]

•

Detroit's race relations had been deteriorating ever since the Great War, when southern blacks had begun flooding into the city. But in the summer of 1925, white supremacy had flared to frightening new levels. The black newspaper, the *Detroit Independent*, reported repeated police assaults on Negroes. Fifty-five blacks had been shot by policemen in the first half of the year alone. A few of them had been executed—there was no other word for it—the way the Johnson brothers had been executed by Arkansas' lawmen. For more than a year, patrolman Proctor Pruitt had harbored a grudge against a colored man, Steve Tompkins. One August evening in 1925, Pruitt's commanding officer asked him to deliver a summons to the Tompkins' home in Black Bottom. Mrs. Tompkins politely invited the officer inside. Pruitt walked up to her husband, drew his service revolver, and fired a single shot into Tompkins's left temple. Pruitt had fired in self-defense, the police department claimed.[29]

Whether Pruitt was a member of the Ku Klux Klan no one knew. But there was no doubt that the police department was thick with Klansmen. The KKK had started recruiting in Detroit in 1921, and since then, their poison had seeped into almost every corner of the city. In private, Klan leaders claimed that there were more members in Detroit than any other place in the country. When ill health forced Detroit's mayor to resign in 1924, the KKK ran one of its own in the special election called to fill his seat. Only a rigged ballot count kept the Klansman from victory. The regular election was set for November 1925, and the Klan was determined not to be defeated again. All summer long, the Invisible Order organized, building its campaign, spreading its message. And one spectacular night in July 1925, it displayed its power. That evening, ten thousand white-robed knights gathered in a field on Detroit's west side, their rally brilliantly illuminated by the blinding light of a burning cross.[30]

Neighborhood violence, though, cut closest to the bone. Five times that summer, crowds of whites attacked blacks who had bought homes in all-white areas. One assault in particular haunted Ossian. Dr. Alexander Turner was one of the foremost colored doctors in Detroit, a widely respected figure who moved easily between the burgeoning black ghetto and the white world. The highly skilled chief of surgery at the colored hospital, Dunbar Memorial, Turner also held appointments at two major white hospitals, both of which barred most black doctors. But none of it meant a thing in June, when the doctor moved into a beautiful home on Spokane Avenue, in an all-white area of Detroit's west side. He had been inside only five hours when a white mob attacked, smashing windows, ripping the phone line, tearing tiles off the roof. Amid the terror, a small group of white men had arrived, claiming to be representatives from the office of Mayor Johnny Smith, an ally of the black community. When the doctor opened the door, thirty or forty members of the mob rushed in to ransack the place. Turner barely escaped, cowering on the floor of his Lincoln sedan as the chauffeur inched the car through the snarling, screaming hecklers. That night, shocked and humiliated, Turner signed the deed for the house over to the neighborhood improvement society that had whipped the crowd into its frenzy.[31]

•

Ossian had spent an anguished summer Sunday in a colleague's office, listening to Turner tell in minute detail the story of what had happened. Afterward, he couldn't keep the ugly scene from preying on his mind. So he sought out the assurances of friends and acquaintances, who invariably cited Turner's failures: the whites were nothing but bullies, Ossian's colleague Carter lectured him—they had meant to intimidate Turner, not kill him. The doctor should have confronted them; he could have made them back down. He had been a damn coward. Others insisted that, had they been in Turner's spot, they wouldn't have retreated. Relaxing in the Dunbar staff room one day, Ossian heard one of the hospital trustees swear: "I made up my mind what I would do if a mob comes to drive me out of my home. I have a revolver and a shotgun. I have a rifle. I'm not going to attack anyone that does not attack me, but the first individual that comes over to tear up my home, he'll pay with his life."[32]

Gladys also refused to be intimidated. She understood the risks, she said; she'd heard her cousins' terrifying stories of living through the Chicago riot of 1919, when rampaging whites had murdered twenty-three Negroes. But hearing stories wasn't the same as seeing the mob take control of the streets or hearing a colored boy's screams. Gladys was a northern girl; she hadn't lived with the daily humiliations of Jim Crow, and she'd never actually confronted the fury of white hatred. She had grown up in a white neighborhood, attended white schools, spent her evenings at the grand white theaters where her stepfather, a musician, performed. In fact, she was almost white herself. Her mother's father was a white man. And Gladys had such light, almost olive, skin she just might have been able to pass, had she been so inclined. There was simply no way she could understand the dangers that might await her on Garland, not the way Ossian understood them. But she wasn't going to be persuaded that the risks were too great. When they talked about the bungalow, Ossian could hear the steeliness creeping into Gladys's voice. You work in the ghetto, she told him, but we don't need to live there. We have a perfect right to live anywhere we please.[33]

Such brave talk stiffened Ossian's resolve. He couldn't stand the thought of his colleagues calling him a coward behind his back, and he desperately wanted to please Gladys, to give her all she wanted, all she deserved. He had to be strong, to prove to himself that he wasn't afraid of a handful of bitter memories and a summer of white hooliganism. "Well, we have decided we are not going to run," he said to an acquaintance in midsummer. "We're not going to look for any trouble, but we're going to be prepared to protect ourselves if trouble arises."[34]

Though Mrs. Smith had agreed to vacate the bungalow by the first of August, Ossian delayed taking possession until September 8, the day after Labor Day. The timing was important: with summer vacation over and school back in session, there was less of a chance his white neighbors would be out on the street when he and Gladys arrived. The Sweets would do their best to stay off the streets as well; better not to be seen too often. Even visiting the local stores would be dangerous, so Ossian had Gladys buy enough food to last a week. He asked his in-laws to keep the baby, Iva, for a while. It wouldn't do to have her underfoot, and he couldn't stand the thought of putting her in danger. No matter how hard he tried, though, Ossian knew he couldn't guarantee his family's safety. He had to be prepared for whites to attack; it was suicidal not to be ready for the worst. A friend asked the police department to provide the Sweets with protection during their first few days in the neighborhood. That was a comfort. But the police couldn't be trusted to put themselves between a Negro and a crowd of angry whites. If the mob should come, there was only one way to keep them at bay: Ossian would have to do it himself.[35]

He understood what it would mean to defend his home. Force was the only thing that a mob respected. Back in college, Ossian had been trained to handle a gun. He had a pistol, a .38 Smith and Wesson a patient had given him a few years back in lieu of payment.[36] But he had to be willing to use it, to point it into a crowd of whites and pull the trigger. If he wanted to save his home, Dr. Sweet had to be willing to kill. He knew that. It was just a fact.

What's more, he had to ask others to do the same. He couldn't possibly defend the house alone: while he was on the front porch, facing Garland, whites could be battering down the side door leading out to Charlevoix. Ossian's brother Otis immediately agreed to join him in the house the first few nights, as did his next younger brother, Henry, who by a stroke of luck was spending the summer in Detroit before heading back to college. Ossian's colleague Edward Carter also promised to be there, as did Ossian's friend and fellow Howard alumnus, lawyer Julian Perry; and an old school chum, William Davis, a battle-hardened veteran of the Great War who now worked as a federal narcotics officer. Henry also lined up another veteran, his cousin and college classmate, John Latting, who had been his roommate that summer. Ossian was gratified—and a bit thrilled—by the response. He wasn't the sort of man who built strong friendships. Yet in his time of need, he could draw around him six of the race's most promising young men, all of them pledged to face down the mob that the best of the older generation had fled in fear.[37]

◆

The Sweets' tiny caravan came rumbling down Garland Avenue shortly after ten o'clock in the morning on September 8, 1925. Ossian, Gladys, and Davis took the lead, sitting in the back seat of their Buick, trying to hide their nervousness, while their chauffeur, Joe Mack, drew up to the curb. Having a driver was a silly indulgence. The Sweets' Buick wasn't exactly a limousine, and family finances were tight enough without having to pay someone five dollars a day to do something that Ossian and Gladys were perfectly capable of doing for themselves. But Ossian loved the touch of ostentation Mack provided, the stares he drew from the sidewalks as the car glided by. Today, he was also glad to have another man around. Otis, Henry, Latting, and Norris Murray, a hired handyman, were right behind, riding in the moving truck.[38] As the day unfolded, the Sweets might need every hand they could get.

Garland was quiet when they arrived. A few housewives stood on the porches, their faces hardened, silently watching the Negroes clamber down from the trucks. But most of the neighborhood men had long since headed off to the factories, and the children, crisp and clean in their new clothes, had been bundled off to the first day of school. Still, Ossian hurried his friends to finish the move as quickly as they could. They hustled to unload the Sweets' few possessions—a bedroom set, a couple of mattresses, a few chairs, some trunks and bags—along with two special bundles: a makeshift package of gunnysack within which Ossian had hidden a shotgun, two rifles, and six pistols, and a bulging brown satchel weighed down by four hundred rounds of ammunition.[39]

The Sweets hadn't been in the bungalow an hour when someone rapped on the door. A police officer, an Inspector McPherson, was standing in the shade of the porch. He was short and stocky, the way a cop was supposed to look, with a shock of thick white hair and a scar running the length of his face. The department had received the doctor's request for protection, McPherson explained, and was pleased to comply. The inspector had four men on the job already, in fact, but he had ordered them to stay out of sight so they wouldn't draw a crowd. McPherson didn't expect any trouble, though; Ossian simply "had to be a gentleman and everything would be all right." Ossian could have taken offense; the last thing he needed was to be lectured on courtesy. But he was so desperate for any reassurance he simply shook the inspector's hand and thanked him for the help. He never mentioned the arsenal hidden in the linen closet in the upstairs hall.[40]

All day long, the Sweets kept waiting for trouble to start. Glancing out the front window, Gladys noticed women shuttling from house to house on the other side of Garland, staring hard at the bungalow as they went. As the children walked home from school at three o'clock, Ossian heard the fractured voices of teenage boys shouting "nigger," their friends' laughter ringing behind them. But the moments passed and the excitement of being in a new house pushed the Sweets' anxieties into the background. Joe Mack and the handyman, Murray, puttered around the house, cleaning floors, moving boxes and trunks. In midafternoon, Dr. Carter stopped by briefly, all good cheer, a set of china he had bought as a housewarming present cradled in his arms. Gladys's dear friend Edna Butler, maid of honor at her wedding two and half years earlier, and another friend, Serena Rochelle, arrived a short time later. Butler was a seamstress, Rochelle an interior decorator; Gladys happily pulled them into the living room, where they sat on the floor talking about curtains, furniture, and paint colors, losing themselves in the fun of planning Gladys's new home.[41]

Always the proper hostess, Gladys insisted that everyone—Butler and Rochelle, her two brothers-in-law, Davis, Latting, even Mack the chauffeur and Murray the handyman—stay for dinner. They ate earlier than was the Sweets' habit, so Butler, Rochelle, Mack, and Murray could leave for home before darkness fell. But somehow they lost track of time. When they finished supper around eight o'clock, the sun had set. The terror was about to begin.[42]

Everyone understood that danger skyrocketed as soon as darkness descended. The police knew it. As the sun set, the inspector had brought his men—a dozen or more—out of hiding and put them on the corner of Garland and Charlevoix, in plain view of the neighbors. Yet, at supper's end, Ossian looked out the living-room window and saw the crowd of white people gathered on Garland.[43] He couldn't tell how many were out there, but it was a huge number; he could see that. The cops weren't allowing anyone onto the sidewalk directly in front of the bungalow. So the whites—a hundred, maybe two hundred, men, women, and children, too—gathered in front of the houses across the street and in the school yard on the other side of the intersection. They were just milling about, that's all, standing and talking, sauntering slowly around. But that's the way it would start, Ossian knew, quietly and peacefully. That was always the way a nightmare began.[44]

Gladys's friends couldn't go out there now, nor could Mack and Murray. A Negro stepping out onto the porch, walking down the sidewalk past the police to the streetcar stop on Charlevoix—that would be the spark right there. There'd be a lynching, here, on Garland, under the amber glow of the streetlight. They'd have to stay, all of them, stay inside and pray.[45]

Ossian tried to calculate their chances. He had Otis and Henry, Davis and Latting; counting himself, that made five men prepared to open fire, should it come to that. Mack and Murray were trapped, too; they might lend a hand. But Ossian was also down two men. Julian Perry had never shown up. And Edward Carter hadn't returned, as he had said he would. Ossian needed them both. Now. But they didn't come. Half an hour slipped by, with Ossian and the others sitting in the darkness, waiting. Finally, the telephone rang, a sudden jangling noise that must have seemed like an explosion within the stillness of the house. It was Carter, wanting to know how the situation looked.

"Bad, very bad," Ossian said. Carter needed to come out right away.

There was a moment of silence. "I could come out," Carter finally said. "But perhaps I would be better able to help on the outside."

Ossian couldn't believe what he was hearing. Carter had told him to buy this house. He'd assured him that he'd be safe, that if worse came to worst, he could face down the mob. Be brave, Carter had said. Coward. Coward. Coward. "If you can't come," Ossian snapped, "you can't do anything." Then he slammed down the receiver.[46]

They would have to do their best. Ossian brought the men upstairs—Mack and Murray, too—threw open the linen closet, and distributed the guns. Standing in the narrow hall, they settled on a plan. They'd establish a watch, sitting at the upstairs widow, lights out, weapons drawn, scanning the street below. That way, they'd be ready when the crowd turned on them.

Evening turned to night. Hour after hour they waited, watching the people come and go, staring at the men who passed in and out of the corner market, which never seemed to close. Some of them smoked to calm their nerves, stubbing out their cigars on the hardwood floors that Gladys had planned to cover with tasteful rugs. Once, just before midnight, a group of men darted out between the two houses on the other side of Garland and threw a few stones at the bungalow. Ossian and his friends stiffened, thinking the moment had come. But the stones bounced harmlessly off the roof, the whites faded into the darkness, and the stillness returned.[47]

Fatigue gradually set in. While others kept watch, Ossian rested for a while in the small bedroom on the north side of the house; Davis stretched out on a mattress they laid in the living room. But even then, they didn't let down their guard. Someone hid a handgun under a radiator in the living room, in case an intruder somehow managed to get through the defenses. The women catnapped on the lone bed during Gladys's first night in the bedroom she dreamed of sharing with her husband. No one really slept. Every noise from the street, every creaking floorboard, every unexpected sound in an unfamiliar house, made them jump. So scared she couldn't lie still, Gladys silently slipped out of bed around four o'clock and wandered through the silent house. She glanced out the window to the street below. Except for the policemen still standing on the corner, it was empty, the crowd gone at last.[48] The Sweets and their friends began September 9 exhausted but unscathed.

•

It was a brilliantly sunny summer morning, without even a hint of autumn about it. After a hurried breakfast, Gladys's friends, Murray the handyman, Otis, and Davis left to start their days. Henry and Latting agreed to keep watch while Joe Mack took Ossian and Gladys on a round of errands. It was wonderful to be out, doing ordinary things, enjoying each other's company. At Lieberman's furniture store, the Sweets bought a dining-room set and several armchairs for the living room— all in mission oak, the perfect complement to the bungalow's arts and crafts style—and two bedroom sets for the boarders' rooms, for a grand total of twelve hundred dollars. From there, Mack drove them over to Gladys's parents so they could spend some time with Iva. Gladys stayed to do some shopping for the night's dinner, while Ossian headed down to his office in Black Bottom to put in an afternoon's work.[49]

As hard as he tried, though, Ossian couldn't stop thinking about the night ahead. Perry and Carter were lost to the cause. Otis and Davis were sure to return, but everyone was going to be so tired, he wasn't sure they could handle the pressure once more. Ossian was already feeling the panic creeping back, and he wasn't even home yet.[50]

He was still turning the situation over and over in his mind when the telephone call came. As part of his practice, Ossian conducted medical exams for the black-owned Liberty Life Insurance Company. When Ossian bought the bungalow, he had one of the company's agents, Hewitt Watson, write up a ten-thousand-dollar policy on the property. An error had been made—something to do with Ossian's birthday—and the home office in Chicago had sent the policy back. Watson was calling to see if he could stop by the doctor's office to make the necessary corrections.

Ossian barely knew the man. But he couldn't help himself. He poured out his troubles, pleading with Watson to come out to the house that evening and bring some friends with him. Maybe the insurance man was moved by Ossian's obvious distress. Maybe he thought of his own neighborhood, where he was the only colored man. Whatever his reasoning, Watson promised to help. They agreed to meet at three o'clock, after the insurance man had some time to talk to his colleagues.[51]

Right on time, Watson drove up to Ossian's office in his dilapidated Ford. With him were two fellow insurance agents, Leonard Morse and Charles Washington. Ossian had a nodding acquaintance with Washington, a fellow Howard alumnus with a wiry build and somnolent eyes. Morse was a stranger. Tall, broad shouldered, and handsome, dressed in a mismatched suit jacket and pants, he spoke in the salesmen's rapid-fire patter, his voice grating, his grammar hopelessly mangled. The trio had discussed Sweet's dilemma, Watson said, and they all agreed to join the defense that night. Ossian probably should have been concerned that three men he barely knew were volunteering to take up arms on his behalf. But in his desperation, the thought never crossed his mind.[52]

The doctor headed home around four o'clock, sitting silently in the Buick while Joe Mack wove his way eastward from St. Aubin to Garland. The traffic was heavy. Downtown businessmen were already beginning their commute to the far reaches of the city; factory workers were packed onto the streetcars, their faces darkened with the day's dirt, their shirts streaked with sweat. The streets that Ossian drove through bore an unmistakable sense of decay. Aged houses sat forlornly

along the curbside, sagging in the sun, decrepit and poorly maintained.[53]

Mack had been driving twenty, maybe twenty-five minutes, before
he swung the car onto Garland and headed up the long blocks to
Charlevoix. Ossian could still hear the rumble of cars and the clang of
the streetcar as the chauffeur approached the corner where the bungalow stood, but Garland was almost deserted. A handful of cars were
parked along the curb. A few men and women were sitting on their
porches; a few kids played listlessly on their lawns. As the Buick
reached Charlevoix, Ossian noted the two police officers standing on
the corner, just as they had been when he and Gladys had left that
morning. Mack pulled the car around the corner, down the alley, and
into the garage, away from the sun and the neighbors' view.[54]

Inside the bungalow, Ossian found Gladys standing by the sink, the
makings of dinner spread on the counter around her. Something was
wrong; Ossian could see it in her face. Before he even had a chance to
ask, she blurted out that Edna Butler had just phoned. Riding the
streetcar home that morning, Butler had overheard the conductor ask
a white woman about the previous night's disturbance on Garland.
"Some 'niggers' have moved in and we're going to get rid of them," the
white woman had said. "They stayed there last night but they will be
put out tonight."[55]

The information staggered Ossian.[56] He knew Garland was empty;
he just seen it himself. But it didn't matter. The house had to be made
secure. He had to protect his family from what he knew was possible.

Since the shades had been drawn all day, the house was almost
completely in shadows. But the foyer was brightly lit and the front
door wide open. When Ossian rushed to close it, he found Henry and
John Latting sitting on the front-porch swing, smoking cigars, the
newspaper spread in front of them. Henry had his own story to tell,
just as terrifying as Gladys's had been. Earlier in the day, one of the patrolmen had come by with a warning. The neighborhood toughs had
met in the corner market last night to plan their attack. "The crowd is
coming back tonight double force," the policeman had said. "You better be on your guard." Henry, proud and determined, had refused to be
intimidated. Just a while ago, in fact, he'd walked straight into the
store himself to buy some cigars. Now he and Latting were just going
to sit and read awhile.[57]

Ossian wouldn't stand for it. "Turn to your own business and don't
bother" anyone, he told Henry and Latting. Don't "be walking out on

the porch . . . so that people would think you're looking for trouble." They were to get out of sight immediately, go into the kitchen, and give Gladys a hand with dinner. Ossian followed them inside, then bolted the front door shut.[58]

His heart was pounding, his pulse racing. Five o'clock. He had a few hours of daylight left, a few hours before—

Ossian turned to Mack. Go down to Black Bottom and get Norris Murray, he said; tell him I'll pay him five dollars if he'll come out to the house tonight. It was a gamble to send the chauffeur away, to reduce their numbers by one. The mob might not wait for nightfall. But Ossian had to take the risk; he had to have more people alongside him. Mack slipped out the back door and was gone.[59]

Suddenly, he was alone. Ossian could hear Gladys and Henry chatting in the kitchen. But he was alone. He walked into the dining room, took a seat at the card table they were using for their meals, and waited.[60]

◆

In some ways, Henry was a better match for Gladys than Ossian. They were about the same age: she was just twenty-three, he twenty-one. And they both had a charm that Ossian simply could never claim. Although he sometimes imagined himself a gregarious man, others found him a bit too aloof, a trifle distant. He attempted to be open and friendly, but it seemed he could never remember people's names correctly. Some said he was formal; others used the word "arrogant." Ossian seemed to expect deference; he was quick to point out the shortcomings of others; he was prone to lecture even casual acquaintances. Dr. Sweet demanded people's respect but didn't easily win their love.[61]

Gladys certainly had some of Ossian's forcefulness. Deep down, she was stronger, tougher, and more confident than he was, but she was better able to blunt her sharp edges. Next to her husband, she seemed slight, a wisp of a woman, with a long, thin face that lit up when she smiled her toothy grin. She wasn't beautiful, at least in a conventional way, but her carefully honed social graces drew people to her. Gladys could chat with acquaintances about books and the theater; she knew how to entertain gracefully; although she was shy, she made friends easily. To all appearances, she was the dutiful wife, standing demurely behind her husband, following his lead. In private, though, she exercised a powerful influence over her family. Ossian considered her his prize, and he desperately wanted to please her. Gladys, in turn, expected to be her husband's confidante and partner. Not once had she considered staying away from the bungalow the first few nights; however great the risks, she would share them with Ossian.[62]

For his part, Henry worshipped Ossian. Nine years younger than his brother, he was only five when Ossian had left home, too young to truly remember sharing their parents' house, young enough to grow up hearing of his eldest brother's triumphs. As soon as he could, he set out to follow the path Ossian had set for him. At Wilberforce University, Ossian's alma mater, he began to train for the life of a professional man, having his hair cut like Ossian's, growing a mustache, even duplicating his brother's glasses. The resemblance was so great that the two could have been mistaken for twins, if Henry only had the fullness, the maturity that so clearly marked Ossian as his senior. But Henry still had the boyish playfulness of a little brother, the exuberance that led him to join every campus club he could, the naïveté that made him take a policeman's warning lightly.[63]

Ossian knew better. Sitting in the heat of the dining room, listening to the idle chatter and the clatter of pots, he knew that they were all in great danger. Tonight, the mob was going to have direction; someone was going to prod them into action, tell them what to do and when to do it. When that moment came, the patrolmen weren't going to be able to stop them, even if they had the courage to try. Only Ossian, his friends, and a trio of men he barely knew were going to prevent the destruction of his home, his life. The day was melting away, nightfall creeping closer. Time was running out. And Ossian was alone, as he felt he always had been.

Then relief arrived in a rush. The back door slammed and Mack walked in with Norris Murray. A short time later—around six o'clock—two of the insurance men, Washington and Watson, pulled into the garage. Leonard Morse wasn't with them; he hadn't been at the pickup spot, so they'd headed over without him. But a few minutes later, Morse surprised them all by sauntering into the house on his own. He'd been delayed by an appointment, he said. So he caught the streetcar out to Garland. It was almost too good to be true.[64] There was still an hour of sun left in the sky. The mob must not have taken over the streets if Morse could hop off the streetcar without any trouble. Only Otis and Davis were missing. But Otis wouldn't let his brother down; Ossian was absolutely sure of that. It was just like Little Doc to be late.

Ossian tried to be businesslike, walking the three insurance men through the house, showing them the upstairs closet where the guns were hidden and the various places established as defensive positions the night before. But he could see that they were jumpy. They needed some distraction, a bit of entertainment. Dinner wasn't ready, though the aroma of baked ham and sweet potatoes was filling the downstairs. So he suggested they play a few hands of whist while Gladys, Henry, and Latting finished cooking.

Morse, Mack, and Washington drew chairs up to the dining room table, while Watson stayed in the living room, trying to read a magazine by the slant of light the drawn shade allowed into the room. Everyone was on edge. Ossian kept getting up from the table and wandering around the house, checking to be sure that the doors were locked, walking to the upstairs closet where the guns were stored. After a while, Mack left the game, saying he wanted to take a bath upstairs before dinner. Murray sat in for a few hands, then he, too, headed up the stairs to check in on Mack, his only friend in the house. The clock inched toward eight.[65]

Suddenly, something slammed against the roof of the house. Henry dashed from the kitchen to the living room windows. "My God!" he shouted, "Look at the people!"[66]

Ossian rushed to the leaded-glass windows that overlooked Charlevoix. Everything looked just as it had the night before. The cops were out on the corner, keeping the sidewalk in front of the bungalow clear. And behind them, in front of the opposing houses and around the school yard, half masked in the dusk, were hundreds of white people, the same white people who'd been out on the street the previous evening. The same, Ossian knew, yet frighteningly different. Somewhere out there, standing among the women and children, lounging on the porches, lurking in the alleys, were the men who would incite the crowd to violence.[67]

All the colored men were up and moving now, though no one had any particular direction in mind. Ossian ran to the side door that led onto Charlevoix for one last check of the lock. He heard someone—in the confusion he couldn't say precisely who—saying, "Go around to the front. We're going to the back and raise some hell." He spun to the kitchen behind him, desperate to see if Gladys were safe. She was standing over a bowl of cake batter, the night's dessert; the ham sat in a pan on the stove top, ready for carving. Brushing past her, he tested the backdoor lock, then pounded up the stairs to the hallway and the guns.[68]

Henry, Latting, Mack, Murray, and the insurance men were all upstairs before him, ducking in and out of the bedrooms. Most of them had already grabbed weapons. Ossian opened the closet door but the hallway was so dim that the dark metal of the guns was indistinguishable in the shadows. Groping around on the upper shelf, he finally pulled out a pistol, then rummaged through the satchel for a fistful of ammunition. Only when he tried to pick out the appropriate shells did Ossian, a man so habitually in control of his emotions, realize how badly his hands were shaking.[69]

Hoping to camouflage his panic and quiet his unsteady nerves, he shoved the remaining bullets into his pocket and slipped into the front bedroom. Rather than resume the watch, he took a seat on the bed, slid off his shoes so as not to scuff the comforter, and lay down in the darkness, the pistol at his side. For the longest time, ten, fifteen, twenty minutes, he didn't move, the sound of his breathing slowly soothing him. Gladys silently entered the room—their room—and for a few moments the two of them talked, their voices hushed. But for the most part he was alone, inside himself. Occasionally, he stole a glance at the street below, peering between the drawn shade and the windowsill to see a considerable crowd of white people standing on the other side of Garland. In the stillness of the darkened room, they were just a distant hum of voices. Ossian could feel himself gradually regaining control.[70]

Then suddenly the window above him shattered. A rock thudded to the floor near the bed while shards of glass skittered across the room. Almost simultaneously, Ossian heard a voice from another room shout, "There's someone coming!"

A taxi had pulled up to the curb in front of the house. "That's your brother," someone else yelled.[71]

Ossian's first thought was of Gladys. The attack was starting; she was in danger. Rushing toward the stairs, he elbowed his way though the pandemonium in the hallway. The men were racing every which way, trying to take up the positions they'd staked out. He thought he saw Henry, Winchester in hand, heading for the front bedroom. There was a quick rush of fresh air: someone had opened the door at the back of the hall and gone out to the airing porch that overlooked the yard. Ossian thundered down the stairs. At the foot of the stairs, he found Gladys, who had been drawn there by the sound of breaking glass. Someone was pounding on the front door. Otis. The door was locked. Otis was trapped outside. Ossian raced through the living room, pulled open the French door that led into the vestibule, unbolted the front door, and threw it open.[72]

And there it was, the scene he'd dreaded all his life, the moment when he stood facing a sea of white faces made grotesque by unreasoned, unrestrained hate—for his race, for his people, for him. Garland was a swirl of light and noise and motion, a blur of bodies moving this way and that, white shirts and summer dresses made stark by a background of darkened houses, the pale skin of the people eerie under the streetlights. Otis and William Davis were standing right in front of Ossian on the porch, terror-struck. The people on the other side of the street were screaming, "Here's niggers!" "There they go!" "Get them! Get them!" Stones were raining down from across the street, smashing into the lawn, crashing onto the painted wooden floor of the porch, and skittering under the swing where Henry and Latting had been sitting a few hours before.[73]

As soon as Otis and Davis stumbled inside, Ossian slammed the door behind them. Otis immediately ran to the phone, which sat in the alcove at the bottom of the stairs, so he could call a friend for help. Senseless with fear, Ossian stood alongside Gladys and Davis in the dining room as more rocks slammed off the roof and walls. "What shall I do?" he asked over and over again, "What shall I do?"

"Don't do anything," Davis replied. "Just take your time and give the police officers a chance." But as he spoke, Davis picked up a rifle that had been lying in the living room, and cradled it in his arms.[74]

A few minutes passed. Another second-story window shattered; the house was filled with the sound of splintering glass hitting the floor upstairs. Then came the deafening roar of gunshots from the bedrooms above, a moment's pause, and another volley, as fierce as the first. Ossian stood stunned, deafened by the report of the guns ringing off the bare walls, the acrid smell of gunpowder beginning to drift down the stairs.[75]

◆

Eric Houghberg was almost done shaving when the landlady's little boy burst in, breathless with excitement. "Eric, come on out," he said, "some guys throwing, small kids—throwing bricks and stones."

Stoning the coloreds' house; Houghberg had to see that. Before the boy could say another word, he bolted down the stairs and onto the porch of his flat, almost straight across from the bungalow. Some of the other renters were out there already: Mr. and Mrs. Dove and their baby; a few others he didn't know. Houghberg started down the steps to the lawn, where the crowd was thicker. Then the shooting started, a single ferocious blast from across the street.[76]

That was gunfire. The coloreds were firing into the street.

Up on the porch, Mrs. Dove was yelling hysterically, her husband scooping up his suddenly squalling baby and scrambling for the door. Some of the folks on the lawn were looking wildly about, as if they couldn't tell where the noise had come from; others were ducking low, falling to their knees, racing for cover. Houghberg didn't even flinch. He just kept going, down off the porch and into the crowd. Why he walked up to the man with the pipe—Breiner, the foreman who lived down the street—he couldn't say. Houghberg just wanted to find out what was happening, do a little commiserating, a touch of socializing. Without a thought, he pulled a cigarette out of his pocket.

Breiner said something about the Negroes shooting. "It is awful they should do that," that's what he said, barely enough to fill the silence before the colored men opened fire again, another vicious volley just like the first.[77]

Breiner screamed—a scream of shock and searing pain—as a bullet ripped into his lower back, clipped off the pelvic bone, and exploded out his belly. For a split second, Houghberg simply stared as Breiner bit down hard on his pipe, as if he were trying to suppress another cry, the way a man should. Then Houghberg felt the burn in his own leg, just above the knee; when he reached down to touch it, he felt blood soaking through his pants.[78]

His instincts told him to run. Houghberg stumbled back from the lawn, down the narrow passageway between his house and the one to the north toward the safety of the alley. But the pain was too great. Before he could reach the rear of the house, his legs buckled and he collapsed in a heap onto the dark, cooling cement.[79]

◆

Inspector Norton Schuknecht couldn't believe it. One second, he was chatting with his brother-in-law, Otto Lemhagen, and Lieutenant Schellenberger, standing on the corner in front of the schoolhouse shooting the breeze, not paying any attention at all to what was going on in front of the Negroes' house. The next thing he knew, guns were blazing from the upstairs windows. The shock of it almost took him off his feet.

Instantly, Schuknecht knew that this was big trouble. The department had a dozen patrolmen out here, but if the situation exploded—if the Negroes kept shooting, if the whites charged the house—twelve cops weren't going to be able to handle it. Someone was going to get hurt, one of his own men, maybe. Call for reserves, he yelled to the lieutenant. Then Schuknecht started across the intersection to the bungalow.

It was hard going. The inspector was a bear of a man—the brass buttons on his uniform pulled and strained across his stomach—and he lumbered more than ran. To make matters worse, he had to force his way through the melee in the intersection, people moving in every direction, pushing and shoving, shouting, cursing, calling for spouses or children. Pandemonium. That's what it was.

By the time he reached the doctor's front porch, Schuknecht was already out of breath. But his adrenalin was pumping and his temper was flaring. The house was pitch-dark. If the Negroes hadn't started shooting, it would have been easy enough to imagine that there was no one inside at all.

Schuknecht punched the doorbell.[80]

•

Ossian was so distraught, so scared, so dazed, he didn't know what to do. He heard Davis screaming at him, "For Christ sake, tell them to cut that damn shooting out there," and he tried to do as he was told, shouting up the stairs, "Keep quiet up there!" When the doorbell rang, Ossian reacted as if a guest had arrived. He stepped to the door, Davis right behind him, and called out, "Who is it?"[81]

"The police," a voice replied. Ossian knew about Alexander Turner's mistake, opening his door to men who claimed to be city officials. Still, he didn't hesitate. A policeman, red faced with rage, stepped into the vestibule. He was an older man, considerably overweight and panting for air. "Jesus Christ," he demanded. "What in hell are you fellows shooting about?"

"Why, they're ruining my property," Ossian said, his first rational sentence since the shooting began.

"What have they done? I have been here right along. I haven't seen anyone throw anything and I haven't seen no disorder. I don't know why you men are shooting."

Ossian was stunned. Hadn't the officer seen? Where was Inspector McPherson? When he'd come by yesterday, he said he would protect the house. Couldn't he speak to McPherson?

"Doctor," the cop interrupted, "I was in charge last night and I am also in charge tonight. We have got men around your house, we got them in the alley, we got them on the side, and we got them on the front."

Ossian didn't argue. He didn't say that the police out front hadn't lifted a finger to protect his house and his family from the mob, that they'd been left to face the terror alone. "There will be no more shoot-ing," he promised. That was enough. Nodding his satisfaction, the po-liceman walked out of the house.[82]

•

Leon Breiner lay at the foot of the steps leading up to the Doves' porch, a widening pool of blood seeping onto the brown lawn beneath him. A flashlight beam split through the shadows as a couple of cops pushed their way through the knot of people gathered around. More shouts came from down the passageway where Houghberg had collapsed: an-other man down.[83]

Already the crowd on Garland was changing. The terrified were clearing away, racing back to their homes, dashing down the alleys. As fast as they left, newcomers took their place, pulled out of their flats by the noise and excitement. If anything, the mob was growing larger, an-grier, more volatile. Not fifteen feet from where Breiner lay, twenty or thirty men stood facing the bungalow, some of them dancing with the jittery energy of prizefighters, trying to build up the courage to rush the doctor's house. All it would take was one of them to stride into the street, to breach the invisible barrier the police had created. Once that happened, they'd all start moving, not just the gang of twenty or thirty but all the thugs and hoods and closet Klansmen the crowd concealed.[84]

As soon as he stepped out of the house, Schuknecht could see that the situation was spiraling out of control. Still, it was a blow when one of his patrolmen sprinted up to him with the news: two men shot. One was wounded, hit in the leg. The other one, over there on the lawn, looked to be dead.

Sweet Jesus. The Negroes had murdered somebody. And they'd done it on his goddamn watch. The inspector quickly ran through his options. The Negroes were going to have to be brought downtown and booked; that was a sure thing. But he couldn't bring them out of the house now, not unless he wanted to see them ripped limb from limb. Better to keep the mob at bay until reinforcements arrived.

Schuknecht barked out a few commands. Set up a perimeter around the house. No one gets past. We'll take care of the coloreds when we can.[85]

It shouldn't have worked. So many people were pouring into the street that the intersection was almost impassable. The more the crowd pushed and jostled and jeered, the darker the mood became. Someone spotted three colored men trapped in traffic at Charlevoix and St. Clair

Avenue, a block east of the bungalow. "There goes some niggers now," came the cries. "Lynch them! Kill them!" A gang of white men surged toward the car, the quickest of them leaping onto the running board and swinging wildly at the trio inside. As the others closed in, the driver slammed his foot on the gas and swung into oncoming traffic, flinging his assailant to the pavement as he sped to safety. When a colored couple drove into the neighborhood a few minutes later, the mob moved more quickly, swarming over the car, smashing its windows, clawing off its cloth top, and pummeling the husband as he sat at the wheel. Only his wife's begging for mercy saved them.[86]

For all its fury, though, the mob stayed back from the bungalow. Once Schuknecht's men had established their ragged line around the Sweets' house, no one had the guts to test their resolve. The crowd kept growing larger, seeping farther and farther into the neighborhood. But the police perimeter held firm—a half-dozen cops standing along the sidewalk trying to keep their knees from shaking too badly, and they didn't break.[87]

Though it seemed much longer, no more than five minutes had passed when the reserve flyer eased its way through the mob with a truckload of reinforcements. While the patrolmen scrambled down from the flatbed, Schuknecht grabbed hold of their sergeant. Put together a squad and follow me, he said. We're going back in to get the Negroes.[88]

◆

Ossian must have known that something was wrong. He had to have heard the furor outside the house, the screams and shouts, the squeal of car tires, the wail of police sirens. But in the darkness of the living room, the terror was dissipating, the paralyzing fear of the previous few minutes loosening its grip. Davis had set down the rifle he'd been holding; Otis had given up trying to phone his friend and was standing beside his brother; someone was heading downstairs. Maybe Edward Carter had been right; maybe whites will back down when colored men show they won't be moved. When the doorbell rang again, Ossian stood by and let Gladys answer it.[89]

The cops burst in. No conversation. No accusations. They just shoved past Gladys and into the living room. One of them snapped on the lights—the first light in the house all day—and pulled up the shades. Ossian must have been momentarily blinded, stunned by the burst of brilliance and the flash of movement.

Gradually, the room came back into focus. There were cops every-where, waving revolvers, shouting commands, demanding that Ossian, Gladys, Davis, and Otis move into the dining room, wanting to know how many other Negroes were in the house, searching around for the staircase, which was tucked away behind the dining room. So many voices, so much activity. No time to argue. Follow orders. Just do what the policemen say.[90]

Boots pounded overhead as the cops moved through the bedrooms rounding up the others. One by one they appeared: Washington and Mack first, then Henry and Latting, Watson, Morse, and Murray, fol-lowed by patrolmen carrying the cache of weapons Ossian had carefully assembled. With every new addition, the dining room grew tighter, smaller, more stifling. The cops patted them all down, searching for more guns. Then they wrenched Ossian's arm to one side, and he felt cold steel snap over his wrist. He was being handcuffed to Davis, the two men bound together like prisoners on the chain gangs that haunted the roads outside his hometown.[91]

The inspector was talking now, the fat one who'd come inside a few minutes before. Something about two white men shot. Killed. Mur-dered. All of them would have to go down to headquarters. It took Ossian a moment to realize what the inspector was saying. He was go-ing to take them outside. Out to the mob.

In that instant, Ossian became a boy again. Not himself. That other boy, his hands bound, his head bowed, spending his last moments sur-rounded by his murderers, wailing, wailing, wailing, as the fire started to crackle.

He began to plead. Bring down the shades; we're on display for everyone to see. Don't take us out the front. They're waiting out there. The alley. Take us out that way. Please God, take us out the alley.[92]

Mack the chauffeur stepped forward. He'd spotted someone he knew standing in the living room, a rail-thin white man dressed in street clothes, his long, narrow face and blond hair blanched by the bright lights. He had to be a cop; every white man in the house was a cop. They talked in quick, hushed tones.[93]

When the conversation ended, the white man walked over to Ossian. He was a lieutenant with the Black Hand Squad, he said, working for Inspector McPherson. And he was here to see to the Negroes' safety. There was a kindness about him that Ossian couldn't have expected. The lieutenant drew the shades again and ordered Ossian's handcuffs removed; the doctor wasn't a threat, he said. Then he sent a patrolman outside to wait for the paddy wagon and send it around back. He'd take the men out first. Gladys would follow when the situation had cooled.[94]

It must have been the most terrifying step Ossian had ever taken, the first step out the back door into the yard. Otis, Henry, and the rest moved in a long single line, patrolmen on either side, the lieutenant in the lead. In the clear night air, the noise on the street was even more intense, more immediate, than it had been inside the bungalow. A wooden fence separated Ossian and the others from the crowd on Charlevoix, so no one knew they were there, moving silently across the grass that Gladys had hoped to turn into a garden. The plainclothesmen led them through the garage, where Ossian's Buick and the insurance men's old Ford were nestled, and into the alley.

Face-to-face with the mob.

The paddy wagon had been backed far enough into the alley so that its back doors were within a few feet of the Sweets' garage. That left the wagon's hood across the sidewalk along Charlevoix. Just to the front of that, all along the street, was a wall of frenzied whites, waiting for the moment when the coloreds appeared. A second passed before the mob realized that the suspects were within reach, a heartbeat before the charge began.[95]

The lieutenant knew exactly what he was doing. He had his gun raised above his head so that the front row of whites could see it, and he was moving straight toward the mob. If anyone makes a move to crash in, he shouted, I'll shoot to kill. The whites seemed to stop— straining to hear, waiting for someone else to act, too intimidated to move.[96]

That was all the time they needed. The patrolmen shoved Ossian and the others into the back of the wagon, slammed shut the metal doors, and slapped the side of the truck to get it moving. Ever so slowly the driver edged the vehicle forward, testing to see how far he could go before the mob stopped him, a few inches, a foot, closer to the cut in the curb and the crowd in the street. One person, then another and another, stepped back, parting to let him pass.[97] The paddy wagon pulled into the street, away from the bungalow and into the sweltering summer night.

TWO

AIN'T NO SLAVERY NO MORE

Ossian Sweet sat shoulder to shoulder and knee to knee with his brothers and the other men as the paddy wagon rumbled toward police headquarters. When the patrolmen had padlocked the door behind him, Ossian must have been relieved. Although the mob's screams pierced the wagon's steel walls, the crowd couldn't touch him, couldn't drag him down Garland Avenue to the school yard, couldn't lynch him from the streetlight that brightened the intersection in front of his new home. In the darkness of the wagon, he was safe.

Yet, as the tumult on Garland trailed away, Ossian's momentary confidence collapsed. It was so claustrophobic inside the steel cage that he could barely breathe. The others were straining, too, more than he was, since their hands were still cuffed behind them while his were free. Every time the paddy wagon lurched over a streetcar track or a sewer grate, they all heard the jingling of the bullets Ossian had jammed in his pockets, damning evidence of his intent to do bodily harm. That's what the cops at headquarters would be looking for: something they could use to build a case against Ossian and his compatriots, to turn them from the mob's intended victims into crazed colored men, criminals, murderers.[1] He would have to make them understand; that's all there was to it. When the police started to question him, he would have to give them a clear and cogent explanation as to why he'd moved into a neighborhood where he wasn't welcome, why he'd filled the house with guns, why he'd been prepared to use them.

But Ossian didn't have a coherent story to tell. He had the shards of his family's history: the legacy of a half-remembered moment when the world was full of promise; the dreams his mother had sustained during the bitter descent into segregation; the weight of his name, the meaning of which he barely knew. And he had his own memories, trailing backward from Garland Avenue to the Jim Crow South, backward to the dusty streets of his boyhood home, to the tidy kitchen of the house his father built, to the tiny school where the black children learned their lessons, to the riot of trees and tropical plants tumbling down the banks of the Peace River, to the smell of burning flesh wafting across the placid water, filling his imagination with the most grotesque of horrors.

◆

Ossian knew his grandfather, Remus DeVaughn, as a wizened old man, bent and bowed, but when Remus was young, he had been at the center of a revolution. In those days, Remus and his brothers—George, Harrison, Hubbert, Edmond, Romulus, and Amos—were poor men, their hands thick with calluses from years of driving hoes into the red clay of other men's land. They had no homes of their own; their landlord supplied the rude log cabins where they raised their families. They had no education; when their children practiced their letters on their slates, their fathers couldn't help them.[2] But it wasn't the desperation of poverty that made the DeVaughns revolutionaries. It was hope.

The brothers had been born to bondage. In the early 1800s, most southern whites were subsistence farmers, tilling their own fields, growing their own food, making their own clothes. Their owner, Alexander Cromartie, was different. A slave owner's son born and raised on a prosperous plantation in the gently rolling hills of North Carolina, Alexander could have stayed home, waiting to inherit his share of his father's estate. But in the 1820s, young men like Alexander weren't settling for what their parents could give them. A man could better his fortune—if only he worked hard and took some chances—and Alexander wasn't afraid to take chances. Packing up his family, he headed to Leon County, Florida, just south of the Georgia border. Among his household goods was a black boy, Edmond DeVaughn, Ossian Sweet's great-grandfather and the father of Remus and his brothers.[3]

Since the last years of the eighteenth century, southern planters had been making themselves rich by selling cotton to the textile mills of industrial England. But these planters had already taken the best cotton land along the eastern seaboard. So ambitious young men like Alexander pushed deeper and deeper into the southern interior in search of new land to cultivate. They found the perfect conditions in the rich red loam that ran through southern Georgia, Alabama, and Mississippi and the northern reaches of Florida. Alexander grabbed his share, buying thirteen hundred acres of prime cotton land on the banks of Florida's Lake Iamonia in newly settled Leon County, fifteen miles north of the territorial capital of Tallahassee.[4]

It was a raw land, its red hills thick with forests, its roads rudimentary, its few settlements spartan. Tallahassee is "a grotesque place," sniffed the visiting Ralph Waldo Emerson, "rapidly settled by public officers, land speculators, and desperados." Small-time farmers here might work the fields themselves, but major planters needed slaves, as many as they could afford: there were twice as many slaves as whites in Leon County by 1840, three times as many by 1860. Keeping with the tradition of American slavery, bondmen had no rights, no legal or social standing. But Florida's lawmakers went further than other states: slaves couldn't leave their plantations, even for a walk, without the written permission of their owners. They couldn't trade goods among themselves or learn to read or gather for prayer meetings. If they committed crimes, their hands were burned by heated irons, their ears nailed to posts, their backs stripped raw by the lash.[5]

Badly outnumbered by their slaves, Leon County planters lived in fear of revolt. Sometimes violence burst to the surface. One evening, a planter dragged a slave into the yard for a flogging. Before the planter could begin, the slave grabbed an axe and split his master's skull. But the ferocity of the law undercut more organized rebellion. So slaves sought other ways out of bondage. Leon County planters were continually searching for escaped slaves who had fled to the swamps south of the cotton belt, where it was difficult for slave hunters to track them. Fugitives would find refuge in the scattered camps of the Seminoles. A few would strike out for the North, so very far away. Alexander's kinsman, Cornelius DeVane, followed him to Leon County in the early 1830s. Shortly after he arrived, a slave couple he owned, Loveless and Pink, stole his shotgun, gathered up their three children, the youngest just five months old, and headed into Georgia, there to begin the long, dangerous journey to the Ohio River and freedom.[6]

Alexander's young slave Edmond may well have dreamed about following their example. But nothing indicates that he ever acted on those hopes. Edmond passed into adulthood working the Cromarties' land, helping to strip the Florida hills of pine, to divide the acreage into fields the slaves filled with row after row of cotton, to make his master and his young wife a comfortable home appropriate to their station. By 1860, Alexander was one of the wealthier planters in Leon County, master of fifty-five slaves, a southern gentleman through and through.[7]

When he came of age, Edmond took a wife, a young slave woman named Gilla, and together they began to build a family. Between 1840 and 1852, the couple had seven sons, beginning with George in 1840 and ending with Amos in 1852. But the tiny, beautiful infants were never completely Edmond and Gilla's children. From the moment they entered the world, the boys became Alexander Cromartie's property, another asset on his ledger sheets, another measure of his success. And when they had children of their own, their bondage would be passed on once again, parent to child, generation to generation, forever and ever.[8]

Or so Cromartie and his fellow slave owners hoped. As the DeVaughn brothers passed through childhood, though, the institution of slavery was plunged into crisis. During the nation's first half century, America's political leaders did their best to keep the slavery question out of public debate. In the 1840s and 1850s, the issue exploded. Edmond and Gilla's fifth and sixth sons, twins Romulus and Remus, were six years old when southern slaveholders pushed Congress to open Kansas to slavery, an act that convinced antislavery forces to organize a new political party, the Republicans, as a counterweight to the slave power. The twins were eight years old when the advocates and opponents of slavery plunged Kansas into guerilla warfare, eleven when the United States Supreme Court affirmed the sanctity of slavery with the *Dred Scott* decision, twelve when the Republicans elected their candidate, Abraham Lincoln, president of the United States. The election became the breaking point. In the months leading up to Lincoln's inauguration, the southern states seceded from the Union and the nation descended into civil war.[9]

Alexander Cromartie dutifully sent his first-born son and namesake to fight for the planters' right to keep human beings in bondage. While young Alexander risked his life, his father did his best to maintain plantation life as it had always been. His rule lasted longer than did most planters'. As northern troops pushed farther and farther into the South, thousands of the enslaved fled their masters for the Union lines, there to claim freedom for themselves. Leon County was far from the main lines of battle so it wasn't until the Confederacy began to crumble in 1864 and early 1865 that the county's slave regime collapsed. Slaves started to talk back to their masters; some refused to work as ordered; many disappeared altogether, fleeing into the woods or slipping away quietly to meet the federal troops at last making their way toward the Florida state line.[10]

The Union Army finally took Tallahassee on May 10, 1865, a full month after Robert E. Lee's surrender at Appomattox courthouse. Word had passed through the plantations that when the slaves heard a gunshot, they were free. The shot came at midday, when they were in the fields. They dropped their plows and hoes where they stood, returned to their cabins to dress in their Sunday best, then joined the flood of black men, women, and children on the road to Tallahassee, hurrying, a participant said, "to go see the Yankees."[11]

◆

Edmond never saw slavery's end. He passed away in 1857, four years before the Civil War began. So Gilla brought her boys into adulthood on her own. When emancipation arrived that day in May, the DeVaughn brothers were young men in their teens and twenties, the perfect age to find their way in a new world of freedom. But freedom had no shape, no substance, in the spring of 1865. Negroes could work for wages but they had no jobs. They could learn to read and write but they had no schools. They could leave their former masters and strike out for themselves but they had no homes, no land of their own. They could plead for government assistance in their time of need. But they had no political power—no vote, no elected representatives—to assure that their voices would be heard.[12]

Across Leon County, former slaves tried to shape freedom for themselves. The vast majority of freedmen were farmers, and they knew they could provide for their families if only they had a few acres of their own. They dreamed of land, not row upon row of cotton, just enough to cultivate some crops. Freedmen also desperately wanted to school their children: free people needed to read and write if they were to manage their own affairs. But it was more than that. Everything their masters had denied them—schooling, family, property, freedom of movement—Negroes were now determined to claim for themselves, whatever the consequences. The mistress of a great Leon County plantation ordered a former house slave, her daughter's "dear black mammy," not to attend a political rally in Tallahassee, but the freedwoman said she would do as she pleased. The planter's wife was livid. "If you disobey me in this matter," she said, "you and your family must leave the place." By night-fall, the "dear black mammy" was gone.[13]

There is no knowing whether the DeVaughns likewise deserted the Cromartie plantation. It's possible that they stayed with their former master. Gilla might have had some distant memory of her North Carolina childhood, but any connection there had been severed long ago; Edmond was buried in Florida soil, and her boys knew no place other than Leon County. If they did leave the Cromarties, the DeVaughns didn't go far. Like most former slaves in the first days of freedom, they would have moved onto a neighboring plantation, close enough to the Cromarties to be familiar, far enough to be independent.[14]

For their part, the masters of Leon County were determined to make sure that the DeVaughns and their fellow freedmen went no further. A few months after Union troops occupied Tallahassee, the federal gov-ernment returned control of the state to the planters. Immediately, the former slaveholders passed a series of laws pushing blacks to the very edge of bondage. Freedmen were to sign year-long contracts to work the planters' fields; those who broke their agreements could be sold into service for a year's time; those convicted of even minor crimes against a planter's property—stealing his cotton or injuring his livestock—were to be whipped and pilloried. Once bound to the planters' land, Negroes were subject to the same casual cruelty their masters had always imposed.

But the planters overreached themselves. The federal government hadn't sacrificed the better part of a generation—360,000 soldiers dead—to assure the former slaveholders' continued domination over southern land and labor. Appalled by the planters' audacity, in 1866, the Republican Congress dissolved the southern state governments formed the previous year, put the entire region back under military control, and launched one of the most extraordinary experiments the nation had ever undertaken, its purposes masked by the bland name of Reconstruction.

The Republicans who controlled Washington pledged to remake the South root and branch. Congress would amend the Constitution to give freedmen all the rights that white Americans enjoyed, including the right to vote. What's more, Republicans would use the power of the federal government to give the South a glittering new economy, where every man, regardless of the color of his skin, could sell his labor in a free and open market. Congress would create opportunity by linking the South, devastated by four years of war, with the vibrant economy of the North. The federal government would encourage industry to build railroads so that southern farms and factories could ship their goods to the cities of the North. Congress would open public schools for southern children, white and black, and it would provide freedmen training in the rudiments of economic exchange—how to negotiate a labor contract, how to work for wages, how to sell crops for a profit—so they could compete for work on a free and fair footing.[15]

Knowing that planters would do all they could to resist such extraordinary changes, Congress dispatched thousands of federal agents across the South to implement Reconstruction programs. Most of these soldiers, teachers, and preachers were white, all aflame with the fire of the free-market gospel, but a precious few were colored. Many of the latter were men of the cloth, missionaries of the northern black churches. All the major black denominations sent ministers to the South in the late 1860s. But none of them was better suited to the Reconstruction project than the ministers of the African Methodist Episcopal (AME) Church.[16]

Methodists preached that even the most humble person could be reborn into God's grace, if only he or she rejected sin and embraced a life of holiness. Believers experienced rebirth in a moment of ecstasy triggered by the tumult of the vast camp meetings that preachers mounted. Once in the flock, the saved proved their virtue by following the strictest of moral codes. Methodists did not drink, swear, gamble, fornicate, or fight. They worked hard, paid their debts, dealt honestly with others. They taught their children to read, write, and do sums. Such discipline was the mark of grace. It was also the perfect match for the free market. "Religion must necessarily produce industry and frugality," Methodism's founder, John Wesley, proclaimed, "and these cannot but produce riches."[17]

In the early days, American Methodists spread the promise of deliverance through circuit riders who traveled the back roads, seeking converts among the poor and downtrodden, regardless of skin color. But like so many other institutions, the church foundered on the rock of racism. In the late 1700s and early 1800s, white congregants in a number of northern cities tried to segregate the free blacks in their midst. Rather than accept second-class salvation, Negroes walked out of the white churches and established their own denomination.[18]

AME preachers maintained the Methodist discipline, but they

enveloped it in a powerful racial consciousness. They would battle the evil of slavery, confront every manifestation of discrimination in the North, and prove to whites—by their thoughts and their deeds—that blacks deserved to be treated as equals. Indeed, they would do the whites one better: they would be more frugal, more hardworking, better educated than their white neighbors. By their accomplishments, they would force whites to acknowledge their equality. It was a heavy burden to bear. "If we are lazy and idle," explained the AME's founder, "the enemies of freedom plead it as a cause why we ought not to be free, and say we are better in a state of servitude."[19]

These AME circuit riders followed the Union troops into the South, determined to proclaim their message of racial uplift to the former slaves. Many freedmen were put off by the condescension and criticism the AME preachers leveled. They flocked instead to the Baptists, who were more willing to accept the freedmen as they were. But a significant minority joined the AME. The very sight of the ministers, forceful black men, brooking no opposition, demanding respect, must have been a draw, but the ministers' message—the wonder of God's word flowing into the promise of liberation—also riveted many to the church. Many more must have been attracted by the churchmen's temporal promises: the freedmen ought to buy land, the ministers preached; hard work and self-discipline would give them the means. Young people needed education if they were to seize the opportunities that would be opening up to them. The AME would build them schools.[20]

Elder Charles Pearce wound his way through the northern Florida cotton district in the spring of 1866. Bearded in the style of Lincoln, Pearce was a muscular man, physically and spiritually. Born and raised in freedom, almost twenty years an AME minister, Pearce was a lion of the church, a missionary zealot. Everywhere he went, he found the spirit of Jubilee drawing the freedmen to him and his church. Revivals burned long into the night: 116 new members in Tallahassee, 453 in neighboring Gadsden County, another 343 in Jefferson County. "It is only necessary for us to name the AME church to them, and they are willing to cast in their lot with us, and they are still coming by the score," Pearce wrote. "We are all looking forward to a glorious future." Religious fervor blended with political organizing. From the start, AME ministers were determined to carve out a role for themselves and their congregations in the Reconstruction government that would eventually replace military rule. Twenty-five hundred freedmen jammed a Leon County meeting ground in May 1867 to hear Pearce and other ministers denounce the evils of slavery and campaign for the Republican Party. Planters were stunned by the turnout, but the ministers were simply tapping into the political passions pulsing through black communities.[21]

The DeVaughn brothers were swept up in the AME's crusade. Gilla's oldest son, George, joined the ministry in 1867, at the age of twenty-seven, and was assigned to the Leon County mission; her third son, Hubbert, followed him a few years later. The family had no trouble adjusting to the discipline that racial uplift required. Gilla and her seven sons drew themselves into a tight circle, all settling together on Solomon Sill's plantation, just a few miles from the Cromarties. As sharecroppers, they tilled Sill's fields and earned a third of the crop they grew. It was a smart strategy: by living and working together, they maximized their earnings and set themselves on the road to buying land of their own. Undoubtedly, they sent their older children to the nearby AME schoolhouse, which was tied to George's mission, where two black teachers taught ninety-three children to read and write. When the federal government created a Freedman's Bank to encourage savings, the DeVaughns opened accounts. They couldn't have had much money to put on deposit. But a minister's family had to set an example, to show the faithful and the prodigal the virtues of hard work, thrift, and sobriety.[22]

It was never easy. The brothers were marrying and having children of their own now: Romulus and his wife, Lisa, had a daughter, Julia, in 1865; the next year, his twin had his first son, Robert; Hubbert had a daughter, Nancy, the year after that. Their growing families needed more food, more space, and more money. Every step was a struggle. In 1867, a drought withered the cotton in the fields, leaving black families so desperate that only the distribution of government rations staved off a winter of complete deprivation. The next growing season began well, but a midsummer plague of caterpillars destroyed much of the crop and left most blacks poorer than when the year began.[23]

Worse, the planters used their power to subvert the freedmen's efforts. Leon County landowners blocked government attempts to settle freedmen on federal land. And they refused to sell even small portions of their plantations to Negroes. Many planters ruthlessly exploited the colored families who rented small plots from them. A few used the slightest pretenses to expel their tenants from the land once the crop was close to harvest.[24]

The threat of violence was constant. Across the cotton belt, planters organized terrorist cells: the Regulators, the Whitecappers, the Ku Klux Klan. Operating under the protection of darkness, the Klan and their fellows targeted anyone who dared to challenge white domination. They forced teachers in colored schools to abandon their posts. They threatened, assaulted, and burned out those few freedmen who managed to acquire land of their own. Mostly, they waged war against the Republican state governments that set Reconstruction's rules. Vigilantes assassinated dozens of Republicans in the late 1860s and early 1870s, as many as seventy in the heavily black county just east of Leon, where the Klan ran rampant.[25]

Great as it was, the terror only pushed the AME's leaders toward an ever more vigorous defense of black rights. They made progress. In 1868, the Republican Party took control of Florida's state government, installing nineteen black state legislators, eight of them AME ministers or prominent laymen, Elder Pearce foremost among them. But the colored delegation was surrounded by a sordid collection of political opportunists more interested in bringing northern business interests into Florida—and fattening their wallets—than in breaking the power of white supremacy. Four years later, when the governor told Pearce that he was powerless to prevent further outrages against the freedmen, church leaders led a coup, overturning the Republican Party's established leaders and handing the 1872 gubernatorial nomination to an avowed reformer, Ossian Hart, to whom they delivered the black vote in the general election. "Elder C. H. Pearce saved this state to the Republican Party," a newspaperman wrote in the election's aftermath. "Florida is destined to become the negro's new Jerusalem."[26]

Hart wasn't quite that radical. Tall and broad shouldered, with a mane of white hair, he had the look of a planter, the unquestioning paternalism of someone to the manner born. He hadn't freed his own slaves until the last days of the Civil War, and he'd only grudgingly supported the freedmen's right to vote. Like his predecessors, Hart was primarily interested in tying the state to northern business; he wanted to see railroad lines brought into the peninsula, so he could link his friends, cattlemen who raised great herds on the open range of Central Florida, to the slaughterhouses of Chicago. But he understood who had put in him in the governor's mansion. And a gentleman always pays his debts.[27]

When antiblack violence broke out in Columbia County, east of Leon, Hart dispatched a contingent of black troops to the area to restore order. He rammed a civil rights law through the legislature, prohibiting discrimination in most public facilities. He named a Negro to head Florida's public school system and committed his administration to dramatically expanding state funding for education. And he appointed AME officials to dozens of minor political posts, from county superintendent to tax assessor.[28]

The DeVaughns got their due. In early 1873, Hart named Edmond and Gilla's third son, Hubbert, justice of the peace, Leon County's primary law enforcement official. The governor undoubtedly thought of the appointment as another political payoff, the price of victory. But the DeVaughns saw it as more than that, much more. When Hubbert claimed the position, he took the place of another promising young man, Alexander Cromartie, his former master's elder son.[29]

So the revolution had come. Eight years earlier, the DeVaughn brothers had been pieces of property. Now they were men who demanded respect: missionaries of the Word, spreading the gospel to their fellow freedmen; aspiring farmers, working to earn a share of the American dream. They were still poor, still landless, still struggling to be equal to whites in fact as well as in name. But they had come so very far, there was every reason to be hopeful. A few months after Hubbert took office, his younger brother Remus and his wife had their fourth child, Dora.[30] What must have run through Gilla's mind as she cradled her granddaughter in her leathery arms? This child wouldn't be like her babies, who had been born into a world now dead and gone. This child would have a future all her own.

•

Hope proved to be a very fragile thing. When Ossian Hart suddenly died in March 1874, his fourteen-month experiment in racial justice collapsed, and the Florida Republican Party slipped back into the hands of the opportunists whom the AME had overturned. The church bloc was broken.[31]

Democrats resumed their attack on "Negro rule." Landlords threatened black voters with eviction. The Klan renewed its terror against black officeholders. Intimidation and fraud peaked during the 1876 presidential and gubernatorial elections, Florida's first since Hart's death. When both the Republicans and Democrats claimed victory in the presidential election, the nation was thrown into a constitutional crisis. Only a Faustian bargain broke the deadlock. The Republican candidate, the ineffectual Rutherford B. Hayes, took the White House. Democrats took control of Florida's state government. Hayes promised them that there would be no more federal interference in their affairs. The Democrats, champions of white supremacy, could do as they wanted.[32]

Florida's Democrats had no intention of reversing the Republicans' economic policies. In fact, they pushed them harder than ever before. The Democratic legislature handed over huge sections of public land to northern railroad companies, which reciprocated by extending their lines south from the Georgia border all the way to the Florida Keys. Florida's economic might had always been centered on the panhandle, but when the tracks linked the peninsula to northern markets, the state's center shifted. Central Florida cattlemen expanded their herds, while farmers planted glorious citrus groves where wild grasses had always grown. Businessmen built lumber and turpentine camps to process the product of the forests they stripped bare. Land speculators platted towns where farmers could sell their goods and workers could spend their wages; shopkeepers and doctors and lawyers filled the new main streets with their stores and offices.[33]

This was the economic opportunity the Republicans had dreamed of bringing to the South. But the Democrats made sure that the New South would be for whites only and set about undoing the racial policies it had taken civil war to create. It took them until 1885 to assure the destruction of the Florida Republican Party and another decade to complete their oppression of the colored race. There were, after all, practical problems to overcome: the fourteenth and fifteenth amendments guaranteed Negroes their rights, and it was no simple matter to subvert the Constitution. The Democrats also had to overcome the limits of their imagination. They knew how to be cruel. But they had to create a social system premised on cruelty. That was a task that took some creativity.

Some steps were obvious. Black voters had made radical Republicanism possible. So they had to be stripped of the right to vote. As a start, the Democrats imposed a poll tax in 1887; voter registration plummeted by 50 percent the first year the tax was imposed. The Democrats followed that triumph by gradually tightening registration further. By 1895, when the last laws were put into place, it was almost impossible for a Negro to vote in the state of Florida.[34]

The next steps were more complicated. The vast majority of whites assumed blacks to be inferior. The trick was to make them act on those beliefs. Democrats began by defending the purity of the white race, not a straightforward matter in a society where interracial sex had a long history. But legislators, insisting that racial lines could be strictly drawn, imposed a stringent definition of who qualified as colored: a person was legally a Negro if just one of his great-grandparents had been black. Legislators also prohibited any further dilution of the white race. Blacks and whites couldn't have sexual relationships, couldn't marry, couldn't even spend a night in the same bedroom. With the groundwork laid, the Democrats gradually moved into the public sphere. Florida's whites had already barred blacks from some public places, such as theaters and hotels. But the segregation didn't have the force of law; it was custom, nothing more. The Democrats mandated the separation and extended it to the places where the New South was being created. Florida was one of the first southern states to require blacks to ride in separate railroad cars. And the legislature made it a crime to teach black and white children in the same classroom.[35]

As the Democrats made it more and more difficult to be black, whites became more and more determined to assert the power of their race. So they piled prohibition on prohibition. Blacks couldn't be buried in the same cemeteries as whites. They couldn't eat in the same restaurants. They couldn't ride in the front of city streetcars. They couldn't drink from the same drinking fountains. Whites also segregated their workplaces. Blacks could be servants and farm laborers, of course, and they could work in the turpentine and lumber camps, where most whites didn't want to go. But whites claimed the vast majority of jobs for themselves. They also demanded privileges that superiority conferred. They expected blacks to step off the sidewalk when a white person approached. They insisted that blacks keep their eyes downcast when they spoke to whites. They demanded that blacks call them "sir" or "ma'am," though they would never dream of reciprocating.[36] They felt free to level any insult, to inflict any injury, without fear of reprisal. Jim Crow taught the great mass of southern whites to see ordinary places and everyday interactions as sacred and to protect the sacred by embracing the profane.

•

Remus DeVaughn's daughter, Dora, grew up as the great hopes of Reconstruction collapsed around her family. As soon as he became governor, Ossian Hart's successor removed her uncle Hubbert as justice of the peace. The family circle that the DeVaughns had drawn around themselves began to break. In 1876, the AME bishop ordered Hubbert to leave Leon County and take up a position at a mission to the south.

Maybe the bishop was trying to protect him; AME ministers had become a particular target of Klan violence. Remus's baby brother, Amos, just drifted away, and his other brother, Edmond, left to take a job teaching school in Jefferson County, a small triumph for the AME's promise of uplift. But for the most part, Jim Crow choked off the advancement the preachers had proclaimed. By Dora's seventh birthday, only her father, Remus, and his twin brother, Romulus, remained in Leon County. Romulus somehow sustained his family on the few dollars he earned as a whitewasher. Remus kept working the land, as he'd always done, but it was harder and harder to eke out a living.[37]

As black political power faded, white landlords were imposing harsher terms on their tenants than they had been able to do during Reconstruction. Each bale of cotton was bringing in less than before, and Remus didn't have a way to increase his production. Dora's older siblings, Robert, Eliza Jane, and Sally, were going to school, so Remus didn't have their help in the fields for much of the year. Dora was old enough to work around the house but too young to spend her days nursing the cotton crop. And she also needed to begin her education soon. Then there were the babies, Maggie and Remus, Jr., to feed and clothe.[38] Dora's father could have pulled the children out of school and sent them to the fields. But that would have meant turning his back on his faith in his abilities and in his church's teachings. It would have meant mortgaging his children's futures, just as he had surely mortgaged his own to land that wasn't and never would be his.

He finally gave up. Sometime in the 1880s, two decades after he'd been freed from bondage, Remus left Leon County and moved his family south, to the Central Florida boomtown of Orlando. Orlando had been nothing more than a frontier town when the Democrats had assumed control of the state. But when the Democrats convinced Florida Southern Railroad to connect it to the northbound lines in 1880, Orlando had become a bustling commercial center. Remus must have believed that there would be work at the railroad terminal, where the citrus farmers piled their oranges for shipment, or in the sawmills, where the pine trees being stripped from nearby forests were planed.[39] Maybe life would be easier there.

It wasn't. If anything, whites were more committed to enforcing Jim Crow in cities and towns than they were in the countryside. Remus did the best he could, settling his family in a small rented home in the black section of town. He tried to find steady work. But he never broke out of the narrow range of jobs to which whites relegated blacks, and after years of struggle, he was discarded. By 1900, he was unemployed; at fifty-two, he was probably too old to find steady work, certainly too old for the backbreaking labor most blacks performed. So he lived on the largesse of his youngest children, now grown to early adulthood. And they, in turn, scraped by on the little that whites were willing to offer them. Remus, Jr., worked as a teacher in Orlando's impoverished black school system; Maggie was a washerwoman.[40]

It would have been easy enough, under the circumstances, to abandon the AME's promises. It was painfully obvious that blacks couldn't raise themselves up in such a society, but for some reason Dora couldn't let go of the great expectations that had swirled around her birth. She had heard the message of uplift and improvement week after week at church, and she couldn't set it aside. A handsome young woman, powerfully built, she carried herself with a quiet dignity that would become her hallmark. But behind it lay a fierce determination to recapture the moment when her family's dreams had been on the verge of fulfillment. Dora wasn't driven by a sense of nostalgia; she didn't want to re-create the past. She wanted to revive its hopes and make them real.[41]

Dora DeVaughn couldn't have been more than sixteen or seventeen when she fell in love with Henry Sweet, an ordinary man, typical of the postwar generation. His family had never found the stability the DeVaughns had enjoyed until Jim Crow came. Henry's parents were enslaved in East Texas, the western reaches of the cotton kingdom. Sometime before the Civil War, they'd been moved to Tuscaloosa, Alabama, a desperate place to spend the war. Union forces slowly choked off the Alabama interior; by 1864, Tuscaloosa was suffering from severe food shortages, and even the most devout rebels dreamed of the day when the fighting would end. Family lore says that by then Henry's parents had escaped their master and fled to the Union lines. If the story is true, the couple had a ferocious desire for freedom. Federal and Confederate raiders waged bitter guerilla warfare all along Alabama's northern border during the last years of the war; the Sweets would have been walking into an area where there were no clear battle lines and no obvious sanctuaries. If they did find safety, they probably would have moved with the troops, perhaps even following them back to Tuscaloosa in the spring of 1865, when the slaves the Sweets had left behind finally won their freedom.[42]

Henry had been born in Alabama on December 16, 1865, a child of freedom. For the next quarter century, the Sweets simply faded from view, lost in the official record until the 1880s, by which time they had followed the railroad to Florida. Tall, thin, and rangy, Henry was the sort of young man who would never fill out, no matter how many years he spent working the fields. If Florida law hadn't maintained such a strict division of black and white, he would have been classified as a mulatto. His light brown skin, sharply drawn features, and wavy black hair put him as close to the American concept of white as black. Maybe Dora was drawn to his looks, maybe to his maturity; he was eight years her senior. Maybe she loved the fact that he shared her determination to make a mark. It was impossible to say where his desire came from. It may have been a reflection of his parents' flight to freedom, perhaps something else, now forgotten. But he had the businessman's drive, an entrepreneurial spirit, fueled by a strong sense of pride and tempered by a dedication to fair dealing.[43] Those were AME values, Dora's values. They were married in 1890 or 1891.

The first few years were very hard. Dora and Henry stayed in Orlando, scraping by and putting aside whatever money they could spare. They had their first child, Oscar, in March 1893. Dora became pregnant again in early 1895. She had another boy on October 30, 1895. They named him Ossian, a tribute to the memory of the Reconstruction governor who had made her uncle a government official, a reminder of what had been lost. Dora must have taken great pride in the name, which was surely hers to give. But the exhilaration of the moment didn't last. Eight days after Ossian's birth, Dora and Henry lost Oscar.[44] It's almost impossible to imagine the burden that the parents bore in those terrible November days, when they had to care for their newborn—so dependent, so insistent—while they buried their toddler.

Hope and despair, the birthright of the baby with the radical name.

•

At long last, land. In the summer of 1898, Henry fulfilled one of the DeVaughns' great dreams: he bought a plot of land. It wasn't much, just a housing lot in the tidy little town of Bartow, halfway between Orlando and Tampa. It was an ordinary town, a bit newer and more prosperous than most but just as dedicated to Jim Crow as any place in Florida. There was white Bartow, the solid respectable center of Polk County. And there was black Bartow, a cache of sun-baked homes separated from the center of town by the railroad tracks and the massive wall of segregation. The Sweets' lot naturally sat on the wrong side of the tracks. But Henry and Dora could afford it; the seller, a white man by the name of Milam, a northerner by birth, had fallen on hard times and was willing to let it go for $250. Henry put down a deposit, Dora packed up their belongings, and they headed the fifty miles west, to their new home.[45]

Bartow hadn't always been sharply divided. With only three hundred people in the entire county, Polk was still very much a wilderness in 1880. Bartow was a tiny trading post of seventy-seven souls, a ramshackle collection of stores barely rising above the dog fennel that flourished in the tropical sun. Blacks and whites didn't live in harmony: Democratic Party vigilantes had operated there in the 1860s, just as they had in Leon County. But the town was too small to segregate and too far out of the way for anyone to care. Then the railroad came.[46]

When Florida Southern extended its line from Orlando to Tampa in 1884, Polk County suddenly became an attractive destination. Aspiring farmers began buying up the land, filling the long empty fields with citrus trees and rows of vegetables. In 1889, prospectors discovered that the river basin of the Peace River, which cut through the heart of the county, was rich with phosphate, the basic ingredient in fertilizer. European investment houses rushed to grab up the tracts with the largest deposits. By the 1890s, the land southwest of Bartow had been slashed into open pits, and the countryside shook with the roar of mill machinery processing twenty thousand tons of phosphate each and every month.[47]

Prosperity made Bartow a substantial place. By the last years of the 1890s, there were close to three thousand people in town. The well-to-do built themselves imposing new homes—all peaks and porches—down Broadway, the elm-lined avenue that ran south toward the phosphate mines. Businessmen lined Main Street with groceries, drugstores, and specialty shops—the bicycle store, the millinery, the jeweler's, the telegraph office—all housed in handsome clapboard and brick buildings fronted by wooden sidewalks and glistening white streets paved with phosphate stone. The new courthouse sat at the corner of Main and Central, the new high school a few blocks to the south, both of them brick-and-mortar proclamations of Bartow's public prominence. There were many more black faces as well. They were drawn there by the ample work on the railroad, on the land, or in the mines. A man could make a living in Polk County; he might even hammer out a measure of the independence so many black folks wanted.[48]

But it just wouldn't do to have blacks mingling with whites, especially given Bartow's new importance. So, as the town fathers put in the sewer lines, the streetlights, and the telephone exchange, they split the town in half. The few blacks who had been able to vote in the 1870s and 1880s were barred by the poll tax; only whites voted by the 1890s, and they always elected Democrats. Blacks weren't welcome in the Orange Hotel, the opera house, or the Main Street stores. They couldn't attend the outdoor entertainments—the county fair in March, the occasional traveling shows—except on specially designated "colored days." They couldn't pray in the fine white churches. They couldn't bury their dead in the white cemetery. But all those prohibitions weren't sufficient. Just about the time the Sweets' wagon rumbled into town, Bartow officials pushed segregation to its logical conclusion. Blacks couldn't even live among whites. Those who owned land in the center of the town—including some of Bartow's founders—would have to sell their homes and move to the other side of the railroad tracks, to the subdivision Florida Southern had laid out ten years earlier, to the other Bartow.[49]

Forced to separate, the people of East Bartow built a thriving community for themselves, poorer than the white side of town, to be sure, but every bit as solid and respectable. Black businessmen opened general stores, barbershops, and restaurants along Wabash Avenue, which became the black downtown. Lawrence Brown, a part-time Bible salesman, built a small real estate empire selling home sites to black customers from the comfort of his handsome Queen Anne home on Second Avenue. East Bartow filled with social clubs and vibrant black churches: Mt. Gilboa Missionary Baptist on Laurel; Burkett Chapel on Third; St. James AME a block over, its grand bell tower rising above the neighborhood.[50]

The Sweets made themselves into pillars of the community. Their lot sat at the corner of Eighth and Bay streets, almost as far from white Bartow as could be. Henry set himself to work building a house, a single-story wood-frame home constructed from the local pine, bounded on two sides by covered porches that sheltered the inside from the noonday sun. Town officials didn't extend utilities into the black neighborhood, so the Sweets' home had no electricity, no running water, and no indoor plumbing. Henry added a barn for the mules he used to break the land he rented beyond the woods to the south. He built coops for the chickens Dora raised. He marked off a garden plot, where they grew the vegetables that filled the family table. And he began building a commercial farm, a farm that could make some money and set his family on its course.[51]

It was endless work. Henry would spend days behind the plow, preparing the fields for planting. Then there'd be the months of tending the cabbages, kale, rutabagas, and peas, hoping that rains would come when they were needed and that the sun wouldn't burn the plants before they could be harvested. He'd sell what he could in the neighborhood; he'd load the mule cart with produce and ride up and down the streets, calling out, "Cabbages," in a singsong voice that might bring the ladies out of their houses to take a look at what he had to offer. The bulk of his produce he'd haul the forty-five miles to Tampa, where the market was bigger and the prices better.[52]

Dora, meanwhile, did the constant round of chores the house required. There was the daily grind of floors to sweep, chickens to feed, meals to prepare, and pots to scrub. There were always clothes to mend and clean; on laundry day, she would have to haul up gallon after gallon of water from the small lake near her husband's fields. And more and more, there were babies to tend. Otis was born in 1899, Deloca, the first daughter, a year later. There were a few years without a newborn. But then Dora was almost continually pregnant. Henry was born in 1904, Parthenia in 1905, Nordica in 1907, Buck in 1908, Cynthia in 1909. Sherman, the tenth and last child, arrived in 1915.[53]

The farmhouse groaned under the weight of the family. But Henry and Dora fused the children into a unit, just as her father's generation had done back in Leon County. As soon as they were old enough, the children were expected to work. The younger ones could care for the animals: gathering the eggs, milking the cows, driving the few head of cattle up from the pasture to the barn each night. And Dora would send them into the woods to pick fruit for canning or to brighten a meal, though the rattlesnakes the children found there terrified them. Ossian and Otis gradually took over the plowing from their father. But Henry was too much of an entrepreneur to rest. As the boys freed him from the fields, he opened a lumberyard on his land as one more venture, one more way to bring the family a few precious dollars he could use to expand his operation.[54]

The Sweets thought of success in financial terms: Henry was too much of a businessman not to believe that hard work paid dividends. But money wasn't the only goal. Henry and Dora were honest, upright people. They wouldn't drink or smoke. They saved what money they could. They strived to live the solidly respectable life the church had taught them to cherish. Every Sunday, after services at St. James, the Sweets would put their round of chores aside. Dora would set the finest table: the china set she somehow pieced together, a freshly ironed tablecloth, a vase of newly cut flowers. The family would sit for a formal meal of the sort served in the grand homes on the other side of town. As they passed platters of food, the family would talk of the past and the future. Sometimes their grandfather would come over from Orlando to join them, and he'd tell tales of his childhood in slavery.[55]

Sometimes, Dora and Henry would lecture on responsibilities. Owning land was a wonderful thing, the great triumph of Henry's generation. But as the AME had taught them, land wasn't enough. The children had to have an education, they said, to take their schooling as far as it would go. For when they reached adulthood, they were duty bound—by their church, by the struggles of the generations that went before them—to be models of Christian virtue and race pride. And only education could give them the tools they needed.[56]

The children learned the lessons well. There wasn't a hint of rebellion; not one of them challenged the course their parents set for them. If all of the Sweet children were willing to take up their burdens, though, Ossian assumed the greatest weight. He was the oldest, after all, and he would have to blaze the trail for the rest. The others would depend on him, not simply as an example but also as the person who could give them the aid they'd need as they tried to fulfill Mama and Papa's exhortations. And he knew—how could he not know—that his parents were also counting on him, to prove them right and to make them proud.[57] He was their hope; their aspirations were his obligations.

But the Sweets' aspirations were inexorably consumed by Jim Crow. In the early 1890s, before the family arrived in town, black children had no school. The town fathers saw no need for it. "It seems to me that attempt at general education of the negroes is an injury rather than a benefit to the race," explained one of Bartow's leading lights. "It tends to pervert his intelligence to a dissatisfaction of his natural and moral condition in life." The pastor of St. James AME, however, refused to accept such an affront to his community. He tried to establish a church-run school, but his congregation simply didn't have enough money to keep the building open. Finally, the year before the Sweets arrived, St. James's elders struck a deal with the town. The church bought a lot in East Bartow and paid for the construction of a grade school, Union Academy, which it then deeded to town officials to operate.[58]

The devil was in the details. State law mandated that white and black schools be separate but equal. But white officials across the state starved black schools of funding. Bartow officials were no exception. Although there were almost as many black as white children in Bartow, the town gave Union Academy only half the appropriation they gave to the white grade schools and far less than they gave to the high school. In its earliest days, the academy could barely afford to keep its doors open: the Sweets' first full year in town, black children attended school an average of twenty-seven days. The situation had improved a bit by the time Ossian started school. The academy was open four months and there was more than one teacher. But the education was still rudimentary. The children learned to read and write, something many of their parents could not do. They were taught basic mathematics. They memorized a bit of history and some snatches of literature. But when the curriculum was completed at the end of eighth grade, the children had nowhere to go but the fields and the phosphate mines.[59]

White Bartow had a high school, of course, a wonderful new school, the pride of the community. Students entered the building through a broad veranda reminiscent of the finest antebellum plantation homes. Double windows six feet high flooded the classrooms with light. A large library filled one corner of the first floor, a laboratory another. An auditorium ran the entire length of the second floor. There was a thirty-foot-long stage at one end, complete with footlights and curtains, where the students could perform and lectures could be held. "With the completion of our new building," the principal told Bartow's newspaper, "we are as well provided with building accommodations as any town in the state. . . ." But Ossian and his siblings weren't allowed in the doors. It would have been illegal for the Sweet children to sit next to white boys and girls, and the good folks of Bartow always did their best to obey the law.[60]

Unless they chose not to. Antiblack terrorism hadn't ended when Reconstruction collapsed. Florida Democrats couldn't very well unleash violence during their election campaigns, then expect it to stop as soon as their victory was secure. Office holders were beholden to the thugs who beat black people into silence; sometimes the thugs and the office holders were one and the same. Violence wasn't just a political tool, though. It was a way of life under Jim Crow. Whites learned to have hair-trigger tempers. If a black person caused the slightest offense—anything at all would do—whites felt free to lash out. It was a right slaveholders once had claimed. Now any white person enjoyed the same privilege.[61]

When Ossian was a boy, the violence escalated to pathological proportions. There were reasons for the upsurge. Decades of sweeping economic change had stripped many southern whites of the security and independence they'd once enjoyed. In the 1890s, a stunning new political insurgency—the Populist movement—sought to rally embattled whites in an assault on the economic order the Democrats had built, even if that meant, as it did in some states, seeking out the support of colored men as well. Desperate to beat back the Populist threat, Democrats tried to redirect whites' anger away from their party and toward their erstwhile colored allies. It was a shockingly bitter campaign, playing on whites' deepest fears of moral decay, economic impotence, and sexual inadequacy. Blacks were poised to attack, speakers proclaimed, to steal honest white men's hard-won gains, to strip them of political power, to rape their women.

"I have three daughters," proclaimed the most fearsome of the demagogues, South Carolina's one-eyed governor, Ben Tillman, "but so help me God, I had rather find either one of them killed by a tiger or a bear and gather up her bones and bury them . . . than to have her crawl to me and tell me the horrid story that she had been robbed of the jewel of her maidenhood by a black fiend." Facing such an imminent threat, no decent white man could desert the party of white supremacy. It was a wholly irrational appeal, politics in its most degraded form, and it worked. As Populism crumbled, darkness descended on the South. Whites waited in fear and anticipation for outrages to begin. Even the rumor of an incident could drive whites into a frenzy of violence, an orgy of retaliation.[62]

Bartow's descent into barbarism began in the phosphate mines. Few white men would take the brutally hard work—breaking stones with pick and ax, sunup to sundown, six or seven days a week—so the mine owners hired large numbers of young, single black men desperate enough to work for a dollar a day. The companies packed the workers into squalid mining camps: rows of wooden shacks, sitting sullenly in the mud. But for all the rank exploitation they faced, the workers also built a world for themselves. It was a rough, often brutal world, built around the "lobbies"—the juke joints, blind tigers, and brothels—that ringed the camps. Come Saturday night, the streets pulsed with life. Miners sat on the porches, drinking and gambling. Prostitutes leaned in the doorways of the shanties, waiting for customers. The music poured out of the bars: "You don't know Polk County lak ah do," the bluesmen sang, "Anybody been dere, tell you de same thing, too."[63]

Whites were fascinated; the perverse alchemy of American race relations was changing the excluded into the alluring. At the same time, though, the allure simply heightened the terror whites felt. "It is said that the life of a decent white man who ventures into these lobbies is in his hands," a reporter warned in 1895. "The awful crimes of Negroes against whites that roused South Carolina . . . are increasing throughout South Florida, and it goes without saying that it is owing to the presence of large numbers of Negroes, lawless, unbridled, and drawing large cash wages, with every means at their disposal . . . for expending the same in riot and debauchery."[64]

White Bartow responded to the threat in the camps by sanctioning the most extreme forms of violence. In January 1899, a black laborer at the Land Pebble mine dared to argue with his foreman, who pulled out a pistol and shot the laborer dead. The foreman turned himself in to the Bartow sheriff. But the sheriff brushed the incident aside. Everyone knew what had happened, he said. The foreman should go back to work. Given such license, mob violence was almost inevitable. A black worker, Sam Smith, killed a white man during an altercation at the Kingsford phosphate mine in June 1900. He tried to flee but a posse tracked him down hiding in a black Masonic lodge not far from the mine. Sheriff's deputies began to bring him back to Bartow, but when a crowd waylaid them, the deputies quickly surrendered the suspect. The whites bound him to a post and riddled him with bullets.[65]

In May 1903, a white man was murdered at one of the blind tigers operating outside the camps. A mob marched on the bar, captured the owner and his two bodyguards, and hung them from the gnarled mulberry tree that curved over the train station nearest the mine, a short walk west of Bartow. Officials actually impaneled a grand jury to investigate the slaughter, but it dismissed the crime as justified. The blind tiger "was an abomination and a curse," the jurors said, "and repeated efforts had been made to have said curse removed, but to no avail." How could the murder of a white man at such a place not be avenged?[66]

East Bartow's respectable black folk tried to insulate themselves from the violence of the mining camps. They agreed with local whites that the camps were a terrible stain on the town. They joined in church campaigns to suppress drinking, gambling, and fornicating. They demanded reform.[67] But their efforts were in vain. Jim Crow didn't discriminate between "good" Negroes and "bad" Negroes; every black person was suspect, every community open to assault. No one was safe.

The violence broke on a glistening morning in May 1901. A white woman, Rena Taggert, the young wife of the town baker, was fishing off the Peace River bridge, less than a mile east of the Sweets' home, when someone dragged her into the thick brush lining the banks. A black man working a short way downriver heard her screams and rushed to town for help. A contingent of whites raced to the scene but Taggert was gone. It took them forty-five minutes to find her body, half buried in the mud of a nearby swamp. She had been raped and her throat had been cut.

In a fury, the whites interrogated the black man who had summoned them. He couldn't have seen much; he was a distance away, and the riverbanks were thick with foliage that time of year. But he said enough to convince his interrogators that Taggert had been murdered by Fred Rochelle, a light-skinned sixteen-year-old Negro, who roomed with his sister in East Bartow while working, like other members of his family, in the phosphate pits. With the interrogation complete, the whites marched en masse to the sister's home but Rochelle was gone, fled into the swampland south of town.

It was an incredibly dangerous moment. More and more whites were gathering as the news spread. And they had no suspect in hand, no one to punish for the outrage. East Bartow's political leaders—including several trustees of St. James AME—desperately tried to distance themselves from the crime. Frantically, they drafted a public declaration condemning Rochelle and proclaiming solidarity with the white mob forming in their streets. "We, the colored citizens of this community," they wrote, "must say that it is a shame and disgrace to our race to allow such brutish conduct [as Taggert's rape and murder] to occur. We should shoulder arms and march to the front and show to our white citizens that we do not uphold such conduct as this. Just to think that a white woman can't go out for air and exercise or fishing without being accosted by a brutish Negro." Colored families like the Sweets, meanwhile, must have been shuttering themselves inside their homes, barring their doors and windows, readying their rifles, waiting for the pogrom to begin.

Rochelle's flight may well have saved East Bartow from destruction. By midafternoon, the mine managers had sent their bloodhounds to town, and most of the able-bodied white men were organizing into posses to begin the manhunt. They spent the night and most of the following day scouring the countryside, vainly trying to pick up Rochelle's trail. Finally, late in the afternoon of the second day, three local black men found him hiding near the phosphate pits a few miles southwest of town. They turned him over to some passing whites, who marched him back to Bartow.

Three hundred townspeople gathered in front of the courthouse to see Rochelle's return. While the sheriff and his deputies stood by, the town's best men interrogated him. He confessed to every detail. The throng decided he should be returned to the scene of the crime. First, they brought him by the victim's house, where her stepfather asked that nothing be done until all of the posses were back from the hunt. Then they marched the victim through the empty streets of East Bartow to the bridge. The mob's leaders delayed until 7:00 P.M. White witnesses said that Rochelle showed no emotion during the ordeal, but the wait must have been agonizing, a sixteen-year-old standing before his executioners, the minutes ticking away, the fear rising and rising. Finally, Bartow's leading citizens placed the young man on a hogshead of flammable material and chained him to a tree. They stacked bonedry wood around the base, poured gasoline on the pile, and invited the victim's husband to apply the flame. He touched a match to the kindling a few minutes after 8:00. The hogshead ignited into a fierce bonfire. Eight minutes later, Rochelle was dead, and the members of the mob began drifting back to their homes. "By midnight," the newspaper reported, "the town was as peaceful as ever."[68]

There would be other mobs. On Christmas Eve 1903, a group of whites tried to lynch a black man imprisoned in the Bartow jail, but the sheriff held them off. Two black prisoners were lynched in Bartow in 1906. And mob violence raced through Polk County in 1909. Two blacks were immolated in February when a suspicious fire burned down the jail in a nearby phosphate town. A few weeks later, whites in the town of Lakeland, just north of Bartow, dragged Jack Wade from police custody, hung him from a tree, and riddled his writhing body with bullets. In April, a Bartow mob lynched Charles Scarborough in a chilling reprise of the rape frenzy eight years earlier.[69]

As appalling as those events were, though, Ossian would always remember Fred Rochelle's death as the most terrifying moment of his young life. As an adult, he'd tell people that he had witnessed the entire scene, that he'd hidden in the bushes near the bridge and watched the burning. He'd recount it with frightening specificity: the smell of the kerosene, Rochelle's screams as he was engulfed in flames, the crowd's picking off pieces of charred flesh to take home as souvenirs. Maybe, just maybe, he did see it all. The bridge was a short walk from his home. He could have been outside—coming back from his father's fields—when the mob drove Rochelle through East Bartow. But he was only five years old in the summer of 1901. And it seems unlikely that Dora would have let him outside anytime that day. More likely, the horrific events imprinted themselves so deeply on Ossian's mind that he convinced himself that he had been there. Either way, the effect was the same. The image of the conflagration—the heart-pounding fear of it—had been seared into his memory.[70]

Dora and Henry already knew. Maybe they talked of it in the stillness of the night, after the children were asleep. Maybe they didn't talk about it at all. But they knew. Their families had struggled for two generations to get this far, to own land, to have a home no one could take from them. But it wasn't enough, not in this place, not at this time. They put off a decision as long as they could. But in the summer of 1909, they were forced to act. It was probably the coincidence of events. Ossian finished eighth grade that spring, just about the time the respectable people of Bartow left Charles Scarborough's broken body dangling from a rope.[71] How could Dora and Henry let their son stay with them? He'd have no hope of an education, no opportunity to make his way in the world, no chance of fulfilling the dreams their family had nurtured since they'd first tasted freedom almost forty years ago. And there was the possibility—almost too horrible to contemplate—that somehow he'd be caught in the terror that so often raced through their streets. It wasn't going to be easy. They'd stressed so much the ironclad bonds of family. Ossian had become a help in the fields, vitally important to a farm family with so many young children. And he was only thirteen, still a boy. But there was nothing else to do. They would have to send him away, to a place where he could pursue his education, to a place where he'd be safe.

The night before he was to depart, Ossian walked over to the parsonage of St. James AME. He was scared to leave Bartow, he said, without God's blessing. "So on the day of his leave," wrote his minister, Ossian "gave his heart to the Lord." Then he boarded the northbound train—and was gone.[72]

THREE

MIGRATION

Xenia was a placid little town, like hundreds of others scattered across the fertile farmland that rolled northward from the Ohio River. A string of shop fronts lined Main and Detroit streets, forming a town square around the county courthouse, its limestone façade shining in the sun. Xenia had touches of urban life—a few small factories, a handful of saloons, dark and mysterious, and a smattering of foreign-born workmen to fill them both—but the town moved with the rhythms of the countryside, gray winters giving way to early springs, blistering summers to muted autumns.[1] As he stepped down from the train at Xenia depot in the first week of September 1909, Ossian Sweet might have found it comforting to see a town that was, surprisingly, so much like the one he'd left behind. But he hadn't traveled a thousand miles in search of what was familiar. He had come to Xenia to take his place in a new world free of Jim Crow's oppression.

Ossian had been given strict orders about what to do. He was to arrive in daylight, not in darkness, but even if the weather were clear, he was not to leave the station on his own. Instead, he was to find the telephone exchange and ring the college office to request "a conveyance." Dad Harris, the venerable maintenance man, would bring his wagon around. Ossian and any other students could put their belongings—clothes, bedding, and Bibles—into the back and scramble aboard for the three-mile ride through the east side, where Xenia's Negroes lived. Out of town, they traveled down curving country roads

past fields and farmhouses to a comfortable cluster of buildings set
into a grove of maples and sycamores, the splendidly isolated campus
of Wilberforce University, the first college in America dedicated to providing Negroes with the blessings of higher education. Here, Ossian
would begin the slow, hard, thoroughly American process of transforming himself.[2]

•

Dora and Henry Sweet were hardly the only southern blacks to send
their son north in the bitter days of the new century. When politicians
and businessmen extended rail lines into the smallest of southern
hamlets in the years after Reconstruction, they had wanted simply to
connect the region's fields and forests to the North's great factories.
But the process also provided Negroes with a thousand escape routes.
It was never easy to leave, to slip free of piles of debts, to shutter homes
and abandon lands, to say good-bye to family and friends. But a hundred thousand colored people did just that between 1900 and 1915,
many of them, like Ossian, very young and very scared.[3]

They were drawn by the promise of equal treatment. In the first few
years after the Civil War, when the Republicans' commitment to racial
change was still strong, most eastern and midwestern states had passed
sweeping civil rights laws that prohibited segregation of public places
and opened ballot boxes to colored men. What's more, white northerners didn't expect Negroes to kowtow the way they were forced to do in
even the most enlightened portions of the South. "Ain't no Mistrus' an'
Marster's up dere, say yes an' no up dere," an Alabama woman explained. "No gwin in de back door. White fo'ks an' 'Niggers' go in an'
out de same door up dere."[4]

The dreams of the vast majority of colored migrants were also in-
extricably tied to hopes for steady work and reasonable pay. Even before the Civil War, the North had more than its share of factories and
mills. In the late nineteenth century, the region had become the work-
shop of the world. From Minnesota's windswept Mesabi Iron Range
to the backstreet shops of Baltimore, nine million working people
transformed the nation's natural abundance into more goods than
any other nation on earth. So insatiable was industrialists' demand
for labor that it couldn't be met by the native-born whites who had
once been the backbone of the American working class. To fill the gap,
employers hired huge numbers of people who had never before set
foot in a mine or factory. Most were immigrants, millions of whom

were arriving each year. But employers weren't quite as open to colored men and women. A few factory owners placed Negroes in the full range of jobs they had to offer, but the son of small-town farmers like the Sweets could expect to fill one of the North's less desirable positions, feeding the blast furnaces of a Pittsburgh steel mill, hauling bricks at a Cleveland construction site, or cleaning offal from the killing floor of a Chicago stockyard.[5]

For Henry and Dora, that wasn't enough. They wanted their children to become men and women of distinction, models of the AME creed. And their oldest boy would show the way. To begin, he would need an advanced education, a college degree, which was an utterly audacious goal. Most Americans of modest means, white or colored, never attended high school, much less university. Southern blacks bore the double burden of poverty and unequal southern school systems; in 1900, half of the Negroes in Florida couldn't read or write. Even those who could stood little chance of further academic achievement. Of the ten million Negroes in America, fewer than two thousand were enrolled in college courses.[6]

Once the Sweets had set their sights on college for Ossian, Wilberforce was the obvious choice. There were better black schools— Atlanta University, Nashville's Fisk University, Lincoln University outside Philadelphia, Howard University, overlooking Washington, D.C.—where doctors, lawyers, teachers, and politicians sent their children. Graduates of those schools thought of Wilberforce as a backwater, provincial and pedestrian, and many of its students as earnest but utterly unsophisticated, well-meaning but not necessarily well educated. One of the century's great intellectuals and most important civil rights activists, W. E. B. Du Bois, spent a painfully long academic year teaching Greek, Latin, German, and history at the college in 1896 and 1897 before moving on to more prestigious postings. The first black man to receive a Ph.D. from Harvard, Du Bois cringed at the pupils who filled his Wilberforce courses. "A struggle with Antigone's struggles by wise and spectacled youths," he wrote acidly in his journal after one class, "all fading away into a dull headache and the bell for noon chapel."[7]

But the Sweets had no inkling of the carefully calibrated hierarchy of the academy. To them, Wilberforce offered extraordinary advantages. It was a northern school, far removed from the terrors of black Bartow. Those who weren't well prepared for the college's demands, such as thirteen-year-old Ossian, were enrolled in a four-year preparatory course before moving on to the university, where they would be given the skills necessary for a career in business or one of the professions. There was another draw as well: owned and operated by the AME, Wilberforce fostered the values that Dora and Henry prized. Such treasures didn't come cheaply; tuition ran $118 a year, far more than the Sweets could possibly pay. But Wilberforce had scholarships set aside for deserving students from the AME's Florida Conference. So at absolutely no cost, Ossian could receive a rigorous education at a college firmly rooted in his family's tradition. It seemed a godsend.[8]

It was a godsend built on desecrated ground. Tucked into the southwest corner of Ohio, a mere sixty miles from slave-owning Kentucky, the campus was originally the site of a grand resort hotel, Tawawa Springs, built for the pleasure of southern planters and the female slaves they claimed as their mistresses. When the resort went bankrupt in the 1830s, a few of the planters remade the property as a school for their mulatto children. But in the 1840s and 1850s, as abolitionism burned across Ohio, the slave masters' largesse came to be seen more and more as an affront to the state's good people. In the mid-1850s, Ohio's white Methodists bought Tawawa Springs, renamed it after the great British abolitionist Bishop William Wilberforce, and transformed it into a college for free blacks. Whites controlled Wilberforce until 1863, when they sold the school to the AME for the princely sum of $10,000. Half a decade earlier, a university run by and for Negroes would have been inconceivable. But in the year of the Emancipation Proclamation, everything seemed possible.[9]

In the sixty years before Ossian's arrival, Wilberforce's great expectations frayed. Chronic underfunding had taken its toll on the campus. There was a fine new library, a gift from Andrew Carnegie, but the older buildings—Shorter Hall, where the male students lived and classes were held; Arnett Hall, the women's dormitory; the small homes that housed faculty members—were starting to decay. Their shutters were going "a little awry," according to a doyen of white Xenia, "steps a little broken, foundations yellow with rain-splattered clay." The university maintained its own electric power plant but it only worked intermittently; most of the time, students worked by the flickering light of gas lamps. The equipment in the laboratories was woefully inadequate. There was simply no money for improvements. Wilberforce was $32,000 in debt in the autumn of 1909, and many of the university's accounts—including the scholarship fund Ossian was counting on to pay his way—were empty.[10]

When Ossian was informed that there would be no scholarship, he must have thought about putting his bags back on the wagon and catching the first train back to Bartow. He was a thirteen-year-old very far from home, and the lack of money would have given him the perfect excuse to head back to his family. But something kept Ossian from leaving. Maybe he didn't want to disappoint his parents. Maybe he felt an obligation to his younger brothers and sisters who were expected to follow his example. Maybe he could feel his own ambitions tugging, telling him that if he left Wilberforce he'd spend his life working his father's fields or breaking his body in the phosphate pits. Whatever his reasons, Ossian decided to stay. To help cover expenses, he took work stoking the college's furnaces and shoveling snow—hard, even humiliating, jobs on a campus where the distinction between scholar and tradesman was of great importance.[11] But Ossian accepted the work because he understood that a young Negro of humble birth would never have a better opportunity than that offered by this small, slightly run-down university. For what Wilberforce lacked in amenities, it more than provided in spirit.

◆

It was a spirit that faith bestowed, not a religious faith, though that was strong enough on Wilberforce's sylvan campus, but a faith in the mission of higher education. Du Bois had said it best: the Negro race, he famously argued in 1903, would move forward only on the strength of its "exceptional" men and women, the handful of scholars and scientists, professionals and poets who he claimed constituted the "Talented Tenth." The black colleges had to be the tenth's training grounds, he said, and to play that role, the schools had to be uncompromising in the education they offered, every bit as demanding as outstanding white colleges.[12]

Had Du Bois said the same thing during the heady days of Reconstruction, a healthy portion of northern whites would have agreed. The North had put great stock in black education in the ten years after Appomattox. Young Yankees had trooped south to help teach freedmen to read and cipher, and white congregations had spent precious sums to create Negro colleges such as Fisk and Howard. Gradually, though, the optimism of those days had faded. Northern whites had a hard time sustaining interest in the fate of freedmen with their own world shaken by economic depression, political corruption, and violent class conflict, all bitter by-products of the North's industrialization. In the 1870s and 1880s, the schoolteachers went home, donations dried up, and Negroes were left to the mercy of southern whites who insisted that colored people were incapable of anything but the most rudimentary learning.[13]

More cruelly still, many northern whites came to agree with the southerners. It wasn't as if northerners had suddenly discovered black inferiority: even the most ardent abolitionists had generally assumed themselves superior to the slaves they sought to free. But as memories of the Civil War grew dim and the humanitarian impulse of the abolitionist generation crumbled under the cudgel of Social Darwinism, white racial thinking ossified. The peoples of the world were set in a rigid hierarchy of development, academics explained, with Anglo-Saxons at its pinnacle, immigrant masses huddled in the middle range, and Negroes at bottom. Ministers, authors, judges, and politicians echoed the argument. "A perfectly stupid race can never rise to a very high plane," concluded Republican Theodore Roosevelt. "The Negro, for instance, has been kept down as much by lack of intellectual development as by anything else."[14]

A few powerful blacks, most notably Alabama's Booker T. Washington, seemed to endorse whites' low opinion of the Negro's potential. A consummate politician, Washington held up his manual training school, Tuskegee Institute, as a model for black education as Du Bois and his Talented Tenth fussed and fumed. But white philanthropists rewarded Washington, the aptly nicknamed Wizard, for his efforts, pouring millions of dollars into Tuskegee so that his students could learn skills deemed appropriate for Negroes, such as shoemaking and carpentry, in the most up-to-date workshops. The leaders of Wilberforce also understood the power of pandering to white prejudices. During one of its periodic fiscal crises, the college convinced the state of Ohio to provide the university with an annual subsidy in exchange for which Wilberforce established its own manual training school, modeled on Tuskegee. By Ossian's first year, the training school had more instructors than the college had faculty members. But the industrial arts students were still considered second-class citizens on campus. They performed the necessary labor—repairing buildings, laying sidewalks, fixing leaky pipes—while the college's men and women set the tone.[15] Wilberforce's new president, William Sanders Scarborough, was determined that it would always remain so.

Scarborough wasn't simply a devotee of the Talented Tenth ideal; he was its exemplar. Born a slave in 1850s Georgia, he was apprenticed to a shoemaker when freedom came. But in the finest AME tradition, Scarborough didn't want to settle for a trade when he could aim for the professions. After two years at recently opened Atlanta University, in the late 1860s, he moved on to Ohio's Oberlin College, a white institution as liberal in its politics as it was demanding in its academics. "I forgot I was a colored boy in the lack of prejudice and genial atmosphere that surrounded me," he remembered in later years, "and enjoyed such life and amusements with others as they presented themselves to me." He also enjoyed a sterling education, eventually earning both his bachelor's and master's degrees in the classics—training sufficient to launch him on a distinguished academic career. The author of a widely used textbook and a well-respected translation of Aristophanes, Scarborough was only the third black man elected to the American Philological Association and one of the finest scholars ever to serve on Wilberforce's faculty.[16]

Few Wilberforce students were going to match Scarborough's achievements, but the college would do everything in its power to give them the opportunity. Like its brother schools, Wilberforce provided its students with a traditional education, rooted in the liberal arts. Ossian spent his first year in the prep school studying Latin, history, mathematics, English, music, and drawing, a daunting program for a youngster from a one-room schoolhouse, made even harder by the demands that his campus jobs must have placed on him. Over the next two years, Ossian added a second language, most likely French, and an introductory science course. And in his final year as a prep student, he was exposed to philosophy and the social sciences. By then, Ossian was beginning to define his interests. When he started the college program in the autumn of 1913, he elected to pursue a degree in science. That meant four more years of chemistry, biology, Latin, and French, three more years of math, and a smattering of additional courses in philosophy, English, and social science. It wasn't a Harvard or Fisk education, to be sure. But it was more than enough to put Ossian into that precious tenth of the race.[17]

For all their emphasis on academics, however, President Scarborough and his fellow administrators didn't believe that higher education was confined to the classroom. The Talented Tenth would also lead the race using the strength of their characters. Wilberforce relied on the AME religious tradition to enforce a moral discipline bordering on monasticism. Ossian and his fellow students were required to attend a scripture service each morning at 8:10, a prayer meeting every

Monday evening, and two services on Sunday, morning and night. Students could have "association with the opposite sex" only when the president granted them written permission; men and women weren't even allowed to walk the same campus paths, lest they fraternize while taking their exercise. The use of profanity was prohibited, and anyone caught indulging in alcohol or tobacco was to be expelled. The only break in the regime came when the campus was swept up in one of its week-long revivals, moments of religious ecstasy that appalled more secular members of the Talented Tenth. During his brief tenure at Wilberforce, Du Bois felt himself driven to "mental imbecility" by the "wild screams, cries, groans and shouts" that shattered the sacred solitude of his rooms.[18]

While the college relied on the spirit of God to shape moral values, it counted on campus life to inculcate a sense of duty and responsibility. Wilberforce maintained the range of activities—the glee clubs, debating societies, and literary groups—typical of colleges across the nation. Students were free to pledge fraternities and sororities, where they could build the bonds of friendship they would need as they ventured into the business world. But for the young men, there was no more important campus institution than the cadet corps. In the 1880s, in one of the last gasps of Reconstruction-era policy making, the War Department had authorized Wilberforce to establish a military training program, the only black school in the country so honored. The United States Army assigned an exemplary string of officers to campus to direct the program. A few years before Ossian arrived, the corps was commanded by Lieutenant Charles Young, the third black to graduate from West Point and a military man of consummate skill and bravery. During Ossian's tenure, the post was held by Captain Benjamin Davis, who in time would become the nation's first black general. The commanders, in turn, built a program of exacting standards. Each morning at 7:25, Ossian joined his fellow cadets of Company A on the practice field for instruction in military drill, first aid, minor tactics, and small-arms fire. Cadets were encouraged to stay in uniform throughout the day, a corps of confident young black men sitting in Wilberforce's classrooms, dressed in the colors of their country.[19]

◆

Wilberforce rounded out its students' education with a heavy dose of racial politics. President Scarborough had never abandoned the radical Republicanism of the postwar years; any form of segregation was an insult to the race, he insisted, and a desecration of American principles. When white Ohioans began tearing down their own discriminatory practices after the war, Scarborough pushed them to go further. In the 1880s, he spearheaded a drive to outlaw the segregation of schools and to repeal state laws prohibiting intermarriage. And as Jim Crow hardened in the South, he fought to isolate the system within Dixie's benighted states. In one furious campaign, he prodded the state legislature to require railroads to remove "whites only" signs from their cars the moment they crossed into Ohio so that colored riders would know that they had passed out of the darkness and into the light.[20]

By the time Ossian arrived at Wilberforce, though, the light was starting to fade. It was galling enough to hear northern academics and politicians declare their belief in the innate inferiority of the colored race and to see white donations pouring into schools that reinforced Negroes' subordination. But it was absolutely appalling to see southern-style racism slither into everyday life above the Mason-Dixon Line. This hatred was spread in part through the power of ideas. While scientists and philosophers published learned studies measuring the chasm between Anglo-Saxons and Africans, an increasing number of ordinary northerners endorsed the racial slanders southern demagogues had perfected. Where whites had once talked bravely of racial justice, they now whispered of Negro workers stealing white men's jobs and colored rapists ravaging white women. And they cheered the demagogues themselves, who traveled the North lecturing on the True South's struggles to contain the black beast.[21]

Demographics turned harsh words into brutal actions. It had been easy enough for northerners to declare fealty to racial equality when more than 90 percent of the nation's colored population lived in the South. As the black migration accelerated, though, northern interest in segregation grew stronger. Many of those white workers lucky enough to belong to unions refused to extend solidarity to Negro workingmen, while a growing number of employers refused to hire colored people for anything but the most menial of jobs, unless they needed to break a strike, at which point Negro labor would do just fine. White homeowners were beginning to object to having colored families live nearby. And more and more white customers were demanding that blacks be excluded from restaurants, hotels, theaters, and other public venues. Neighborhoods and businesses weren't the only places where Negroes were increasingly unwelcome: at Scarborough's beloved Oberlin, there was talk of black and white students taking their Bible studies in separate classes. None of this segregation had the sanction of law—state civil rights statutes remained on the books—and it wasn't consistently applied: it was a patchwork of practices, differing from place to place and even street to street. But for colored people, the trend was frighteningly familiar.

Racism's rising tide inevitably reached Wilberforce. Half a century before, Xenia's whites had taken pride in the colored college just outside of town. Now they treated the campus community with derision, refusing to extend to the university any of the town's facilities or services, not even fire protection. They twittered at the parents who arrived in town each graduation day, amused at the very thought that colored families would try to dress well and carry themselves with elegance. No one came in for more disdain, though, than President Scarborough's wife of twenty-five years. Sarah Scarborough was a woman of high breeding and distinction. But on the rare occasions when she ventured into Xenia, she was shunned by the town's best people, not because she was black—they could have withstood that—but because she was white.

As painful as they were, insults and indignities were easier to endure than the most fearsome of southern imports, the race riot. Since before the Civil War, blacks and whites had shared the streets of Springfield, Ohio, a grim-faced factory town fifteen miles north of Wilberforce. Then, in 1886, the city's largest employers had used black strikebreakers to destroy Springfield's powerful all-white iron molders union, an action white workers never forgot and never forgave. One cold night in March 1904, tensions exploded: the violence began when a colored man, recently arrived from Kentucky, killed a white policeman down at the Levee, a dingy row of saloons and brothels hard along the railroad tracks. Enraged whites dragged the murderer from his cell and lynched him, then turned on the Levee itself, burning it to the ground. In the process, they destroyed the homes of the town's poorest Negroes as well. Colored people had just rebuilt when the mob struck again. Several minor confrontations in February 1906 triggered two days of terror, as whites rampaged through Springfield's colored quarter, beating those who dared to be on the streets and burning out those who hid indoors. "The North has reached the point where it is ready to echo almost anything the South chooses to assert," Scarborough raged in the aftermath of the second pogrom. "It thinks the early education of the Negro a mistake, the ballot a blunder, the Negro a fiend. . . . It has become hypnotized by the assiduous efforts of . . . men who have succeeded in muzzling the press, muzzling the pulpit, muzzling the platform—muzzling the mouths of nearly all those who in the past saw any good in the Negro people."[22]

Scarborough understood that outrage wasn't sufficient; if black America were to retain the rights it had struggled so mightily to attain, the Talented Tenth had to organize against the racist juggernaut. He became a charter member of the Du Bois–led Niagara Movement, founded in 1905 to counter the appeasement of the Washingtonians and to mount a vigorous defense of racial equality. The movement rang with the same militancy that the AME ministers had spread through Leon County back when Ossian's grandfather was a young man. "We claim for ourselves every single right of freeborn Americans, political, civil, and social," Du Bois proclaimed during the movement's second conclave, held at the abolitionist Gethsemane of Harpers Ferry, Virginia, "and until we get those rights we will never cease to protest and to assail the ears of America." Brave words, but they were hard to pair with vigorous action. Crippled by lack of funds and torn by infighting, the Niagara Movement limped along for several years, until another night of bloodshed galvanized a new round of activism.[23]

•

The paroxysm of violence that convulsed Springfield, Illinois, on August 14, 1908, was induced by the familiar toxic blend of economic conflict and racial hatred. That most explosive of events, a rumor of rape, led the white citizens of Illinois' capital on a rampage against their black neighbors. National Guardsmen restored order the following dawn, but by then six Negroes had been shot dead, two more had been lynched, and two thousand driven from town. Northerners had come to expect such atrocities in the South. But there was something truly shocking about the violence in Illinois. Springfield wasn't just another place on the map, after all. It was the home and final resting place of Abraham Lincoln.[24]

The symbolism of the Springfield pogrom was so stark that progressive whites couldn't help but take notice. The southern race war was moving north, the indefatigable reformer William English Walling wrote in New York's influential newspaper, the *Independent,* and it cannot be stopped until "a powerful body of citizens" revived "the spirit of the abolitionists." Du Bois, Scarborough, and their colleagues in the Niagara Movement had been saying precisely the same thing for

several years. But whites such as Walling brought resources and connections that the Talented Tenth couldn't match. Throughout the balance of 1908, a gradually expanding group of New York liberals began
discussing ways of fulfilling Walling's charge. In the early months of
1909, they announced plans for a new organization of "fair-minded
whites and intelligent blacks" who together would fight for the rights of
Negroes across the land.[25]

If Scarborough was put off by the white progressives' sudden
discovery of racial hatred, he didn't show it. When he received his invitation to attend the inaugural meeting of the new civil rights organization, to be held in Manhattan on the last day of May 1909, only
a few months prior to Ossian Sweet's arrival on the Wilberforce
campus, he was pleased to accept. The overwhelming majority of
attendees were white, men and women of sure social standing and
enormous goodwill, drawn to the black cause for a host of deeply
personal reasons. They were the progeny of the abolitionist generation, led by Oswald Garrison Villard, millionaire grandson of the
great William Lloyd Garrison, who saw in the new racial terrors the
destruction of his ancestor's lifework. Walling brought along a number of his fellow reformers, many of them, like the young social
worker Mary White Ovington, drawn from the ghetto settlement
houses that had become the seedbeds of social justice in industrial
America. They were joined by a solid contingent of Jewish liberals,
who understood the profound dangers of injecting racial supremacy
into the body politic. For their part, the black participants were
drawn heavily from the Niagara Movement. Du Bois was in attendance, of course, as were William Monroe Trotter, the fiery Boston
publisher; antilynching crusader Ida B. Wells; esteemed Mary Church
Terrell; and, sitting in silent fury, Scarborough, the slave-born philol-
ogist. It would take another few months to settle on a permanent
name for the new organization. But in the course of one long day,
the National Association for the Advancement of Colored People was
born.[26]

Ossian entered Wilberforce three months after the NAACP's founding meeting. Over the next eight years, he would be repeatedly exposed to the association's principles of uncompromising opposition
to segregation, North and South, and unremitting struggle to secure
equality before the law. He sat in his assigned seat in the chapel as a
steady stream of speakers—academics, ministers, and politicians—
lectured on the state of race relations. On special occasions, he shared

the campus with some of Scarborough's best-known associates in the fight for justice: Terrell's National Association of Colored Women came to campus for its annual meeting in the spring of 1914, and that summer, Du Bois, by then editor of the NAACP's monthly magazine, the *Crisis*, spent several weeks at the college teaching economics. Ossian attended the monthly "rhetoricals," where students debated the issues of the day. And within the cozy confines of the Carnegie Library, he could find the best of Talented Tenth thought. Du Bois's brilliant book *The Souls of Black Folk* sat on the shelves, as did his newly published biography of John Brown, the abolitionist who sought justice through the barrel of a gun.[27]

◆

Ossian couldn't help but be affected by it all. He was little more than a child when he first stepped off the train at the Xenia depot. He had never met a black man or woman as accomplished as the professors who taught his classes or the soldiers who directed him in drills. And no one back in Bartow dared to speak so forcefully, so publicly, of justice and rights as did President Scarborough and his distinguished friends. It must have been very exciting to move into this new world.

Ossian didn't find it easy to adjust. The work he performed on campus put him in the margins between the prized college students and the second-rank industrial arts students; one year, in fact, university officials inadvertently listed him as enrolled in the shoe department, a simple clerical error, no doubt, but also a stinging reminder that Ossian wasn't a substantial figure on campus. He worked hard at his studies, but others were better prepared and more capable. He joined a few clubs, pledged a fraternity, Kappa Alpha Psi, and did his duty as a member of the cadet corps. But he wasn't the sort of person who attracted his fellow students' attention or won their admiration. Others were elected president of their clubs or named company commanders; Ossian remained one of the crowd, a reliable member of the fraternity, a dependable private in the cadet corps, but never a star.[28]

Only once did he make his mark, and it wasn't a proud moment. One spring day in 1914, Ossian was spotted in Xenia with two of his fellow cadets from Company A. None of the three had been given permission to go to town, a serious enough infraction. Worse, one of Ossian's companions was drunk. The faculty disciplinary committee charged all three with having gone to Xenia "to partake of the whiskey," an offense punishable by expulsion. Ossian was devastated. "I will admit I was in bad company," he wrote the committee in desperation. "I will admit that I left the campus without . . . permission. And again I will admit that I did not go to town for the purpose of buying intoxicating drinks and I firmly say, I am a 'total abstainer.' After having been part of this institution for three years and having to face this worthy body under no circumstances. And then to be brought to you for such an offense is indeed very grievous unto me, as I am wholly innocent as far as the intoxicants are concerned. I humbly beg that you reconsider my case."[29]

Ossian's pleading worked: although one of his friends was expelled, the faculty committee let him off with a public reprimand. But the incident and Ossian's response reveal that, despite his five years on campus, he remained an insecure young man, determined to please his superiors, to say just the right thing, even if it meant turning on his friends.[30]

Money concerns added to his insecurity. Rather than head back to Bartow when the 1909–10 school year ended, Ossian decided to spend the summer working in the North. His younger brothers Otis and Henry were old enough to help their parents bring in the crops, while he could use three months' work to add to his meager savings. There were plenty of places for Ossian to go. It was only a dozen miles from Wilberforce to Dayton, which was filled with factories, and thirty miles to bustling Cincinnati. But Henry and Dora's son had too sharp an eye for money to settle for the sort of job he could find in a second-tier city. Instead, he chose to spend his summer in big, booming Detroit, where bosses were begging for workers. Three months' work there could earn Ossian more than he'd make almost anywhere else.[31]

It didn't work out quite that well. Detroit was the first big city Ossian had ever lived in, and he must have enjoyed the excitement of walking in the shadows of towering downtown buildings and sharing sidewalks with polished businessmen. But he had a lot to learn about making a living in the big city. A man working in one of Detroit's brand-new auto factories might be paid as much as $2.50 a day; that much was true. But those jobs weren't going to fourteen-year-old colored boys. Though practices differed from plant to plant, the best positions generally went to native-born whites: craftsmen, farm boys, and former miners who knew how to tinker with machines and didn't need a translator to follow the boss's orders. For the huge middle range of jobs that didn't require any special skill—increasingly Detroit's specialty—most of the big employers hired the foreign-born. For a few years, the Board of Commerce went so far as to pay a hiring agent to work the great hall of Ellis Island, recruiting workers for Detroit's factories before they even cleared customs. Once in a while, a Negro managed to slip his way in alongside a foreigner—Henry Ford in particular liked to hire a colored man now and again—and there were a small number of black professionals and businessmen. But most members of the city's small colored community ended up doing service work: unloading the Great Lake steamers that drew up to the Detroit docks, waiting tables, shining shoes, doing white folks' laundry, or minding their children.[32]

Ossian couldn't do any better. He spent his first two summers in the city, 1910 and 1911, washing dishes and selling sodas to the throngs of pleasure seekers who crowded onto Bob-Lo Island, a whirligig of amusements and sideshows a few miles downriver from Detroit. His wages began at a dollar a day, not much more than he would have earned working the fields for a white farmer back home, then gradually rose to dollar and a half. In the summer of 1912, he took a job as a bellhop at the Hotel Norton, a small downtown establishment catering to out-of-town salesmen and other small-time operators; the next year, he moved on to the Fairfax Hotel a few blocks away. Finally, in 1914, he began a four-summer run as a waiter, working on the excursion boats that ran between Detroit and Cleveland.

Each job was an improvement, with better working conditions and slightly higher wages and tips. Though many of his coworkers were older, stretching meager wages to keep their families fed, Ossian also found friends much like himself, driven young men such as Caribbean-born Vollington Bristol, head bellhop at the Fairfax Hotel, who had come north filled with dreams of doing great things. Northern cities had their edges, Bristol told Ossian the summer they worked together. But they were still the only places in America for colored men who wanted to better themselves. Down south whites feared blacks with ambition, and a Negro who tried to get ahead had to spend most of his time watching his back. In a city like Detroit, Bristol insisted, white folks respected ambition, and a Negro who worked hard, saved his money, and had a head for business was going to be rewarded. Bristol already had his plans plotted out; one day, he was going to open his own funeral parlor, as respectable and profitable an undertaking as anyone could imagine. Ossian could do just as well if he put his mind to it. This was the sort of talk Ossian took to, but it didn't quite square with his day-to-day experiences. Lugging someone's bags down a hotel corridor or carting away the remains of a roast beef dinner, it was hard to think of oneself as a member of the Talented Tenth.[33]

More than anything else, it was the financial struggle that shaped Ossian. A decade later, that was what he remembered of his college days: not the classes he took, not the friendships he made or the speakers he heard, not the halcyon days he spent walking on the leaf-strewn campus, but his constant battle to make ends meet. There was an edge of bitterness, an unspoken resentment, in his memories. But deprivation also gave shape to his ambitions.[34]

From childhood, he'd been taught the virtues of entrepreneurship and the pleasures it could buy: he'd seen how his father had squeezed every penny he could out of his land and how his mother had taken such pride setting the Sunday table with fine china of the sort East Bartow's Negroes weren't supposed to have. But, at some point in his Wilberforce years, Ossian decided that he wanted more than a solid living and a few creature comforts. He made it his goal, he told a reporter years later, "to rise in his profession and to amass a substantial fortune."[35] A Du Bois or a Scarborough might look on those ambitions as unworthy of the Negro elite, since they were driven by the pursuit of Mammon rather than the advancement of the race. But to a struggling student shoveling snow off the walkways so that his classmates wouldn't ruin their boots, such goals were noble enough.

By the time he entered the college program, Ossian had selected his path to success: he had decided to become a doctor. Of all the professions open to him, he couldn't have made a more extraordinary choice. Not so long before, it had been perfectly reasonable for someone of Ossian's social standing to consider a career in medicine: there were any number of barely trained practitioners prescribing nostrums from inconspicuous offices and backroom clinics. But times had changed. Stricter standards and tighter regulation had driven marginal doctors out of business; by the 1910s, medicine had become the preserve of the highly educated and the well-to-do. The more exclusive the profession became, the more status it accrued. Americans might still joke about quacks and con artists, but in the end no one commanded more respect than a doctor. Therein lay its attraction for Ossian. A life in medicine would give Ossian the status he dreamed of—and the money he craved: a doctor could easily take home fifteen hundred dollars a year, an almost unimaginable amount to a young man whose father probably earned a fifth of that figure. If Ossian should rise in the profession, as he intended to do, his income could go even higher: the director of

Washington's foremost black hospital earned a staggering four thousand dollars a year. But it wasn't the money alone that mattered. A high income would give him the outward signs of success: the dapper clothes he never had the chance to wear, the fashionable home so different from the farmhouse his father had built. But to be called doctor—Doctor Ossian H. Sweet—that would be the greatest mark of respect he could imagine.[36]

It was also wildly unrealistic. There were fewer than twenty-five hundred Negro doctors in the United States, and the profession's new standards threatened to cut the number further. Few black men had the luxury of devoting four years of their lives to the classes and clinical work the profession now required. To make matters worse, most of the nation's medical schools had stopped admitting colored candidates at all, one more sign of the racism spreading through the North, and the handful that would consider allowing a Negro within their halls enrolled one or two such students a year. Black colleges didn't fill the void. There were only two black medical schools in operation—one at Howard University in Washington, D.C., the other at Meharry Medical College in Nashville—and neither admitted more than forty or fifty new students at any one time. Most of the available slots went to the best graduates of Lincoln, Howard, or Fisk, not to average students from schools like Wilberforce.[37]

Just as Ossian was completing his undergraduate education, though, world events shook black America to its core. For two and a half years, the United States had watched in mounting horror as the European powers slaughtered their peoples in what was coming to be known as the Great War. Finally, in the winter and spring of 1917, Woodrow Wilson could stand no more. On April 2, 1917—just two months before Ossian's graduation—the president asked Congress for a declaration of war against Germany. The United States fought not for territorial gain, Wilson said in his achingly eloquent address to the nation, but "for democracy, for the right of those who submit to authority to have a voice in their own Governments, . . . for a universal dominion of rights by . . . a concert of free peoples."[38]

For the Talented Tenth, it was a siren call. The NAACP's white president, Joel Spingarn, scion of a wealthy Jewish family and a lauded literary scholar at Columbia University, secured the army's permission to establish a training camp for black officers in faraway Des Moines, Iowa. In the pages of the NAACP's magazine, the *Crisis*, W. E. B. Du Bois pleaded for volunteers. The leaders of the race would fight for democratic principles abroad, he argued. And by their blood sacrifice, they would force white America to recognize the rights of black people at home.[39]

War fever raced across Wilberforce. There was talk that the former commander of cadets, now Lieutenant Colonel Charles Young, living just outside the campus, would be given command of black troops and perhaps even be elevated to general. The current corps commander, Ben Davis, had already been called to active duty. His cadets rushed to join him. In the spring of 1917, thirty of the ninety-three students in the college passed the qualifying exam and headed to Des Moines to join the fight for democracy. Ossian wasn't among them. He had dutifully taken the army's test, but his eyesight was so poor that he was placed in Class 5, disqualified for service.[40]

It was a very lucky break. As the army drained away college men, the competition for the few slots in medical schools became much less keen. Sometime that spring, Ossian received word that he had been accepted into Howard University's College of Medicine. It must have been a triumphant moment, a vindication of his parents' faith and his effort, as well as a huge stride toward the fulfillment of his ambitions. Another summer waiting tables in Detroit, then, come September, as many of his classmates were heading into the charnel house of Europe, Ossian would move on to the nation's capital, itself awash in war.

◆

The lights of official Washington burned late every night in September 1917. Not since the Civil War had the United States undertaken such a thoroughgoing mobilization. There was a massive army to raise, train, and ship to the trenches of France: the military was expecting some four million young men to serve, the vast majority of them draftees. There were thousands of factories to be converted to the production of military material. Great sprawling complexes like the Ford Motor Company's Highland Park plant in Detroit had to be made part of the American war machine, as did tiny sweatshops hidden down alleyways and in tenement garrets from New York to Seattle. And there was a polyglot nation to be rallied. Government spokesmen fanned out across the country to explain to farmers and factory workers that America was fighting to preserve freedom and democracy, while government agents rooted out those who dared to dissent. Socialists and pacifists were censored and even imprisoned when they questioned the wisdom of war. German-Americans, Irish-Americans, and other immigrant groups were harassed because they didn't live up to the new government standard of "100 percent Americanism."[41]

Washington's drive for unity halted at the color line. Southern-born Wilson had already done a great deal to advance segregation during his first four years in office, having extended Jim Crow into Washington's offices, cafeterias, and lavatories and purging thousands of Negro civil servants from government payrolls. Now he dashed the Talented Tenth's hopes that they might win civil rights by serving their country. There was never any question that the army would be segregated, but no one was prepared for the flagrant insults the military leveled. The young men training in Des Moines were told that when they went to war they would all serve in a single division commanded by whites; not one of them would be commissioned at field rank. The very best black officers were simply shunted aside. When a white Mississippian wrote to his senator to object to serving under Charles Young's command, the War Department conveniently classified Wilberforce's finest officer as medically unfit to serve, even after the lieutenant colonel proved his stamina by riding horseback from Xenia to the nation's capital.[42]

Wartime changes, moreover, raised racial tensions to frightening new heights. In the spring and summer of 1917, the steady stream of colored people out of the South suddenly became a torrent. It was a classic economic migration. With the Atlantic Ocean turned into a battlefield and the nations of Europe feeding an entire generation of young men into the slaughter, immigration to the United States was all but cut off. The American military draft, meanwhile, drained factories of workers at precisely the time industrialists were desperately trying to fill the flood of military orders. Facing a labor shortage of unprecedented proportions, employers sent word south that long-standing racial barriers were being torn down for the duration. The news had an electric effect on sharecroppers, day laborers, and domestics desperate to escape grinding poverty and decades of unrelenting brutality. Almost half a million southern blacks left the South for industrial centers like Detroit, Chicago, and New York in 1917 alone, an exodus so great that southern whites feared the economy of their region might well collapse from want of workers.[43]

Instead, the North lurched ever closer to southern-style violence. The first sickening incident came in East St. Louis, Illinois, in July 1917. Blacks had been migrating to the grimy town alongside the Mississippi

River for the better part of a decade, but the influx had suddenly shot upward in late 1916 and early 1917. Democratic Party politicians, including President Wilson himself, declared that the black migration was a Republican plot designed to flood Illinois with GOP voters. White workers, meanwhile, became convinced that black newcomers were about to steal their jobs. When the city's employers crushed a series of strikes—a replay of the dynamic that had underlay the Springfield pogrom a few years earlier—union members blamed the defeat on blacks who they said crossed their picket lines. East St. Louis teetered on the edge of violence throughout the early summer.

On July 1, 1917, it toppled over the precipice. For days, rumors of an impending white attack had swirled through the black neighborhood. Late on the first, jittery blacks mistakenly opened fire on a police car, killing two plainclothesmen. In retaliation, white mobs rampaged through the black part of town in an explosion of violence that made the Springfield riots seem like minor affairs. Whites killed at least forty Negroes and perhaps many more; some victims were hurriedly buried in unmarked graves, while others were dumped into the creeks that fed the Mississippi. Hundreds were injured, thousands made homeless as the mob burned block after block to the ground. The Talented Tenth pleaded with the president to condemn the outrage, but Wilson refused to say a word. So the NAACP responded with a stony silence of its own. In New York City's burgeoning black enclave of Harlem, the association's recently hired field secretary, poet, composer, journalist, lawyer, politician, and diplomat James Weldon Johnson, organized a massive protest parade, ten thousand Negroes—women and children in white, men in black—marching down Fifth Avenue without a sound except for the tramp of boots and the tattoo of muffled drums. At the head of the column waved the Stars and Stripes and a banner reading "Blood Is On Your Hands."[44]

◆

The ruins of East St. Louis's ghetto were still smoldering when Ossian arrived in Washington, D.C., in time for the 1917–18 school year. Most likely, he had read Du Bois's searing editorial on the summer's barbarism. "Russia has abolished the ghetto—shall we restore it?" Du Bois had roared in the just-published September issue of the *Crisis*. "India is overthrowing caste—shall we upbuild it? No land that loves to lynch 'niggers' can lead the hosts of Almighty God." Ossian must have noticed how Washington itself was swollen with migrants:

southern-born job seekers, of course, but also bureaucrats and soldiers drawn to the capital by the wartime emergency. Perhaps he realized that the crush of people was stretching city resources and straining tempers. It wouldn't have taken him long to hear word of Jim Crow's mounting popularity in the capital. Even as the Supreme Court was striking down Louisville, Kentucky's ordinance requiring the segregation of its neighborhoods—the NAACP's first great legal victory—southern Democrats were calling on Congress to impose similar laws on the district. But when Ossian arrived at the wrought-iron gates of Howard University, it was almost possible to forget just how dire the state of race relations was becoming.[45]

Like Wilberforce, Howard had been born in the great rush of hope that emancipation had engendered. But there the similarity ended. Created by an act of Congress in 1867 and supported by federal appropriations, Howard didn't struggle to pay its bills or sustain its ideals. The graceful campus, an eclectic mix of Victorian display and classical understatement, sat upon a hill in northwest Washington. To the south and west lay a struggling neighborhood of row houses backed by the capital's infamous alleys, where Negro servants and laborers lived in crushing poverty. But Howard preferred to look to the elegant houses northeast of campus, home to many of America's most elite Negroes—the "Black 400"—highly accomplished, extraordinarily cultured, and invariably light-skinned men and women such as Robert and Mary Church Terrell; the brothers Grimke, who headed the NAACP's Washington branch; and the Langston family, which would produce the finest poet of the Harlem Renaissance. At its best, Howard's faculty was just as accomplished. Kelly Miller, dean of the Liberal Arts College, spent his career trying to build the discipline of black studies; his young colleague, professor of philosophy Alain Locke, the first Negro to win a Rhodes scholarship, acted as midwife to a new generation of black artists and aesthetes; at the law school, James Cobb, a former assistant U.S. attorney, helped to set the groundwork for a legal assault on segregation north and south.[46]

The medical school was the jewel in Howard's crown. When the school opened its doors in 1868, medical education in the United States was very much a haphazard affair. Determined to raise the quality of care—and the status of its members—in 1910, the American Medical Association imposed strict new standards on medical schools. Students had to have at least a highschool diploma before they could be accepted into medical school, the AMA ruled. They were to have four years of training, at least part of which was to be clinical work in a teaching hospital. And when their education was complete, they had to pass comprehensive examinations before they would be licensed to practice.[47]

There had been seven black medical schools in operation when the AMA set its standards; five of them couldn't possibly comply with the new rules and were forced to close, while the sixth—Meharry—barely survived. Howard thrived. It easily met the AMA's benchmarks for admission, since most of its incoming students held college degrees. It maintained an exhaustive and exhausting course of study. In their first two years, students took classes in anatomy, histology, physiology, pharmacology, pathology, bacteriology, therapeutics, diagnosis, and preventative medicine. Then they moved on to a two-year round of clinical experience, much of it completed at Freedmen's Hospital, right next door to the medical school's imposing four-story building. Founded a few years before Howard, Freedmen's had been little more than a barracks where Washington's indigent could go for emergency care. But in 1908, the federal government spent six hundred thousand dollars to build a new three hundred-bed facility, as well-appointed as almost any city hospital of its day. Freedmen's still treated the poor, but it also gave Howard's medical students exposure to a full range of specialties, from surgery to ophthalmology. The AMA was very impressed. "The future of Howard is assured," the association announced when it issued its standards. "Indeed the new Freedmen's Hospital is an asset the like of which is in this country extremely rare."[48]

Ossian also must have been impressed—and a bit intimidated. Coming from Bartow, he had thought Wilberforce was such a grand place; it must have been something of a shock to see how much more imposing Howard looked, how much more professionally its laboratories were equipped, how much more cocksure its students seemed to be. His entering class was small, twenty-two in all. Almost half of them were northerners, and more than a few were coming from first-rate schools where the Negro elite sent their sons: a number were Howard men, one was a graduate of Northwestern University, outside of Chicago, and another had received his degree from Williams College, the elite school tucked away in Massachusetts's Berkshire Hills. Wilberforce had trained Ossian well enough—he had his Latin, his chemistry, and his biology—but he was surrounded by better students, by and large, more comfortable with the rigors of the first year: the long days in the classroom trying desperately to master the flood of information presented by Professors Bartsch, Just, Lamb, and Mitchell, each more distinguished and more demanding than the last; the hours spent dissecting cadavers under the meticulous instruction of angular Doctor West, peeling back the skin, exploring the musculature, and probing the organs of the black corpses the District of Columbia provided from among those too destitute to afford burial.[49]

Ossian's finances made the work all the harder. In its early days, Howard's medical school had expected its students to hold down jobs; all of its classes were held in the evening so the students could work during the day. But in its determination to meet the AMA's benchmarks, Howard had reversed its policy. University officials made it quite clear that medical students should come with funds sufficient to cover the three hundred dollars in tuition and fees; the curriculum was too demanding, they said, to permit students to have jobs during the school year. But Ossian simply had to be employed. The money he had saved from his work in Detroit wasn't enough, not with rent at a local rooming house adding to the bills. So he took a part-time job serving at social events. Ossian would spend evenings waiting on guests at local soirees, pocket a dollar or so, then head back to his room for a long night pouring over massive textbooks, memorizing conditions and prescriptions, so that he could perform for his professors the following morning.[50]

He was no more a standout at Howard than he had been at Wilberforce. Some of his classmates were less capable, to be sure; a few were asked to leave at the end of the first year, their performance was so poor. But Ossian didn't do well enough to attract particular attention. When it came to choosing class officers, others were selected; when the professors identified the most promising students, others were mentioned. It was a familiar enough position for Ossian, a repetition of his undergraduate experience. If he had felt the sting of marginality at Wilberforce, though, at Howard, he experienced the thrill of soaring status. No matter what his academic standing, a graduate of Howard's medical school was never average. He was a professional of the highest order, a young man who deserved and demanded respect.[51] As he learned the intricacies of the human body, therefore, a Howard man also had to learn how to carry himself with towering confidence. He couldn't simply be a doctor. He had to act like one.

A few of Ossian's colleagues were naturals. Even in their first year, they had the proper air about them: the brow knitted in concentration, a pipe clenched between the teeth. Ossian must have found it harder to adopt the physician's proper pose; he'd been taught to do as he was told, to keep his eyes downcast when his superiors talked to him, to answer them with all the politeness and deference he could muster. Bit by bit, Howard transformed him. Ossian was made to dress as a doctor should, pressed shirts and tasteful ties peaking out from beneath crisp white lab coats. In the lecture hall and the laboratory, he was taught to answer questions with all the authority he could manage, as if he harbored no doubts about his abilities. When he moved on to Freedmen's, he learned the proper way for a doctor to act around the infirm. He was to be understanding but not overly sympathetic, friendly but never a friend, a bit distant, a bit detached. That was the demeanor his patients would expect and his colleagues would demand.[52]

For a poor boy determined to make good, it was hard to keep such lessons in perspective. Once acquired, professional detachment slid easily into haughtiness, self-assurance into arrogance. Ossian grew more forceful, more brusque, more judgmental. Even those closest to him no longer measured up. His younger brother Otis devotedly followed Ossian's example, completing his degree at Florida State College, a third-rate Negro college, then advancing to dental school at Meharry. Ossian openly criticized the shortcomings of the schools, so obviously inferior to Howard.[53] Others might well bristle. But they had to understand that Ossian wasn't the country boy he had once been. He had become learned, highly skilled, poised to achieve great things.

Dreams of greatness inevitably collided with the bitter reality of racism. Ossian was used to the sting of segregation. He had never even been inside most of Bartow's public buildings; he'd ridden back and forth from Xenia in Jim Crow railroad cars; he'd worked in hotels where Negroes weren't welcome as guests. His parents had taught him, in their own quiet way, not to accept the humiliations that such discrimination imposed. Time and again, he had heard the same message from President Scarborough and his NAACP colleagues. But only now, in the middle of his medical-school years, did Ossian squarely face the enormous injustice of white supremacy.

It was partly the way that discrimination struck at the professional pride that he was so eagerly embracing. Ossian had no doubt that he was going to be a more talented doctor than most graduates of white medical schools. But almost no white hospital in the country would welcome him as an intern. The AMA wouldn't permit him to be a member. Virtually no white patients would have him as their physician. So for all his training, all his hours of study, all his skills, chances were good that he would have to build a practice among people too poor to pay his fees, that he'd have to serve as an attending physician in an ill-equipped and underfunded black hospital, and when one of his patients needed the sort of care that only a superior facility could provide, Ossian would have to turn over the case to a white doctor who was his inferior in everything but the color of his skin.[54]

Ossian wasn't shaken solely by his confrontation with the medical profession's discriminatory practices, as galling as they were. Halfway through his time at Howard, he also had to face the terror buried deeply inside him. In the summer of 1919, the racial tensions that the Great War had triggered exploded in an unprecedented surge of violence. This time, the bloodshed didn't occur in some distant place like Springfield or East St. Louis. It swept through the streets of Washington itself, from Pennsylvania Avenue all the way to Howard's gates. As it did, all the newfound confidence faded away in a blinding fog of fear.

◆

Ossian was in military dress, drilling alongside his fellow students, on the day the Great War ended. At the beginning of the 1918 school year, Howard had required its medical students to enlist in the Student Army Training Corps, established on campuses across the nation to prepare college men for active duty. There was very little risk of them actually seeing combat. The United States had its massive army built by the summer of 1918, and more than three hundred thousand Americans were already in France, preparing for battle. In August, British, French, and American troops launched their first combined offensive, and the German lines buckled. Three months of bloody fighting followed. Then, on November 11, 1918, Germany sued for peace and the guns fell silent.[55]

Victory in Europe didn't restore harmony at home. Instead, it seemed to feed division. The government's wartime crackdown on dissent fostered a blinding hatred of anyone thought to threaten the American way of life. In the months after the war, workers worried about the security of their jobs mounted a massive wave of strikes. Determined to defeat their workers and destroy their unions, employers condemned the strikers as communists, intent on bringing the recent Soviet revolution to American soil. As the fear mounted, the Wilson administration launched a fevered campaign against left-wing politicians and activists, the nation's first Red Scare. Radicals were swept up in government dragnets, held without trial, and in many cases deported. The government's panic, in turn, stoked the furnace of Anglo-Saxon supremacy. Long a power in American politics, nativists argued that the only way to prevent further subversion was to cut off the flow of foreigners into the United States. Anti-Semites and anti-Catholics rushed to support immigration restriction. "When the Bolshevists in Russia are overthrown there will be a great massacre of Jews," one prominent American coolly explained, "and I suppose we will get the overflow unless we can stop it."[56]

Racial hatred was even more vicious. For its part, the Talented Tenth greeted the peace with a surge of militancy. "We are returning from war!" Du Bois wrote in the *Crisis*. "This is the fatherland for which we fought! But it is *our* fatherland. . . . The faults of *our* country are *our* faults. Under similar circumstances, we would fight again. But by the God of Heaven, we are cowards and jackasses if now that the war is over, we do not marshal every ounce of our brain and brawn to fight a sterner, longer, more unbending battle against the forces of hell in our own land." But the forces of hell proved very strong. The South had its share of outrages. A score of Negroes were lynched in the first half of 1919, including one veteran hung for wearing his uniform in public. There were two major antiblack pogroms, one in Charleston, South Carolina, in May, another in Longview, Texas, in June. When news of the latter incident reached New York City, the NAACP's white executive secretary, John Shillady, hurried to Austin to demand an investigation. His second day in town, a gang of whites assaulted him. A pacifist, Shillady didn't fight back and was beaten senseless. His body recovered. But his spirit never did. He resigned from the NAACP within the year.[57]

The violence reached Washington, D.C., in mid-July 1919. Like so many cities, the capital had been stretched to the breaking point. The city's three black areas—the section around Howard in the northwest, a neighborhood to the southwest, and Foggy Bottom close to downtown—were overflowing with southern migrants, who continued to pour into the city even though the promise of wartime jobs had ended. Washington had another influx as well: thousands of white soldiers were billeted on the outskirts of town, waiting to be mustered out of service. Boredom was itself a hazardous thing. A series of sexual assaults, all attributed to black men, heightened the danger, as it had in Bartow all those years ago. When word reached the military camps that a soldier's wife had been raped, the conflagration began.[58]

Saturday night, July 19, a hundred soldiers, sailors, and marines marched on the colored neighborhood to the southwest and attacked blacks unlucky enough to be on the streets. The violence spread on Sunday, as more soldiers and sailors joined the mobs roving the city in search of victims. Brutality swirled around the seats of power: several black men were pummeled in full view of the White House, where President Wilson, exhausted from his efforts on behalf of world peace, lay ill in bed. Anarchy peaked the third day. The *Washington Post* opened the morning with a call to arms: "Every available service man stationed in or near Washington or on leave here" was to gather at Pennsylvania and Seventh avenues at nine that evening, the newspaper reported, for a "'clean-up' that will cause the events of the last two evenings to pale into insignificance." By nightfall, more than a thousand white men crowded the downtown area. Military authorities tried to pen them in with a hastily assembled corps of four hundred cavalrymen. But the mob surged through the lines and fanned out toward the Negro sections.[59]

Foggy Bottom was quickly overrun and the southwest neighborhood again imperiled. But in northwest Washington the mob met massive resistance. All day long, the area's Negroes had been preparing to defend themselves. Residents bought up any gun that was for sale, and when the stock ran out, they grabbed free weapons that had been rushed in from Baltimore. Many families barricaded themselves inside their homes to await the mob's attack, while groups of men organized themselves into neighborhood defense units. Whites arrived as darkness descended. Down the side streets, gunfire blazed from upstairs windows; passing automobiles were riddled with bullets and members of the white mob scattered for cover. Main thoroughfares became battlegrounds. The intersection of Seventh Avenue and T Street, a few blocks south of Howard, saw the most fearsome fighting. Blacks and whites engaged in hand-to-hand combat throughout the night. Dozens were seriously injured, including two policemen, and one black man was shot to death. Only exhaustion and the approaching dawn ended the bloodshed.[60]

Violence finally ended on the fourth day. From his sickbed, Wilson ordered two thousand federal troops into the capital to secure the streets. And a furious rainstorm drove both whites and blacks indoors. Negro spokesmen insisted, however, that neither federal action nor a fortuitous turn in the weather had quelled the attack. James Weldon Johnson, soon to be named Shillady's successor as NAACP executive secretary, arrived in the city just as the soldiers were taking up positions. "The Negroes saved themselves and saved Washington by their determination not to run, but to fight," he concluded after two days of consultation and investigation, "fight in defense of their lives and their homes. If the white mob had gone on unchecked—and it was only the determined effort of black men that checked it—Washington would have been another and worse East St. Louis."[61]

There's no sign that Ossian joined in the defense that Johnson celebrated, though he undoubtedly had more training with firearms than most of those who stood their ground on Seventh Avenue. He couldn't have helped but hear the screams of the combatants, the report of the guns, and the wails of the injured during the long night's battle. He was then living at the Chi Delta Mu fraternity house at Third Avenue and T Street, four blocks from the intersection where black Washington made its stand. But he didn't venture out.[62]

Perhaps he was paralyzed by fear. Sometime in the first few days of the riot, Ossian had been walking down the street when a gang of whites descended on a passing streetcar, pulled a black passenger down to the sidewalk, and beat him mercilessly. It is easy enough to imagine the terror of the scene: the sickening sound of fists and boots slamming against bone, the victim curling his body into the fetal position to avoid the blows, the stream of blood filling the cracks in the cement. After two years of medical school, Ossian would have known the details of the damage the thugs had inflicted, the way a skull cracked, the ways internal organs hemorrhaged. But it would have been the memories that the attack evoked—those terrible childhood memories—that would have been most frightening. It was a visceral emotion, a wrenching deep down in the gut. He could bury his past under years of education. He could live hundreds of miles from his parents' home, in the heart of a great city. But no matter what he achieved or where he went, he was never safe from the mindless fury of the mob.[63]

As it happened, the summer's savagery was just beginning. Less than a week after peace was restored in the nation's capital, whites on Chicago's South Side stoned to death a black boy who mistakenly had gone swimming at a beach whites considered their own. Rumors of imminent black retaliation sparked yet another assault, this one much worse than either East St. Louis or Washington. In the course of five days, twenty-three Negroes and fifteen whites were murdered, five hundred were injured, and millions of dollars in property was destroyed. Fears of sexual violence, that most potent of provocations, triggered smaller riots in Knoxville, Tennessee, in August, and Omaha, Nebraska, in September. And in October 1919, whites in eastern Arkansas slaughtered a hundred or more black sharecroppers they feared were going to form a union. With such a staggering series of offenses to occupy the public mind, most Americans soon forgot about the Washington riot. But for Ossian, the violence on the streets of the capital had reopened the wound cut in Bartow years before. The wound was sure to close; he was young and resilient. Yet there was always the chance of another rupture, should the terror come again.[64]

◆

The most fearsome violence abated late in 1920. Northern riots came to a sudden halt, the worst fears subsided, and the national mood began to swing toward an optimism that in a few years' time would create the Jazz Age. But the forces the war unleashed were never really contained. The Red Scare of 1919 shattered the union movement and destroyed radical political organizations. Those victories didn't satisfy the nativists, who continued to assail the immigrants in their midst. If anything, the intellectual attack on the foreign-born grew even more shrill as the 1920s got under way. "Our country, originally settled by the Nordics, was toward the close of the nineteenth century invaded by hordes of immigrant Alpines and Mediterraneans, not to mention Asiatic elements like Levantines and Jews," Boston lawyer Lothrop Stoddard wrote in one of 1920's most widely read books, *The Rising Tide of Color Against White World Supremacy*. "As a result, the Nordic native American has been crowded out with amazing rapidity by the swarming, prolific aliens, and after two short generations he has in many of our urban areas become almost extinct." Bitter rhetoric blended seamlessly with political action. In the course of 1920, the Ku Klux Klan, reborn in Georgia five years earlier, began its race into the North by adding anti-Semitism, anti-Catholicism, and xenophobia to its traditional appeal to white supremacy. In the wells of Congress, meanwhile, the nation's representatives pushed relentlessly toward closing the country to further immigration, a fundamental reversal of the policy that had made the nation's industrialization possible.[65]

Race relations in the cities of the North likewise remained tense. The informal segregation of public places continued to metastasize. "As a colored woman," Mary Church Terrell reported from Washington, D.C., "I may walk from the Capitol to the White House ravenously hungry and supplied with money to purchase a meal without finding a single restaurant in which I would be permitted to take a morsel of food if it were patronized by white people, unless I were willing to sit behind a screen. And in some places I wouldn't be allowed to do even that." Farther north, segregation wasn't yet so advanced. But the situation continued to be dangerously unstable. On Chicago's bloody racial frontier, whites bombed eight separate properties bought by Negroes in the first three months of 1920. Ongoing guerilla warfare wasn't enough, though, to stem the flow of migrants out of the south; it was better to risk a sudden outburst on the streets of a major city than to face perpetual poverty and oppression in the cotton fields of Alabama or Mississippi.[66]

◆

Ossian also felt the fever fade and his hopes revive. He spent most of his last two years in medical school, 1920 and 1921, sharpening his skills at Freedmen's Hospital. It wasn't quite the glowing place the AMA had thought it to be. The hospital's appropriations had been cut during the war, so the administration couldn't afford to maintain the building properly: when Ossian began his clinical work, paint and plaster were peeling in two of the three wards, floor tiles were cracked, and even in the main operating room there were broken windows. Freedmen's nevertheless provided an excellent experience for senior medical students. Since its founding, the hospital had never turned away patients simply because they couldn't afford to pay for care. Washington's poor therefore flocked to Freedmen's; most of the patients the hospital accepted were on charity, their fees paid by the federal government at the princely sum of two dollars a day. As the poor arrived, they brought with them a staggering array of conditions and diseases. So Ossian saw the routine cases—expectant mothers, injured workmen—and the cases he never would have seen had he been working in a hospital treating more prosperous patients: children suffering from malnutrition, men whose untreated wounds had turned gangrenous, families devastated by diphtheria or typhoid.[67] By the end of his two years in the wards, Ossian had the kind of experience most medical students would have envied.

Ossian received his medical degree in the spring of 1921. At twenty-five years of age, he still had a young man's face. His rich brown skin was smooth and clean, his eyes bright and alert; the furrows and crow's-feet that came with age and worry had yet to appear. His high hairline hinted that one day soon he would go bald but the process had yet to begin. He had his mother's tight dark hair, which he kept carefully trimmed. He had taken to wearing round horn-rimmed glasses, his version of the academic look that was de rigeur on campus. And he had learned to effect an appearance that made him seem not simply serious but stern. He arched his eyebrows, set his lips, and glowered, a pose meant to impress a professor, intimidate a patient, and just perhaps, to convince himself that he had become a member of the most esteemed profession possible.[68]

He wanted more. Every year, Freedmen's Hospital offered eleven year-long internships to recent medical-school graduates. No post was more coveted. Internships weren't yet a required part of American medical education, though for white doctors they were becoming much more common. For colored doctors, unwelcome in most white hospitals, internships were a mark of distinction; those who undertook additional study were considered the crème de la crème of the profession, its rising stars. So winning an extra year's study at Freedmen's was a particularly great honor. For Ossian, it would be the first marker that he was in fact on his way to becoming a physician of the first rank.[69]

Ostensibly, the internships were awarded purely on merit: applicants took a competitive exam in May and those with the highest scores were appointed the following month. Behind the scenes, however, candidates used whatever influence they could to secure a spot. One of Ossian's classmates had a United States senator write on his behalf; another applicant had an important local politician intervene. In such a competition, Ossian never stood a chance. Somehow he managed to secure an extra two months' work at Freedmen's, an abbreviated internship. But the year-long posts went to others. It must have been terribly disappointing to receive his rejection, an unmistakable indication that despite all his labors he had yet to work his way into the elite of the race.[70]

Ossian didn't have the time to brood over his defeat, though. The completion of his brief internship would bring to a close his student years; come September 1921, a new class would arrive at Howard, fresh faces from Fisk and Lincoln, and his classmates would move on, leaving the capital for careers across the nation. Without an additional year at Freedmen's to occupy him, Ossian, too, would have to set out on his own. He could have gone back to Bartow, back to the embrace of his family. It would have been a victorious return, twelve years in the making. How his parents would have beamed with pride as their neighbors clucked over the fine young man their son had become; how the community would have rejoiced to finally have a colored doctor who could deliver their babies, treat their children, and help the elderly gently pass; how whites on the other side of town would have bridled at the impressive home he could have built on Second Avenue, facing the railroad tracks so all the Crackers could see its splendor. Or Ossian could have moved to a small town in the North, a place like Xenia perhaps, where he could have set up a general practice, bought one of the best houses in the black part of town, and settled into a quiet life, the beloved county doctor growing gray among a generation of townspeople he'd nurtured into adulthood. There were appeals in pursuing such paths. But Ossian still held to the pledge he'd made himself at Wilberforce—to rise in his profession and make his fortune—and he wasn't about to surrender it for a career of comfortable obscurity. To be the sort of man he wanted to be, he needed a bigger stage.

Perhaps he'd always thought of returning to Detroit when his training was complete. But Ossian claimed, later in life, that it was the summer he'd spent at the Fairfax Hotel in 1913 that brought him back. The wonderful promise the head bellhop had dangled before him—Detroit rewarded the ambitious—that was the draw. Of course, it would be hard to start a practice in a city where he had no relatives to support him, where most of his acquaintances were servants of one sort or another, where life moved at the relentless pace of the assembly line rather than to the rhythm of the seasons. But ambition—since the day he'd stepped off the train at Xenia station and scrambled aboard Dad Harris's cart, he'd been driven by ambition. It was the gift his family had given him and the burden it had placed on him. It was the lesson he'd learned best at Wilberforce and Howard; not languages or biology or anatomy or even racial militancy but dogged determination. That's what drew him down to Washington's Union Station in the late summer of 1921 for one more move, one last migration, one more train ride to a new beginning in the Motor City.

FOUR

UPLIFT ME, PRIDE

When Ossian Sweet arrived in Detroit late in the summer of 1921, he had two hundred dollars in his pocket, his diplomas packed away in his bags, and a few tenuous connections left over from his days working as a bellhop and waiter. Beyond that, the new doctor had nothing: no home, no office for a practice, no real friends, no family to give him a start.[1] He was on his own.

The first time Ossian had seen Detroit, in the summer of 1910, it was already a brawny manufacturing center elbowing its way into the front ranks of urban America. Eleven years later, the city had arrived as an industrial colossus, a modernist metropolis of steel, smoke, and sinewy assembly lines. Auto factories that a few years before had been hailed as engineering marvels were already being dwarfed by new facilities. Just behind the train station on the west side, Wall Street's latest conglomerate, General Motors, was putting up a brand-new factory for the production of its luxury line of Cadillacs; on the narrow streets of the east side, the Dodge Brothers were feverishly expanding their elegant Albert Kahn–designed plant, already one of the nation's largest. For sheer audacity, though, none could outdo Ford. The incredible Highland Park plant was only a decade old, but along the banks of the placid Rouge River, just west of Detroit, the company was building a complex five times the size that would eventually cover over a thousand acres and employ almost a hundred thousand workers.[2]

Such dramatic economic expansion fueled massive migration: more than a million people now lived in Detroit, twice as many as in 1910. No matter how furiously officials tried to annex more land, they couldn't make room for all the people. In the city center, where empty lots had once sat waiting for development, neighborhoods had become so crowded they were beginning to resemble Manhattan's Lower East Side or Chicago's infamous Back of the Yards. "A city which is built around a productive process . . . is really a kind of hell," wrote a young Detroit minister, Reinhold Niebuhr. "Thousands in this town are really living in torment while the rest of us eat, drink, and make merry. What a civilization!"[3]

The tenor of the streets was rough and sometimes shocking. In the boom's early days, the automakers thought they could create a model industrial city, full of hard-working, patriotic, efficient workmen, and for a few heady years, they seemed to have their way. In 1914, when Ford raised wages to five dollars a day, he sent a team of one hundred inspectors out to his workers' homes to assure that they were living according to the highest standards of decency and frugality. Those who didn't measure up had their wages cut in half. The following year, Detroit's largest firms launched a citywide Americanization campaign, designed to teach immigrant workers the English language and the manufacturers' definition of citizenship: "Each one in his sphere keeping busy, doing honest work, and contributing to the sum total of wealth for the support of the nation." To break the power of the ethnic political bosses, the automakers and their allies remade city government, putting power in the hands of upright Anglo-Saxon businessmen. The first mayor elected under the new charter, in 1918, was Henry Ford's bookkeeper. And to clear the city of workingmen's saloons, city fathers pushed through a prohibition law two years before the nation went dry.[4]

But by 1921, dry, decent Detroit, with its fine new government and its strict moral laws, had split wide open. There wasn't a time of day or night when liquor wasn't flowing somewhere: the swells patronized speakeasies on Grand Boulevard, and those looking for an edgier experience went down to the black and tans along Hastings Street, where jazz bands played, drinks were first-rate, and slumming was all the rage. But there were thousands of other places in the city, joints the slummers didn't even know existed: blind pigs offering teacups of fine whiskey smuggled in from Canada and Mason jars full of white lightning made in basement stills; tenderloin jukes jumping with the piano blues of Speckled Red, Big Maceo Merriweather, and Tupelo

Slim; back-room dives hidden in the rear of cigar stores and sweet shops; and dingy apartments where locals sat at beat-up tables downing shots and home-brewed beer. And breaking Prohibition was only the beginning. Drugs, gambling, prostitution were sweeping the city— if a person had a vice, Detroit had a venue for it.[5]

Detroit's newfound license extended to brutality. Bootleggers, numbers runners, drug dealers, pimps, and assorted mobsters waged war for their share of the city's illicit trades, but viciousness wasn't limited to hoodlums. Businessmen's faith in their ability to remake the city was crumbling, and in its place was rising an increasingly bitter and repressive politics. Once again, Henry Ford led the way. Determined to explain moral decline, he latched onto *The Protocols of the Elders of Zion*, purportedly the Jewish blueprint for undermining Christian civilization, but in truth a rambling, nearly incoherent forgery created by czarist agents at the turn of the century to justify Russians burning shtetls and pillaging synagogues. By the summer of 1921, the automaker had already mass-produced some half million copies.[6]

Ford's extremism fed fires of xenophobia smoldering among the city's Anglo-Saxon minority, blending anti-Semitism with anti-Catholicism, nativism, and a deepening racism. Detroit's cops, themselves overwhelmingly native-born whites, were almost as likely to rough up foreign-born and colored suspects as they were to arrest them. In the poorer districts, more than a few innocent citizens felt the whack of a billy club in the course of a year. Down on the factory floor, meanwhile, Ford and his fellow manufacturers turned a blind eye to the dictatorial regimes of their foremen, who forced out ever-increasing production by threatening their men hour after hour, day after day. Worst of all, there was no saying when the pressures of life in a boomtown—too much drink, too much work, too much worry about making ends meet— would trigger an outburst: the back of a hand across a spouse's face, the flash of a fist in a packed barroom, the flame of a pistol shot in the midst of a neighborhood dispute. In 1920 alone, ninety-four people had been murdered in Detroit, many of them gangsters slain on back streets or dumped into the Detroit River, others just ordinary folks, victims of the city's growing penchant for solving problems with brutish force. "That's a hard-boiled burg all right. . . . Lots of tough muggs in Detroit, lots of whorehouses and tough joints," remembered one migrant who fled for home the first chance he got. "It was too goddamn hard working for Ford. That assembly line stuff is a sonofabitch, I'm telling you. That's nothing but slavery."[7]

Ossian Sweet could have been excused for taking his time to adjust. Instead, he moved into the heart of the city, renting a room on Clinton Street, half a mile east of downtown. It was a dingy place, squeezed in alongside Walter Green's trucking depot in a block of well-worn houses on the edge of the toughest, most desperately overcrowded neighborhood Detroit contained. But that was exactly where Ossian wanted to be. For inside this area were forty thousand Negroes, an entire generation of southern migrants jammed into a four-square-mile section of squalor, the very people the newly minted doctor hoped would make him his fortune.[8]

•

Ossian was no stranger here. Most of his summers in the city, he'd lived just a few blocks east of Clinton Street, in one of the many boarding houses that dotted the area everyone called Black Bottom. Well-to-do colored families lived scattered around the city, but most of Detroit's poorer Negroes—the laborers, waiters, shoeshine boys, and domestics—lived nearby. At the time of Ossian's first visits, it was still a tiny community: in 1910, there were only fifty-seven hundred colored people living there, not that many more than in Bartow and its surrounding countryside. And despite its name, Black Bottom wasn't really a colored area. Most of its residents were immigrants, not Negroes. A few were Germans, half-forgotten old men and women left behind when their prospering sons and daughters moved into other, more comfortable parts of the east side years earlier. More came with the huge wave of foreigners from eastern Europe and the countries of the Mediterranean rim, the kind of people America's Anglo-Saxons were convinced lay somewhere between black and white. In the center of Black Bottom, along Hastings and St. Antoine streets, Negroes lived alongside recently arrived Russian Jews, refugees from the czar's pogroms. On the neighborhood's fringes, blacks shared streets with Italians, Greeks, and Syrians, refugees from grinding poverty.[9]

Only in Ossian's final two years in Detroit, the cataclysmic summers of 1916 and 1917, had the neighborhood begun to change, the transformation beginning with the same dynamic that altered so many parts of the North—the cutting off of European immigration, the coming of war, industrialists' desperate need to find new workers to fill factories humming with military orders. But true to form, Detroit made the process more intense, more furious than anywhere else. News of high-paying jobs up in the Motor City shot through every portion of the South, carried from town to town, farm to farm, by labor re-cruiters, colored newspapers, word of mouth, and even the blues. "I'm goin' to get me a job, up there in Mr. Ford's place," they sang in road-houses deep in the delta and across the Black Belt, "Stop these eatless days from staring me in the face. When I start makin' money, she don't need to come around, 'Cause I don't need her now, Lord, I'm Detroit bound."[10]

So they were, by the trainloads. Some thirty thousand colored people came to Detroit during the Great War, thousands more in its immediate aftermath. The vast majority were working people, sharecroppers, lumber-camp hands, and maids. But they were looking for exactly the same thing that had drawn Ossian to Detroit: the promise of opportu-nity, the chance for something better. "I was reading the paper," remem-bered one migrant, "and it say where the plumbers were making twelve dollars a day and the brick layers and plasterers, too. . . . Well, that's more I ever made in a regular job during off season down in Georgia. Down there when the crop was in and it was wintertime pay over two dollars a day. So I just know I could make big money in Detroit."[11]

Most migrants didn't find those fabulous tradesmen's wages. By southern standards, though, typical Detroit pay rates were nothing short of spectacular: assembly-line workers earned up to six dollars a day during the war years, some of the highest industrial wages any-where in America. No wonder Detroit's black population shot up at such an extraordinary rate: between 1910 and 1920, Detroit's black population had increased by 600 percent. No other colored commu-nity above the Mason-Dixon Line, not even Harlem, had grown so fast.[12]

The results were drearily predictable. Like so many other parts of the North, Detroit's race relations had been decaying since the turn of the century. The Great Migration dramatically accelerated the decline. There was no serious attempt to repeal the state's long-standing civil rights statutes, which outlawed discrimination in public places, pro-hibited segregated schools, and even sanctioned interracial marriage. But in practice, white Detroiters grew more and more insistent on keeping Negroes in their proper place. Segregation came in fits and starts, imposed by random acts of cruelty. The owner of an auto-parts plant set up separate toilets for his white and colored workers. The management of a tire factory strung a thick iron chain across the cafe-teria so that white men could eat their sandwiches without fear of amalgamation. A white high school teacher required colored students

to sit apart from their Caucasian classmates. Government officials rejected appeals to put more than a handful of Negroes on city payrolls,
no matter how menial the jobs. Whites bludgeoned a colored man because he sat in the wrong seat at a baseball game in a neighborhood
park.[13]

Segregation spread into the job market, too. To be sure, the Great
War opened auto-factory jobs to Negroes, but colored workers faced a
bewildering array of discriminatory practices. A few automakers, Henry
Ford foremost among them, sometimes hired Negroes for the full
range of production positions, though almost never for the skilled
work that native-born whites had always controlled. The precious few
colored men who were placed on the assembly line faced repeated
harassment. From the minute he punched in to the minute he punched
out nine hours later, an assembler worked at breakneck speed, doing one simple job—putting a side panel into place or screwing on a
bolt—over and over again. He'd feel his muscles screaming at him to
stop, to just sit down and rest. But the foreman was always behind
him, yelling at him to keep going, to get the production out. Not a
word of respect, just "nigger do this" and "nigger do that," barked over
the relentlessly throbbing machinery. When the foreman wasn't riding
him, his fellow workers often were. Colored men had to guard against
their workmates sabotaging their machines, breaking their tools, even
taking a swing at them when they weren't looking. Most manufacturers didn't allow such conflicts to develop. Instead, they restricted colored men to specific jobs, mostly those so dangerous or so miserable
only the most desperate migrants were willing to take them.

At the Dodge Brothers factory, Negroes spent their days in the toxic
cloud of the spray rooms, applying the black paint that made the road-
sters shine. At Cadillac Motors, they were slotted into the wet-sanding
department. And in plant after plant, even Ford's, they were dispropor-
tionately assigned to the foundries, feeding iron into the face of furnaces so large they dwarfed the mighty monsters of Birmingham,
Alabama's steel plants, drawing out buckets of molten metal and pouring the contents into the castings from which parts were made, hoping
and praying that this time there'd be no accident, because foundry
workers didn't recover from accidents.[14]

At least a man could get a factory job. Auto manufacturers wouldn't
so much as think of hiring a colored woman. So a young lady coming
out of the South had to take whatever work she could get. If the color
of her skin wasn't too dark, she might land a job in a second-rate store

or downtown hotel. More likely, she went into domestic service. Wages were a lot higher than in the South; working in one of the big houses in suburban Grosse Pointe, a woman could bring home thirteen, maybe fourteen dollars a week. But the work was as demanding as anything a factory hand endured. A maid had to be up before the sun so she could have "her" family's breakfast on the table before they came downstairs to begin their day. By the time she headed home on the streetcar, hollow eyed from exhaustion, the sun was long gone and the streets passing by were draped in darkness.[15]

Most likely, she went home to Black Bottom. Detroit wasn't like Bartow or other southern towns, where officials tried to mandate where Negroes could live. In Detroit, the neighborhood color line was drawn in the same jagged way that segregation was imposed everywhere else in the city, through a host of individual actions arbitrarily imposed. Many migrants, like Ossian, headed to Black Bottom of their own accord, knowing that was the place where they'd make connections and find friends. Other newcomers were steered into the neighborhood the moment they got off the train, pointed in the right direction by the women who staffed the Visitors Aid desk or the Black Bottom landlords who prowled the station's cavernous hall looking for potential renters.

But it was mounting discrimination in the real estate market that increasingly sealed Negroes into Black Bottom. Since the early 1910s, white real estate agents and landlords in Chicago and New York had refused to so much as show Negroes homes in white neighborhoods, saying that the presence of colored people depressed property values. In the course of the Great War, those practices spread to Detroit. Not every real estate agent or landlord signed on: if colored folks were willing to pay a premium for a piece of property in a white part of town, some real estate men were happy to oblige them. But to defy the new racial conventions took more courage—or more avarice—than many real estate agents and landlords had. So discriminatory practices passed from office to office, property to property, and racial hatred gradually turned into common business practice, the way things were done.[16]

Where the market failed to keep colored people contained, white homeowners sometimes threatened to do the job themselves. Detroit never experienced the racial conflagrations that exploded in Chicago in 1919, but there were certainly brushfires during the war years. Well-to-do whites tried to buy out a black doctor who moved into their neighborhood. A contingent of property owners threatened another colored man with expulsion unless he and his family abandoned their newly rented apartment.[17] Then there was the trouble on Harper Avenue, just north of Black Bottom. It began when a white landlord couldn't resist the thought of raising the rents in his four-family flat to the usurious level colored people paid. In August 1917, he offered one of the apartments to a group of Negro workingmen and their families. The new tenants weren't in the flat more than an hour when a mob of two hundred whites gathered in the street.

Speaking for the crowd behind them, two former aldermen informed the colored men that they wouldn't be allowed to stay the night. The Negroes appealed to a policeman they spotted walking by, who told them it would be "best to leave and not to have any trouble." Before the migrants could figure out what to do, the mob surged past them, gathered up their clothes and furniture, carried all of it off to the four trucks they had waiting, and drove the goods back to Black Bottom, where they dumped them in the street. "Before we'll stand for these niggers staying here," one of the whites said as he dragged the Negroes' belongings down the stairs, "we'll turn this house upside down." Strange thing was, a colored family lived just two doors down from the flat. They'd been there for years, and no one seemed to mind until the segregationist fever raced through the neighborhood.[18]

Thus did the rough walls of segregation begin to rise around Black Bottom as Ossian settled into Clinton Street at the end of summer 1921. Wealthier blacks still lived in different sections of Detroit, many of them in otherwise completely white neighborhoods, some in tiny black enclaves miles from the inner city. And there were still plenty of foreigners on the streets of Black Bottom. When Ossian took a walk down his block, more than half the neighbors he passed were immigrants: Joseph Saprenza, right next door; the Catalanos, a few houses up; Frank Gidzie, Sam Monecatto, and Alex Schuwalow, living together closer to the corner of St. Aubin Avenue, where the business strip lay. But if Ossian kept walking east to the blocks just beyond St. Aubin, from the edge of Black Bottom to its center, the concentration of colored people became dramatically more intense, street after street filled with southern migrants who, because they were black, had no choice but make their new home in Detroit's emerging ghetto.[19]

•

Black Bottom buckled under the weight of thirty-five thousand colored newcomers. Like many of Detroit's older neighborhoods, the area was a long, narrow strip running several miles north from the Detroit River. Downtown, full of glittering new skyscrapers, movie palaces, and swanky hotels, served as the neighborhood's western border. The area's central section ended seven blocks to the east, at the Grand Trunk Railroad lines that ran just behind St. Aubin, though the population pressure was so great that more and more Negroes were moving to the streets on the other side of the tracks, where Ossian was living.[20]

Black Bottom's worst section was down by the river, where beat-up boardinghouses catered to sailors trying to find some action and winos willing to sleep in a roach-infested room rather than spend the night huddled in a warehouse doorway. Conditions slowly improved as one moved toward the white neighborhoods that formed Black Bottom's northern boundary. The flophouses became fewer and farther between, replaced by blocks of dilapidated wood-frame homes, each of them no more than a couple of feet from the one next door, without so much as a touch of greenery front or back. The only open space came from the alleyways that ran along the back of the houses, where little girls jumped double Dutch amid the piles of refuse that hid the nests of rats.

As depressing as it was to walk Black Bottom's streets and back ways, it was worse to climb up a set of broken steps, push open a door, and begin the search for a place to sleep. A migrant from the Mississippi delta was used to making do; sharecropper shacks didn't come with amenities. But Black Bottom pushed the limits of endurance. Landlords knew there were far more Negroes looking for places than the neighborhood had to offer. So they ratcheted up rents as high as they would go.

To get a couple of dingy rooms barely big enough to house a family would cost a man and wife fifty or sixty dollars a month. And groups of rooms were hard to come by. Many landlords wanted to squeeze in tenants until they were stacked like cordwood. A sign reading "Room for Let," pasted up on a house window might well mean that there was nothing more than a bed available—a tangle of threadbare sheets and blankets resting on a soiled mattress, the head and foot pushed up against other beds, ten, twelve in a room that at one time had been the parlor of the house. Day or night, there'd be men trying to rest, still dressed in their sweat-stained overalls, blankets pulled up around them to block out the talk and the chill of the room.[21]

With demand so high, landlords didn't see the need to make repairs. There were houses in the central section of Black Bottom where the water cascaded through the ceiling every time it rained; houses where the walls were so sodden the tenants had to pull their beds into the center of the room so they wouldn't spend the night drenched to the skin; houses where the plaster on the walls had crumbled so that the wind whistled through the exposed laths; houses without glass in the window frames all winter long. Bathtubs turned black from overuse. Toilets stopped up and overflowed. Kitchen sink spigots that spewed rust red water. And in half the houses of Black Bottom, there was no running water at all. To fill a cooking pot, a tenant had to prime the backyard pump. To relieve himself, he had to endure the outhouse, fending off the swarm of flies in the summertime, the cutting cold in the winter, and the stomach-churning stench any time of year.[22]

Some migrants had to settle for even worse. For a fee, the owners of the pool halls on Hastings Street allowed men to bed down on top of the tables. Down on Mullet Street, where Ossian had roomed in 1917, two men paid twenty-five dollars a month to sleep in a sagging shed hammered together in the backyard of a rooming house. A couple and their baby lived in a single windowless room off a barbershop; the outhouse was so close to the well that both mother and child were poisoned by the drinking water. A family from Tennessee—husband, wife, and a gaggle of children—crowded into a tarpaper shanty, which they lit with kerosene lamps, insulated with scrap paper, and heated with the embers from the kitchen stove. The family dreamed of owning the place one day, if only they could come up with the fourteen hundred dollars the owner was asking for it.[23]

Official neglect reinforced Black Bottom's burdens. City Hall spent Detroiters' tax dollars putting sewer lines and proper lighting into the new housing developments being built out near the suburbs, while many Black Bottom folks lugged pails of pump water through dimly lit yards. The neighborhood's working people had to rely on inadequate streetcar lines to carry them to their jobs; maids with plum positions in Grosse Pointe could count on almost an hour's ride to work, while men lucky enough to get jobs at Ford's new River Rouge plant figured on twice that long squeezed onto overcrowded trolleys.[24]

Detroit policemen treated Black Bottom's colored residents with absolute contempt; it was common practice for patrolmen to stop black men at random and subject them to searches, often at gunpoint, and those taken into custody sometimes spent days in jail just waiting to be charged with a crime. At the same time, the police department did nothing to check Black Bottom's illicit trade. On weekend evenings, when pay packets were full, white men crowded the streets of Detroit's most notorious vice district, which overlapped with Black Bottom's eastern edge. The most entrepreneurial brothels had their prostitutes stand in the front windows, trying to lure the johns inside. But those in the know—white or colored—found the best deals in Black Bottom's numerous buffet flats, where pimps and madams provided customers with a full range of services: liquor, dope, cards, dice, sex, the buffet flats had it all, even a bit of the blues. "There's a lady in our neighborhood who runs a buffet flat," the incomparable Bessie Smith sang of a Detroit dive she knew well, "And when she gives a party she knows just where she's at." The cops knew, too, but they didn't care, unless they saw a colored man walking in the company of a white woman. Then they ran him in.[25]

Of all the problems that afflicted the neighborhood, none was greater than disease. Contagion was a constant threat, partly because everyone lived in close quarters, partly because no one was vaccinated: a migrant carried smallpox up from the South a few years before Ossian arrived and in short order Black Bottom faced an epidemic. Syphilis, the plague of the vice district, also was widespread. But dramatic illnesses weren't the real threat. Straightforward diseases—those that afflicted the poor, that flourished in dirt and fetid air—those were the ones that devastated Black Bottom. Pneumonia was twice as likely to kill a Negro as it was a white person, tuberculosis three times as likely. Parents buried children lost to afflictions as simple as diarrhea and enteritis, malnutrition and exposure. In 1919, 595 colored babies were born in the city; 89 of them were dead by 1920.[26]

Rudimentary care would have saved some of them. But Black Bottom didn't get even that. Visiting a doctor was a luxury for a working person when there was rent to pay and food to buy. In any case, there were only twenty-seven colored doctors in the entire city in 1921, one for every fifteen hundred Negroes. A truly desperate person might drag himself to one of Detroit's white hospitals, far outside Black Bottom. But chances were, he'd get no more than a quick once-over in the outpatient clinic, since most white institutions wouldn't admit Negroes, no matter how sick they were, unless they could pay their own way, and not many migrants could do that.[27]

The city welfare office was willing to pick up the tab for particularly poor Negroes, but only a few white hospitals were willing to provide them with beds, and even then, they restricted colored patients to segregated wards and prohibited their physicians from seeing them; it wouldn't do to have a colored doctor darkening the hospitals' pristine white halls. So in 1919, only 3 percent of Detroit's ill Negroes went to hospitals for treatment, while the rest tried their best to get by. They bought up the patent medicines that drugstores kept on their shelves. They brewed home remedies from recipes they'd carried up from the South. They relied on midwives to deliver their babies and, in some case, root doctors and faith healers to cool fevers and quiet tremors. But mostly, they suffered.[28]

With his sharp businessman's eyes, Ossian knew that the desperation that stalked Black Bottom would give him the opportunity he wanted. He wasn't in an ideal position to open a practice. The few months he spent preparing for the state medical exam slowly ate away at his small savings, so that by the time he received his license in November 1921—the only colored man to qualify that year—he couldn't afford rent on an office of his own. But around the corner from his house, along St. Aubin Avenue, was a small pharmacy, the Palace Drug Company, owned and operated by Cyrus Dozier, a southern-born colored man just about Ossian's age. Maybe it was affinity, maybe economic necessity, but Dozier was open to a deal. Ossian agreed to invest one hundred dollars in the pharmacy, in exchange for which he received office space in the back. Palace Drugs was an ordinary storefront, long, dark, and narrow, sharing a wall with Sam Delisli's dance studio next door. But the location was first-rate, an easy walk from anywhere in Black Bottom, and the customers who came in to pick up a cold remedy or a stick of candy were sure to spread the word about the handsome new doctor looking for patients. All in all, Ossian had gotten himself off to a very good start.[29]

Years later, he still recalled his first case. Lucius and Elizabeth Riley were fairly typical Black Bottom folks—he worked as a barber, while she kept house for her husband and two boarders in a cramped flat just around the corner from Palace Drugs—and the problem that brought them to Ossian was a typical Black Bottom malady. Mrs. Riley's jaw had grown stiff, and the couple suspected that she had contracted tetanus. The disease was terribly simple to acquire—the bacteria thrives in dirt and passes into the body through the smallest of punctures—but the consequences were fearsome: the infection races through the nervous system, triggering spasms so severe that the victim's malfunctioning body literally chokes her to death. A careful examination convinced Ossian that there was no infection: Mrs. Riley had simply dislocated her jaw. The relieved couple gave him five dollars to reset the bone. And they started to spread the word that the young man in Palace Drugs knew what he was doing.[30]

Through the balance of 1921, Ossian's practice grew at a steady pace. Most of the work was routine. Parents arrived with sick children in their arms; factory workers came looking for treatment of blistering burns they'd received in the foundries; men and women sat at his desk and mumbled about the excruciating pain of venereal diseases. Once in a while, something unusual came his way. Patching up a patient battered in a Christmas Eve brawl—another victim of Detroit's mean streets—brought in fifty dollars, a staggering sum for a few hours' work. In celebration, Ossian treated himself to a fine holiday dinner, then banked the balance.[31] Most of the time, though, his patients couldn't afford to pay more than a dollar or two for treatment, and sometimes Ossian had to settle for nothing more than a thank-you and a vague promise that the cash would be on its way as soon as payday came.

Still, the fees added up. On a reasonably busy day, Ossian could make twice as much as Black Bottom's best-paid factory workers and far more than he had ever earned toting suitcases at the Fairfax Hotel and waiting tables on the D & C Lines. As cash came in, he squirreled it away. It was his nature to be disciplined about money matters, like his parents before him, to think of the future rather to indulge in the immediate gratification that Detroit provided in abundance. There would be time for extravagances later. But in the early going, it was more important to set his practice on a firm foundation, to build a reputation for dependability and prudence. So through the gray winter of 1922, Ossian worked as hard as he could treating the physical burdens that poverty imposed on his patients, letting his reputation spread through Black Bottom, his office grow busier, his bank account fatten. And in his precious spare moments, he began to look beyond the poor people who filled his days to the professional class he'd spent the previous twelve years preparing to join.

•

Ossian knew any number of people like him, ambitious young entrepreneurs who saw in the flood of southern peasants the chance to make their fortunes. He spent most days at Palace Drugs in the company of Arkansas-born Cyrus Dozier; occasionally he ran into his old friend from the Fairfax Hotel, Vollington Bristol, now proud owner of a funeral parlor on Division Street; walking along St. Aubin, he passed

A. G. Wright's real estate office and Harry Nuttall's drugstore. Ossian had no trouble easing his way into that world. Black Bottom's businessmen were ebony Babbitts, spending their days wheeling and dealing, their evenings slapping backs and trading jokes in a dizzying array of social clubs and service organizations. Ossian did his share of joining, taking membership in the Benevolent and Protective Order of Elks, in the Free and Accepted Masons' Hiram Lodge No. 1, and in Kappa Alpha Psi's graduate chapter, where he rose to the exalted position of Polemarch. He couldn't have been all that comfortable with the mandatory conviviality of the lodge hall—not exactly his style—but a businessman had to have connections. In much the same spirit, Ossian joined a church, Ebenezer AME, which prided itself on being one of the more progressive congregations in Black Bottom. It must have been an obvious thing to do; no son of Dora and Henry Sweet was going to put aside his religion. But the step had its practical side, too. Church folks expected to see their doctor sitting in a pew on Sunday morning, and if they didn't, they'd be quick to take their business elsewhere.[32]

All his effort paid dividends. It was probably through one of the lodges that Ossian was named a medical examiner for Liberty Life Insurance, an appointment that assured him a steady stream of patients he might not otherwise have acquired. He even made a few friends, no easy matter for a man of Ossian's studied reserve. He came to enjoy the company of Julian Perry, a fellow Howard man struggling to set up a legal practice in Black Bottom. Slight, quiet, and serious like Ossian, Perry made an amiable companion for the occasional evening out. When he needed advice, though, Ossian increasingly turned to his fellow Elk, Mason, and fraternity brother, Dr. Edward Carter, whose office was several blocks north of Ossian's on St. Aubin.[33]

Though Carter was ten years Ossian's senior, there was a real affinity between the two. A shared profession drew them together, but it was more than that. Both of them were sons of humble southern families who had worked their way through school—Carter was the first black doctor to graduate from the University of Iowa's College of Medicine—an experience that gave them a fierce determination that Perry never really had. Like every other Black Bottom businessman, Perry wanted to do well for himself. Carter encouraged Ossian's desire to go further, to work his way beyond the lodge hall and into the upper reaches of black society.[34]

There must have been times in 1922 when Ossian wondered whether such a leap was possible. The elite of colored Detroit wasn't as rarified a circle as Washington's fabled Black 400—no one in Detroit had roots that deep in the American aristocracy—but it was imposing enough. Most members of the black upper class were northerners by birth, a healthy portion of them Canadian-born progeny of fugitive slave families that had prospered in the safety of Ontario's flat farmlands. With their families' money to support them, they had attended the best colleges. Some of them went to Howard, naturally, but many others graduated from white schools: abolitionist Oberlin, the University of Michigan, Columbia, even Harvard. Most of them preferred the quiet elegance of St. Matthew's Episcopal Church to the intensity of the Baptists and the AME. Though they sometimes held leadership posts in the Masons or the Odd Fellows, they rarely went to meetings. And they certainly weren't shopkeepers. The men were invariably doctors, lawyers, and ministers. The women devoted themselves to the social clubs that were the backbone of black philanthropy.

And though they often worked in Black Bottom—even the most skilled colored professionals had a hard time securing white clients—they almost never lived there. A few, such as Dr. Cleague and Dr. Young, owned handsome homes in the small black area nestled among the solidly middle class, native-born white neighborhoods of Detroit's west side. Most of the colored elite, though, settled in otherwise exclusively white parts of the city. Dr. Charles Green, so light skinned he could have passed for white, lived on a gracious side street north of Black Bottom, not far from the grand homes of Boston Boulevard, where Henry Ford had lived when his first Model Ts were rolling out of his factories. Rev. Robert Bradby, the enormously powerful pastor of Second Baptist Church, had a house in a comfortable east-side neighborhood miles from his church, while regal Dr. Albert Johnson, son of one physician and brother to another, lived even farther east, well on the way to Grosse Pointe, a world away from Ossian's room on Clinton Street.[35]

But Sweet and Carter had one entrée into the charmed circle that wasn't open to most of Black Bottom's aspiring entrepreneurs. When the Great Migration reached floodtide in the spring of 1918, eleven of Detroit's foremost colored doctors decided that the city simply had to have a hospital that accepted black patients without discrimination. The city government certainly wasn't going to provide it. So the physicians took it upon themselves to build an appropriate facility. Rather than look for a building in Black Bottom, they bought a rambling old house on Frederick Street, three blocks beyond the ghetto's northern boundary.

The physicians gave their new hospital an appropriately grand name, Dunbar Memorial. It was much harder to make it into a grand institution; Dunbar survived on donations from white charities and the continual effort of its founders. It wasn't enough: the hospital was so small it could admit only twenty-seven patients at a time and so underfunded it could maintain only a single ill-equipped operating room. Still, the doctors took enormous pride in their achievement. They had given the colored people of Detroit their own hospital, a place where they could be treated with care and dignity. They'd hired an entirely black staff of nurses. And they had given themselves a place where they could practice their craft without suffering insults and exclusion, a place of their own.[36]

It was about two miles from Palace Drugs to Dunbar Memorial, just far enough to be inconvenient. But Ossian made the trip as often as time would allow, climbing into the rattletrap of a Model T he bought in the spring of 1922 and bumping through the streets. After years of working at Freedmen's Hospital, he must have found Dunbar's facilities disappointing and the medicine practiced there utterly routine; if a colored doctor encountered a genuinely difficult case, he'd invariably swallow his pride and send the patients off to a white hospital. But the hospital's social opportunities were sterling. Undoubtedly, the contacts Ossian made were casual: standing on Dunbar's broad stone steps, perhaps, chatting with the chief of surgery, Alexander Turner, while the good doctor's chauffeur kept the sedan idling at curbside; trading stories of Howard University with Dr. Ames, the last colored man to serve in the state legislature; asking H. Peyton Johnson, Tufts Medical Class of '96, for his opinion on a puzzling case.[37] It was through such moments—so ephemeral as to seem almost meaningless—that a young man of no pedigree brought himself to the attention of the elite and taught himself their ways.

There is no way to recover all the pieces of information Ossian must have gathered as he listened to his senior colleagues: the name of a tailor who knew how to give a suit coat the right cut, perhaps the merits of one school, one neighborhood, or one church over another; the way the midwesterners' nasal twang altered the pronunciation of a medical term Ossian had learned to say with his deep southern drawl. But there is no doubt that once he made his way into Dunbar's cramped wards, Ossian was again enveloped in the fervid politics of the Talented Tenth, as he had been at Wilberforce years earlier.

◆

Times had certainly changed. By the early 1920s, the Bookerite movement that had so enraged Scarborough and his associates in the first decade of the century had been thoroughly routed, and Booker T. Washington himself was gone from the scene, killed by an unspecified disease—syphilis, some whispered—in the closing days of 1915. The tectonic shifts brought on by the Great War, meanwhile, opened new fissures within colored America. NAACP liberals found themselves under attack from a new generation of radicals, while integrationists such as W. E. B. Du Bois turned on the black nationalists who were surging to the flamboyant standard of Jamaican-born Marcus Garvey.[38] However deep their difference, though, civil rights activists shared a sense that the war had fundamentally altered the terms of combat in the battle for racial justice.

While Du Bois pledged that Negroes would return from Europe ready to fight for equal rights, socialists A. Philip Randolph and Chandler Owen preached the power of armed resistance. "We are . . . urging Negroes and other oppressed groups confronted with lynching and mob violence to act upon the recognized and accepted law of self-defense," the pair wrote during the bloody summer of 1919. "Always regard your own life as more important than the life of the person about to take yours, and if a choice has to be made between the sacrifice of your life and the loss of the lyncher's life, choose to preserve your own and to destroy that of the lynching mob." Garvey's fellow Jamaican Claude McKay captured the same sentiment in a verse that swept through black communities like a sudden summer storm. "If we must die, let it not be like hogs / Hunted and penned in an inglorious spot. . . . Like men we'll face the murderous, cowardly pack / Pressed to the wall, dying, but fighting back!" The black press personalized the new militancy with a telling name. "The NEW NEGRO . . . does not fear the face of day," proclaimed the *Kansas City Call*. "The time for cringing is over."[39]

The crosscurrents of civil rights cut through Detroit, as they did most major urban centers. The Motor City had a handful of black radicals struggling mightily to organize the proletariat. And for a few seasons, Garvey made deep inroads among Black Bottom's working people, some five thousand of whom joined his United Negro Improvement

Association in the early 1920s.[40] The medical men of Dunbar, however, had no truck with such newfangled movements. They were steadfastly devoted to the ideals Du Bois had articulated almost a generation earlier, committed to the principle of integration through agitation and convinced that they, colored Detroit's leading lights, were obligated to take the lead.

The effort was shot through with condescension, the dark side of racial uplift. Most of Detroit's elite were convinced that the city's race relations had declined partly because whites were appalled by the bad manners migrants had brought with them from the rural South. "Why is segregation increasing?" sniffed the head of the Detroit Urban League, a graduate of Tufts and Harvard. "Chiefly on account of the loud, noisy, almost nude women in 'Mother Hubbards' standing around on the public thoroughfares. . . . There are dirty white people of course, but white people are the judges and colored people are being judged."[41] It must have been comforting to think that the Talented Tenth might break down the growing wall of segregation by scrubbing clean the face of the ghetto. Dunbar's physicians were certainly willing to give it a try.

The Detroit Urban League, which had Dr. Green and Dr. Johnson on its board, sent its members into Black Bottom to hand out pamphlets instructing the poor on how to carry themselves with the necessary decorum. "Don't crowd inside of a street car filled with people in your dirty, greasy overalls," the leaflet helpfully suggested. "Wear a coat over your clothes when you are going back and forth from the foundry." Under the direction of Dr. Turner's wife, the colored YWCA on St. Aubin Avenue brought working girls off the streets and into sewing circles. For their part, Dunbar's senior staff organized its own Health Week, during which the hospital's doctors traveled across Black Bottom denouncing folk practices carried up from the South and urging those crowded into rooming houses and dilapidated flats to keep their homes neat and clean. The doctors found it an edifying experience. "It has been found," they reported, "that in a great many homes in Detroit that rats enjoy as much care and comfort in the house as do some of the members of the family."[42]

As they preached to the poor, the elite struggled to maintain the militancy that the New Negro was supposed to embody. In the 1910s, Detroit's black professionals had built one of the more vibrant NAACP branches in the country. The branch's guiding force was Father Robert Bagnall, pastor of St. Matthew's Episcopal, the colored elite's church of choice. In typical NAACP fashion, Bagnall and his Talented Tenth associates used the full force of law to batter away at the discriminatory practices spreading across the city. The branch filed dozens of legal suits against businesses that refused to serve colored customers. When trains leaving the Michigan Central Terminal for points south required Negro passengers to ride in separate cars, Bagnall demanded that the railroad companies rescind the practice. With the branch's backing, lawyer Charles Mahoney, a Republican of some influence in Detroit politics, forced the nearby town of Ypsilanti to abandon the school segregation it had practiced for half a century. And in a singular act of solidarity, Bagnall's branch waged a long campaign on behalf of a luckless Georgia farmhand, Thomas Ray, who in June 1920 had murdered his abusive landlord.

After the fatal shooting, Ray had fled north toward Canada, but before he could cross the border, the Detroit police had taken him into custody. The branch's attorney, W. Hayes McKinney, quickly launched a series of legal maneuvers to block Ray's extradition to Georgia; should he be sent back, McKinney argued, he'd surely be lynched. The case generated enormous passion in the black community: when a rumor passed through Black Bottom that a white mob was going to seize Ray during a court appearance, a phalanx of Negroes threw a protective cordon around the courthouse. The branch finally sealed the victory in June 1921, a full year after the shooting, when Michigan's governor declared the homicide justifiable.[43]

By then, though, the branch had also suffered a crushing loss. Perhaps it was the surging militancy of the New Negro, perhaps just a matter of timing, but in June 1920, the white progressives who ran the NAACP's Executive Board finally decided to place the association's day-to-day operations in the hands of a colored man, James Weldon Johnson. As soon as the appointment was made, the new secretary set out to build a black staff. Du Bois was already an institution unto himself in the offices of the *Crisis*. But Johnson added three more men. For the position of assistant secretary, he hired Walter White, a twenty-seven-year-old blond-haired, blue-eyed bantam with a genius for self-promotion. William Pickens, a longtime NAACP activist, signed on as field organizer. And Robert Bagnall agreed to serve as national director of branches. Bagnall resigned his pulpit at St. Matthew's in January 1921 to take up his post at the NAACP's New York headquarters.[44]

The Detroit branch couldn't function without him. Bagnall's successor, attorney McKinney, launched a few initiatives of his own, including a half-hearted attack on police harassment of interracial couples, but the branch quickly became engulfed by infighting so vicious it all but ceased to function. McKinney eventually resigned, turning the organization over to a businessman who wouldn't even answer his mail, much less confront segregation's steady advance. From Manhattan, Bagnall raged at the destruction of his handiwork, but at such a distance, he couldn't pull the branch back together.[45]

By the time Ossian integrated himself into Dunbar in 1922, the coordinated civil rights campaigns of the 1910s had devolved into a series of ad hoc actions, sporadic protests hastily conceived by friends and colleagues in response to the latest affront to the race. A handful of doctors, tired of having women in the throes of labor turned away from Detroit's best maternity hospital because they were colored, tried to have the facility's public funding cut. When rumors of a Negro crime wave pushed police repression in Black Bottom to frightening new heights, the Talented Tenth threw together a committee to plead with city hall to hire more colored officers. A prominent Negro attorney, caught up in the force's crackdown, was dragged out of his car and searched at gunpoint by a snarling cop. The lawyer sued the officer for fifty thousand dollars in damages. Such forays were brave enough—it was riskier to confront discrimination without the protection an organization provided—but against the consolidating forces of white supremacy, they had a quixotic air about them, the colored elite imitating, in their way, Claude McKay's tragic hero, fighting back against an enemy that in the end was destined to win.[46]

It wasn't a role that came naturally to Ossian. Though he bridled at the discrimination spreading across the city, he'd never participated in any sort of challenge to white supremacy. Under his colleagues' influence, though, he took an increasing interest in racial affairs. He never got around to joining the NAACP, perhaps because the Detroit branch was moribund, but he took out subscriptions to all the black publications favored by the Talented Tenth: Du Bois's *Crisis*, Randolph and Owen's *Messenger*, the *Chicago Defender* and the *Pittsburgh Courier*, two of the nation's largest and most influential black newspapers. Poring over the pages of those papers, he came to fancy himself a student of the nation's racial problems, a specialty he'd never claimed at Wilberforce or Howard. He was even drawn into a few of Dunbar's initiatives. During Health Week in 1922, he walked over to Macedonia Baptist Church to deliver the doctors' prepared lecture on cleanliness and proper garbage removal. It didn't take much effort on Ossian's part, since the church was only a block away from Palace Drugs. But Ossian took one step more. He actually joined one of the small protests that his senior colleagues mounted.[47]

One day, Charles Green approached Ossian with an invitation, a precious thing to a young man striving to be noticed. A local college group planned to host a testimonial dinner in honor of the city's greatest sports hero, the Detroit Tigers' brilliant outfielder, Ty Cobb. The best hitter the game had ever seen, Cobb was a baseball genius and, in Ernest Hemingway's delicate phrase, "an absolute shit": a bully, a thug, and, thanks to a childhood spent in backcountry Georgia, a racist of frightening ferocity. The venom of lynch law surged through his veins; even the slightest violation of the color line was an insult to his honor and a cause for violence. When a Negro worker yelled at him to stay off the tar he had just laid on a Detroit street, Cobb assaulted the man. When a colored groundskeeper tried to shake his hand, Cobb knocked him to the ground and kicked him in the head, then tried to choke the man's wife. When a colored elevator operator mistakenly took him to the wrong floor of a Cleveland hotel, Cobb slapped him; the hotel's black security guard intervened, and Cobb responded by pulling a knife and slashing him in the face.[48]

What a delicious thought, to have Cobb sitting on the dais watching in horror as a squad of black men strode into the auditorium to join the festivities. So Green bought a table's worth of tickets. Then he asked Ossian and eight other colored men to join him for the evening's entertainment. It is easy to imagine that Ossian hesitated to accept; this would be his first involvement in any protest, and the dinner was going to be a very public affair. To refuse Green's invitation, though, was to risk being thought a coward, unworthy of a place among the city's Talented Tenth. In the end, the risks were small. Though the white crowd stirred as the group made their entrance, no one tried to stop Ossian and the others from taking their seats, not even Cobb, who for once managed to keep his temper.[49]

Ossian relished the moment enough to remember the details several years later. Undoubtedly, he reveled in the sense of solidarity that the ten men felt that evening, the slap on the back from a senior colleague when the dinner was done, the raucous laughter in the staff room when the tale was retold, the slightly more vigorous nod the next time he passed Green in the wards, the way that just a little bit of courage opened up the charmed circle of Detroit's elite, if only for an evening. But he also must have realized just how small a protest it had been. Going through the race papers stacked up in his Black Bottom rooms, Ossian couldn't miss all the brave talk about the New Negro, the exhortations to self-sacrifice on behalf of the race, the glorification of confrontation, a politics for young men who knew no fear. No matter how enjoyable the experience had been, spoiling the color scheme at Cobb's testimonial certainly didn't measure up to such great expectations.

But Ossian did know fear. In his nightly reading, Ossian inevitably focused on the most recent installments in the nation's long history of racial horrors. There was the unusual litany of lynchings, fifty-one in 1922, including three black men murdered on the same day in a small Texas town. It was the larger cruelties that most often caught his attention, though. He brooded over Tulsa's epic 1921 pogrom, still a raw wound the following year. More than a hundred colored people had died in two days of white rioting, all of it brought on by a Negro teenager accidentally brushing up against a white girl in a downtown elevator. But Ossian fixed on a single death, which Walter White had movingly chronicled for the *Nation*. Dr. A. C. Jackson was one of Tulsa's most promising young men, a skilled surgeon who, White carefully noted, had done advanced study at the Mayo Clinic. On the first day of the riot, Jackson exhausted himself treating the wounded, and when darkness finally came, he hid in the basement of his substantial home, which by some miracle the rioters had yet to set ablaze. Early in the morning of the second day, Jackson smelled whiffs of smoke from the fires that were beginning to consume his block. Facing immolation, he came out of his hiding place to surrender to the vigilantes filling his street. "Here I am," the doctor yelled out, his arms upraised. "Take me." But one of the mob, a teenager out for a night of fun, lowered his rifle and pumped two bullets into Jackson's chest. Then another white boy stepped over the doctor as he writhed in pain on the sidewalk and shot him again.[50]

A year and a half later, Ossian's attention was riveted by another southern riot. On New Year's Day 1923, news of a rape shot through the hamlet of Sumner, Florida. Enraged whites marched on the nearby colored town of Rosewood, though they had no proof that the rapist was hiding there. Like the black men of Washington, D.C., in 1919, Rosewood's Negroes tried to defend themselves from the assault, but they were overrun. At least seventeen of Rosewood's residents were murdered that day, and the rest were driven into the countryside while the mob burned the town to the ground. The story cut into Ossian partly because the attack took place just seventy miles north of Bartow.[51] But there was more to it than that. In Tulsa and Rosewood, Ossian could see the reflection of the fires that had burned above the banks of the Peace River and along the streets of Washington, D.C., and in those flickering flames—searing light dancing off the deepest blackness—he knew that the terror that balled up inside him at the thought of truly confronting white supremacy was entirely justified.

◆

Maybe it was the color of her high yellow skin, maybe the way the lights above the dance floor brought out the hints of auburn in her hair. It could have been her self-assurance, the deeply ingrained confidence he never quite secured, or her gracious manner or her warm toothy smile that drew him to her. Whatever the reason, when Ossian met Gladys Mitchell one evening in 1922, he felt an immediate attraction.[52]

It's hard to believe that Ossian hadn't been in love before. If he'd had other infatuations, though, there hadn't been much opportunity to act on them. Wilberforce maintained such high walls between its male and female students it would have taken tremendous effort to scale them. Though Howard's co-eds were some of the race's most accomplished young women, Ossian spent his days in the medical school's almost exclusively male world and his nights either hunched over textbooks or working to pay his bills. In any case, the timing was never right. Ossian had degrees to earn, a practice to establish, a career to build. There hadn't been room for a wife. By 1922, though, he'd made such great strides that whatever reservations he had felt melted away.

The moment wasn't completely free of calculation. With all the diversions and entertainments Black Bottom had to offer, from smoldering nightclubs and red-hot dance halls, Ossian went looking for companionship at one of the most respectable venues in all of black Detroit, a formal dance at the St. Aubin Avenue's colored YWCA, a favorite charity of Dunbar's doctors and their wives. Gladys was precisely the kind of young woman he would have expected to find there. A slender, almost frail twenty-year-old with a long, thin face and weak chin, almond skin, deep brown eyes, and luxuriously long hair that flowed to her waist when she uncoiled it, Gladys carried herself with the charming reserve and sure grace that the middle class bestowed on its daughters.[53]

They were gifts she almost didn't receive. Gladys's mother, Rosella, was only seventeen, a native of Washington, D.C., living in Pittsburgh, when she gave birth to her only daughter; if Gladys's father was a presence in the early days, he apparently didn't remain so, though it's not clear what happened to him. In a city as rough-hewn and unforgiving as Pittsburgh, it would have been simple for a teenage mother without a husband's income to slip into the miasma of poverty. But Rosella had the great fortune to meet and marry Benjamin Mitchell, a musician by trade, just barely out of his teens himself. When Gladys was seven, the family moved to Detroit, where her stepfather built a successful career playing for pit orchestras in downtown theaters while teaching piano on the side.[54]

Rosella and Benjamin handed their only daughter every advantage they could. They joined St. Matthew's, Bagnall's prestigious church, where Gladys was surrounded by the colored elite that Ossian scrambled to join. They moved to the northeast side of the city, settling into a pleasant two-story house on Cairney Street, directly across from The Nativity of Our Lord Catholic Church, a massive edifice built to serve the immigrants who filled the surrounding streets. There was one other colored family on the Mitchells' block, a doctor and his wife; otherwise, the neighborhood was completely white, not wealthy certainly, but solidly working class, a safe, stable area full of hardworking families.[55]

Comfort didn't come cheaply—Rosella had to take in boarders to meet the mortgage—but the extra work was worth it. Gladys was able to go to the local grade school, where she was the only black child in her class, and to Northeastern High, where the education was far better than it would have been in the colored part of town. The Mitchells trained Gladys in the social graces that a young lady should have when she ventured into the world: the soft handshake, the ready smile, the ability to carry a casual conversation without so much as a trace of effort. And they gave her a home filled with books and music; études and nocturnes drifted through the parlor, a world away from the rough sounds of the roadhouses and the buffet flats.[56]

A secure childhood made Gladys a strikingly poised young woman. Unlike Ossian, she felt no need to impress acquaintances by overpowering them. Instead, she drew them in with her impeccable manners, so carefully cultivated as to be almost invisible. Having extended courtesy, she expected courtesy in return, even when dealing with whites. Gladys certainly wasn't naive enough to think that race didn't matter. Sitting in her family's pew at St. Matthew's, she heard Bagnall continually condemn the discrimination that marred Detroit. And white violence had brushed by her family; some of her cousins had been trapped in the Chicago Riot of 1919 and one of them, a policeman, had almost been murdered by a mob. But racism hadn't scarred her the way it had Ossian. She was comfortable in the presence of whites, was, in fact, a quarter Caucasian herself. The auburn in her hair was an inheritance from her grandfather, a Scotsman transplanted to Virginia. So when whites didn't treat her as the equal she knew herself to be, she assumed a steeliness—so hard-edged it cut to the quick—that Ossian, for all his bitter memories, couldn't manage.[57]

Comfort also made Gladys less focused than her husband. Ossian had marched through his schooling with the single-mindedness ambition creates. Gladys drifted. After high school, she enrolled at Detroit City College but she was not a serious student, moving from teachers' education to nursing without settling on any course.[58] It wasn't a matter of intellect but rather of expectation: Gladys didn't need education's imprimatur the way Ossian did. On the contrary, she must have understood that any time she spent in front of the classroom or in the hospital ward was likely to be temporary. Her parents had trained her to follow the middle-class path, to be a wife and mother; they assumed that managing a household would be her life's work, not teaching schoolchildren or caring for the sick.

There were other differences as well. Ossian was almost seven years older than Gladys and much more experienced: he had been on his own for a dozen years, whereas she had never lived outside her parents' home. Within the Mitchells' world, though, Gladys had the advantage; for all of his mother's attempts to bring an air of refinement to the Sweets' home, Ossian was still too much of a country boy to be completely at ease amid the flowered divans and fine lace doilies of a formal sitting room. For Ossian, such contrasts must have only added to the attraction. When this charming young woman slipped her hand into his, he knew he had found the sort of mate a young doctor of such obvious promise ought to have. After a few months of dating, Ossian summoned up the courage to propose. The wedding was a small but gracious affair, held at St. Matthew's—her church, not his—five days before Christmas 1922. Ossian's friend Julian Perry stood by his side while Gladys made her way up the aisle on the arm of her stepfather. Father Bagnall's replacement, Everard Daniels, read the vows. Then the best man and Gladys's maid of honor, her friend Serena Rochelle, handed the couple the wedding bands they were to place onto their spouse's finger, a permanent sign of devotion, a moment of triumph for both bride and groom. Though she probably didn't know it, it's very likely that Gladys was pregnant.[59]

There was never any possibility of Ossian taking his bride to live in Black Bottom. Naturally, Gladys had spent plenty of time in the neighborhood; St. Matthew's was in the heart of the district, and the Y where she'd met Ossian was on its eastern edge, close to Palace Drugs. But a middle-class northern girl couldn't be expected to live among the migrants and the foreigners, to shop in the same stores as foundry workers and maids, to share the sidewalks with bootleggers and numbers runners. And with Gladys's light skin, it was only a matter of time before a beat cop pulled the couple over, slapped Ossian up against a wall, and demanded to know why he was keeping company with a white woman. So, instead of settling into the Clinton Street apartment or even searching for something better nearby, Ossian packed up his rooms and moved with his bride into her parents' house.[60] For the first time in his life, he was going to live among white people.

•

They didn't plan to stay with the Mitchells for long. Sometime during their brief courtship Ossian told Gladys that he intended in the near future to spend a year in Europe studying the latest medical advances. Perhaps he dangled the idea as an extended honeymoon: pleasing Gladys is one of the few explanations for why the usually practical young doctor wanted to shut down a practice that was just beginning to thrive. Maybe, since being rejected for an internship at Freedmen's Hospital, he'd been hoping to obtain postgraduate training that was better than anything Washington could provide. The notion of studying in Europe, rather than looking for a domestic program, may well have come from listening to his colleagues at Dunbar; Alexander Turner's wife had spent six years studying music in Leipzig, a fact sure to impress someone the first dozen times she said it. Perhaps the idea reflected a touch of sibling rivalry. When Ossian's brother Otis completed his dental training at Tennessee's Meharry Medical School in 1922, he went on to an advanced course in the treatment of pyorrhea at Canada's McGill University; studying in Europe would certainly outdo that achievement. Surely it was important to Ossian that there Negroes were actually treated with respect, dignity, and even, at times, a touch of honor. "For what am I thankful for this night?" W. E. B. Du Bois wrote from France in the April 1919 issue of the *Crisis*. "For nothing but the most commonplace of commonplaces: a table of gentlewomen and gentlemen—soft-spoken, sweet-tempered, full of human sympathy, who made me, a stranger, one of them." It wouldn't be easy to pay for such pleasures; no matter how much money Ossian had managed to put away in his first year of practice, his bank balance couldn't have been high enough to pay for a transatlantic voyage and a year's living expenses. But a few months living rent-free would help to top off his accounts and make such an extraordinary adventure possible.[61]

Gladys's pregnancy must have complicated matters. By springtime, she was showing, by early summer well along. Surely she would have had some reservations about leaving the country shortly after giving birth. But Ossian seems to have forged ahead, plotting out a course so grandiose it would have taken a great deal of advance planning. The couple would spend their first few months at the University of Vienna, where he could attend lectures by surgeon Anton von Eiselsberg. Once the fall semester was complete, he, Gladys, and the baby would spend a few weeks touring the Mediterranean, then settle in Paris for the winter and spring, when Marie Curie would be teaching at the Sorbonne.[62]

Ossian couldn't have chosen more impressive names. Baron von Eiselsberg had helped to create the field of neurosurgery: he'd been the first doctor in the world to resect tumors of the spinal cord and the brain, accomplishments widely considered two of the most amazing medical feats of the age. For her part, Curie was an international icon: the meticulous scientist who first isolated radium; the brilliant theorist whose work on radiology promised to transform medical practice; twice winner of the Nobel Prize. During her triumphant tour of the United States in May 1921, about the time Ossian was applying for a Freedmen's internship, a New York magazine had hailed Curie with only slight exaggeration as "the greatest woman in the world." Word of Ossian's agenda would have left Dunbar's doctors—and anyone else even slightly acquainted with the scientific world—in open-mouthed awe.[63]

As it turned out, the Sweets didn't have a newborn to take with them. On July 17, 1923, Gladys went into premature labor. It's impossible to say precisely how far the pregnancy had advanced. If Gladys had become pregnant on her wedding night, her baby boy was born two days short of thirty weeks, old enough to have opened his eyes but too young to breathe without a struggle. Chances are he was a few weeks older, since he managed to survive three days. Ossian and Gladys's firstborn died at three o'clock in the afternoon of July 20 and the next day was buried in Roseland Park Cemetery, in an all-white suburb north of Detroit. Having expected the worst, his parents hadn't given him a name.[64]

The Mitchells' house must have been wrapped in mourning. Even if the pregnancy hadn't been well-timed, the Sweets surely had indulged themselves in the excitement of anticipating parenthood. With the death of his boy, moreover, Ossian had to have heard the echo of his parents' experience losing their first son as a toddler years ago. Under the circumstances, the European trip probably took on added meaning. Traveling abroad would have offered a chance to get some distance from Detroit, to begin to forget, to put the tragedy behind them. Exactly one month after the baby's birth, Ossian and Gladys completed their passport applications. The itinerary was already set, passage booked. All that remained was packing trunks and leaving home.[65]

The Sweets set sail for Europe aboard the S.S. *Carmania* on October 6, 1923. It must have been a bit frightening watching New York harbor fade into the distance. Neither Gladys nor Ossian had ever been outside the United States, except perhaps for a day trip across the Detroit River to Ontario, hardly an experience in world travel. But the couple also must have been exhilarated by it all. It had been fourteen years since Ossian boarded the train out of Bartow, a terrified child sitting alone in a filthy car reserved for colored people. A decade and a half later, he and his wife were standing on the glistening deck of an ocean liner, the chill wind whipping their faces, heading toward the sort of experience most Americans, white or black, could only dream of having. The first fine surprise came when the couple went below deck to find that their stateroom lay between two cabins occupied by whites. On the Cunard Line, there was no Jim Crow.[66]

The trip from New York harbor to Vienna took Ossian and Gladys through a world still shuddering from the horrors of the Great War. The *Carmania*'s first port of call was in Queenstown, Ireland, a nation engulfed in civil war, the final fratricidal act of the revolution begun in high drama during Easter week 1916. The Sweets disembarked in Liverpool, where years of deprivation had given way to waves of working-class protest and a leftward swing in public life. Once on the Continent, the couple passed through land made desolate by the most merciless combat the world had ever seen. Paris's glittering streets were haunted by the maimed, blinded, shell-shocked veterans of the trenches and by the too-young widows of those who didn't return. Vienna, capital of the fledgling republic of Austria, had lost three hundred thousand of its inhabitants during the war, but still the city confronted a severe shortage of decent housing that the new socialist government was desperately trying to fill. It must have been so strange, so shocking, to see a new Europe struggling to be born.[67]

Settling into a daily routine created challenges that at times had to have seemed more than daunting. Whenever they walked into a shop or encountered a neighbor, Gladys and Ossian had to rely on the less-than-polished German and French they had learned in school. Though Vienna and Paris weren't expensive cities by the standards of boom-town Detroit, the Sweets still had to make do without an income, so they undoubtedly counted every schilling and franc. But the greatest test was personal. Shortly after arriving in Vienna, Gladys discovered she was pregnant again. The realization must have opened up all sorts of fears. Should something go wrong this time, Gladys wouldn't have family and friends to comfort and console her, and should the baby die, it would have to be buried in foreign soil. Even if all went well, if she carried to term, the child would be born toward the end May 1924, before the Sorbonne's term ended, so she would have to deliver in Paris, itself an intimidating prospect.[68] It was comforting to have a doctor for a husband, of course, but there must have been times when Gladys longed to have her mother hold her hand.

For Ossian, though, the year was magical. Attending lectures didn't put him at the center of the academic world; the truly innovative work was being done not in university amphitheaters but at the Eiselsberg Clinic and the Curie Institute, where doctoral students toiled away under their supervisors' intimate direction. Still, Ossian could pick up information on the latest medical innovations, as long as he could follow complex technical presentations in languages that weren't second nature to him. The knowledge Ossian acquired wasn't going to be transferred back home easily. No matter how well he understood the details of Eiselsberg's neurosurgeries, it was inconceivable that he would replicate the procedures in Dunbar's rudimentary operating room. And while Curie lectured on radium therapy's curative powers—her presentations delivered to the throng of students in her elegant Polish-accented French—Ossian knew that patients in Black Bottom weren't about to gain access to expensive experimental treatments, not when something as simple as an X-ray was hard to come by. But Ossian wasn't really looking for practical training. He wanted the imposing credentials that studying with Eiselsberg and Curie bestowed, credentials most American physicians only dreamed of having. In that regard, the trip was enormously successful. Though Ossian didn't earn a degree during his year abroad, the Sweets would always think of his European education as his greatest accomplishment, a point of unending pride.[69]

Ossian also reveled in the lack of racial discrimination. European nations had their deep, disturbing prejudices: cosmopolitan Vienna sustained an anti-Semitic current strong enough to have swept along its most infamous prewar resident, Adolf Hitler, while republican France showed no interest in the liberty of its colonial subjects in Africa and Indochina. On the side streets and boulevards of the two capitals, though, dark skin simply didn't bear the stigma that it did in the United States. Along Franz Josef's magnificent Ringstrasse, a colored couple was something of a rarity, worth a second glance but hardly a cause for concern. The world war had brought many more blacks to Paris, most of them Africans serving in the French military but a sizable number of them American soldiers, members of the black battalions raised in the spring of 1917. The French were fully aware of Jim Crow—the U.S. military made sure of that—but they insisted that it would not be imported. Colored Americans were free to go into any public establishment, to live wherever they wished, to socialize with whites, even to keep company with members of the opposite sex. Some Parisians went beyond openness to admiration. Immediately after the war, black culture became all the rage in the quarters of the avant-garde. Intellectuals embraced the "primitivism" of African art, literature, and dance, while the city's sophisticates fell head over heels for American jazz. The combination of equality and fraternity made Paris into a mecca for Negro artists. When the Sweets arrived in early 1924, the greatest migration was still a year or so away. But there was already a small thriving community of black Americans in Montmartre, the bohemian neighborhood that lay in the shadow of Sacré Coeur. At night, young Parisians crowded into its nightclubs and filled its black-owned restaurants, where haute cuisine gave way to downhome cooking.[70]

Ossian and Gladys were no more interested in the Montmartre scene than they were in the nightlife of Black Bottom. Most likely, they settled in the Latin Quarter, where Ossian could walk to the university and Madame Curie's lectures. However far they were from the smoky clubs, though, they shared in the freedom that drew jazzmen and poets to the City of Lights. For the first time in his life, Ossian experienced what it was like not to be branded an inferior. Small pleasures must have been so invigorating: to walk into a café off the Boul'Mich without having to wonder whether he would be turned away; to be called "monsieur" by a shopkeeper; to have a white man surrender his seat on the streetcar to Gladys, now uncomfortably large with their baby; to have a white woman smile at him as he held open a door to let her pass. Simple courtesies that in the United States he would never have received: that's what Ossian remembered from his springtime in Paris.[71]

Only one incident marred the Sweets' time abroad. As Gladys's due date drew closer, Ossian set out to make arrangements for a hospital stay; better to have her surrounded by professionals in case of emergency. The obvious choice was the American Hospital in the nearby suburb of Neuilly-Sur-Seine, an excellent private institution founded by well-to-do expatriates to care for Americans living in the city. Knowing that the hospital depended on donations to pay its operating expenses, Ossian contributed three hundred francs—not a major sum but generous enough for a couple of a tight budget—on the assumption that administrators would reciprocate by assuring Gladys a bed. He was wrong. Shortly before his wife's delivery date, Ossian was informed that the hospital couldn't accept Gladys. The white Americans who made up the vast majority of patients, he was told, wouldn't be comfortable with the idea of sharing a ward with a colored woman.[72]

Luckily, Gladys didn't need any special medical care this time. On May 29, 1924, she gave birth to a healthy baby girl, the first daughter of freedom's third generation. The Sweets gave her a suitably Gallic name, Marguerite, though they soon took to calling her Iva. Even as he rejoiced in the safe arrival of their child, however, Ossian couldn't bring himself to forgive the hospital's insult. Here was the truly cutting pain of Jim Crow. With its casual rejection, handed down simply as a matter of course, the American hospital had imperiled the health, and perhaps the life, of his wife and child, and there was nothing he could do but endure the affront. Timing made it all the worse. By late May, the Sorbonne's academic year was drawing to a close; Ossian and Glady had already booked passage aboard the S.S. *Paris*, sailing out of Le Havre on June 21. During the Sweets' last precious weeks in Paris, while Gladys fussed over the baby, Ossian had time to dwell on the hospital's callous reminder of the world awaiting his family when they went back home.[73]

FIVE

WHITE HOUSES

Through most of June 1925, the rumor passed up and down Garland Avenue. It was handed off in casual conversations, tossed across kitchen tables, turned over on front porches, where people liked to gather when the weather turned warm. The bungalow on the corner had been sold, neighbors told each other, and a colored man had bought it. Right off, people had been concerned, but they knew better than to believe every bit of gossip that came their way. The couple who owned the bungalow kept to themselves mostly—folks didn't even know their names—and no one dared to ask them whether the story was true. So there was no panic until Sunday, July 12, when the posters were nailed to the lampposts.[1]

The posters' tone was temperate enough, as such things went: there was none of the wild ranting of the Klan broadsides plastered around town, no skull-and-crossbones warnings crudely copied out. This message read as if a real estate agent had written it. "Do you want to maintain the existing good health conditions and environment for your little children?" the flyer asked. "Do you want to see your neighborhood kept up to its present high standards?" Those who shared those goals were invited to organize "in self-defense" at what the Waterworks Park Improvement Association was calling a mass meeting. It was to be held at the schoolhouse on Tuesday evening, two nights after the signs went up. No one had ever heard of the Waterworks Park Improvement Association, but the message was clear enough. Standing on the sidewalk, staring at the poster hanging limply on the rough wood, people knew the Negroes were coming.[2]

There was no stopping the panic then. In the privacy of their flats, husbands and wives talked nervously of fragile family budgets, mortgages years from being repaid, and the specter of plummeting property values. Children heard the fear in their parents' hushed voices and spun out the horrors that the Negroes would bring to their homes, terrifying and thrilling themselves with thoughts of assault and pillage. Out on the streets, there was rage at the audacity of the coloreds, moving where they didn't belong, buying the best goddamned house on the block.[3]

Seven hundred people turned out on Tuesday night, July 14, for the meeting at the elementary school, far more than organizers had expected. Despite its size, it was a polite, orderly crowd: foremen washed and groomed after a day's work; salesmen and clerks in their crisp white shirts; young mothers; teenage boys with arms crossed and faces set, all gathered on the schoolhouse lawn. The chairman of the Waterworks Park Improvement Association, a local man named Harold McGlynn who lived a dozen doors up from the bungalow in question, said a few words about the need for neighbors to band together. Then he turned the meeting over to the keynote speaker, and the attitude of the evening changed.[4]

He was a stranger, an outsider, and the moment he began talking everyone knew he was a hard case. He had come to tonight's meeting, he said, as a representative of the Tireman Avenue Improvement Association, and that alone riveted folks' attention. For weeks, the violence in and around Tireman had been front-page news: three times in the past month Negroes had tried to move into that neighborhood, and three times whites had driven them out. So heated had the conflict been that the mayor publicly appealed for calm, saying that Detroit was heading down the same bloody path as East St. Louis, Chicago, and Washington, D.C. But the speaker on that summer evening hadn't come to Garland to preach the peace the mayor hoped for. He shouted so that even those on the far reaches of the crowd could hear him say how vital the fight was that lay ahead. Tireman's homeowners didn't want coloreds in their neighborhood: Negroes were a pestilence, a plague. The Tireman Avenue Improvement Association had done its duty. Now Garland should do the same. Use legal means if possible, force if necessary. But put the niggers out. Put them out.[5]

The assembly cheered. Not just a few rabble-rousers, not just the

Klansmen, but all of them, although some standing amid the crush were ashamed afterward. Before the speaker could even finish his address, the entire crowd, seven hundred decent, hard-working, sober citizens cheered harder than they had the entire evening, their applause rolling across the schoolyard, rumbling through the clear summer night, and echoing off the bungalow on the opposite corner not a hundred feet away.[6]

·

"If I had known how bitter that neighborhood was going to be," Ossian said later, "I wouldn't have taken that house as a gift." It was the sort of thing he had to say then, when his life depended on striking just the right tone. But it wasn't true. To be sure, Ossian and Gladys didn't have an intimate knowledge of the surrounding area. But in the summer of 1925, there was no missing the hatred seething through the streets of Detroit. And there was no reason to think that Garland Avenue was immune from its contagion.[7]

The Sweets had returned to the States on June 28, 1924 and within a day or two were back at the Mitchells' cozy house on Cairney Street. It was a triumphant homecoming, with a baby to show off and, when Gladys needed a rest, to hand off to doting grandparents. Ossian had his sparkling new credentials: no new degrees to add to his name, but his stories of Baron von Eiselsberg and Madame Curie were more than enough to impress anyone who cared to listen. And the Sweets undoubtedly had their tales of travel—the wonderful details of the exotic sights they'd seen, the strange foods they'd eaten, the tourists' misunderstandings and mistakes that seemed so funny in the retelling. Gladys seemed to have acquired an air of sophistication in her year abroad, acquaintances remarked, and Ossian seemed to stand just a bit taller, if such a thing were possible.[8]

In many ways, 1924 was a pivotal year for Ossian, a moment of passage from one age to another. It wasn't simply that his twenties were coming to a close—he turned twenty-nine on the thirtieth of October—or that he now had the responsibility of fatherhood. It was more a matter of expectations. With his reputation secure and his credentials now dramatically enhanced, the time had come to move beyond the strict frugality of his early days in Detroit. He could demand a new status. Rather than driving his old Model T, which was hopelessly out of fashion, he bought a brand-new Buick touring car, an automobile to match the fine machines his senior colleagues parked outside Dunbar

Memorial. There wasn't any question that, after his time away, he'd re-build his practice in Black Bottom. But instead of moving back to Palace Drugs, he rented space a few blocks north of the pharmacy. It was just a storefront, right next door to a funeral home, hardly a reas-suring sight for sick folk making their way into his waiting room, but for the first time in his career, Ossian had an office of his own, an in-dulgence perhaps, but also a sure sign of upward mobility.[9]

The year saw another shift as well, more subtle but even more pro-found. Ever so slowly, Ossian was beginning to replace his parents as the center of the Sweet family. Dora and Henry had nurtured the change each time they'd regaled their younger children with stories of Ossian's successes. Now the older ones were beginning to follow the path Ossian had made for them. In the summer of 1923, Dora and Henry's second boy, Otis, arrived in Detroit to begin his career as a den-tist. A few months later, their third son, Henry, left his parents' farm for Wilberforce, the first step in his march to be just like the elder brother he barely knew.

Living apart for the past fourteen years, Ossian and Otis weren't close friends. Their personalities widened the gap between them. They shared the businessman's touch: within a few months of coming to Detroit, Otis was running a promising practice ("Dr. O. O. Sweet, Pain-less Dentist") not far from Palace Drugs, in an office he shared with the president of the Detroit branch of Marcus Garvey's Universal Negro Improvement Association. Unlike his brother, though, Otis didn't com-bine dedication to his profession with a relentless drive to excel. A friendly, engaging man with a guileless, boyish face, he loved to take in the baseball games at Mack Park, where the Negro League played; to go dancing on colored nights at the glittering Graystone Ballroom; to while away the hours at the Nacrima Club or one of the other lodges he rushed to join. Ossian cringed at Otis's lack of sophistication, and he was not one to hold his tongue when he saw something to criticize. An acquaintance once remarked that Otis wasn't as articulate as his older brother. "The difference," Ossian bitingly replied, "is the differ-ence between a Negro who has been educated in the North and one who has been educated in the South." Had they not been brothers, Ossian wouldn't have chosen Otis as a friend.[10]

For their part, Ossian and Henry were almost complete strangers. Four years old when his brother first went north, Henry had grown up seeing Ossian only a few times a year. But the distance between them only intensified Henry's determination to match his brother's accomplishments. Temperamentally, Henry was more like Otis. Genial and gregarious, he'd made more friends in one year at Wilberforce than Ossian had in eight. Young women enjoyed his gentle teasing, and campus groups appreciated his earnestness and reliability: in addition to his membership in Ossian's old fraternity, Kappa Alpha Psi, Henry played on the football team, performed with the choral club, managed the military corps' band, and kept the books for Wilberforce's YMCA. But in other respects, he was Ossian's double. When Ossian traveled down to Xenia one Saturday in 1924 to watch Henry play football, he found a younger, more solidly built version of himself, almost every detail an imitation. In academics, too, Henry was following his brother's example, pursuing a bachelor of science in anticipation of graduate school, hopefully at Howard, and a life in the professions.[11]

If Ossian's recollections can be trusted, he and Henry also shared an interest in racial affairs. But while Ossian stood on the fringes of New Negro activism, Henry was more than likely drawn into the thick of it. A few weeks after Wilberforce's 1924 school year opened, night riders began to terrorize a local sharecropper, William Martin, shooting into his house and setting his hayrick on fire. The first few nights, Martin faced the attacks alone. Then Wilberforce's cadet commander decided to intervene. One evening, a contingent of college men, rifles in hand, marched across the harvested fields and with military precision established a defensive perimeter around the sharecropper's house. The night riders didn't dare challenge them; from that point on, William Martin slept in peace. Whether Henry was among those who stood guard isn't clear, though a popular, eager young man active in the college military program seems a likely candidate for frontline duty on behalf of the race. In any case, he must have been caught up in the militancy that burned across campus that month, and it's hard to believe he didn't share his enthusiasm with his brother in the course of their weekend together. Ossian was impressed enough to invite Henry to come live with him in Detroit the following summer, by which time, Ossian must have assumed, he'd have a new home base for the generation of Sweets that was starting to circle around him.[12]

The timing didn't quite work out. Detroit's manic boom had become even more intense by late 1924 than it had been before Ossian and Gladys went to Europe: the population had soared to a million and a quarter, far more than the city's already strained housing stock could absorb, and home prices were skyrocketing, up 67 percent from the year before. To make matters worse, the Sweets would have to buy above the market rate, since colored families were always expected to pay a premium for property. With all the other expenses Ossian was incurring, it took more time than expected to put aside a decent down payment. Through the winter of 1924–25, Ossian, Gladys, and baby Iva stayed with the Mitchells while they saved what they could. Only in the spring did they begin to scour the city for a house of their own. They couldn't have picked a more volatile moment.[13]

•

It had begun with the smallest of tremors, the first rumble in what would become an earthquake so great it would reconfigure the American political landscape. When the Anglo-Saxon elite took control of city government in 1918, they made it a priority to restructure Detroit's criminal court, long known as Recorders Court, which they considered hopelessly soft on crime. To toughen it up, they increased the number of judges from five to seven, put control of case assignment in the hands of a presiding judge, then made sure that hard-nosed conservatives won election to four of the seven seats on the bench, enough to assure them a permanent hold on the presiding judgeship and thus on all the court's activities. In short order, the conservatives launched a massive crackdown on petty crimes and the poor people who committed them, a judicial complement to the police brutality rampant in the foreign-born and colored districts of the city.[14]

When the judges came up for reelection in the spring of 1923, the lower classes struck back. In February, just two months after Ossian and Gladys's wedding, Frank Murphy, a thirty-two-year-old Detroit lawyer and Democratic Party activist, announced that he was joining the court's three progressive judges in a campaign bloc expressly designed to take control of Recorders Court away from the conservatives. The campaign had its cynical side: one of Murphy's key supporters, Irish-born criminal attorney Tom Chawke, specialized in keeping mobsters out of prison, and another, *Detroit Times* editor Red Mulcahy, another Irish American, saw in his candidacy a way to boost circulation and take a swipe at the paper's conservative competition. But it was also a genuinely liberal crusade, backed by reform-minded clubwomen, liberal ministers, and trade unionists determined to reverse justice's decline into repression.[15]

In Murphy, the campaign found its ideal spokesman. Handsome in an Irish American sort of way, with a long, sharp, serious face made dramatic by thick eyebrows and a shock of deep red hair, Murphy was charming, devout, well educated, and ambitious to a fault. Although he enjoyed being seen in Detroit's toniest clubs and cabarets, Murphy had never so much as touched a drop of liquor, an abstemiousness he learned watching his father's descent into alcoholism. He dated a string of starlets and society girls, but those closest to him knew he'd never marry; he reserved his deepest passions for his career, which he was convinced would take him to the White House, and for his mother, Mary, to whom he wrote ardent, painfully Oedipal love letters. Mary Murphy had given her beloved son a Catholicism so fervent—a faith of pilgrimages, prayer cards, and the sweet smell of incense floating above a golden sanctuary—some of his contemporaries thought him literally suited to the priesthood. But Frank was sure that he had been called to public service. He also knew precisely how to tap into the deep resentment the court had created among foreign-born and colored voters. Detroit's legal system favored "political grafters, exploiters of the poor, and profiteers," he proclaimed as he crisscrossed Detroit's working-class wards, while "the friendless and the penniless have less than an equal chance of justice." As word of his attacks spread, the crowds swelled. "I have gone among the humble of Detroit," he told a throng of five thousand at one rally, "and it is their great desire to free this city from the shackles of judicial tyranny." If elected, he shouted above the cheers, "I will try to have a temple of justice, not a butcher shop."[16]

The business elite and its political allies shot back with the full force of moral righteousness and fearmongering. The conservatives' newspaper, the powerful blue-blood *Detroit News*, gleefully quoted a well-known madam saying she was for Murphy and his running mates "heart and soul," then for good measure added a dose of anti-Semitism, tracking down two aged political fixers, Abe Ascher and Abe Ackerman, so that they could be put on record in support of the liberals. As the election approached, the *Detroit News* and its reactionary rival, the *Detroit Free Press*, played the race card, running simultaneous exposés purporting to show that "underworld characters" were "herding" twenty thousand Black Bottom Negroes into the registrar's office so that they'd be eligible to vote for Murphy. "Do we want to discourage crime in Detroit?" the *Detroit News* asked on its front page. "Or shall we adopt the theory that every stranger to a bathtub, clean collar, and upright life, who has committed a crime, is a victim of modern society and should be treated very tenderly? They are voting heavily in the tenderloin districts—Can you do less as a citizen?"[17]

For the most part, Detroit's Talented Tenth reacted to the campaign with an understandable confusion. Here was a new kind of politics, centered around an ethnic Democrat, the product of a party that had long championed white supremacy, appealing to the masses, black and white, with promises of equal rights before the law while the most respectable people in the city raged against him. Black Bottom's ordinary folks understood. On election day, April 2, 1923, Detroit split right down its ethnic, racial, and economic fault lines. The conservative judges carried the heavily white, native-born, more middle-class west side. But Murphy and his running mates swept through the east-side wards crowded with colored and foreign-born working people, piling up such huge margins that they crushed the conservatives in the overall vote. "We have met the enemy and we are theirs," a dejected member of the city's elite wrote a few days later, as Detroit faced "an entirely new deal in the court." He couldn't have picked a more prescient phrase, for Murphy had pieced together the coalition that in another nine years would make Franklin Roosevelt president of the United States.[18]

◆

If the spring of 1923 belonged to Murphy and his supporters, the Ku Klux Klan controlled the summer. The first Klan organizer had come to Detroit in 1921, just as the organization was trying to push its base into the urban North. He spent the next year spreading the carefully crafted message of moral renewal, 100 percent Americanism, anti-unionism, anti-Catholicism, anti-Semitism, and racism: a more overt, cruder version of the politics that the *Detroit News* had vainly employed against Murphy. So great was the reception, the Klan could barely keep up with the flow of recruits. By 1923, there were twenty-two thousand Klansmen in Detroit, and the Invisible Order was ready to go public. Throughout that summer, the KKK held nighttime rallies on the far west side, complete with cross burnings so spectacular and speeches so incendiary they drew upward of eight thousand. Klan newsboys took to selling the organization's newspaper, the *Fiery Cross*, on street corners. And on Christmas Eve 1923, Klansmen marked the season by burning a six-foot-tall cross in front of city hall, then cheering a hooded Santa Claus, come to entertain the kids.[19]

Perhaps the Klan would have remained happy torching lumber and rallying the faithful had it not been for a peculiar turn in city government. In early 1924, Detroit's businessman mayor announced that he was too ill to complete the second half of his two-year term, and a special election was called for November 1924 to select a replacement. When a local politician, John Smith, emerged as the front-runner, the fissures that had split the city during Murphy's campaign cracked wide open again. It wasn't just that Smith was sure to appeal to the same alliance of Negroes and foreigners that had put Murphy on the bench. Johnny Smith was actually *from* the east side's working class, a genuine product of the streets. And that made him anathema to the militant Anglo-Saxons who spent their nights draped in Klan sheets.[20]

The youngest of seven children raised by his widowed Polish Catholic mother, Smith had gone to work at age five, hawking newspapers on downtown streets mornings and evenings, setting pins in a bowling alley at night. With only a fourth-grade education, he had no hope of entering the professions. Instead, he became a soldier— a wounded veteran of America's imperial adventures in Cuba and the Philippines—a steamfitter, a trade-union activist, and, bit by bit, a politician of considerable reputation. Smith had the manner of an old-fashioned political boss who seemed happiest when puffing on a good cigar in the backroom of a corner saloon. When it came to public policy, though, he was a fierce progressive. Murphy could talk about helping the humble people of Detroit; Smith had done it, battling for strict enforcement of Michigan's child labor and tenement improvement laws. Murphy could talk about checking police aggression; Smith had actually confronted the cops, in one famous episode literally facing down a squad sent to break up a strike in a Detroit-area chemical plant, an intervention that cost him a broken nose that forever after made him look like a second-rate boxer. As mayor, he promised more confrontations. He'd put an end to arrests for drunkenness, he said, unless the suspect was dangerous; he'd stop illegal raids on neighborhood speakeasies; and, most controversially, he'd see to it that the police department hired more colored officers.[21]

A Catholic, a labor sympathizer, and a wet who promised to put Negroes in uniform and give them guns: to a Klansman, there was no more horrifying combination. For the previous three years, the Klan had been storming through northern politics, winning control of state governments in Indiana, Colorado, and Oregon. As Smith's candidacy gained momentum, the Kluxers decided they had to take charge of Detroit as well. Their campaign was painfully amateurish. As their candidate, they chose a complete unknown, lawyer Charles Bowles, whose only qualification for office was a successful term as president of the

Masonic Order's youth league. As if their man wasn't weak enough already, the KKK then failed to get his name on the November ballot and had to hope he could be elected as a write-in candidate. But none of that really mattered. The Klan's forte wasn't polished politics; it was thuggery and intimidation. At times Bowles's campaign seemed more suited to Mussolini's Rome than to the fourth-largest city in the United States. At one point, the KKK torched a cross on the front lawn of Smith's west-side home. When an anti-Klan group tried to stage a rally at a downtown arena late in the campaign, six thousand Klansmen massed in front of the venue, chanting "Bowles! Bowles! Bowles!" and intimidating anyone who tried to enter. The weekend before the election, the Klan mounted an even more frightening display. That Saturday night, upwards of fifty thousand gathered under a flaming cross in the western suburb of Dearborn—Henry Ford's hometown—to hear last-minute exhortations and the usual round of condemnations. Klan pickets kept nonmembers away, so no outsider knew precisely what was said. But the message was clear enough. The KKK was preparing for power.[22]

Johnny Smith, however, didn't mind going toe to toe with the Invisible Empire; in fact, the Klan's crusade strengthened his appeal. The KKK's slurs won Smith the allegiance of the Talented Tenth, who closed ranks behind him in a way they hadn't with Murphy the year before. What's more, it solidified the mayor's support among both the middle-class progressives who had long anchored reform and the most ambitious of Detroit's up-and-coming ethnics—some of them now-seasoned politicians such as Frank Murphy and his tough-minded backers, Tom Chawke and Red Mulcahy, others political newcomers, like the brilliant young pastor of the west side's Bethel Evangelical Church, Reinhold Niebuhr. The son of German immigrants whose intellectual gifts had carried him from tiny Lincoln, Illinois, through Yale Divinity School, Niebuhr saw in the Klan's militant Anglo-Saxonism a repudiation of the assimilation he worked so hard to achieve and the Social Gospel he was determined to preach. Supporting Smith wasn't a perfect fit for a man of Niebuhr's sobriety: "It seems to me rather unfortunate that we must depend upon 'publicans' for our social conscience to so great a degree," he wrote in his diary, but it was better than draping city hall in the white robes of the Klan.[23]

Best of all, Smith traded on the fears the KKK engendered to energize his political base. While the Kluxers lit up the western sky, he worked his old east-side neighborhood, visiting as many synagogues,

Catholic parishes, and black churches as would have him. Klansmen "have robbed Catholic churches and attempted to burn them," he told a crowd at St. Stanislaus, one of the sacred sites of Polish Detroit. "They have tortured and slain Negroes and Jews." The tactic worked to perfection. With Mulcahey's *Detroit Times* trumpeting every charge and the mayor's ethnic and black backers working the streets on his behalf, Smith swept the immigrant and colored wards by margins even greater than Murphy had managed: 99 percent of Black Bottom went his way. But the west side's Anglo-Saxons did even better for Bowles. A record 325,000 people cast ballots in the 1924 mayoral election, and when the polls finally closed, the Klan candidate had a majority of seven thousand votes.[24]

Or he would have, had Smith been the sort of politician who suffered defeat gracefully. But he was too much of a street fighter not to take one last punch. A review of the ballots showed that Bowles's backers weren't always sure how to spell their man's name: by official count, voters tried 120 variations. Most of the mistakes were minor—a missing letter, the wrong middle initial—but Smith's cronies on the Detroit election commission threw out every vote that wasn't precisely right, seventeen thousand in all, more than enough to strip Bowles of his victory and make a former pin setter and pipe fitter mayor of Detroit.[25]

No one was under the illusion that the war was over. Because he was only serving out his successor's term, Smith had to stand for reelection in a year's time, November 1925. And the KKK was dead-set on having its revenge. At the end of 1924, the Klan's national leadership dispatched to Detroit one of its more effective political operatives, Ira Stout, an owlish former boy scout and fundamentalist preacher, who was to prepare the groundwork for the fall campaign.[26] Michigan's frigid gray winter wasn't prime time for political organizing. But with the coming of spring—just as Ossian and Gladys were beginning to hunt for a house—the Klan headed into its marching season, when crosses could be burned and the emotions of a hundred thousand nativist voters could be set aflame. And in Detroit, there was no better way to fuel savage anger than to raise the specter of the Negro masses pouring across the color line into white man's land.

◆

Gladys insisted that, as far as she was concerned, they could live in either a colored neighborhood or a white one. But the chances of finding a suitable house in a black area were slim. There were several small Negro enclaves on Detroit's west side, one of which was home to several of Ossian's colleagues. If the Sweets had settled in that area, though, Ossian would have had a terrible commute to his office, while Gladys would have been very far from her parents. On the east side, the only colored neighborhood was Black Bottom, where life was increasingly intolerable. In the first few months of 1925, cops working the Black Bottom beat had shot a dozen or more colored people, several of them fatally. In one of the most egregious cases, a patrolman opened fire on a truck that failed to obey his order to stop. One of the bullets shattered the jaw of the truck's passenger, a twenty-five-year-old expectant mother. She died seven days later, having given birth to her baby. An investigation found the patrolman completely justified in his actions, and he was returned to duty. No, Ossian couldn't possibly take his family back to Black Bottom.[27]

Neither was it a simple matter to move beyond its boundaries. Ossian's senior colleagues had moved into white neighborhoods before discrimination had started to course through the housing market. Even in the early 1920s, Detroit's growing wall of segregation still had its gaps. But in 1923 and 1924, as Ossian and Gladys enjoyed the freedom of Vienna and Paris, developers, real estate agents, and bankers sealed the wall shut, so that now a Negro family looking to live outside the ghetto faced an almost impossible task.

For the developers who were furiously building housing tracts on the edge of the city and in the suburbs, the job was simple, a matter of a few words inserted onto all the development's deeds. For years, builders had placed restrictions on properties when they first went on sale, in order to give an area a certain character; it was common practice to say that a house couldn't be changed into a business, say, or be subdivided into apartments. In Chicago and other cities, developers regularly added racial restrictions as well: property owners could not sell their homes to colored buyers or, at times, to Jews. But that wasn't common practice in Detroit until the early 1920s, when suddenly developers blanketed the new houses on the city's outskirts with restrictive covenants, a practice they turned into a selling point. "We have carefully restricted this section to include only the kind of people you would be glad to have next door," one of the biggest firms proudly proclaimed as it unveiled its newest development on the far west side. "Here you can feel free to make friends with your neighbors."[28]

In established neighborhoods, too, the Sweets would immediately run up against a whole new series of prohibitions. Ever since the Great War, many white real estate agents had refused to show colored families properties outside Black Bottom. But it wasn't until 1924 that the real estate agents' trade association absolutely barred its members from selling houses in white neighborhoods to Negro customers and imposed sanctions on those who dared to break the rules. At almost exactly the same time, housing appraisers made it official practice to downgrade the value of any neighborhood that had even a single black resident, a requirement that immediately transformed even the most well-to-do colored homebuyers into credit risks, since the moment a purchase was complete the property wasn't worth as much as it had been. And because blacks drove down property values, there wasn't a bank in Detroit willing to give Negroes a mortgage.[29]

Ossian and Gladys ran into the restrictions right away. Three times, they found promising houses on the east side, and three times, they were turned away as soon as they made inquiries. One can imagine how much the rejections hurt; Ossian with his fine education and studied air of authority, Gladys with her lifetime living among whites, staring into the impassive face of a real estate agent while he shook his head and told them nothing was available. Friends urged them to stop searching on their own and hire a white agent to buy a house for them. Ossian wouldn't hear of it; he had no intention of skulking into a neighborhood, as if he didn't belong there. Instead, the Sweets found the tiniest of cracks in the wall that real estate agents and bankers had built, and they squeezed their way through.[30]

The break came in a completely unexpected way. One day in May, Lucius Riley stopped into Ossian's office with a bit of news. Riley had been a devoted patient of Ossian's ever since the day he'd brought his wife into Palace Drugs fearing she had lockjaw. Now Riley extended his own professional courtesy. He knew of a fine house just about to go on the market, he told Ossian, a nine-year-old bungalow, well built and well maintained, in a white neighborhood a few miles east of Black Bottom. The house sat on a corner lot, so it had a bit more land than most, and it was right across from an elementary school. Best of all, Riley was absolutely sure that the owners would be willing to sell to a colored family.[31]

When the Sweets first went out to the house on Garland Avenue in late May 1925, they had to be a bit disappointed in the neighborhood. It was a workingman's area, by and large, certainly not poor but not imposing either, filled with modest houses and two-family flats. But the location was just about ideal. Ossian would have an easy twenty-minute drive to his office on St. Aubin, while Gladys would be about fifteen minutes south of Cairney Street. The intersection in front of the house was busy. Though Garland Avenue was a quiet residential street, the cross street, Charlevoix Avenue, was a major thoroughfare, complete with a streetcar line. As long as they were newcomers and their presence might stir resentment, though, the Sweets had no intention of spending much time in the front of the house. They could get all the fresh air they needed in the backyard, which was safely hidden by a high wooden fence.[32] All in all, the bungalow was a very attractive home.

For their part, the owners were more than pleased to find the Sweets. By all appearances, Ed and Marie Smith were a completely conventional white couple, hardly the sort one would expect to shatter the neighborhood's color line. But the Smiths weren't exactly what they appeared to be. Mrs. Smith was indeed Caucasian. But her husband was a light-skinned colored man who had spent most of his adult life passing for white. The deception had given him the ability to build a successful business selling real estate in areas no black real estate agent could operate, while his brother, who was just as light skinned, had risen to the rank of sergeant in the Detroit Police Department.[33]

They saw the Sweets as a couple of easy marks. Had the Smiths sold to whites, the bungalow probably would have gone for $12,000 or $13,000, the standard for the neighborhood. But Ossian and Gladys had nowhere else to go, so the Smiths upped their asking price to $18,500. To make sure the Sweets couldn't walk away, they offered to finance the purchase themselves. Ossian and Gladys would put down 20 percent of the asking price and pay the balance directly to the Smiths in 120 monthly installments of $150 each. Of course, there were a few catches. The Smiths would keep the title to the house until the final payment was made, so Ossian and Gladys wouldn't actually own the bungalow until 1935. In the intervening ten years, they would pay the Smiths an extraordinary 18 percent interest on the balance they owed, so far above bank rates as to be almost criminal. Then again, there was no way the Sweets were going to get a bank loan. They had to take what they could get.[34]

That's exactly what they did. On June 7, 1925, Ossian and Gladys handed over their down payment of $3,500 and signed the purchase agreement. The Smiths needed a few months to move out, but come August 1, the Sweets would have their home.[35]

Yet Ossian's fears persisted. When the papers were signed and the real estate agents were packing up their briefcases, Ossian took Marie Smith aside for a quick word. Was the neighborhood safe for colored people, he asked her? Would he have to worry about the Klan?

Oh no, she said, there weren't any Klansmen in the area. Garland was a nice quiet street. The Sweets would be very happy there.[36]

◆

The rumor started right away. Someone saw Ossian and Gladys sitting on the front porch swing during one of their visits to the bungalow. "It just isn't right," said Ray Dove, the factory worker who lived in the upstairs flat directly across from the bungalow, and he didn't need to say any more. Some of the men must have feared for the safety of their wives and children, knowing that the black beast was moving into their midst. George and Alvina Hamming, just two doors north of the corner, had two teenage daughters, fifteen-year-old Ruth and Grace, the thirteen-year-old; a couple of doors beyond them lived nine-year-old Margaret Rudge, and on the opposite side of the street were Leon and Leona Breiner's girls, fourteen-year-old Evelyn and twelve-year-old June. Surely it crossed the parents' minds that their daughters soon would be sharing the street with brooding Negro men and sitting in classrooms next to colored boys whose passions knew no restraint. At least some people also felt in the rumor a blow to their pride. Having Negroes in the neighborhood would ruin standards, Harry Monet insisted, dragging whites down to the coloreds' level, degrading everything people up and down the block had worked so hard to achieve.[37]

But it was the marketplace that really induced panic along Garland Avenue. Once the Negroes arrived, real estate agents would start steering white customers elsewhere, banks would downgrade home values, some of the neighbors would try to sell as quickly as they could, and the downward spiral would begin, housing prices tumbling, family budgets crumbling, disaster looming. It was a process shot through with irony, whites suddenly being victimized by the very practices that were supposed to protect them from Negro invasion. The thought was simply terrifying.

It hadn't always been like this, a family's fate hinging on the value of its house. Just a generation earlier, working-class Americans had considered owning a home the ultimate form of security, a bulwark against the vagaries of life, not an investment to be protected. Instead of taking out mortgages, they saved every penny they could until they could buy a house free and clear, or they'd do what Ossian's parents had done: pay for a lot, then put up the house themselves. That's how the cottages of Black Bottom had been built in the nineteenth century, home by home, until the neighborhood was full. It wasn't always easy. Though land was cheap enough—two hundred dollars would buy a lot in turn-of-the-twentieth-century Detroit—and houses could be constructed for a thousand dollars or less, many parents sacrificed their children's future, sending them off to work as newsies or maids, so that they could put together the cash they needed. But once a purchase was completed, a family forever after had a roof over its head, and come what may—an economic depression, an accident at the plant, a sudden illness, a tragic death—nothing could take it away.[38]

But boomtown Detroit had no place for security. The fields that became Garland Avenue had been bought up at the turn of the twentieth century by one of the city's large real estate developers, the Bewick Company. When the developer carved the fields into narrow lots, he wrote into each deed that no house built on a plot would be worth less than two thousand dollars, a figure expressly set to shut out workers who planned to build their homes the old-fashioned way. Instead, the Bewick Company and a handful of contractors put up most of the houses along Garland, slapping the flats together in a rush in the first half of the 1910s, then setting prices high enough that no one could get by without a mortgage. The piano tuner and his wife, John and Della Getke, had to borrow two thousand dollars to buy their home next door to the bungalow in February 1915. A few years of frenzied growth later, that seemed a steal. When the Smiths bought the bungalow on the corner in July 1923, they had to go five thousand dollars in debt to make the purchase possible.[39]

That's where the trouble began. By working-class standards, the people who lived on Garland were to be envied and just a little feared. They were the carpenters, streamfitters, and electricians who roamed the factories as if they owned them, skilled men standing proudly above the mass of common laborers. They were the salesmen in the cheap suits who breezed through the plants, sample cases in hand, on the way to having a chat with the manager up in the front office. Mostly, they were the foremen who spent the day stalking the assembly lines, breathing down the workers' necks, cursing and threatening and cajoling to make sure that the chassis kept moving inexorably toward the factory doors. Fourteen foremen lived within a block of the bungalow, an imposing concentration of hard-nosed men making their living in an unforgiving job. There was no doubt that they had risen in the ranks because they weren't immigrants or Negroes, because they came from Ohio or New York or small-town Michigan instead of Alabama or Galacia or Lodz, because they wore a Masonic pin on their lapels when they went to see the boss who did the hiring, and the bonds of brotherhood extended to the factory floor. Still, it hadn't been easy climbing into the upper reaches of blue-collar life. Before he landed his job at Continental Motors, before he moved to Michigan and met Leona, before he was even old enough to vote or serve in the army, a teenage Leon Breiner had done the most brutal work of all, mining coal far beneath the hard earth of Carbon County, Pennsylvania. After that, a man had to feel that he'd earned whatever safety and comfort a foreman's wages could bring.[40]

But solid wages weren't enough, not when a mortgage dangled around a man's neck like a noose waiting to be pulled tight. It was bad enough that families had to borrow more than their incomes could bear simply to get into Detroit's raging market. The pressure was compounded by the crippling terms financial institutions had to offer. The major downtown banks, rock-ribbed conservatives that they were, wouldn't allow their customers to borrow more than 50 percent of a house's value, and they required that loans be repaid in the briefest of periods, often within three to five years. With housing prices so high, most families couldn't possibly put down 50 percent of a purchase, so they had to take out second and even third mortgages just to piece together a down payment. Because banks refused to make such deals, borrowers were forced to turn to mortgage companies and local moneylenders, who gouged their desperate customers with usurious interest rates. Even if homeowners did manage to make their multiple payments, loan periods were so short that they were constantly refinancing. By the summer of 1925, ten years after they bought the tiny house next to the bungalow, the Getkes had already taken out three mortgages and were in negotiations for a fourth, a thousand dollars larger than the original.[41] It was a terrible burden to place on the money a man could make tuning pianos.

And it couldn't withstand the shock that the coming of the Negroes would bring. It was easy enough to spin out the economic consequences of Garland's color line giving way. When property values started falling, lenders wouldn't refinance, and loans would come due. Some families would try to pull themselves out of the morass by trying to sell their houses, but that would only trigger a price war, pushing values down even faster and making it that much harder to earn enough on a sale to pay off the mortgage holders or to start over in a city where houses in decent neighborhoods were so expensive. Others would stay put, hoping they could scrape together enough money to pay off the mortgage when the loans came due and refinancing fell through. But if they failed, the cost would be extraordinarily high. There'd be a few months of grace before the bank or mortgage company came calling. But sooner or later, they'd show up on the doorstep demanding their due, their workmen standing behind them, itching to begin piling the furniture at the curb for all the neighbors to see. When that happened, a good-paying job as a foreman or a craftsman wouldn't mean a damn thing.

As worried as they were, though, no one on Garland Avenue did anything at first. They didn't know what to do. The neighborhood didn't fit neatly into Detroit's polarized political communities: it was too full of the native-born to share in the sense of oppression that united the east side's foreign-born and colored populations, too far from the west side to participate in the politics of rage that fueled the Ku Klux Klan. Nor was it a street that lent itself to organizing. Some neighbors were tied together by personal connections—Ray Dove and Leon Breiner belonged to the same Masonic Lodge; Albert Suppus's son played with the Arthur boy—but otherwise people tended to keep to themselves. The neighborhood didn't give folks a chance to develop deep friendships: work was too demanding to leave much time for socializing; renters came and went; and even the most long-term resident had only been there a decade. Much of Detroit was like that; "A city of strangers," a journalist called it. On Garland Avenue, that description was just about right.[42]

Then the west side exploded.

•

The clashes came as a shock, they flared so quickly and in such an unexpected place. For years, several thousand Negroes had been living in a small triangle of streets wedged between two of the near west side's largest thoroughfares, West Grand Boulevard and Tireman Avenue. Compared to Black Bottom, the west-side enclave was prosperous and stable, and the whites who surrounded it had never seen it as threatening. Though the neighborhood's borders were clear enough, they had also been somewhat porous. Dunbar Memorial's head of surgery, Dr. Alexander Turner, had been living in a nearby white area for the previous fifteen years, caring for Caucasian patients, without so much as a complaint. But in the summer of 1925, the whites who encircled the enclave suddenly became passionately, violently committed to preventing Negroes from crossing the color line.[43]

The first incident occurred in the spring of 1925, just as Ossian and Gladys were about to begin their search for a home. On March 7, two young colored couples, Aldeine and Fleta Mathies and their friends, the Burtons, all recent migrants from Georgia, rented a flat just one street west of the black neighborhood's traditional boundary. Almost immediately, the families received a series of frightening letters from the local KKK, demanding that they surrender their lease. When they didn't respond, the neighbors came calling. Twice in the first week of April, mobs gathered in front of the flat, and twice the men of the house faced them down, standing on the porch with rifles in their hands. But it was twenty-two-year-old Mrs. Mathies who eventually pulled the trigger.

Monday night, April 13, she and Mrs. Burton settled themselves in the side bedroom, the safest part of the house, since it didn't face the street or the alley but rather the home next door, where a policeman and his wife lived. The two women had just nodded off when a rock shattered the windowpane. Without a moment's hesitation, Fleta Mathies grabbed the pistol lying on her bedside table and fired two shots through the gaping hole of shattered glass, hitting the frame of the window directly opposite. The police rushed to the scene. But instead of restoring order, they took Mathies into custody, charging her with careless use of a firearm. When the patrolmen brought her in, the Mathies' next-door neighbor was waiting for her. "If I had been home," he told her, "your husband would have been going down to the undertakers after a coffin for you instead of coming down to the police station to get you. You people have got more privileges than you're entitled to. You want to spoil our street." Another cop took a cat-o'-nine-tails off a shelf and dangled it in front of her. "You see this," he said. "If you were a man, I'd give you a sound thrashing."[44]

Still, the families refused to be intimidated. To defend his wife, Aldeine Mathies hired two colored lawyers, W. Hayes McKinney, the former president of Detroit's NAACP branch, and criminal attorney Cecil Rowlette. When the case went to court in May, McKinney and Rowlette convinced the judge that Fleta Mathies had fired in defense of her home and therefore had committed no crime. Afterward, young

Mrs. Mathies was as defiant as ever. "I'm not afraid and will not move until I am positive that I have made it possible for some other colored person to live here after I'm gone," she told the Negro press. "The race needs people who are not afraid to die to defend their pride."[45] With that, the threats and intimidation stopped, and for the better part of three months, the area was as calm as it had ever been. Then Dr. Alexander Turner grew tired of the traffic noise on his street and decided to move his family to a new home a mile away.

As was his habit, Turner bought the very best he could afford, an impressive two-story brick home on Spokane Avenue, eight blocks north of Tireman Avenue. Had it not been for the Mathies' troubles, the doctor wouldn't have given a second thought to moving onto an all-white street. Certainly his situation was different: the Mathies had barely crossed out of the black neighborhood whereas he was moving a considerable distance from it; they were newcomers, whereas he was an established member of the community. Still, it was better to be cautious. Shortly before Turner moved, a small group of his colleagues met with Mrs. Mathies's lawyer, Cecil Rowlette, to ask whether they could join the doctor in his house on the first night so that he might have some protection. Absolutely not, Rowlette said. A man had the right to defend his own home. But it would be a serious mistake to have others defend it for him.[46]

So the Turners moved to their new home on their own. They took possession on the morning of June 23. Within a few hours, a mob of two hundred, most of them women and children, had gathered out front. First, they stoned the colored painters Turner had hired to touch up the trim, then they started smashing windows. The escalating violence brought the police, who arrested one fifteen-year-old boy as he stood on the sidewalk, rock in hand. But the cops did nothing to stanch the flow of people into the street. By dusk, the mob had swelled to more than a thousand, far more than the forty policemen on the scene could possibly control. The doctor and his wife were cowering inside, every escape route hopelessly blocked, when they heard a rap on the door and the voices of several white men calling to them, saying that they had been sent by Mayor Smith to provide the couple with the protection they needed. In his desperation, Turner opened the door.

Dozens of people surged past the doctor into his house. While the police stood by, the mob trampled through the downstairs rooms, wrenching open closet doors, pulling up rugs, grabbing furniture and unpacked boxes full of precious belongings to cart outside. The ringleaders took hold of Turner. They were representatives of the Tireman Avenue Improvement Association, they said, and they wanted the deed of the house signed over to them. It was an utterly audacious demand, robbery in the midst of pillage, and under normal circumstances, Turner, a man of supreme self-confidence, never would have given in to it. But there was no saying what would happen next: whether the mob would destroy everything he owned; whether they'd turn on him and his wife; whether he'd ever escape this accursed neighborhood alive. More people were trying to push their way inside every minute, and those outside cheered as the first pieces of furniture were dumped into the street. Turner choked out his agreement.

Satisfied that the problem was solved, the police agreed to escort the doctor and the men from the improvement association back to Turner's office, where they could complete the property transfer. The Turners managed to make it safely into the back seat of their sedan. But the sight of the chauffeur firing up the engine enraged the mob again. A barrage of stones and bricks hit the car, smashing the windows. A piece of flying glass struck Turner above the eye, gashing his forehead. Blood trickling down his face, he pulled himself and his wife down to the floor of the car and ordered the chauffeur to get through the crowd as quickly as he could. Somehow they managed to move forward, slowly, then with real speed. Within a few minutes, they were free of Spokane Avenue. The Turners raced to his office, where they summoned lawyer Rowlette and signed away the house they had lived in for less than a day.[47]

Precisely two weeks later, the Tireman Avenue Improvement Association struck again. This time, they made their target one of Ossian's oldest friends in Detroit, Vollington Bristol. The Bristols had long owned a house on American Avenue, ten blocks east of Turner's place on Spokane Avenue. They had never lived in the home—it was simply too far from their funeral parlor in Black Bottom—but instead had rented it out to a secession of white tenants. But the tenants had been nothing but trouble: rents went unpaid; apartments had been damaged. Figuring that whites were defying them because they were black, the Bristols decided in the spring of 1925 to rent to colored families. Several times, they found suitable tenants, but as soon as they moved in, the newcomers received notes so threatening that they moved out again. Finally, on July 4, Vollington Bristol reached his breaking point.

He arrived at the property that day with four families in tow. A delegation of twenty-five white neighbors met him there. This was his last warning, they said. He was not to rent to coloreds anymore, and if he tried again, he'd regret it. All right, Bristol replied, he wouldn't rent to Negroes. He'd live there himself.

Unlike the Turners, Bristol asked for police protection before he moved in, and the day he arrived, July 6, two cops were on duty in front of the house. As he was taking his belongings into the building, Bristol's next-door neighbor came by to ask if he really intended to go through with his threat. When Bristol said he was, the man turned on his heels, growling, "You will hear from us later." Nothing happened the first night. But the next evening, July 7, all hell broke loose.

The police had a small contingent of five patrolmen and an inspector surrounding the house when the mob began to form. Initially, the crowd kept its distance, not daring to test the police line. Then, a woman who lived across the street from Bristol's house mounted her porch and launched into a harangue. "If you call yourselves men and are afraid to move these niggers out," she screamed, "we women will move them, you cowards!" That was it. Almost instantaneously the mob began stoning the house. Someone approached the police to ask if they would step aside for five minutes; it wouldn't take any longer to drive the coloreds away. When the inspector refused to move his men, the mob stoned them, too. Fearing that at any moment they would be overrun—perhaps killed—by the hundreds of people in front of them, the cops fired a volley of warning shots into the air. Members of the mob returned fire, rifles blazing from so many directions it was impossible to tell where in the crowd the gunmen were standing.

The patrolmen could have been mowed down right there, but by pure luck no one was hit. They could have broken ranks and run, but for some reason they held their ground long enough for reinforcements from precincts around the city—two hundred or more—to arrive. Such a massive show of force tipped the balance. The cops waded into the mob, pushing those they could all the way back onto Tireman, arresting those who resisted. In all, nineteen white men were jailed that evening, and the police seized thirty-five guns, two knives, and hundreds of rounds of ammunition. But it took several more hours to realize just how dangerous the situation had become. Around midnight, patrolmen stopped eight colored men making their way through the neighborhood and found that they, too, were armed. When word of the melee had spread into the black neighborhood, the men had decided that they would provide Bristol with the defense he needed. Had the mob still been in the street, American Avenue might have run red with the mingled blood of blacks and whites.[48]

Blood did flow finally, but not on American Avenue. The police were still providing round-the-clock protection to Vollington Bristol when the violence shifted several blocks northeast to 9428 Stoepel Avenue. John Fletcher, a waiter, bought the house on July 1 and, with extraordinarily bad timing, moved his wife, children, and two boarders into the home a week later, on July 9, two days after the chaos in front of Bristol's house. The family had just seated themselves at the dinner table on the tenth when they heard a commotion outside. Across the street, a woman was going door to door, urging her neighbors to come get "the niggers." Fletcher hurriedly called the police. But to his amazement, instead of driving the whites off the street, the seven cops who showed up stood and chatted with them.

The mood remained light enough until the sun began to set. In front of the house next door sat a ton of coal, a recent delivery from the coal dealer. Around eight, the mob started raiding the pile, throwing chunks at the Fletchers' place. In short order, every window was broken, a mirror cracked, and two prized pieces of furniture destroyed. The sudden assault brought another forty policemen to the scene, but by then, the mob had worked itself into such a fury it wasn't going to be stopped. Through the shattered windows, Fletcher could hear the shouts from the street: "Lynch him! Lynch him!" Trapped inside the house, the walls around them cracked and blackened by the lumps of coal now scattered at their feet, the four adults could barely contain their panic. Fletcher picked up a rifle he had brought with him, went to the upstairs window, and opened fire on the mob below. Fifteen-year-old Leonard Paul collapsed on the pavement, two gaping holes in his hip.

Instantly, the mob's exuberance drained away, the joy of destruction, the promise of an evening's brutal excitement, replaced by wild-eyed fear. While the teenager lay writhing on the ground, most of his neighbors fled, racing to the safety of the surrounding streets. The cops took advantage of the opening to get Fletcher safely down to the local precinct. The next day, Saturday, July 11, he made bail, returned to Stoepel Avenue and, under heavy police guard, moved his battered belongings onto a truck and out of the neighborhood. "I couldn't live in the house anyway, because all the windows and screens were smashed and the paint on the outside was all marred up," he explained, adding, as if an afterthought, "I was afraid of my life."[49]

That night, calm finally returned to the area around Tireman Avenue. The Turners were gone; the Fletchers were gone. Only Vollington

Bristol remained, and he barely dared to go outside, so intense was the hatred on his block; already his mailbox was jammed with death threats, and the one time he'd tried to leave his home, a passing car had swerved onto the sidewalk and tried to run him down. It had been a terrible three weeks, the worst in Detroit since the Great Migration began. But the members of the Tireman Avenue Improvement Association were proud of the work they'd done. The neighborhood had been saved from a Negro invasion, property values preserved, the walls of segregation shored up, the streets cleansed with only a little blood. The stain that the wounded boy left on Stoepel Avenue would fade eventually, but the color line would remain inviolate.

•

From the moment they heard of the attack on the Turners, Ossian and Gladys watched events on the west side with a sickening sense of dread. The assaults would have been frightening enough had they happened to complete strangers. But to think of friends and associates being mobbed—less than a month before the Sweets themselves were scheduled to move—was utterly terrifying. Had he been willing to try, Ossian probably could have gotten out of the deal he'd made for the bungalow, trading his down payment for his family's safety and his own peace of mind. To back down, though, would be to admit that he wasn't willing to live up to the principles that had been preached to him ever since Wilberforce, that he had no claim to a place among the Talented Tenth. It would have been a very public humiliation. Gladys and Otis would have seen it, of course, as would Henry, who had recently arrived in Detroit for the summer and was rooming at the Mitchells'.[50]

What's more, Ossian would have had to face his Dunbar colleagues at the worst possible time. After two years of inactivity, the local branch of the NAACP was finally being revived. In March, the national officers had taken it upon themselves to appoint a new branch president, Rev. Robert Bradby, the extremely powerful pastor of Second Baptist. Bradby, in turn, had named several Dunbar men, including Ossian's friend Edward Carter, to the executive board. Aflame with the NAACP spirit, they were anxious to push against the color line, not surrender to it.[51]

In fact, Carter had almost dragged Ossian into the middle of the melee at Turner's house. The night of the assault, the two men were out with several of their colleagues. Carter tried to convince the group to drive over to Turners', just to be sure that all was well. In the end, they decided against it, and the four physicians had drifted to their homes, having enjoyed an evening of bravado. Ossian must have felt his stomach clench as he read the newspaper's bare-boned account of the incident the following morning. And he couldn't help but cringe when, over the next few weeks, Turner was vilified. "The dirty coward got down on [the] floor of his car and made his chauffeur drive thru the mob," one man said, repeating a refrain heard across Black Bottom. "He knew when he moved in he was going to have trouble and he should have gone prepared to stay or die." No doubt they'd say the same thing about Ossian, if he decided to give up the house on Garland.[52]

It wasn't until Fletcher was driven out, though, that events truly closed in on the Sweets. That weekend, Detroit shuddered with talk of segregation and the implicit threat of violence. On Friday night, the Ku Klux Klan opened its bid to channel white anger. While a group of Klansmen burned a cross in an empty lot not far from Bristol's besieged home, their fellow Kluxers posted huge placards around the neighborhood inviting "every free-minded citizen of Detroit" to a mass rally the next evening. The event turned into a frightening show of force, ten thousand white-robed knights and assorted hangers-on gathering before a blazing cross to hear Klan leaders denounce the Negro invasion and demand legislation barring blacks from moving beyond the ghetto.[53]

Sunday morning's newspapers carried Johnny Smith's carefully crafted reply. The mayor began with a warning. "The condition which faces Detroit is one which faced Washington, East St. Louis, Chicago, and other large cities," he wrote. "The result in those cities was one which Detroit must avoid, if possible. A single fatal riot would injure this city beyond repair." Then he tried in as circumspect a way as possible to turn the west troubles against his opponents. He blamed the violence on "malign influences which are willing to go even to the limits of bloodshed to gain their ends." He called the cops to task for letting the mobs take control of the streets. "The police department can have but one duty in connection with all such incidents," he said. "That is, to use its utmost endeavors to prevent the destruction of life and property. . . . The law recognizes no distinction in color or race." Had he stopped there, Johnny Smith would have placed himself squarely in defense of equal rights and integration. But he didn't. Instead, he urged black "leaders of thought" to back down, to accept the color line as it stood for the sake of peace and order. In the furies of the street, the mayor had found the limits of his electoral coalition.[54]

Dunbar's doctors and their associates in the Talented Tenth barely had time to read the mayor's statement before they gathered that afternoon in Herbert Sims's Black Bottom office to discuss the crisis. Ossian listened intently as Alexander Turner described the desecration of his home and justified his surrender to the mob's demands. There was no missing the defeat in his voice. He and his wife planned to take a trip, Turner said, to get out of town for a few months. They were trying to put behind them the memories of that night on Spokane Avenue, no doubt, but also to escape the sniping that the doctor couldn't help but overhear.

In the midst of the conversation, the telephone rang. Marie Smith was on the line—undoubtedly Gladys had given her the phone number—and she had to speak to Dr. Sweet right away. Posters had just gone up around Garland, she told him; the neighbors were organizing. Ossian must have returned to his colleagues shaken. But they bolstered him up, the room bristling with a militancy made all the stronger by Turner's presence. Attorney Cecil Rowlette expounding on a man's absolute right to protect his home just as his client, young Mrs. Mathies had done, while Edward Carter and Julian Perry boldly promised to be by their friend's side come moving day. If any doubts drifted through Ossian's mind—if he thought back to the days of the Washington riot, when he stayed off the street while others took up arms; if he saw himself walking from Carter's car into the safety of his mother-in-law's house the night of the attack on Turner—he didn't express them. It was so much easier, so much more satisfying to be enveloped in his colleagues' unquestioned confidence, to become, in that moment, the man that Turner had failed to be.[55]

⋅

It's not clear who on Garland Avenue first thought of mimicking the Tireman Association. The idea probably started with someone hunched over the morning newspaper, the *Detroit Free Press,* reading the story of the Turners' expulsion. From there, it must have spread the way the rumors of the Sweets' arrival had spread, through casual talk out on the street. Harry Monet, a tire-factory worker who lived half a block north of the bungalow, volunteered his garage for the first meeting. It must have been stultifying, two dozen people crowded into a one-car garage on a hot summer night. But the group did its job, officially forming the

Waterworks Park Improvement Association, named after a majestic public park at the foot of Garland Avenue, a few long blocks away. As chairman, they selected one of Monet's neighbors, Harold McGlynn, a thirty-six-year-old husband and father who worked as an inspector in a nearby auto plant.[56] Perhaps McGlynn got the nod because the association had been his brainchild. But it wasn't completely his to run. From the start, the organization bore the unmistakable imprint of a more seasoned hand in the real estate game.

Most likely, the driving force behind the Waterworks Park Improvement Association was the man elected secretary the night of the first meeting, a thirty-five-year-old real estate agent by the name of James Conley. Like Monet and McGlynn, Conley lived within a block of the bungalow, in a modest home he shared with his wife, Lillian, their two children, Margaret and Eddie, and his maiden aunt, Alice. But Conley had a second stake in the neighborhood that set him apart from the others. He and a partner ran a real estate office on the corner of Charlevoix and St. Clair avenues, not a minute's walk from the Smiths' house. So word that the Negroes had bought the bungalow was doubly devastating: once the sale was final, his property values would tumble and his client base would dry up. More than anyone else on Garland, Conley needed to keep the coloreds out.[57]

Conley also brought an expertise to the task that his neighbors simply didn't have. Within a week or two, the association had adopted and printed up a constitution and bylaws filled with real estate agent boilerplate: members would "render constructive civil and social service," would "assist to maintain a clean and healthy condition in our streets and alleys," would "cooperate with the police department, that the rule of 'law and order' shall be maintained." More important, he began to direct its energies into the proper channels. Members agreed to undertake a campaign to blanket the neighborhood in restrictive covenants, something they undoubtedly wouldn't have thought of without a real estate agent to guide them. In the meantime, the association's leaders would try to convince the owners of the bungalow to call off the sale. Someone suggested that they begin both efforts with a rally at Howe Elementary, an event that could spread news of the association's existence and send a message of the neighborhood's resolve. Conley likely used his connections to make it a spectacular event. Like the Waterworks group, the Tireman Avenue Association was run by a real estate agent whom Conley undoubtedly knew. A friendly phone call and the rally had its featured speaker.[58]

There couldn't have been much doubt about what he would say. The invitation must have gone out just about the time the mob attacked Vollington Bristol's house, and the posters were nailed to Garland's lampposts the same day the mayor's message was printed in the newspaper. But Conley, McGlynn, and the others had no intention of heeding Johnny Smith's call for calm. They wanted neighbors to feel the power of numbers. And they needed the couple in the bungalow to hear the frenzied cheers of the mob, to see what the future would hold if they dared to go through with the sale. To keep Garland Avenue safe from invasion, the Waterworks Park Improvement Association had to be willing to dance with the devil.

In the end, the rally was a stunning success. The skies threatened rain Tuesday night, July 14. But the crowd began arriving early, hundreds of people streaming into the elementary school with the proud abolitionist name. Leon Breiner was there, as were Ray Dove, the Getkes, and so many other neighbors that the school auditorium couldn't hold them all. Rather than turn anyone away, the association moved the rally out to the school-yard lawn, in full view of the Smiths' house. From a makeshift platform, the speaker delivered his incendiary speech. The crowd roared. And the rally organizers stood by and listened to the message ring out. When the Negroes came to Garland Avenue, there was going to be trouble.[59]

•

The undercover cops sprinkled through the crowd that night took no notes and when they were done, they prepared no report. They simply sat down with their commanding officer, Inspector Norton Schuknecht, and told him everything they'd seen and heard. The inspector didn't need any more than that. He'd spent his lifetime on the east side of Detroit, growing up on St. Aubin back when it was a German neighborhood instead of a district full of Negroes and Italians; walking the beat as a rookie back at the turn of the century; settling with his wife, Emma, in their house off Gratiot Avenue, two miles due north of the school yard; visiting his sister Matilda and her husband, Otto Lemhagen, in their house a block away from the bungalow where the colored man was supposed to be moving; running the precinct that covered all the territory in between. Those streets were his streets, the people in the school yard his people. He knew them better than any of his men ever would.[60]

Schuknecht also knew the ins and outs of the force. The police

department had 2,660 cops on the payroll, most of them just as likely
to have ended up working in a factory as to be wearing the blue. If
Norton hadn't gone into the force, he might have followed the same
path. Once his brother Alfred took charge of their father's bookbinding
business, Norton's other brothers had settled into working-class jobs:
Walter was a trucker, Elmer, a foreman living less than a mile from the
Garland house. Norton had done better for himself. Being a beat cop
didn't pay well, but Schuknecht had moved slowly and steadily up
through the ranks until, six years before, he was named a precinct commander, a desk job suitable for a fifty-five-year-old man with a stomach
that stretched over his belt, an extra chin or two to strain his collar, and
half a year until he could take a pension. Other cops were flashier, filling
their records with commendations for bravery that Schuknecht never
came close to winning. But having the city treasurer for a brother-in-law
had helped his career no end, as had the gaudy Masonic ring
Schuknecht squeezed onto his pudgy finger. Police departments were
all the same: a little pull and the right pedigree went a long way. In New
York, Chicago, or Boston, a man couldn't rise in the ranks unless he had
an Irish name, a lifetime membership in the Hibernians, and a mon-
signor's imprimatur. To make it in Detroit's force, a cop had to have ties
to the white, native-born Protestants who had always run the city.[61]

Now Schuknecht was in a hell of a spot. Ever since the mayor's
statement criticizing the force for its handling of the west-side violence,
the brass down at police headquarters had been making it clear that they
wouldn't tolerate any more incidents. Not that they cared for Johnny
Smith; most men in the department, from the top officers down to the
traffic cops, couldn't stand the way the mayor had made them a target
in the previous campaign while playing up to the Negroes and the foreigners. But the patrolmen's complicity in the mobbing of the coloreds
was an embarrassment, even on a force where discipline was perpetu-
ally paper-thin, and the mayor was right to say that the city was spinning toward a repetition of Chicago and Washington. To make matters
even worse, there were rumblings of revolt in the ranks; word had it
that a lieutenant in the Vinewood Station had resigned rather than
"protect niggers." So the higher-ups had to assert themselves, to prove
that they had control of the situation and to make sure that, the next
time there was trouble, Johnny Smith couldn't pin it all on them.[62]

Personally, he felt for the people of Garland Avenue. He had a
teenage daughter at home and he had a mortgage to repay, too. He also
felt for the men under his command, who would hate being assigned to

protect that colored family while they moved into the bungalow. Some of his officers were Klansmen; no one could say for sure how many men on the force had joined the Invisible Empire, but the number was high. But it wasn't just the Klan's influence that made his cops angry. They had signed on to defend these neighborhoods, to keep them clear of trouble and free of crime, not to stand down people just like themselves so a Negro could live in a place where he didn't belong.[63] Come moving day, it would be easy enough to drive the coloreds out. All Schuknecht would have to do was wait for the mob to form, then tell his men to stand back. It would be over within a matter of minutes. People in the neighborhood would love him for it, and every precinct in the city would hail him as a hero. But the brass would have his head.

◆

In the weeks after his Sunday afternoon meeting, Ossian grew into the role his silence had won him. His fears remained as strong as ever, a primal pull away from the terror he knew he was walking into. But to see how friends and family admired him was nothing short of intoxicating. He loved the feeling that came when, in the course of an ordinary conversation, he told the head of Dunbar's board of directors that he wasn't going to run, and it was thrilling to see how Vollington Bristol looked at him with respect the day the two met in a bank lobby, and Ossian said he, too, was willing to face the mob.[64]

It was the reaction on Cairney Street that really mattered, though. When Ossian told Gladys that he wanted to see the sale through, she no doubt set her jaw and said she would join him in the bungalow the first night it was theirs to own, and when Gladys made up her mind, no one in the world was going to dissuade her. Henry pledged to be by his brother's side, whatever might happen; Otis, too, promised his support. Even Gladys's mother approved of his decision, though it would put her daughter at grave risk. One day she took her son-in-law aside and put a pistol in his hand, telling him that he should be ready to use it.[65]

There were times when his courage began to crack, but friends were always there to pull him back. The worst moment came when Marie Smith called to report that she was receiving anonymous phone calls: someone said that her house was going to be dynamited; another said that they planned "to kill the nigger." Putting down the receiver, Ossian's commitment collapsed, shattered by confirmation of a lifetime's nightmares. Edward Carter calmed him down. Whoever was saying such things was simply trying to intimidate her into revoking the contract, he insisted. The people who lived around the bungalow weren't the type to commit violence. It was tough talk, nothing more, and Ossian shouldn't be afraid of it.[66] It was the weakest of assurances, based on nothing but instinct, and Ossian must have known it. But he wanted to believe it was true.

Mostly, though, Ossian was swept up in the fervor of the moment. Throughout the balance of July and August, the question of neighborhood segregation remained white-hot. When members of the Detroit real estate board gathered in a west-side library to discuss ways of restricting Negroes to Black Bottom, several dozen colored men stormed the meeting, demanding to be heard; the terrified real estate agents summoned the police, who shoved the black men outside and locked the doors.[67]

From his pulpit, the associate pastor of Second Baptist urged those black homeowners threatened by mobs to seek legal redress; one of the city's leading papers shot back that the minister "prefers a race riot to the surrender of a single legal right by a few Negroes." That exchange, in turn, brought a sharp reply from one of the most powerful voices in black America. The NAACP's national officers had been keeping tabs on the Detroit situation ever since the *Pittsburgh Courier* reported the west-side violence in late July.

The first week of August, James Weldon Johnson fired off an open letter reprinted around the country. "In Detroit," he wrote, "Negroes have been driven from their homes by mobs, those who refused to go having defended themselves in the absence of adequate police protection. We now have the spectacle of white . . . newspapers taking sides with the mob and warning Negroes that if they cleave to their citizenship rights they are inviting a 'race riot.' . . . It is a frightful commentary upon American civilization that any editor should dare to threaten any group of citizens with riot because they will not 'surrender a single legal right.' " Privately, the NAACP took an even tougher stand. "Whenever the price of our rights is made to be a riot or death in another form," field secretary William Pickens wrote the new branch president, Robert Bradby, "we would prefer to pay the price rather than give up the rights of men." Detroit's Talented Tenth didn't need the exhortations, Bradby replied; branch meetings, which a few months before had been all but deserted, were now drawing four or five hundred people.[68]

Ossian wasn't among them. Not once that summer did he present himself to the branch as a symbol of resistance, nor did he ask for its help, though Carter and other members of his circle must have informed him of the NAACP's commitment to make a fight of it. But in the end, Ossian confronted the terrors awaiting him on Garland the way he'd tackled so many other challenges in his life, hefting other people's expectations and marching relentlessly forward. He worked methodically all through the balance of July and into August, trying to anticipate the most volatile moments, to compensate for his vulnerabilities, to prepare for the worst. Gladys bought extra food, enough for a week's siege, and stored it away, while he carefully assembled the cache of weapons they'd need and sought out a few more men to join the Sweets, Perry, and Carter in defending the house the first few dangerous nights. Full of enthusiasm, Henry talked a college friend and fraternity brother, John Latting, into signing on, while Otis recruited one of his numerous friends, an army veteran and federal narcotics agent by the name of William Davis, dangling the offer of a room in the bungalow as compensation. Ossian, meanwhile, hired a young Black Bottom man, Joe Mack, to serve as his chauffeur, an idea he undoubtedly took from Turner, and he made arrangements for another hired man, Norris Murray, to help around the new house. Mack and Murray weren't explicitly asked whether they were willing to take up arms, but neither did Ossian tell them of the dangers that would be facing them on moving day. So, by default, they, too, joined the defense. By mid-August, the contingent was complete: eight young men, Ossian and Gladys, a makeshift Talented Ten.[69]

The final few weeks were given to last-minute details. When they met in the bank, Vollington Bristol urged Ossian to inform the police of his plans. Ossian was skeptical, so Otis, who seemed to know all the ins and outs of Black Bottom, took it upon himself to contact Detective Inspector Robert "Bert" McPherson, head of the department's flamboyant Black Hand Squad, the office in charge of policing Italian mobsters and Negroes of every description. McPherson promised to give the Sweets the protection they needed. Ossian, meanwhile, thought through defensive tactics—guns in the upstairs windows where the sightlines were better, a couple of men out on the rear porch to protect the flank—the way he'd learned to do on Wilberforce's parade grounds.[70] Then, when everything was in place, he waited for summer to end and the confrontation to come.

•

But the summer didn't end. The heat of July carried through the dog days of August and into the first week of September. City hall all but shut down as Johnny Smith rested in anticipation of the autumn's bruising campaign, when Detroit would again be up for grabs. The Klan kept its crosses burning, and by the first week of September, they'd gathered the signatures they needed to put their man, Charles Bowles, back on the ballot in November's mayoral election. So sure was kleagle Ira Stout of the Klan's eventual success, he announced plans to put a brilliant neon sign atop the Invisible Empire's downtown headquarters, so that white, native-born Detroit could see the letters "KKK" blinking bloodred in the night and know where the city's center of power was soon to be. At the McClellan Station, Norton Schuknecht kept his eye out for trouble, waiting for word that the Negroes were about to move.[71]

And on Garland Avenue, the neighborhood's meager lawns turned from green to brown and the weeds that had poked up through the cracks in the sidewalk withered and died. Immediately after the Improvement Association's school-yard rally in mid-July, there'd been a flurry of activity. A thousand people signed membership cards and handed over their dollar dues. Encouraged by the flood of support, Conley and McGlynn appointed block captains to go door to door getting neighbors to add restrictive covenants to their deeds. But the campaign ran up against the reality of life along Garland. The Doves, right across the street from the bungalow, would have been happy to restrict the sale of their flat to whites, but they were renters: the owner lived miles away, far beyond the Improvement Association's reach. More troubling was the response of most of those who did own their homes. Time and again, the block captains were told that families wouldn't dare sign away their right to sell to Negroes without the assurance that everyone else in the neighborhood would do the same. The logic was unassailable. Just a few exceptions, a few people doing like that woman in the bungalow did and selling out to Negroes, and everyone else would be trapped, prohibited from accepting an offer from coloreds and stuck with a house whites wouldn't buy. It was all well and good to talk about banding together. But in the end, a man had to look out for himself and his family. After weeks of work, the Waterworks Park Improvement Association managed to convince 150 people to restrict their deeds.[72]

Intimidation also failed miserably. While the memory of the rally was still fresh, a three-man committee called on Marie Smith to see if she were willing to renege on her deal with the Negro and sell the bungalow to the association instead. She certainly was, she replied, as long as they were willing to pay her new asking price of thirty thousand dollars, a figure so ludicrously high they had no choice but to walk away. When the threatening phone calls began, Smith lost some of her moxie. One threat left her so rattled she blurted out that she hadn't sold her house to a Negro after all; she'd sold it to a Jew, and the Jew sold it to the colored man. Instead of giving in to the pressure, though, in early August, Smith packed up her belongings and fled—gone to California, some said—leaving the house dark and empty. That was about the time silence descended on Garland. The association called no more meetings; the block captains, defeated by their neighbors' self-interest, abandoned their rounds; and news of the Negroes dried up. There was still plenty of talk out on the porches and the street, bad feelings made worse by the incessant heat, but no one knew for sure when or if the coloreds were going to arrive.[73]

♦

Norton Schuknecht also spent the balance of the summer waiting for word of the Sweets' intentions. Twice in the weeks after the July rally, he sent men out to ask the bungalow's owner when the Negroes were going to move in, but she insisted that she didn't know anything. It never occurred to him to track down the coloreds themselves, though it wouldn't have been hard to do. Then again, the Negroes hadn't come looking for him, either. When they put in their request for police protection, they went to Bert McPherson, the inspector in charge of the Black Hand Squad. That decision alone was enough to make Schuknecht livid. McPherson was a high flyer— fourteen meritorious mentions in his first eight years on the force, a full inspector at forty-three—but he was too undependable for Schuknecht's taste. It wasn't clear how long McPherson had news of the Negroes' plans, but he didn't pass it to Schuknecht until the evening of September 7, just twelve hours before the coloreds showed up on Garland Avenue. Schuknecht was so angry he didn't even ask the Black Hand boys for assistance, though they knew a thing or two about dealing with Negroes.[74]

Instead, he scrambled to put together a plan he hoped would keep the peace. The Sweets would have around-the-clock protection, he decided: four cops at the bungalow in the morning, eight in the afternoon, ten or more by nightfall. To make sure that everything was done right, Schuknecht would personally direct operations on the street. In case of emergency, he arranged to have two hundred men held in reserve at the precinct house during the first few nights the Negroes were in their new neighborhood.

Almost immediately things went wrong. Late on the night of the seventh, as Schuknecht was making his final arrangements, two patrolmen spotted a Negro chasing a white man down one of the west side's major thoroughfares. When they tried to intervene, the Negro pulled a gun and opened fire, killing one of the cops and wounding the other. By the time Schuknecht's men gathered for roll call the next morning, word of the murder must have spread across the police department, and emotions were undoubtedly running high. He tried to be tough. Those officers assigned to the doctor's house should avoid using excessive force, he said; simply keep the crowds from congregating. But, he insisted, "we're there to preserve peace and order, and that man, Doctor Sweet, can live there, if we have to take every man in the department to protect his home."[75] In private, though, Norton Schuknecht must have known that in a department thick with Klansmen, this wasn't a day to count on his men to do their duty.

◆

Tuesday, September 8, began with the small shivers of excitement that the break of seasons brings. Most men and a few women were up and off to work early that morning, anxious to punch in on time after the long holiday weekend. Mothers and the few fathers who stayed behind wrestled wriggling children into brand-new dresses and sharply creased shirts and marched them down the street to the first day of school. By midmorning the bustle had eased and Garland had settled into a blessed quiet. Those who worked at home such as Kathleen Dove, with the baby to care for, were in the midst of their morning chores when the Sweets' touring car passed slowly down the block and pulled up to the curb just short of Charlevoix.[76]

Most of the day, the neighbors kept watch surreptitiously, peering out from behind blinds or glancing over to the bungalow, anxious to see every move the coloreds made. They watched as a gang of Negroes drew in behind the sedan with a truckload of trunks and suitcases, a few packages of gunnysack, and a couple of pieces of furniture. They saw the cops arrive—that was a surprise—two patrolmen idling on the corner, another officer walking right up to the front door and standing in the shadow of the porch talking to one of the colored men for a minute or two. In the course of the afternoon, some of the movers left and other Negroes showed up, jauntily striding up the steps and disappearing into the house.[77]

It wasn't until late afternoon that the neighbors began to move outdoors. The kids came first, drawn to the corner by the sight of policemen and the frightening, thrilling news that at long last the Negroes were on their block. But the cops had no trouble shooing the youngsters away, and by suppertime, the street was largely clear. Once meals were finished and dishes cleared, though, the crowd began to gather. There were a lot more cops on the street by then, a dozen or so, a few on each of the four corners of the intersection where the bungalow stood, several more in the alleyway behind.[78]

Nothing happened. No one from the Waterworks Park Improvement Association—not Conley the real estate agent or McGlynn the autoworker or Monet the rubber worker—went among the men exhorting them to challenge the police line. No neighborhood woman mounted the Doves' front porch and dared the men to attack. No one picked up a stone and lobbed it across the street. No one did anything to pull the crowd together, to transform the curious into the murderous, to make a mob. The sun set, the streetlights blinked on, and still the neighbors stood on the street until the hour grew so late that they started to think of the following day's work and, one by one, drifted home to bed.

◆

The next day, September 9, Garland was again rife with rumors, the way it had been back in June. The Negroes were to be put out, people told each other. There'd been a meeting in the corner market where the attack had been plotted; some of the men from Tireman Avenue were on their way over to lead the assault; tonight was the night. There was a lot of angry talk that day, so much that the cops stationed at the corner heard it, the motorman on the Charlevoix Avenue streetcar heard it, residents on nearby streets heard it, and the Sweets heard it, too.[79]

By eight, the crowd was as thick as it had been the night before, maybe thicker. As the streets grew clogged, the police officer in charge—the obese fellow over near the school yard—huddled with a couple of his men, who then closed Garland to traffic a block north and south of the bungalow. Without the occasional car rumbling past, the street grew empty, only a few feet of asphalt still hot from the day's sun separating the patrolmen in front of the Negroes' house from the people gathered on the lawns and porches on the opposite side. The Getkes came out onto their porch to sit for a while. Across from them, neighbors filled the Doves' front yard from the sapling planted next to the curb all the way up to the porch where Ray Dove stood leaning against the railing, his wife and their roomers behind him. Eric Houghberg strode past, slipping into his flat so that he could grab a quick supper and get back out onto the street. Leon Breiner sauntered down to the corner store, then, as he headed back home, stopped by the Doves' to chat and smoke his pipe. Bored with the view from the corner, thirteen-year-old Ulric Arthur and his friend George Suppus squeezed through the men and women gathered on the Doves' lawn and planted themselves on the porch steps, where their view of the bungalow was just about perfect.[80]

No sign of the corner-market conspirators or the men from Tireman Avenue. Darkness coming, cover of night. Maybe then. Maybe never. Rumors. Bitter words filling a summer evening. Put the niggers out. Dancing with the devil.

They came from opposite directions, the taxi rattling past the police checkpoint down Garland toward the corner and the gang of teenagers—six or seven local boys, neighborhood kids—spilling out from the half lot between the Doves' flat and the grocery store next door. But it was as if their movements were choreographed. The first stones flew as the cab came to a stop, rocks and chunks of coal grabbed from the alleyway arching gracefully over the policemen's heads and thudding onto the bungalow's sloping roof. A dormer window shattered, though in the sudden noise and confusion the sound of breaking glass was hard to hear. As the cab door swung open the cries went up, "Here's niggers!" "There they go!" More stones—aiming at the porch, at the other windows, at the two coloreds racing for the bungalow's steps. The front door suddenly opened and another Negro appeared. For a fraction of a second, he stood stock-still in the doorway, staring beyond the coloreds running toward him to the people on the Doves' front lawn. Then he was gone, faded back into the darkness of the house.[81]

The stones kept coming a minute more, maybe two. Then the bungalow's upstairs windows slid open and the guns blazed, brilliant flashes of light illuminating the blackening sky.

SIX

THE LETTER OF YOUR LAW

The paddy wagon pulled up in front of the police department's downtown headquarters, its back door creaked open, and a patrolman signaled for the ten men to climb down. Enough time since the shooting had passed for the force's high command to confirm the worst: the Negroes' fusillade had struck two white men. Eric Houghberg, rushed to Receiving Hospital bleeding profusely from a bullet wound in the thigh, was expected to survive, but Leon Breiner had been killed by what appeared to be a single bullet in the back.

As news of the murder spread, Garland Avenue was teetering on the edge of a riot. An hour after the shooting, there were five thousand people thronging the intersection in front of the bungalow, a crowd greater than anything the west side had seen that summer, and though its members still seemed leaderless and unsure of themselves, the risk of a rampage was dangerously high. Desperate to impose order, Norton Schuknecht rushed the entire force he'd put on reserve, two hundred men, into the neighborhood, their authority bolstered by a new weapon, the department's own whippet tank.

As Ossian and the others uncurled themselves from the wagon's benches and gingerly stepped down to the street, they had only the most basic sense of what was happening. Someone in the mob had been killed and they were in deep, deep trouble.[1]

Police headquarters loomed above them. Opened just two years earlier, it was a monumental building, with the force and grandeur to disquiet a powerless man. Its architect, Albert Kahn, had made his reputation designing Detroit's auto factories, spare utilitarian structures of glass and concrete, but for this commission, he had drawn on classical forms. To report to duty, the city's men in blue passed through a vaulted entranceway flanked on either side by four soaring arched windows. Above them rose eight four-story-tall faux Doric columns ostensibly supporting a final floor of crisp, clean lines: seventeen Tuscan columns capped by a frieze decorated with bas reliefs. The building was nothing less than a civic temple, an evocation in stone and sculpture of the Western tradition's highest ideals.[2]

But it was nothing more than a façade, as inside the police headquarters, corruption was rampant, and every Negro in the city knew that justice received here would be tempered at best, lethal at worst. Colored people raised in Alabama, Mississippi, or Florida hardly expected justice to be blind, but still they despised the blinding prejudice that seemed to consume Detroit's cops. Colored men were two and a half times more likely to be arrested than whites, colored women almost seven times as likely as their Caucasian counterparts. Once they were in custody, Negroes routinely were held for days without being formally charged and often were denied access to lawyers— sometimes suspects were moved from precinct to precinct so they couldn't be found, then were threatened and even beaten until they confessed. And those were the colored people lucky enough to have been spared cops' summary justice.[3]

So when Ossian and the others followed Lieutenant Blondy Hayes of the Black Hand Squad into the police headquarters, they were under no illusions. Hayes had been incredibly kind in the terrifying moments after the shooting, taking off Ossian's handcuffs, calming his fears, and arranging for the back-alley exit from Garland. His willingness to confront the mob in the alleyway behind the bungalow may well have saved the Negroes' lives. But when the colored men were delivered to the officers who were going to take on their case, they had to be prepared for accusations to be leveled and intimidation to begin. They could assume no degree of sympathy; they couldn't risk an errant word. And they had to fear, as the lieutenant led them up flight after flight of stairs until they reached the fourth-floor offices of the homicide squad, whether they would ever be free again.[4]

It was about ten o'clock when Hayes settled Ossian and the other nine men into a long, narrow anteroom in the Detective's Bureau.

Gladys arrived a short time later, escorted by a patrolman from the reserve unit. All of them must have felt ragged and worn, drained by the stifling heat of the room—at the end of a summer's day, the air had to have hung heavy and still—the lateness of the hour, and the surreal sense of watching a nightmare unfold. Somehow Davis, the narcotics agent, managed to fall asleep, the skill of a military man who'd learned in the course of combat how to grab rest whenever he could have it. The others sat hollow eyed around the room's large table or against the wall, waiting for something to happen.[5]

As soon as the opportunity presented itself, Ossian and one of the insurance men, Hewitt Watson, asked for the chance to call their lawyers. Although he was surely still angry at his friend's failure to show up at the bungalow the previous night, Ossian phoned Julian Perry, while Watson talked to Charles Mahoney, one of the most able black attorneys in the city. Precisely what the lawyers said isn't known, but most likely they urged the prisoners not to give the police any incriminating information. Not that the eleven needed that advice. In the time they spent together in the anteroom, Ossian and the others agreed on a makeshift defense they would share when the police starting asking questions. As they whispered out their alibis, though, they had to have wondered whether the story they assembled would hold through eleven separate interrogations, or whether one of them—too tired to think, too scared to keep the details straight, too anxious to save himself—would say something that condemned the rest. When no one was watching, Ossian squeezed his hand around the bullets he still had in his pocket and silently slipped them into the cuspidor that sat on the floor next to his chair.[6]

There was still no sign of the lawyers when, at 10:45 P.M., two hours after the shooting, Hayes asked Ossian to follow him into the interrogation room. In a panic, Ossian got to his feet, and this strange and terrifying night entered its next dangerous phase.

◆

As he walked into the tiny room, Ossian must have expected intimidation, perhaps even the threat of violence. Instead, he found the makings of a formal legal procedure. In front of him sat Assistant Prosecuting Attorney Ted Kennedy, dispatched by his boss, Wayne County Prosecutor Robert Toms, to personally conduct the interrogations in an effort to make sure the record wasn't contaminated by the force's usual abuses.[7]

Kennedy began gently enough, introducing Ossian to the stenographer and to the two officers, Blondy Hayes and Lieutenant William Johnson of the Homicide Squad, who sat around the table with him, then inquiring about the details of the doctor's move. As he tried to answer, Ossian grew agitated, talking too fast, stumbling over words. And when the prosecutor moved onto dangerous ground, Sweet offered painfully clumsy denials, so transparent they defied belief. Kennedy asked him whether Garland Avenue was a white neighborhood. Ossian said he didn't know.

"Well, I mean, before you bought it, you investigated, of course," Kennedy replied in genuine surprise.

"No," insisted Ossian, "the house was for sale; and I simply asked her would she sell it."

His other answers were no more believable. He hadn't asked the other men to help him defend his home, he said; they were just visitors, boarders, there on business. They weren't huddled inside waiting for attack; he had invited them all to dinner and they were waiting for the ham to finish cooking. They had only started shooting once the rocks started hitting the house and the windows were smashed. He couldn't say who fired when. "I was so excited," he explained, "I wasn't normal then; I don't know what was there." But they had been provoked; he knew that. They'd had to shoot or the mob would have destroyed the house.

Kennedy took it slowly at first, letting the doctor put together his version of events, not probing too much. But the closer it got to midnight, the more aggressively the prosecutor pushed. Why had Ossian filled the house with guns? Sweet backtracked ever so slightly, saying he had heard "rumors" that the whites were going to drive him off and he wanted to protect himself. How did the men know where to find the guns once the attack began? He had showed them the weapons in the upstairs closet. When did Ossian buy the guns? "Oh, when the trouble started around here, sometime ago," Ossian answered. "About a month ago."

Kennedy knew he was close to getting the answer he wanted. One more step and Ossian would admit that he had planned his defense, had conspired with the other Negroes. "Now, doctor," he said, "isn't it a fact, you moved up in the neighborhood, knowing it was a white neighborhood; if you went up there, there was going to be trouble?"

"No."

That had been too direct. Kennedy tried again. "You say that certain things developed, after the place [was] bought, which led you to believe there was going to be trouble after you moved in?"

"Yes."

"When you moved in, you had the arsenal up there with you. . . . You took them up there, knowing you were going to have trouble, didn't you?"

Ossian tried to hedge. "No," he said, "I didn't know [I was] going to have trouble." But Kennedy wouldn't let him slip away that easily. "You had a pretty good reason to believe it," he asked, "didn't you?"

"Yes."

"Why did you move in there, then?"

"Because I bought the house," Ossian said, "and it was my house, and I felt I had a right to live in it."

Principle. After an hour of evasion, Ossian fell back on the fundamental point of the entire affair. The house was his, and he wasn't going to be driven from it. At midnight, Kennedy sent him back to the anteroom and started working his way through the others one by one.[8]

The differences between them were dramatic. Insurance man Charles Washington had the salesman's touch, shaking hands all around when he walked into the interrogation room, while his colleague Leonard Morse was so desperate to please he came across as obsequious. "Have I threatened you in any way?" Kennedy asked as the interrogation came to a close. "No," Morse replied. "I believe you too much of a gentleman for that, Mr. Kennedy." William Davis was much more guarded, his answers brief, his words carefully chosen, his participation in the Sweets' defense edited down to a minimum; not once did he mention that he'd spent the night of September 8 trapped inside the bungalow, waiting for an assault that didn't come. Small John Latting, Henry's college friend, was so terrified he had trouble putting words together. And poor Joe Mack, the chauffeur, had to stop in the middle of his interview so he could gather himself. He had been sick for quite some time—heart trouble—and the pressure was too much to bear.[9]

When Kennedy moved them through the evening's events, though, almost all of the suspects told the same story Ossian had offered. No one had gone out to Garland to help the doctor protect his house. Mack was doing his job, and handyman Norris Murray had come by hoping to get paid for the work he'd put in the previous day. Davis and Latting were to look at rooms they were hoping to rent. And the three insurance agents agreed that they were there to correct a mistake on the doctor's policy. Once they had assembled inside the bungalow, there'd been no talk of a mob attack, no discussion of tactics, no distribution of the guns hidden upstairs. Washington and Morse described a casual evening of cards and conversation. "Why I didn't do anything but sit down and went to talking," Morse said, "principally joking." Murray said he set to work in the basement, getting the boiler heated up so Mrs. Sweet could finish cooking the dinner. Joe Mack went up to the bathroom to "take a bath and a crap."[10]

As quickly as the suspects assembled their alibis, Kennedy tore them down. Sometimes, he played one witness off another. Did you hear any water running into the bathtub in the hour before the shooting, he asked Latting, or notice anyone go into the basement to start the boiler? No, the young man said, bewildered by the questions. Other times, Kennedy confronted the suspect directly. Was it necessary for three insurance men to deliver news about a mistaken policy, he asked Watson. Do you always devote so much time to your clients, he said to Washington. You couldn't have spent the whole evening lighting a boiler, he pressed Murray. What else did you do?[11] Once or twice, the prosecutor came tantalizingly close to breaking the weakest of the group. "When did you start to talk about the trouble out there, that might arise there," Kennedy asked Joe Mack. "You started to talk about that, didn't you?"

Mack tried to stall. "Sir?"

"You started to talk among yourselves, about some trouble you might have?"

"Yes," the chauffeur replied. "They says they might run us away from out here tonight."

"They might what?"

"The white people says, going to run us away from here tonight."

"Was the doctor talking about that, too?" Kennedy said. "What I mean is, when you were playing cards with these men in the room there, weren't you talking about this trouble you might be having tonight?"

But there was something in the question—the doctor's name, perhaps, or the hint of excitement in Kennedy's voice—that reminded Mack of what he was supposed to say. "No, I didn't hear," he said, suddenly adamant. "There wasn't nobody saying anything about no trouble; wasn't paying no attention."[12]

If the suspects had trouble keeping all the pieces of their story together, though, on the two most pivotal points there was complete agreement. In the moments before the shooting, the bungalow was under intense assault. "Stones. [They] started throwing stones," Latting insisted. "Bricks and so forth being throwed against the house and bricks comed through the window," agreed Morse. "I wasn't in the room but I heard the breaking of the glass." Davis, the narcotics agent, heard the glass shattering as well. "Bricks or rocks or something, some kind of missiles, hitting the house . . . from all sides," he said. "Then there came a big crash upstairs, a window going through, something like that." And when the guns went off, none of the suspects were any-where near the upstairs windows. Mack was still in the bathroom, Murray in the basement. Latting was cowering in the upstairs hallway, away from the shards of glass flying across the bedrooms. Morse stayed downstairs, hiding in the alcove right behind the front vestibule. Davis was standing in the living room. Otis Sweet was at the phone near the back staircase. Washington kept moving from room to room. And Watson couldn't recall where he was. "I'm sure I don't know," he told Kennedy. "You know, [there was] quite a lot of excitement." Ten guns, two hundred rounds of ammunition, fifteen or twenty shots fired, and no one pulled a trigger.[13]

So through five hours of interrogation, the feeble story arranged in the anteroom held together—but for two moments when caution gave way to defiance.

Gladys Sweet was tougher than Ossian and the other men, a lot tougher. She wasn't intimidated the way Kennedy must have expected her to be, the way her husband had been. She didn't have excuses to offer or an unlikely story to tell. On the contrary, she seemed proud of what she and her husband had done, that they'd taken a stand. And she resented being questioned, as if there were no reason to investigate the night's events, as if it were painfully obvious what had occurred, as if the Negroes had a right to shoot into a crowd of white people.

Kennedy asked her whether she knew she was moving into a white neighborhood. "Certainly did," she replied.

"You knew and expected if you went out there, there was going to be trouble?"

"Possibly, yes," Gladys said. "They informed us they was going to be trouble."

"Why did you go up there?" Kennedy asked.

"I think it is my perfect right to move where I please," she said.

"You brought all those guns up there, didn't you?"

"Well, yes."

"And talked about using them, too, if necessary?"

"If necessary."

But she'd go no farther. For the better part of an hour, Kennedy tried to get her to re-create the evening, to describe the conversations her husband had with the other men, to retrace their movements immediately before the shooting, something, anything, that he could use to show that the men planned the shooting. Gladys couldn't recall a single moment, not a word spoken, not a step taken. Kennedy tried to shake her. He showed her the guns. He brought a couple of extra cops into the room, to make her feel small and vulnerable. But Gladys still stonewalled. Finally, Kennedy couldn't contain his frustration. "Do you want this attitude throughout the entire statement," he snapped. "You don't remember anything, is that right?"

"I don't remember what I don't remember," she fired back. "You can't make me."

"No. Is it because you don't want to remember?"

"It is because I don't remember."

He didn't need this, not from this little colored woman barely out of her teens. "Will you remember tomorrow morning?" he asked.

"No, I won't."

"Will you remember a week from now?"

"No."

It was useless. She wasn't lying, at least not in the way that the others had lied. They had tried to fool Kennedy by misdirection and obfuscation of the most obvious sort. She was defying the prosecutor, taunting him by withholding the information they both knew she had. He wouldn't break her, no matter how much of the night he wasted. Kennedy sent her back to be with her husband.[14]

Henry Sweet's answers were even more startling—and much more dangerous. A few minutes into his interrogation, Kennedy asked him what happened when the stones began hitting the house. For some reason, Henry didn't follow the script. He went upstairs, he said, picked up his rifle, walked into the front bedroom, knelt at the window, and scanned the mob standing across the street.

It took Kennedy a second to realize where Henry was going with his story. The prosecutor started to ask about the rifle. Which gun was it? Could Henry identify it? But that wasn't the line to follow. Not yet. Kennedy had the weapons, all piled up outside the interrogation room, waiting to be tagged as evidence. What he didn't have was the suspects' actions, the key to establishing their intentions, the foundation for the prosecution's case. What did you do then, once you were at the window, he asked.

"I didn't do anything until the stones began coming in on me," Henry replied.

"Then what happened?"

"I tried to protect myself."

"What did you do?"

"I fired the rifle," Henry said.

"Where did you fire it?"

"The first time in the air."

"Then what did you do?"

"I fired again in the crowd." He hadn't aimed at anyone in particular. He'd tried to fire a foot or two above the mob, to "frighten them so they would leave us alone."

He said it without a hint of braggadocio or remorse. Henry was just setting out the facts, putting himself on record. He was also giving up his best alibi, his surest hope of avoiding conviction. Kennedy had the sudden hope that he would hand over the others as well. Was anyone else in the room with you, he asked. There were two or three men kneeling alongside him, admitted Henry. Perfect. Kennedy pushed as hard as he had all evening. Who were they? Which window was the doctor at? Had the others fired into the street as well? But Henry wouldn't take the next step. He couldn't say. The room was dark; he couldn't make out their faces. There had been too much confusion; Henry couldn't recall who was doing what.

That was ludicrous. The others must have been standing a foot or two away from you, Kennedy said. You had to have seen them or at least heard their guns going off. But Henry was adamant. He would implicate himself, but he wouldn't implicate anyone else. So Kennedy tried a different tack. When did the group plan the defense? They must have talked over what each man would do if trouble started. "Never to my knowledge," Henry said. They all intended to shoot the moment they picked up the guns, didn't they? "Not necessarily," Henry replied. There wasn't a mob, was there? Henry saw the policemen on the street, didn't he? He knew the police had the situation under control. He didn't need to fire into the crowd.

Henry stiffened. "Before I made the first shot," he said, "the stones pouring down like rain."

Kennedy wouldn't let up. "Did any of them hit you? How close they come to you?"

"Very close."

"If you stayed out of the front room," Kennedy said, "you wouldn't have been hit, would you?"

"Probably I would have been dead by now," Henry answered, "if I hadn't gone out there."[15]

He'd pulled it back to self-defense. Henry had been moving right toward a confession. Then he had pulled it back to self-defense.

It was almost three thirty in the morning when Kennedy finished the interrogations, packed up his notes and transcripts, and headed home to prepare the report for his boss's desk first thing in the morning. When the young man was gone, the cops clasped manacles onto the eleven Negroes and led them outside into the stillness of the deep city night, across the street to the decrepit Wayne County Jail. Gladys, again separated from the others, was taken to the women's ward. Ossian was escorted into one of the men's cellblocks, his brothers and the seven others into a different section of the jail.[16] It must have been almost dawn by the time all the cell doors were finally slammed shut.

◆

News of the Sweets' arrest rocketed through Detroit's Talented Tenth. Ossian's panicked call to Julian Perry got the word out. As soon as Sweet was off the line, Perry phoned his fellow lawyer, Cecil Rowlette, to ask for help. Having represented both Fleta Mathies and Alexander Turner, Rowlette had an intimate understanding of the legal and political issues the Sweets would be facing. He also had the temperament any defense counselor was going to need. Perry, a short, slight, light-skinned young man five years out of Howard University's law school, embodied the physical attributes and educational achievements the colored elite most prized, but he had no real fighting instinct. Brawny, dark-skinned Rowlette made up for what his colleague lacked. The youngest of eleven children born to former slaves outside Richmond, Virginia, he was weaned on stories of oppression; when she was just twelve, his mother used to tell him, she was sold three times in one day. Like Ossian, Rowlette pulled himself into the Talented Tenth by taking advantage of the opportunities black colleges provided, graduating from Virginia Union University in 1908 and Howard Law four years later. In his ten years of practice in Detroit, he'd established himself as a first-rate criminal lawyer—tough-minded, relentless, extraordinarily confident in his abilities, and a bit of showman. As soon as Perry explained what had happened on Garland, Rowlette signed on to the case. They agreed to meet at police headquarters right away.[17]

Hewitt Watson's call to attorney Charles Mahoney, meanwhile, went instead to William Osby, a Negro engineer who lived across the street from Mahoney in an otherwise white neighborhood not far from Tireman Avenue. Mahoney, it turned out, didn't have a phone, so Osby took his evening calls. The arrangement put the Sweets' news into the heart of the Talented Tenth. Head of the Dunbar Board of Trustees, a member of the executive board of Detroit's fledgling NAACP branch, and a founder of the Detroit Urban League, Osby was a powerhouse in black Detroit. Mahoney was every bit his equal. The son of a business-man, Mahoney had grown up the only colored child in a small Michigan town. When he reached college age, his parents sent him to Fisk Univer-sity, one of the finest black colleges in the country. He received his law degree from the University of Michigan in 1911 and immediately set up a successful practice in Detroit, taking civil rights cases for the NAACP on the side. His work in breaking the segregation of nearby Ypsilanti's school district won him widespread attention, even from white politi-cians: he already had three years on the city's planning commission be-hind him, and Mayor Smith had made him one of his closer advisers, a prelude, many thought, to Mahoney seeking office himself. The moment he heard what had happened, Mahoney also headed downtown, while Osby started contacting his NAACP colleagues across the city.[18]

Most likely, Perry, Rowlette, and Mahoney ran into one another at po-lice headquarters that night; they certainly ran into the same stone wall. In 1925, criminal suspects had no legal right to have their attorneys present during questioning, and Detroit's cops weren't in the practice of erring on the side of leniency toward Negroes. It was an indication of Mahoney's stature that he managed to get all the way up to the Homi-cide Squad offices before being booted out the door, but Lieutenant Johnson came out of the interrogation room to personally send the lawyer packing. "Get the hell out of here," he growled. So the attorneys headed home that night without so much as a glimpse of their clients.[19]

But they knew that the battle was just beginning. As always, the cops had brute force on their side, but the Talented Tenth had the weight of politics, or so they thought. Colored voters had helped to give progres-sive judges control of the criminal court in 1923 and had put Smith in the mayor's office the following year. It was time to call in some debts. By Thursday morning, September 10, Perry, Rowlette, and Mahoney had agreed to create a joint defense team. Their first order of business was to gain access to their clients; every hour that passed heightened the risk that one of the suspects would say something incriminating, and in any case, the prisoners deserved to know that someone was working on their behalf. The key step was to secure a writ of habeas corpus, forcing the prosecutor either to surrender the suspects or file charges. Already the bench's progressives were incensed about the department's abuse of procedural rights: just a few weeks before, the criminal court's leading liberal, Frank Murphy, had released thirty-six accused gamblers because the cops had held them a day and half before any charges were lodged. By the time the lawyers' plea reached the bench, Ossian and the others would be closing in on twenty-four hours. As long as Mahoney, Rowlette, and Perry put their case before one of the four liberal judges, there was no way the court was going to turn them down.[20]

By itself, the writ wouldn't release the eleven suspects. In fact, it would probably do nothing more than force the prosecutor to present charges against them. But the lawyers were convinced that the court wouldn't let the charges stand. When Fleta Mathies had taken a potshot at her neighbor on Northfield Street, Rowlette had argued that she had acted in self-defense, and the judge had agreed, quashing the warrants before the young woman ever faced a jury. The court had also thrown out charges against John Fletcher, the last victim of the Tireman mobs, and he had actually shot a white boy. Again, the pivotal step was to get the case put before one of the progressives. As luck would have it, Murphy was the presiding judge for the month, in charge of assigning all cases. It would take some time and a lot of effort, but Rowlette was sure the eleven could be freed.[21]

In the meantime, Osby had pulled the NAACP branch into the action. The branch's former president and current legal counsel, W. Hayes McKinney, put his considerable political weight to the task of prying open the Sweets' jail cells. What's more, the branch president, Rev. Robert Bradby, pledged to open his church, Black Bottom's Second Baptist, for a mass rally in support of the Sweets after Sunday morning services. Three months before he stood for reelection, Johnny Smith would have no choice but to pay attention. And if he did, the course of the battle would shift and the forces of reaction would suddenly be on the run.[22]

Instead, the Talented Tenth was blindsided.

◆

The intersection of Garland and Charlevoix was still in chaos when the reporter from the *Detroit Free Press* arrived an hour or so after the shooting. So he avoided the corner and headed to the victim's modest home farther up the block, where a stunned Leona Breiner and her girls kept a death watch. Then he met with the leaders of the Waterworks Park Improvement Association, gathered in an emergency meeting at Joseph Rudge's house, seven doors north of the Sweets'. Only around midnight did he venture down to the bungalow, hoping to have a few minutes with the cops' commanding officer.[23]

By then Norton Schuknecht must have been utterly exhausted. As soon as McPherson's man, Blondy Hayes, led the Negroes to the paddy wagon, Schuknecht had turned his attention back to the massive mob gathered around the bungalow. There had to have been four thousand, maybe five thousand people on the street, he guessed, though in the pandemonium of the moment, it was impossible to get an accurate estimate. It took no more than a few minutes for the two hundred patrolmen he had put on reserve to pour into the neighborhood—truck after truck of heavily armed cops ready for riot duty. Immediately, Schuknecht reinforced the hastily arranged cordon he'd put around the coloreds' house, and when the department's tank rumbled down the street, he ordered it to protect his men's vulnerable flank along Charlevoix. For a while, he had to have wondered whether the line would hold; several times, gangs of men tried to push their way through to the bungalow, but the cops drew their billies, and the sickening sound of wood whacking against skull bone drove even the most fearless back down the block. Gradually, Schuknecht could feel the balance tipping his way. Passions spent, most folks drifted home as midnight closed in, until only a few hundred troublemakers remained, too angry or too stupid to know that the battle was over, too gutless to risk taking on cops they no longer outnumbered twenty to one.[24]

It was about that time that the reporter showed up on the bungalow's rock-strewn porch. Schuknecht could have begged off, citing all the work he still had to complete—the reports to file, the evidence to catalogue—before he could go home to bed. But it seems he wanted to talk, to make clear who was responsible for putting that white man into the morgue. So he invited the reporter inside for a tour of the house and a few words of explanation. He'd been on the street himself right before the shooting, Schuknecht said, and he knew the truth: there hadn't been any mob threatening the Negroes, no one surrounding the house, no one throwing stones. Garland Avenue was perfectly peaceful when the coloreds opened fire.[25]

By sunup the next morning, September 10, the spectacular story lay on stoops and newsstands across Detroit. "Shots poured without warning and seemingly without provocation last night at 8:30 . . . from the upstairs windows at 2905 Garland Avenue, into which Dr. and Mrs. Ossian H. Sweet, a Negro couple, had moved Tuesday, cost one man his life [and] put another in the hospital with a bullet in his leg," the front-page story began under a blaring headline. "A police inspector, a lieutenant, and a patrolman had been standing within 35 feet of the house which was lighted only in the upper window. They had been talking over the potential trouble that might result from Sweet's moving into the white neighborhood. A rain of bullets ended the conversation. As if the triggers of a dozen guns were being pulled simultaneously, the firing started. It stopped with the same suddenness that it began. While the police ran up the steps and hammered at the door, the gathering throng counted the casualties."

From there the story moved into the poignant details of a senseless death. In the course of the summer, the Waterworks Park Improvement Association had tried to talk the previous owner out of selling to Negroes, but she wouldn't cooperate. The Sweets themselves seemed to have come to Garland looking for trouble: they brought almost no furniture into their new home—not even enough chairs for all the Negroes who gathered inside—but they made sure the house was stocked with guns and ammunition. Leon Breiner posed no threat; he was simply strolling down the street when a bullet from the bungalow hit him in the head. All evening long, the victim's wife and daughters waited for Breiner to return from his walk. "Both girls heard rumors that their father had been hurt but did not suspect that he was killed," the story ran. "From time to time, as anxiety swept over them, they cried out, 'Daddy, daddy, where's my daddy?' When at last she learned that her husband wouldn't be coming home, his widow collapsed and by press time had yet to be revived."[26] Altogether, it was a damning story, sure to inflame passions all over the city.

The afternoon papers, the *Detroit News* and the *Detroit Times*, followed the *Detroit Free Press* onto the newsstands a few hours later. Normally, the papers were fierce competitors. For the better part of a century the *Detroit Free Press* and the *Detroit News* had split the Detroit market, the former claiming the workingman's penny with a host of homey touches and a dependable racism, the latter serving as the august voice of the business class, champion of Prohibition, good government, and Anglo-Saxon virtue. In 1921, William Randolph Hearst had taken control of the city's third paper, the long moribund *Detroit*

Times, transforming it from a staid sheet almost no one read into a champion of the working class, which it entertained with lurid stories of romance gone wrong and murder most foul. With the city's readership suddenly split three ways, the newspapers tried desperately to distinguish themselves, disagreeing on almost every issue, endorsing opposing candidates for elective office, spinning the same stories in dramatically different directions. But when it came to describing the tragic events on Garland Avenue, the three newspapers reached a remarkable unanimity.[27]

Like the *Detroit Free Press*, the *Detroit Times* took its lead directly from Schuknecht. "The outbreak occurred," the paper reported, "at a time when police, already guarding the house around which a hostile but orderly crowd had gathered, were congratulating themselves on having the situation well in hand. Without the slightest warning, and without any overt act from the outside, police said, a volley of shots burst from the upper window." The *Detroit Times* repeated some of the *Detroit Free Press*'s damning details: the lack of furniture in the Sweets' house; the abundance of weapons. And it added yet another fact even more condemning of the coloreds. According to assistant prosecutor Ted Kennedy, one of the Negroes, Henry Sweet, had confessed to shooting into the street.[28]

The *Detroit News* could have taken a very different tack. One of its reporters, Philip Adler, was heading home from a dinner party on the evening of the ninth, driving along Charlevoix Avenue a few blocks east of Garland, when he was stopped by a police roadblock. Curious, he parked on Goethe, the cross street north of Charlevoix, left his wife and baby in the car, grabbed his notebook, and walked past the barricade into the mob. When he asked a woman what was happening, she said, "A nigger family has moved into the neighborhood and they're going to put them out." Adler mingled with the mob momentarily, until things turned ugly. He saw stones hitting the house, the shots exploding from the upstairs window, and the police rushing the bungalow. Scared for his family, he ran back to his car and got them safely home. Then he headed to the newsroom.[29]

His editors, though, weren't interested in what he had seen. Perhaps they feared readers' response to an article describing rocks hitting the Negroes' house "like rain" just before the shooting; maybe they feared the political implications of a report that shifted the blame for Breiner's death from black to white. Whatever their reason, the editors tossed Adler's story into the wastebasket and went instead with a thoroughly professional account contradicting everything their own reporter had observed. "The shooting was not provoked," the *Detroit News* explained, again citing Shucknecht. "A small crowd was in front of the house, on both sides of the street, but no threats were made and no missiles were thrown. Suddenly an attic window was thrown up and a rifle was fired. A score or more shots followed in quick succession." By the afternoon shift change at the auto plants, the three papers had half a million copies flooding the city, each and every one of them turning the Sweets into killers.[30]

◆

By all accounts, Wayne County Prosecutor Robert Toms was a decent man. He came from the solid midwestern stock that in the years before the Civil War had championed abolitionism; Toms's grandfather had been a founding member of the Republican Party in the 1850s, when Abraham Lincoln was still an unknown backwoods lawyer. Unlike many other big-city prosecutors, Toms didn't measure his office's performance by the number of convictions secured. He didn't want to prosecute a case, he claimed, unless he deserved to win. And he absolutely dreaded the thought of sending an innocent man to prison. Better to let ninety-nine criminals go free, he told the press in a surge of sanctimoniousness, than to condemn one man for a crime he didn't commit.[31]

Yet as soon as he finished reading the previous night's interrogation transcripts, Inspector Schuknecht's brief report to his superiors, and Thursday morning's papers, Toms knew he had to bring those eleven Negroes to trial. It wasn't a matter of principle, at least not obviously so. It was politics. At thirty-eight years old, Toms had years of public life ahead of him, dozens of election campaigns to wage, and a spate of offices to win. There was no saying how far he might go. He had the standard good looks—the forceful square jaw, the deep blue eyes—voters loved. He held degrees from the best midwestern schools, the University of Chicago and the University of Michigan, and belonged to the right church and clubs: he was a Methodist and a Mason, an Odd Fellow and a Son of the American Revolution. Years ago, a politician with such a pedigree could have been magnanimous with Negroes. But these were bitter times. When the press ran stories that he was a member of the Klan, Toms vigorously denied them. With the KKK whipping racial tensions to a fevered pitch, though, Toms would squander every one of his advantages if he failed to prosecute the Sweets and their accomplices.[32]

But the interrogation transcript showed Toms the obvious weakness in his case. Time and again, the suspects said that the house was, in fact, under attack when the fatal shot was fired. Even Henry Sweet, who virtually confessed to the crime, was adamant that he was acting in self-defense. By saying that, the Negroes were handing their lawyers one of the most firmly established principles of common law. Hundreds of years of precedent granted a man an absolute right to defend himself and his property—even by deadly force—as long as he had reasonable cause to believe he was in imminent danger. The assessment didn't even have to be correct; according to the law, self-defense was all a matter of perception, not reality. To justify their actions, the Negroes simply had to say that they *believed* they were about to be attacked by a mob.

Toms would have only one effective reply. The Negroes had no reason to be afraid, he would have to say, because there was no mob in front of the doctor's house and therefore there was no threat. But that was the rub. Laymen might think of a mob as a howling mass of humanity waving torches and pitchforks. According to the State of Michigan, however, a mob existed when twelve or more armed people or thirty unarmed people assembled to intimidate or inflict harm. To make matters even more difficult, the legal definition of "harm" set an extremely low threshold: as soon as those thirty unarmed men and women caused twenty-five dollars in damage to a piece of property, they were breaking the law.[33]

According to the *Detroit Free Press*, there had been several hundred people out on Garland the night before, precisely the same number the Negroes cited during their interrogation. The suspects also told Kennedy that the rocks the mob had thrown shattered a window, and Schuknecht's report confirmed that one of the panes upstairs had been broken. Given these facts, Toms was going to have a very difficult time arguing that the Sweets hadn't faced a situation well beyond the legal requirements justifying self-defense.

Of course, Toms wasn't naive enough to believe that jurors decided cases according to fine points of law. When they went to trial, the Sweets would face an all-white jury—Toms would see to that—and the prosecutor didn't deserve his salary if he couldn't convince twelve Caucasians to convict eleven Negroes who invaded a white neighborhood armed to the teeth. There was every chance, though, that the case wouldn't get that far. At the preliminary hearing, the Negroes' lawyers would move to have the indictments quashed. When they did, the judges weren't going to overlook the legal technicalities, particularly if Toms ended up with one of the liberals hearing the motion. There were no two ways about it. To move his case all the way to trial, the prosecutor had to find some way to bring his argument within the letter of the law.

So before Toms had his office prepare indictments, he sent Assistant Prosecutor Kennedy out on more rounds of interviews. Kennedy had to have known that he was looking for any information his boss could use to downplay the threat the Negroes faced from the street, anything at all that would cast doubt on the whites' intent to do harm. But even he seemed surprised by what he heard when he went down to Garland that afternoon.

•

The Sweets' bungalow was quiet when Ted Kennedy, the stenographer, and Lieutenant Billy Johnson from Homicide arrived in the early afternoon of September 10. Norton Schuknecht had cordoned off the house while detectives photographed the scene, gathered the empty shell casings strewn upstairs, and scoured the closets and cabinets for whatever shards of evidence remained. Kennedy couldn't help but notice that the police hadn't catalogued the dozen stones littering the front porch and its overhanging roof.[34]

Schuknecht was waiting for him inside, his brother-in-law, Otto Lemhagen, still by his side. Kennedy began by reviewing the details the inspector had put in his report. Schuknecht confirmed them all. He was standing at the intersection when the shooting occurred, just as he told the newspaper reporters. The Negroes weren't being threatened; his men were in charge of the situation, and the firing began "without any warning. It was such a surprise to us," he said. "It rather took us off our feet." Then Kennedy asked the first critical question. "Did you observe any people standing in front of the house, directly across from the Sweets?" Shuknecht said he did.

"How many would you say there were?"

"I would say twelve or fifteen people across the street there."

It was the precision that was startling. Twelve or fifteen was a figure perfectly pitched to keep the crowd below the legal definition of a mob. Schuknecht had never before claimed that the gathering on Garland was so small, not when he talked to the press, not when he filed his incident report at police headquarters.[35] It was too unlikely a number to be coincidence; the inspector must have read the statute books and learned the law.

Kennedy gently probed the soft spots in Schuknecht's story, using an approach that was certainly softer than the one he had taken with the Sweets the night before. "It appeared there were a few missiles on top of the roof of the porch there, seven or eight," he pointed out. "Did you see those thrown?"

"Right after the shooting," Schuknecht said, "when I got across the street and ran to the front door, there were several missiles thrown then, because I know one or two struck the porch."

"After the shooting?" Kennedy asked.

"After the shooting, yes."

It was too good to be true. No crowd, no stones thrown until the Negroes opened fire, the physical evidence of the assault accounted for: it was the perfect testimony. Kennedy tested one more area. The papers were reporting several hundred people in the streets around Garland in the hours after the shooting. Did the inspector see a crowd gather after the shooting?

Absolutely, Schuknecht said. The moment the Negroes opened fire, he rushed into the bungalow. He wasn't inside for more than a minute or two. When he came out, a crowd "was closing up into the house." But Schuknecht's men held them off.

Here was a potential problem. If there were only a dozen people in front of the bungalow before the shooting, how could several hundred people be there seconds later? "How many would you say were out in front or across the street there," Kennedy said, "when you came out on the porch?"

"Oh, there may have been twenty-five," Schuknecht replied, "twenty-five, thirty people across the street then, when I got out there."

Twenty-five or thirty: just the right number again. Even after the shooting, after the Negroes killed Breiner, the whites had stayed within the law.[36]

Kennedy turned to Schuknecht's brother-in-law for confirmation. Everything the inspector had said was absolutely true, said Lemhagen. But his brother-in-law left out one telling observation. He had tagged along with the policemen when they entered the bungalow to arrest the coloreds. He took a good long look at Gladys, standing in the kitchen. Then she did the oddest thing. "She just laughed. I looked at her and [she] laughed, and I thought to myself: hard boiled." A perfect little detail, the sort of thing a jury was sure to remember when it came time to convict.[37]

As soon as Kennedy was finished with Shucknecht and Lemhagen, he crossed Garland to the flat opposite the bungalow, where Ray and

Kathleen Dove, their boarders, and the Sweets' next-door neighbors, the Getkes, were waiting for him. Homicide detectives would interview most of the people on Garland, but Kennedy needed to take these statements himself.[38] The Getkes had spent the evening sitting on their porch, not twenty feet from the Sweets' front door; if the Negroes' house had been stoned, they would know it. And the entire Dove household was an arm's length from Breiner when he'd been hit. They'd watched him die.

The interviews started on a promising note. The neighborhood was absolutely calm, not a bit of trouble, Ray Dove said in the soft, slightly southern drawl of his native Indiana. When Kennedy asked him whether there was a crowd in front of his house, though, Dove didn't give the right answer. "Oh yes," he replied, "quite a crowd." His wife, Kathleen, agreed. "There was more than fifty, I would say."[39]

Kennedy couldn't have been surprised by the Doves' estimate, which seemed more realistic than Shuknecht's. But at this point, the prosecution didn't need the truth seeping into the record. So Kennedy let the question drop; no point in being precise if the facts were going to undermine the state's case. When he interviewed the Doves' boarders and the Getkes, Kennedy didn't ask them how many people were on the street when the shooting began. Instead, he concentrated on whether the crowd, whatever its size, was threatening the Negroes.[40] But even that line of questioning spun off in the wrong direction.

"Did you see anything strike the Sweets' house," Kennedy asked John Getke, as he had asked the others.

"Different times seems as though we heard something," Getke said, "but yet we couldn't tell what place it was."

This was potentially damaging, an eyewitness account of stones hitting the house. Kennedy tried to find out how much the piano tuner had seen. He tried to exaggerate the attack to see if the man would back down. "Did you hear any great tumbling of rocks, stones, anything like that, on the house? Did you hear any crashing of glass?"

Getke seemed to realize that he'd said the wrong thing. "Absolutely no," he answered, there was nothing like that. It was just that—well— he had heard something right before the coloreds started shooting. "While we were sitting on the porch, my wife asked me what was that noise? I says, 'I don't know what—I can't hear it.' She says, probably throwing a pebble, you might call it; in fact, much lighter than a pebble. I scarcely heard it myself. Then two or three others [were thrown] and I heard them, and there was a volley [from the Sweets' house] immediately after that."[41]

That was better—not perfect but encouraging. The neighbors clearly knew what they were supposed to say, even if they didn't have the details down the way Schuknecht did. With a little bit of luck and maybe a few words to the wise, they could be counted on to testify that the Negroes had faced no threats, no stones, no mob. That's all the prosecutor's office would need to push the case through the preliminary hearing. And when that hurdle was cleared, the way would be clear for Toms to put the Sweets' fate before a jury of their Caucasian peers.

◆

Day or night, the Wayne County Jail rattled with noise. By Detroit standards, it was an ancient building, a four-story rattrap built thirty years earlier, now utterly inadequate to house the hundreds of suspects who passed through the city's overburdened legal system. The jail had a few individual cells, primarily in solitary, a dank dungeon hidden away in the basement, but most prisoners were placed in the upstairs cell blocks—long, cramped holding pens that housed a dozen or more suspects each. The guards set the cell blocks rules. But behind the bars, the prisoners were on their own. Many whiled away the days lying in a stupor on the tiny metal cots. But there was always someone up and about: drug addicts screaming through withdrawal pains or alcoholics suffering the d.t's; young people too scared to settle down; the guy who had been waiting months for a hearing and simply couldn't stand to be caged anymore; the woman who'd been through it all before and enjoyed needling the newcomers.[42]

It wasn't the clamor that bothered Ossian, Gladys, and the others, though. It was the silence. All Wednesday night and through the day Thursday, the eleven had waited for some word from their lawyers, from friends, from anyone who would be willing to fight for them. But they had heard nothing but silence, the burden of which grew heavier and heavier as the hours passed. Gladys, for all her bravado, felt it most. Alone in the women's block, sharing a cell with hardened criminals— one of her cell mates was awaiting trial for murder, or so she said, another for bootlegging—separated from her husband and toddler, Iva, Gladys was so sick with worry she couldn't even manage to eat, though her stomach was raw with hunger.

Ossian also felt the isolation crushing him. Put in a separate cell block from the others, he sat surrounded by pimps, thieves, and thugs, tortured by the thought of Gladys and his brothers, whom he had pledged to help and protect, whom he had failed. At least Henry and Otis had each other. By a stroke of luck, the guards had put them in the same cell, along with Davis, the narcotics agent. So they had the comfort, small as it was, of sharing the silence as it dragged through the meager lunch and into Thursday afternoon.[43] Almost a day gone by since the shooting and not so much as a hint of what was to come.

William Davis was the first to break under the pressure. He'd been true to the others during the interrogation the night before, sticking to the story the ten terrified men had thrown together in rushed whispers. But the more Davis thought, the more he must have realized how much he had to lose. He was a federal officer, whom his superiors considered a credit to the department; he earned a good paycheck; he had a government pension to look forward to. This threatened it all. He hadn't done a thing out at Sweet's house, hadn't been there more than a few minutes before the gunfire started. He had to extricate himself. He had to talk to the prosecutor again, before it was too late.

Ted Kennedy brought Davis back to the Detectives' Bureau in the middle of the afternoon Thursday, shortly after he completed the interviews on Garland. Davis opened the session with an apology. During the previous evening's interrogation, he said, he had forgotten to mention that he had been at the bungalow the evening before the shooting; in fact, he'd spent the night with Sweet and his wife, protecting the house, as had Otis and Henry, their cousin Latting, the chauffeur, and the handyman. If Kennedy hadn't been so tired himself, he might have leapt at the new information, additional evidence of conspiracy. Instead, the interrogation slogged along, Kennedy repeating his standard questions, half listening to the responses. Finally, he asked whether Ossian had given Davis any instruction on defending the house. Davis let his guard slip away. "Here's what he told me," he said. "That he was going out there; he wasn't looking for any trouble. But he was prepared to look after himself if he didn't get protection."

Kennedy suddenly revived. "Well, didn't you ask him what he meant by that, or how he was going to protect himself?"

"No, I didn't ask him other than to say to him, what do you mean? Just like that. He says—oh, he says: The boys will take care of things."

"Didn't you ask him how they are going to take care of things? Or did he tell you he had plenty guns and ammunition there to take of things with?"

"He says he had sufficient arms to look after things."

Kennedy could see it now, Davis's determination to be helpful. He fumbled for the right words, he was so anxious for more. "Was there anything—do you know—did any of these men tell you who fired the shots upstairs?"

"Now, you mean," Davis began, stopped, started again. "I will tell you when I did hear that? Was afterwards, after we were, after we were taken down to police headquarters."

"What did you hear?"

"I heard, it sounded like the voice of the insurance man, the bald-headed man, light one."

Kennedy had to get this right. "What's his name," he prompted. "Leonard C. Morse, was he the man with the gray suit, and kind of bald?"

"Yes," Davis replied. "I heard him make the remark that Henry— Henry Sweet, that is, the doctor's brother . . . I heard him say he was on the back pumping the rifle, something like that now; he spoke of Sweet being on the back [porch]."

"Did you hear anything more?"

"Well," Davis replied, "I heard Joe, Joe Mack. . . . Joe says, 'I shot that damn pistol three times, and then it hung up on me, and the police officer was shooting back at me.'"

"Is that what Joe Mack said?"

"That is what Joe Mack said."

It was done. Kennedy asked if Davis had heard anyone else talking about the incident, but he had no more information to share. So the assistant prosecutor brought the interview to a close and sent him back to the jail.[44] It wasn't going to be easy for Davis, sitting with the others in their cells, pretending to be one of them, waiting for the silence to break. He knew better than to tell them what he had done; they'd never forgive him. But it was better to deceive his fellow suspects than to have the previous night's lies come crashing down around him in a court of law. The authorities would have to treat him fairly now that he had told the truth, now that he had given them Sweet and Morse and Mack. He had betrayed them; there was no other way to look at it. But a Negro couldn't expect to be handed justice as a matter of right. One way or another, he had to pay for it. And it never came cheaply.

◆

For Julian Perry, Cecil Rowlette, and Charles Mahoney, the first hint of trouble came on Thursday afternoon, September 10, when they presented their petition for a writ of habeas corpus to Judge John Faust. A dedicated member of the court's liberal majority, Faust should have been happy to approve the petition. Instead, he turned it down flat. A mad scramble secured the writ from a sympathetic circuit court judge, but that only led to the next round of shocks. As expected, the prosecutor's office responded to the defense lawyer's move by presenting its warrants to the criminal court's presiding judge, Frank Murphy. Toms sent his assistant, Lester Moll, to make the presentation. "The evidence shows no act of violence or provocation on the part of the victims or any other persons," he told Murphy. "The prisoners were found in a room filled with deadly weapons. As we are unable to say who fired the fatal shots we must charge them all with the same crime." Ossian, Gladys, and the nine others "did make an assault, with intent, [against] Erik Hougberg [sic] . . . feloniously, wickedly and of their malice aforethought, to kill and murder," and "feloniously, willfully, and of their malice aforethought did kill and murder one Leon C. Breiner." The pivotal phrase was imbedded in the text: "malice aforethought." The black lawyers had expected their clients to face serious charges, perhaps even manslaughter. But the prosecutor was going for the maximum, assault with intent to commit murder and murder in the first degree. If convicted, all eleven suspects would spend the rest of their lives in prison.[45]

By all rights, Murphy should have been skeptical of such a scattershot approach to the most serious of crimes, submitted to his court at precisely the same time the three dailies were declaring the accused guilty in twenty-four-point type. In the two years since his election, he'd proved to be every bit the liberal he'd claimed to be on the stump. So devoted to saving souls that the officers of the court called him "Father Murphy" behind his back, he had limitless patience for the procession of drunks, prostitutes, gamblers, drug addicts, and petty thieves whom he saw as victims of an unjust social system. "I want mercy," he wrote his brother in the cloyingly pious style to which he was given. "I don't believe in [punishment] much and I do a great deal in mercy." Like Judge Faust before him, though, Murphy showed absolutely no sympathy toward the suspects. He simply took the warrants under advisement and ordered the lawyers to return the following day.[46]

That night the city seethed. After a month of inaction, the Waterworks Park Improvement Association called a mass meeting for Thursday night, September 10, at the Amity Lodge Hall a few blocks west of Garland. A thousand people showed up, filling every inch of the auditorium and spilling out into the street. Real estate agent James Conley ominously shared the podium with two avowed Klansmen, one of them a former kleagle running for a seat on the Detroit City Council, the other a spokesman for the KKK's campaign to segregate the city's public schools, a sure way, said the latter, to keep Negroes in their place. Later that night, the Klan held its own rally, an open-air affair filled with the fiery rhetoric and ringing endorsements of Charles Bowles's mayoral campaign that had marred the summer. In one important respect, though, the meeting was dramatically different than the dozens of others the Klan had staged in previous months. This time, the Invisible Empire didn't gather in its west-side stronghold. Instead, it met in Waterworks Park itself, just three blocks south of the Sweets' bungalow, in the center of Mayor Johnny Smith's east side. The message couldn't have been clearer. In the murder of Leon Breiner, the Klan believed it had found the wedge it needed to crack open the coalition of black and white that had denied it the mayor's office the previous November.[47]

Facing such fearsome anger, the courage of Detroit's progressive bloc seemed to buckle, as Perry, Rowlette, and Mahoney learned when they filed back into the courtroom Friday morning. Without a word of explanation or apology, Murphy handed down the warrants, now affixed with his florid signature, and ordered a hearing Saturday in Judge Faust's chambers on the defense lawyers' hurried request that their clients be released on bail.[48]

•

There was only one bright spot in the entire proceedings. Now that the charges were set, the attorneys finally had a firm legal right to meet with their clients. It took until Saturday afternoon—almost three days past the shooting—to arrange a jailhouse conference. Perry, Rowlette, Mahoney, and their NAACP associate, W. Hayes McKinney, brought the defendants the only positive news of the day. After a furious round of organizing, McKinney grandly announced, the Detroit NAACP was committed to underwriting the entire defense, no matter the cost.[49]

Fund-raising was to begin with the Sunday rally at Second Baptist, which everyone expected to be wildly successful. Ossian wept at the thought of his Talented Tenth colleagues rallying to his side. Even at such a crucial moment, though, he couldn't completely let down the guard he'd built around himself. When the lawyers had him make a formal statement explaining what had happened in the bungalow, Ossian repeated the unlikely story he had told Prosecutor Kennedy the night of the interrogations. All of the defendants had been there by coincidence, he insisted; there had been no planned defense, no principled stand. The attorneys dutifully wrote it all down but they couldn't have believed a word of it.[50]

Nor could they have hoped that such a painfully weak alibi could withstand an opposition that was growing stronger hour by hour. Saturday morning, Judge Faust rejected the defense's request for bail, the third time in three days the court's liberal bloc had failed to come to the Negroes' aid. Even Gladys, who everyone agreed had never so much as picked up a gun, was to be held indefinitely. Worse, Detroit was rife with the sort of shadowy rumors that every Negro knew proceeded pogroms. Colored men were on the march, whites whispered to each other all through the weekend. A Negro had murdered a white man just up the street from Garland Avenue, they were saying; another colored man shot a Caucasian through the chest; a gang of Negroes assaulted three whites, putting them in the hospital with fractured skulls. The attacks were unprovoked; no one was robbed; it had to be the beginning of a race war. "The situation is very tense in Detroit," McKinney wrote that evening as the stories swirled around him.[51]

Then came the last brutal blow of the week. Ever since the shooting, Mayor Smith had kept his peace: not one word of condemnation for the cops who had failed to protect the Sweets from attack; not one reply to the blast of biased newspaper reporters; not one response to the Klan's bold incursion into his territory. It almost seemed as if street-fighting Johnny, pin boy turned progressive, had been frightened into silence.

Finally, on Saturday night, September 12, Smith issued an open letter to the police commissioner, his first comment on the crisis that was threatening to split the city. Sunday morning's newspapers carried the full explosive text. "The outrage" on Garland, the mayor said, was not a singular event but rather a culminating point in the KKK's campaign to establish "a dictatorship" in Detroit. All summer long, the Invisible Empire had been trying to "induce Negroes to go into districts populated entirely by persons who would . . . resent such an invasion," hoping that as blacks broke through the color line, Detroit would be consumed by racial violence so severe the city government would topple, a white supremacists' beer-hall putsch. Of course, Negroes had a legal right to live wherever they wished. But, insisted Smith, "it does not always do for any man to demand to its fullest the right which the law gives him. Sometimes by doing so he works irremediable harm to himself and his fellows." In fact, segregation was a social good and those who dared to challenge it an enemy to their people and their city. "I deprecate the moving by colored persons into districts in which their presence would cause disturbance," Smith concluded. "I shall go further. I believe that any colored person who endangers life and property, simply to gratify his personal pride, is an enemy of his race as well as an incitant of riot and murder. These men who have permitted themselves to be the tools of the Ku Klux Klan in its effort to fan the flames of racial hatred into murderous fire have hurt the cause of their race in a degree that cannot be measured. I feel that it lies with the real leaders of the colored race in Detroit to dissipate this murderous pride."[52]

The Talented Tenth was still seething at the mayor's broadside when they gathered at Second Baptist for the NAACP's three o'clock rally. The mammoth church was filled to capacity, the pews jammed not only with Ossian's colleagues from the professional and business classes but also with ordinary Black Bottom folks, who felt the burden of neighborhood segregation every time they paid the rent on a decrepit apartment or felt the wind whistle through a broken windowpane the landlord refused to replace. Even as they surveyed the crowd in front of them, though, Bradby, McKinney, Edward Carter, and the other branch leaders had to have felt the city closing in on them. The Klan was in the ascendancy; the Negroes' white allies on the bench had deserted them; the mayor they had helped to elect had endorsed injustice and declared the pursuit of civil rights a threat to peace and liberal democracy. No longer was this simply a question of whether the Sweets were justified in firing into the mob on Garland Avenue. Now the Talented Tenth was locked in combat against segregation itself, battling to preserve some shred of the promise that brought almost a million people out of the South in the previous ten years, to show that the North was different, to prove that there were places in America where Jim Crow would not be allowed to rule. This had become a fight over fundamentals.

SEVEN

FREEDMEN, SONS OF GOD,
AMERICANS

James Weldon Johnson saw the potential right away. Each year the NAACP's Manhattan headquarters received so many reports of racial incidents that even some of the most tragic stories were simply set aside, new additions to black America's ever-expanding archives of unanswered injustices. But the paragraph-long wire-service article tucked into the back pages of *New York World* on Friday morning, September 11, was different. As soon as he finished reading about the Sweets' arrest, Johnson knew he was on to something big.[1]

It wasn't that the arrest of eleven Negroes was more outrageous than the other news. Both Philadelphia and Gary, Indiana, had opened the new school year by segregating colored children; a New York City theater was launching a run of D. W. Griffith's incendiary 1915 film, *Birth of a Nation;* and the city council of Norfolk, Virginia, had passed an ordinance prohibiting Negroes from living in "white communities" unless a majority of Caucasians gave their express approval. But the timing of the Detroit story was exquisite. And James Weldon Johnson wasn't the sort of person who let a promising moment pass him by.[2]

"He was a tall graceful man, always immaculately attired, calm and uneffusive," said his friend and associate Arthur Spingarn. "The first impression on strangers was one of extraordinary urbanity and poise. In fact it has been said that when he first came in contact with white men of position he was at ease several minutes before they were." Johnson saw no reason for it to be otherwise. "I will not allow one prejudiced person or one million or one hundred million to blight my life," he explained. "I will not let prejudice or any of its attendant humiliations and injustices bear me down to spiritual defeat. My inner life is mine, and I will defend and maintain its integrity against the forces of hell."[3]

Such supreme self-confidence had its source in a Florida childhood far removed from the brutalities of Bartow. Johnson's father was a freeborn Virginian, a headwaiter at an exclusive Jacksonville hotel. His mother, a West Indian—daughter of a Bahamian politician of some note—held the distinction of being the first colored woman hired by a Florida public school. From birth, James defied racial convention: while his mother recovered from a difficult delivery, his father hired a neighbor to serve as his son's nursemaid. "In the land of black mammies," he often said, "I had a white one." As boys, James and his brother, Rosamond, were wrapped in a cocoon of middle-class gentility: Johnson's earliest memories were of the serenity of the family parlor, with the Bible opened on a marble tabletop, the piano standing majestically in a shaded corner, and his mother sitting by the fireplace, reading *David Copperfield* to her sons.[4]

When he was old enough, Johnson's parents sent him to Atlanta University's preparatory school and then to the university itself, a tiny bastion of New England Congregationalism on a hill rising above the quintessential New South city, "a spot fresh and beautiful," Johnson recalled, "a rest for the eyes from what surrounded it, a green island in a dull, red sea." Yet venturing out inevitably brought him face-to-face with Jim Crow. He was seventeen years old in the spring of 1888, taking the train home from his freshman year in Atlanta, when he had his first real encounter with white supremacy. As always, he rode in the first-class car. This time the white passengers objected. At first there were murmurs against him, then "the remarks in the car became . . . open and loud. Threats began to reach our ears." There was talk of a mob waiting at the next station, armed with guns and rope. Terrified, Johnson abandoned the car. But by then, it was too late to teach Johnson his proper place. Upon graduation, he returned to Jacksonville to begin what would be a lifetime of breakthroughs. By the turn of the century, he had established the first Negro daily newspaper in the United States, had become the first colored lawyer admitted to the Florida bar, and had founded the first black public high school in the state, which he served as principal. In his spare time, he wrote poetry, composed an opera with his brother, a classically trained musician, and dreamed of a life in the arts. When his opera received encouraging reviews, he decided to put aside the academic life. In 1902, he packed his bags and headed to New York, one more aspiring songwriter starry-eyed with thoughts of finding success along the Great White Way.[5]

In typical Johnson fashion, he surpassed all expectations. Within a few years, he and his collaborators, brother, J. Rosamond, and friend Bob Cole, had a string of hits to their credit, wonderful Tin Pan Alley confections that filled their bank accounts and made them international stars. Still, he wanted more. Even as his songs swept Broadway, Johnson proclaimed his fealty to the high arts, both as a hallmark of civilization and as a weapon in the struggle for equal rights. "No people that has produced great literature and art has ever been looked upon by the world as distinctly inferior," he insisted. "And nothing will do more to . . . raise his status than a demonstration of intellectual parity by the Negro through the production of literature and art." It was an extremely roseate vision, to imagine that a finely crafted poem or well-told tale might help to break down white supremacy, but Johnson committed himself to pursuit of the ideal. His stirring "Lift Every Voice and Sing" became the "Negro national anthem," sung by hosts of children too young to understand its subtle blend of mourning, celebration, and ongoing struggle. His 1912 novel, *The Autobiography of an Ex-Colored Man,* exposed the bitter ambiguity of the color line whites took to be inviolate. The *New York Times* published his celebratory 1913 poem marking the fiftieth anniversary of the Emancipation Proclamation—"Far, far the way we have trod/From heathen kraal and jungle den/To freedmen, freedmen, sons of God/Americans and citizens"—while Du Bois's *Crisis* printed his searing 1916 verse giving voice to the lynch mob: "Stop! To each man no more than one man's share/You take that bone, and you this tooth; the chain/Let us divide its links; this skull, of course/In fair division, to the leader comes."[6]

What would have been a brilliant career for most men was for Johnson a springboard to even more success. Theodore Roosevelt so enjoyed a ditty Johnson wrote for the 1904 presidential campaign he appointed the composer to the consular service. He spent seven years living abroad, first in Venezuela, then in Nicaragua. Reserved, quietly charming, and preternaturally politic, he proved to be a gifted diplomat. When Woodrow Wilson took control of the White House in 1913, he had Johnson fired. Three years later, after a spell of editorial work and a stint as a speechwriter for the Republican Party, he joined the NAACP's staff, beginning as an organizer and moving up in 1920 to executive secretary, the first black man to be given responsibility for the association's day-to-day operations. It was a superb appointment. With his finely honed diplomatic skills, Johnson captivated the whites who dominated the association's board of directors and soothed the NAACP's notoriously contentious staff; even the imperious Du Bois was willing to listen to his advice. He also filled the association's New York headquarters with vigorous recruits, most notably peripatetic Walter White as assistant director, and devoted himself to building up the NAACP's membership, so that by the mid-1920s the association had branches in more than three hundred towns and cities, many of them south of the Mason-Dixon Line, where before the Great War the association had hardly made a ripple. And he infused NAACP activism with an extraordinary dramatic flair, beginning with his masterpiece, the 1917 Silent Parade down Fifth Avenue, a peerless example of protest as performance art, and reaching full flower in the literary renaissance of 1920s Harlem, when Johnson helped to make art into a performance of protest.[7]

Now the *New York World* had placed the précis for another piece of racial theater in Johnson's hands. With nothing more than a hundred-word story to go on, it was impossible to say whether Ossian Sweet's was the case Johnson was looking for, but it seemed extremely promising, with a perfect protagonist; a sharp, clear, and compelling conflict; and a final act miraculously undecided. So Johnson fired off a telegram to the officers of the Detroit branch asking for details.[8]

The first reply from Detroit was guarded, as if local officials were wary to have outside interference. "Will get full details from Dr. Sweet today which will be given in letter," W. Hayes McKinney wired early Saturday, before the full force of events came crashing down on him. "Branch handling matter." Johnson responded with his customary cool, graciously offering "all cooperation possible," then waiting for circumstances to break his way. It didn't take long. He and a few friends were spending their Sunday morning on a New Jersey golf course when the clubhouse man rushed across the greens with word of a long-distance phone call "We would like to have Mr. White leave for Detroit if possible tonight," Johnson jotted down as he listened to McKinney's frantic plea for help. "Very urgent." He didn't record his answer. But within an hour or two, Johnson was back home in his 135th Street brownstone, ready to launch the NAACP's next great campaign.[9]

•

For Johnson, the increasing segregation of the cities was a personal affront. In the two decades since he left steaming Jacksonville, he'd

come to think of himself as a "cosmopolite," happiest when he was
caught up in cultural Manhattan's dizzying swirl, perfectly content in a
darkened theater or an elegant uptown cabaret. He had long since settled in Harlem, which he adored for both its vitality—its "movement,
color, gayety, singing, dancing, boisterous laughter and loud talk"—
and its passionate respectability. "Harlem is indeed the great Mecca for
the sight-seer, the pleasure-seeker, the curious, the adventurous, the en-
terprising, the ambitious, and the talented of the whole Negro world,"
he wrote. "It is a city within a city, the greatest Negro city in the
world." And New York, he concluded, was the greatest city for Negroes. "New York guarantees its Negro citizens the fundamental rights
of American citizenship and protects them in the exercise of those
rights," he proclaimed. "In return the Negro loves New York and is
proud of it, and contributes in his way to its greatness."[10]

But Johnson simply couldn't ignore the precipitous decline in
northern race relations. The Klan's stunning success above the Mason-
Dixon Line was devastating to the NAACP's officers. New York remained
largely immune from the KKK's contagion, a fact Walter White attributed to the city's polyglot peoples. "Its Jewish, Italian, German, French
Greek, Czecho-Slovakian, Irish, Hungarian quarters with their teeming thousands and hundreds of thousands form so great a percentage
of the city's population," he argued, " 'white, Gentile, Protestant' Nordics
have but little opportunity to develop their prejudices as they do, for
example, in Mississippi or the District of Columbia." Yet there was also
no denying that whites were carving the color line deeper and deeper
into the urban landscape. The NAACP was painfully aware that blacks
weren't welcome in many restaurants, clubs, and theaters in northern
cities. But it was the relentless segregation of neighborhoods that was
most frightful. "Lynching has been the peculiar institution of the
south," declared a colored newspaper in an editorial circulated through
NAACP headquarters. "Forceful residential segregation has taken root
and is spreading so fast till if it's not soon checked it will become the
peculiar institution of the North."[11]

Not even Johnson's beloved New York could avoid that particular
curse, as he explained in a scintillating 1925 analysis. Colored families
first moved to the area around 134th Street and Lenox Avenue, in the
heart of Harlem, in the early 1900s, he said. In response, nearby whites
unleashed the real estate market's arsenal of discriminatory practices,
creating neighborhood improvement associations, trying to impose restrictive covenants, convincing banks not to extend Negroes mortgages.

The efforts failed. Using their own capital, a handful of black businessmen, among them Johnson's brother-in-law, bought up a few un-
derpriced apartment blocks, which they opened to colored tenants.
Once their defenses were breeched, whites "became panic-stricken
and began fleeing as from a plague. . . . House after house and block
after block were deserted. It was a great demonstration of human beings running amuck." And a textbook example of the power of the
marketplace. By the mid-1910s, property values had plummeted, thousands of whites had departed for other sections of the city, and Harlem
had been transformed into New York's colored quarter, a ghetto gilded
by the presence of men like Johnson, who lived in one of his brother-
in-law's properties, but a ghetto nonetheless.[12]

The NAACP struck its first blow against residential segregation in
1917, Johnson's first full year in the association's employ. During the
course of the 1910s, a number of southern cities passed ordinances
barring blacks citizens from living anywhere but in carefully pro-
scribed colored neighborhoods. In response, the NAACP decided to
mount a Supreme Court challenge, taking as its target Louisville,
Kentucky's segregation law. The case was presented by Beacon Hill's
august Moorfield Storey, head of the NAACP board of directors, former president of the American Bar Association, and, in an era long
past, personal secretary to one of the greatest abolitionists of them all,
Massachusetts's fiery senator Charles Sumner. Even a court ill disposed
to equal rights couldn't withstand the force of Storey's argument, or
perhaps the justices were just offended by the thought of a city government limiting the ability of landowners to sell their property to
whomever they pleased. Either way, the Supreme Court struck down
Louisville's ordinance, and by extension, all other such laws, handing
the NAACP the first of what would become a half century of landmark
constitutional victories.[13]

Although the pressure to segregate northern cities was beginning to
grow, no city government tried to follow Louisville's example and segregate by statute. But the dramatic surge in discriminatory market
mechanisms in every major urban center threatened to have the same
effect. So, in 1923, the NAACP went back to court, this time to test the
right of individual homeowners to prohibit the sale of their property to
Negroes. Howard University law school professor James Cobb found
the perfect test case when Helen Curtis, wife of a colored surgeon
and professor at Howard's medical school, bought a home just off
Washington, D.C.'s Dupont Circle, not knowing that a few years

before, the seller, a Caucasian woman, and thirty of her neighbors agreed to keep their block lily-white by adding restrictive covenants to their deeds. When the white neighbors secured an injunction against the transaction, the colored couple turned to the NAACP's Washington branch for help. Cobb, chairman of the branch's legal committee, carried the fight to Johnson, arguing that it was "the most important case of its kind ever handled by the Association." Johnson pledged the NAACP's support.[14]

A disciple of Booker T. Washington who had worked his way up from tiny Arcadia, Louisiana, to a post as Howard University's professor of negotiable instruments, Cobb directed the case's first test before the District of Columbia Court of Appeals. He argued, reasonably enough, that by using restrictive covenants, white property owners were contravening the principles established in the Louisville ruling and therefore were in clear violation of public policy. The stakes were enormous, warned Storey from his home in Back Bay. Should the association's appeal fail, similar cases pending in Baltimore, St. Louis, Los Angeles, St. Paul, and Detroit would be lost, and the NAACP's chances of stemming the segregationist tide would be dealt a devastating, perhaps mortal, blow. What's more, southerners would take the association's defeat as a signal that they could have the Louisville decision itself reversed; already New Orleans had passed a segregation ordinance designed to get the ruling back before the Supreme Court. Come that day, Storey concluded, "Heaven help us all!" It arrived all too quickly. In June 1924, the D.C. court ruled against Cobb and his clients, saying it couldn't compel white people to sell to Negroes. The Howard professor immediately appealed to the Supreme Court. And the NAACP promptly handed the case to a stellar legal team led by Storey and his eminent associate, the great constitutional lawyer and longtime Jewish activist Louis Marshall, relegating Cobb to a supporting role for the final confrontation in a battle he had made possible.[15]

By the time it agreed to hear the case, the high court's docket for the upcoming year was full, so the NAACP wouldn't have the opportunity to present its argument until the autumn of 1925, at the earliest. In the meantime, James Weldon Johnson prepared to make the fight into a nationwide crusade. Of course he wanted publicity, but he also needed the money. The association's most recent Supreme Court case—a defense of six Arkansas sharecroppers convicted of murder without so much as a vestige of due process—had cost fifteen thousand dollars, enough to push the association to the brink of insolvency.

Even with Marshall and Storey working pro bono, the Washington case and a second challenge, this one against Texas's exclusion of black voters from its state Democratic Party primaries, would eat up ten thousand dollars, twice what the NAACP had in its bank accounts. To see the fight through, Johnson simply had to get the association an infusion of cash, and that meant convincing black Americans that the cause was important enough to be worth donating five, ten, or twenty dollars that many of them couldn't afford to spare.[16]

There was more to it than money, though. If New York City had been saved from the most rabid forms of racism simply by the overwhelming presence of ethnic Americans, as Walter White believed, then an explicit coalition of such peoples might have the power to beat back the white supremacists' advance through the rest of the urban North. Du Bois had raised the possibility in 1922, the first year the Klan's crosses burned under city lights. "The Anglo-Saxon cult" sought nothing less than "the disfranchisement of Negro, Jew, Irishman, Italian, Hungarian, Asiatic, and South Sea Islander—the world rule of Nordic white by brute force," he said, and it had to be countered by its opposite, an alliance of Negroes "and disadvantaged groups like the Irish and the Jews and between the working classes everywhere. . . . And in that battle the triumph of Democracy for the darker races, for the segregated groups, and for the disadvantaged classes is written in the everlasting stars."[17]

The logic of the alliance was unassailable, as politicians such as Frank Murphy and Johnny Smith understood when they went trolling for votes in the immigrant and colored quarters. But blacks and the ethnic masses were also divided by decades of fierce competition for a share of industrialism's dregs, a tortured history of mutual distrust, and the poison of the American racial ideal, which made the swarthiest of immigrants desperate to prove himself a white man. For all his optimism, even Du Bois had to admit that the workers of the world showed little inclination to unite across the color line. Negro laborers "are not part of the white proletariat," he wrote elsewhere. "We are the victims of its physical oppression, social ostracism, economic exclusion and personal hatreds." And he bridled against the United States' "'new' white people"—"Irish and German, Russian Jew, Slav and 'dago'" who are trained "to [the] despising of 'niggers' from the day of their landing."[18]

With its fight against restrictive covenants, though, the NAACP believed it had a way to show its erstwhile allies that in the era of the

KKK they were not assured of being on the safe side of the color line. Already the NAACP had reports of builders barring Jews from new housing developments. And there was every reason to believe that Anglo-Saxons would soon extend such prohibitions to Catholics and immigrants as well. Every opportunity they had, association officials hammered the message home. Agreements that denied blacks access to the homes of their choice were "the entering wedge of the Ku Klux Klan program of elimination," insisted Louis Marshall, who had seen firsthand the expansiveness of white supremacy in 1915, when a southern mob lynched his client, Leo Frank, for the crime of being a Jew. Johnson also emphasized the point. "Of course it's not the Negro alone who is concerned in this fight," he said. "There is no minority group in this country that will be unaffected. If it is possible to segregate Negroes, then why not Catholics and Jews, or Italians or Irish?"[19]

But for all the association's efforts, the NAACP's campaign didn't catch on. The white press paid no attention whatsoever, and in the first half of 1925, Johnson's fund-raising stuttered, then stalled. It was a problem of dramatics, Johnson concluded. "Colored people of America are not awake to the danger which threatens them," he complained. "So long as the mob is not at their door ordering them to move into another neighborhood, threatening them with death if they do not give up their home and sell their house, they seem to think the danger a distant one." So all through the summer of 1925, he scoured the nation's newspapers for an incident he could make into a rallying point. He looked into the case of Lola Turner, driven from her new house in Los Angeles by a white mob. He asked for details on a string of bombings against black homeowners in Kansas City. He had his Legal Committee meet with Samuel Browne, a colored postman who refused to abandon his Staten Island home despite repeated death threats. And he paid particular attention to the month-long violence on Detroit's west side that July, when Alexander Turner, Vollington Bristol, and the Fletcher family came under attack. Perhaps it was the intensity of the troubles that piqued his interest, or perhaps it was the fund-raising possibilities he saw in Detroit's huge black community. By the end of July 1925, Johnson had decided to intervene. Not only did he send a blistering open letter to newspapers across the country condemning the violence, but he also told the branch officers that come autumn the entire NAACP high command would travel to the Motor City for a series of "great meetings." Johnson intended to kick off the campaign personally as soon as the summer was over. Then he headed off to a much-needed vacation in western Massachusetts's bucolic Berkshire Hills.[20]

While he was relaxing in the shade of the Berkshire pines, he struck upon a marvelous solution to the association's money problems. In 1922, twenty-three-year-old Charles Garland had inherited a million dollars from his father, a highly successful Wall Street broker. But young Garland didn't want the money, pointing out quite rightly that he hadn't earned a penny of it. At first, he thought about simply refusing his inheritance. But the timely intervention of a couple of cash-starved radicals, muckraking journalist Upton Sinclair, and Roger Baldwin, chairman of the newly formed American Civil Liberties Union, pushed him in another direction. With Baldwin's help, Garland established a philanthropic organization, the American Fund for Public Service, which he put under the guidance of a board full of prominent civil libertarians, trade unionists, and one civil rights activist, James Weldon Johnson. Over the next few years, Johnson managed to secure the NAACP several thousand dollars in grants. Now he decided to ask for much more. He sketched out a proposal to create an NAACP Legal Defense Fund of fifty thousand dollars, more than enough to cover both the Washington and Texas cases. Garland might contribute half that amount, he believed, if black America could raise the other half.[21]

As a member of the American Fund's board, Johnson couldn't submit the proposal himself. So as soon as he returned to Manhattan after Labor Day, he wrote to Moorfield Storey asking if he would approach the board on the NAACP's behalf. But even in the excitement of the moment, Johnson had to admit that, given his dismal experience with the residential segregation crusade, he couldn't guarantee the twenty-five thousand dollars in matching funds that the proposal required. "I face the actual fact that it will not be possible to raise any such amount," Johnson admitted, "unless [association members] have a tremendous incentive that they can pass over to the people whom they solicit."[22]

Then the Sweet-case clipping passed across his desk. And Johnson knew he had exactly the story he had been looking for.

◆

Detroit was the last place Walter White wanted to be. While his boss was taking his August holidays in the Berkshires, White had hammered away at his second novel, *Flight*, the highly anticipated follow-up to his widely praised inaugural effort, *The Fire in the Flint*. Once the new manuscript was in the hands of his good friends, Alfred and Blanche Knopf, White had resumed the rounds of parties that occupied his nights. To launch the Labor Day weekend, he and his wife, Gladys, had filled their apartment at 90 Edgecombe Avenue, which peeked over Harlem's glorious Strivers Row, with a glittering array of literary lights. It had been a riotous time, Sinclair and Grace Lewis and a bevy of friends sharing drink, music, and gossip almost until dawn. White was the most indefatigable of men. But even he couldn't keep up such a furious pace without his body claiming some of the attention denied it. So he was battling a cold—and planning the following weekend's soirees—when James Weldon Johnson called on Sunday afternoon, September 13, to tell him that he was to be aboard *The Wolverine* out of Grand Central Station as soon as possible Monday.[23]

As much as he disliked the idea, White knew the assignment was a perfect fit. When Johnson recruited him for the NAACP staff in 1918, White had been a twenty-four-year-old Atlanta insurance salesman, but Johnson was drawn by his boundless energy and peerless background. The son of a postman and a schoolteacher, White was raised in a home very much like Johnson's, where good manners, strict rules, and educational excellence were prized above all else. In the years since Johnson came calling, White had made himself into the association's indispensable man, a public relations genius particularly skilled at communicating the terror of racial violence to white audiences. It was a talent built partly on the electricity he brought to any task, partly on his unquestionable courage, and partly on a family inheritance that set him apart from most of black America. To look at White was to see a man of decidedly Anglo-Saxon features, a Caucasian through and through. "I am a Negro," he once wrote. "My skin is white, my eyes are blue, my hair is blond. The traits of my race are nowhere visible upon me."[24]

Had he wished to, White easily could have spent his life passing. But one terrifying evening in September 1906 foreclosed that possibility forever. Jim Crow's fervor was at its height that autumn, and Atlanta was shot through with rumors of the Black Beast hunting down white women. Thirteen-year-old Walter and his father were downtown on the afternoon of the twenty-second when the tensions exploded and whites took control of the streets. They rushed back to their home on the edge of the black neighborhood. Hidden inside, the Whites could hear the mob moving toward them, could see the flickering light of their torches in the distance, could hear their shouts ripping through the night: "That's where the nigger mail carrier lives! Let's burn it down! It's too nice for a nigger to live in!" Walter's father took him into the parlor, handed him a rifle, and positioned him at a window. "Son," he remembered his father saying, "don't shoot until the first man puts his foot on the lawn and then—don't you miss." Walter never had to pull the trigger. As the mob come upon the house, friends of his father's who had barricaded themselves into a nearby home opened fire, driving the whites back into the darkness. But the moment had changed Walter forever.

"I was gripped by the knowledge of my identity," he said, "and in the depths of my soul I was vaguely aware that I was glad of it. I was sick with loathing for the hatred which had flared before me that night and had come so close to making me a killer; but I was glad that I was not one of those who hated; I was glad that I was not one of those made sick and murderous by pride. I was glad I was not one of those whose story is in the history of the world, a record of bloodshed, rapine, and pillage. I was glad my mind and spirit were part of the races that . . . had still before them the opportunity to write a record of virtue as a memorandum to Armageddon."[25]

Still, like many Negroes, White couldn't quite set aside the standard American equation of light skin and virtue. One night in the 1920s, he sat down for a heartfelt talk with Joel Spingarn, a former Columbia professor of literature who had devoted much of his life to the NAACP's causes. Spingarn recounted the conversation a few days later in a private letter to his wife. "I asked him frankly if he thought men of unmixed Negro blood capable of the highest achievement and character," Spingarn said. "At first he hedged. . . . But finally he admitted that he had virtually never met a pure Negro whom he really could trust, that he didn't believe it was in them, that they *were* inferior, infinitely inferior now, whatever they might possibly become in the future. So there's the conflict—nine-tenths white loathing the one-tenth black, one-tenth black hating the nine-tenths white. The passionate pro-Negro loyalty is a conflict, a whirlpool, and a mask." Over the years, White's opponents would level the same charges publicly. "In the first place, Walter White is white," Du Bois would say about his colleague during one of their many bitter feuds. "He has more white companions and friends than colored. He goes where he will . . . and naturally meets no Color Line, for the simple and sufficient reason he isn't 'colored.'"[26] At the start of his career, though, White's ability to move freely in a Caucasian world was his, and the NAACP's, greatest asset.

When Dr. Ossian Sweet bought a house in an all-white section of Detroit in the summer of 1925, he knew his move might trigger white violence. "Well, we have decided we are not going to run," he told a colleague a few weeks before taking possession of his new home. "We're not going to look for any trouble, but we're going to be prepared to protect ourselves if trouble arises." (Walter P. Reuther Library, Wayne State University)

In May 1901, a white mob lynched a black teenager steps away from the Peace River Bridge in Bartow, Florida. The incident scarred young Ossian Sweet, who forever after remembered hiding in the bushes, a terrified five-year-old watching the mob set its victim ablaze. (Florida State Archives)

So that their son might escape the brutality of Jim Crow, Ossian Sweet's parents sent him north. At Ohio's Wilberforce University (above), he was immersed in the politics of Black America's Talented Tenth. Howard University's medical school vaulted Sweet, fifth from right (below), into the highest rank of professionals. (Ohio Historical Society / Moorland-Spingarn Center, Howard University)

"Detroit is El Dorado," said a Jazz-Age visitor to the city. "It is staccato American. It is shockingly dynamic." Inside Detroit's burgeoning black ghetto, though, living conditions were desperate, poverty pervasive. (Wolff Family Photograph Collection, Bentley Library, University of Michigan / Walter P. Reuther Library, Wayne State University)

Having lived among whites all her life, Gladys Sweet (upper left) saw no reason why she and Ossian should be forced to buy a home in the ghetto simply because they were black. The bungalow at 2905 Garland Avenue (bottom) had the stylish touches she loved, and she looked forward to her daughter, Iva (upper right), growing up in a safe, secure neighborhood. (Walter P. Reuther Library, Wayne State University / Walter P. Reuther Library, Wayne State University / *The Chicago Defender*)

A bullet fired from the bungalow on the evening of September 9, 1925, killed Leon Breiner (upper left), a former coal miner who lived half a block north of the Sweets' house. (*The Chicago Defender*)

As soon as news of the Sweets' arrest crossed his desk, NAACP secretary James Weldon Johnson (upper right) knew he had found a case he could turn into a national crusade. (Carl Van Vechten Photograph Collection, Library of Congress)

Ten of the eleven defendants (below), all charged with Breiner's murder. Top row (from left to right): Otis Sweet, John Latting, Norris Murray, Joe Mack, Charles Washington. Bottom row (from left to right): Ossian Sweet, Henry Sweet, Hewitt Watson, William Davis, Leonard Morse. Not pictured: Gladys Sweet. (*The Chicago Defender*)

Walter White (upper left), Johnson's indefatigable assistant secretary, spent months shaping the Sweets' story as if it were one of his Harlem Renaissance novels. (Library of Congress)

When he first met trial judge Frank Murphy (upper right), White was amazed by Murphy's determination to give the defendants a fair trail. "It is so seldom that those of us who are trying to secure even-handed justice for Negro citizens encounter one like yourself," he wrote the judge, "you may well imagine our joy when that experience does come." (Walter P. Reuther Library, Wayne State University)

Park Avenue lawyer Arthur Garfield Hays so enjoyed fighting alongside Clarence Darrow in the previous summer's "Monkey Trial" in Dayton, Tennessee, he volunteered to join Darrow in defending the Sweets and their friends in November 1925. (Seeley G. Mudd Library, Princeton University)

When the case went back to trial in May 1926, the principled Hays was replaced by Thomas Chawke (second from right), a criminal lawyer best known for his association with Detroit's many mobsters. Chawke stands alongside Henry Sweet (far left), Ossian Sweet's friend Julian Perry, and Darrow. (Walter P. Reuther Library, Wayne State University)

Before settling on the twelve men who would decide Henry Sweet's fate, defense attorneys demanded that potential jurors reveal whether or not they were prejudiced against blacks. (*Detroit News*)

"I've heard about lawyers making a judge cry," said an attorney who witnessed Clarence Darrow's closing plea in the Sweet case, "but Darrow was the first man I ever saw do it." (Walter P. Reuther Library, Wayne State University)

White wasn't on the NAACP's staff two weeks when he was dispatched to Tennessee to investigate a horrific lynching. Johnson had done such work before, but White's Nordic face gave him access to information his boss couldn't have secured. Posing as a traveling salesman for an Atlanta hair-straightening company, White spent a few days chatting up Caucasians, who were more than glad to tell him all about the recent excitement. His searing exposé of the victim's crimes—among other things, he'd returned from a stint living in Detroit unwilling to bow to Jim Crow—was so original and immediate it won the association widespread attention in the popular press and set White on a path that would make him famous.[27]

Over the next few years, he exposed lynch mobs across the South, walked the streets of riot-torn South Chicago, uncovered the perfidy behind the 1919 pogrom in Phillips County, Arkansas, exposed electoral violence in 1920 Florida, and revealed the gruesome details of the infamous 1921 race riot in Tulsa, where he went so far as to join a white posse patrolling the burned-out black section of town. It was extremely dangerous work. As he was gathering information in the tiny town of Helena, Arkansas, in 1919, a colored man took him aside to say that whites had discovered his identity. Walter raced to the nearby depot and leapt onto the first train heading north. The conductor couldn't understand why he was in such a rush to get out of town. "But you're leaving, mister, just when the fun is going to start," the man said. "There's a damn yellow nigger down here passing for white and the boys are going to get him." "What will they do with him?" White asked, all innocence. "When they get through with him," said the conductor, "he won't pass for white no more!"[28]

Such daring made for marvelous copy, a traditional trickster tale dressed up for the Jazz Age. Northern newspapers, black and white, regularly recounted White's exploits, and leading liberal journals such as the *Nation* and the *New Republic* published his firsthand accounts of racial terrors, told in clean, clear prose made all the more chilling by their crispness.

Although James Weldon Johnson reveled in the publicity that White's reporting provided the NAACP, he wanted more for the young man he increasingly considered his protégé. He tried unsuccessfully to temper White's frenetic enthusiasm with a touch of diplomacy, gently tutoring him on the power of a quiet word and a well-placed compliment. He introduced him to the highest level of politics, bringing White with him to Capitol Hill while he lobbied for an ill-fated antilynching bill, and even sending him to Paris as one of the NAACP representatives to the 1921 Pan-African Congress. More than anything else, he drew White into the world of the arts, the new frontier of civil rights advocacy. As with everything else he did, White responded to Johnson's instruction with gusto. In a city rapidly filling with young people of extraordinary talent, Walter made himself one of the great promoters of the Harlem Renaissance—and its first star.[29]

Just as he had ingratiated himself into southern lynch mobs, so did White charm his way into the inner circle of Manhattan's cultural avant-garde. The moment was ideal. From the cutting-edge publishing houses clustered near the NAACP's Fifth Avenue headquarters to the jazz clubs of Harlem, from Greenwich Village salons through Broadway all the way to Provincetown, white artists were scrambling to claim a share of the vibrant black culture they saw as an antidote to the banalities of white society. "What American literature decidedly needs at the moment is color, music, gusto, the free expression of gay or desperate moods," gushed editor and critic Carl Van Doren. "If the Negroes are not in a position to contribute these items, I do not know what Americans are." Ziegfeld girl Gilda Gray put it more succinctly in a 1922 show tune: "You must black up to be the latest rage."[30]

Walter White wasn't given much to blacking up. But he was more than willing to exploit the avant-garde's sudden interest in the race. Johnson provided some of the necessary introductions, and Walter's conviviality did the rest. By the mid-1920s, White knew just about everybody worth knowing. Sinclair Lewis, H. L. Mencken, and Carl Van Vechten—three of the most acerbic critics of middle America— were particular friends. But at one time or another, George Gershwin, Dorothy Parker, Eugene O'Neill, Heywood Broun, Rebecca West, George Jean Nathan, Horace Liveright, Andre Siegfried, Nancy Cunard, and a host of others partook of White's hospitality. All he asked in return was that the cultural elite lend a hand to the remarkable collection of colored artists he had helped to assemble. Langston Hughes, Countee Cullen, Claude McKay, Paul Robeson, short-story writer and graduate of Howard University College of Medicine Rudolph Fisher, tenor Roland Hayes, and baritone Jules Bledsoe all made valuable contacts via White, who relentlessly trumpeted their skills and shopped their manuscripts. He also didn't hesitate to inform them when they didn't measure up to his rigid standards of racial uplift. After her debut at New York's Town Hall, the sublime Marian Anderson received word that while White very much enjoyed her operatic performance he thought her willingness to sing popular songs during the encore was in "bad taste."[31]

In 1922, H. L. Mencken suggested that White try his hand at a novel. It took the better part of a year for Walter to carve out the necessary time, but after twelve feverish days and nights of writing in the summer of 1923, he had a draft. On the strength of Mencken's endorsement, Knopf snatched up *The Fire in the Flint*, which it published in September 1924. It was, as Somerset Maugham said, "a terrible book, but a very powerful one, and it gives one a tragic feeling of truth." In breathlessly melodramatic style, White told the story of young Dr. Kenneth Harper, a Negro graduate of an unnamed northern medical school and a Great War veteran, who returns to his Georgia hometown to open a clinic. At first, Harper is determined to avoid racial politics. But the hostility of local whites, who hate his family's success, and the tutelage of Jane Philips, the beautiful, accomplished young woman with whom he falls in love, gradually break down his reserve. "It's men with your brains and education that have got to take the leadership," she tells him in a moment of transformation. "That's just the reason they try to make it hard for men like you—they know if you ever get going, their treating the Negro as they have has got to stop!" In the novel's climactic closing scene, Harper becomes the exemplar of the heroic New Negro, facing a murderous, cowardly pack, pressed to the wall, dying, but fighting back.[32]

The novel's publication was one of the signal events of the Harlem Renaissance's breakthrough year. Sinclair Lewis called it one of the two most important books of the autumn—E. M. Forster's *A Passage to India* was the other—while Heywood Broun gave it a glowing review in *New York World*, Freda Kirchwey did the same in the *Tribune*, and Konrad Bercovici gushed in the *Nation* that the novel was nothing less than "the voice of the new Negro"; there was even talk of Eugene O'Neill mounting a stage adaptation, with Paul Robeson playing the lead. Alfred Knopf made sure to send copies to the most rabidly racist southern newspapers so that the predictable cries of outrage could fuel sales. But it was Du Bois who, as usual, got it just right, hailing the book in the *Crisis* as "a stirring story and a strong bit of propaganda against the white Klansman and the black pussyfoot," the ideal combination of form and function, in the editor's utilitarian vision of racial art.[33]

•

Detroit's Talented Tenth wasn't expecting the whirlwind that pulled into the Michigan Central Depot at 8:15 Tuesday morning, September 15.

The NAACP branch officers had asked Johnson to send White their way hoping he'd do a bit of his legendary investigating, perhaps even slipping by the police cordon that was preventing the black lawyers from scouring the Sweets' bungalow for any evidence that would help their clients.[34] Instead, they were swept up in White's frenetic stage management.

White planned to be on the train back to New York on Friday, so as not to miss the weekend's parties. That left him four days to get the Sweet case into the proper shape, more than enough time for a man who could write a best seller in less than two weeks. A round of conferences with branch officials on Tuesday gave him all the information he needed to craft the scenario of the Sweet case that the NAACP would need to attract attention and support. In his telling, the characters bore a remarkable resemblance to those in *The Fire in the Flint*: Ossian was a "very highly respected" doctor just a few weeks back from a year's study in Vienna, White reported to Johnson, while Gladys "is from one of Detroit's oldest and most respected colored families." When it came to scripting the next part of the drama, though, the performance threatened to unravel.[35]

Trouble started in the segregated dining room of downtown Detroit's most elegant hotel, where White had arranged a late breakfast with Ira Jayne, the only NAACP executive board member living in Detroit. A forty-three-year-old circuit court judge, Jayne was, in a colleague's words, "an incorrigible public servant," a former schoolteacher and social worker who relentlessly championed the rights of the poor and the powerless. Like his fellow NAACP board members, he was anxious to combat the spread of residential segregation, so he was pleased to hear that the NAACP wanted to make the Sweets the centerpiece of its crusade.[36]

But Jayne wanted White to understand that the case wasn't lining up the way the association wanted to. Since the shooting, the city had cracked straight down the color line, and the chasm was widening by the day. The mayor and the Ku Klux Klan were locked in a venomous exchange of race-baiting: when the Sunday papers printed Johnny Smith's broadside linking the Sweets and the Klan, the Invisible Empire immediately issued a bitter response—stuffed into mailboxes across white Detroit that very afternoon—charging that the mayor himself had triggered "the negro agitation" with his promises to the coloreds of equal treatment in city affairs. The east side's white neighborhoods, meanwhile, still teetered on the edge of violence. All weekend long, the police had battled rumors of rampant colored criminality. And on Monday, the day Leona Breiner buried her husband, the police department had held hundreds of officers in reserve, fearing that the sight of the deceased's Masonic brothers bearing his casket down Garland Avenue might trigger renewed rioting, perhaps even the long-feared pogrom. Under such dire circumstances, there was simply no way for the association to save the Sweets from a sure conviction—as long as Negroes were doing the talking. Hire the most prestigious white attorney the NAACP's money could buy, Jayne insisted, and hope that his presence might win back the city's progressives and ease the blood lust coursing through the working-class wards.[37]

White must have seen Jayne's proposal as no more controversial than handing the Washington case to Marshall and Storey or passing a brilliant piece of Harlem art to Knopf or Mencken. But that afternoon when he informed the Sweets' three colored attorneys that they were to be demoted, he met a firestorm of resistance. The defense couldn't be derailed now, the lawyers insisted, not with their clients facing a preliminary hearing the very next day. Cecil Rowlette heatedly argued that there was no need to change course; legal precedent was clearly on their side, and in time, the court would dismiss the charges. The attorneys even raised the specter most likely to terrify the NAACP's national office. The black community was fully aroused, they said, money was pouring in—the branch already had eleven hundred dollars in a defense fund, seven hundred dollars alone from the Sunday afternoon rally at Second Baptist—and donors would expect to see black men leading the fight. White, they pointed out, had been in Detroit less than half a day; he couldn't possibly understand the situation.

White tried to counter with Johnson's diplomatic touch. The decision "cast no reflection" on the lawyers' legal skill, he said, "but [the Sweet case] was bigger than Detroit or Michigan . . . for it was the dramatic climax of the nation-wide fight to enforce residential segregation." What's more, politics demanded a change. "As even the best white sentiment of Detroit was against Sweet," he said, drawing on the ammunition Judge Jayne had given him, "the retention of an eminent white lawyer would serve to win over this alienated opinion, alienated because many white people believe the killing was unwarranted." But the attorneys wouldn't hear a word of it. Should the association hire a white man ahead of them, Rowlette and Mahoney pledged to tender their resignations, a move sure to cause so much controversy that the NAACP's campaign would be thrown into complete disarray. In the end, White had no choice but to back down, promising to postpone any decision until after the next day's hearing.[38]

In private, though, he was livid. Sitting in the quiet of his hotel room early Wednesday morning, he ripped off a blistering letter to Johnson, filtering the fight through a scrim of quick assumptions and unspoken prejudices. All three attorneys were shysters, he said, out for a cut of the defense fund. Mahoney, with his soft voice and northern ways, seemed able enough. But Julian Perry was dismissed with a wave of the hand: the young man had "no personality and commands no respect as far as I can see either as a man or as an attorney."

For Rowlette, White pulled out the knife. He "is a blustering, noisy, pompous individual, with a very inflated opinion of his own ability," he wrote. "You may judge his ability as a lawyer from the fact that yesterday, when I pointed out to him that in the trial of this case as in most criminal cases, the issue was of fact and not so much of law. He flatly contradicted me and declared that this case was wholly a matter of law."[39] White didn't seem to know that a few months earlier Rowlette had saved Fleta Mathies from prison simply by invoking her fundamental right of self-defense. Nor did he notice that he'd saved his worst invective for the rough-edged, dark-skinned son of a slave, the one attorney farthest from the face White was determined to put on the NAACP's crusade.

◆

Tensions were so high as the preliminary hearing got under way Wednesday afternoon that the police commissioner sprinkled a whole squad of undercover cops among the spectators jammed into Judge John Faust's courtroom. He needn't have worried. Though five hundred Negroes showed up to support the Sweets, there were no demonstrations or confrontations, just a peaceful assembly gathered in silent witness to the promise of justice. It was White's first chance to see the defendants, Ossian dapper in a tasteful suit and sober gray and red tie, sitting at the head of two long rows along one wall, Gladys hidden away at the far end of the second row, next to Hewitt Watson, the insurance man.[40]

But it was Assistant Prosecutor Lester Moll's masterful manipulation of the proceedings that truly caught White's attention. Technically, the prosecutor's job was to establish that he had a strong-enough case to take to trial. But Moll neatly sidestepped the state's central assertion of whether Ossian and the others conspired to shoot into the crowd, which he had no way of proving. Instead, he zeroed in on the technical question of whether the Negroes had cause to open fire, assuming that once he'd established the peacefulness of Garland Avenue, the judge would make the critical connection on his own. If the coloreds were in no danger, they must have moved into the neighborhood looking for a confrontation: conspiracy by implication, conviction by assumption.[41]

Within the first few minutes, Norton Schuknecht was in the witness box, recounting his painstaking preparations to keep the Sweets safe, the complete calm on Garland Avenue, and his shock at the shooting. Ray Dove followed with a perfectly matched testimony. A few days earlier, he'd told prosecutors that the night of the shooting there was "quite a crowd" directly across the street from the Sweets' bungalow; now he recalled seeing only "a few" people in his yard, certainly no more than ten or fifteen, a figure precisely set to be just below the legal definition of a mob.[42] When Ossian's next-door neighbor John Getke took the stand Thursday morning, his memory had also taken a turn for the better. The day after the shooting, he recalled hearing stones hit the Sweets' house right before the Negroes opened fire. Prosecutor Moll asked him to revisit the moment. "Was there anything happened in the ten or fifteen minutes in which you were on your porch that would attract your attention to that house? Was there anything to call your attention to the Sweets' house?"

"No, sir," Getke replied. "Not particularly."

Moll asked again, as if to underscore the point. "Was there anything at all before the shooting . . . that would attract your attention to the Sweets' house, that would cause you to notice it particularly as you sat on your porch?"

Getke answered more emphatically. "No, sir, absolutely nothing."

A third time Moll asked. "It was quiet around the house?" Absolutely quiet, Getke said.

"You saw nothing thrown?"

"No, sir."[43]

For its part, the defense was prohibited by the hearing's rules from presenting evidence of its own. So Perry, Rowlette, and Mahoney faced the extraordinarily difficult task of using hostile witnesses to break the state's case. While Schuknecht was on the stand, Rowlette slammed away at the logical inconsistency of pursuing murder charges without having any sense of who the murderer was. Do you know of your own knowledge whether Doctor Ossian Sweet fired the shot that killed Leon Breiner, Rowlette asked. "I don't," the inspector admitted.

"Do you know whether Doctor Otis Sweet fired those shots?" Rowlette asked. Schuknecht started to say that one of Ossian's brothers had confessed to shooting into the crowd, but the lawyer cut him off. "I am not asking you about that. Stand up, Doctor Otis Sweet. Do you know whether this man fired those shots there or not?" Shucknecht had to say that he didn't. Down the line Rowlette went. "Morse, stand up. Do you know whether this man fired those shots?" "Latting, stand up. Do you know whether this man fired those shots?" Ten times he asked—only Henry wasn't ordered to stand—and ten times Schuknecht had to say that he wasn't sure. "Do you know of your own knowledge whether any of those people fired those shots or had anything to do with firing those shots or not?" Rowlette persisted.

"All I know," Schuknecht replied weakly, "[is] those shots came out of the house."

Rowlette also focused on the pivotal question of crowd size. His first approach was too strong. How many people were in front of the flat where Breiner was shot, he asked Schuknecht. Ten or twelve, the inspector said. "Wasn't there more than twenty there?" Rowlette fired back. "Isn't it a fact, inspector, that there were two hundred people there at 8:25 on the evening of September 9?" But the figure was too high and Schuknecht shrugged it off with an emphatic "absolutely not."[44]

By the time Ray Dove took the stand for his cross-examination Thursday morning, Rowlette had honed his technique. "You said yesterday there were fifteen people in front of that place, didn't you?" he began, inching the previous day's estimate to its upper limit. When Dove agreed, Rowlette started jabbing. Who were these people? Could you name them? Surely you can recall fifteen names? Were they all neighbors? Don't you know your neighbors? Was there anyone in the vacant lot between the flat and the corner grocery store? How many? Gradually, Dove began to raise his estimate. Maybe there were fifteen people on his lawn and a few more in the lot next door. Seeing his opening, Rowlette pounced. "There must have been thirty-five or forty people there, weren't there?" It was a perfectly chosen number, just enough beyond the legal definition of a mob to slip by a layman. But Dove knew better than to concede the point. "No, sir, there wasn't that many," he said.

"How many would you say?"

"Maybe fifteen to twenty."

There was no missing Rowlette's disappointment. "Altogether?" he tried again.

"Yes, sir, altogether."[45]

But if Dove could withstand Rowlette's badgering, Getke was no match for Mahoney's stern authority. As soon as Moll finished quizzing the piano tuner, Mahoney unfolded his lanky body from the defense table and approached the witness box. He opened with a gentle question. "Where did you say you lived, right next door?"

"Next door, yes," Getke said.

Suddenly, Mahoney took the offensive. "You understand you are under oath in this matter?"

"Yes, sir."

"And you understand, too, you could be punished for perjury in a case of this kind?"

Only Moll's immediate objection and a rebuke from the bench drew Mahoney back. But the attack had its desired affect. When the attorney pressed Getke to repeat his testimony that all had been quiet before the shooting, the witness wasn't quite as confident as he had been. "And you want to testify there were no stones thrown on the night of the ninth," he asked. "I do," Getke ventured. "You do," Mahoney repeated with a trace of exasperation—or was it disgust—in his voice.

Getke folded. "I will recall that," he said. "I want to testify that there was or wasn't, because I don't know whether there was or not."

"That's better," Mahoney replied.[46]

It was an impressive performance under terribly unfavorable circumstances. By the time the hearing ended Thursday afternoon, September 17, Judge Faust must have realized that prosecutor Moll hadn't explicitly tied any of the defendants to Breiner's murder, and it would have taken a profound act of will not to see that the prosecution had coached its witnesses. But in the end, neither White nor Rowlette had understood the true dynamic in the courtroom; the case didn't pivot on the facts or on the law. It was all about politics. In the superheated atmosphere that Breiner's death had created, even a judge as progressive as Faust didn't dare side with the Sweets. Friday morning, he ruled that the prosecution's case was strong enough to advance to trial. Then he passed it on to the court's presiding judge, Frank Murphy, for assignment.[47]

The decision wasn't two hours old when White swept into Rowlette's Black Bottom office for one last meeting before heading back to Manhattan. Since his confrontation with the three colored lawyers on Tuesday afternoon, Walter had shelved every other activity—even his investigations fell by the wayside—so he could focus on remaking the defense team to his satisfaction. He'd prepared a legal agreement for the eleven defendants to sign, ceding "ultimate choice of attorneys" to the NAACP. He'd lined up the branch officers behind him. And with the help of Judge Jayne, he'd drawn up a list of prestigious replacements, topped by the longtime president of the Detroit Bar Association. All that stood in his way were the lawyers themselves, and surely their opposition would have weakened now that they had given the case their best effort and been utterly defeated.[48]

Sure enough, Faust's ruling had robbed Rowlette of his earlier confidence; perhaps it would be best to add a white lawyer, he agreed, so that the Talented Tenth wouldn't take complete blame for the conviction that now seemed almost inevitable. But even with the sting of his loss still smarting, he refused to bow out of the case. As Perry scribbled notes on the back of an envelope, Rowlette laid out his terms for changing the defense team. He and his cocounsels would select the white attorney, who was to receive five thousand dollars for his services. The three colored lawyers would split another five thousand dollars between them. And the only acceptable addition would be Thomas Chawke, the most skilled criminal lawyer in Detroit.

White was stunned. He had planned to offer the colored lawyers no more than five hundred dollars for their services; to demand anything more was nothing short of blackmail. The association certainly wasn't going to give a no-name "rough and tumble artist" like Rowlette dictatorial control over its case. Worst of all, White couldn't countenance having Chawke fronting the defense. By all accounts, he was a "corking lawyer"; even Jayne had told White that. But Chawke's specialty was keeping the guilty out of jail—rumor had it that a coalition of mobsters had pooled their cash to keep him on retainer—and that wasn't the image the NAACP planned to put before the public. This was meant to be a drama of injustice fairly fought and soundly defeated, not a sordid tale of legal manipulation. Jamming Perry's envelope into his pocket, White turned on his heels and headed for the door.[49]

On the train ride home, White's fury began to fade, replaced by his natural enthusiasm. Sometime in that long evening, as the sun set and the landscape of farms and factories faded into the darkness, he tried out a few tentative lines of publicity for use in one of the dispatches he intended to send the following day, when he was safely back in Manhattan's glowing embrace. "Doctor Sweet and the others are martyrs to the cause of freedom for the Negro," he wrote, his rhetoric rising to the cause. "The eyes of America are on Detroit." But even as he eased himself back into the joy of literary creation, White couldn't stop himself from thinking about one pugnacious lawyer—and a story that was not yet what he wanted it to be.[50]

◆

James Weldon Johnson wasn't concerned. As soon as he had White's confirmation that Dr. and Mrs. Sweet were the symbols he was looking for, he set the NAACP's crusade in motion. And like any first-rate publicist, he wasn't about to be knocked off message by a few messy details.

News of the Sweets' arrest was already spreading, thanks to the Associated Negro Press, the Chicago-based wire service that provided copy to the hundreds of weekly newspapers published across colored America. The ANP's Detroit correspondent cobbled together his first report largely from the white newspapers' accounts of the shooting, though he gave the story the militant twist that was the service's trademark. "A bitter legal battle with far reaching significance is about to be fought here as a result of the fatal wounding of one white man and the wounding of another in a segregation clash in this city on Wednesday night," the story opened, "a thing that had long been calculated the inevitable outcome of the wave of prejudice that has been sweeping the country. . . ." Colored editors snatched it up, plastering the report on front pages from Dallas to Boston, St. Louis to Baltimore. Even the biggest papers, less dependent on the wire service for their news than were the smaller sheets, gave the story prominent play. The mammoth *Chicago Defender*, with a circulation stretching from the Windy City's sprawling South Side ghetto all the way to the Mississippi delta, made the tragedy its lead story for the week of September 19, the account accompanied by a bitter editorial demanding to know "what's wrong in Detroit?"[51]

Johnson, however, had to make sure that the story was spun in just the right way. For a campaign created on the run—its strategy and publicity shaped in the snatches of time the association's frenzied schedule permitted—it was very effectively fashioned. Beginning with the press release announcing that the NAACP "will throw its entire power to the defense of Dr. O. H. Sweet," sent out the day the defendants lost the preliminary hearing, Johnson never failed to link the Sweet case and the Washington supreme court challenge, companion pieces in a seamless struggle against residential segregation. At first, he also tried to tie in the other incidents he'd learned of in the course of the summer, in hopes of bringing the campaign home to as many Negroes as possible. As the Sweets' story gained traction, though, the focus sharpened. In early September, Johnson had arranged for a Sunday rally at Harlem's Abyssinian Baptist Church on behalf of the Staten Island postman whose home had come under repeated attack a few months earlier. By the time the rally was held at the end of the month, the postman's plight was pushed to the periphery, as Johnson regaled the audience with details of the battle for Detroit. Once he was back in New York, White fed to the black press the Sweets' own stirring jailhouse declarations, which miraculously matched the themes the association wanted to highlight. "For a good cause and for the dignity of my people," Ossian was quoted as saying in late September, "I am willing to stay indefinitely in the cell and be punished. I feel sure by the demonstration made by my people that they have confidence in me as a law-abiding citizen. I denounce the theory of Ku Kluxism and uphold the theory of manhood with a wife and tiny baby to protect." Tough as nails on the night of the shooting, Gladys became in White's hands a black Madonna, her arms aching for the child she could not hold. "Though I suffer and am torn loose from my fourteen-month-old baby," she said, "I feel it is my duty to the womanhood of the race. If I am freed I shall return and live at my home on Garland Avenue."[52]

The manipulation of pride and pathos slipped smoothly into appeals for financial support. The directors of the Garland Fund weren't scheduled to meet until the last week of October, so there was plenty of time to put the final touches on the association's proposal for a permanent Legal Defense Fund. In the meantime, Johnson tried to embarrass Negroes into giving. "Do you want to be a segregated race?" he demanded to know in one press release. "Do you want the Jim Crow system extended to the residential streets of northern cities? Or will you fight residential Jim Crow through the courts and before the tribunal of public opinion? The answer rests with colored Americans. The NAACP stands ready to carry out their mandate. It is already embarked upon this immense struggle with shamefully inadequate funds."[53]

Johnson hoped that the excitement of mass meetings also might get the money flowing. Each Sunday in September and the first weeks of October, colored Detroiters trooped to a different Black Bottom church to hear the Talented Tenth plead for contributions to the defense fund they had established for the Sweets, while Johnson and White arranged for companion rallies not only in Harlem but in New Jersey and Washington, D.C., as well, each event to be headlined by one of the NAACP's stars. Johnson even considered White's extravagant proposal that the association send a letter of solicitation to each of the nation's seven hundred thousand colored homeowners, a suggestion that no doubt sent the NAACP's miniscule secretarial staff to the want ads in search of alternative employment.[54]

Money didn't pour in. Even in Detroit, donations didn't keep pace with expenses, so the local defense fund ended September with a lower balance than the NAACP branch had after its first rally. Still, Johnson had to be pleased with the way the association's message was taking hold. By early October, the black press was beginning to fall into line. "The heroic defense of their homes exhibited by those brave and fearless Detroiters . . . makes every Negro in this country their debtor," insisted the editors of Philadelphia's race paper. "And so it ought to be left to that splendid organization, the National Association for the Advancement of Colored People, to undertake their defense. . . . Every Negro in the United States should pay the debt we owe them. We helped with our lives to pay Germany for the horrors of the Belgian invasion. Should we do less in the face of what our own citizens inflicted upon our own flesh and blood in Detroit?"[55]

Selling the Sweets' story to white audiences was a tougher proposition, as there was no sign that the NAACP's publicity blitz was reaching beyond colored America to the ethnic masses whose support the association dreamed of having. To make matters worse, Johnson picked up indications that white liberal opinion was starting to break in exactly the wrong direction. White's reports of the progressives' full-scale retreat in Detroit were worrisome enough, but at least they could be discounted as political maneuvers, cynical but understandable. Other opinions were harder to dismiss. In late September, the editor of the journal *Christian Work*, one of the leading voices of the Social Gospel, sent Johnson his most recent editorial. In light of the tragedy in Detroit, the editor argued, "neither the whites nor the Negroes seem to get any advantage from living next to each other. . . . In Anglo-Saxon lands, at least, the social mixture of white and black leads to unhappiness." Johnson was quite taken aback. It was bad enough to think that liberal Christians could see the separation of God's children as a social good. But he couldn't have missed the stinging irony of this particular publication decrying the integration of urban neighborhoods. *Christian Work*, after all, had its editorial offices directly across the street from NAACP headquarters.[56]

The association countered, as usual, by turning to powerful friends for support. The editor of the *Nation*, NAACP cofounder Oswald Garrison Villard, was pleased to accept White's long piece on the case, written in a rush the week White returned from Detroit. Though it lacked the immediacy of White's earlier reports from the darkest regions of Jim Crow, the article hit all its marks. White opened not with the violence on Garland Avenue but with the NAACP's defeat of city ordinances requiring neighborhood segregation and the subsequent rise of restrictive covenants, both of which he claimed were pieces of "a nation-wide effort on the part of certain groups backed by the Ku Klux Klan" to lock Negroes into ghettos. The attack on the Sweets wasn't simply an outgrowth of that campaign but "its dramatic high point," the tragic culmination of a Klan conspiracy, a lineage of hatred so pure it was sure to appeal to the *Nation*'s invariably progressive readers, "the better class of white citizens" that White insisted were already joining with Negroes to defend the Sweets.[57] But James Weldon Johnson knew his job too well to imagine that one strategically placed article was anything more than a good start. To take the cause across the color line, he had to draw out all the dramatic potential he'd seen in the tiny clipping that had first caught his attention, to make whites feel the injustice that Negroes felt, to make them care. For all his skill, Johnson hadn't found a way to push the campaign to that level. Then the situation in Detroit reached a crisis point, and everything suddenly fell into place.

•

As soon as he was back at his desk Monday morning, September 21, White had renewed his offensive against the colored lawyers. The safety of distance gave his efforts a harder edge. He sent Judge Jayne a detailed account of Cecil Rowlette's demands and a plea for help "in checking the rapacity of these lawyers." His closest ally in the Detroit branch, meanwhile, received strict orders to ratchet up the pressure. "I do not think it would be a bad idea for you to hint gently that . . . if necessary we will make public all of the various things these lawyers have said and done which will end them for all time in the eyes of the colored people," he said. "They have got to know that we are doing the employing in the case and we are going to pay the bill and it's not for them to dictate to us what we shall do." By week's end, he had the response he wanted. Julian Perry, who had been all but silent throughout White's time in Detroit, stopped by Jayne's chambers to say that he, too, wanted a "first-class white attorney" to take over the defense. He would insist that his co-counsels follow his lead. What's more, he would personally offer the job to the NAACP's first choice, the former Bar Association president. "The situation is simmering along nicely," Jayne reported Friday.[58]

He couldn't have been more wrong.

All week long, word of White's pressure on the defense team had been spreading through colored Detroit. Friday night the backlash hit, striking at the true heart of the NAACP's campaign. That evening, Reverend Joseph Gomez, pastor of powerful Bethel AME, told a packed meeting at the colored YMCA that he was launching his own Sweet Defense Fund, explicitly intended to be "a local organization, uncontrolled by outside politics." Gomez himself was probably doing a bit of ministerial maneuvering, setting himself up against Second Baptist's control of the NAACP branch, perhaps even exacting a bit of revenge for Bradby imperiously shutting Gomez out of the branch's executive board earlier in the year. Whatever his motivation, Gomez tapped into a deep well of resentment at the association's high-handedness. By meeting's end, some of the most important organizations in the black community—including Gladys's home church, St. Matthew's Episcopal—had joined Gomez's campaign, and plans were under way for a competing series of Sunday rallies that were sure to drain money away from the NAACP.[59]

That news, in turn, gave Cecil Rowlette all the leverage he needed to derail White's offensive. In the course of a bitterly fought conference with the branch officers Saturday afternoon, Rowlette tossed aside his earlier concessions to White and instead demanded the right to take the case to the next stage the following weekend, when the defendants would be arraigned before Judge Murphy and the defense would have its last opportunity to have the charges dropped. To make sure that the branch was listening, he resurrected his promise to resign if he didn't get his way, a threat that suddenly seemed much more dangerous than it had the week before.

So the NAACP's local officers threw themselves into full retreat. Not only did they promise Rowlette control of the case through the arraignment, but at the next day's church rally, they also passed a resolution promising "that the matter of defense attorneys be left entirely to the persons imprisoned and the present defense attorneys, and that there would be no interference by the association in this regard."[60] Those concessions, though, simply triggered another sharp reaction, this time from the defendants themselves.

◆

In the course of September, life inside the Wayne County Jail grew more comfortable for Ossian, Gladys, and the others. The prominence of the case made it impossible for jail officers to maintain the isolation they had imposed on the Sweets the first few days after their arrest, and by midmonth, the defendants were seeing a steady stream of visitors. The NAACP's Detroit branch, meanwhile, took to providing the eleven with catered meals, sure to be better than prison fare, and to covering some of their more pressing debts, including the $150 a month the Sweets owed on the bungalow's land contract. Still, it must have been terribly difficult for the defendants to endure weeks of imprisonment—suffering the continual taunts of the guards and the perpetual company of their fellow prisoners, trying to remain optimistic even as their attorneys' maneuvers failed again and again, fighting back the terrifying thought that they might never be freed. As the month came to a close, one of the Sweet brothers suddenly decided that it was time to fight back.[61]

It's impossible to say what caused the outburst, but there's no doubt that it was an emotionally wrenching time. For on the last weekend of September, the Sweets received the most important visitor of them all: their father.[62]

Three months shy of sixty, the elder Henry Sweet must have begun showing the signs of age. To his boys, though, he was still a commanding figure—the stern man who had taught them the virtues of hard work and respectability—and they hated the thought of him coming all the way from Bartow to see his sons behind bars, charged with the most serious of crimes. When the guards brought Henry Sweet into the detention pen to talk to his second son, Otis tried to apologize. No explanations, no rationalizations, no appeals to principles that he wanted his father to understand. He simply said he was sorry for the embarrassment he and his brothers had brought to the family.

But Henry Sweet, himself a son of runaway slaves, wasn't angry; he was proud. "You have nothing to be embarrassed about," he said to Otis. "You know who runs? Only rabbits run."[63]

Maybe those words—that blessing—had no affect on the events of the next few days; maybe the cause lay solely in the Detroit branch's decision to abrogate responsibility for finalizing the selection of defense attorneys. But on Tuesday, September 29—at most two or three days after his father's visit—Otis Sweet took his only public stand during the entire Sweet affair.

Along with two of the insurance men, Charles Washington and Leonard Morse, and the narcotics agent William Davis—whose attempts to incriminate his fellows remained unknown to his cell mates—Otis drafted a pair of long letters to the NAACP Detroit branch and the association's national office. Gone were the equivocations the defendants had employed on the night of their interrogations, replaced by a fierce determination to stand up for the cause they now represented. "We feel," they wrote, "that this is a case in which more is involved than the liberties of the eleven persons concerned; it is a case that boldly challenges the liberties, the hopes, and the aspirations of fifteen million colored Americans. If the prosecution should win, in that very act, they erect over the head of every Negro not only in this city but in every community in this country a very formidable threat of residential proscription whose consequences none of us can now predict. He would be forced to face the future with only the feeblest hope as to the positive maintenance of his inalienable right under the Constitution to live without molestation and persecution wherever he may. We feel that the prosecution realizes this and will spare no cunning in the prosecution of their dastardly program."[64]

Given the stakes, Otis and his three associates insisted, the NAACP must assume complete control of the case immediately, rejecting Rowlette's machinations and putting in his place "the best legal talent available." The four defendants admitted that the rest of the accused didn't necessarily agree with their demand for a complete change in the defense team—"the other seven concerned . . . have been just a bit more gullible than we," emboldened Otis wrote in an uncharacteristic rebuke to his brothers—but "we feel this is no time to permit the sordid efforts of narrow self-seekers [such as Rowlette] . . . to place in jeopardy an issue of such vital moment to the race." Then, just to be sure that their message received the attention it deserved, they had Morse's wife send an urgent telegram to the NAACP's office, care of Du Bois, whom they assumed ran the association. "We the undersigned prisoners in the Sweet Case want to know if the Legal Department of the NAACP [is] in complete charge of the defense," the telegram read. "If not, please do same at once."[65]

♦

The moment the messenger boy dropped the telegram off Thursday afternoon, Walter White flew into action. If the colored attorneys couldn't be threatened into following the NAACP's script, perhaps they might be awed into compliance. After a flurry of phone calls and a hastily arranged Saturday morning meeting, White convinced the chair of the association's Legal Committee, influential Arthur Spingarn, to come with him to Detroit the following weekend to lay out the NAACP's bedrock demands. Spingarn prepared the brief they would carry. "[The] color line should be put aside in this case," he wrote, "and . . . the very best lawyer we can afford to retain with the highest professional and personal standing should be secured at the earliest possible time." Then came the hammer blow: "In the event that this very definite opinion of the National Legal Committee is not adopted by the defense, it is recommended that the NAACP decline to accept full responsibility for the ultimate outcome of the case."[66]

Even as he and Spingarn finalized arrangements, though, White knew that the color line wasn't about to break. While Rowlette and Mahoney prepared for the arraignment, Perry had quietly visited the prominent attorneys on the NAACP's list, asking if they might be interested in taking on the case, and one after another, they turned him down. All of them had reasonable excuses: they weren't taking new clients; their schedules were full; they weren't sufficiently skilled in criminal law. But there was no doubting the real reason they wouldn't sign on. The Klan's flame was burning brighter than ever as September came to a close. The four glistening new printing presses in the basement of KKK headquarters were spewing out reams of campaign literature; Klansmen were going door-to-door soliciting votes; there was to be another giant KKK rally on the west side the same day that the Negroes were to be arraigned, Saturday, October 3. Three days after that, Detroit was scheduled to hold its primary election, when the field of candidates would be set for the November general election, and there was every reason to believe that those men who had the Invisible Empire's backing would do very well indeed. Under the circumstances, any white man interested in having a future would be a fool to stand up for the Sweets and their friends. Only Thomas Chawke was willing to take on the challenge, for the gold-plated price of seventy-five hundred dollars, far more than the association's suddenly beleaguered defense fund could bear.[67]

Perhaps White's irrepressible optimism prevented him from admitting the truth even to himself. But there would be no white lawyers. The fate of the Sweets and of the NAACP's fledgling crusade rested in the ebony hands of Cecil Rowlette and his two colored colleagues.

The next few days played out with dreadful predictability. Having staked his hopes on the power of the law, Rowlette arrived at the arraignment on Saturday, October 3, armed with a briefcase full of precedents. Because the witnesses at the preliminary hearing had refused to concede that there had been a mob in front of the bungalow, Rowlette was forced to back off from the argument for self-defense that had proved so successful in the Fleta Mathies case. Still, his nine-page motion to quash was a fine piece of work, striking first at the same soft spots he'd attacked in the preliminary hearing, then citing almost a dozen state Supreme Court rulings to show that those weaknesses made the charges unsustainable. He tacked on a particular plea for Gladys, arguing that according to common law, a wife was not to be implicated in her husband's crimes simply because she shared his household. As quickly as that point was entered into the record, he swung back to general principles. Without an identifiable murderer and compelling evidence of conspiracy—without showing malice aforethought—the prosecution had no grounds for bringing forward a charge of murder. To preserve the dignity of the judicial system, the Sweets and their friends had to go free.[68]

Judge Murphy paid Rowlette the compliment of taking his motion under advisement for the balance of the weekend. No doubt he agonized over the brief; he was too fine a student of the legal process not to see the strength of the argument the defense was making and too sensitive a soul not to be bothered by the possibility of Ossian, Gladys, and the others spending the balance of their lives behind bars. But he also understood the play of city politics, the coursing of emotion on the street. So the balance of justice tipped as it had time and again since the night of the shooting.

On Monday, Murphy announced that he was willing to grant Gladys bail of ten thousand dollars, a balm, perhaps, to a troubled conscience. But Rowlette's motion was denied. Court would convene two weeks hence to begin hearing *The People v. Sweet*. The following day, Tuesday, October 6, the Ku Klux Klan swept the city primary, rolling up imposing majorities for its candidates in district after district, from the west side's Anglo-Saxon strongholds to the rows of working-class flats on the east, where the Invisible Empire was thought to be anathema. Whites of every description, it seemed, were consolidating behind the Klan and its program of racial purity. One more month, one last election, and Detroit would become the Invisible Empire's latest prize, the world's most modern metropolis turned into the Great White City.[69]

◆

If it hadn't been for the trouble with the lawyers, the letter from Chicago probably wouldn't have made such an impression. Had he not slipped his business card into the envelope, no one at NAACP headquarters would have known that N. K. McGill served as general counsel for the *Chicago Defender*. Nor would they have been so intrigued by his extraordinary offer. "I am interested in the procedure in the case of Dr. Sweet in Detroit and I would thank you to let me know if I can assist your efforts in that case," McGill said. "I have free access to such minds as Mr. Darrow's and other great lawyers here and it may be that we could use their knowledge and experience without actually paying the regular fee that they charge in such cases."[70]

As it was, the letter sat in Walter White's in-box all day October 5 as he occupied himself with more pressing matters. It wasn't until the next day, while Klansmen were filling polling places across Detroit, that he found time to reply, and even then he was more concerned with getting the NAACP's campaign bigger play in the *Chicago Defender* than in tapping McGill's legal connections. Not until the day after that, October 7— four weeks since the shooting, twelve days to trial—did someone in the office pull the name off the page.

Clarence Darrow was for a quarter century the most brilliant defense attorney in the country, counsel for Debs and Haywood, Leopold and Loeb, and a Tennessee schoolteacher named Scopes; perhaps he could be convinced not simply to offer his advice but his services. If the idea wasn't Johnson's—if it came instead from White or Du Bois or another member of the staff—he saw its potential right away, just as he had seen the potential in the Sweets' story from a few paragraphs of newsprint. It would be such a marvelously theatrical turn, classic in its form, riveting in its imagery: Clarence Darrow lumbering to the defense table in a Detroit courtroom, the NAACP's faltering racial drama saved by a deus ex machina resplendent in red suspenders and a rumpled suit.

EIGHT

THE PRODIGAL SON

James Weldon Johnson's invitation to Clarence Darrow's Chicago office rang with the staccato rhythm that Western Union imposed: two sentences summarized the specifics of the Sweets' arrest, then Johnson broadened his appeal. "Case is dramatic high point of nationwide issue of segregation in which National Association for Advancement of Colored People has case now pending in United States Supreme Court. *Stop*. This issue constitutes a supreme test of the constitutional guarantees of American Negro citizens. *Stop*. Defense requires ablest attorney of national prestige that we can possibly secure who would be willing to undertake such a case. *Stop*. Please wire us collect if you would consider favorably request that you assume charge of the case. *Stop*." The next morning, October 8, Johnson received a reply. Darrow wasn't at home, reported his secretary. He was in Manhattan, visiting his friend and fellow attorney, Arthur Garfield Hays. Within a few hours, Johnson had put his sterling connections to use and had an invitation to meet with Darrow that very day.[1]

The NAACP secretary arrived at Hays's Greenwich Village home with Walter White, Arthur Spingarn, and Spingarn's law partner, Charles Studin, in tow. They were ushered into the guest room, where they found Darrow propped up in bed, fully clothed but still looking exceedingly comfortable. Despite his advancing age, he retained the broad-shouldered, barrel-chested body of the workman he'd never been. His face, though, had grown old, his dappled skin sagging from his high cheekbones, the furrows around his mouth and eyes deeply etched. A forelock of unruly hair, gray and thin, fell over his forehead. As the celebrated attorney's gray-green eyes locked on his visitors and his brow knitted in concentration, though, there was no doubt that his mind remained as agile as it had ever been.[2]

As head of the NAACP's National Legal Committee, Spingarn took the lead in laying out the details of the case, a presentation he handled with expertise. A decade later, Darrow would recall how Spingarn's words had stirred the idealism of his youth, when the great abolitionists had graced his father's humble Ohio home. "I made the usual excuses that I was tired, and growing old, and was not physically or mentally fit," he recounted. "I knew that I would go when I was making the excuses. I have always been interested in the colored people. I had lived in America because I wanted to. . . . The ancestors of the negroes came here because they were captured in Africa and brought to America in slave ships, and had been obliged to toil for three hundred years without reward. When they were finally freed from slavery they were lynched in court and out of court, and driven into mean, squalid outskirts and shanties because they were black, or had a drop of negro blood in their bodies somewhere. I realized that defending negroes, even in the north, was no boy's job, although boys were usually given the responsibility."[3]

The others in the room that evening remembered the conversation differently. When Spingarn was finished talking, Darrow offered him the subdued sympathy for which he had become famous. "Yes, I know full well the difficulties faced by your race," he said.

"I'm sorry, Mr. Darrow," replied Spingarn, whose naturally swarthy skin had grown even darker after a summer in the sun at his Dutchess County estate, "but I'm not a Negro."

Embarrassed, Darrow turned to Studin, whose face was the same shade as Spingarn's. "Well, you understand what I mean," he said.

"I am not colored either," Studin answered.

Finally, Darrow took a look at Walter White. "I wouldn't make the same mistake with you," he said.

"I am a Negro," White replied.

Darrow broke into a smile. "That settles it," he said. "I'll take the case."[4]

◆

The response was vintage Darrow, a rage for justice combined with an adoration of irony, the absolute and the ambiguous fused together and presented to the world as dark-edged humor. His critics thought him nothing more than a cynic. "He is never happy except at a funeral," a prominent social reformer complained, "and not then unless . . . the deceased had committed suicide." To see Darrow in such a light, though, was to assume that he believed everything he said. Poet Edgar Lee Masters, who knew and despised Darrow, understood his complexity. "This is Darrow," he wrote three years before the Sweets' arrest, "Inadequately scrawled, with his young, old heart / . . . And his artist sense that drives him to shape his life / To something harmonious, even against the schemes of God."[5]

The harmony Darrow sought was built on the discordant notes of metropolitan modernism. Like the self-styled bohemians who filled turn-of-the-century Greenwich Village, Darrow wanted to shatter what he saw as the smug self-satisfaction—he'd say self-delusion—of mainstream America and to build in its place a society free, open, and savagely honest. Darrow's route to cultural revolution was typical, if somewhat circuitous, his rebellion nurtured by a childhood spent on the radical fringe of the small-town Midwest and given shape by a young man's encounter with the full force of urban life.[6]

Born on the eve of the Civil War, he came of age in the northeast Ohio hamlet of Kinsman, where his father served as furniture maker, undertaker, and, in Darrow's words, "village infidel." An agnostic in a town filled with pious Presbyterians and Methodists, a Democrat in an area dominated by Republicans, a workingman who preferred to spend his days reading his well-worn volumes of Voltaire, Paine, and Jefferson than practicing his craft, the elder Darrow relished the role of freethinking outsider. At first, Clarence seemed determined not to follow in his father's footsteps. After an abbreviated college career and a year at the University of Michigan Law School, he established a conventional small-town practice in Kinsman, married a conventional small-town girl, and settled into what seemed to be an utterly conventional small-town life. But the pull of ambition and ideas was too strong to resist. In 1887, at age thirty, he abruptly drew up stakes, moving his family, which now included a son, and his practice to the place his hometown newspaper called "the wickedest city in the United States."[7]

Late-nineteenth-century Chicago had its share of sin, doled out in dingy working-class saloons and first-class sporting clubs, steaming Turkish baths and smoke-filled gambling dens. Mostly, though, Chicago had the throbbing energy of a great industrial center, where the natural bounty of the West met the manufacturing might of the East and

the two were transferred in a massive tangle of railroad lines. Just sixteen years removed from the cataclysmic Great Fire, Chicago had become "the heart of the nation," as Frank Norris said, "brutal in its
ambition, arrogant in the new-found knowledge of its giant strength,
prodigal of its wealth, infinite in its desires." It was teeming with people,
a million in 1890, almost 80 percent of them immigrants or their progeny. It roiled with class conflict, the byproduct of industrialists' relentless drive for profit. And it absolutely seethed with ideas. Social
Darwinism, populism, progressivism, socialism: Darrow raced through
them all, an intellectual drunkard on a decade-long binge. Eventually,
he found his place not in any of the city's political circles but rather in
the slightly seedy salons of the artistic avant-garde, where the icono-
clasm of his father's generation was being updated for the Machine
Age. It proved a perfect fit.[8]

Of course the avant-garde were themselves highly political, but
theirs was a cultural rather than electoral politics, a battle for the soul
rather than the ballot box. They took as their enemy bourgeois respectability, which they saw as the polite face of oppression. Through
their art, they sought to strip away the middle class's illusion of decency and to expose the "real" America, at once more bleak and, in the
raw simplicity of its immigrant working class, more beautiful. At the
same time, they tried to turn themselves into respectability's shocking
antithesis, doggedly determined to flaunt convention in their work,
their dress, their living arrangements, and their relationships—to subvert the established order by emancipating themselves. There was a
good deal of artifice to it all: small-town transplants, late of Davenport
and Terre Haute, sitting on well-worn Persian rugs in Jackson Park
studios, drawing tea from samovars and talking of free love, free
speech, and the impending revolution. But Darrow adored it. In 1897,
the year he turned forty, he began the first of a series of seductions, divorced his wife, moved into a cooperative apartment building tucked
in among the immigrant slums of Chicago's west side, and created his
own bohemian salon filled with writers, painters, and assorted hangers-
on. "A more interesting group of peculiar people could not be brought
together," a rattled visitor reported after a night in Darrow's digs.
"Their points of agreement are first, weariness with life as lived by normal society and a desire to live a strained abnirmal [sic] life. . . . Both
male and female members of the club smoked and used profane language as they discussed politics and political leaders; lauded extreme
socialism and anarchy, and cheered anarchists."[9]

For a while, Darrow thought of abandoning the law to become a writer. He even published two novels: *Farmington*, a scalding portrayal of his boyhood hometown disguised as a rural idyll; and *An Eye for an Eye*, a pitch-black portrait of life in Chicago's working-class wards. But his facility with the written word couldn't match his brilliant artistry in the courtroom. He'd burst onto the national scene during one of the worst of Chicago's periodic outbreaks of class conflict, the epic 1894 Pullman strike, when he'd taken up the cause of Eugene Debs, the dynamic president of the American Railway Union. Debs hadn't started the strike—the men and women who made Pullman railroad cars did that—but he had escalated the confrontation dramatically by convincing the members of his union to boycott work on any train that contained a Pullman car. As the nation's rail system all but ground to a halt, the federal court issued an injunction ordering the railway men back to work. When they refused, Debs was charged with contempt of court. Darrow took his case all the way to the United States Supreme Court, which ruled against him. Debs was dispatched to a federal penitentiary to serve out a six-month sentence. And Darrow was transformed into the Great Defender, champion of the embattled working class.[10]

For close to twenty years, Darrow fought for labor's cause. There were the predictable confrontations with capitalist power, fighting for the Amalgamated Woodworkers Union, threatened with conspiracy because they dared to call a strike; for Chicago's switchboard workers, facing imprisonment unless they abandoned their walkout; for the United Mine Workers, desperate to improve their abysmal working conditions. Then there were the truly spectacular cases, which bathed Darrow in the national spotlight. He devoted most of 1906 to defending one-eyed Big Bill Haywood, the excruciatingly romantic, indisputably radical leader of the Western Federation of Miners, who stood accused of murdering Idaho's bitterly antiunion former governor. Five years later, in a case that almost destroyed his career, he waged a fierce battle to save a pair of Irish-American ironworkers, John and James McNamara, from the hangman's noose. The McNamara brothers had dynamited the *Los Angeles Times* building, prosecutors claimed, killing twenty and injuring hundreds. Champions of labor knew it was a frame-up, perhaps orchestrated by the *Times'* owner himself, the bitterly antiunion Harrison Gray Otis. "When the weak and friendless masses clamor for the sweat of his very soul in their behalf," gushed one of his lovers, "Clarence Darrow will appear again and yet again, with flaming sword."[11]

As much as he was moved by the plight of the masses, though,

Darrow was truly driven by the attention that controversial cases won him. Once he embraced the avant-garde, he lost all faith in the legal system—"society is organized injustice," he insisted—and grew bored with the intricacies of legal procedure. But he continued to practice law because in the glare of a high-profile case he found the perfect opportunity to attack the status quo and proclaim the modernist creed. "This meant more than the quibbling with lawyers and juries, to get or keep money for a client so that I could take part of what I won or saved for him," he said in his old age. "I was dealing with life, with its hopes and fears, its aspirations and despairs. With me it was going to the foundation of motive and conduct and adjustments for human beings, instead of blindly talking of hatred and vengeance, and that subtle, indefinable quality that men call 'justice' and of which nothing is really known."[12]

Darrow never presented himself as a sophisticate. In personal appearance, he remained very much a country lawyer, his clothes slightly disheveled and with each year increasingly old-fashioned, his shoulders slumped, his voice tinged with a soft drawl that listeners found endearing. When he rose from the defense table, though, trials were transformed into great social dramas. Prosecution witnesses were turned into symbols of society's stupidity and corruption, defendants into victims of its cruelty, avarice, and ignorance. His closing statements became legendary: no carefully constructed argument, no review of precedent, just cascades of images, emotions, cheap sentiments, and complex ideas, jabs of sarcasm, hints of philosophy, and snatches of poetry, presented in shouts and whispers and sometimes in tears. For eleven hours, he held the Haywood jury spellbound, pleading, preaching, and cajoling, until the trial had become a test of capitalism itself, "that accursed system upon which the favored live and grow fat" while "the poor, the weak, and the suffering of the world stretch out their hands in mute appeal." It was all so convincing, so moving, so tragic, the twelve Idaho farmers who finally trooped into the jury room couldn't bring themselves to convict the anarchist miner sitting by Darrow's side.[13]

Over the decades, Darrow's passions shifted and changed. Six years after his divorce, Darrow married again, taking as his wife Ruby Hamerstrom, a journalist twelve years his junior. Although Clarence maintained his artistic friends and occasional lovers, Ruby shut down his west-side salon, eventually enveloping Clarence in an opulent cocoon of an apartment near the University of Chicago campus. For all his talk of liberation, he happily accepted his new wife's perpetual attention to his needs and comforts. Lincoln Steffens once asked him how his marriage was faring. "Fine," he replied, "because Ruby and me, we both love Darrow." His love affair with the labor movement, in contrast, came to a bitter end during the 1911 McNamara case. Hired to clear the movement's bloodied reputation, Darrow instead pled his clients guilty in exchange for the state's promise not to put them to death. It was a reasonable trade, given that the McNamara brothers had actually committed mass murder. But union leaders were convinced that Darrow had betrayed them, a sentiment made all the stronger when the Great Defender himself was brought up on charges of bribing a juror shortly before the plea bargain was completed. Darrow managed to keep himself out of jail. But his days as the hero of the working class were over.[14]

No matter how much his life twisted and turned, though, Darrow's dedication to modernism didn't waver. With the collapse of his labor advocacy, in fact, the scope of his attacks on the existing order widened. He spent more and more time on the lecture circuit, enthralling audiences with his marvelously sharp assaults on religion, Prohibition, criminal justice, capital punishment, and the very meaning of life. Inside the courtroom, he took up a new string of cases and causes, each more spectacular than the one before. As the fever of "One Hundred Percent Americanism" burned through the nation in the aftermath of the Great War, Darrow defended Italian-born anarchists, Irish-born socialists, and Russian-born communists thrown into jail for preaching revolution on street-corner soapboxes and in radical papers almost nobody read. Their ideas might not stand the test of time, he said, but the nation dare not deny "the right of men to think; to speak boldly and unafraid; the right to be master of their souls; the right to live free and to die free," for "there is no other cause so worthwhile." In 1924, in the wildly publicized case of child killers Nathan Leopold and Richard Loeb, Darrow abandoned his defense of unlimited freedom to argue that his clients were compelled to kill by their damaged psyches, traditional notions of crime, sin, and personal responsibility swept away by the dark art of modern psychoanalysis.[15]

Then came the most brilliant performance of them all. For a man who had participated in so many capital cases, the stakes in the Scopes "Monkey Trial" were ludicrously small. But the case was so furiously spun, so expertly promoted, it became the "trial of the century." In early 1925, the Tennessee state legislature prohibited the teaching of evolution in public schools, lest students come to question the unerring truth of holy scripture. Appalled by what it took to be an assault on academic freedom, Roger Baldwin's American Civil Liberties Union announced that it would defend any Tennessee schoolteacher willing to test the new law. Hoping for a windfall of publicity for their tiny town, the good folks of Dayton, Tennessee, promptly offered up their high school science teacher, twenty-four-year-old John T. Scopes. At first, it was assumed that Scopes's defense would be led by the ACLU's favorite attorney, forty-three-year-old Arthur Garfield Hays. The son of a German Jewish businessman, Hays made himself rich practicing corporate law. He kept himself happy by lending his considerable legal talent to the defense of civil liberties. Hays's list of pro bono clients read like a who's who of the dispossessed: imprisoned unionists, silenced radicals, and two poor immigrants named Nicola Sacco and Bartolomeo Vanzetti, living out their days on death row.

As Hays and the ACLU's directors began preparing for their careful constitutional challenge, though, the Scopes case slipped out of their hands. First, three-time presidential candidate William Jennings Bryan, once the champion of populist politics, now the defender of fundamentalism, announced that he would join the prosecution. Then Darrow elbowed his way onto the defense team. Suddenly, everyone forgot about the core issue of academic freedom. Down in Dayton, Tennessee, in July 1925—just as the streets of Detroit's west side exploded into racial violence—the Old Time Religion went on trial.[16]

Some ACLU officials were appalled at the change of emphasis. Hays embraced it, reveling in the dark-hued idealism he and Darrow shared and in the frenzy of attention the Great Defender inevitably attracted. More than two hundred reporters trailed the pair into the Bible Belt, Hays to take care of the trial's legal issues, Darrow to provide the drama. As newsreel cameras captured the excitement, Chicago's WGN broadcast back to the big city every word uttered in the sweltering courtroom. Darrow gave them all a brilliant show. In his two-hour opening, he pillaged the Temple: "We are marching backward to the glorious age of the sixteenth century," he proclaimed, "when bigots lighted fagots to burn the men who dared to bring any intelligence and enlightenment and culture to the human mind."[17]

His masterstroke came on the seventh day, when he asked Bryan himself to take the stand as an expert on the Good Word. For two interminable hours, Darrow battered away at Bryan's simple faith, daring him to defend the Bible as literally true, laughing at him when he tried, humiliating him when he faltered. At one point, Bryan grew so flustered, he blurted out, "I do not think about things I don't think about." Darrow shot back, "Do you think about things you do think about?" "Well, sometimes," Bryan meekly replied. When the judge finally put a stop to the assault, Bryan stepped down from the witness stand a broken man.[18]

Darrow's dismantling of fundamentalism didn't help Scopes, who was convicted in a mere nine minutes' deliberation and fined one hundred dollars. But Darrow returned north more famous than he'd ever been before, his mailbox bulging with accolades, invitations, and condemnations, his reputation as modernism's ageless warrior burnished to a blinding sheen. "When [Darrow] confronted Bryan at last, the whole combat came to its climax," wrote Walter White's friend and literary mentor, H. L. Mencken, the enfant terrible of the next generation's smart set. "On the one side was bigotry, hatred, superstition, every sort of blackness that the human mind is capable of. On the other side was sense. And sense achieved a great victory." Now that he had reached the pinnacle of his extraordinary career, Darrow talked of retirement, although he knew he didn't mean it. "I had practiced almost fifty years," he recalled, and for a long time wanted to stop. "But it's not easy to follow one's inclinations." In his heart, he knew there'd be another trial, another cause, another engagement in the battle for the American mind.[19]

Then, just three months after the Monkey Trial ended, the NAACP came calling.

As Darrow listened to Spingarn tell of the Sweets' dilemma, he recalled the radical abolitionists who had tramped through his father's door when Clarence was a boy: William Lloyd Garrison, Wendell Phillips, Charles Sumner, Frederick Douglass, and, most of all, John Brown, who in 1859 had gathered his ragtag troops just fifteen miles from the Darrows' home in Kinsman before marching on to fulfill his destiny at Harpers Ferry. The elder Darrow wasn't himself a participant in the abolitionist crusade. Although the Underground Railroad ran through that area around Kinsman, there's no record of the Darrow family ever secreting escaped slaves to freedom. But Clarence's father loved to hear the abolitionists talk, and to repeat their sweet words to his son; many Sunday evenings, the town agnostic gathered his family around the dinner table and read sermons to them from the most progressive Protestant ministers, such as abolitionist Theodore Parker, with his glorious promise of a universe arching toward justice.

Clarence feigned indifference, but the lectures marked him deeply. The abolitionists were, he wrote, "poor, sensitive, prophetic souls, feeling the suffering of the world and taking its sorrows on their burdened backs," as honest a self-portrait as Darrow would ever put into print. He often mourned the abolitionists' passing, even when it wasn't entirely appropriate to do so. "Whilst a black man was lynched in the shadow of the monument built to the memory of Abraham Lincoln and in the town where he lived and was laid to rest . . . where were the Garrisons?" he roared from the stage of the NAACP's second annual conference in 1910, as the Liberator's grandson, association cofounder Oswald Garrison Villard, sat in red-faced fury. "The Garrisons were preaching in rich pulpits and pointing their aristocrats to an aristocratic heaven. . . . And the voice of humanity and justice was still. What has happened in fifty years?" Until the Sweet case came his way, though, Darrow had never truly stood against the segregationist tide that had swept away so much of the abolitionists' work. Now, in his advancing age, it was time to be about his father's business.[20]

But there was also calculation in the decision to accept the NAACP's offer. When his host, Arthur Garfield Hays, announced that he also was willing to join the defense—"freedom of residence" was at stake, he thought—Darrow leapt at the opportunity to re-create the publicity juggernaut that had been built in Dayton, Tennessee. Better still, Darrow loved the idea of turning the juggernaut against the most sacred of American creeds, more beloved even than the Good Word that he had battered the previous summer. With the Sweet case, Darrow would have his chance to make Americans confront the sheer stupidity of white supremacy.[21] So he smiled at the splendid confusion of hues he saw in the earnest faces gathered around him. And he pledged to go to Detroit.

•

Had they given it much thought, James Weldon Johnson and Walter White would have recognized the risks of bringing Darrow into their employ. For all his courtroom skills, he hadn't amassed an enviable record in high-profile cases: Debs, the McNamara boys, Leopold and Loeb, all had gone to prison, and even Scopes, whose crime was so miniscule it didn't merit jail time, had paid his fine and handed the school board his resignation, his teaching career ended forever. Darrow hardly bore sole responsibility for the defeats—it was a miracle that some of his clients hadn't ended their days dangling from the gallows—but there was no doubt that he cared more for the fight itself than for victory. And when the heat of battle grew intense, Darrow often indulged in the sort of provocations that the association's habitually respectable leaders considered anathema. Not only had he insulted Villard at the NAACP's 1910 convention, he'd horrified a number of the association's members by urging Negroes to fight for "social equality," including the right to marry white folks, and arguing that miscegenation offered the best solution to the nation's race problem. Colored men had been lynched for saying less.[22]

But Johnson and White weren't worried about how Darrow's penchant for the outrageous might be received in the dangerously enflamed streets of white Detroit. It was the publicity that mattered to them, the phosphorescence of celebrity, which illuminated the black cause so brilliantly that white America couldn't help but take notice. Spending evenings with Mencken, Lewis, Knopf, or Van Vechten meant enduring the occasional idiocy—sharp tongues loosened by liquor and the thrill of being uptown after dark—but discomfort was a small price to pay for the benefits the Harlem Renaissance bestowed on the fight for civil rights. So, too, was it worth risking a bit of Darrow's bombast for the opportunity to cast this particular story, and the crusade it was meant to dramatize, in the dazzling light generated by his incomparable star power.

It took another week to settle the details. There was, as always, the matter of money. Because of the principles involved, the lawyers were willing to reduce their usual fees to rock-bottom prices: Darrow would take the case for five thousand dollars and expenses—a tenth of his typical fee to defend those charged with murder—while Hays would work for a token three thousand dollars and expenses. But even such marginal costs were too much for the NAACP's depleted defense fund. So Johnson couldn't guarantee payment until he convinced his executive board, full of flinty New Englanders, that retaining the services of the nation's most famous attorney was worth the investment.[23]

While Johnson waited for the board's approval, Walter White set out to solve the tangle of problems that had led him to Darrow in the first place. A day after the meeting in Hays's guestroom, he and Arthur Spingarn headed to Detroit on the overnight train for the consultations they'd scheduled with the Sweets' three lawyers. When they'd planned the trip a few days earlier, White and Spingarn had expected a weekend of acrimony, the two of them pressuring the colored lawyers to surrender the case to an unknown white attorney, Julian Perry, Cecil Rowlette, and Charles Mahoney resisting, both sides growing even more frustrated and angry. But the promise of Darrow's and Hays's intervention had restored White's enthusiasm. Although he now had the leverage he needed to force the Negroes out of the case, he no longer cared to do so.

Darrow had made it clear that he wouldn't take the case unless he were welcomed by the local attorneys, and in any case, the defense now had its white face, and the presence of a few black men in the background would do no harm. So White swept into Detroit on Saturday morning, October 10, determined to settle the conflict as quickly and amicably as possible. A few broad hints of Darrow's coming and a suddenly replenished well of goodwill worked wonders. By noontime Sunday, White and Spingarn had promised to keep all three attorneys on the case at a fairly generous fee of fifteen hundred dollars each, to be paid not by the national office—White wasn't in that agreeable a mood—but by the Detroit NAACP branch. In exchange, Perry, Rowlette, and Mahoney agreed to surrender control of the defense to an officially unnamed white counsel whom White coyly referred to as "one of the most prominent lawyers in the United States."[24]

Putting to rest the problem with the attorneys, in turn, promised to resolve the conflict over fund-raising that had exploded a few weeks earlier, when a considerable portion of the city's Negro leadership, angry at White's insistence that the association control the case, had created its own Sweet Defense Fund in competition with the local branch's effort. Now that Perry, Rowlette, and Mahoney were to stay on the defense, the main point of friction was removed. But to be on the safe side, White launched a diplomatic offensive that would have made James Weldon Johnson proud. Though his schedule was filled to bursting, he took the time to meet with the rival fund's director, Reverend Joseph Gomez of Bethel AME, and "by the use of a little judicious flattery," he reported a few days later, tried to convince him that the association desperately needed his help—and the two thousand dollars Gomez had already collected. "To nullify any feeling that we outsiders are interfering and contributing only advice," he and Spingarn made a dramatic appearance at the Detroit branch's regular Sunday afternoon rally, Black Bottom's Macedonia Baptist ringing with cheers as the pair grandly presented Bradby with a five-hundred-dollar contribution from the national office to the branch's coffers, a considerable down payment on the colored lawyers' fees. By the time White boarded a train for a Chicago rendezvous with Darrow Tuesday afternoon,

Detroit's Talented Tenth was awash in warm feelings for the association's selfless efforts on their behalf, a month's worth of conflict seemingly forgiven and forgotten.[25]

Finally, on Thursday, October 15, James Weldon Johnson sent word
to the nation's newspapers that Darrow and Hays had been retained.
Except for the fact that the trial was set to open the following Monday,
the timing was perfect. The NAACP's legal campaign against residential segregation was about to reach its climax: though the clerk of the
Supreme Court had not yet given the association's legal team a firm
date for oral arguments on the Washington, D.C., restrictive covenant
case, everyone assumed the session would be held sometime in
November. In preparation for that day, Louis Marshall had put the finishing touches on the association's brief; copies lay in stacks around
NAACP headquarters, waiting for the press to take notice. What's
more, the meeting of the Garland Fund's board of directors was only
two weeks away. Johnson had his application for seed money to create
a permanent Legal Defense Fund nearly ready for Moorfield Storey's
approval and submission.[26] Now all he needed was the rush of publicity that would make the progressives on the board take notice of the
association's battle to beat back the segregationist tide.

There was no press conference to announce Darrow's joining the
defense team, just a page-long announcement crafted with the skill of
a veteran publicist who knew the importance of framing a breaking
story. First came a quick recounting of the shooting, justified as an act
of self-defense, followed by an explicit linking of the violence on steaming Garland Avenue with the fight about to be waged in the Supreme
Court's velvet-draped chamber. Finally, Johnson made his pitch to the
masses he'd been trying to rally to the cause for the better part of a
year. To colored men and women, he offered the same warning he'd
been issuing since the association first took up the Sweets' case in
September: "If in Detroit the Negro is not upheld in the right to defend
his home . . . then no decent Negro home anywhere in the United
States will be safe." To white progressives, he appealed to principle, to
ethnics, he presented self-interest, the two arguments blended together in the message he'd been honing ever since the KKK's brand of
Anglo-Saxon supremacy had spread across the urban North. "This
practice of segregation must be faced in a common sense way," he argued. "The practice is absurd and un-American. If you begin by segregating members of one race, you may easily come to the point where
segregation is made into a matter of creed as well as race. . . . Of

course America is not going to stand for it. It would undermine the very foundation of American citizenship."[27]

The result was electric. After a month of maddening silence, the Sweets' story suddenly raced across the color line, virtually all the major dailies down the east coast urban corridor giving the story prominent play while the wire services flashed the association's announcement to smaller papers nationwide. Understandably, most of the press focused on Darrow taking up the defense of Negroes, race substituted for religion in the autumn version of the summer's Tennessee extravaganza. But in a few cases, slices of James Weldon Johnson's message came through as well. Having recounted the NAACP's version of the shooting in graphic detail, Darrow's hometown newspaper, the *Chicago Daily News*, dismissed the prosecutor's presentation of the same events as "peculiar," while the Pulitzer family's prized possession, *New York World*, called on the Detroit courts to immediately dismiss the case. "Unless there have been flagrant misrepresentations in the press reports of the incident this is a clear case of self-defense, and the Negroes had a right to protect their own lives by firing on those who sought to kill them," insisted the *World*'s editors. "The law in America is presumably broad enough to cover the Negro as well as the white man."[28]

In Detroit, Walter White punctuated the news by leading Darrow into a perfectly staged surprise appearance at the downtown courthouse to ask for a two-week delay in opening the trial. Filing the motion for a continuance was a routine matter—any of the colored lawyers could have done the job without a fuss—but when word of Darrow's presence shot through the hallways, lawyers, judges, clerks, and secretaries dashed up to Judge Murphy's fifth-floor courtroom to catch a glimpse of the nation's most famous attorney in action. An impromptu press conference followed, with a hastily assembled pack of reporters clamoring for a good quote for the early editions, photographers' flashes exploding around them, passersby stopping to point and stare. Darrow stood casually amid the chaos, surprisingly dapper in a dark pin-stripe suit and stylish pale tie, spinning the case into his personal crusade against racial intolerance. That afternoon, the story was splashed across the front pages, filling the space the Klan's mayoral candidate had hoped would be devoted to his first major appearance since the Invisible Order's sweep of the city primary ten days earlier. But a long-winded speech on the need for economy and Christian morality in city government simply couldn't compare to news that, on

Frank Murphy's order, the next trial of the century was to open in the Motor City on October 30.[29]

•

The news seeped into the Wayne County Jail the way a crisp autumn morning of incarceration began, a wan shaft of sun breaking through the darkness, gradually spreading into a pool of brilliant light dancing off the filthy gray of the cellblock walls.

The first few days of October had been particularly cruel. Cecil Rowlette had given the eleven defendants some hope that at the October 3 hearing Judge Murphy would grant his carefully argued motion to dismiss the charges. So when the proceedings ended like the ones before, with Murphy denying the motion and the defendants marching back to their jail cells, the defeat seemed particularly crushing. Amid the depression of the next days, the conflicts between the defendants flared again, most of the group desperately clinging to their faith in their lawyers' ability, the three insurance men and Davis, the federal agent, again complaining that Rowlette, Perry, and Mahoney were incompetent, their failures "almost criminal." So deep was their anger that the four sent off yet another telegram to the NAACP's New York office, all but demanding new representation, the absence of the others' signatures a silent condemnation of their foolishness.[30]

Almost as soon as the telegram was dispatched, however, the situation began to improve. On Tuesday evening, October 6, Gladys was released on bail, her ten-thousand-dollar bond secured by friends of her parents. For Ossian, the news must have come as a great relief. At last she could have a taste of the comforts he desperately wanted for himself: a decent night's sleep, a measure of privacy, a few moments of peace, the chance to cuddle with their daughter. Three days later, Ossian received an enigmatic telegram from Walter White, saying that the association was "conducting negotiations with one of the most eminent criminal lawyers in [the] country." A week passed without any elaboration. Then, on October 15, Bradby arrived at the jail with word that Clarence Darrow would be taking control of the defense. The news seemed so unlikely that the defendants didn't quite believe it at first. Late the next morning, though, the guards escorted the ten men out of their cells and down to the visitors' room, where they found Darrow waiting for them, Walter White beaming by his side.[31]

Darrow remembered the moment in his memoirs. "On my way

home from New York," he wrote, "I stopped in Detroit to find out what I could about the case. I found my clients all in jail, excepting one, the wife of one of the defendants, who had been admitted to bail; the rest were men and boys." That wasn't quite the way it happened. Darrow came from Chicago, not New York; before he arrived in the jailhouse, he had already spent the better part of a day with White, poring over the case's details; and from that discussion, he knew all of the defendants still imprisoned were men, not boys.[32]

"Did the defendants shoot into that mob?" Darrow had asked White in the course of their conversation. White hesitated, fearing the Great Defender might be put off if he thought his clients responsible for a white man's death. "I am not sure—" he mumbled. Annoyed, Darrow cut in. "Don't try to hedge. I know you weren't there. But do you believe the defendants fired?" White reluctantly admitted that in his opinion they had. Good, growled Darrow. "If they had not the courage to shoot back in defense of their own lives, I wouldn't think they were worth defending."[33]

"I have seldom seen such joy in the faces of any persons as appeared on those of the defendants when I introduced Mr. Darrow to them," White recalled a few days later. For the longest time, Darrow sat with Ossian and the others, listening to them recount the evening on Garland Avenue, gently pressing them to admit to the shooting rather than cling to the unlikely stories they had concocted the night of the police interrogation, quietly reassuring them that the case could be won even if they had fired into the crowd, bridging the chasm between the famous white lawyer and ten desperately afraid colored men with his remarkable gift for empathy. As he strained to hear Darrow's words, spoken so softly they seemed a whisper, Otis Sweet felt the numbness that had afflicted him—the sickening sense of inevitable defeat—begin to fade. "He talked to you and tried to [see] just how you felt," Sweet remembered years later, "then he'd fill in to show you there wasn't nothing to be afraid of."[34]

A month of perpetual fear wasn't dissipated that easily. But the defendants couldn't help but be caught up in the excitement triggered by Darrow's presence. Otis and most of the others felt it in the cell block. "The whole atmosphere of the jail changed" in the days after Darrow's appearance, he recalled. "Even the turnkeys spoke to you. . . . That's when you built up a little hope. Then they started to bet in jail between an acquittal and a conviction. Before it had been ten to one for conviction."[35] For Ossian and Gladys, the flicker of hope quickly flamed into something more. It took a few days for the Negro press, dominated by weeklies, to pick up the news of Darrow's hiring. When the story finally broke, Ossian—the cowering boy in the bulrushes, the medical student hiding in his rooms as gunfire filled the streets of the capital, the ambitious doctor determined to secure his place among the Talented Tenth—suddenly found himself not simply one of eleven defendants but a national symbol of New Negro militancy, while his charming young wife was swept into the marvels of celebrity.

Not even James Weldon Johnson and Walter White had anticipated just how vigorously colored newspapers would support the Sweets once Darrow had drawn their attention to the cause. From the South came uncharacteristically forthright calls for equal justice, editors emboldened by the fact that they were writing about a northern outrage. "As goes Dr. Sweet," Houston's black weekly shouted, "so goes the American Negro! Selah!" "The case affects every Negro in America, whether he lives in Detroit, Chicago, Jacksonville, or Bartow," echoed the *Florida Sentinel.* "If a group of people can band themselves together and exclude a Negro from one particular section in any American [city] they can bind together and keep a Negro out of every section." For the colored paper in Little Rock, Arkansas, an hour's train ride from the ruins of black Tulsa, the cause was even broader. "Dr. Sweet and . . . his friends have set an example worthy to be followed by all true American citizens," the paper read. "The question is deeper and farther reaching than . . . whether Negroes shall be secure in their inalienable rights but a question as to whether American citizenship shall be robbed and pillaged of their most sacred heritage, a heritage vouchsafed in the constitution; the question whether prejudice and hatred shall rule our nation or whether a pure democracy shall prevail. . . ."[36]

The more influential big-city sheets were just as enthralled with Ossian's courageous stand. "If it is true that Dr. Sweet fired into the crowd of whites to keep them from rushing his home . . . then he was certainly within his rights, and should be supported by every law-abiding citizen in Detroit," wrote the *Chicago Defender's* fearsome publisher, Robert Abbott, in an editorial Ossian was almost sure to have read. "White people in Detroit, as well as other cities, may as well know now as later that our Race will no longer run from our homes because they object to us. They may as well learn, also, that we will live where we can afford to live if we have to keep an armed guard posted continuously. If the police cannot protect us from mob violence, then we must be prepared to protect ourselves."[37]

Washington, D.C.'s colored paper seconded the *Chicago Defender*'s militant righteousness. "We have learned through the years since slavery passed to fight our enemies with their own weapons. If physical violence is offered we kill in self-defense." The *Amsterdam News*, Harlem's hometown newspaper, likewise rang with pride in Ossian's actions. "Possibly the most important court case the Negro has ever figured in all the history of the United States is [about to be] heard out in Detroit Michigan," proclaimed the paper with a touch of hyperbole. "Thank God Dr. Sweet moved in! Thank God that his noble wife moved in with him! And thank God nine of his relatives and friends came in with him! . . . This is the spirit of unity the Negro must more and more evidence if he is to survive. He must face death if he is to live! He must be willing to die fighting when he is right! When police authorities fail to protect him and his family; when courts of law desert him; when his own government fails to take a stand in his behalf, he faces death anyway, and might just as well die fighting!"[38]

Publicity begot money. Johnson waited for the initial rush of news to abate before announcing that the NAACP's accounts were empty and donations were desperately needed to pay even the reduced fees of Darrow and Hays. Almost instantly, the cash came pouring in. The Detroit defense fund, which had been slowly dwindling since the Sweets' arrest, shot upward. The first Sunday mass meeting after Johnson announced Darrow's hiring brought in two hundred dollars, a very solid showing; the second—held amid the crush of stories in the Negro press—netted three times as much. "It's a pity I had not laid out ten days for Detroit," the NAACP's field secretary, William Pickens, reported back to New York after a furious weekend of fund-raising. "We just have things HOT now." The heat spread to other cities as well. NAACP branches in Chicago, New York, Philadelphia, Cleveland, Toledo, and Washington, D.C., organized rallies on the Sweets' behalf, as did the students of Howard University, who packed the campus's spiritual center, Rankin Chapel, in a stirring demonstration of support for one of their own. Wilberforce could claim three of the defendants, two of them current students, but there wasn't quite as much money in Xenia's glens as there was on Howard's hill. When the faculty passed the hat, the most generous donation—five dollars—came from the commander of the campus cadet corps, on whose parade ground the Sweets had learned the skills of self-defense.[39]

Now that she was free, Gladys became the defendants' public face. Rather than move back to her parents' house, she rented a flat four long blocks away from her mother, on another completely white street a little more than a mile northwest of the deserted bungalow. It was a small but comfortable place, well-appointed with the furniture that was supposed to have gone into her family's new home. But in the weeks before the trial, Gladys was too busy to spend much time there. Her days were filled with requests from Darrow and Hays, filtered through Walter White, for information to track down and witnesses to secure, and with appearances at NAACP meetings, Sunday rallies, and, for one poignant evening, a benefit at the Arcadia Ballroom, where she sat with the other defendants' wives watching couples twirl around the dance floor as she and Ossian had done the night they met. She found all the attention thrilling. "I consider it quite an honor and of no little importance to be noticed by a person as busy and so much in demand as yourself," she wrote White with just a touch of flirtation the last week of October. "If things keep on I shall soon believe myself to be quite a personage."[40]

The outpouring of support turned Ossian's head, too. Gladys packed her visits to the jail with news of the latest rallies, and no doubt she handed over the most recent issues of the *Chicago Defender*, the *Courier*, and the other Negro publications to which the couple subscribed so that her husband could see the tributes being lavished upon him. How extraordinary it must have been for Ossian to read the great Du Bois's searing treatment of his case in the November *Crisis*, which arrived in the mail at the tail end of October, to have the very man who coined the term "Talented Tenth" hold him up as a model for the young men of the race to emulate, in explicit contrast to Alexander Turner, whose decision to flee from the rabble the editor bitterly recounted. "Which [example] would you follow," Du Bois asked his forty thousand devoted readers, "if you were 'free,' black and 21?"[41]

To be the object of such praise was so heady an experience it was easy for Ossian to let slip the memory of his own hesitations and prevarications. He couldn't forget the paralyzing terror he'd felt the night of the shooting: the uncontrollable shaking of his hands as he tried to load the pistol he never fired; the sight of the mob as he opened the door to let Otis and Davis inside; the moment the guns went off above him and the very walls seemed to shudder. But he began to see the road he had followed to Garland Avenue as much straighter, his steps more purposeful, than they had actually been. Over time, Ossian would find just the right words. He had dared to move into the bungalow, he would say again and again, "only because my group had been chased all over town and there didn't seem to be anyone left to take the lead in the great fight to secure a decent place in which to live." The reluctant hero standing for principle when all others had failed: it was a worthy image for a man who so desperately wanted to make his life exemplary and a comforting thought when the light of day faded and Ossian was forced to contemplate the weeks ahead, when his future would depend on Clarence Darrow's ability to tell a story as inspiring as the one Ossian had come to believe.[42]

◆

"It is a thrilling situation," a buoyant Walter White wrote one of his many friends a week before the trial was to open. "We have got a very hard fight on our hands. [But] with Mr. Darrow as our chief counsel, we have got a fighting chance to win out." Obviously, the Great Defender was the key. White loved being in his company, listening to the old man talk of philosophy and politics, gossiping about their mutual friends among the literati, watching him map out the defense in his mind, adding the occasional suggestion, for which Darrow seemed genuinely grateful. White also adored the swirl of excitement Darrow brought in his wake. Walter's schedule was crowded with speaking engagements at rallies and forums devoted to the Sweets, while his mailbox overflowed with congratulatory messages: bringing Darrow into the case was "a great stroke," wrote James Cobb, himself immersed in the upcoming Supreme Court challenge; it was "a masterstroke," said another lawyer who'd fought his share of race cases; even the young poet Langston Hughes, hidden away in a Montmartre garret, sent a note saying that Darrow's hiring "is certainly fine."[43]

But it wasn't Darrow's presence alone that gave White hope that the case might be won. There were also surprising signs of movement in Detroit, where the white progressives seemed at last to be shaking off their month-long stupor. White picked up the first hints of change during the weekend he spent settling the NAACP's conflict with the colored lawyers, when he squeezed in an hour or so to chat with Frank Murphy about the trial. White didn't know much about the man before the meeting, but what his informants had told him wasn't particularly encouraging. Word was that Murphy had maneuvered the Sweet case into his courtroom because he hoped his unbiased handling of the trial would solidify his support among colored voters, whom he had to have on his side when he ran for mayor in two years' time. But then Murphy had rejected Cecil Rowlette's motion to dismiss the charges against the Sweets, a bitter disappointment, and now a lot of colored men—and not a few whites as well—doubted whether Murphy would have "the grit to stand boldly" against the prosecution's framed-up case.[44]

As soon as White settled into the judge's rooms, though, he was bathed in Murphy's self-conscious compassion. He didn't record the judge's precise words. But White was struck by his seemingly deep sympathy for Negroes ("I like them," he told a girlfriend, "because they are so out of luck and get the worst of each deal"), his commitment to maintaining a color-blind courtroom, and his obvious relish in taking on a case that would put his principles to the test. "The question of how to secure a fair trial for the eleven colored defendants is constantly on my mind," Murphy said to his sister a few weeks later. "Above all I want them to know that they are in a court where the true ideal of justice is constantly sought. A white judge, white lawyers and twelve white jurymen are sitting in judgment of eleven who are colored black. This alone is enough to make us fervent in our effort to do justice. I want the defendants to know that true justice does not recognize color." No doubt White heard much the same speech, Murphy's matinee-idol face soft with emotion, his blue eyes glistening. The performance was so impressive that as soon as he arrived in Chicago, where he was to spend the day with Darrow, White rushed off to Marshall Field's and bought a thumbed-through copy of *The Fire in the Flint*. The book arrived in Murphy's mailbox a few days later. "It was a very real pleasure to meet you, and a most pleasant surprise to find one with such lofty ideals," read the inscription. "It is so seldom that those of us who are trying to secure even-handed justice for Negro citizens encounter one like yourself you may well imagine our joy when that experience does come."[45] Obviously, White was indulging in his incomparable gift for flattery. But the note also expressed a genuine sense of awe—and not a little relief. In a city full of Klansmen, White had found St. Francis.

Murphy's almost ethereal sense of fairness was complemented by a suddenly surging, uncompromisingly aggressive campaign to crush the Ku Klux Klan's drive for control of city hall. Once the enormity of the KKK's sweep of the October 6 primary sank in, Mayor Johnny Smith shunted aside his race baiting of early September—the hints of a colored-Klan conspiracy, the promises to keep Detroit's white neighborhoods racially pure—and again embraced the muscular street politics that had been his hallmark.

Day after day, he worked to ignite the passions of his electoral base in the ethnic neighborhoods of the east side, rubbing his voice raw with speeches at the Holy Name Society, the Weinman Settlement House, and St. Margaret Mary's Hall; swapping war stories with the grizzled men gathered at the VFW post; pumping hundreds of calloused hands as the afternoon shift trooped through the gates of the Dodge Brothers' mammoth factory. Everywhere he went Smith hammered at Klan intolerance, his square jaw firmly set, his fist slamming into his open palm in his signature style. The city's foreign-born, its Catholics, its Jews—they were all victims of the Invisible Order's attacks, he insisted. He, too, felt the sting. "I was born in this country," he told a banquet hall full of Lithuanian businessmen on the day Darrow's hiring was made public. "My father fought in the Civil War. I myself fought in the Spanish War and the Philippine Insurrection. I have done nothing but work hard all my life. . . . Yet they say I am not an American." He wouldn't let such a slander stand. Neither should they. "Those who have made America great are the men and women of all races who have mingled in this country," he proclaimed from the dais. "I venture to say there is not a person at this table who does not better understand and more truly follow the concepts of America than any of these self-styled '100 percent Americans' who goes around with a hood over his head."[46]

Smith worked Black Bottom the same way, slashing away at the Klan's campaign, using its expansive hatreds to build a bond between himself and his audiences, whose sufferings he shared and whose dignity he was determined to defend. Though he arrived an hour late for a Sunday rally sponsored by a host of Negro organizations, including the NAACP branch, he had the crowd on his side within moments of beginning his remarks.

"Mr. Chairman," he said, "I was going to say 'my fellow countrymen,' but there is a question about my being a countryman of yours. They say I'm a foreigner, despite the fact that I was born in the city of Detroit and twice raised my right hand and swore to bear honestly and faithfully the arms of my country. But they tell me I'm a foreigner so I will have to say 'ladies and gentlemen,' I guess." As laughter rippled across the room, Smith drew his audience in. "I come to you as a candidate for mayor, not of any secret organization, but as a candidate of all the people, without regard to race, religion, or creed. . . . I feel as mayor of the city of Detroit—and it is my wish as an American citizen—that we could understand these foolish yokels who pay ten dollars apiece to hate you and me, and we could do more by trying to understand them than by abusing them and . . . preaching hate. I have not any malice in my heart for any of them; I feel sorry for them."[47]

Smith did feel malice toward Klansmen, though, deep personal malice—and as he talked his audiences felt it, too. The crowds that came to the mayor's east-side rallies hadn't necessarily experienced the Klan's chauvinism firsthand. But many of them understood what such hatred could mean. Some of them had felt it in other forms and other places. They'd seen the cossacks riding to the synagogue's steps, heard the tattoo of the Orangemen's drums coming down the road, or felt the pulse-pounding terror of the night riders' arrival at their door. For others, it was a bitter memory passed from previous generations. It was the smug landlord in Calabria, Connemara, Macedonia, or Louisiana who put out his tenants after years of faithful service. It was the petty official in some half-remembered village who said a Russian Jew couldn't own property, an Irish Catholic couldn't vote, a Negro couldn't walk the roads without a white man's permission. It was the boss at the Ukranian iron mill, the Belfast shipyard, or the North Carolina textile mill scowling at a grandfather, then a young man desperate for work, and saying, "We don't hire your kind here."

Then there were all the insults and injuries that Detroit imposed: the way a Polish-born autoworker could give Ford thirty years' labor and still never make foreman because that job was reserved for real Americans; the way a colored man had to painstakingly plot a day's outing with his sweetheart so as to avoid all those places where he wouldn't be welcome; the way a child's face looked when he had been taunted with one of the ubiquitous school-yard epithets—kike, dago, wop, mick, hunky, nigger—and knew in the very sounds of the words that he was hated. The humiliation, frustration, and fury of such moments: that was what Johnny Smith wanted his audiences to feel when he mocked the Klan.[48]

Once the mayor made the Klan his target, the city's progressive bloc rallied round him, as they had the year before. Liberal lawyers, judges, businessmen, clubwomen, and leaders of the city's fragile trade unions, all of them took to the attack, their charges invariably reprinted by the proudly partisan *Detroit Times* and normally reactionary *Detroit Free Press*, which had swung its support behind Smith. A vote for Bowles was a vote for prejudice, insisted wealthy Harriet McGraw, the doyenne of Detroit's progressive reformers, as she launched a "Women for Smith" club from the ballroom of a fine downtown hotel. If the Klan won the mayor's office, a prominent attorney said at another rally, Detroit would become "a leper colony in the eyes of the rest of the nation." From his pulpit, the minister of prestigious First Presbyterian slammed the

Klan's racism: "The blond Nordic," he proclaimed, "has no barter from the Almighty to dominate the rest of humanity."[49]

Of all the Protestant voices, though, none spoke with more authority than thirty-three-year-old Reinhold Niebuhr, whose eloquent addresses on social issues over the past few years had won him widespread attention among the city's progressive bloc. "We fair-minded Protestants cannot deny that it was Protestantism that gave birth to the Ku Klux Klan, one of the worst specific social phenomenon which the religious pride and prejudice of peoples has ever developed," he preached in a Sunday sermon that so impressed the editors of the *Detroit Free Press* they put it on the front page. "I do not deny that all religions are periodically corrupted by bigotry. But I hit Protestant bigotry the hardest at this time because it happens to be our sin and there is no use repenting for other people's sins. . . . We are admonished by Scripture to judge men by their fruits, not by their roots; and their fruits are their character, their deeds and accomplishments."[50]

Smith's opponent, Charles Bowles, tried desperately to escape the pummeling, claiming over and over that he wasn't a Klansman, that the candidates should be debating Detroit's rampant vice and criminality rather than the KKK, that Smith was heightening the fears of foreigners and Negroes to obscure his failings in office. But Bowles had drawn around himself a circle of supporters who weren't about to be silenced by their papist opponent and his progressive allies. When Bowles wasn't at the podium, his rallies shook with condemnations of the immigrant "rabble with their thumb-worn creeds," with warnings of black-robed priests engaged in papal plots to destroy American liberty, and with dark threats to "pure womanhood."[51]

Just beneath the surface lurked the danger of violence. From the sanctuary of her husband's church, a minister's wife proclaimed that any woman who voted against the Klan candidate should be "tarred and feathered." From his downtown headquarters, kleagle Ira Stout warned the newspapers to send over only Protestant reporters, since the safety of Catholics and Jews could not be assured. And when the workingmen of the Kelsey Wheel plant declined to spend their lunch break listening to one of the Klan's candidates for city council harangue them, the man pulled a pistol from his jacket and demanded that attention be paid. Such talk simply played into the hands of Smith's supporters.[52]

Bowles is undoubtedly a decent man, said the editors of the *Detroit Free Press*. "Nevertheless, about him have joined all the elements of intolerance, the haters of Catholicism, the haters of the Negro, the haters of cosmopolitanism, hundreds of sincere people who believe in the Christianity exemplified by Bryan. . . ." There was the central conflict of the campaign just as Darrow might have framed it: crabbed champions of indefensible traditions battling the heterogeneous masses of modern America; the prejudices of the old order pitted against a new vision of openness and justice.[53]

But justice had its limits. Twice during the campaign, Johnny Smith came face-to-face with those most responsible for the summer's violence: on October 16, he met with a large group of real estate men in the office of James Conley, the driving force behind the Waterworks Park Improvement Association, and four days after that, he made a foray to the city's west side—"into the very heart of the district that is reputed to be the stronghold of his Ku Klux Klan opponent," the *Detroit Times* breathlessly reported—where a mass meeting of the Tireman Avenue Improvement Association was waiting to hear him speak. It would have been easy enough to confront both those groups—surely their votes were already lost—to lecture them on rights and justice and respect for the law. But Smith didn't so much as mention the racial tensions roiling the city's neighborhoods.[54]

Nor did he find another, less volatile venue in which to make a principled stand. Not once in the many appearances that the newspapers reported did Smith defend the right of colored families to live wherever they pleased, as he had done during the July disturbances; not once did he criticize banks, insurance companies, builders, and real estate agents for hemming Negroes into Black Bottom, nor did he condemn mobs for assaulting those few who managed to break through its boundaries; not once did he talk about the Sweets, although the story was white-hot as the mayoral campaign came to a climax. It was a politic silence, given white Detroit's hostility to Negroes crossing the neighborhood color line, a simple act of omission—and an unrepentant sin of commission in the ongoing construction of a segregated city.

♦

Clarence Darrow saw it all unfold in front of him.

Frank Murphy had given him just two weeks to prepare for trial, two weeks to gather whatever evidence he could and to make of it a solid defense. Most attorneys would have been overwhelmed by the thought of it. But Darrow simply sat in his office, watching the information pile up around him, waiting for inspiration to strike.

News of Detroit's maelstrom arrived in fragments. From his lone jail-house visit, he had his clients' own version of the fatal night on Garland Avenue. Perry, Rowlette, and Mahoney also provided Darrow with the evidence they'd accumulated of the summer's violence: clippings from the *Detroit Independent* detailing the mob attack on the Mathies' home; a statement by Vollington Bristol recounting the assaults he endured; newspaper stories of the Turners' expulsion and Johnny Smith's subsequent plea for peace, all of which he filed away. During his stop in Detroit, he took the time to visit a few old friends—a venerable anarchist who once dominated Detroit's left, a judge made sympathetic in a long-ago encounter—who brought him up to speed on the mayor's furious battle to swing the ethnic masses against the Klan, while the Chicago papers provided him periodic updates on Detroit's mayoral campaign.[55] He didn't need much more. Having spent half a career defending desperate workingmen and three decades slipping in and out of Chicago's electoral cockpit, he knew better than most men how fiercely the flames of ethnic, racial, and class politics could burn once the fuse was lit.

Arthur Garfield Hays and Walter Nelson, a white Detroit attorney who was added to the defense team on Darrow's suggestion, balanced impressionistic political reporting with a cache of precise legal analyses. Although he liked to strike the same cynical pose toward his profession that Darrow had perfected, Hays was by all accounts a marvelous lawyer, a brilliant logician—as a young man he'd tutored a teenage Walter Lippmann on the fine art of debating—who was much more likely to exploit precedent and procedure than to dismiss them, in Darrow's fashion, as garroting the pursuit of justice. His talent showed in the crisp, concise material he prepared for Darrow's perusal. Many of the memos dealt with strategic issues: whether the defense would be better demanding separate trials for each of the eleven defendants, as the law allowed; how to prevent the prosecution from blurring the charges of murder and conspiracy, a tactic that had hamstrung the defense during the preliminary hearing. Most importantly, Hays and Nelson took up the painstaking work of fashioning the defense's basic brief.[56]

Using Cecil Rowlette's well-crafted motion to dismiss as a reference point, they continued to home in on the critical point of whether the people who had filled Garland the night of the shooting constituted a mob. But they stripped away the colored lawyers' concern for who fired the fatal shot, which Rowlette had seen as the weakest point in the prosecutor's case, and instead focused on whether the defendants had cause to shoot into the crowd. Rowlette's motion provided the defense with the precedent that Prosecuting Attorney Robert Toms had feared they would find: in the 1860 case of *Pond v. The People of Michigan*, the state supreme court ruled that a man threatened by mob assault had the right to defend his life and property, even if his perception of the mob's intentions proved to be incorrect. Rowlette had buried the ruling among a dozen citations; Hays and Nelson turned it into the centerpiece of the defense team's new brief, incontrovertible proof that the law was on their side.[57]

Walter White, meanwhile, handed Darrow reams of information on the perilous state of American race relations. At Hays's request, White gathered together a primer on mob violence that included James Weldon Johnson's summary of the 1919 Washington riot, a wrenching expose by the NAACP field secretary of an Arkansas field hand's immolation in 1921, White's compelling account of the Tulsa horror, and the association's careful tally of the previous year's lynchings. It was powerful material, but almost all of it dealt with southern atrocities, and none of it touched on the crusade against residential segregation that had brought the NAACP into the Sweet case in the first place. To be sure that Darrow understood that the battle of Detroit was but one part of that crusade, White also sent on copies of Louis Marshall's brief against restrictive covenants and Du Bois's long article in the November *Crisis*, two brilliantly intense analyses of the very institutional arrangements that Johnny Smith so assiduously avoided mentioning.[58]

A constitutional scholar of the first rank, Marshall built his case on a careful balancing of public policy and legal precedent. Having time and again committed itself to the principle of equality before the law, he argued, the nation cannot condone private agreements that brand one segment of its citizenry as inferior, nor can it endorse—or worse yet advance—economic arrangements that, once put into practice, would eventually balkanize the nation. For his part, Du Bois combined the rigor of the sociologist he had once been with the outrage of the propagandist he had become. In slashing strokes, he exposed the deadly interplay between prejudice and the "organized real estate interests" that controlled the modern urban housing market. White men wail that Negroes depress property values, Du Bois wrote, but it was "an ancient and bearded lie" manipulated by profit-hungry real estate agents, bankers, and builders to codify racial exclusion and by so doing to create the fetid ghettos that even "decent, quiet, educated" colored families cannot escape. And when, "by bribery, politics and brute force," a few brave

Negroes manage to break through the barriers erected against them, they had to face white homeowners transformed into murderous mobs by the fears that these interests induced. "Dear God! Must we not live?" he roared so that heaven and Harlem both would hear. "And when a whole city full of white folk led and helped by banks, Chambers of Commerce, mortgage companies and 'realtors' are combing the earth for every bit of residential property for whites, where in the name of God are we to live and live decently if not by these same whites?"[59]

A more disciplined mind might have moved methodically through such a jumble of material, fitting facts into the law's rigid rules, organizing ideas and arguments into logical sequences, building an ironclad case. That wasn't Darrow's way. He didn't see the need for painstaking preparation, not when he had at his command forty years' worth of words and images that he was sure could hold a courtroom transfixed, not when he knew that there was always a way to make a jury want nothing more than to set his clients free, not when he intended to transform the trial into yet another engagement in his life-long battle against the established order. It was enough to have a feel for the case and its context, and to rely on wit, manipulation, and his incomparable persuasive powers to do the rest. A fellow lawyer, anxious to see how Darrow constructed "the steelwork" of another murder case, once asked to see the file the Great Defender had assembled to lead him through the trial. Clarence showed him "four or five little half line notes on a yellow pad, which he then proceeded to throw down and leave behind him on the desk when the court said, 'Very well, you may proceed now, Mr. Darrow.'" The Sweets deserved no less of his attention, and received no more.[60]

By Friday morning, October 30, Clarence Darrow was ready to go to court.

◆

Walter White had taken the overnight train to Detroit so often in the past two months that the trips had started to blend together. But this time, the journey had a special edge. It must have been difficult to say good-bye to his wife and baby daughter knowing that he might not see them again for a month or more, to watch out the train window as Manhattan gradually faded into the dusk, and to awaken the next morning to the sight of smog-shrouded Detroit drawing into view, its skyline particularly bleak in the weak light of dawn. The burdens of the assignment were eased, though, by the thought that within an hour of his arrival he'd be sitting at the press table of Frank Murphy's courtroom watching Darrow open the drama that he and James Weldon Johnson had helped to create, and that whatever happened over the next few weeks, the NAACP's triumph was all but assured.[61]

The news had come shortly before White left headquarters to catch his train. After careful consideration, the board of directors of the Garland Fund had voted to support James Weldon Johnson's proposal to create a permanent Legal Defense Fund. The decision wasn't surprising. Johnson's position on the board assured the proposal a full hearing, while the hiring of Darrow and Hays, both close friends of board chairman Roger Baldwin and champions of the causes other Garland Fund members held dear, made approval all but automatic. Still, the announcement was extraordinarily exciting.

The NAACP was to receive five thousand dollars of Charles Garland's fortune immediately—enough to cover Darrow's entire fee—to be followed by an additional fifteen thousand dollars as soon as the association raised twice that sum on its own. A few months earlier, Johnson would have despaired at the thought of having to secure thirty thousand dollars in donations. But now that the Sweet case was riveting black America, even such a demanding goal seemed well within reach. Naturally, the fund-raising would require a great deal of organizing. But there was every reason to believe that by the time the jury rendered its verdict and White finally headed home to Harlem, the NAACP would have an astounding fifty thousand dollars endowment, "the munitions of war," as Johnson put it in his first blast of publicity, "for such a fight in behalf of justice for the Negro as has not been fought since the Civil War."[62]

When White walked into the downtown courthouse sometime after nine o'clock, the corridors were already packed with people—two hundred or more, the vast majority of them Negroes, a boisterous mob crowded outside the courtroom's closed doors, jostling for position so that when the specially posted guards opened the way, they were ready to make a mad dash for seats. Gradually, White pushed his way to the front, flashed the press pass Murphy had provided him, and with a nod to the policemen slipped inside.[63]

It was a compact space, much smaller than the cavernous courtroom from which the Scopes trial had been broadcast to the world, but it had a simple elegance unusual in a city that valued speed of production over quality of workmanship. Its floor was a slick marble, as was the six-foot-high wainscoting that ran along all the walls. Above the white wainscoting, the plaster was painted a tasteful gray, its dark hue softened by the light that streamed in through three large windows. White passed by the six or so rows of chairs reserved for spectators—all of them sure to be filled as soon as the guards allowed the crowd in the corridor to stream in—pulled back the low gate in the railing that ran the fifty-foot length of the chamber, and stepped into the courtroom's overcrowded well. Directly in front of him stood the judge's towering mahogany bench, beside it the witness box, and in front a long, narrow table where the clerk of the court and the stenographer would sit. To White's left, along the far wall, was the bench reserved for the defendants and to his right the still-empty jury box. Somehow the court had managed to fit in two more substantial tables as well, one to be shared by the prosecution and the defense, the other set aside for the press. White squeezed in among the other reporters and within a matter of minutes was working his charm, chatting happily about the editors he knew back in Manhattan, all of whom he was sure would love to read the novels his fellow newsmen had tucked away in the bottom drawers of their desks, awaiting discovery of their genius.[64]

Prosecuting attorney Robert Toms, tall, handsome, and dignified, arrived first, accompanied by his assistant, Ted Kennedy, and together they took possession of the half of the lawyer's table nearest the jury box. Then the quiet of the courtroom was broken by a burst of cheers in the hallway. Again the doors creaked open and in ambled Darrow, seemingly oblivious to the applause that had greeted him, more an old man come to do another day's work than the acclaimed champion of the poor, the dispossessed, the weak, and the erring. A few minutes later, the clerk called the court to order, Frank Murphy took the bench, and *The People v. Sweet, et al.* was called to the bar of justice.[65]

Most of that first day struck White and his fellow reporters as terribly tedious. In his determination to be scrupulously fair, Murphy had summoned a particularly large panel of one hundred and twenty potential jurors. Almost half of those called failed to show up. But that still left sixty-five men and women for the opposing lawyers to sift through in search of the perfect twelve. Prosecutor Toms began the process. All morning and well into the afternoon, he stood before the jury box, methodically quizzing each of the dozen men and women picked at random from among the sixty-five, while Darrow sat silently at the far end of the lawyer's table, one arm slung over the back of his chair, his head hunched between his broad shoulders, his eyes fixed on the middle distance. Toms tinkered with the panel, excusing four men for cause, questioning their replacements as he had the others in his unfailingly professional manner. It was close to three o'clock when he declared the jurors in the box acceptable to the prosecution and turned the twelve over to the defense for examination.[66]

Darrow slowly got to his feet, jammed his hands into his pockets, and sauntered over to the front rail of the jury box. When he began to speak, his voice was so soft that the reporters on the other side of the room strained to hear him. His questions were equally intimate. He wanted to know the jurors' birthplaces, nationalities, professions, and political affiliations. He asked them whether they owned their homes, what they thought of Negroes moving into their neighborhoods, and whether a man had a right to defend his property from mob attack. It was almost always done in a casual way, as if Darrow and the juror he was questioning were two strangers standing in a corner bar making conversation. There were moments, though, when the tone would change. Frank Buell's answers seemed ordinary enough: born and bred in the United States, just like his parents before him, he was in his sixty-fourth year; over the course of his life he'd held a number of jobs—the best of them working as a clerk in a factory—but now that he was getting older, he was scraping by on a night watchman's wages and living under his son-in-law's roof. Darrow heard something, though— a phrase, a word, perhaps just an inflection—that he didn't like. "Are you a member of any secret societies which you do not care to discuss here?" he suddenly said, and everyone in the courtroom knew he was asking about the Ku Klux Klan. Buell admitted that he was.[67]

You may step down, Darrow snarled, and in that unexpectedly sharp command rang the righteousness of Garrison, Douglass, Brown, and their abolitionist brethren.

The first great battle in James Weldon Johnson's newly proclaimed war against racial injustice had begun.

NINE

PREJUDICE

All of Friday afternoon and Saturday morning, October 30 and 31, Clarence Darrow interrogated the jurors that the prosecution had passed. Slowly, the faces in the jury box changed. A second juror was dismissed because he held membership in the Ku Klux Klan, two others because they made their living as real estate agents. When a colored man was called, Darrow sent him off without a single question, saying that the prosecutor was sure to discharge him. A white woman was asked to step down when she revealed that she had recently served on a jury that had convicted a defendant of manslaughter. A second woman said that if Negroes moved into her neighborhood she would fear for her property values; she, too, was dismissed. As the overcrowded courtroom grew restive, a few colored spectators took to heckling the whites eliminated; prospective jurors complained that they were being intimidated; Frank Murphy, bristling, issued a sharp rebuke to the spectators from the bench. Still, Darrow kept up his exhaustive examination, lingering over each juror as if the entire proceedings depended on the answers he received. "Two days of the trial have already passed," Walter White told James Weldon Johnson on Saturday night, "most of the regular panel . . . is exhausted—and additional panel of 65 has been called—and thus far there are only two of the twelve jurors in the box who are at all satisfactory."[1]

Darrow wasn't concerned. In virtually every U.S. criminal court, lawyers were given two ways to remove a potential juror. If the venireman, as he was called, made it clear he couldn't be objective, either the prosecution or the defense could ask the court to dismiss him "for cause." Or an attorney could exercise a peremptory challenge, which allowed dismissal for no reason whatsoever. Most of the time, courts imposed strict limits on both. A hostile judge—and Darrow had met more than his share of those—could refuse a lawyer's request to dismiss for cause. And the law typically restricted the number of peremptory challenges at an attorney's disposal: when Darrow defended Big Bill Haywood, he had just ten such challenges. A defense attorney had to press each juror hard in hopes that, as the pressure mounted, the venireman would expose any biases: Darrow worked over the jurors in the Haywood trial, Big Bill said, as if he were "killing snakes." Peremptory challenges, meanwhile, were hoarded, to be used only for those jurors an attorney didn't trust but couldn't crack.[2]

This time, the circumstances were much more favorable. From Walter White's reports, Darrow understood that Frank Murphy was determined to give the defense every advantage he could, so challenging a juror for cause carried virtually no risk of judicial veto. Better still, under Michigan law, an attorney defending a client charged with murder received a generous thirty peremptory challenges. Since Darrow had not one but eleven clients, he went into jury selection with an extraordinary three hundred and thirty challenges, enough to reject three entire jury pools single-handedly. Securing that tremendous advantage was one of the key reasons he and Arthur Garfield Hays had decided against demanding separate trials for each of the defendants. Now the defense had the power to shape the perfect jury.[3]

Darrow knew what he wanted. A national magazine once asked him how to pick just the right juror. "Let us assume we are representing one of 'the underdogs'" in society, he replied. In that case, never accept a wealthy man: "He will convict, unless the defendant is accused of violating the anti-trust law, selling worthless stocks or bonds, or something of that kind. Next to the Board of Trade, for him, the penitentiary is the most important of all public buildings." A prohibitionist was just as poor a choice. "He is too solemn and holy and dyspeptic. He knows your client would not have been indicted unless he were a drinking man, and anyone who drinks is guilty of something, probably worse than what he is charged with, although it is not set out

262 • ARC OF JUSTICE

in the indictment." All women should be dismissed, since they have only recently been allowed to serve on juries "and take their new privilege seriously." Avoid any Presbyterian—"He believes in John Calvin and eternal punishment; get rid of him in the fewest possible words before he contaminates the others"—and reject all Baptists, as "they too are apt to think that the real home of all outsiders is Sheol." If a defense attorney must choose a religious man, pick a Catholic, since "he loves music and art; he must be emotional and will want to help you." An Englishman is acceptable: "He comes from a long tradition of individual rights and is not afraid to stand alone; in fact, he is never sure he is right unless the great majority is against him." So, too, a German, though he "is not so keen about individual rights except where they concern his own way of life. . . . Still he wants to do what is right, and he is not afraid." And then there were the Irish, Darrow's ideal jurors. "An Irishman is called into the box for examination. There is no reason for asking about his religion. He is Irish; that is enough. We may not agree with his religion, but it matters not, his feelings go deeper than any religion. You should be aware that he is emotional, kindly and sympathetic. If he is chosen a juror, his imagination will place him in the dock; he is trying himself. You would be guilty of malpractice if you got rid of him, except for the strongest of reasons."[4]

That was Darrow the court jester, standing the social order on its head, laughing all the while. The humor must have struck younger sophisticates as a tad old-fashioned: florid Catholics, freethinking Germans, and misty-eyed Irishman may have seemed the shocking antithesis of polite society in the small towns of nineteenth-century Ohio, but the avant-garde had long since passed that honor to the Bohemians, Italians, Russians, Poles, and Negroes who filled the modern city's poorest quarters. If Darrow's cultural criticism wasn't quite up-to-date, his understanding of social conflict remained as sharp as the day he set aside his regular practice to defend the saintly Eugene V. Debs. Across America, there were millions who knew that the powerful and the pious looked down on them because they'd been born in the wrong country, they worshipped in the wrong church, they belonged to the wrong class, or their skin was too dark a shade. Those who recognized these bitter realities were just the sort of people Darrow wanted to fill a jury box, because when he put society's bigotry and brutality on trial, those were the citizens whom, he believed, would take his side.[5]

And in the trial's brief weekend recess, it became clear to Darrow that Detroit was full of the people he wanted to find.

•

Johnny Smith's voice was reduced to a rasp as he headed into the final few days of the mayoral campaign. With the election scheduled for Tuesday, November 3, he maintained a feverish pace, barnstorming through the east side, his entourage enveloped in ever-larger crowds wherever he appeared. Hundreds gathered at St. Hedwig's Church, in Black Bottom's Masonic hall, and at the Moose Temple. Fifteen hundred greeted him at the Elks headquarters, two thousand at the Dom Polski Hall, and a reported six thousand at the downtown Detroit armory, just three blocks from Hastings Street. Yet however weak his voice, however much fatigue his face revealed, when Johnny Smith started to speak, he pulled them all to their feet—the workingmen, the ethnics, the Negroes, and the middle-class reformers—with his uncompromising attacks on the enemy they shared. "Kill forever this unholy, un-American thing—the Ku Klux Klan," he told the throng at Dom Polski. "Go to the polls. See to it that your wives and sisters and brothers, your friends and your neighbors go to the polls. You have a sacred duty to perform. It is not to elect John Smith mayor. That is of little importance. Your duty is to serve notice for all time upon the forces of intolerance and bigotry that they have no place in an American community. . . . Keep Detroit an American city!"[6]

For those who didn't find their way into Smith's rallies—two thousand were turned away from the armory because there wasn't an inch of space in which to put them—the mayor's supporters spread his message through a furious last-minute assault on the Invisible Empire. Both the *Detroit Times* and the *Detroit Free Press* reached their overwhelmingly working class readerships with front-page editorials so fierce they seemed almost incendiary. "When a Catholic or a Jew or a Negro of the A.E.F. went slogging in the mud beneath the Flanders stars to hellish death beyond," sneered the editor of the *Detroit Free Press* in an open letter to the Klan's campaign manager, Ira Stout, "some people called it Americanism, but you and I, Ira, refused to be misled. We had small sympathy for those women back home who cried over the O'Reillys, the Cohens and the Bert Williamses in the roll of casualties. Americanism, we know, is a special monopoly of native-born white Protestants."[7]

A phalanx of religious leaders rallied the faithful. Once again, Reinhold Niebuhr led the attack. "The tragedy of today is that so many Protestants are being corrupted by prejudice instead of using their influence to dispel intolerance," he declared in a perfectly timed Sunday evening address. "Prejudice has supplanted the American ideal of brotherhood and good will. The bestial attitude of our jungle ancestry flames up anew." At Temple Beth El, the oldest and most prestigious synagogue in the city, Rabbi Leo Franklin pleaded with Detroit Jewry to stand up for "the American ideal of freedom and equality and the rights of men which you wish to hand down unsullied and unstained to your children." And imperious Bishop Michael Gallagher, the son of an Irish-born boilermaker, fairly shook with fury as he condemned the Klan's attempt "to make Detroit the 'Atlanta' of the north, in preparation to undo the work of Grant, Sherman and Lincoln, who preserved . . . the unity of the nation and the equality of all citizens—black or white, Jew or Gentile, native or foreign born."[8]

Black Bottom, meanwhile, was flooded with copies of the Saturday, October 31, issue of the *Chicago Defender*, which proclaimed that twelve million Negroes were waiting for their brothers and sisters in Detroit to "deal the death blow to the Ku Klux Klan." Colored men and women hardly needed the encouragement. When Smith's opponent, Charles Bowles, tried to deliver a long-planned address at a hall on Sherman Street, not far from Otis Sweet's empty office, he was all but driven from the stage. By Monday night, emotions were running so high the police department was readying its riot squad, should Election Day descend into violence.[9]

There was no violence, though, just a massive outpouring of voters, a quarter million of them, filling polling places from the moment they opened Tuesday at 7:00 A.M.—slightly too late for those who worked the auto factories' morning shifts—until they closed at eight o'clock that evening. The Klan vote slipped somewhat on the west side, while Johnny Smith swept through the east side with extraordinary force. In the heart of Black Bottom, Smith won 2,048 votes, Bowles just 94, while the precinct around Clinton Street, Ossian's first home on the ghetto's edge, gave Smith 447 votes to Bowles's 43. The near east side immigrant wards went for Smith by margins of two or three to one. And even in the Garland Avenue area—bloody Garland—Smith beat Bowles by 68 votes. By midnight, word was leaking out of city hall. Smith had been reelected by a 31,000 vote margin.[10]

Only then did trouble flare. Some thirty Klansmen were gathered on the sidewalk outside the Invisible Empire's headquarters north of downtown when a motorcade of three hundred Smith supporters rumbled into view. In panic, the Kluxers fled inside, where they huddled together awaiting assault. A few rocks were thrown, some windows smashed. Then one courageous Klansmen, J. S. White, strode out the front door cradling a rifle and threatening to shoot into the crowd. A squad of policeman arrived before he had the chance to open fire, and with a quick, efficient show of force, order was restored. The next day's newspapers buried the incident beneath an avalanche of election news. But perhaps Fleta Mathies, Vollington Bristol, or the Sweet brothers noticed it—and smiled.[11]

Clarence Darrow must have smiled, too, in his silent way. He never commented on the election—not to the pack of reporters who followed his every move in the courtroom, not in the numerous lectures he gave while he was in Detroit, not in the memoir he wrote a decade later. But he had to have read at least some of the weekend's papers, which put the initial accounts of the trial right alongside detailed reports of the campaign's final furious days. On Saturday, he heard the assurances of his lunchtime companion, one of the city's most generous Jewish philanthropists, who said that the bitterness that had gripped Detroit throughout the long summer had in the last few weeks begun to give way.[12] And he was confident that the time was right to pick a jury.

When Darrow returned to court Monday morning, Arthur Garfield Hays finally at his side, his mood was positively buoyant. To squash the heckling of the previous session, White had stacked the gallery with members of the Talented Tenth, including two of the most powerful pastors in Black Bottom, Joseph Gomez and Everard Daniels. As it turned out, the spectators had few opportunities to give the jurors a hard time. Though he still had 307 of his peremptory challenges remaining, Darrow and Hays dismissed only eight veniremen that day, six of them for cause, before declaring that they were satisfied. Prosecutor Toms spent the balance of Monday undoing most of the defense's handiwork, clearing out nine jurors with his peremptory challenges and another fifteen for cause. Even that didn't seem to bother Darrow, who seemed more intent on winning over the courtroom with his gentleness than in crushing whatever snakes may have been lurking in the jury box. "[He] is the most amazing figure I've ever seen," Walter White wrote, one master manipulator admiring the work of another. "He's got the . . . judge, clerk, [and] attendants all with him. Most of the jurors are eager—too eager in view of the strength of the Klan here—to serve, and he every so often makes some droll remark that sets the entire court to laughing and instantly all tension is relieved." By the close of court Monday, the jury was still completely in flux, but Darrow headed off to dinner confident that after Tuesday's election he would have no trouble settling on twelve men and women to his liking.[13]

Robert Toms opened Wednesday as he had finished Monday, moving veniremen in and out of the box in search of the perfect combination. Three potential jurors he dismissed for cause and four others, the only women on the panel, he eliminated with his peremptory challenges, so that by the time he was done, shortly after lunch, half the jurors who had begun the day in the box had been replaced. Although they had the ability to reject all of Tom's choices, Darrow and Hays asked just one to step down: a clerk at Studebaker who defiantly admitted to being a member of the Klan, the third member of the Invisible Order that the defense had ferreted out of the jury pool. A substitute was selected. Then Darrow signaled to the bench that he would ask no more questions. The jury was set.[14]

The panel wasn't as cohesive as it might have been had Darrow taken more time with the selection process. All the jurors were white, as everyone in the courtroom knew they would be. But beyond that obvious similarity, the differences among them seemed great. A handful spoke with immigrants' accents—a Scot's burr, a German's throaty rumble—though most had the flat twangs of native midwesterners. Seven were Catholic, the others, presumably, from various Protestant denominations or of no faith at all. Many of them were family men with children at home, though John Welke, at seventy-three, was well beyond that stage of life, while twenty-one year old John Moralle, who still lived with his parents, was yet to enter it. They came from all across the city, from the relentlessly grim factory district on the southwest side, not far from where Henry Ford was building his monumental Rouge Plant, to within walking distance of the bungalow on Garland Avenue, and one man, Harold Anderson, lived so close to Spokane Avenue that he would have heard the mob's cheers the night they drove out Alexander Turner. Some were homeowners, others renters, and several boarded with relatives.

Even in his haste, though, Darrow hadn't neglected what he considered the basics. The jury had the class bias he hoped to see. John Welke and William Whalen had retired, and poor John Zang couldn't seem to keep a job. All the others were working men: six were factory hands, one a housepainter, another an electrician, yet another a streetcar conductor. Though most of the twelve were native-born, every one of them was related to immigrants. Zang's parents had come to the United States from Alsace-Lorraine, his wife's people from Ireland. William Irvine's parents were Scots—dreaded Presbyterians, most likely—John Geis's wife was French Canadian, and Charles Naas's in-laws Bohemian, born and raised in Prague. There was no saying whether any of the jurors had voted for Johnny Smith. But they were the sort of people who had packed the mayor's rallies, cheering as he condemned intolerance, jeering the Klan. One day after Smith's victory, Darrow had twelve of them in the jury box.[15]

As the clerk of the court prepared to administer the jurors their oath, the Great Defender leaned over the press table on the opposite side of the room. "The case is won or lost now," he said sotto voce. "The rest is window dressing."[16]

◆

When the proceedings resumed at half past nine on Thursday, November 5, the courtroom had been transformed into a tableau of American justice. On a simple bench along one wall sat the eleven defendants, Ossian and Gladys side by side on the far end, exchanging occasional whispers but otherwise watching events with grim-faced concentration. Against the opposite wall sat twelve of their peers—in name if not in fact—arranged in two neat rows of chairs set behind a low railing. Between the two groups in the well of the courtroom stood the representative of the people, the accuser facing the accused as the finest of Anglo-Saxon traditions required, a handsome young white man come to say why eleven Negroes should spend the rest of their lives in prison paying for their crimes.[17]

The thought of squaring off against Clarence Darrow would have terrified many prosecutors, but Robert Toms refused to be intimidated. At the preliminary hearing, his office had presented just enough testimony to assure that the case would move forward. Now he wanted to overwhelm the court with witnesses willing to say that there had been no hint of violence on Garland until the Negroes started to strafe the street with gunfire. Twenty policemen were scheduled to appear for the prosecution—a parade of blue sure to impress the jury—as were forty-one of the Sweets' Garland Avenue neighbors. It wasn't a random sample of neighbors, either. To finalize the list, Toms had worked hand in hand with the officers of the Waterworks Park Improvement Association, who knew far better than he did which of the people who lived along Garland's row of houses could be trusted to say just the right thing. The association's officers themselves—James Conley, Charles Garrett, and Harold McGlynn—were kept off the witness list, so as to protect the prosecution from the secrets they might reveal under Darrow's withering cross-examination.[18]

Toms also prepared himself. Like almost everyone else in the country, he had followed the Scopes trial the previous July, and he knew that if he pushed his case too hard, Darrow would turn on him the way he'd turned on William Jennings Bryan, making him into the foil for whatever countercase the defense intended to make. So Toms decided that there would be in his performance no imitation of brilliant William Borah, Darrow's opponent in the Haywood trial, who could make the courtroom shake with his thunder, nor of the late lamented Bryan, filling Dayton, Tennessee, with bombast and bluster. Instead, Toms intended to move calmly through his witness list, piling fact upon fact, impression upon impression, a thoroughly professional, incessantly polite young man preparing to debate a point of law rather than a crusading prosecutor bringing eleven murderers to justice. "I began a studied course of humility," he said years later. "I was almost obsequious at times, and I showed [Darrow] the utmost deference." All the better to throw the old man off his stride.[19]

So when Arthur Garfield Hays demanded that the prosecution not be allowed to call its first witness until it presented to the court a bill of particulars—a maneuver designed to constrict the state by forcing it to define precisely the charges it intended to prove—Toms replied with a presentation so bloodless the jurors' eyes must have glazed over: "The theory of the people in this case," he told them, as if they were a panel of particularly strict professors of law, "is that the defendants premeditatedly and with malice aforethought banded themselves together and armed themselves with a common understanding and agreement that one or more of them would shoot to kill. . . . Further, the deceased came to his death by a bullet fired by one of the defendants, aided and abetted by all the others, in pursuance of their common understanding as set forth above." And when Darrow, slouched nonchalantly in a chair he'd pulled alongside the jury box, interrupted his examination of the first few witnesses with a string of offhand comments, Toms let the remarks pass him by while he concentrated on putting the preliminary pieces of evidence into place. A neighbor who had identified the victim's body at the morgue testified that it was indeed Leon Breiner, and the county coroner explained how the bullet that had killed him had ripped through the body from back to front, a passage he illustrated by tracing a line across the torso of the assistant prosecutor, Lester Moll.[20]

Then, shortly before noon the first day, Toms turned to the core of his case. He called Norton Schuknecht to the stand.

In his sharp dress uniform, brass buttons gleaming, gold-braided hat neatly positioned on his lap, the inspector cut a surprisingly impressive figure. Toms knew better than to expect an equally impressive performance once Schuknecht started talking. For most of the first morning, he led the inspector through the events of September 9, and with Schuknecht's terse answers, he laid the foundation upon which the state would rest its argument for conviction. Yes, his men had the situation under control that evening. No, there was no crowd on the street, "nothing more than the ordinary person walking by." Yes, there had been a few people standing on the lawn directly across from the Sweets: "I daresay there were ten or twelve," but they were "simply standing there and talking, as far as I know, I didn't see them do anything." No, those folks hadn't been throwing rocks or yelling or threatening the bungalow in any other way before the Negroes opened fire. Yes, immediately after the shooting he had gone into the pitch-black house, where his men found an arsenal of rifles and pistols but very little else, just "a few chairs and a very small table," a couple of mattresses, and "a roast of some kind standing on the oven." It was an ominous image—eleven heavily armed Negroes hidden away in an all but empty house, waiting for the opportunity to commit evil acts—and Toms let it linger as he turned from Schuknecht and stepped back toward the lawyer's table, the prosecution's most difficult task successfully completed.[21]

•

Over the next week, Toms built on his first day's work. From his parade of policemen, the prosecutor gathered a host of damning details that rounded out Schuknecht's account. Ranking officers told of the protective cocoon that surrounded the Sweets as soon as they arrived on Garland Avenue. Within an hour of Ossian and Gladys moving into the bungalow on September 8, detective inspector Bert McPherson said, he was at their front door, telling the couple "that any time of the day or night that [they] seen anything that looked suspicious to call me."[22]

From that point on, Sergeant Clayton Williams explained, the Negroes were under continual guard, provided by himself and four other patrolmen during the day and by Inspector Schuknecht each evening. And Deputy Superintendent James Sprott, second in command in a force of twenty-six hundred, described how he had personally reviewed the protective measures just an hour before the incident and found them wholly satisfactory. The men in Schuknecht's squad recalled the shooting itself. The inspector's right-hand man, Lieutenant Paul Schellenberger, saw the gunfire blaze from the bungalow's front windows; Sergeant Joseph Neighbauer heard the bullets whistle over his head as he raced across Charlevoix Avenue to call for reserves, and patrolmen Frank Lee Gill, posted in the alleyway behind the bungalow, watched two black men burst onto the second-story airing porch at the back of the house and squeeze off eight or ten shots into the street; Gill returned fire but the colored men slipped back inside unscathed.[23]

The officers who followed Schuknecht into the bungalow after the shooting told of the sparsely furnished rooms—that image again—and of the guns they found hastily hidden under mattresses and inside dresser drawers. When the patrolmen finished testifying, Toms had them come down from the witness stand to identify the weapons he'd piled up on the lawyers' table as those they'd brought out of the Sweets' home on the night Breiner died.[24]

The most dramatic testimony, though, came not from those who swarmed into the Sweets' home after the shooting but from one of the officers who stayed out on the street. Sergeant William Grohm arrived on Garland with the reserves that Schuknecht's men had summoned. No sooner had he and his fellow officers hopped down from the truck than he heard someone screaming that a man had been shot. Grohm rushed over to the Doves' front yard, where he found Leon Breiner sprawled on the porch steps, his shirt drenched in blood. "Did you see anything in the hands of the deceased?" asked Toms. "Not in his hands," Grohm answered, "not in his hands, no."

Toms led the witness to the place he wanted him to go. "Did you see anything in his mouth?" he said. "Yes, sir," replied the officer. "He had a pipe." The memory seemed so poignant—a glimpse of an ordinary life destroyed in a burst of inexplicable violence—that the moment she heard it, the widow Breiner, sitting beside her teenage daughter in the front row of the gallery, caught her breath and fainted dead away.[25]

When he turned from the cops to the Sweets' neighbors, Toms abandoned the compilation of specifics for a kaleidoscopic re-creation of the moments surrounding Breiner's death. Around the bungalow he moved, from in front of the school yard opposite the house, where seventeen-year-old Dwight Hubbard was waiting for the truck that would take him to the night shift at the Hudson Motor Car Company; to the intersection of Charlevoix and Garland, where Otto Lemhagen stood chatting with Norton Schuknecht; over to the corner market, where Edward Wettlaufer had gone to buy a loaf of bread, a bottle of milk, and a couple of bananas; to the steps of the house next door to the Sweets, where John and Della Getke were relaxing after their supper; back across the street to the Doves' front porch, where Ray Dove played with his baby, thirteen-year-olds George Suppus and Ulric Arthur were settled to watch for any excitement, and Eric Houghberg strode into a hail of gunfire; and north up Garland, where Bruce Stout was strolling on the way to visit his girl. No matter who was in the stand, Toms's questions remained the same. Was there any sort of crowd on the street before the shooting started? If a small group did gather, did the policemen move them along? Was there any threat to the peace—epithets shouted, rocks thrown, windows shattered in the doctor's house? From your angle, did you see or hear gunshots coming from the bungalow? Did you see the victim fall or hear him cry in pain?[26]

There were times when the witnesses stumbled. John Getke's recollection of events had been shaky enough when he'd spoken to Toms's assistant the day after Breiner's death. Under the pressure of the courtroom, his memory seemed to fail completely. Even the simplest facts escaped him—whether he'd been home for dinner on September 9, what time he heard the gunfire, whether he and his wife stayed inside all night after the shooting—and on crucial details, such as how many shots he heard fired from the bungalow, he refused to even venture a guess until Toms snapped, "Well, can you remember anything you sa[id], felt or heard," at which point Getke stopped talking altogether.[27]

Several others said too much. While you were waiting for your ride to work, Toms asked Dwight Hubbard, "what did you see happen?" "Well, there were a great number of people and the officers ..." Hubbard began. Then he caught himself. "I won't say a great number— there were a large—" Again he stopped. "There were a few people there," he said, more sure of himself on the third try, "and the officers were keeping them moving; suddenly there was a volley of shots."[28]

Edward Wettlaufer started his testimony much more strongly. A poolhall proprietor who lived around the block from the Sweets, Wettlaufer described coming out of the corner grocery and turning up Garland toward the knot of people gathered on a nearby lawn. He was twenty feet from the Doves' porch, he said, when he heard the roar of the guns and saw Leon Breiner crumple to the ground. Toms was moving smoothly toward the last of his standard questions, quizzing Wettlaufer about conditions prior to the shooting, when things went wrong. "Did you hear any sound of broken glass?" he asked. "Yes," the man admitted, "I heard; I heard something sounded like glass breaking." Quickly, Toms tried to repair the damage. "Where did the noise come from," he pressed, "which direction?" "Well, I don't know just where it came from," Wettlaufer said, backtracking furiously. "I know it sounded like broken glass; it might have been the house and it might not." Toms ventured another question. "Was the glass broken before or after the shooting?" Wettlaufer hesitated. "Well," he finally said, "it was before."[29]

But such missteps were few and far between. It was often painful to watch the people of Garland struggling to keep their composure on the stand. Some were so scared they could barely get their stories out. Others tripped over their own tongues. Still others mangled words beyond all recognition: it took Toms several tries to understand that when his witnesses said they lived near "Gothee," they were talking about Goethe Street, one block north of the bungalow.[30]

For all their rough edges, though, the state's witnesses gave Toms precisely what he wanted. In the minutes before the shooting, there had been a group of five or ten people gathered around the Doves' house, swore witness after witness, while a few other folks meandered around the neighborhood or stood in the school yard. But there was no mob, and there hadn't been a hint of trouble—"everything was in peace and quiet," said Edward Belcher—until the Negroes started shooting.[31]

Some saw flames flashing from the upstairs windows; others heard the report of the guns; one or two swore they noticed the gunmen themselves in the shadows. Almost all agreed that there were fifteen or twenty shots, a brief pause, and then another, less intense blast of gunfire. It was the second volley that brought down Breiner, said those who hadn't run for cover after the first fusillade. "My God, I'm shot!" Eric Houghberg heard him say. But everyone else thought he just hollered, his hands clutching his chest, before he toppled onto the porch steps. By the time the cops came running over, pushing back the bystanders and pointing their flashlights into the victim's face, the man looked to be dead.[32] That's what they remembered, almost forty people repeating the same story, the same sequence of events, the same tragic climax, until the consistency of the telling became almost mind-numbing and the prosecution's case started to seem ironclad.

But for Hays and Darrow.

◆

They worked in an exquisite choreography. On legal questions, Darrow invariably deferred to Hays, who time and again used his intimate knowledge of precedent and finely honed debater's skills to knock Toms off stride. When the prosecutor asked a police detective to say whether the weapons found in the bungalow had been fired any time close to September 9, Hays objected; too imprecise, he said. When Toms tried to supplement Ray Dove's testimony with photographs of the bullet-pocked front porch, Hays objected; the material was prejudicial, he insisted. And the moment Leona Breiner fainted, he leapt to his feet, arguing that such a tawdry attempt to play on the jury's sympathies was grounds for a mistrial.

Judge Murphy almost always sustained Hays's objections—even the defense must have been surprised when he agreed that photos of the crime scene weren't admissible—though he stopped short of declaring a mistrial over an incident that eight of the twelve jurors hadn't so much as noticed. But Hays wasn't counting victories. He was breaking the momentum of Toms's questioning, shattering the jurors' concentration on the witness stand, and reminding everyone that he was the foremost legal authority in the room. "He never asked the court," recalled Otis Sweet, who along with the other defendants took to celebrating whenever Hays won another challenge. "He demanded the court and brought up law to prove that he had a right to demand it. He'd give citations on every [point] . . . sometimes for as long as fifteen minutes in cases similar, from Florida to California. In fact, in my opinion he was a little too smart for the court."[33]

Once Toms turned his witnesses over to the defense for cross-examination, Hays slipped into the background and Darrow stepped forward. It was the sort of challenge he loved, taking on the prosecution's witnesses and finding a way to turn them into spokesmen for the defense. "The trying of a case in court calls for an acute intelligence, the capacity for instantaneous thought and for deciding what to do in the twinkling of an eye," he explained in his memoirs. "Most of the men in the [jury] panel have some sense, plenty of charity and understanding, and often have made mistakes themselves; in short, they generally are human and, after all, if a jury wants to save the client they can find a good reason why they should, and will. The problem is to bring about a situation where court and jury want a lawyer's client to win."[34]

Like Toms, Darrow adopted a professional appearance that surprised those who had come to know him through the Scopes extravaganza, but his demeanor remained as casual as it had always been. "The 'galluses' which featured in his appearances in the hot court house of Dayton are not on view," wrote a reporter that first week of the trial, "but their place is taken by the armholes of his vest, the place of repose for his thumbs when things are proceeding more or less normally." Some witnesses he dismissed with a question or two. There was no point in keeping Eric Houghberg on the stand a moment longer than necessary, for instance, so Darrow asked him whether the bullet that passed through his leg had ever been found, and when he had the answer he wanted—no, it hadn't—he sent the young man on his way.[35]

When Darrow saw an opportunity to deal the prosecution a blow, though, his homey manner gave way. Once on the offensive, noted the reporter, "his left arm hangs limp by his gangling figure while his right is thrust directly out from the shoulder, his index finger moving convulsively as he punctuates his questions," his soft voice suddenly replaced by a rattle of piercing questions.[36]

He began late in the morning of the first day, when Toms finished spinning out Norton Schuknecht's story and Murphy nodded for the defense to begin its interrogation. Darrow must have been tempted to go for the jugular, to bring down the prosecution's case with a slashing attack on its first significant witness. But this case required a more subtle touch. For close to four hours, Darrow kept Schuknecht on the stand, until the defender himself, too tired to continue, asked for a recess shortly before five o'clock. In the course of the long afternoon's questioning, he gradually transformed the inspector from the authority figure he had been under Toms's handling into the sort of sullenly indifferent cop at least some of the jurors would have recognized from their own dealings with the Detroit police.

In the month before Sweet moved into the house, Darrow asked, did you ever contact him to tell him he would have protection? When you heard that the people on Garland had formed the Waterworks Park Improvement Association, did you try to uncover the organization's intentions? On the nights of September 8 and 9, did you ask any of the bystanders on the street why they were there? When you had the traffic on Garland diverted shortly before the shooting, did you stop any of the motorists to ask what brought them into the neighborhood on a supposedly quiet Wednesday night? Did you so much as overhear any conversation on the street? Did you notice a taxicab with two Negroes pulling up to the house a few moments before the shooting began? Did you react in any way? No, no, no, Schuknecht answered again and again, always no, until, as the *Chicago Defender* reported, "Darrow gave a toss of his head and a shrug of his shoulders as if to ask, 'What did you do?'"[37]

There were moments, moreover, when Darrow forced Schuknecht to give the jury a glimpse of something worse than incompetence. As the day was winding down and exhaustion setting in, Darrow asked the inspector to describe again his search of the bungalow on the night of the shooting. Reinforcing the most powerful image of the morning's testimony seemed to be a tactical error, until Darrow brought Schuknecht back to the bungalow's front bedroom. Besides a bed and a few chairs, he asked, did you find anything else in the room? Schuknecht hesitated for a moment before replying, "I found a small stone." If Darrow was surprised by the concession, he didn't show it. "Did you find any broken glass?" he asked. Yes, the inspector admitted, there were shards scattered about the room. "Why didn't you mention finding broken glass on the floor?" demanded Darrow more sharply. "Why didn't you ask me?" Schucknecht fired back, his response so aggressive it made the omission seem all the more suspect. Darrow could have answered with a burst of righteous anger, but he chose a cooler approach. Would the fact that the glass was inside the house, he asked, "lead a policeman to the idea that [the stone] was thrown from outside?" "We found the stone on the inside, and I believe it was thrown from the outside," said Schuknecht. "I do not doubt that at all." Back at the lawyers' table, Toms slumped in his seat. "You cannot ask for anything better than that, can you?" he muttered loud enough for those in the well of the court to hear.[38]

But Darrow was just getting started. All that first week, he tried different angles of attack. There were the personal questions, quick and cutting. I suppose you didn't want Dr. Sweet as your neighbor, he said to Ray Dove. "I cannot say I am prejudiced against anyone," Dove answered. "Well, I am not talking about that," said Darrow. "You didn't want him in your neighborhood, did you—any colored man." Dove ventured another evasion—"I don't own property there myself," he said—but Darrow wouldn't let him slip away. "Is there any trouble about your answering that question," he demanded, so that Dove felt he had to give a proper response. "I don't believe in mixing people that way," he replied, "colored and white." "Well now," Darrow said, "with that preface you can answer it, can't you? You didn't want him there?" "No," Dove admitted at last.[39]

Then there were the questions intended to shatter the silences the prosecution's story imposed. Are you a member of the Waterworks Park Improvement Association, Darrow asked witness after witness, hoping that the question would open to the jury the series of threats that had terrorized his clients in the months before they moved to Garland Avenue. No, said Russell Burns, who lived a block north of the bungalow, though his sister, who owned the house, belonged. No, said real estate agent Raymond Alf, without mentioning that his business partner was the association's leading figure. Yes, said Della Getke, while she furiously chewed a wad of gum; both she and her husband, silent John, had signed up. But as soon as she had made that admission she was struck with the same amnesia that had afflicted her husband when he testified. "Did anyone stop by to talk about the organization before you joined," Darrow asked. "I don't remember," she replied. When did you join? "I can't remember." Where were you when you joined? "I couldn't say." Did you attend any meetings? "Not that I know of." His frustration rising, Darrow tried a different approach. "Do you know what the group was for," he asked. "Sure," Mrs. Getke answered. "Improvement."[40]

It was harder still for Darrow to crack the witnesses' accounts of the fatal night. No matter how long he kept the policemen on the stand, he couldn't shake their testimony the way he'd rattled Schuknecht. In fact, their stories seemed to harden under pressure: every time he asked an officer how many people were on the street before the shooting, the number seemed to shrink. There had been "eight or ten" at the Doves' place, said Sergeant Neighbauer, and another "eight or ten" on the school-yard lawn. There wasn't anyone at all in the school-yard, said patrolman Walter Doran, though there were "seven or eight" people out along Charlevoix. Doran's partner, Ernest Stanke, saw six people on Charlevoix; officer Roy Schaldenbrand saw only three or four; and Deputy Superintendent Sprott didn't notice anyone anywhere in the neighborhood. "No one standing north of Charlevoix on Garland?" Darrow asked. "No sir." "Nobody standing around the schoolhouse corner?" "No sir." "And nobody on the south side of Charlevoix?" "I didn't see anybody," Sprott insisted. "Well, you looked to see, didn't you?" sneered Darrow, but Sprott remained adamant. "I didn't see anyone," he repeated, as if Darrow hadn't heard him the first time. But Darrow was already moving the interrogation in a different direction. If Garland was deserted, he demanded, why did you order your men to close the street to traffic a half an hour before the shooting occurred? "Precaution," Sprott laconically replied.[41]

Most of the witnesses from Garland Avenue were just as stiff-necked. Like Ray Dove, Harry Monet, Otto Eberhardt, Florence Ware, Abbie Davis, and Eban Draper all admitted to Darrow that they didn't want coloreds in their neighborhood. But even under the Great Defender's most relentless cross-examination, they wouldn't concede that anything more than idle curiosity brought them onto the street the night of the shooting, or that while they were there they saw even a hint of danger for the Negroes barricaded inside the bungalow. Finally, Darrow's patience snapped. "You understand these eleven people are on trial, charged with murder, don't you?" he thundered at Draper, whose house was opposite the Howe School. "Are you reluctant to tell what you really know, where a life sentence is in danger?" Toms's assistant, Lester Moll, shouted out an objection but Darrow ignored him. "Are you reluctant to tell us what you know, fully and frankly," he said again. "Are you reluctant to tell it?" "What do you mean?" Draper stammered. "Well, I don't think I could explain the word," Darrow fired back. "You know the meaning of the word, don't you?" "No," said Draper, and Darrow threw up his hands in exasperation, started to say something to Murphy, thought better of it, then silently turned his back on the witness.[42]

There were other witnesses, though, who couldn't stand up to Darrow's assault, and when they fell, the prosecution's carefully constructed case threatened to tumble with them. Dwight Hubbard had already tripped over Toms's question about the size of the crowd on Garland when Darrow walked slowly up to the young man to begin his cross-examination. "When you first started to answer the question," Darrow began, "you started to say you saw a great crowd there, didn't you?" "Yes, sir," Hubbard responded. "Then you modified to say a large crowd, didn't you?" "Yes, sir." "Then you said a few people after that?" "Yes, sir." "Do you know how you happened to change your mind and whittle it down so fast?" "No, sir," said Hubbard. "You have been talked to a great deal about it, haven't you?" "No, sir." "Any [police] officers talk with you about it?" Darrow asked as he gazed distractedly out the window. "Just Lieutenant Johnson" (the detective in charge of the investigation), said Hubbard, "if you consider him an officer." "Well, I suppose he does," Darrow said, "and I haven't any reason to think otherwise. . . . How many times did he talk with you about it?" "Once." "And you kind of forgot you were to say a few people, didn't you, when you started in?" Toms tried to object—"Just a minute," he shouted, "that is an innuendo. . . ."—but Murphy overruled him. Darrow repeated the question: "When you started to answer [Toms's] question, you forgot to say a few people, instead of a great many?" "Yes, sir," said Hubbard, and the courtroom burst into laughter.[43]

No one laughed when Alf Andrews broke. The forty-four-year-old foreman undoubtedly found his way onto the witness list because the officers of the Waterworks Park Improvement Association knew he was dependable: he and his wife, Mabel, owned the home next door to the association's president, Harold McGlynn, and it's hard to imagine that the two men hadn't stood at the backyard fence some warm summer night in 1925 discussing how much they hated the thought of Negroes living down the block from them; when the association's membership cards were passed up and down the street that July, he'd signed his name and handed over the dollar it cost to join. But Andrews, tough enough to make his living whipping factory hands into shape, wasn't tough enough to withstand Darrow's most vigorous cross-examination. Almost all afternoon Thursday, November 12, Darrow pushed and pushed, until Andrews revealed the secrets the prosecution had hoped to keep hidden from the jury. He did indeed belong to the Waterworks Park Improvement Association, he said; he'd been at the association's mid-July rally at Howe Elementary; and the crowd that night had been huge—six hundred people was his guess—an entire neighborhood came out, as Andrews himself had come out, to demand that Garland remain lily-white.[44]

When thirteen-year-olds George Suppus and Ulric Arthur were on the stand, Darrow took a softer approach. The defender's looming presence so scared the boys that he took a few steps back from them, moving almost to the lawyers' table, then with the utmost gentleness, he walked them through the evening of the shooting: finishing dinner, walking down to the corner to see the policemen, settling onto the Doves' steps. Gradually, the boys relaxed—it was so hard to resist the old man's charm—and as they did, the truth came tumbling out. Everybody on the porch was talking about the colored family, George and Ulric agreed; that's how they passed the time as darkness fell.

Then a taxi pulled up in front of the bungalow and let off two colored men, who dashed into the house. "Did you see anyone throw any stones," Darrow asked Ulric. "Well," he answered, "there was four or five kids between the houses, they were throwing stones." "Where were they throwing them?" "They were throwing them at the house where the colored people moved in," Ulric said. "Did you hear the stones hit the house?" "Yes, sir." Do you know whether any of them broke any glass?" "I heard glass break," said the boy. "I guess it was the stones." "And the shooting occurred right after it, didn't it," Darrow said. "Well . . ." Ulric began before Darrow cut him off with a commanding, "What?" "Yes, sir," the boy meekly replied.[45]

There it was, a simple, honest account shining through a thousand lies. And all Darrow could do was hope that the twelve men sitting in the jury box would take hold of it like the precious thing it was.

◆

All through the first stages of the trial, Walter White pushed himself as hard as he had ever done before. From the moment James Weldon Johnson had heard that the Garland Fund was willing to help the NAACP create its longed-for Legal Defense Fund, he had set his staff to work full-time on the fund-raising circuit. So White spent the first two weeks of November scrambling from courtroom to train station, city to city, rally to rally across the Midwest, constantly talking of the trial and the principles for which it was being fought. The outpouring of support was nothing short of phenomenal. White's swing through the old abolitionist stronghold of northern Ohio—one bleary night in Cleveland, the next in Toledo—earned the fledgling Defense Fund almost seventeen hundred dollars in donations. After a quick stop back in Detroit to see Darrow complete jury selection, White was off again, this time to Chicago, where more than nine hundred NAACP stalwarts jammed a mass meeting to protest the Sweets' incarceration and the recent bombing of a South Side Chicago church, the latest in a string of terrorist attacks against Negroes stretching back almost eight years. From there, he raced to Minneapolis and St. Paul for a whirlwind of appearances that brought in another five hundred dollars. "Eighteen speeches since last Sunday!" he boasted to Johnson as he prepared to board the train back to Detroit to watch Darrow and Hays conduct their cross-examinations.[46]

The pace in Detroit was even more frenetic. Up at seven o'clock each morning, by half past nine White was at the courtroom, joining the stream of lawyers, politicians, and reformers who had angled the special passes they needed to sidestep the line of ordinary people—working stiffs with lunch pails in hand, church folks in their Sunday best, the young woman with a ukulele under her arm—who waited hours to catch a glimpse of the proceedings. "To get a seat without danger of personal injury," wrote one of the dozen reporters who crowded alongside White at the press table, "one almost has to be a friend of somebody who is 'somebody' in the court." Ruby Darrow attended every day, sitting close to the defense team so that she could keep a hawk's eye on her husband. Arthur Garfield Hays also brought his new wife, Aline, and Frank Murphy invited the young socialite he was then dating, who arrived chastely chaperoned by her mother, as the judge preferred her to be. All day long, White watched the quietly furious battle between Toms and Darrow, straining to hear the witnesses over the buzz of conversation from the overflowing gallery, adding to the cacophony by continually offering his fellow newsmen editorial suggestions that, more often than not, found their way into the next day's papers.[47]

When the workday was done, White joined Darrow and his oversized entourage as they headed out for long nights of talk, drink, and, when Ruby wasn't looking, a few flirtations. Almost every evening, it seemed, Darrow was on a stage somewhere in the city, preaching the modernist creed. At prestigious Orchestra Hall, he lectured on evolution; to the Detroit Federation of Labor, he talked of crime and punishment; at the swanky Penguin Club, he spoke on birth control; and at the colored YMCA, in the heart of Black Bottom, he addressed the problem of race. He never restricted himself to a single topic, though. Once he had his audience's attention, he roamed across the social questions of the day, slashing away at fundamentalists and self-styled patriots—"one hundred percent Americanism is a slogan for selling prunes," he told one gathering—eugenicists and white supremacists, capitalists, socialists, anarchists, anyone who fooled himself into believing he was wiser, better, more decent than the common run of humanity.[48]

Darrow "made everyone writhe as he pictured the injustices and immoralities of our present industrial system," Reinhold Niebuhr wrote after attending one lecture. "The tremendous effect of his powerful address was partially offset by the bitterness with which he spoke . . . [but] I suppose it is difficult to escape bitterness when you have the eyes to see and the heart to feel what others are too blind and too callous to notice." For his part, Darrow did what he could to keep from becoming too depressed. When he was finished speaking at an event, two or three hours after taking the stage, it was back to his hotel room for cocktails and conversation, Hays reciting verse, the Great Defender holding forth, their entourage of friends and hangers-on sitting entranced, too content or too tired to be bothered to call it a night.[49]

There were times when seeing Darrow in action must have made White wince. At the Penguin Club, the defender spotted a young woman, Josephine Gomon—a married mother of five, as it turned out—who had been in the courtroom several times during the first weeks of testimony. Gomon was a political activist in her own right, an associate of Harriet McGraw, Detroit's foremost progressive, and through McGraw, a friend and ally of Frank Murphy and Johnny Smith. All that mattered to Darrow, though, was that Gomon had a pretty face. The first chance he got, he sidled up to her, slid his hand around her arm, and guided her into the lobby. "Do you mind if I walk to the streetcar with you," he asked. "I'd be delighted," she replied, "but I'm driving." "Then you'll drive me home," he said, smoothly moving her out the door. As they headed toward the car, the seduction began. "Come up to my room," he told her. "I'm expecting a couple of interesting fellows and we'll read poetry." As soon as the invitation was extended, though, Harriet McGraw swooped down upon them, saying that she, too, could use a ride home. Darrow smiled and let his hand slip away. "You seem to be well protected," he whispered with obvious disappointment, an old reprobate suddenly condemned to spend another night in the company of his wife.[50]

His performance at the colored Y was even more embarrassing. As the session opened, it looked to be a triumph. Fifteen hundred people filled the cavernous auditorium; Detroit's Talented Tenth lined the dais; the press was there to record whatever Darrow had to say. But the guest of honor was in a particularly pessimistic mood—a particularly honest mood, he would have said—and his presentation quickly veered off in all the wrong directions. Had it not been for slavery, he lectured the crowd, "you might still be savages in Africa, and at that you might be better off there. But I still think civilization is worth the price we pay for it; what the white man paid in his upward struggle, what you are paying today." But Negroes shouldn't expect too much. Hope was an illusion, after all, conflict a constant. "If the race problem is solved, there will come along new maladjustments," he insisted. "Always the man on the ground has feared the newcomer, because he didn't understand him. If a white man went to the Congo he would be hated and misunderstood. That is your lot here. You have a long, hard road to travel, an arduous foe to fight, and that foe is prejudiced, a fact we have always had with us."

At last, he turned to the Sweets themselves, and for the briefest of moments, he seemed to get back on the message the NAACP wanted him to deliver. "I shall not discuss the case now being tried," he said, "but it is certain that a district built to house five thousand Negroes will prove a bit too small to accommodate the eighty thousand now in Detroit. Obviously they have to live somewhere." Then came the qualification: "And yet if they move into white neighborhoods they depreciate property values. That's true—and . . . I don't know what can be done about it." It was more than a qualification, really. It was a capitulation to the forces that were most responsible for segregating the great cities of the North and, worse yet, a confession that even the most sympathetic of white Americans couldn't imagine a nation truly defined by justice.[51]

Still, the Great Defender's star power was such that when the collection plates were passed through the crowd they came back filled. That day, $378.65 was taken in, 1 percent of the total the NAACP had to raise to create its Defense Fund paid in a pile of coins and crumpled bills that a lot of folks in the audience probably couldn't afford to surrender. So if White grimaced at Darrow's remarks, he didn't say anything.[52] He simply gathered up the donations and headed on to the next rally, the next speech, the next wearying train trip, knowing that the association was one step closer to the day when it would be able to fight its legal battles the way it saw fit rather than relying on those who, for all their goodwill, didn't understand just how much was at stake.

◆

By all rights, Walter White should have skipped the morning session in court on Saturday, November 14, and spent the time catching up on his sleep. Thursday night's Penguin Club meeting had kept him out later than expected; Friday night he hadn't gotten to bed until four in the morning; and he had to be on a train by half past one Saturday afternoon so as not to miss his scheduled appearance at a rally of colored physicians in Chicago that evening. Despite what must have been crushing exhaustion, though, White was in his place at the press table when court convened at nine o'clock, waiting for the moment when

Robert Toms rested his case and the trial moved to its most challenging phase.[53]

White was sure that Darrow's cross-examination had shattered the
state's improbable version of events: "Every witness for the past three
days put on by the prosecution has helped the defense," he reported to
NAACP headquarters the previous evening. "Contradictions so glaring
as to be unmistakable have abounded and numerous of those testifying have been so obviously lying. . . ."[54] Now the truly hard work began. Over the next few days, the defense would have to replace the
prosecution's splintered story with another tale, so well told, so compelling that it would convince twelve white men that they should not—
could not—convict eleven Negroes of murdering a man very much like
the jurors themselves.

There were so many ways the defense's case could be constructed.
Darrow and Hays might have turned the courtroom into a classroom,
as they'd tried to do in Dayton the previous summer, filling the witness
stand with experts on the race problem—Du Bois, perhaps, or the brilliant sociologist Charles Johnson, author of the epic 1922 study *The
Negro in Chicago*—who could speak with authority on how the pressures of a segregated housing market pitted white homeowners against
black house hunters and, through that conflict, fostered in whites a
murderous rage. They could have overwhelmed the court with the
most imposing of character witnesses—the doctors of Dunbar Hospital, the businessmen who ran the Liberty Life Insurance Company,
professors from Wilberforce and Howard, the vicar of Gladys's church,
St. Matthew's Episcopal—who together might have convinced the jurors that the defendants were incapable of conspiring to commit a
heinous crime.

The cocounsels also thought seriously of trying to misdirect the
jury, arguing that the fatal shot came not from inside the bungalow
but from the alleyway, where patrolman Frank Lee Gill, a white south-
erner just five months on the force, had tried to shoot at the black men
he saw on the back porch but instead had fired wildly into the night.[55]
But each approach had its weakness: too bloodless, too indirect, too
far-fetched. And all of them ran the same terrible risk. Perhaps Darrow
had misjudged the jurors, made the wrong choices, acted too quickly
and too impulsively in putting them on the panel. Perhaps those
twelve men couldn't set aside the prejudices they carried with them
into the jury box. Perhaps they'd vote to convict no matter what.

To be safe, Darrow and Hays agreed that they would begin their case not with the grand opening statements of which they were capable but with a motion to the court to dismiss all charges against their clients. Only if the motion failed would the defense place before the jury the story it wished to tell, the pieces of which Hays was still assembling Thursday night.

White wasn't entirely pleased with the strategy. "There will be great advantage for us in putting in our testimony and finishing the job of education which gives the trial its greatest ultimate value," he complained to Johnson, and in "getting a verdict of acquittal by a jury which will influence public opinion infinitely more than a dismissal of the case by the judge." But Hays and Darrow were adamant. Of course, prolonging the courtroom battle would make for more dramatic political theater. But a conviction would be catastrophic, both for the defendants and for the cause for which the NAACP was fighting. Better to let the trial end with a whimper than with a crushing defeat. "So," said White with a resigned shrug, "we won't refuse a dismissal if Murphy should see fit to do it."[56]

Half of Saturday's session was finished before Toms's last witness completed his testimony and Hays rose to make his motion. Murphy immediately ordered the jury removed from the courtroom, then invited the defense to argue the motion's merits. For the balance of the day, the Sweets' counsel held the courtroom in their hands. For his part, Hays tripped the legal trap he had set on the first day of testimony, when he'd demanded that the prosecution present a bill of particulars. That document clearly stated that the state's case rested on a charge of conspiracy, he pointed out, yet, in nine days of testimony, the prosecution hadn't presented the court a single shred of evidence establishing that the defendants had joined together to plan Leon Breiner's murder. What's more, all the evidence they had presented—the large number of people inside the bungalow, the lack of furniture, the collection of guns—was not only circumstantial "but consistent with a lawful purpose." So, by the standards it had set for itself, the state had no case at all. Hays leavened the relentless logic of his argument with flattery so perfectly suited to Murphy's self-perception as to be utterly shameless. "I am aware of the responsibility and courage required of the court, especially in view of the prejudice of the community against the defendants," he said, "but the defense has the greatest confidence not only in your honor's learning and knowledge but also in your honor's courage." And just in case that appeal wasn't enough, he turned to a classic bit of courtroom razzle-dazzle. As the court sat hushed, trying to follow the tight twists of Hays's presentation, a baby suddenly burst into tears. Murphy asked the bailiff to have the infant taken out into the hall, but Hays objected. "That is the Sweet baby," he said with a flourish. "We had her brought in here as an illustration. Had she been in that house that night, she might well have been arrested and tried and the evidence here would condemn her to the same extent it does the defendants." Two decades later, Hays still relished baby Iva's exquisite timing. "What inspired that child to break out at that special moment, I don't know," he wrote in the 1940s. "The mother[-in-law] of Doctor Sweet had the baby in charge but I am certain that my instructions were merely to bring the child into the courtroom."[57]

When Hays was done, Darrow took over. He, too, hit at the logical gaps in the state's case. "It is very evident," he said, "[that] one bullet killed Mr. Breiner. It could have been fired by only one man and from only one gun. Suppose excitement should occur in this courtroom and someone was shot. Would everyone be charged with murder?" Mostly, though, he unleashed the righteous anger that had been building ever since Norton Schuknecht took the stand on the trial's first day. "It has been evident that the state's witnesses have purposely and consistently misstated the facts in this case," he insisted. "There was a meeting of five hundred or more persons of a society pledged to keep Negroes out of the district. A house had been bought by a Negro in a district that hitherto had been given over to the Noble Nordics. I know what racial and religious prejudices are. There was an organization in the neighborhood long before this family moved into their home. The police had escorted them into their home on the day of the moving. On September 8 people gathered around the home. [The Sweets] were besieged. On the ninth they were penned in. The crowds began to gather. That number grew larger. I am not maligning the police but I want to say here that they misstated the facts in this case. It was night. Out in the streets people moved. The worst and best we can say is that they had white faces."[58]

"I have never in my life heard such magnificent presentations," gushed White that evening, his reservations washed away in a wave of ebullience. "Hays the logician, relentless, keen, incontrovertible; Darrow the great humanist, pleading with fervor for decency and justice and tolerance, breathing into the law romance and beauty and drama. The jury was excluded during the motions but I am sure that had they heard Darrow they would have voted at once for an acquittal though they had heard none of our evidence."[59]

The weekend's optimism spiked even higher when the proceedings resumed on Monday. For the first time since the trial began, Toms came into court ready to make the defense a concession: the state was willing, he quietly informed Darrow and Hays, to drop all charges against Gladys Sweet. Although Gladys wouldn't even consider the possibility— she wanted no special favors, she said—the very fact that Toms had made the offer told the defense that the prosecutor's confidence was starting to crack. That impression had to have hardened during the morning session, as Toms struggled through his argument against the defense motion, his chain of thought repeatedly broken by Murphy's searching questions. By the time Toms stumbled to a finish, Walter White must have believed that victory was a hair's breadth away.[60]

It wasn't. Murphy never explained his decision to rule against the defense. Some thought it was a political move; Father Frank was planning to run for mayor himself one day soon, they said, and he didn't want to be known in white neighborhoods as the judge who freed the Sweets. Others claimed he'd been thinking of the Negroes: a verdict of not guilty would be much stronger coming from a jury rather than from the bench, that's what they said. Still others thought he'd made a principled stand. The prosecution hadn't proved conspiracy; that much was true. But neither had the defense proved the necessity of the Negroes firing thirty some shots into Garland Avenue. So Murphy listened politely to the lawyers' arguments, gave the question a few minutes' consideration, then set the defense's motion aside. The bailiff brought the jurors back to the courtroom, and Murphy signaled to Darrow that he was to begin making a case for the innocence of his clients. The defender deferred to Hays, who again stepped forward from the defense table, the defeat already shrugged off, and started to tell his tale.[61]

•

Ossian was alone once more. Gladys was at his side, Henry and Otis a few feet down the defendants' bench, supporters and associates scattered in among the strangers who filled the gallery. Yet Ossian was alone, the thirteen-year-old on the train to Wilberforce, the medical student picking his way through the bloodied summer streets of Washington, D.C., the promising doctor sitting in the gloom of his new dining room, trying to beat back the fear welling inside him so that he might act like the man he thought he ought to be.

The story Hays told the jury was Ossian's story. His presentation had the requisite flights of oratory: an opening citation of William Pitt the Elder, authoritative and uncompromising, championing the ancient Anglo-Saxon right of self-defense; a closing recitation of the Harlem Renaissance's most gentle protest poem, Joseph Cotter's elegiac "And What Shall You Say?" But the balance of Hays's opening statement belonged to Sweet. Hays told Ossian to stand "so the jury can look you over"—an unfortunate choice of words, with their echoes of the slave market—and while the jurors stared at the handsome young man on the opposite side of the courtroom, the attorney talked of the doctor's rise from poverty, his years of hard work, his marvelous academic achievements, his loving marriage. He took the jury through the summer of 1925—through the terrors that confronted Bristol and Turner and Fletcher—and from there, he moved to Garland Avenue, into the bungalow on the night of the shooting, as Ossian thought not only of the mob on the street but of "lynchings . . . in various parts of the country, of negroes taken from policemen said to be guarding them and burned at the stake by slow fire, even of women mistreated by mobs . . . of East St. Louis and Tulsa and Chicago and Washington and Arkansas, where the lives of negroes have been wantonly taken." It was as if there were no other defendants, no other lives hanging on the jurors' decision, just this solitary man shouldering the brutal burdens of Black America.[62]

For the next two days, Ossian sat in silence as the defense used a dozen witnesses to flesh out Hays's account. John Fletcher and Vollington Bristol both took the stand to describe the attacks on their homes. Ossian's associate, Edward Carter, spoke of Sweet's agonizing decision to go through with his move after he learned of the west-side violence, and of the threats he received as word of his coming spread along Garland Avenue. Gladys's friends Serena Rochelle and Edna Butler told of the night they spent trapped inside the bungalow on September 8, so scared of the crowd gathered outside that they didn't dare go home. And in a riveting round of testimony, the defense led the jurors out onto the street on the night of the murder, out into the mob that the prosecution said didn't exist. Philip Adler, the white *Detroit News* reporter who happened on the troubles a few minutes before the shooting, said that at the intersection in front of the Sweet house the crowd was so thick—"between four hundred and five hundred people," he estimated—he had to elbow his way through it.

The number was confirmed by Bruce and Mary Spaulding, a handsome young black couple who were driving down Charlevoix shortly before the shooting; when they first saw the crowd milling around Garland, Mary Spaulding said, they assumed there must have been some sort of terrible accident. A young colored man, James Smith, and his uncle Alonzo recalled how they were out for an evening drive when, moments after the shooting, they ran into the police roadblock. They tried to turn around but before they knew it, a "considerable mob" was racing toward them, screaming racial epithets and throwing stones. Though the windshield was shattered, the Smiths managed to escape unscathed. Charles Shauffner wasn't so lucky. He, too, drove into the neighborhood by accident, he told the court, and when a mob swarmed his car, he was so panicked he stalled the engine. Somebody hit him in the head with a brick—he pointed to the scar above his left eye—but amid the blood and blinding pain, he somehow managed to get the car moving again. How many people were in the mob, asked Hays. "It seemed to me like five thousand," Shauffner said.[63]

Then, on Wednesday afternoon, November 18, Ossian heard Arthur Garfield Hays call his name. He rose from the defendants' bench, leaving Gladys and the others behind him, and walked the few paces to the witness stand, where the bailiff was waiting for him, Bible in hand.

Ossian didn't have to testify. No one could have objected to his refusing, so great was the responsibility: if he said the wrong word, put the wrong inflection in his voice, sat in a way that struck the jurors as too casual or too confident, grew rattled under cross-examination, succumbed to a single flash of anger, whatever sympathy Darrow and Hays had won for the defendants could be lost, the entire defense destroyed. But Ossian didn't refuse. Undoubtedly he agreed out of pride—the intoxicating sense that in the past few weeks he had become the representative of his race and the champion of its rights—and, as always, out of obligation. He would do what his lawyers wanted him to do, what his wife and brothers and friends needed him to do, what his colleagues surely expected him to do. He had no choice, really, but to take the stand.

Most of the examination was devoted to retelling the tale Hays had sketched out in his opening statement. In his precise and methodical way, the attorney walked Ossian through his life story from Bartow to Howard, Detroit to Paris, and back again. When that work was done, Hays asked the doctor to recall, one by one, the racial incidents that scarred him most. "Without hesitating for word or phrase," said a reporter, Ossian began to recite his litany of horrors: Fred Rochelle burning at the stake, the nameless colored man pummeled during the

Washington riot, the stories he'd heard of the Chicago pogrom. Toms tried to object to the line of questioning—certainly all this information was of no relevance to the case, he said—but Darrow, who had remained silent the entire afternoon, immediately countered with a response adapted from his defense of Leopold and Loeb. "This is the question of the psychology of the race," he argued, "of how everything known to a race affects its actions. What we learn as children we remember—it gets fastened to the mind. . . . Because this defendant's actions were predicated on the psychology of the past I ask that this testimony be admitted."

Murphy granted him the point, and the litany resumed: Ossian described the mob murder of Alexander Jackson in Tulsa and the Johnson brothers in the Arkansas countryside, the assault on Rosewood, Florida, and, finally, with Hays's prompting, of his reaction when he learned of the attacks on the west side the previous July. Though the information wasn't new, the presentation was absolutely gripping. Looking about him, Walter White thought the courtroom had been made "breathless" by Sweet's terrible accounting. A reporter from one of the Detroit dailies agreed. Sweet's intimate description "of morbid details," he said, "held the jury and spectators silent and immovable." Ever so slowly, Hays took Ossian back to Garland Avenue on the night of September 9. "Then began one of the most remarkable direct examinations to be found in all the records of criminal cases," wrote another reporter, young David Lilienthal, come to cover the trial for the *Nation*, "a vivid picture of the fear-ridden mind of a black man, terrified by a hostile crowd of whites outside his home."

"When did you first observe anything outside?" Hays asked.

"We were playing cards," Sweet said. "It was about eight o'clock when something hit the roof of the house."

"What happened after that?"

"Somebody went to the window and I heard them remark, 'People, the people!'"

"And then?"

"I ran out to the kitchen where my wife was. There were several lights burning. I turned them out and opened the door. I heard someone yell, 'Go and raise hell in front; I am going back.' I was frightened and after getting a gun ran upstairs. Stones kept hitting the house intermittently. I threw myself on the bed and lay there a short while—perhaps fifteen or twenty minutes—when a stone came through the window. Part of the glass hit me."

"What happened next?"

"Pandemonium—I guess that's the best way of describing it—broke loose. Everyone was running from room to room. There was a general uproar. Somebody yelled, 'There's someone coming.' They said, 'That's your brother.' A car had pulled up to the curb. My brother and Mr. Davis got out. The mob yelled, 'Here's niggers! Get them! Get them!' As they rushed in, the mob surged forward, fifteen or twenty feet—"

Ossian faltered—a second, no longer—and his hand slipped over his eyes. Darkness, like the darkness that had enveloped him as he lay in the bedroom that evening, soothing and terrifying. His body shuddered slightly, just enough for the men of the press to notice. Then his hand fell away and he glanced over to Gladys, tried to smile, and started to speak again.

"It looked like a human sea. Stones kept coming faster. I was downstairs. Another window was smashed. Then one shot—then eight or ten from upstairs. Then it was over."

"What was your state of mind at the time of the shooting," asked Hays softly.

"When I opened the door and saw the mob," Ossian said, "I realized I was facing the same mob that had hounded my people through its entire history. In my mind I was pretty confident of what I was up against, with my back against the wall. I was filled with a peculiar fear, the fear of one who knows the history of my race."[64]

Ossian Sweet, standing alone.

◆

It was done. The final four days of testimony had their dramatic moments: Ossian fending off Robert Toms's uncharacteristically aggressive cross-examination, his answers delivered with a dignity so fierce it was inspiring; Hays fighting with every legal weapon available to prevent the prosecutor from introducing into evidence Henry Sweet's admission on the night of the shooting that he had indeed fired into the crowd, only to suffer a rare defeat; the defense countering by calling Lieutenant William Johnson as a witness, then battering him with questions about the interrogation that night, which was intended, Hays implied, to force the defendants into confessing to a crime they didn't commit; Walter White making a surprise appearance on the stand to describe his extensive research into mob violence, a threat so pervasive, he explained, every Negro lived in terror of it. All of that testimony, though, was denouement. The moment Ossian opened the bungalow door for the jurors and let them see the Garland Avenue crowd through his eyes, Clarence Darrow had everything he needed to bring the trial to its conclusion.[65]

The final witness stepped down on Monday, November 23—the start of Thanksgiving week—but some last-minute legal wrangling prevented closing statements from beginning until the following morning. Although Detroit's most powerful radio station, WJR, intended to broadcast the proceedings so that the entire city and much of the Midwest could hear Darrow's plea to the jury, the crowds arrived at the courthouse even earlier than usual, knowing that the chance to watch the Great Defender at his finest would make the competition for seats particularly intense. As soon as the doors swung open, the crowd surged in, spectators pushing and shoving past one another; fistfights broke out, and a few of those who came to watch justice unfold instead found themselves spending the day in jail. Hundreds never even got inside. So they stood in the packed corridor for hours on end, determined to catch a fraction of the day's orations.[66]

The morning's session belonged to the prosecution. For two and a half hours, Toms's assistant, Lester Moll, led the jury through the facts of the case, "building a gigantic structure of reason," according to one of the numerous newsmen there that day, interspersed with "short sarcastic darts" at his esteemed rivals. "The defense has advanced a fear complex theory," he sneered. "It's poppycock; it's bunk. What a situation—a premeditated murder. If that's a fear complex . . . then give me something else."[67]

The defense took its turn after lunch. Arthur Garfield Hays led off with a slashing, sometimes rambling attack on the state's argument, complemented by the recitation of yet another Harlem Renaissance poem—a piece by Countee Cullen this time—and a final, soaring appeal to principle. "Gentlemen of the jury, the opportunity doesn't come often in life to do a great act," he said. "The writing of the Emancipation Proclamation for a nation is given to few. And yet you men here have an opportunity to write a charter of freedom, not for eleven men but for a race, for an oppressed race; you have an opportunity to write that charter of freedom by your verdict . . . and if you do that, gentlemen of the jury, you will do more to end all of the outrages than all the race commissions appointed by all the mayors of all the cities, of all the states, of these United States."[68] It was Hays's weakest performance of the trial, too highbrow for a jury full of workmen—one can only wonder what juryman John Zang thought of Cullen's poetry—and too convoluted to be convincing. But everyone knew that it was nothing more than a prelude. At three o'clock sharp, Darrow sidled up to the rail in front of the jury box. Instantly, the normally clamorous courtroom fell into a deep silence, so that the only sound came from the defender's gentle, weary voice. "If the court please and gentlemen of the jury," he began, "I wish it was not my turn, that I didn't feel it was my duty to talk to you in this case. It is not an easy matter to talk about a case of this sort, and I am afraid it won't be an easy matter to listen but you can't help it any more than I can."[69]

With that, Darrow was off and running. He spoke until half past six that evening, spent another night on the town, and when court resumed the next morning at nine o'clock, he started up again, sweeping the courtroom with a great torrent of softly spoken words. There were almost no histrionics; Darrow "just chatted with [the jurors]," Toms said later, drawing them and the audience gathered around them into his confidence, challenging them as he'd challenged so many before them to abandon the self-deceptions that gave them comfort and to face the world as it truly was.[70]

First, he talked of "the everlasting problems of race and color and creed that have always worked their evil in human institutions." He talked of prejudices "that have been taught to us and that began coming to us almost with our mother's milk, and they stick almost as the color of the skin sticks." He talked of the evils that prejudice produces, the way "it will take good, kindly, human men and women and make them fiends [who] throw reason to the wind and throw justice to the wind and throw mercy to the wind." And he admitted, the way only a man of Darrow's confidence could admit, that the jurors surely were prejudiced themselves, as was he, though he liked to think otherwise. "I would guess that some of you—maybe most of you—believe that colored people should have one neighborhood and white people the other," he said. "If you ask me what I think about it, I would say I don't know. That is an idea—I have an idea that that is not the right way, but I can very well understand that many very rational and considerate white people believe it; I can very well understand it." As he spoke, wrote David Lilienthal, "the old man with the unalterably sad face and the great stooped shoulders seemed no mere lawyer pleading for hire. He seemed, instead, a patriarch out of another age, counseling his children, sorrowing because of their cruelty and hatred, yet too wise in the ways of men to condemn them for it."

When Darrow turned to the weeks of testimony, though, his sorrow

became tinged with gall. He understood, he said, that the seventy people who testified for the state were "in the ordinary affairs of life honest and decent. . . . But in this case man and woman and child alike
have come into this court and under oath have deliberately lied to
send eleven people to the penitentiary for life . . . and there is not an
officer who has testified in this case that is not partially guilty of this
murder and who to shield himself has not perjured himself on account
of the character of this case." No one was fooled, though, because
there wasn't a person in the courtroom, "whether he be a policeman, a
neighbor, a prosecutor, a juror, a mere spectator, that does not know
what happened" on Garland Avenue that terrible night.

Then with the seasoned lawyer's dexterity, Darrow smoothly slid the
tragedy into the political conflict that had roiled Detroit for the past
year, transforming the people of Garland from ordinary folks into prox-
ies for the Klansmen that the men of the jury—all of them members of
the city's sprawling working class, all of them connected in some fashion to the immigrant masses—were likely to despise. "Up and down the
street were the lines of these Noble Nordics"—that phrase again, so
perfectly chosen—"father and mother and child, a lodger, a boarder, a
tenant, and friends coming from far and near, lined up on their front
porches and cast a glassy eye over toward the Sweet house and waited
to see what happened. . . . They were gathered together just the same as
the Roman Coliseum used to be filled with a great throng of people
with their eyes cast to the door where the lions would come out; they
were gathered together just as in the old days a mob would assemble to
see an outdoor hanging and waiting for the victim with their eyes set
on the gallows. . . . And they were gathered together to awe and to intimidate the poor black family which had bought the corner house and
who had a right to buy it under every law of the land. That is why they
were there." And they'd done it all—the conspiracy, the mobbing, the
perjury—"in behalf of what they think is their noble Nordic race."

And that, said Darrow, was the story's bitter irony. For the testimony proved that the ignoble Nordics of Garland Avenue were determined to purge from their neighborhood—"not especially a high-toned
neighborhood at that, nothing swell about it"—people who were
clearly their betters. "We have presented witnesses that are as intelligent, as attractive, as good-looking as any white man or woman," he
insisted, "and who are as far above the bunch which testified against
these men as the heavens are above the earth and you know it and they
know it." Think of Gladys's friends Edna Butler and Serena Rochelle,

he commanded the jurors, "bright, intelligent, cultured, truthful, modest" young women, so much more impressive than the white women who testified for the state. Think of Walter White, "the peer of any man in this courtroom." Think of the defendants sitting across from the jury box, "half of them are at least college graduates or attending college. . . . They would compare almighty favorably with anybody who lives around the corner of Garland and Charlevoix."

Think, most of all, he continued, of brilliant Dr. Sweet, seeing in the mob the history of his race, "loaded like sardines in a box in the middecks of steamers and brought forcibly from their African homes, half of them dying in the voyage. He knew they were sold like chattels as slaves and were compelled to work without pay; he knew that families were separated when it paid the master to sell them; he knew that even after he had got liberty under the Constitution and the law he knew that . . . in every state of the Union telegraph poles had been decorated by the bodies of Negroes dangling to ropes on account of race hatred and nothing else." He had the jurors with him now, moving through Sweet's terrors, back to Bartow, up to Garland, into the face of hatred. "He knew they had been tied to stakes in free America and a fire built around living human beings until they roasted to death; he knew they had been driven from their homes in the north and in great cities and here in Detroit, and he was there not only to defend himself and his house and his friends but to stand for the integrity and the independence of the abused race to which he belonged . . . a hero who fought a brave fight against fearful odds, a fight for the right, for justice, for freedom, and his name will live and be honored when most of us are forgotten." Judging by men and women such as these, Darrow archly asked, wouldn't any reasonable person conclude that it was not the Nordic but the Negro who belonged to the superior race?

The question was meant to be shocking, both in its audacity and in the sudden realization that it had to be answered in the affirmative. Darrow had taken on the Sweet case for just this moment of terrible honesty, when, with a twist of the evidence and a flash of eloquence, he made the courtroom see that white supremacy was an illusion, a poisonous, ruinous fantasy, just as it was an illusion to believe that capitalism was just, that men were responsible for the evil that they did, and that there was a God in Heaven.

As soon as the illusion was shattered, he presented the court with the harrowing, beautiful truth. "I know," he told the jurors, "that back of me and back of you is an infinite ancestry stretching a way back at least five hundred thousand years, and we are made up of everything on the face of the earth, of all kinds and colors and degrees of civilization, and out of that come we. Who are we, any of us, to be boastful above our fellows?" A world made one by miscegenation: to say such a thing in 1925 America was an act of startling insight and singular courage. But that was Darrow's genius, drawing a new understanding and a new humility out of the violence that Americans inflicted on one another.

Then something—caution, calculation, the limits of his own imagination—drew Darrow back. He could have pressed the logic of his argument, demanding, in the spirit of the abolitionists, that the jurors see segregation as illusion's folly, a social system built upon a bold-faced lie. As he drove toward his closing, though, idealism gave way to the same tired realism he'd demonstrated at the colored YMCA the week before. "Ask yourself this question, gentlemen," he said, "if you could settle [the race problem] as you wanted to, not this case but this infinitely troublesome problem that is back of it, how would you do it? How would you do it? If I were asked the question as to how I would do it, I could not answer it. I know that trouble and sorrow are incident to human life. . . . I know that many of our deepest problems are worked out in the secret travail of body and of mind. I know that nature takes time, infinite time, and the adjustment of races, the adjustment of religions, and the understandings of human beings by each other is the question of infinite time. I see no way that we can help it."[71]

Darrow was all but shouting now, his voice ringing out "like a brass gong," according to David Lilienthal, "his eyes . . . hard and grim, every muscle of his huge body tense and strained." But his message was soothingly soft. He wouldn't demand that the walls of segregation be brought down, that whites welcome blacks into their neighborhoods, or that they acknowledge Negroes as the brothers they were. Like Johnny Smith before him, he asked for nothing more than tolerance. "I ask you gentlemen in behalf of my clients," he boomed. "I ask you more than everything else, I ask you in behalf of justice, often maligned and down-trodden, hard to protect and hard to maintain, I ask you in behalf of yourselves, in behalf of our race, to see that no harm comes to them. I ask you gentlemen in the name of the future, the future which will one day solve these sore problems, and the future which is theirs as well as ours, I ask you in the name of the future to do justice in this case."[72]

Lilienthal understood what Darrow had done. "He seemed to be pleading more that the white man might be just than that the black be free," the young man said, "more for the spirit of the master than the body of the slave." But the rest of the courtroom was simply swept away by the power of a presentation so brilliantly concluded. "I've heard about lawyers making a judge cry," one of the colored attorneys, Charles Mahoney, recalled of the moment the plea was finished, "but Darrow was the first man I ever saw do it." "It was wonderful, eloquent, logical," wrote the young woman from the Penguin Club, Josephine Gomon, in attendance at Darrow's request. "People wept and [the] jurors were moved." The Great Defender himself wiped a tear from his eye, quickly scanned the courtroom to find if his beloved Ruby was in attendance, then seeing that the coast was clear, slipped over to where Gomon was seated and asked if she might be interested in joining him for a very private lunch.[73]

◆

By the time Darrow had finished his plea midway through Wednesday morning, Frank Murphy could see the court's Thanksgiving break looming before him. So he pushed the trial to a speedy conclusion. Robert Toms cooperated by keeping his address to the jury mercifully short: an hour spent reviewing the facts one more time, another hour trying to counter Darrow's closing with a series of sarcastic jabs. "How little attention is paid to poor Breiner," he said at one point. "Poor Breiner? Breiner? Oh yes, yes. Breiner. Why yes, oh yes, he is the man who was killed. I had forgotten about him. We have gone to Orlando, we have gone to Tulsa, we have gone to Washington, we have gone to Vienna, we have gone to Paris. . . . And we have left poor Breiner dead here in Detroit."[74]

Murphy took another hour to read to the jurors legal instructions so learned and precise—at one point he provided them the Latin derivation of the word "homicide"—it's hard to imagine that they followed half of what he told them. As soon as the judge's instructions were complete, at 3:20 P.M., the bailiff escorted the jurors into a small room directly off the court. The door was locked from the outside. And the waiting began.[75]

At first Gladys, Ossian, and the other defendants were positively buoyant, chatting and laughing among themselves as if the verdict were a foregone conclusion. Their defenders also seemed hopeful of an early victory. Rather than head back to his hotel, Darrow lingered at the lawyers' table, while Arthur Garfield Hays and Walter White made plans to be aboard the seven o'clock train back to Manhattan, so as to be home in plenty of time for Thanksgiving dinner. As the afternoon slipped away without so much as a sound from the jury room, though, optimism began to fade. Darrow, Hays, and their wives drifted off to dinner; White's train left without him. Shortly after ten o'clock, someone from inside the jury room rapped on the door, and suddenly the courtroom, still crowded despite the hour, was transfixed.[76]

But the jurors didn't have a verdict to deliver; they simply needed to clarify a few points. Could they convict some of the defendants and not others? Could the murder be justified if Dr. Sweet thought he was in danger, even if his perception proved to be wrong? Murphy reread the appropriate portions of his complicated instructions—yes, the jury could convict one or more of the accused, as they saw fit; yes, perceptions could be taken into consideration—and sent the jurors back to their deliberations. This time there wasn't silence. For the rest of the evening, those dogged enough to stay in the courtroom could hear the jurymen shouting at one another, though no one could quite make out their words. And when, at 2:10 A.M., Murphy finally sent the jurors off to the courthouse's sixth-floor dormitory for what remained of the night, the dozen men trudged out of the jury room looking angry and utterly bedraggled.[77]

Although it was a holiday, the crowds filled the courthouse again Thursday morning. With Murphy closeted in his chambers rather than on the bench, spectators spilled all over the courtroom, some perching on the rail that divided the gallery from the well, others dozing in the jury box, still others loitering about the witness stand. Ossian and the other male defendants remained in jail, where they were to be treated to the county's traditional turkey dinner, but Gladys kept vigil, continually pacing the length of the courtroom in a vain attempt to relieve the tension. Darrow and Hays sat glumly at the lawyers' table, playing cards, while White forced down a Thanksgiving meal of "two sandwiches and a bottle of skimmed milk so thin it was blue instead of white," his thoughts no doubt on the fine celebration he could be hosting in the comfort of 90 Edgecombe Place. As the day dragged on, cigarette smoke grew so thick that the bailiffs had to throw open the windows, though the day was cold and raw. A newsboy arrived with a bundle of papers, which in short order were strewn about the floor, rustling underfoot as the restless stood up to stretch their legs or wander into the corridor. Otherwise, the room was remarkably quiet, as everyone strained to pick up some scrap of the conversation going on behind the bolted door of the jury room.[78]

What they heard wasn't encouraging. The jury resumed deliberations at half past nine, and almost immediately the shouting began again, accompanied this time by the crash of furniture being tossed about the tiny room. The jurors seemed to settle down after that, but as noon approached, there was another outburst. "Damn it," one of the twelve yelled so loudly his voice rang throughout the courtroom, "I am a reasonable man, I tell you!" Obviously, the other eleven didn't agree. All afternoon, the arguments continued, occasionally punctuated by the hammering of fists upon tables and the shoving of chairs against walls. At six o'clock, Murphy, making his one concession to the day, sent the jurors off to a downtown hotel for a fine Thanksgiving dinner, which they ate in sullen silence. As soon as the meal was done, the bailiffs brought them back to the jury room for another interminable evening in one another's company.[79]

Darrow and Hays, meanwhile, took their holiday dinners as honored guests of the colored YMCA, a nice diversion on an otherwise dismal day. Considerably brightened, the pair returned to the court ready for a night's entertainment. Murphy's clerk, already awash in the spirits of the day, happily agreed to unlock an adjoining courtroom so that the defender might have a private space for entertaining; someone purloined a few bottles of scotch; and Darrow and a handful of his closest friends—including the ubiquitous Josephine Gomon, miraculously free of her husband and five young children—passed the evening in conversations made exciting by a deepening alcoholic haze. ("Something was said about newspapers and prohibition," Gomon recorded in her diary. "I don't recall [what] but my retort was that it made me so damn mad. Mr. Darrow reached over and took both my hands. 'We are affinities. To think I should ever hear such an opinion from a woman.'") The party was still going strong at 11:10 P.M., when word came that Murphy was bringing the jury out.[80]

The judge had to clear the crowd from in front of the bench so that there was room for the jurors to gather before him. "Are you unable to reach agreement?" he asked the foreman, thirty-eight-year-old Charles Naas.

"We can't agree," answered Naas, visibly shaking.

"Do you think you will be able to reach an agreement at any time?" Murphy pressed.

"No," the foreman admitted.

Murphy paused for a moment to consider his options. Then he spoke. "My duty is plain. This trial has been running almost a month at great expense to city and defendants, and it is absolutely necessary that I keep you here some time more. You may go to bed and resume deliberations at 9:30."[81]

At Murphy's decision, almost everyone in the courtroom sagged with weariness. But the frustration of the moment struck Gladys particularly hard. From the first, she had been the most iron willed of all the defendants, always defiant, always confident in the justice of the cause. Now she buried her face in her mother's shoulder and wept.[82]

◆

The jurors slogged back into deliberations as ordered the next morning, but they had nothing left to discuss. At lunchtime Thursday, foreman Naas had polled the others. All agreed that eight of the defendants should be acquitted. But they split on the guilt of the remaining three: Ossian, Henry, and, for some inexplicable reason, insurance salesman Leonard Morse. Five of the jurors thought that Morse and the Sweet brothers should be acquitted as well. But seven other jurors wanted them convicted of murder in the second degree, not quite the crime Toms was after but serious enough to merit its perpetrators fifteen years imprisonment. For the balance of the day, each group had tried to sway the other to its position, but no one had budged. A second night of tossing and turning on the courthouse's cots did nothing to soften opinions. Once they had been locked inside the jury room for the third day, Naas polled the men again. The votes remained the same.[83]

Murphy kept them sequestered from 9:30 Friday morning to 1:30 that afternoon, long enough to break a deadlock if it were to be broken. Then, forty-six hours after he'd put the case in their hands, he had the twelve brought back to the bench. Was there the slightest chance of the jurors rendering a verdict, he asked twice, and each time Naas gave the same weary reply. No, there wasn't. So Murphy surrendered to the inevitable. With great regret, he dismissed the jurymen from their duty and declared *The People v. Sweet* a mistrial.

Immediately, Darrow and Toms were on their feet, clamoring for the court's attention, ready to renew the battle that after four ferociously fought weeks no one had won.[84]

TEN

JUDGMENT DAY

Clarence Darrow and Arthur Garfield Hays stayed in Detroit just long enough to ask that their clients be released on bail, to inform Frank Murphy that when the case was resumed they wanted separate trials for each of the defendants, and to talk to the press one last time. Then they were gone, Clarence and Ruby back to the amiable confusion of their Chicago apartment, Hays and his young wife, Aline, off to Manhattan in the company of Walter White, who couldn't wait to end his month-long exile from the East Coast.[1]

The jury had been out too long for the mistrial to come as a surprise, but the lack of acquittal still stung. Unlike many other battles they had waged over the years, everything had gone just right this time. The judge had been remarkably sympathetic; the accused had held themselves with dignity and grace while the prosecutions' witnesses had repeatedly stumbled; on the stand Ossian Sweet had been nothing short of magnificent; and in his closing, Darrow had brought the case together as brilliantly as any advocate could. Yet all of that wasn't enough to convince twelve white men that the defendants deserved to go free. "I have had a strenuous time of it at Detroit in the biggest legal battle we have ever handled," a disgusted White wrote a friend during his first weekend home. "After thirty days of trial the jury still could not agree . . . necessitating a new trial though the State's case fell down completely and the defense proved beyond the shadow of any reasonable doubt that if a member of the mob who was killed was shot by one of the eleven defendants, there was ample provocation." The jurors' "stubbornness is going to cost us about $25,000 more," he told another friend. "Thus six thousand years of civilization reaches its finest flower!"[2]

A few days free of the courtroom's all-consuming combat helped restore perspective. Obviously, the Sweets' defenders had wanted an acquittal, but no one had gone into the case simply to win it. This had been a show trial, a piece of political theater, and as such, it had been spectacularly successful. The fight had riveted black America. Mention anywhere in the country that you are from Detroit, wrote a newspaperman the first week of December, "and immediately Negroes . . . inquire, 'How about the Sweet case?'" The mainstream white press had proved much tougher to crack. After an initial flurry of interest in Darrow's latest battle, the major East Coast newspapers had become transfixed by the story of wealthy New Yorker Kip Rhinelander, who married the daughter of a cab driver, then sued for divorce when he discovered that his new bride was a Negro. One spectacular race trial was as much as the white press could handle, it seemed, and sex sold better than murder, so the Sweets' story had faded from many of the most important papers, much to Walter White's annoyance.

Still, the drama in Detroit had breached the color line in a few strategic places. David Lilienthal's marvelously evocative account of the Sweets' trial in the *Nation* brought the story into the headiest circles of white progressivism, though, like Darrow, Lilienthal seemed more concerned with exposing the power of prejudice than exploring the forces dividing urban neighborhoods along the color line. And White's shameless stroking of Detroit's reporters had almost completely reversed the way their papers portrayed the Sweets. There were still a few bitter voices. "Noble Nordic Darrow . . . exhibited in numerous ways the most degenerate form of race prejudice," snarled Henry Ford's weekly newspaper, *The Dearborn Independent*, "prejudice against the race that bore him. Negroes don't respect white men who fawn upon Negroes." But such sentiments were all but drowned out by a chorus of praise for the defendants: by the trial's close, even the *Detroit Free Press*, the most blatantly racist of the dailies, was writing glowing stories of Ossian's courage. Such a remarkable turnaround seemed to be softening white opinion across white Detroit. "From the comments that have come to me since the Sweet trial, I am satisfied that a great deal of good was accomplished," an unnamed "prominent Detroit attorney," most likely Judge Ira Jayne, wrote James Weldon Johnson a week or so after the mistrial was declared. "One man who used to live in the neighborhood of Garland and Charlevoix told me that he believed that the people of that locality have a new understanding of the right of the colored people to buy property and live in it." Weighing the evidence, Arthur Garfield Hays began to wonder whether the mistrial had been a defeat after all. "From the public point of view, both as concerns negroes and whites," he mused in a private note at the end of December, "a disagreement was perhaps better than would have been a verdict either way."[3]

Walter White wasn't willing to go that far. It pained him to hand out the raft of payments that the first trial required—a total of $12,400—when he knew that the same bills would have to be paid numerous times as Darrow fought through the eleven separate trials he'd demanded. And it took all of White's congenital conviviality to nurture the personal relationships that the NAACP would need when the defendants returned to court. White targeted Hays for particular attention that December: there was a tasteful get-together one night at White's apartment on Edgecombe Place, another evening at the theater to see *Hamlet* performed in modern dress, and a somewhat more raucous night touring Harlem's hotspots. Frank Murphy, meanwhile, received a series of letters so chummy that in his replies the judge began referring to White as "uncle" and "Walt old dear." White's friends from the press table also were informed that the résumés and draft novels they had entrusted to White's care were being passed around Manhattan's best publishing houses. Even Robert Toms got a generous thank-you note for his kindnesses during the trial, pointedly accompanied by an NAACP pamphlet on the horrors of lynching and an autographed copy of *Fire in the Flint*.[4]

For all the duties it imposed, though, the mistrial also bestowed one great benefit on the NAACP. A month of rallies and appeals on behalf of the Sweets had brought the association tantalizingly close to completing its long-sought Legal Defense Fund. As always, the association's well-heeled allies had come through: reformer Florence Kelley wrote the campaign a two-hundred-dollar check; Joel Spingarn gave five hundred dollars; and longtime benefactor Julius Rosenwald, newly named chairman of Sears, Roebuck and Company, contributed two thousand dollars. But it was the passionate interest of ordinary black folk that made the difference. They'd done what they could, dropping fifty cents into a collection plate, stuffing a dollar into an envelope and mailing it to Manhattan, cajoling lodge brothers or sorority sisters to raise fifty or a hundred bucks, tiny sums that, put together, amounted to a stunning twenty-three thousand dollars. Just another seven thousand dollars to raise and the NAACP would receive the fifteen-thousand-dollar matching grant pledged by the Garland Fund. Maybe the euphoria of a court-room victory would have brought in the balance. Or it might have stopped the campaign dead in its tracks, as the case faded off the front pages and out of the public mind. Now the Sweets' story was sure to stay bitterly, wonderfully alive at least until the new year.[5]

Through all of December, the association's officers raced to push the campaign to its triumphal conclusion. James Weldon Johnson tried to use his peerless connections to wheedle a few more substantial dona-tions, while W. E. B. Du Bois imperiously commanded Negroes to pay the balance as the price of racial pride. "No listless foolishness, no carp-ing criticism," he barked in the Crisis, "but to work! Pay! Sacrifice! Be men and women! Be free!" Walter White, meanwhile, cast the campaign in the glow of Renaissance Harlem. Some gentle persuasion convinced Charles Boni, publisher of Alain Locke, Jessie Fauset, and Jean Toomer, to host a Park Avenue fund-raiser. The company of Mooching Along, the newest revue from the team that gave America the Charleston, donated the entire box-office receipts of a special midnight performance. New York World accepted White's long piece on the trial, while H. L. Mencken, Blanche Knopf, and Sinclair Lewis received chatty notes informing them of the latest battle against the Nordic Neanderthals and discreetly inquiring whether they might be interested in seeing something on the Sweets put into print. And for the campaign's crescendo, White brought the heroes of Detroit home to Harlem with him.[6]

Darrow came in mid-December 1925. His social schedule was too full to fit in Walter White's offer of an evening's entertainment. But the NAACP made sure that Darrow was suitably feted during the after-noon rally at Salem Methodist Episcopal, the Harlem church pastored by Countee Cullen's adoptive father. With J. Rosamond Johnson lead-ing them, the crowd of three thousand joined together on "Lift Every Voice and Sing." Tenor Taylor Gordon, fresh from his highly praised performance at Town Hall, performed a few spirituals. Donations were presented from black fraternal organizations, church groups, women's clubs, and the colored schoolchildren of Yonkers, Manhattan, and Staten Island. Then James Weldon Johnson introduced the Great Defender—"a champion of causes that need a champion"—and the au-dience leapt to its feet, cheering wildly as the old man made his way to the pulpit. For the next hour, he flayed his favorite targets, the church rocking with applause as he condemned prejudice, religion ("You're too blooming pious," he told the crowd as the ministers sitting him be-hind him squirmed) and his new bête noir, the "Noble Nordics" of

Garland Avenue. When the day was done, the Legal Defense Fund was $5,057 closer to completion.[7]

Three weeks later, White put the newest NAACP stars on the New York stage. On January 3, 1926, Ossian and Gladys made their Harlem debut.

◆

At first, Gladys was livid with White for deserting Detroit without seeing to it that her husband was released from jail. Frank Murphy had been more than willing to grant the request from Darrow and Hays that their clients be granted bail, but he'd set the bar very high: five thousand dollars for each of the seven defendants that the jurors had wanted to free, ten thousand dollars for Ossian, Henry, and Leonard Morse, over whom the jurors had disagreed. As it turned out, Gladys didn't need White's help; while some of the defendants, such as chauffeur Joe Mack and handyman Norris Murray, had a terrible time securing the necessary funds, Sweet had much of Detroit's Talented Tenth clamoring for the honor of posting his bond.[8]

Ossian came home on December 3, eighty-two days after the gates of the Wayne County Jail doors first shut behind him. Hays desperately wanted him to move directly into the bungalow on Garland, but he was too weary to face the anger still seething through the streets around the house. With the trial completed, the Waterworks Park Improvement Association had resumed meetings. Already there had been one ugly incident: just the week before Ossian's release, someone had tossed gasoline-soaked rags into the bungalow's garage and tried to set them ablaze. Had the police guard not been in place, the structure, and perhaps the house as well, would have burned to the ground. To make matters even worse, Inspector Norton Schuknecht sent word that as soon as Sweet was released, he would withdraw the guard, since the doctor could protect the property himself. So, instead of claiming his house, Ossian moved into the flat Gladys had rented among the foreigners on Belvidere Avenue, a mile northwest of Garland. The new neighborhood wasn't prepossessing, the apartment a small, unattractive flat in a nondescript building the Sweets shared with a white waiter and his unemployed roommate. However much the surroundings disappointed him, though, it must have been a relief for Ossian to finally stand in the tiny sitting room that Gladys had filled with a few of their favorite things, holding his beaming wife and squealing daughter in a luxuriously long embrace, knowing how close they'd come to being separated forever.[9]

Decades later, Otis Sweet claimed that his older brother and the other defendants had taken the mistrial philosophically; "we kind of expected something like that," he said. Perhaps. But any sense of resignation Ossian may have felt disappeared as the first reviews of the trial came in. The December issues of the *Crisis*, the *Nation*, and Harlem's militant *Messenger* all praised Ossian's unparalleled courage, while the Negro weeklies—almost universally incensed at the jury's inability to reach a verdict—proclaimed him the latest in a noble line of heroes and martyrs. To the *Arizona Times*, he was an exemplar of the New Negro ideal: "The Sweet case has positively proved to the world at large," the paper said, "that the American Negro will fight and stand up for his rights as a citizen until every ounce of blood is spilled from his veins." Having witnessed Ossian's performance on the witness stand, the editor of the *Cleveland Call* stretched for a greater point of comparison. "The newspapers commented on Doctor Sweet's poise, evident refinement, lucidness and fearlessness in his quick and accurate replies," he wrote. "One was proud of Sweet, yet there was a pathos, a scene like . . . one other scene two thousand years ago when One Who Opened Not His Mouth was being baited." People clamored to see Sweet in the flesh. Just three days after his homecoming, the Detroit NAACP branch made him the keynote speaker at its regular Sunday rally. Although it was a bitterly cold afternoon, a huge crowd filled every inch of Black Bottom's Ebenezer AME to hear the famous doctor. Shortly thereafter, Ossian's college fraternity invited him to address its annual conference in New York City. James Weldon Johnson all but ordered him to decline. The association's leaders had big plans for the good doctor. And they weren't about to be trumped by the men of Kappa Alpha Psi.[10]

Walter White timed Ossian and Gladys's visit to New York to coincide with the NAACP's annual business meeting, which was always capped by a mass rally in Harlem. It proved to be an intoxicating experience. Advertisements in New York's leading black newspaper, the *Amsterdam News*, announced their arrival in the city. Ossian was invited to sit in on the business meeting, and listen to such towering figures as James Weldon Johnson, W. E. B. Du Bois, and Arthur Spingarn discuss the state of the antisegregation campaign that the Sweets had made a success. When he and Gladys walked into the sanctuary of Lenox Avenue's Mount Olivet Baptist Church for the public rally, the crowd of fifteen hundred Harlemites broke into sustained applause. Elegant Mary White Ovington, the most devoted of the association's white members, introduced the couple. The church choir sang "America" while ushers passed through the aisles gathering donations. Arthur Garfield Hays, appearing uptown at White's personal request, capped the event by turning the day's major address into a soaring tribute to his client. "I presume no man has ever had a greater opportunity to do more for his race or for mankind than Doctor Sweet," Hays said, "and never in his life will he ever have a greater opportunity to do a bigger thing than to lead the fight against segregation. . . . It would be a glorious thing for a people whose ancestors only a few generations ago were slaves, if they could lead the fight for emancipation from ignorance, bigotry, prejudice, such as exists today. . . ." For Ossian, sitting proudly beside his wife, facing the throng come to cheer him, Hays's address must have been an extraordinary confirmation that his greatest hopes had come true. By his bravery, Dr. Sweet had become a leader of his race.[11]

Ossian's sense of himself soared with all the acclaim. When the Harlem rally was finished, Walter White dispatched the Sweets on a six-day tour of NAACP branches. The association wanted the couple simply to appear at each venue, say a few words of thanks, and stand by quietly while the association's director of branches, Gladys's former pastor Robert Bagnall, appealed for contributions. But whenever Ossian saw the people waiting for him—twenty-five hundred in Philadelphia; twelve hundred in Pittsburgh, despite a blizzard; two thousand in Cleveland, with hundreds more turned away for lack of space; five hundred at a badly managed affair in Chicago's cavernous Eighth Regiment Armory—he began to hold forth like the luminary everyone said he was. "Each day he got more egotistic," Bagnall grumbled as the trip wound down. "He draws crowds—but—!!" It was a fair complaint. Although he claimed to be no orator, Ossian "thundered" at his audiences, according to the *Chicago Defender,* trying to impress them with a mix of exaggeration, self-righteousness, and more than a touch of arrogance. "I have had the good fortune to have traveled in Europe and in many parts of Africa," he proclaimed at the tour's last stop. "Even in the jungles where the so-called barbarians and semi-civilized people live, a man's home is his castle. It was then that the thought came to me that the least we who claim to be civilized and more progressive can do is to uphold this principle at the cost of our very lives. I am thoroughly convinced that we have the best people everywhere with me in this fight, as I believe no man who thinks highly of himself and his own household can in any way disregard my stand by saying that there was another way out."[12]

In private, too, Ossian's usual assertiveness descended into a persistent abrasiveness. "I averted no fewer than four scenes," reported

Bagnall, "[and] abated five quarrels between the Sweets. . . ." The couple's clashes may have been rooted in family matters: both Gladys and one-and-a-half-year-old Iva were wracked by coughs that winter—the family was convinced that Gladys had caught a bug during her weeks confined in an overcrowded cell block, then passed it on to Iva—and there could have been some conflict over the decision to be separated from the toddler for almost two weeks. But Bagnall thought he saw "hero complexes" at play. Since November, Gladys had been the defendants' spokesman, appearing at dozens of rallies, smiling shyly as attention was lavished on her, impressing everyone with her poise and charm; now she was cast back into the shadows—Ossian's "girl-wife," the *Chicago Defender* called her—while her husband stood in the spotlight, telling tales about himself that she knew weren't always true. It's easy to imagine Gladys taking her husband aside for a few words, his bristling at her challenge to his authority, tempers flaring, voices rising, and the two of them saying things that would have seemed unimaginable a month before, when Ossian was satisfied to cradle his wife in his arms. "When I saw them off this morning it was a relief beyond description," Bagnall wrote to the NAACP's headquarters on the day he sent the Sweets home to Detroit. "Tell Walter—never again!"[13]

Bagnall had nothing to fear; the tour was such a smashing success there was no need to consider an encore. When news of Ossian and Gladys's arrest first passed across his desk back in September, James Weldon Johnson was dreaming of the day when the NAACP might have a fifty-thousand-dollar Legal Defense Fund at its disposal. Thanks to the Sweets' compelling story, the fund stood at a remarkable seventy-six thousand, an endowment large enough to carry the association not only through its pending cases but into battles so distant they had yet to be imagined.[14]

◆

The first test came with the perfect timing that James Weldon Johnson so loved. All though November, as the dispatches from Detroit piled up on his desk, Johnson waited for word that the United States Supreme Court had placed on its docket the NAACP's case testing the constitutionality of restrictive covenants. Nothing would have been finer than to have the two cases culminate at precisely the same moment, but it wasn't to be: the Sweet trial was two weeks past when the clerk of the court finally set a date for oral arguments. Nevertheless, the timing was superb. If the justices accepted the association's argument that homeowners be prohibited from placing restrictive covenants on their properties, the Court would strip from the marketplace one of the segregationists' most potent weapons. The association's lawyers were to present their case to the justices on January 8, the same day that Ossian and Gladys appeared before an overflow crowd in snowbound Pittsburgh. Thus did Johnson and his fellow officers mark the creation of the Legal Defense Fund by bringing before the nation's highest tribunal the case that might just halt Jim Crow's grim march through the streets of urban America.[15]

Swaddled in tradition and decorum, the Supreme Court didn't permit the sort of theatrics that had made the Sweet trial such a gripping story. But with the stakes infinitely higher, the court's cramped chamber crackled with intensity. At precisely two o'clock, the chief justice, former president William Howard Taft, settled his great weight into the center seat at the justice's ornate bench and signaled for the attorneys to begin their presentations. Although the NAACP had a considerable contingent on hand—James Cobb, the Howard professor of law who had seen the challenge through the lower courts; Arthur Spingarn, the head of the association's legal committee; several former United States attorneys—only the two most senior and august members of the group addressed the court. Eighty-year-old Moorfield Storey struggled through a brief introduction, his once formidable skills blunted by age and illness. Then he surrendered the podium to his colleague, Louis Marshall, who carried the NAACP's case for the balance of the afternoon.[16]

At sixty-nine, Marshall was himself slowing down, and some in the courtroom thought his performance lacked vigor. But he was at his best when tracing for the justices the frightful logic of segregation in the nation's most heterogenous places: first blacks would be banished to the ghetto, he said, repeating the NAACP standard warning, to be followed by Catholics, Jews, indeed anyone the majority considered undesirable. And when that day came, "that which has been most noble and exalted and humane in American life will have been shattered. Great as are the mental and spiritual sufferings of those against whom the shafts of prejudice and intolerance are aimed, the lasting injury is, however, inflicted upon a civilization of a country which connives at a covenant such as that which has been enforced by the decrees here sought to be reviewed." It was a judicial jeremiad delivered with the grand old lion's customary eloquence, certainly enough to offset Storey's fumbled opening.[17]

As he turned to the legal basis for the association's case, though,

Marshall lost his edge. His argument was, by necessity, complex. The most obvious position would have been to say that restrictive covenants violated the equal protection clauses of the fifth and fourteenth amendments. But because the covenants were private agreements rather than government mandates, they fell outside the amendments' purview.

So Marshall had to approach the question of constitutionality through a flanking attack. Individuals may be free to add discriminatory provisions to their deeds, he argued, but judges should be prohibited from enforcing those provisions, since to do so would be to give government sanction to neighborhood segregation, something that the Louisville case said was unconstitutional. "The legislature may not segregate," he said. "The governing body of a city or village may not do so. Can a court, acting as a branch of government, by its mandate bring about segregation without running foul of the [Louisville] decision? . . . I think not."

The justices clearly weren't convinced. Marshall was peppered with questions from the bench, most of them concerning not his legal argument but whether the Court had the right to decide the case at all. Perhaps because he'd entertained those doubts himself, Marshall seemed to be thrown off stride; his answers were so hesitant and unsure, said Cobb with a twist of the knife, "that we who knew the case were greatly alarmed." When Taft gaveled the session to a close at four o'clock, it almost seemed a relief.[18]

"I do not feel very much gratified by what occurred," Moorfield Storey confided to James Weldon Johnson. "Mr. Marshall spoke for about three-quarters of an hour and I hope made an impression on the court. The feeling however among our friends seemed rather to be that we had not succeeded in persuading the court, and I am afraid they will find some way of dodging the question on the ground that the court has no jurisdiction in the case." But in the end, he remained hopeful, unable to put aside his faith in the justices' willingness to see the righteousness of the cause. "In the [Louisville] segregation case I was given to understand we should probably lose the case, but the result was favorable and it may be again," he told Johnson. "We can only wait and hope," a fragile coda for a campaign that would decide the future of the millions of Negroes who had come to call the nation's cities their home.[19]

•

The Sweets also waited that winter. Ossian and Gladys came home from their January tour expecting to head back to court within a few weeks. But there were delays. First, Robert Toms begged off, citing his commitment to prosecute another major case. Then there wasn't space on the court's calendar. When open dates finally were found, Frank Murphy canceled them; his father had fallen ill and he needed to be by his side. January, February, and early March drifted past, deep winter giving way to a tentative spring, and still the defendants' fate hung precariously before them.[20]

The anxiety of those long, dreary months should have been unrelenting. For Ossian, though, the power of celebrity transformed them into a peculiarly promising time. With his storefront office on St. Aubin Avenue continually packed with people wanting his care, there was more work than he could possibly handle—and more money coming into his accounts than ever before. So dramatic was the increase he considered expanding his business. There was talk that Garafalo's Pharmacy, a substantial corner shop on one of the busier streets on the eastern edge of Black Bottom, might be for sale; with its fine location and established reputation, the store would give Ossian the firm foundation upon which he could build his fortune. Money also gave him the opportunity to enjoy the sweet taste of avenging a wrong, albeit indirectly. Although there was still the bungalow's mortgage to pay, he moved his family out of the dismal flat Gladys had found them and into a bright, airy, third-floor apartment in an immaculately maintained sixteen-unit building due north of Black Bottom. Probably he chose the place because it was an easy stroll to Dunbar Memorial. But more than geography went into his choice of homes. The building wasn't exclusive, any more than Garland Avenue had been, but when Ossian and Gladys made their way up the narrow staircase with their boxes of books and satchels of clothes, all the other tenants they passed were white.[21]

His success led to whispers against him—Sweet was getting too big for himself, some said—but Ossian paid no mind. When a man rose above the average, he had to expect petty jealousy from those he left behind. He moved in different circles now: when Walter White came to town, lawyers and judges trooped to his hotel room to pay their respects, but when White needed to see Ossian, he came down to the doctor's office. Where it mattered most, moreover—inside the Sweet family circle—Ossian reigned supreme. Tensions remained, of course. Baby Iva's winter illness seemed so impervious to treatment her parents must have known that something was seriously wrong. And it's impossible to believe that Gladys set aside the fierce resolve that was central to her personality. But at the appropriate moments, she knew to defer to her husband's authority. One early spring Sunday, an out-of-town reporter, a friend of Darrow's, accepted an invitation to dinner at the Sweets' new apartment. Family and friends had gathered—brother Henry, cousin John Latting, lawyer Julian Perry—all but Ossian, who was occupied with pressing business. So when the meal began, Gladys sat at the head of the table she'd draped in linen, chatting amiably with her guests. The moment the doctor walked in, though, she surrendered the seat to him, and for the rest of the evening sat in silence at the table's far end while he described his triumphal tour on behalf of the NAACP, dropped the names of famous people he'd met, and expounded on the problems of the race, the undisputed head of the family exercising a hero's prerogatives.[22]

There must have been moments during the months of waiting when Ossian's confidence threatened to break. Friends and associates certainly gave him reasons to worry. Through Julian Perry, he learned of the colored lawyers' angry analysis of the first trial. Darrow and Hays were brilliant, they admitted, but because they had refused to share even a sliver of the spotlight, the defense never had a local face; all the jurors saw were high-priced outsiders talking about principles that didn't have much meaning on the grimy streets of Detroit.

More distressing was the continual criticism of Darrow's decision to seek separate trials for each of the defendants. Almost everyone in Detroit's Talented Tenth said the same thing: as long as the eleven were kept together, the prosecutor would have to confront the conspiracy charge that had tied him into knots during the first trial. Once they were split apart, that pivotal protection would evaporate, leaving the most vulnerable of the defendants dangerously exposed to a jury's whims. And that, said one colleague, "would be suicidal to the cause."[23]

If Ossian shared those fears, he refused to express them. Maybe he thought it his responsibility to maintain a courageous face; perhaps he couldn't admit even to himself that a future that suddenly seemed so bright might come to a bitter, brutal end. But he didn't protest when Walter White renewed his efforts to purge the colored lawyers from the defense team, saying they were an unnecessary expense. Nor did he flinch—publicly, at least—when he learned that, contrary to all expectations, he wasn't going to be the first defendant brought back to trial. In early February, Robert Toms announced that he would bypass Ossian in favor of prosecuting the one man who on the night of Leon Breiner's death had admitted to shooting into the street: Henry Sweet, the doctor's little brother. The news had to cut deep. Henry was Ossian's charge, after all; his parents had entrusted him with the duty of leading the young man to a better, safer life. And instead, he'd led Henry into the face of a mob, only to leave him alone in the defendant's chair and, if his associates in the Talented Tenth were correct, dangerously vulnerable to conviction. Yet Ossian remained unfailingly optimistic. "When I get out from under the criminal [charges]"—that's the way he put it when people asked him about his future; not "if" or "whether" but "when," as though he were simply waiting for an acquittal that was sure to come.[24]

He even reacted with equanimity when, on March 22, Walter White arrived at the office to say that Henry's trial date was set at last. Jury selection would begin on April 1. There was one more thing, added White. Now that the trial was a week and a half away, the defense team had fallen apart.

•

Clarence Darrow didn't devote much time to the Sweet case during the prolonged delay of the second trial. After his Harlem appearance, he headed off to Colorado to spend Christmas—"the hollow-days," he called them—with his grandchildren, after which he occupied himself with his normal round of public appearances, lambasting all his favorite targets for the entertainment and edification of the great unwashed. On the few occasions that the Sweets came to his attention, he was every bit as confident as Ossian that the next round of prosecutions would end in complete victory for the defense. He said it in early December, when Arthur Garfield Hays and Walter White were still licking the wounds that the mistrial had inflicted. And he repeated it in February, when White dutifully reported the Talented Tenth's fears about holding separate trials. "There is practically no chance of convict[ing] Henry Sweet," he reassured the NAACP, "and . . . despite pressure that might be brought on the prosecutor by the Ku Klux Klan, Mr. Toms would not try more than one or two [of the defendants, once] the first tried was acquitted."[25]

Darrow never explained what made him so uncharacteristically optimistic. No doubt he was buoyed by Detroit's political situation, which in the run-up to the second trial seemed to be breaking just the right way. On January 1, 1926, Johnny Smith recited the oath of office that made him mayor for two more years. Almost immediately, it became clear that bluenoses no longer set the rules. From city hall came orders that beat cops were to stop rousting workingmen just because they'd imbibed too much at the corner speakeasies. There was to be more money for neighborhood parks and additional construction to ease overcrowding in city schools. And to address Detroit's festering racial problems, the mayor appointed a blue-ribbon commission, to be headed by one of his most loyal supporters in the previous campaign, Reinhold Neibuhr. It was understood that the appointment was a political payoff. But for Niebuhr, it was also a marvelous opportunity to study race relations in a systematic way. So he packed the committee's board with Sweet supporters—the bishop of the Detroit-area AME was named vice-chair, Ossian's friend Edward Carter secretary—then turned the commission's real work over to a specially arranged team of social scientists, who were to investigate every aspect of black life in Detroit and to propose specific policies the mayor might pursue.

The recently fearsome Ku Klux Klan, meanwhile, plunged into freefall. After its humiliation in the mayoral campaign, the KKK's national office—itself scarred by a sex scandal so vicious polite society couldn't discuss the details—ousted Detroit's kleagle, Ira Stout, amid accusations of incompetence and embezzlement. Rather than go quietly, Stout fought back. Account books disappeared; warrants were issued; ever more venomous charges and countercharges were exchanged, each bitter turn splashed across the front pages of the city's newspapers until even the most devoted Klansmen must have wondered what had become of the brave-hearted men who had promised to purify America. "Bob [Toms] is a nice fellow and I can't for the life of me see why he is connected with that bunch of hoodlums," Walter White's friend on the *Detroit Times* wrote him as the sorry story spun out. "Besides he should know that the Klan is a dead flower in this community populated by Ethiopians, Jews and followers of the Roman Catholic church."[26]

Darrow also seemed convinced that he could exploit the situation in Detroit more effectively than he had in the first trial. Not that the defense had done a poor job the last time round. But mistakes had been made, and with a second trial, he had the opportunity—rare even in his long career—to correct them. That was the reason he had asked for separate trials. Others thought he was simply trying to intimidate the prosecution into dropping the charges against some of the defendants. In fact, Darrow was righting what he saw as a fundamental error. By allowing all eleven defendants to be tried together, he had given the jurors the freedom to divide their votes in any number of ways; little wonder deliberations had dragged on for days without producing anything close to consensus. Better to present a jury with a single defendant and a simple choice: send him to prison or let him go free.[27]

There were to be other changes, too. But all that winter, the Great Defender kept his confidence—until a Jazz Age gem of a story forced him to reveal a bit of the hand he was planning to play.

Through the first weeks of March, the national press had been salivating over the salacious tale of Vera, Countess Cathcart, come to New York for the debut of her first play, only to be denied entry into the United States because, once upon a time, she had a very public affair with the Earl of Craven and thus was guilty of the unpardonable crime of "moral turpitude." Every day, the front pages were filled with the countess's tragic plight, trapped on Ellis Island while her high-priced Park Avenue attorney, Arthur Garfield Hays, gallantly fought for her release. Had Vera's incarceration occurred just a few weeks earlier, Hays might have managed to settle the case in time to return to Darrow's side by April 1. As it was, he had to pick between two great causes. On March 13, Hays summoned Walter White and James Weldon Johnson to his brownstone to offer his regrets. He desperately wanted to come back to Detroit but, well, he couldn't bring himself to abandon the countess in her moment of need.[28]

White waited until a March 21 strategy session in Detroit to give Darrow the bad news. The Great Defender must have seen it coming, since he had already settled on a replacement. If he couldn't have Hays as his cocounsel, he wanted Thomas Chawke.[29]

White almost choked on the idea. He had investigated Chawke back in September, when the NAACP was desperate to find any white lawyer willing to take the Sweets' case, and the reports hadn't been good. It wasn't a question of skill—by all accounts Chawke was the best criminal lawyer in Detroit—but of appearances. Chawke tried to strike the sophisticated pose that Hays held as a matter of course, draping his six-foot frame in a two-hundred-dollar suit, the crease in his pant leg so sharp it could draw blood, the French cuffs of his silk shirt perfectly positioned below the sleeve of his jacket. But there was no masking the truth. At thirty-eight, Chawke remained rooted in the parochial world of working-class Detroit: an Irish-born immigrant who still lived with his widowed mother and spinster sister in the east-side neighborhood that had been his home since childhood; a devout Catholic with a brother in the priesthood; a backroom politico admired for his ability to make or break careers; and worst of all, a trusted associate of the boys who kept the booze flooding across the border and the blood flowing in the streets of Detroit.

Rumor had it that the big-time mobsters—the locals with ties to

Johnny Torio and Scarface Capone—loved Chawke's bruising court-room style: his intimate knowledge of the law's tricks and turns; his re-lentless attacks on hostile witnesses, whom he sometimes subjected to questioning so intense they'd say just about anything to escape him; the outsized oratory he used to manipulate jurors into acquitting even those obviously guilty of the crimes lodged against them—and a few more besides. For his part, Chawke saw such work as nothing more than business. His clients put up a considerable amount of cash to keep him on retainer. And he provided the services they needed, no questions asked, no excuses necessary. Not the sort of man Walter White imagined representing the NAACP in the climactic battle of its fight for justice in the urban North.[30]

An afternoon conference hardly eased White's concerns. Chawke lis-tened politely as White described the NAACP's mission, his presentation sprinkled with the names of the distinguished attorneys who had bat-tled for the association's causes. Then the lawyer laid out his terms. He was willing to take the case, he said crisply, but it had to be handled cor-rectly. Each potential juror would be investigated beforehand so that when jury selection began, the defense would know precisely whom to choose. If there were new evidence to be had, he wanted it. He wouldn't be Darrow's lackey; the two men would share equal time before the court. And he expected to be paid properly. Darrow might be willing to settle for five thousand dollars, but Chawke would expect half again as much. Should that prove to be too high a figure, the NAACP could look elsewhere. White was aghast. "I found [Chawke] . . . obviously a shrewd lawyer with a pleasant personality but with none of the idealism of Darrow or Hays," he reported to NAACP headquarters. "So far as I can judge he has no prejudice against Negroes but he is going into this case as a business proposition and because, as he phrased it, it is a case that can be won." Darrow had made it clear that he had to have a cocounsel, however, and the association had nowhere else to turn. After a few days of dickering, the deal was struck. A week to trial and the NAACP had placed the fate of Henry Sweet in the hands of the Detroit mob's favorite front man. Darrow couldn't have been more pleased.[31]

◆

As it happened, the trial didn't begin on April 1 but almost three weeks later, on Monday morning, April 19, 1926. Although it was an unusu-ally cold day for early spring, with temperatures hovering in the low thirties, the streets outside the courthouse seemed, said one observer,

to be in "half holiday." For days, the Detroit newspapers had been announcing the trial's renewal, stoking the anticipation of another dramatic Darrow performance. But it was the morning's surprising
announcement that gave the day a particular edge. According to the
Detroit Free Press, Robert Toms had decided to stake his entire prosecution on the outcome of the case, just as Darrow had predicted he
would. If the jurors convicted Henry Sweet of murder, Toms would try
the remaining ten defendants, each in his turn. Should Henry be acquitted, the charges against all the others would be dropped.

Inside the sun-streaked courtroom, the tension was palpable. Henry
Sweet sat silently at the lawyers' table, stiff and serious in a dark suit,
Thomas Chawke by his side, Darrow lounging in a chair off to the side.
Ossian, Gladys, and their eight compatriots squeezed into the visitors'
gallery, relegated to being spectators in a trial that would decide the
course of their lives. Around them gathered hundreds of their supporters, the "the same tense [black] faces," Darrow later said, "watch[ing]
every move in what to them represented a part of the tragedy of the
whole race." Walter White was noticeably absent—he'd begged off a return visit, saying he was too busy preparing for the NAACP's upcoming
convention—but Josephine Gomon was back in her seat, waiting for
the Great Defender to stop by, and Ruby Darrow in hers, prepared to
pounce the moment her husband made his move.

Frank Murphy had lost his father the week before—one of the reasons the proceedings had been delayed yet again—and he took the
bench in a subdued, somber mood. Robert Toms matched him with an
opening performance so predictable it became tedious. Although the
state's entire case now rested on this one prosecution, Toms intended
to call precisely the same witnesses as in the first trial and to make precisely the same argument: there had been no mob on Garland Avenue
the night of September 9; the Negroes had been perfectly safe inside
their home; the shooting of Leon Breiner was premeditated, an act not
of self-defense but of murder in the first degree. Then Toms began the
soporific process of jury selection, laboriously sifting through the pool
of a hundred prospective jurors, most of them the sort of stolid white
workingmen who in the first trial had proved impervious to persuasion, carefully doling out a few of the ten peremptory challenges he
had to command. By the time he had assembled a preliminary panel—
again all white and male—the once animated crowd had slipped into a
late afternoon stupor.[32]

When Toms turned the panel over to the defense for review, Darrow didn't even bother to get out of his chair. Instead, he stretched out his legs, slipped his hands into his pockets, and casually began quizzing each of the jurors the prosecution had put in place. Most of the questions were the same as those he'd asked in the first trial, questions about the jurors' families, their birthplaces, their religion, their political beliefs, though he added a new set of inquiries, too, delivered in the same offhand way. "Well you've heard of this case, I suppose?" a reporter recorded him as asking, "Read about it? Talked about it? Formed an opinion? Got it yet? Ever had any association with any colored people? Understand, Doctor Sweet's a colored man—bought a house in a neighborhood where there were no colored people. Well, that's the background. My client is a colored man. . . . Now you wouldn't want not to be fair. You just tell me yourself whether any views you have or surroundings you have would handicap my client or the state." When Chawke took his turn, the questioning was considerably sharper, a cross-examination rather than a conversation, but the focus was precisely the same. Background. Experience. Prejudice; again and again, prejudice.[33]

Gradually, the prosecution realized what was happening. However consistent his style, this wasn't the Darrow of the previous trial, searching for appropriate jurors by instinct and assumption; this was a disciplined defense transforming jury selection into a prolonged opening statement, repeatedly presenting its central argument for all the jurors to hear, winnowing out those least likely to listen.

On Tuesday morning, the assistant prosecutor, Lester Moll, tried to break the momentum. One of Toms's choices had just admitted to Darrow that he wouldn't want Negroes moving into his neighborhood, and the defense had asked Murphy to dismiss the man for cause. Moll suddenly broke in. "This is not a trial of race prejudice," he objected. "We are not trying to determine whether or not a colored man has the right to move into a white neighborhood. . . . The state is trying Henry Sweet for murder. His guilt or innocence on that charge is the only issue." But it was a pointless appeal. As soon as he heard Darrow's sharply honest reply—"I think we're trying the race question and nothing else"—Murphy endorsed it. There was no room for prejudice in the jury box, he ruled; the defense could proceed as it saw fit.[34]

With that, Darrow and Chawke assumed control of the selection process. For the rest of the week, they methodically moved through 4 jury pools, 198 people in all, searching for the 12 men most likely to sympathize with the defense's cause. Sometimes it was enough to hear a hint of personal identification. George Small was a young Catholic of the professional class—a man much like Chawke—who, when asked about his contact with colored people, spoke affectionately of his family's maid. Eighty-five-year-old Charles Thorne had put in half a century working for the Detroit and Cleveland Navigation Company, the same steamship line that had employed Ossian as summer help when he was a student at Wilberforce, while twenty-three-year-old Edward Bernie was just starting his career as a druggist; perhaps he would see something of himself in a defendant so close in age and ambition.

At other times, the defense was attracted to a juror's self-description. With eleven years' service in the navy, much of it abroad, Ralph Fuelling considered himself a man of the world, comfortable in the company of people from varied backgrounds Then there was ancient Louis Sutton, night watchman at Detroit's Catholic seminary. The old man hadn't heard a word about the previous trial—his reading tended toward church history and poultry science, not newspapers—but he knew he could be objective, he said, because "all my life I have tried to love my neighbor as myself." Not until noon Saturday did they settle on their final man, a middle-aged factory worker who had long lived alongside Negroes on the ragged edge of Black Bottom and couldn't quite see why one colored man had caused such a fuss on Garland. At Judge Murphy's order, the bailiff led the dozen jurors up to the courthouse's sixth-floor dormitory to be sequestered until 9:30 Monday morning, when the prosecution was to begin making its case against Henry Sweet.[35]

Toms intended it to be the day he took back the jury. For his opening statement, he planned to combine the circumstantial evidence upon which the previous prosecution had been built—the bungalow's lack of furniture, Gladys's stockpiling of food, Ossian's gathering of ten men inside the house on the night of the shooting—with Henry's damning admission to the assistant prosecutor that he'd aimed his rifle toward the street and squeezed off at least two shots. Toms hoped that with the young man's mumbled words eight months earlier—"I fired the rifle . . . the first time in the air," then "again in the crowd"—the rickety framework of the state's case would seem much more firm and reliable.

If he followed his pattern from the first trial, Darrow would then defer his opening statement, preferring to wait until the state closed its case and the defense was ready to begin presenting its evidence. So Toms would be free to move straight to his first witnesses, Inspector Schuknecht and his lieutenant, Paul Schellenberger, who'd finish the day with detailed descriptions of quiet, pacific Garland in the moments before the Negroes started shooting. Words alone wouldn't do, though. Before the jury was brought into the courtroom Monday morning, Toms stacked onto the lawyer's table the entire cache of weapons the police had found in the Sweets' house the night Breiner died so that when the jurors glanced at Henry Sweet, sitting directly behind his lawyers, they'd see the murder weapon, too, defendant and rifle reunited in a single indelible image.[36]

But again the defense moved in an unexpected direction. When Toms finished his opening statement, Murphy invited the defense to offer its response. Rather than demurring, Darrow rose from his seat, and, leaning on the jury box rail, told the jurors that the prosecutor was right: most likely a bullet from one of the guns now spread on the table killed Leon Breiner, and it was entirely possible that Henry Sweet pulled the trigger. But that tragic fact didn't make the young man into a killer, for he had been driven to his desperate act by the real villains of the story: the "average people"—"not any more than average," he added, "[As] you'll see"—who were now waiting to testify on the prosecution's behalf.[37]

Then the assault really began.

·

There were times when it was painful to watch. Every day for a week and a half, Toms would carefully lead his witnesses through their testimony, ordinary folks unaccustomed to public appearances nervously recounting for the packed courtroom the events of September 9 precisely as the prosecutor needed them told. Then Darrow or Chawke would start the cross-examination, alternating the task between them. Except when children took the stand, there would be no gentle buildup, no attempt to beguile witnesses into saying something damaging, the way the defense had sometimes done during the first trial. The questions would come hard and fast, as they'd come for William Jennings Bryan in the stifling heat of Dayton, Darrow's typically gentle voice dripping with sarcasm, Chawke's deep bass raised in anger, the two men daring Toms's witnesses to hold their ground, pressing them to crack.[38]

Of course, they wanted to squeeze from the witnesses the critical admission that would bring the prosecution's version of events tumbling down—on the night of the murder, Garland was in the grip of a mob; the air was thick with threats; the bungalow was being pelted with stones— and they tried hard to get it. In the first trial, Darrow had allowed some of the state's witnesses to slip by with only perfunctory cross-examinations. Now, almost every witness was subjected to an intense interrogation, every detail pressed and probed, any equivocation a cause for attack. His hands clasped behind his back, his body leaning slightly toward the witness like a hawk looking for prey, Chawke asked Lieutenant Schellenberger whether he saw "an unusual number of automobiles" on Garland in the hour before the shooting. "I should say not," the young officer replied. Then why did you stop traffic on Garland but not on the streets immediately east and west of it, Chawke said.

Schellenberger hadn't seen that question coming and he tried an evasion. "I think the streets are wider and can accommodate more cars." Chawke pounced. How wide is the street to the east? How wide is the street to the west? Schellenberger said he didn't know. Then why did you stop the cars on Garland, Chawke demanded, the questions fired so rapidly now there was barely time for a reply. Were there strangers in the autos pouring into Garland, people who didn't belong in the neighborhood? Who were they? Why were they there? Thoroughly flustered, Schellenberger fumbled out an answer. "It appeared to me that people were getting curious, more so than anything else, and there was an unusual amount of traffic." That was what Chawke had been looking for. "Then there *was* an unusual amount of traffic [on Garland]," he said, "wasn't there?" Schellenberger gave Toms a desperate look, then said in as firm a voice as he could manage, "There was."[39]

Most of the witnesses proved tougher than Schellenberger. If a man or woman's lies couldn't be exposed, though, the liar could. In the trial's first fierce confrontation, Darrow took on Norton Schuknecht, "the veteran attorney fac[ing] a veteran police officer," as one reporter put it. The inspector struck a nonchalant pose, one arm draped over the witness chair, his hand dangling limply, his Masonic ring glinted toward the gallery. For an hour or more they battled, Darrow digging into every detail of the inspector's two nights on Garland. How many people were on the street on September 8? September 9? What did you hear them saying? How heavy was the traffic? Did you see the taxi bringing Otis Sweet to the bungalow? Did you see rocks thrown? Glass broken?

Doggedly, Schuknecht stuck to the story he'd been telling since September—no crowds, no violence, no cause—but that simply gave Darrow the opportunity to press the witness all the harder. If the Sweets were in no danger, he asked, why did you have a dozen men around the house and a reserve squad at the ready? Why did you order Garland closed to cars shortly before the Negroes opened fire? If the shooting were unprovoked, why was your first response to run straight toward a house filled with homicidal colored men, without bothering to take his gun out of its holster? With each question, the contradictions became more glaring, the inspector's answers more labored, until Darrow finally turned to the jurors, let out an audible "humph," and shrugged his shoulders in weary disbelief.[40]

Thomas Chawke subjected small, scared John Getke, the piano tuner who owned the house next to the Sweets, to the same treatment, albeit with a more combative edge. During the state's examination, Getke told Toms that Garland was deserted right before the shooting, but under Chawke's persistent questioning, he changed his mind, saying he might have seen a few people gathered on the sidewalk. "Did you surmise why a crowd was there?" demanded Chawke, and Getke said he did. "And your surmise had something to with the colored people who had moved into the neighborhood?" Again, Getke said it did. Desperate to put the witness back on track, Toms broke in to ask what Getke understood "surmise" to mean. The question seemed to remind the piano tuner of what he was supposed to be saying. "Since the last trial, I guess I kind of visualized a crowd," he explained. "I haven't a very good memory anyway." "Then you really didn't see a crowd?" said Toms. "No, I didn't," Getke replied and, that settled, stepped down from the witness box and started back to his seat. Instantly, Chawke blocked his way, towering over the man and thundering, "Will you see if you can tell us the truth? Was there or was there not a crowd?" Getke pulled himself to his full height, still far below that of Chawke, and screamed, "No!" while Toms, also on his feet, shouted his objection to the bench.

For a split second, it seemed as if a brawl were about to break out, but Murphy gaveled for order and the bailiff ushered Getke, red faced and fuming, back to the stand. Immediately, Chawke returned to the attack. "You 'surmised,' didn't you, that Mr. Toms wanted you to say no? You saw between five hundred and a thousand people there, didn't you?" "No," Getke insisted. "Do you know what a crowd is?" the attorney snarled. "Well," said the witness, "they say that one is company, two is a couple, and three is a crowd. I saw three policemen in front of the Sweet home." "At which," wrote a friend of Darrow's, "Mr. Chawke, with wrathful sardonic eyes and a look at the jury, dismissed him."[41]

To make sure that the jurors didn't miss the meaning behind all the glances their way, Darrow found a moment to make his condemnation of the witnesses perfectly plain. It was late in the first week and the defender was putting yet another Garland Avenue resident under a furious cross-examination. The witness was in the midst of making a slightly damaging admission when Lester Moll objected to his answer being admitted into evidence. Darrow exploded. "I don't believe the State has put on one witness who was present at the shooting who told the truth," he shouted, as heated as he'd been all trial. "Their own statements show they are hedging, quibbling and lying." On Toms's objection, the outburst was purged from the official record. But the jury had heard every word.[42]

Nor were the state's witnesses simply liars. With sneers so sharp they would have made H. L. Mencken proud, Darrow transformed those who took the stand from the decent men and women the prosecution claimed them to be into idiots, city cousins of the slope-browed simpletons he and his fellow sophisticates had humiliated in the backwoods of Tennessee the summer before. Patrolman Roy Schaldenbrand was trying to answer a question about the size of the crowd on Garland when he forgot what he was about to say. "I didn't think—" he hesitated. "What do you mean you didn't think?" shot Darrow. "Don't policemen think?" "No, a policeman is not supposed to think," the patrolman replied.

The people of Garland fared far worse. Time and again, Darrow mocked the witnesses' unconvincing answers, their lack of polish, their mangling of grammar and pronunciation. He knew from the first trial that the Sweets' white neighbors habitually mispronounced the cross street due north of Charlevoix, Goethe Street, calling it "Go-thee," but he hadn't made anything of it. This time he did. Marjorie Stowell, fifteen years a high school teacher, had already drawn laughs from the gallery by telling the clerk of the court her name and address not once but twice, both times in a voice so booming it rattled off the court's marble walls. Darrow began his cross-examination with a taunt. What's your name again, he asked. "You heard it the first time," she snapped. "What do you do?" Darrow drawled. "I am a teacher," she replied. "And you live near what street?" "Go-thee," she said for the third time. "You mean to tell me," Darrow scoffed, "anyone is fit to teach school in this city who pronounces 'Goethe' that way?" The next day, Stowell's humiliation made headlines in every one of Detroit's dailies.[43]

Of the various impressions the defense tried to create during cross-examination, though, one took preeminence. With almost every neighborhood witness, Darrow and Chawke circled their questioning back to the Waterworks Park Improvement Association. They never asked about the mundane activities that had filled much of the previous summer: the meeting in Harry Monet's garage at which the founding members talked of the association's rules and purposes; James Conley's consultations with other real estate agents to find the proper form for the restrictive covenants that he promised would protect the street from a Negro invasion; the association's going door to door in a fruitless search for neighbors willing to add the covenants to their deeds. Instead, Chawke and Darrow struck at individual motivation. Are you a member of the Waterworks Park Improvement Association, they'd begin. Yes, a witness would say, and the lawyers would ask the inevitable follow-up: why did you join? What did you hope to accomplish?[44]

Most of the witnesses tried to dodge the questions. "I joined because my husband did," said Della Getke, and no matter how hard Darrow pushed, she'd say no more. Edward Wettlaufer refused to remember a single thing about the association—who invited him to join, why he'd paid his dues, whether he'd ever attended a meeting. But there were breakthroughs, too. Florence Ware, who lived on the block south of the bungalow, told Darrow she joined the association "to protect my property." "Do you mean from colored people?" Darrow asked. "For the betterment of the community," she began to say, but Darrow cut her off. "Do you mean from colored people?" he asked again, his tone more insistent. Immediately, Toms objected. "Now don't interrupt the witness," he said. "You won't let her answer, and she is trying to answer your question." "She is trying not to answer," Darrow barked back, "just like the others." The objection was overruled and Murphy instructed the witness to respond. Yes, said Mrs. Ware at last, she was trying to protect her property from colored people. Edward Miller, a foreman who lived on the far end of the Sweets' block, tried a similar evasion, with even more miserable results. What was the purpose of the Waterworks Park Improvement Association, Darrow asked him. "Oh, we wanted to protect the place," he said. Against what? "Against undesirables," Miller answered. "Who do you mean by undesirables?" "Oh, people we don't want," Miller said, thinking himself cagey, but the defender demanded specifics. "Against Negroes," the witness admitted. "Anyone else?" Darrow asked, readying his knife. There was a pause while Miller thought about it. "Eye-talians," he finally said. Anyone else? Then "the witness with a Germanic name and the face of a moron," in James Weldon Johnson's scalding words, said that the people of Garland didn't want "anybody but Americans" living on their street. In went the blade. Do you know that Negroes have been in America for more than three hundred years, snarled Darrow, and that America was discovered by an "Eye-talian"?[45]

It wasn't sufficient to expose the association's discriminatory intent, though. Once a witness admitted his membership, Darrow and Chawke invariably led him back to the lawn outside Howe Elementary School in the heat of a July night, back to the moment when discrimination and the threat of violence first began to blend together. Several times, they came close to uncovering the full story of the association's mass meeting at the school yard, only to have the witness stop talking. By Saturday, May 1, they were running out of time; almost all of the prosecution's seventy-one witnesses had testified, and Toms was planning to bring his case to a close within a day or two. So when Alf Andrews took the stand, Darrow launched as vigorous a cross-examination as he could manage. Andrews wasn't any more friendly a witness than the others had been. But in the first trial, he'd been the one to say that the midsummer rally had attracted six hundred or seven hundred people. Now, under Darrow's relentless questioning, he revealed more.

The break began when Andrews said that the featured speaker that evening had been from the Tireman Avenue Improvement Association. What did the man say in his speech, Darrow asked? "He called a spade a spade when he talked," said Andrews. "Why can't you say it?" Darrow demanded. "Why can't you put it the way he did?" Andrews struggled for words. "He said that they—he offered the support of the Tireman Avenue Improvement Association to the Waterworks Improvement Association to handle the problem it was up against." "Did he say that they—the organization—made the Turners leave the[ir] house?" "Yes, he did," the witness said. "They didn't want colored people in their neighborhood and proposed to keep them out. He was very outspoken in his statements." "And you felt the same about not letting them out there?" said Darrow. Andrews admitted that he did, "if by legal means we could restrict them."

By now, the courtroom was riveted. Darrow "shoved his hands way down into his pockets," wrote a reporter who watched the exchange unfold, "let his face fill with withering scorn, hunched his shoulders. He was in full cry after his quarry."

"Did the speaker talk about 'legal means'?" he asked.

"I admitted to you that this man was radical," said Andrews.

"Answer my question. Did he talk about legal means?"

"No."

"He talked about driving them out, didn't he?"

"Yes, he was radical—I admit that."

"You say you approved of what he said and applauded it, didn't you?"

"Part of his speech," Andrews conceded.

"In what way was he radical?"

"Well I don't—I myself do not believe in violence."

"I didn't ask you what you believe in," Darrow snapped. "I said in what way was he radical? Any more you want to say about what you mean by radical, that he advocated?"

"No," said Andrews, almost pleading. "I don't want to say any more." But Darrow wasn't about to stop.

"You didn't rise at that meeting and say, 'I myself don't believe in violence,' did you?"

The thought seemed to horrify the witness. "No," he said. "I'd had a fine chance with six hundred people there!"

"What?" Darrow bellowed. "You would have caught it yourself, wouldn't you? You wouldn't have dared do it at that meeting?"

From behind him came Toms's desperate interruption. "Don't answer it!" he commanded Andrews. "I object to [the question] as very, very improper," and for once, Murphy agreed. But Darrow simply ignored the bench. "What did you mean by saying you had a fine chance?" he asked again. Toms grabbed Darrow by the arm, as if to restrain him. "Wait a minute!" he yelled. "Didn't you get the court's ruling?" Darrow shrugged him off. "What did you mean by that?" he asked again.

"You imagine I would have made myself heard with six hundred people there?" Andrews replied. "I wasn't on the platform."

Darrow shifted ground ever so slightly. "Did anybody—did *anybody* in that audience of six hundred people protest against advocating violence against colored people who moved into the neighborhood?"

"I don't know."

"You didn't hear any protest?"

"No."

"You heard only applause?"

"There was—as I stated—this meeting was in the school yard—"

Darrow broke in. "You heard nobody utter any protest, and all the manifestation you heard was applause at what he said?"

"Yes, that is all."

Again, Toms interrupted. "Did he *advocate* violence?" he asked, trying to hand the witness the answer he needed to escape Darrow's attack. But Andrews was too rattled to notice. "I said this man was radical," he told the prosecutor, seemingly annoyed that someone else was asking him questions he'd already answered. Toms tried a second time. "I know you did. Did he advocate violence?"

Andrews sat silently for a moment, then said the one word Toms didn't want to hear.

"Yes."[46]

The defense couldn't have asked for anything more than that. Ten days of dogged cross-examinations every bit as disciplined as jury selection had been, ten days of battering the prosecution's witnesses, and Darrow and Chawke had done precisely what they set out to do. By the time Toms closed his case on May 4, everyone in the courtroom knew that prejudice had a home. It lived in the cramped, crabbed houses that lined Garland Avenue.

◆

After the ferocity of its cross-examinations, the defense's presentation of its case opened in a subdued and predictable way. Darrow and Chawke brought in the requisite character witnesses—the president of Wilberforce's board of trustees, the Rev. Dr. Joshua Jones, and the college's football coach—and for an hour or so one afternoon, the director of the Detroit Urban League, John Dancy, provided an explanation of the city's racial problems so calm and judicious that even the prosecutor applauded his presentation.[47] Otherwise, the defense kept the court circling in and out of the Sweets' bungalow, just as they had in the first trial, showing the jurors snatches of two nights of terror.

Gladys's friends Edna Butler and Serena Rochelle returned with their story of seeing the mob gathered outside on the evening of September 8 and of the long night they spent huddling inside the house, too scared to go home. White reporter Philip Alder and the light-skinned colored couple, Bruce and Mary Spaulding, again told of wading through the crowd on Garland in the minutes before the shooting, their stories corroborated by the defense's one surprise witness, Thomas Chawke's cleaning lady, Theresa Hinties, who, as luck would have it, lived right across the alley from the Sweets' bungalow. Hinties set out to walk her dog on the evening of September 9, she explained in her thick German accent, but the mob in front of the Sweets was so large—at least three hundred people strong—the sidewalks were impassable, and she turned back; "I stepped me by the alley door," she said, just in time to hear the guns go off behind her. James Smith picked up the story there, describing the rampaging gangs of whites that engulfed his car as he tried to make his way down Charlevoix in the shooting's immediate aftermath.[48]

And with that the defense was complete—but for one witness. Friday morning, May 7, Darrow and Chawke brought Ossian back to the stand. By all rights, it should have been Henry, but the defense wasn't confident he could hold his own during what was sure to be a rigorous cross-examination, so the young man sat in silence—all but forgotten, thought a reporter—while his older brother took the jury on the long, bloody road from Bartow to Garland, from his hiding place in the bulrushes along the Peace River to the moment he opened his front door for Otis and Davis and saw a rabid mob across the narrow street. One man's story slotted into the nation's torturous history of race relations, an American dream darkened by nightmarish memories of rope and kerosene and a sudden, sickening confrontation with hatreds so deep they seemed bred in the bone.[49]

By early afternoon, the story was told. So Darrow returned to his seat, wearied from the day's exertions and a nagging cold, while Toms rose to begin his questioning. The rest of that day and most of the next, he kept Ossian on the stand, searching not for new information—there was none to find—but for the one misstatement, admission, contradiction that would destroy his credibility. Chawke and Darrow did what they could to protect their client, blocking Toms's most aggressive questions with objections that Murphy almost always sustained. When he had to answer, Ossian tried to be as cautious as he could; "most of the time," wrote an observer, "[the cross-examination] reminded one of a duel with swords," the prosecutor's thrusts parried by the doctor's carefully calibrated replies. At one point, Toms brandished the NAACP's tally of lynchings that Walter White had provided him. Have you read this report, he asked. Ossian said that he had. Why, then, did you fear for your life on Garland, said Toms, if you knew that there hadn't been a lynching in Michigan since 1889? "I thought that if Michigan mobs could find Negroes to lynch when there were comparatively few here," Ossian answered, "there was a good deal of danger now that there are eighty thousand of us."[50]

But there were also a few moments—the most perilous moments of the trial—when Ossian let down his guard. It wasn't that he stumbled, although after hours on the stand, he must have been exhausted. In fact, he seemed to straighten in his seat as the questions were asked. How was it that the men who were in the house on the night of the shooting all had guns? I supplied them, Ossian said, no hint of hesitation in his reply. That's not what you told the assistant prosecutor at police headquarters that evening, Toms pointed out, his chance at impeachment never better. I lied, said Ossian, "because I was scared and bewildered and denied the right of having an attorney. I thought they wanted to get me to make an incriminating statement so they could send me to prison." Now the fear was gone, replaced by unbending pride, the terrified little boy of Bartow given way to a New Negro willing to risk everything in defense of his family, his home, and his principles.[51]

"I was in Detroit last week and attended the Sweet trial," longtime activist Charles Edward Russell wrote his friend W. E. B. Du Bois after watching the scene unfold. "My dear Doctor, that was one of the great revelations—I wish you could have seen it. You would have thought better than ever of your people."[52]

◆

When the defense rested its case Saturday afternoon, Darrow left court ill and irritable, an old man feeling all of his sixty-eight years. But a day of rest and a surge of righteousness revived him, so that by the time closing statements began at half past nine Monday his blood was in full boil.[53]

The day did nothing to cool him. Assistant prosecutor Lester Moll filled the morning with an unexpectedly bitter screed against the defense, dismissing Ossian as "quasi-intelligent," scoffing at Serena Rochelle and Edna Butler as "so-called artists," and, most of all, mocking Darrow and Chawke for their misdirection of the jury. "God, how they hate to stand in front of the Dove house," he roared as his presentation reached its climax. "Breiner is dead and gone. We are interested in the right of the negro to live where he chooses. We are interested in the proposition that a jury of twelve men in this court of record will give them their due. Now let us forget about Breiner. Let us forget about that hail of lead bullets, gentlemen. Let us talk about intolerance. Take a trip down with me to the South. Take a trip back with me through the ages of history; take a trip with Doctor Ossian Sweet and stand by his side in Orlando, Florida, when he was a child seven years old. Register that remote impression of the negro instinct of which you know nothing. . . . We will put in a beautiful historical background. We will have a beautiful drop curtain. We will have a beautiful side curtain. We will have the beautiful music of Mr. Darrow's sweet lullaby, waving aside anything that bears on malice and on felonious homicide. Oh, that is beautiful. The accompaniment to this case has been beautiful. It has been soothing, and it has been pleasant until we talk of Breiner, and then the music of the voice transfers itself to the basso of the funeral march. . . ." But Moll wouldn't be seduced by the defense's performance, and neither should the jury. "Now I am carrying the brief of Leon Breiner," he said in his peroration, "and I am putting the case of Leon Breiner right on your doorstep . . . and alongside the dead body of Leon Breiner I am placing the fate of Henry Sweet. Now you can judge him, giving both their due."[54]

That afternoon, Thomas Chawke spoke in rebuttal, Moll's maudlin closing countered with a rococo condemnation. "Why deny that the greatest asset that the State has in this case is prejudice and the greatest handicap that we have on this side of the table is prejudice," he told the jurors. "I thought this case was fraught with nothing but disastrous things, and apart from the testimony, when I viewed here the sinister figure of prejudice, sitting before you twelve men in a dispensary of justice, but as I sat here this morning, and I saw an attempt made to arouse that prejudice, in order to becloud the issue here, so that you twelve men would not decide this case upon the testimony . . . I was amazed to think that a public prosecutor at this eventual hour should go to the burial place of Leon Breiner and drag his helpless body before you in order that you might send Henry Sweet to jail because Leon Breiner is dead and Henry Sweet is black instead of white."

Chawke's central goal wasn't to batter the prosecution, though, but to make the jurors see the case as part of the bitter divisions that had roiled Detroit's politics for the past two years. Darrow and Hays had tried to tap into that conflict's deep emotions during the first trial, but they'd done it with a subtlety that Chawke had no intention of repeating. "I say that this case marks an epoch in the history of the city," he said. "To those of you who have been lifelong residents of this town, as I have, the memory of your yesterdays must present a picture to you of a happy and contented citizenry, a citizenry that respected the right of the others in the town, without regard for color or creed or nationality." But the forces of hatred had been unleashed, the rights of the minority threatened by the tyranny of the mob, not just on Garland but across the city that Chawke was proud to call his home. As the afternoon wore on, the mobsters' man sounded more and more like Johnny Smith. "Now have we come to a point in the history of our city when a majority can ride roughshod and ruthlessly over the rights of a minority?" he shouted. "Is this the kind of government you prefer, or do you prefer . . . a government that would stay the hand uplifted for the injury of another? Do you prefer law and order to bloodshed and violence? Which? What will your answer be?"

It wasn't a question of principle alone but of self-preservation for all those people, like Chawke himself and at least some of the men watching him from the jury box, who didn't match the Nordic ideal.

"May the day never dawn when neighbor will be arrayed against neighbor in this city where I have spent the best part of my life and, please God, I hope to die. Here, where I have rubbed elbows with my fellow townsmen, all of these now nearly forty years; here where I have partaken of the hospitality of Jew and Gentile, colored man and white man; here, where I have grown amidst an atmosphere surcharged with liberality; that this place that I have selected as my home should ever become a place where the victims of mob fury and race hatred should be slaughtered like innocent children in the streets. Tell me, where will this lead? Today it is the colored man that is the victim of this particular kind of intolerance. Tomorrow, who will be the citizen, what portion of our citizenry will it be said to that you have rights under the law but that you dare not exercise them?"

Then, in his last few minutes before the jurors, Chawke tied the mayor directly into the case. "You have chosen as your chief executive officer a man who has denounced . . . bigotry and intolerance, and who feared that this race hatred might be a lasting stain upon the good name of the city," he said, as if it were the previous November and he were on the stump, pleading for votes. "I summon you to the side of the chief executive officer of this city. I ask you to let him lead the way, under the standard of tolerance and charity and good will toward all men that he has raised, above the strife, the turmoil, the hatred and enmity which some professional agitators would bring into this community to cause hate to run its riotous way. . . . Tell me, my fellow townsmen, what will your answer be? You have justice on the one side and injustice on the other. You have hatred and enmity, as against love, charity, and good will. These will dominate your deliberations, one or the other. We will permit you to go now, conscious of the fact that this verdict will be a righteous one; that Detroit will take its place among the fair cities of this country, as a place where government prevails under an orderly administration; where bloodshed and riot are denounced as pernicious things, things like a cancer, they eat their way into the body politic and bring about its ruin." The day was done. Almost six hours of oratory, and the Great Defender hadn't said a word.[55]

The next morning, the courtroom was as packed as it could possibly be, the gallery a jumble of black and white, the well of the court filled with spectators that Murphy had permitted to sit beyond the rail. Still there wasn't enough room, and hundreds of people remained standing in the hallway, hoping for a chance to squeeze inside. With all the noise and confusion the crowd caused, it was ten o'clock before the judge was able to get the proceedings under way. The nation's most famous agnostic ambled over to the jury box and began to preach a jeremiad for the modern age.[56]

He started in the same soft voice he'd used in his previous closing, the weight of a harsh and dangerous world resting on his slumped shoulders. "Now, gentlemen, I say you are prejudiced," he told the twelve men chosen precisely because they claimed to be open-minded. "Who are we, anyway? A child is born into this world, without any knowledge of any sort. He has a brain which is a piece of putty; he inherits nothing in the way of knowledge or ideas. If he is white, he knows nothing about color. He had no antipathy to the black. The black and the white both will live together and play together, but as soon as the baby is born we begin giving him ideas. We begin planting seeds in his mind. . . . We tell him about race and social equality and the thousands of things that men talk about until he grows up. It has been trained into us, and you, gentlemen, bring that feeling into this jury box, and that feeling which is a part of your life long training. You need not tell me you are not prejudiced. I know better."

Having exposed the sin buried in their American souls, Darrow then showed the jurors the darkness that lay at the end of the road to perdition. It was a bravura performance, sentimental, caustic, blatantly manipulative, and marvelously entertaining. "Now dropping to a whisper, now swelling until the very walls of the building seemed to vibrate in unison, his voice went on and on," wrote Josephine Gomon, "always interesting, always fascinating, always holding the attention of Judge, jurors and audience." For hours on end, he meandered through the testimony that had filled the previous few weeks, slipping in and out of the bungalow, up and down Garland, continually playing off black and white. He talked of Mary Spaulding, "modest, intelligent, beautiful; the beauty in her face doesn't come from powder or paint or any artificial means, but has to come from within; kindly, human feeling" and of her husband, Bruce, "a real gentleman" with "a good mind" and courteous manner. He spoke of Henry Sweet, "a boy, working his way through college, and he is just as good a boy as the boy of any juror in this box; just as good a boy as you people were when you were boys," and of the others who joined him in the bungalow on the fatal night, men who wanted nothing but "a chance to live; who asked for a chance to breathe the free air and make their own way, earn their own living, and get their bread by the sweat of their brows."

Most of all, he talked of Ossian, the embodiment of the American dream. "Gentlemen," he said, "a white man does pretty well when he does what Doctor Sweet did. A white boy who can start from nothing, and put himself through college, study medicine, taking postgraduate work in Europe, earning every penny of it as he goes along, shoveling snow and coal, and working as a bellhop on boats, working at every kind of employment that he can get to make his own way, is some fellow."

He spoke, too, of the people who populated "this highly cultured community near Goethe Street." Back came Marjorie Stowell, "fifteen years a school teacher and in common with all the other people in the community she calls it 'Go-thee' Street." Back came "wonderful mathematical geniuses" like John Getke who couldn't manage to count how many people gathered on the street in front of his house the night Leon Breiner died. Back came Edward Miller, "who thinks he's the only kind of American. The Negroes and the Eye-talians don't count. . . . Christopher Columbus was an Eye-talian, but he isn't good enough to associate with Miller. None of the people of brains and courage and intelligence, unless they happen to live around those four corners, are good enough, and there are no brains and intelligence to spare around those corners." Back came the "neighborly, visiting crowd" that gathered in front of the Sweets' home, "bringing them greetings and good cheer! Our people were newcomers. They might have needed their larder stocked. The crowd probably brought them ice cream and soda." Back came Alf Andrews at the school-yard rally listening to the speaker come over from Tireman Avenue—and suddenly all of Darrow's vicious wit disappeared.

"Six or seven hundred neighbors in this community listened to a speaker advocating the violation of the constitution and the laws and calling on the people to assemble with violence and force and drive these colored people from their homes," Darrow roared. "Gentlemen, in a school yard paid for by your taxes, paid for by the common people of every color, and every nationality, and every religion, that man stood there and harangued a mob and urged them to violence and crime . . . and nothing was done about it. And what else did Andrew say? He said the audience applauded this mad and criminal speech, and he applauded it, too." From that moment on, the benighted people of Garland Avenue were set on destruction. So when night fell on the eighth of September, "the mob gathered with the backing of the law. A lot of children went in front and threw the stones. They stayed for two days and two nights in front of this home and by their threats and assault were trying to drive the Negroes out. Those were the cowardly curs, and you know it. I suppose there isn't any ten of them that would come out in open daylight. . . . Oh no, gentlemen, their blood is too pure for that." And when their efforts failed—because the doctor and his friends dared to defend themselves—the Sweets' neighbors and the cops who supported them went into court and "lied and lied and lied to send these defendants to the penitentiary for life, so they will not go back to their home." Think of it, he thundered: this unconscionable cabal "violated the constitution and the law, they violated every human feeling and threw justice and mercy and humanity to the winds, and they made a murderous attack upon their neighbor because his face was black." And there was no reason for it, no cause—except for the terrifying power of racial prejudice.

There it was: a darkness so deep it made men blind. "Prejudices have burned men at the stake," Darrow told the jurors, "broken them on the rack, torn every joint apart, destroyed people by the million. Men have done this on account of some terrible prejudice which even now is reaching out to undermine this republic of ours and to destroy the freedom that has been the most cherished part of our institutions. These witnesses honestly believe that it is their duty to keep colored people out. They honestly believe that the blacks are an inferior race and yet if they look at themselves, I don't know how they can. If they had one colored family up there, some of the neighbors might learn how to pronounce 'Goethe.' It would be too bad to spread a little culture in that vicinity. They might die. They are possessed with that idea and that fanaticism, and when people are possessed with that they are terribly cruel. They don't stand alone. Others have done the same thing. Others will do the same thing as long as this weary world shall last. They may do it again, but, gentlemen, they ought not to ask you to do it for them. That is a pretty dirty job to turn over to a jury, and they ought not to expect you to do it."

By now, Darrow had been speaking for more than six hours, and those who knew him best thought him too drained to continue. "Twice he almost concluded," said a friend, "and then, as if some deep instinct warned him that he had not yet said quite all—that perhaps he had left uncovered in the minds of those men before him some tiny point upon which might hinge that kind, splendid young colored chap's whole future—he would go on." He recounted the horrors of slavery, just as he had in the first trial—ancestors trapped by slavers, the Middle Passage with its clank of chains and stench of death, generations spent in the sun-baked fields making other men rich—and as he spoke, the spirit of his beloved abolitionists seemed to surge through him. "Now that is their history," he said, every bit his father's son. "These people are the children of slavery. If the race that we belong to owes anything to any human being, or to any power in this Universe, they owe it to these black men. Above all other men, they owe an obligation and a duty to these black men which can never be repaid. I never see one of them that I do not feel I ought to pay part of the debt of my race—and if you gentlemen feel as you should feel in this case, your emotions will be like mine."

And he stretched his arms out toward the jury box, palms lifted upward in a gesture he often used, and offered redemption, thin and frail as it was. "I do not believe in the law of hate," he said. "I may not be true to my ideals always, but I believe in the law of love, and I believe you can do nothing with hatred. I would like to see a time when man loves his fellow man, and forgets his color or his creed. We will never be civilized until that time comes. I know the Negro race has a long road to go. I believe the life of a Negro has been a life full of tragedy, of injustice, of oppression. The law has made him equal—but man has not. . . . I know there is a long road ahead of him, before he can take the place which I believe he should take. I know that before him there is suffering, tribulation, and death among the blacks, and perhaps among the whites. I am sorry. I would do what I can to avert it. I would advise patience; I would advise toleration; I would advise understanding; I would advise all those things which are necessary for men who live together. . . . This is all. I ask you, gentlemen, on behalf of this defendant, on behalf of these helpless ones who turn to you, and more than that—on behalf of this great state, and this great city which must face this problem, and face it fairly—I ask you in the name of progress and the human race, to return a verdict of not guilty in this case!"[57]

For a moment, the court was silent, no one moving, no one talking as Darrow turned to take his seat. Then the crowd began to surge around him. James Weldon Johnson pushed his way through to offer his thanks. "His eyes were shining and wet," reported Johnson. "He placed his hands on my shoulders. I stammered out a few words but broke down and wept, and I was not ashamed of my tears."[58]

◆

Robert Toms led off the next morning with his closing statement, the last before Murphy handed the case to the jury. Like the defender, he talked for the better part of a day, pleading with the jury not to be fooled by all the beautiful words they'd heard from the other side.

"Back of all your sophistry, gentlemen of the defense," he said in closing, "back of all your transparent philosophy, back of your prating of
the civil rights, and your psychology, and your theory of race hatred,
and fear, and slavery, back of all that rises the dead body of Leon
Breiner with a bullet hole in his back. . . . Leon Breiner, just a poor, insignificant American citizen, just one man in thousands, but a living
human being with a right to live, without aspirations and with hopes
and with ambitions, and with the God-given right to work them out,
Leon Breiner, chatting with his neighbor at his doorstep, is shot through
the back, from ambush, and you can't make anything out of those facts,
gentlemen of the defense, or gentlemen of the jury, but cold-blooded
murder." It was a solid enough performance, suitably dramatic, relentlessly aggressive, and occasionally bitter, but it was no match for the
previous day's oration. One of Darrow's associates captured the tenor
perfectly. "Somehow," she said, "it reminded one of the clatter of folding chairs after a symphony concert."[59]

Since the afternoon was spent by the time Toms finished, Murphy
delayed instructing the jury until the following morning, Thursday,
May 13. The more pedantic elements of his earlier charge had been
stripped away, and the statement now read like a long discourse on
the concept of justifiable homicide, capped by a warning that Darrow
himself could have written: "Now gentlemen of the jury," he said, "I
consider it my duty to especially caution you and warn you against
prejudice or intolerance in your deliberations. . . . You will remember,
gentlemen, that under the Constitution of the country, as well as the
Anglo-Saxon concept of justice, all men are equal before the law. Real
justice does not draw any line of color, race, or creed or class. All
charged with crime, rich or poor, humble or great, white or black, are
entitled to the same right and the same full measure of justice. It may
be possible, human as we are, we cannot create perfect justice; but the
ideal is plain, and it is our duty to strive and reach for it as sincerely as
it is in our power do so."[60] So instructed, the jurors filed into the jury
room to begin their deliberations.

If the previous trial were any guide, there was no point in waiting
for a verdict to be reached. Someone suggested that Darrow might
enjoy a quiet little speakeasy not far from the courthouse. Off they
went, Clarence and Ruby, Thomas Chawke, the ever-present Josephine
Gomon, and nine of their closest friends, to while away the afternoon
deep in drink and conversation. They were still there three hours later—
Darrow sipping port and reciting bawdy poetry to his increasingly

inebriated entourage—when an officer of the court dashed in. They had to return to the court immediately, he said: the jurors were asking for a point of clarification, and before he could answer them, Judge Murphy needed to consult with counsel.[61]

It was almost four o'clock before they managed to find their way back to Murphy's chambers. Chawke and Toms prepared a reply, the two of them trading a yellow pad back and forth, wrangling over details. Just as Toms agreed to the last correction, word arrived. No need to finish; the jury was in.[62]

For the first few minutes, there was nothing but confusion. No one had seen the clerk of the court since he'd headed off with Darrow earlier in the afternoon, and while Murphy scrambled to find a replacement, the courtroom filled to suffocation—reporters, lawyers, judges, and assorted observers rushing in to hear the verdict rendered. Henry Sweet stood at the defense table, his hands clasped in front of him, his lower lip quivering ever so slightly; when Chawke leaned in to whisper a few words of encouragement, he didn't seem to notice. Darrow sat beside them, his mouth drawn in a thin line, his head leaning forward, his hands holding tight to the arm of the chair.[63]

Finally, Murphy took the bench and, with a nod, told the police officer nearest the jury room to escort the jurors into the well of the court. They came in single file, silent and somber, the foreman, young George Small, in the lead. Once they had assembled, the newfound clerk asked the required question: "Have you gentlemen in the course of your deliberations reached a verdict in the case of Henry Sweet? And if so who will answer for you?"

"We have and I will," said Small. A second's pause, an instant for the foreman to compose himself.

"Not guilty."[64]

A single clap of hands burst from the gallery, a single cheer. Then everyone seemed to move at once. Chawke and Darrow, both fighting back tears, reaching over to congratulate a stunned Henry; Toms, ashen faced, shouting for the verdict to be read again; Josephine Gomon and James Weldon Johnson joining the crowd of well-wishers rushing forward to offer their congratulations; Murphy gaveling for order that he couldn't hope to maintain.

In the midst of it all, no one seemed to notice Ossian Sweet sitting alone in the row behind his brother, his face buried in his hands.[65]

REQUIESCAM

A month after its triumph in the Sweet case, the NAACP held its annual convention on Chicago's South Side. It was a celebratory affair, as befitting a summer of hope. James Weldon Johnson spoke of the legal challenges to Jim Crow that the new Legal Defense Fund would make possible; majestic A. Philip Randolph, president of the Brotherhood of Sleeping Car Porters, made an impassioned plea for his nascent campaign to unionize the race men who worked on the Pullmans; W. E. B. Du Bois lectured on the trajectory of the Harlem Renaissance, now at the apex of its influence; and Walter White roamed through the assembly promoting his latest novel, *Flight*, just published and in need of glowing reviews. The convention didn't really begin to rock, though, until Clarence Darrow took the stage of the Auditorium Theater for a Sunday afternoon mass rally. So electric was the attraction that two thousand people had to be turned away. Those lucky enough to gain admission stood and cheered him for the brilliance of his work in Detroit, cheered again when he invoked the immortal spirit of John Brown, and again when he spoke of the course of American race relations.

Among "the new generation of white men," there were those who dared to speak of tolerance and understanding, he told the crowd, and in that generation, Darrow saw the future. Prejudice was still a mighty force, he admitted, but its decline had already begun, and in time it would be defeated.[1]

It was a remarkably upbeat message for a man who liked to dwell in darkness. But Darrow had sensed something in the Sweet trial— something in the way his words were heard, perhaps, or in the mix of people he came to know during those days or in the passionate politics that swirled around the case—that gave him hope. And he was right. In the first quarter of the twentieth century, there was no dishonor in believing that white, Anglo-Saxon Protestants stood atop an inviolate hierarchy of the races, no shame in saying that blacks, Jews, Catholics, and the immigrant masses—Italians, Irishmen, Greeks, Slavs, Poles, Turks, Russians, Mexicans, Chinese, and so many others—were by their very nature inferior beings. But, over the course of the 1930s, 1940s, and 1950s, the voices of toleration slowly pushed those ideas toward the dark corners of metropolitan America.

Not that racial and ethnic hatred disappeared. But they became disreputable, a sign of crudeness, stupidity, and moral failing, a product of the prejudice that, as Darrow had said, made men terribly cruel. As attitudes changed, the virulent racism that had swept across the urban North in the 1910s and 1920s faded away. The intelligentsia exchanged its grand theories of racial evolution for a subtle understanding of the brotherhood of man. The Ku Klux Klan shriveled to nothingness, until even the memory of its meteoric rise was lost. Shops and theaters and even some workplaces gradually abandoned the color lines they had hastily erected when the Great Migration began.

Only once, in the fevered days of World War II, were northern cities wracked by large-scale antiblack pogroms the way they'd been in Chicago, Washington, D.C., and so many other places in early days of the century. The easing of the extraordinary tensions of the 1910s and 1920s, in turn, convinced more and more northern whites that they were in fact a tolerant people, a perception reinforced by the persistence of the most blatant forms of discrimination below the Mason-Dixon Line. That's where the nation's racial problems lay, northerners concluded: in the daily humiliations of segregation, the obvious wrong of disenfranchisement, and the habitual injustice of southern courtrooms, not in the streets of New York, Chicago, and Detroit, where a black woman riding in the front of a bus was no cause for concern.[2]

In the time left him, Darrow did what he could to hurry the day when America would become a tolerant place. There were other issues he tackled in the years after Detroit: a battle against the banning of books in Boston and a defense of radicals accused of murder in the Bronx, both fought alongside Arthur Garfield Hays. But the race problem remained a passion. In 1926, Darrow joined the NAACP's executive board, and from that position became one of the most devoted of the association's white champions, contributing a portion of his considerable lecture fees to the organization, regularly consulting with James Weldon Johnson and Walter White, writing an occasional piece for the *Crisis*. And once, in the bitter winter of 1932, he and Hays tried to recreate the Sweet defense in the heart of Jim Crow, traveling at the NAACP's behest to Alabama to defend nine desperately poor black teenagers accused of raping two white girls. But the Scottsboro Boys, as they were known, already had representation provided by the American Communist Party, and they couldn't be convinced that they'd be better off with the seventy-four-year-old Great Defender. The rebuff didn't bother him much. Darrow understood that his time has passed, that the causes he'd championed now belonged in the hands of that younger generation he'd celebrated at the NAACP convention in 1926. Although he could never retire, illness eventually slowed him down, and on March 13, 1938, he passed away. To the end, said Ruby, "[Clarence] maintained that he didn't care whether he went to heaven or hell because he had so many good friends in either place."[3]

◆

Not everyone involved in the Sweet case fulfilled the expectations Darrow had for the next generation. Though he talked of his role in the defense with obvious pride, Thomas Chawke showed no inclination to pursue public service. When the trial was over, he happily returned to his usual lineup of unsavory clients. That work was stimulating enough, he said—during the recess of one trial, an opponent whacked him over the head with a tire iron—and when he grew too old for its demands, he eased himself into a profitable civil practice.

Mayor Johnny Smith, meanwhile, watched his promising political career crumble beneath him. For a while after the Sweet trial, there was talk of his running for governor, but Detroit's elite were determined to see him toppled. For the next two years, they assailed Smith as a front man for Detroit's rampant vice trade, and when he stood for reelection in 1927, they found an appropriately upright candidate to oppose him. The progressive bloc again tried to rally around him, but this time there was no Klan menace to make the campaign into a crusade: Smith lost the 1927 mayoral election by eleven thousand votes. Never again did he hold an office higher than city councilman.[4]

To a remarkable degree, though, the people who circled through

the Sweet case did help move America away from the brutal intolerance of the 1920s. For a quarter century after the trial, Arthur Garfield
Hays continued his peripatetic campaign to secure justice for those the
nation made marginal. He was in Boston pleading for clemency on
the night Sacco and Vanzetti were executed; in Jersey City defending
free speech when that town's brutal boss tried to silence striking union
men; in Puerto Rico protesting oppression when colonial authorities
sought to crush the nationalist movement with force of arms; in Harlem
demanding justice when police brutality reached such obscene levels
it triggered nights of rioting. And when he looked back on it all late
in life, he thought of no better epitaph for his career than the words
Darrow had used whenever he introduced one of his friend to Hays:
"Dear Art, he's one of our kind."[5]

Reinhold Niebuhr spent a year coming to understand the depths of
Detroit's racial problems on behalf of the mayor's commission. "It has
been a rare experience to meet with . . . white and colored leaders and
talk over our race problems," he wrote in his diary. "The situation
which the colored people of the city face is really a desperate one and
no one who does not spend real time can have any idea of the misery
and pain which existed among these people. . . ." When it was finally
presented to Johnny Smith in March 1927, the commission's report
was a marvelous piece of social research, minutely detailing the
depths of discrimination black Detroiters faced in health care, housing, employment, and criminal justice. As a call to action, however, it
was sadly lacking, its recommendations restricted to requesting that
whites be fairer in dealing with their colored neighbors. But the experience of confronting Detroit's multiple divisions had already started
to move Niebuhr beyond the mild Christian liberalism the report embodied. In 1928, he left his Detroit pastorate for a teaching position at
New York's prestigious Union Theological Seminary. Four years later,
he published the first of a series of pathbreaking theological treatises
grappling with the problem of man's duty to confront society's sins.
Condemned by conservatives as dangerously radical, Niebuhr's work—
at once deeply analytical and profoundly engaging—inspired two generations of politically involved students, foremost among them a young
man named Martin Luther King, Jr., who read Niebuhr's books when
he was twenty-one years old and forever after considered himself a
disciple.[6]

Josephine Gomon and Robert Toms, meanwhile, quietly built distinguished careers. In the depth of the Great Depression, Gomon took

charge of Detroit's struggling welfare system, transforming it into a national model of well-managed generosity. Like Hays, she made civil liberties her life's passion, supporting the right of working people to organize unions and women to receive equal treatment before the law, struggles that made her, in the words of one admirer, "the conscience of Detroit." No one would have expected Toms to follow a similar path, given his political commitments in the 1920s. As the Anglo-Saxon fever faded, though, the prosecutor moved in a new direction. With Darrow's endorsement to boost him, Toms was elected circuit court judge in 1929. Once he was on the bench, he proved to be a solid supporter of civil rights. In the 1930s, he joined the Detroit branch of the NAACP. And in the signal achievement of a surprisingly well-spent life, he devoted all of 1947 to confronting the greatest of racial evils, presiding over the prosecution of Nazi war criminals as a trial judge for the United States Military Tribunal at Nuremberg.[7]

It was another member of that young generation of Detroiters, though, who brought the principles espoused in the Sweet case to the highest levels of public life. When Detroit's elite defeated Johnny Smith in 1927, they undoubtedly thought they were taking their city back from the Negroes and foreigners who had put the half-deaf former pipe fitter into office in the first place. Just three years later, Frank Murphy used the same coalition of working people—black and white, Low Church Protestant, Catholic, and Jew—to make himself mayor. The election itself wasn't particularly important. But the voting bloc Murphy had assembled was of the greatest significance, for it was the same coalition that in the desperate year of 1932 elected Franklin Roosevelt president. When Roosevelt took power, he saw in "young, red-headed, idealistic" Murphy a tribune to the urban masses who anchored America's new political order.[8]

Thus began Murphy's extraordinary climb to national prominence. During the 1930s, he served as governor-general of the Philippines, governor of Michigan, and attorney general of the United States, always with the studied sympathy for the underdog he'd proclaimed when crisscrossing Detroit's east side in search of votes in 1923. His last promotion came in 1940, and it was the greatest of them all, to a seat on the United States Supreme Court. Being on the court, he said, gave him "the rarest of all opportunities to evangelize for tolerance and all things that are just." During his nine-year tenure, he did just that, defending the right of Jehovah's Witnesses not to salute the American flag, of Communist Party members to speak their minds without fear of reprisal, of protesters to picket peacefully, of accused criminals to receive fair trials. He abhorred "the ugly abyss of racism," he wrote in his searing dissent condemning the internment of Japanese Americans during World War II. And when NAACP lawyers came before the court, as they did in several critically important cases during his tenure, Murphy always gave them his vote.[9]

James Weldon Johnson was gone by then. For all his self-possession, he couldn't prevent the NAACP's incessant demands from eating away at his health, and in the summer of 1929, he opted for a calmer life as professor of literature at Fisk University. Walter White stepped into the position his mentor had vacated. He stayed for twenty-six tumultuous years, guiding the association through Depression and war with a hand so firm his critics feared he was giving the NAACP rigor mortis. There were new initiatives under his watch, of course: attacks on discrimination in government employment during the New Deal, alliances with the emerging labor movement, a long battle to desegregate the military.

Above all else, though, White's NAACP doggedly pursued the legal strategy Johnson had put in place. In his early years as secretary, White built up the Legal Defense Fund made possible by the Sweet trials until it could support a full-time staff of attorneys. Headed first by Howard law school dean Charles Houston, then by his star pupil Thurgood Marshall, the NAACP's legal department spent more than two decades using Supreme Court challenges to chip away at Jim Crow. Ever so slowly the justices flaked off pieces of the southern system: the white primary, the barring of blacks from juries, the segregation of interstate transportation, all were declared unconstitutional in the 1930s and 1940s. Then in May 1954, a year before White's death, the association's campaign reached its climax. In *Brown v. Board of Education*, the Court shattered one of Jim Crow's foundation stones, the legal segregation of schools, and by so doing fundamentally weakened the entire structure of southern apartheid. It would take another decade of struggle—and much blood—for black activists to topple the structure completely. But with the NAACP's extraordinary victory in *Brown*, Jim Crow's destruction was set in motion.[10]

◆

The North moved in a different direction. Two weeks after Henry Sweet walked out of the courthouse a free man, the Supreme Court ruled against the NAACP in the Washington, D.C., restrictive covenant

case, as Moorfield Storey feared it would. With that defeat, the association lost its last hope of stopping the color line from being drawn
across urban America. Over the next few decades, racism and the forces
of the marketplace, which had only begun to intertwine in the 1920s,
thoroughly fused together. Developers placed restrictive covenants
on their deeds as a matter of course; real estate agents invariably steered
colored customers away from white neighborhoods; banks and insurance companies made it ironclad policy to refuse services to blacks
buying homes in white areas; and in a cruel turn of politics, the New
Dealers who depended on the black vote gave these discriminatory
practices government sanction by writing them into the many housing
programs they created in the 1930s, so that in every one of the nation's
great cities the once disconnected walls of segregation were made
complete.[11]

As the walls went up, there was no outcry from even the most liberal of northern whites, no calls for an end to the obvious injustices
that the marketplace inflicted. Like Darrow in Detroit, they simply
shrugged their shoulders and said that they didn't know what could be
done about it. Racism was a personal failing, after all, to be solved by
understanding, by civility, by a softening of the human heart. When
white mobs took to the streets to drive out black families that somehow managed to cross the color line, an event that happened time and
again in the 1930s and 1940s, liberal whites offered swift condemnation, as they would of southern lynchings, for such heinous acts were
clearly the work of prejudice. But it never occurred to them to attack
the economic structures that transformed hatred into organized violence, as that wasn't where they believed the problem lay. Intolerance
was wrong. But the separation of whites and blacks was to be expected, since, as Darrow said as he stood before the jury in Frank Murphy's courtroom all those years before, "the adjustment of races, the
adjustment of religions, and the understandings of human beings by
each other is the question of infinite time. I see no way that we can
help it."[12]

Eventually, black activists forced whites to recognize the role that the
marketplace played in maintaining the color line. The NAACP finally
won a reversal of the Washington decision in 1948, the victory secured
in a case brought to the association by a black man who had been
barred from buying a home just six blocks from the house Alexander
Turner had tried to make his in the summer of 1925. It took another
twenty years—until the cataclysmic summer of 1968—to push through

federal legislation prohibiting discrimination in the selling and financing of homes. By then, it was too late. Segregation had become so deeply entrenched in urban America it couldn't be uprooted, no matter what the law said. To this day, the nation's cities remain deeply divided, black and white neighborhoods separated by enduring discriminatory practices, racial fears and hatreds, and the casual acceptance by too many people that there is no problem to address. And of all the cities in the United States, none is more segregated than Detroit.[13]

•

When Ossian Sweet bought the house on Garland Avenue in the spring of 1925, he imagined his family living a life free of segregation's most crushing burdens. But there was no escape.

In the days after the acquittal, the accolades poured into the Sweets' apartment, just as they had after the first trial. The most welcome report, though, come from the prosecutors' office. Now that Henry was acquitted, Robert Toms let it be known that there would be no more trials; *The People v. Sweet* would never come to court again. The joy of the moment was tempered, though, by very grim news: the reason Gladys and Iva had been unable to shake their illnesses that winter was because they were afflicted with tuberculosis, contracted, they were sure, during Gladys's incarceration in Wayne County Jail. More than likely the Sweets knew of the diagnosis before the April trial. But it wasn't until Henry was safe that they sought a cure. Early that summer, Gladys took her daughter to Tucson, Arizona, where the hot, dry air was better for their damaged lungs. It didn't help. At the end of August, two months past her second birthday, Iva passed away. Gladys brought the baby home so that she might be buried beside the son she and Ossian lost in 1923. When the funeral cortege arrived at the gates of Roseland Park Cemetery, the white groundskeeper ordered them to go through the back entrance, as Negroes were expected to do. Ossian reached into his pocket, drew out a gun, and demanded that the gates be opened to him.[14]

Ossian and Gladys spent the next two years living apart, he in the apartment near Dunbar Memorial, she back in Tucson nursing her health. Finally, in the middle of 1928, he took possession of the bungalow, which had been shuttered since the shooting. A few months later, Gladys came home to die. Ossian buried her on a dark November day. She was twenty-seven.[15]

Sweet stayed in the bungalow for a quarter century. In that time, he experienced the financial success he'd dreamed of having when he was sweeping sidewalks back at Wilberforce. Shortly after the second trial, he bought Garafalo's Drugstore, the fine corner property a few streets east of his St. Aubin office. He moved his practice to the building's second floor, while on the first, he maintained a steady trade in pharmaceuticals and sundries. Although his fame assured him a permanent position on Dunbar's staff, in 1929 he left his post to run the first in what would be a series of small, rival hospitals in the heart of the ghetto. Though none of them flourished, they must have provided Ossian a healthy income, for there was money to indulge in a marvelous affirmation of his rise into the professional class. As he approached his fiftieth birthday, he began to buy tracts of land in East Bartow— enough to eclipse his father's tiny lot—and to spend part of his winters there, tending the citrus crop and enjoying the honor bestowed on a native son everyone on the colored side of town called "Big Doc."[16]

But there were losses as well, many of them bitterly hard to endure. With Gladys's death, Ossian's personal life spiraled downward. He married two more times, but both marriages ended in divorce, the second amid accusations of physical abuse. Over the years, he opened his home to several Black Bottom teenagers, at least twice offering to make the boys his sons, but those relationships also ended badly, as he demanded of them the sort of backbreaking labor he'd performed when he was young.

The public role that Ossian had adored during the trials crashed around him as well. In his insensitive way, he made an ill-advised bid for the presidency of the Detroit branch of the NAACP in 1930, running against the very men who'd rushed to his defense five years earlier; the city's Talented Tenth never forgave him for the effrontery. Twice, he ran for elective office, once for a seat in the state Senate, another time for U.S. Congress, his campaigns built on a fierce pride in his accomplishments and a touching faith in what he called "the American way of life." Twice, he was defeated.

Henry Sweet helped recoup some of the family honor. After his acquittal, he went on to Howard University—as always following his big brother's example—to earn a law degree. Upon graduation, he returned to Detroit, where he used the charm that Ossian never had to work his way up the NAACP hierarchy. By the late 1930s, he had become president of the association's Michigan conference. Then, in the summer of 1939, Henry learned that he, too, had contracted TB; six months later he was dead, another victim of the inadequate health care available to even the most accomplished of black Detroiters.[17]

At last, even Ossian's finances failed him. Not until 1950 did he pay off the land contract and assume ownership of the bungalow. Almost immediately, the property taxes fell into arrears. There's no saying what caused the problem—maybe it was the increasingly intense arthritis slowing his practice, maybe the slow decay of his tiny hospital on St. Aubin—but the debt mounted year after year, until he faced foreclosure. Rather than lose the house, Ossian sold the property in April 1958. When he left, thirty-two years after that terrible night, the neighborhood around Garland Avenue was still largely white. But Ossian passed on the bungalow to a black family, southern migrants who had come north in search of opportunity, good honest people looking for a place to raise their family in peace.[18]

With nowhere else to go, Ossian made an apartment for himself in his office above Garafalo's. It had to have been a terribly painful move, to exchange the house on Garland for the ghetto that as a young man he had sacrificed everything to leave behind. When Robert Toms saw him at a social event about that time, he was shocked by the decline; the doctor had put on weight, and the agile mind he'd displayed on the witness stand had slowed. There developed about him "a bitterness, a darkness," said another acquaintance. He never said what haunted him in those years. Maybe it was nothing more than memories: of a night dancing with Gladys at the colored Y, perhaps; of their newborn's feeble cry in a Paris apartment; of a spring evening walking through the house on Garland for the first time, seeing Gladys's face glow with happiness as she imagined it being hers; of lying on their bed, a pistol beside him, waiting for night to fall. Finally, on March 20, 1960—just as the civil rights movement was about to sweep through the South—Ossian Sweet went into his tiny bedroom, picked up a handgun, and put a bullet in his brain.[19]

NOTES

Prologue: America: 1925

1. Keith L. Bryant, Jr., "Cathedrals, Castles, and Roman Baths: Railway Station Architecture in the Urban South," *Journal of Urban History* 2 (February 1976): 195–230.

2. National Association for the Advancement of Colored People [hereafter referred to as NAACP] press release, June 4, 1925, frame 195, reel 3, part 7, NAACP Papers [microfilm edition]; "Mississippi Mob Lynches Two More Men," *Chicago Defender*, March 21, 1925, clipping in frame 722, reel 13, part 7, NAACP Papers; "Negro Burned to Death Near Scarboro, Ga.," *[Atlanta?] Journal*, March 4, 1925, frame 1172, reel 10, part 7, NAACP Papers.

3. James Grossman, *Land of Hope: Chicago, Black Southerners, and the Great Migration* (Chicago: University of Chicago Press, 1989), pp. 3–4, 11; William Tuttle, *Race Riot: Chicago in the Red Summer of 1919* (New York: Atheneum, 1970).

4. W. Hawkins Ferry, *The Buildings of Detroit: A History*, rev. ed. (Detroit: Wayne State University Press, 1980), p. 329; Sally Chappell, "As If the Lights Were Always Shining: Graham, Anderson, Probst and White's Wrigley Building at the Boulevard Link," in John Zukowsky, ed., *Chicago Architecture, 1872–1922: Birth of a Metropolis* (Munich: Prestel-Verlag, 1987), pp. 291–301; Barbara Diamonstein, *The Landmarks of New York* (New York: Harry N. Abrams, 1988), p. 308.

5. On urban America's hegemony, see Ann Douglas, *Terrible Honesty: Mongrel Manhattan in the 1920s* (New York: Farrar, Straus and Giroux, 1995). "The joy cry of wealth and power," wrote the German architect Erich Mendelsohn upon visiting 1920s New York, "the victory cry over Old Europe and the whole world. Loud beyond measure." Quoted in Robert A. M. Stern et al., *New York 1930: Architecture and Urbanism Between the Two World Wars* (New York: Rizzoli, 1987), p. 589.

6. Ellis W. Hawley, *The Great War and the Search for Modern Order: A History of the American People and Their Institutions, 1917–1933* (New York: St. Martin's Press, 1979), pp. 81–87; Alfred D. Chandler, Jr., *The Visible Hand: The Managerial Revolution in American Business* (Cambridge, Mass.: Harvard University Press, 1977), pp. 456–476; William Leach, *Land of Desire: Merchants, Power, and the Rise of a New American Culture* (New York: Alfred A. Knopf, 1993), pp. 340–341.

7. Detroit's African-American population figures from Mayor's Inter-Racial Committee, *The Negro in Detroit* (Detroit: Bureau of Governmental Research, 1926), section 2,

p. 4; New York City's population figures from Gilbert Osofsky, *Harlem: The Making of a Ghetto* (New York: Harper and Row, 1963), p. 128.

8. Jane Addams, *Twenty Years at Hull-House* (1910; repr. New York: New American Library, 1960), rep. 170; Christine Stansell, *American Moderns: Bohemian New York and the Creation of a New Century* (New York: Henry Holt, 2000), p. 334; Douglas, *Terrible Honesty*, p. 112.

9. David Levering Lewis, *When Harlem Was in Vogue* (New York: Alfred A. Knopf, 1979), p. 98.

10. "Detroit Stations," http://www.nationalmuseum.org/stations/detroit.htm, last accessed on December 13, 2001; "Jazz Age Chicago—Illinois Central Station," http://www.suba.com/~scottn/explore/sites/transport/cent_sta.htm, last accessed on December 13, 2001; Bradford Gilbert, "The Architecture of Railroad Stations," *Engineering Magazine* (1895), quoted in Ric Burns and James Sanders, *New York: An Illustrated History* (New York: Alfred A. Knopf, 1999), p. 354.

11. John Higham, *Strangers in the Land: Patterns of American Nativism, 1860–1925* (1955; repr. New York: Atheneum, 1971); Matthew Frye Jacobson, *Whiteness of a Different Color: European Immigrants and the Alchemy of Race* (Cambridge, Mass.: Harvard University Press, 1998); Iver Bernstein, *The New York City Draft Riots: Their Significance for American Society and Politics in the Age of the Civil War* (New York: Oxford University Press, 1990); Elliot Rudwick, *Race Riot in East St. Louis, July 2, 1917* (Carbondale: Southern Illinois University Press, 1964).

12. Lynn Dumenil, *The Modern Temper: American Culture and Society in the 1920s* (New York: Hill and Wang, 1995), chapters 4–6, for an excellent introduction to the tensions of the 1920s; Robert Sobel, *Coolidge: An American Enigma* (Washington, D.C.: Regnery Publishing, 1998); Calvin Coolidge, "Whose Country Is This?" *Good Housekeeping* (February 1921): 109.

13. Dumenil, *The Modern Temper*, p. 237; David M. Chalmers, *Hooded Americanism: The First Century of the Ku Klux Klan, 1865–1965* (Garden City, N.Y.: Doubleday, 1965) for an introduction to the second Klan; Detroit and Chicago Klan figures are from Kenneth Jackson, *The Ku Klux Klan in the City, 1915–1930* (New York: Oxford University Press, 1967), pp. 103, 129. A brilliant analysis of the Klan, albeit in a southern setting, is Nancy Maclean, *Behind the Mask of Chivalry: The Making of the Second Ku Klux Klan* (New York: Oxford University Press, 1994).

14. Chalmers, *Hooded Americanism*, pp. 286–288.

15. Higham, *Strangers in the Land*, chapters 10 and 11.

16. Oscar Handlin, *Al Smith and His America* (Boston: Little, Brown, 1958), p. 123.

17. Victoria W. Wolcott, *Remaking Respectability: African American Women in Interwar Detroit* (Chapel Hill: University of North Carolina Press, 2001), p. 1; Jervis Anderson, *This Was Harlem: A Cultural Portrait, 1900–1950* (New York: Farrar, Straus and Giroux, 1981), p. 142.

18. Lewis, *When Harlem Was in Vogue*, p. 165.

Chapter One: Where Death Waits

1. "The Weather," *Detroit Free Press*, September 10, 1925.

2. On the early history of Detroit, see Silas Farmer, *History of Detroit and Wayne County and Early Michigan* (Detroit: Gale Research, 1969). A brilliant analysis of Detroit's transformation is Olivier Zunz, *The Changing Face of Inequality: Urbanization, Industrialization, and Immigrants in Detroit, 1880–1920* (Chicago: University of Chicago Press, 1982), parts 1–2.

3. Allan Nevins, *Ford: The Times, the Man, the Company* (New York: Charles Scribner's Sons, 1954); Douglas Brinkley, *Wheels for the World: Henry Ford, His Company, and a Century of Progress, 1903–2003* (New York: Viking, 2003), pp. 3–160; Lindy Biggs, *The Rational Factory: Architecture, Technology, and Work in America's Age of Mass Production* (Baltimore: Johns Hopkins University Press, 1996), chapters 4 and 5.

4. Zunz, *The Changing Face of Inequality*, pp. 292–309; Robert Conot, *American Odyssey* (New York: Morrow, 1974), pp. 193–195.

5. Stephen Meyer III, *The Five Dollar Day: Labor Management and Social Control in the Ford Motor Company, 1908–1921* (Albany: SUNY Press, 1981), pp. 74–77; Steve Babson et al., *Working Detroit: The Making of a Union Town* (New York: Adama Books, 1984), pp. 22–28; "City 1,242,044 Census Shows," *Detroit Free Press*, September 27, 1925; reporter quoted in Peter Gavrilovich and Bill McGraw, eds., *The Detroit Almanac: 300 Years of Life in the Motor City* (Detroit: Detroit Free Press, 2000), p. 76.

6. Zunz, *The Changing Face of Inequality*, pp. 342–371; Richard W. Thomas, *Life for Us Is What We Make It: Building Black Community in Detroit, 1915–1945* (Bloomington: Indiana University Press, 1992), pp. 89–102; Kevin Boyle and Victoria Getis, *Muddy Boots and Ragged Aprons: Images of Working Class Detroit, 1900–1930* (Detroit: Wayne State University Press, 1997); Thomas Sugrue, *The Origins of the Urban Crisis: Race and Inequality in Postwar Detroit* (Princeton, N.J.: Princeton University Press, 1996), p. 22; Robert Dunn research notes, n.d. [c. 1926], box 1, Robert Dunn Collection, Archives of Labor and Urban Affairs, Walter P. Reuther Library, Wayne State University, Detroit, Mich.

7. Specifics on Garland Avenue are drawn from Sanborn Map Company, *Fire Insurance Map of Detroit, Michigan* (New York: Sanborn Map Company, 1929); a review of R. L. Polk and Company, *Detroit City Directory* (Detroit: R. L. Polk and Company, 1910–1920) and of Garland Avenue building permits, Detroit Building and Safety Department Index, v. 3, Burton Historical Collection, Detroit Public Library, Detroit, Mich.; and from a series of personal visits from 2001 to 2003.

8. For a snapshot of Garland Avenue, see sheets 3–10, e.d. 629, 1920 U.S. census manuscript, Detroit, Michigan, and R. L. Polk and Company, *Detroit City Directory*, 1925–1926 (Detroit: R. L. Polk and Company, 1926). On routes into the upper reaches of the working class, see Steve Babson, *Building the Union: Skilled Workers and Anglo-Gaelic Immigrants in the Rise of the UAW* (New Brunswick, N.J.: Rutgers University Press, 1991), pp. 85–94, and Dunn research notes, n.d. [1926].

9. Dunn research notes, n.d. [1926–1927]; Polk, *Detroit City Directory*, 1925–1926; 1920 U.S. census manuscript; David Montgomery, *The Fall of the House of Labor: The Workplace, the State, and American Labor Activism, 1865–1925* (Cambridge, England: Cambridge University Press, 1987), chapters 1 and 4; Nelson Lichtenstein, "'The Man in the Middle': A Social History of Automobile Industry Foremen," in Nelson Lichtenstein and Stephen Meyer, eds., *On the Line: Essays in the History of Auto Work* (Urbana: University of Illinois Press, 1989), pp. 73–99.

10. Walter Clyde, *A Million Dollar Secret* (Detroit: Walter Schulte Corp., 1927); Joyce Shaw Peterson, *American Automobile Workers, 1900–1933* (Albany: SUNY Press, 1987), pp. 72–85; Committee on Negro Housing, *Negro Housing* (1932; repr. New York: Negro Universities Press, 1969), p. 44.

11. David Alan Levine, *Internal Combustion: The Races in Detroit, 1915–1926* (Westport, Conn.: Greenwood Press, 1976), p. 158; transcript of *Detroit Free Press* story, n.d. [September 10, 1925], box 5, Clarence Darrow Collection, Library of Congress, Washington, D.C.; Marcet Haldeman-Julius, "Clarence Darrow's Defense of a Negro," *Haldeman-Julius Monthly* 4 (July 1926): 23–24; "Put Guard on Home of Negro," *Detroit Times*, September 10, 1925.

12. Transcript of Ossian Sweet statement to police, September 9, 1925, Detroit Police Department records, copy in author's possession; Gladys Sweet to Walter White, n.d. [September 1925], frames 353–360, reel 3, part 5, NAACP Papers [microfilm edition]; transcript of Norton Schuknecht testimony at the preliminary hearing, September 16, 1925, box 1, Ossian Sweet Collection, Burton Historical Collection.

13. In the course of the first trial, most witnesses from Garland Avenue demonstrated virtually no knowledge of their neighbors; most couldn't even recall their names. Time and again witnesses said they came out to the street on September 9 because of curiosity. See, for example, testimony of Edward Wettlaufer, Otto Eberhardt, Eben Draper, and Fred Benoit. Trial transcript, November 5–13, 1925 [microfilm edition], Michigan Historical Collection, Bentley Library, University of Michigan, Ann Arbor.

14. Transcript of police statements made by Ray Dove, Kathleen Dove, George Strauser, and William Arthur, September 10, 1925. On Ray Dove's profession, see transcript of his trial testimony, November 6, 1925.

15. George Suppus and Ulric Arthur trial testimony, November 10, 1925.

16. "Victim's Wife in Collapse, Is Near Death," *Detroit Free Press*, September 10, 1925; Ray Dove trial testimony. Description of the Breiners' home comes from personal observation.

17. Otto Lemhagen statement to police, September 10, 1925; Lemhagen trial testimony, November 11, 1925.

18. Norton Schuknecht to superintendent, September 9, 1925, Sweet case file, Detroit Police Department records, copy in author's possession; Eric Houghberg testimony, November 11, 1925; "Home Row Victims," *Detroit Free Press*, September 10, 1925; Houghberg statement to police, September 10, 1925.

19. "Two Principals in Riot Case," *Detroit News*, November 19, 1925, clipping at frame 66, reel 3, part 5, NAACP Papers; undated description of Ossian and Gladys Sweet, box 5, Clarence Darrow Collection, Library of Congress, Washington, D.C.; Marcet Haldeman-Julius, *Clarence Darrow's Two Great Trials* (Girard, Kan.: Haldeman-Julius Company, 1927), pp. 34–35.

20. Sweet's story is detailed in chapters 2–4.

21. On Ossian Sweet's personality, see Haldeman-Julius, *Clarence Darrow's Two Great Trials*, pp. 35–38; oral history interview with Arthur Boddie, M.D., July 13, 1998, box 2, Kellogg African-American Health Care Project, Reuther Library; oral history interview with Sherman Sweet, February 27, 2002, notes in author's possession. Particular incidents and assessments of Sweet, from which this portrait is drawn, are available throughout the notes.

22. Sanborn Map Company, *Fire Insurance Map of Detroit, Michigan;* Gladys Sweet to Walter White, n.d. [September 1925]; Haldeman-Julius, *Clarence Darrow's Two Great Trials*, pp. 29–30; Arthur Garfield Hays opening statement, November 16, 1925, frames 920–938, reel 3, part 5, NAACP Papers; 2905 Garland Avenue National Registry of Historic Places Inventory, Nomination Form, November 28, 1984, copy in author's possession; Clifford Edward Clark, Jr., *The American Family Home, 1800–1960* (Chapel Hill: University of North Carolina Press, 1986), chapter 6.

23. 2905 Garland plat book legal description, June 1, 1916, Wayne County Registrar of Deeds, Detroit, Mich.; building permit entry 587, June 16, 1916, building permits 1909–1924, Detroit Building and Safety Department Records, Burton Historical Collection; sheet 9A, a.e.d. 629, 1920 U.S. census manuscript, Detroit, Michigan; personal tour of 2905 Garland, October 20, 2001.

24. Gladys Sweet statement to police, September 9, 1925.

25. Gladys Sweet statement to police, September 9, 1925; Arthur Turner and Earl Moses, eds., *Colored Detroit, 1924* (Detroit: n.p. 1924), p. 121, for home addresses of African-American physicians; "The Dr. Sweet Case: A Milestone in Civil Rights," *Detroit News*, August 15, 1965.

26. "The Dr. Sweet Case"; "Race Psychology Told in Sweet's Testimony," *Detroit Free Press*, November 19, 1925; Haldeman-Julius, *Clarence Darrow's Two Great Trials*, p. 33; Robert Toms closing statement, May 10, 1926, p. 58, Bentley Library; "Police Officer, Two Negroes, and One White Killed," *Washington Post*, July 22, 1919.

27. Arthur Garfield Hays opening statement to the jury, November 16, 1925, frame 937, reel 3, part 5, NAACP Papers; Philip Dray, *At the Hands of Persons Unknown: The Lynching of Black America* (New York: Random House, 2002), pp. 240–241; Tim Madigan, *The Burning: Massacre, Destruction, and the Tulsa Race Riot of 1921* (New York: St. Martin's Press, 2001), pp. 179–182; Mark Robertson Schneider, *"We Return Fighting": The Civil Rights Movement in the Jazz Age* (Boston: Northeastern University Press, 2002), pp. 354–356.

28. "Sweet to Describe Riot Fear," *Detroit Times*, November 18, 1925; Hays opening statement November 16, 1925; Ossian Sweet statement to police, September 9, 1925. For

comparisons of housing prices in the neighborhood, see classified advertisements, *Detroit News*, September 4, 5, 8, 17, 1925.

29. Cosmopolitan League circular, n.d. [1925], frame 947, reel 2, part 5, NAACP Papers; Mayor's Inter-Racial Committee, *The Negro in Detroit* (Detroit: Detroit Bureau of Intergovernmental Research, 1926), section 9, p. 33; "Cop Kills Man Court Wanted," *Detroit Times*, August 21, 1925.

30. Kenneth Jackson, *The Ku Klux Klan in the Cities* (New York: Oxford University Press, 1967), p. 140; Levine, *Internal Combustion*, pp.157–158.

31. "Sweet to Describe Riot Fear"; Hays opening statement November 16, 1925; Gladys Sweet to White, n.d.; Turner and Moses, *Colored Detroit, 1924*, p. 24; oral history interview with Elsie Smith, June 24, 1997, box 2, Kellogg African-American Health Care Project, Archives of Labor and Urban Affairs, Wayne State University, Detroit, Mich.; Levine, *Internal Combustion*, pp.153–157.

32. "Sweet Takes Stand Today," *Detroit News*, November 18, 1925, frame 0000597, reel 4, part 5, NAACP Papers; "Sweet to Describe Riot Fear"; "Other Race Troubles Figure in Sweet Trial," *Detroit Free Press*, frames 000055–56, reel 4, part 5, NAACP Papers; oral history interview with Cecil Rowlette, August 1, 1960, Alex Baskin Collection, Michigan Historical Collection, Bentley Library, University of Michigan, Ann Arbor; oral history interview with William Osby, Sr., July 27, 1960, Baskin Collection.

33. Gladys Sweet to Walter White; sheet 4, e.d. 600, 1920 U.S. census manuscript, Detroit, Michigan, shows the racial makeup of the neighborhood where Gladys lived and the ethnic makeup of her family. On Gladys's commitment to the move, see her statement to police and Haldeman-Julius, *Clarence Darrow's Two Great Trials*, pp. 28–30.

34. "Race Psychology Told in Sweet's Testimony," frame 000059, reel 4, part 5, NAACP Papers; Osby interview, Baskin Collection.

35. Gladys Sweet to White, n.d.; trial testimony of John Hayes, November 9, 1925.

36. Wilberforce University, annual catalogue, 1911–1912, Wilberforce University Archives, Xenia, Ohio; Ossian Sweet statement to police, September 9, 1925.

37. Respondents' statements, *The People v. Sweet*, October 3, 1925, box 1, Ossian Sweet Collection, Burton Historical Collection; oral history interview with Rowlette; list of military officers, book notes, frame 931, reel 84, W. E. B. Du Bois Papers, University of Massachusetts, Amherst; "Sweet Takes Stand Today."

38. Davis's second statement to police, September 10, 1925; Ossian Sweet statement to police, September 9, 1925; Ossian Sweet statement to Frances Dent and W. Hays McKinney, September 12, 1925, frame 924, reel 2, part 5, NAACP Papers; Haldeman-Julius, *Clarence Darrow's Two Great Trials*, p. 31.

39. Haldeman-Julius, *Clarence Darrow's Two Great Trials*, p. 32; Schuknecht to superintendent; evidence list, ammunition, April 22, 1926, Detroit Police Department records, copy in author's possession; "Sweet Says He Provided Guns," *Detroit Free Press*, May 8, 1926, copy at frame 265, reel 4, part 5, NAACP Papers; Clarence Darrow, *The Story of My Life* (New York: Charles Scribner's Sons, 1934), p. 305.

40. Hays opening statement November 16, 1925; Haldeman-Julius, *Clarence Darrow's Two Great Trials*, p. 31; Bert McPherson testimony, trial transcript; Ossian Sweet statement to police.

41. Haldeman-Julius, *Clarence Darrow's Two Great Trials*, p. 32; Norris Murray statement to police, September 9, 1925; "Witness Tells of Sweet 'Mob,'" *Detroit News*, November 17, 1925, clipping at frame 49, reel 4, part 5, NAACP Papers; Hays opening statement.

42. Marriage license 240625, December 18, 1922, reel 166, Return of Marriages Recorded in Wayne County, 1922, Library of Michigan, Lansing; "Witness Tells of Sweet Mob"; Elsie Smith interview, June 24, 1997.

43. Paul Schellenberger trial testimony, November 5, 1925; Norton Schuknecht trial testimony, November 5, 1926; Hays opening statement; "Sweet Takes Stand Today."

44. Haldeman-Julius, *Clarence Darrow's Two Great Trials*, p. 32; "Defense Opens in Sweet Case," *Detroit Free Press*, May 6, 1926.

45. "Doctor Sweet Goes on Stand," *Chicago Defender*, November 28, 1925; Murray statement to police; Ossian Sweet statement to police.

46. "Other Race Troubles Figure in Sweet Trial," *Detroit Free Press*, November 18, 1925.

47. Preliminary hearing testimony, September 16, 1925, box 1, Sweet Collection; Schuknecht trial testimony, November 5, 1925; Davis statement to police, September 10, 1925; "Sweet Takes Stand Today."

48. Davis statement to police, September 10, 1925; Schellenberger preliminary hearing testimony, September 16, 1925; Gladys Sweet statement to police.

49. Gladys Sweet statement to police; Ossian Sweet statement to police; Joe Mack statement to police, September 9, 1925; Davis statement to police, September 10, 1925; Hays opening statement; Haldeman-Julius, *Clarence Darrow's Two Great Trials*, p. 33; Robert Toms closing statement, May 12, 1926, Michigan Historical Collection.

50. "Witness Tells of Sweet 'Mob'"; Haldeman-Julius, *Clarence Darrow's Two Great Trials*, p. 33; Hays opening statement.

51. Hays opening statement; Levine, *Internal Combustion*, p. 163; Harry H. Pace, "The Business of Insurance Among Negroes," *Crisis* (September 1926): 219–224; Haldeman-Julius, *Clarence Darrow's Two Great Trials*, pp. 33–34; Hewitt Watson entry, sheet 6B, e.d. 479, 1920 U.S. census manuscript, Detroit, Michigan.

52. Davis statement to police, September 10, 1926; "Dr. Sweet Wanted Home for Baby," *Chicago Defender*, December 5, 1926; Charles Washington statement to police, September 9, 1925; Hewitt Watson statement to police, September 9, 1925; Leonard Morris statement to police, September 9, 1925; Ossian Sweet statement to police; Hays opening statement; "Race Psychology Told in Sweet's Testimony."

53. Polk, *Detroit City Directory*, 1925–1926, Mack statement to police, Thomas, *Life for Us Is What We Make It*, p. 91, show the boundaries of the ghetto. I traced Sweet's likely route home on the *New National Authentic Map of Detroit and Environs* (Detroit: National Lithograph Co., 1925), available in the Map Collection, University of Michigan Graduate Library, Ann Arbor.

54. Mack statement to police; Ossian Sweet statement to police; Schuknecht trial testimony, November 5, 1925.

55. Hays opening statement; Gladys Sweet statement to police; "Race Psychology Told in Sweet's Testimony"; "Other Race Troubles Figure in Sweet Trial"; "Doctor Sweet Goes on Stand."

56. Ossian Sweet statement to police.

57. Henry Sweet statement to police, September 9, 1925; "Race Psychology Told in Sweet's Testimony."

58. Mack statement to police.

59. Ibid.; Murray statement to police.

60. Robert Toms opening statement to court, November 5, 1925; Schuknecht trial testimony, November 5, 1925; Ossian Sweet statement to police.

61. Walter White to James Weldon Johnson, September 16, 1925, frames 943–946, reel 2, part 5, NAACP Papers; Ossian Sweet statement to police; Haldeman-Julius, *Clarence Darrow's Two Great Trials*, p. 35; Ossian Sweet to Julian Perry, April 28, 1931, box 1, Ossian Sweet Collection; Sweet to Ruby Darrow, n.d., box 5, Darrow Collection; Walter White memo, December 12, 1930, box G-96, group I, NAACP Papers, Library of Congress, Washington, D.C.; Arthur Boddie interview; oral history interview with Sherman Sweet.

62. Gladys Sweet statement to police; Haldeman-Julius, *Clarence Darrow's Two Great Trials*, pp. 27–31; Gladys Sweet to White, n.d. [October 1925]; oral history interview with Otis Sweet, August 1, 1960, Baskin Collection; oral history interview with Robert Toms, November 28, 1959, Baskin Collection.

63. Oral history interview with Sherman Sweet, sheet 24A, e.d. 134, 1910 U.S. census manuscript, Bartow Town, Polk County, Florida; Haldeman-Julius, *Clarence Darrow's Two Great Trials*, pp. 27–28, 37; sixty-fourth annual report of the president, June 14, 1927, Wilberforce University Archives; Wilberforce University *Forcean* (1925), Wilberforce University Archives.

64. Norris Murray, Joe Mack, Hewitt Watson, Charles Washington, Leonard Morse statements to police.

65. Ossian Sweet, Gladys Sweet, Henry Sweet, Hewitt Watson, Joe Mack, Norris Murray, Charles Washington statements to police; Hays opening statement.

66. Haldeman-Julius, *Clarence Darrow's Two Great Trials*, p. 40; Norris Murray statement to police. There are various versions of what was said at that moment. Some accounts have Henry shouting, "The people! The people!" Others have him saying, "We'd better get up. They're coming!" Still others report him saying, "Look at that gang out there now." See "Race Psychology Told in Sweet's Testimony"; "Sweet Depicts Fear in Court."

67. Levine, *Internal Combustion*, p. 163; "Dr. Sweet Goes on Stand"; "Sweet Depicts Fear in Court"; "Race Psychology Told in Sweet Testimony."

68. "Race Psychology Told in Sweet's Testimony."

69. Ibid.; "Sweet Depicts Fear in Court"; Hays opening statement.

70. Ossian Sweet, Gladys Sweet statements to police; "Race Psychology Told in Sweet's Testimony"; "Sweet Depicts Fear in Court."

71. "Race Psychology Told in Sweet's Testimony"; "Sweet Depicts Fear in Court."

72. Ibid.

73. Ibid.; "Dr. Sweet Goes on Stand"; Otis Sweet statement to police, September 9, 1925; Davis statement to police; Otis Sweet oral history; Ossian Sweet statement to W. Hayes McKinney, September 12, 1925, frame 924, reel 2, part 5, NAACP Papers; Hays opening statement.

74. Ossian and Otis Sweet statements to police; Davis statements to police, September 9 and 10, 1925.

75. "Race Psychology Told in Sweet's Testimony"; "Sweet Depicts Fear in Court"; Ossian Sweet statement to police; Davis statement to police, September 9, 1925.

76. Eric Houghberg statement to police, September 10, 1925, copy in author's possession.

77. Houghberg statement to police; Ray and Kathleen Dove statements to police, September 10, 1925; Houghberg trial testimony, November 11, 1925.

78. Mary Henley trial testimony, November 10, 1925; William Ryan testimony at preliminary hearing, September 16, 1925; Ryan trial testimony, November 5, 1925; Houghberg statement to police; "Darrow Hints at Demand for Another Jury," *Detroit Free Press*, November 10, 1925.

79. Houghberg statement to police; Houghberg trial testimony.

80. Schuknecht statement to police; Schuknecht statement at preliminary hearing, September 16, 1925; Schuknecht trial testimony, November 5, 1925; Otto Lemhagen statement to police, September 10, 1925; "Put Guard at Home of Negroes"; "Victim's Wife in Collapse, Is Near Death."

81. Ossian Sweet statement to police; Davis statement to police, September 9, 1925.

82. Schuknecht testimony at preliminary hearing, September 16, 1925; Schuknecht trial testimony, November 5, 1925; Ossian Sweet statement to police.

83. "Sweet's Trial Will Continue," *Detroit Free Press*, April 30, 1926; Bruce Stout trial testimony, November 10, 1925.

84. Schuknecht statement to police; "Put Guard on Home of Negroes"; "Victim's Wife in Collapse, Is Near Death"; "Slaying Leads to Night Riot," *Detroit News*, September 10, 1925.

85. Schuknecht statement to police, September 10, 1925; Schuknecht testimony at preliminary hearing, September 16, 1925; Schuknecht trial testimony, November 5, 1925.

86. "Dr. Sweet Goes on Stand"; "Other Race Troubles Figure in Sweet Trial."

87. Schuknecht statement to police, September 10, 1925; "Put Guard on Home of Negroes"; "Victim's Wife in Collapse, Is Near Death"; "Slaying Leads to Night Riot."

88. Schuknecht statement to police; George Fairbairn trial testimony, November 9, 1925; Bernard Mahlmeister testimony at preliminary hearing, September 16, 1925.

89. Davis statement to police, September 9, 1925; Otis Sweet statement to police; Ossian Sweet statement to police; Mahlmeister testimony at preliminary hearing; "Dr. Sweet Goes on Stand."

90. Ossian and Otis Sweet statements to police.

91. Schuknecht trial testimony and Paul Schellenberger testimony, both on November 5, 1925; George Fairbairn trial testimony, Almarion Wolfe trial testimony, and Marvin Leach testimony, all on November 9, 1925.

92. "Dr. Sweet Goes on Stand"; Otis Sweet oral history.

93. Joe Mack statement to police; Hayes testimony at preliminary hearing, September 16, 1925; "Death Calls Troubleshooter," *Detroit News*, October 14, 1943, copy in Detroit News clipping morgue, Detroit.

94. Hays trial testimony, November 9, 1925; Otis Sweet oral history; Ossian Sweet statement to police; "Dr. Sweet Goes on Stand."

95. Otis Sweet oral history; Mahlmeister testimony at preliminary hearing; Hayes trial testimony, November 9, 1925.

96. Otis Sweet oral history.

97. Ibid.

Chapter Two: Ain't No Slavery No More

1. "Dr. Sweet Is Cross-Examined," *Detroit News*, November 19, 1925, frames 64–66, reel 3, part 5, NAACP Papers [microfilm edition], Library of Congress, Washington, D.C.; "Sweet Verdict Due This Week," *Detroit Free Press*, May 9, 1926; "Sweet's Fate to Jury Soon," *Detroit Times*, May 9, 1926.

2. "Race Psychology Told in Sweet's Testimony," *Detroit Free Press*, November 19, 1925. The DeVaughn brothers are listed in Gilla Devoud [*sic*] application, application number 737, October 2, 1869, reel 5, Freedman's Bank Records, Tallahassee Branch, National Archives, Washington, D.C.

3. For details on the Cromarties, see the family entry, p. 148, 1820 U.S. census manuscript, Bladen County, North Carolina. Most likely, young Edmond came to Alexander through Alexander's mother, Elizabeth DeVane, whose father was a slaveholder. The DeVane family entry is available at p. 282, 1820 U.S. census manuscript, Sampson County, North Carolina. The Cromartie–DeVane connection is available at http://worldconnect.rootsweb. com, searched under either "Alexander Cromartie" or "Elizabeth DeVane." Last accessed March 15, 2004. When Elizabeth's father died in 1810, his property—including slaves—was divided among his children. See George DeVane will, February 10, 1810, at http://ftp. rootsweb.com/pub/usgenweb/nc/sampson/wills/gdevane.txt, last accessed March 15, 2004.

4. Clifton Paisley, *The Red Hills of Florida, 1528–1865* (Tuscaloosa: University of Alabama Press, 1989), p. 134; Alexander Cromartie entry, p. 123, 1830 U.S. census manuscript, Leon County, Florida.

5. A. J. Hanna, *A Prince in Their Midst: The Adventurous Life of Achille Murat on the American Frontier* (Norman: University of Oklahoma Press, 1946), pp. 79, 113. Larry E. Rivers, "Slavery in Microcosm: Leon County, Florida, 1824 to 1860," *Journal of Negro History* 56 (fall 1981): 237; Julia Floyd Smith, *Slavery and Plantation Growth in Antebellum Florida, 1821–1860* (Gainseville: University Press of Florida, 1973), chapter 6.

6. Paisley, *The Red Hills of Florida*, pp. 175–180. Loveless can be traced directly to Elizabeth's father, who passed the slave to his wife in his 1810 will. Most likely, Loveless was passed on to Cornelius upon his mother's death in 1822.

7. Alexander Cromartie entry, p. 72, 1860 U.S. census manuscript, Leon County, Florida. A list of the Cromarties' slaves is available in p. 279, 1860 U.S. census, slave schedule, Leon County. Though the slaves are not listed by name, there is listed among them a pair of twelve-year-old boys the age of twins Remus and Romulus DeVaughn.

8. The ages of the DeVaughn children are taken from p. 571, 1870 U.S. census manuscript, Leon County, Florida.

9. For an introduction to the coming of the Civil War, there is no better starting point than David Potter, *The Impending Crisis, 1848–1861* (New York: Harper and Row, 1976). Also see Michael Holt, *The Political Crisis of the 1950s* (New York: Wiley, 1978) and Eric Foner's brilliant book, *Free Soil, Free Labor, Free Men: The Ideology of the Republican Party Before the Civil War* (New York: Oxford University Press, 1970).

10. Edward E. Baptist, *Creating an Old South: Middle Florida's Plantation Frontier Before the Civil War* (Chapel Hill: University of North Carolina Press, 2002), pp. 278–279.

11. George P. Rawick, ed., *The American Slave: A Composite Autobiography*, v. 17 (Westport, Conn.: Greenwood Publishing Company, 1972), pp. 246–247.

12. Edmond's death date comes from Gilla DeVaughn's application to Freedman's Bank, October 2, 1869.

13. Eric Foner, *Reconstruction: America's Unfinished Revolution, 1863–1877* (New York: Harper and Row, 1988), particularly chapter 3; Susan Brandford Eppes, *Through Some Eventful Years* (Macon, Ga.: J. W. Burke, 1926), pp. 284–285.

14. Foner, *Reconstruction*, p. 81; sub-assistant commissioner's monthly report, October 1868, frames 691–692, reel 15, RG 105, Freedman's Bureau Field Office Records, National Archives. When the DeVaughns first appear in the record after the Civil War, in 1869, they lived on a plantation close to the Cromarties'. Gilla DeVaughn Freedman's Bank application, October 2, 1869. Many freedmen did move, of course. See Leon Litwack, *Been in the Storm So Long: The Aftermath of Slavery* (New York: Random House, 1979), chapter 6.

15. The standard work on Reconstruction is Foner, *Reconstruction*. Also see W. E. B. Du Bois's path-breaking *Black Reconstruction in America* (New York: Harcourt Brace, 1935), and Steven Hahn's important new study, *A Nation Under Our Feet: Black Political Struggles in the Rural South from Slavery to the Great Migration* (Cambridge, Mass.: Harvard University Press, 2003).

16. Litwack, *Been in the Storm So Long*, pp. 450–455; James T. Campbell, *The African Methodist Episcopal Church in the United States and South Africa* (New York: Oxford University Press, 1995), pp. 53–54.

17. Rhys Isaac, *The Transformation of Virginia, 1740–1790* (Chapel Hill: University of North Carolina Press, 1982), pp. 260–264. On the connection of Methodism and the marketplace, see Charles Sellers, *The Market Revolution: Jacksonian America, 1815–1846* (New York: Oxford University Press, 1991) pp. 160–161. Wesley quoted in E. P. Thompson, *The Making of the English Working Class* (New York: Random House, 1963), p. 355. Wesley feared the effects of such success. "But as riches increase," he said, "so will pride, anger, and love of the world."

18. Sellers, *Market Revolution*, pp. 160–161; Clarence E. Walker, *A Rock in a Weary Land: The African Methodist Episcopal Church During the Civil War and Reconstruction* (Baton Rouge: Louisiana State University Press, 1982), pp. 4–11; Campbell, *The African Methodist Episcopal Church in the United States and South Africa*, chapter 1.

19. Clarence E. Walker, *A Rock in a Weary Land*, p. 13.

20. Foner, *Reconstruction*, p. 92; Litwack, *Been in the Storm So Long*, pp. 470–471; Stephen W. Angell and Anthony B. Pinn, eds., *Social Protest Thought in the African Methodist Episcopal Church, 1862–1939* (Knoxville: University of Tennessee Press, 2000), p. 5.

21. Larry Eugene Rivers and Canter Brown, Jr., *Laborers in the Vineyard of the Lord: The Beginnings of the AME Church in Florida, 1865–1895* (Gainesville: University Press of Florida, 2001), p. 46; Joe M. Richardson, *The Negro in the Reconstruction of Florida, 1865–1877* (Tallahassee: Florida State University Press, 1965), pp. 84–85. "On political subjects [the freedmen] are easily excited and the more . . . radical the address made to them the better they seemed pleased," reported a federal agent from Leon County. "In Tallahassee most of the freedmen have adapted themselves to politics as a calling." W. Martin to Allen Jackson, October 22, 1868, box 15, Freedmen's Bureau Florida Field Office Records, RG 105, National Archives, Washington, D.C. [microfilm edition].

22. Charles Sumner Long, *History of the AME Church in Florida* (Philadelphia: A.M.E. Book Concern, 1939), p. 65; Rivers and Brown, *Laborers in the Vineyard of the Lord*, p. 95; Tallahassee Branch; p. 571, 1870 U.S. census manuscript, Leon County, Florida. Edward West to Colonel Sprague, March 1867, frames 726–728, reel 9, Freedman's Bureau Field Office; teachers' monthly school report, April 1868, frame 386, reel 13, Freedman's Bureau Field Office; Gilla DeVaughn Freedman's Bank application, October 2, 1869; Romulus DeVoud [*sic*] Freedman's Bank application, application number 726, September 11, 1869, reel 5, Freedman's Bank Records; Edward West to Colonel Sprague, March 1867, frames 726–728, reel 9, RG 105, Freedman's Bureau, Field Office, National Archives.

23. DeVaughn family entry, 1870 census; sub-assistant commissioner's monthly

report, Leon County, June 1868, frame 100, reel 13, Freedman's Bureau Field Office; sub-assistant commissioner's monthly report, August 1868, frame 133, reel 13, Freedman's Bureau Field Office.

24. Paul Ortiz, "'Like Water Covered the Sea': The African American Freedom Struggle in Florida, 1877–1920," Ph.D. dissertation, Duke University, 2000, p. 25; S. I. Halliday to Jacob Ch[ ], April 19, 1869, frame 312, reel 10, Freedman's Bureau Field Office; sub-assistant commissioner's monthly report, October 1868.

25. The Joint Select Committee to Inquire into the Condition of Affairs in the Late Insurrectionary States, *Testimony* (Washington, D.C.: Government Printing Office, 1972), p. 273; Jerrell H. Shofner, *Nor Is It Over Yet: Florida in the Era of Reconstruction* (Gainesville: University of Florida Press, 1974), chapter 13.

26. Joint Select Committee, *Testimony*, p. 171; William Watson Davis, *The Civil War and Reconstruction in Florida* (1913; repr. Gainesville: University Press of Florida, 1964), pp. 526–528; Rivers and Brown, *Laborers in the Vineyard of the Lord*, p. 83.

27. Canter Brown, Jr., *Ossian Bingley Hart: Florida's Loyalist Reconstruction Governor* (Baton Rouge: Louisiana State University Press, 1997).

28. Brown, *Ossian Bingley Hart*, pp. 275–294; Canter Brown, Jr., *Florida's Black Public Officials, 1867–1924* (Tuscaloosa: University of Alabama Press, 1998), pp. 25–27.

29. Brown, *Florida's Black Public Officials*, p. 85; for Cromartie as justice of the peace, see p. 603, 1870 U.S. census manuscript, Leon County, Florida. It seems there was a good deal of dissatisfaction with Cromartie's tenure as justice of the peace among blacks in Leon County. See sub-assistant commissioner's monthly report, October 1868.

30. E.d. 483, p. 12, 1880 U.S. census manuscript, Leon County, Florida; Dora L. Sweet gravestone, Evergreen Cemetery, Bartow, Fla. The gravestone lists Dora's birthday as December 29, 1873.

31. Brown, *Ossian Bingley Hart*, pp. 293–299.

32. Foner, *Reconstruction*, pp. 575–583; Shofner, *Nor Is It Over Yet*, chapter 19.

33. Jerrell H. Shofner, "Reconstruction and Renewal, 1865–1877," in Michael Gannon, ed., *The New History of Florida* (Gainesville: University Press of Florida, 1996), pp. 263–264; Edward Ayers, *The Promise of the New South: Life After Reconstruction* (New York: Oxford University Press, 1992), p. 45; Charlton Tebeau and William Marina, *A History of Florida*, 3rd ed. (Coral Gables: University of Miami Press, 1999), chapter 18.

34. Ayers, *The Promise of the New South*, p. 52; *General Statutes of the State of Florida* (St. Augustine: Records Company, 1906), pp. 307–308; J. Morgan Kousser, *The Shaping of Southern Politics: Suffrage Restriction and the Establishment of the One-Party South* (New Haven, Conn.: Yale University Press, 1974), pp. 91–103.

35. *General Statutes of the State of Florida*, pp. 165, 213–214, 1305–1306, 1376; Ayers, *Promise of the New South*, pp. 142–146.

36. There is a vast literature on the creation of Jim Crow. Among the most influential and insightful studies are C. Vann Woodward, *Origins of the New South, 1877–1913* (Baton Rouge: Louisiana State University Press, 1951); Joel Williamson, *The Crucible of Race: Black-White Relations in the American South Since Emancipation* (New York: Oxford University Press, 1984); Ayers, *Promise of the New South;* Leon Litwack, *Trouble in Mind: Black Southerners in the Age of Jim Crow* (New York: Random House, 1998).

37. Brown, *Florida's Black Public Officials*, p. 85; Rivers, *Laborers in the Vineyard of the Lord*, p. 111; e.d. 95, p. 18, 1880 U.S. census manuscript, Liberty County, Florida, for Hubbert DeVaughn; e.d. 76, p. 36, 1880 U.S. census manuscript, Jefferson County, Florida, for Edmond DeVaughn; e.d. 88, p. 18, Leon County, Florida, for Romulus DeVaughn; e.d. 483, p. 12, for Remus DeVaughn and his family.

38. Gavin Wright, *Old South, New South: Revolutions in the Southern Economy Since the Civil War* (New York: Basic Books, 1986), pp. 75–76, 99–106; Litwack, *Trouble in Mind*, pp. 130–138; Remus DeVaughn entry, 1880 U.S. census.

39. On Orlando and its economic context, see Benjamin D. Brotemarkle, *Beyond the Theme Parks: Exploring Central Florida* (Gainesville: University Press of Florida, 1999), pp. 12–13, and Charles W. Tabeau and William Marina, *A History of Florida* 3rd ed. (Coral Gables: University of Miami Press, 1999), chapter 18.

40. E.d. 116, p. 2; 1900 U.S. census manuscript, Orange County, Orlando, Florida; *Orlando City Directory*, 1915–1916 (no publication information), p. 134, copy available in Library of Congress, Washington, D.C.

41. Dora L. Sweet funeral program, September 1, 1957, box 2, Dovie Sweet Papers, Western Reserve Historical Society, Cleveland, Ohio; oral history interview with Sherman Sweet, February 27, 2002, Bartow, Fla.; oral history interview with Charlie McNeill, February 26, 2002, Bartow, Fla., notes of both interviews in author's possession.

42. Sherman Sweet telephone interview, January 11, 2002, notes in author's possession; Sherman Sweet interview, February 27, 2002; Henry W. Sweet gravestone, Evergreen Cemetery, Bartow, Florida; "A Special Tribute to the Sweet Family," July–August 1997, copy in author's possession; William Warren Rodgers, Robert David Ward, Leah Rawls Atkins, and Wayne Flint, *Alabama: The History of a Deep South State* (Tuscaloosa: University of Alabama Press, 1994), p. 220.

43. Henry Sweet gravestone; e.d. 132, p. 18, 1900 U.S. census manuscript, Bartow Town, Polk County, Florida; Sherman Sweet interview, February 27, 2002; Charlie McNeill interview, February 26, 2002; description of Henry Sweet is from a photograph in Sherman Sweet's possession.

44. Sherman Sweet interview, February 27, 2002; Oscar and Ossian Sweet gravestones, Evergreen Cemetery, Bartow, Fla.

45. *Sectional map of Polk County, Florida* (Buffalo, N.Y.: Associated Railway Land Department of Florida, 1890); record of transaction, May 10, 1898, Deed Record, v. 53, p. 45, Polk County, Fla., court house; for Milam family, e.d. 132, pp. 6–7, 1900 U.S. census manuscript, Bartow Town, Polk County, Florida; "City Locals," *Bartow Courier-Informant*, November 15, 1899; "Milam Closed Out," *Bartow Courier-Informant*, September 3, 1902. Indiana-born Milam, a grocer by trade, was a dabbler in real estate. For details, see grantee index, pp. 176–178, Polk County court house.

46. Canter Brown, Jr., *In the Midst of All That Makes Life Worth Living: Polk County, Florida to 1940* (Tallahassee: Sentry Press, 2001), pp. 121, 127–128, 140–146; Canter Brown, Jr., "'Bartow Is the Place for Our People to Go': Race and the Course of Life in Southern Polk County, 1865–1905" (unpublished essay in author's possession), pp. 3–8.

47. Brown, *In the Midst of All That Makes Life Worth Living*, pp. 154–159, 179–183, 194; Samuel Proctor, "Prelude to the New Florida," in Michael Gannon, ed., *The New History of Florida*, p. 277; Ayers, *Promise of the New South*, pp. 109–110.

48. Brown, *In the Midst of All That Makes Life Worth Living*, pp. 143–144, 155–156, 197–198; Sanborn Map Company, *Fire Insurance Map of Bartow, Florida* (New York: Sanborn Map Company, 1906); *Bartow: Where It Is a Pleasure to Live* (Bartow: Bartow Board of Trade, 1914).

49. "Registered and Qualified Electors, Polk County, FL, October 8, 1989," Polk County Historical Library, Bartow, Fla.; Patricia Merritt, "Fighting from Within," *Polk County Ledger*, n.d., copy available in "African American" vertical file, Polk County Historical Library; advertisement for county fair, *Bartow Courier-Informant*, March 15, 1899; "'Blind Tom' at Armory," *Bartow Courier-Informant*, April 10, 1901; minutes of town council, April 19, 1892, minute books, Bartow town hall, Bartow, Fla.; ordinance 37, Bartow Ordinance Record, v. 1, Bartow town hall; oral history interview with Claude Woodruff, February 25, 2002; "City Council," *Bartow Courier-Informant*, August 15, 1900.

50. Brown, "'Bartow Is the Place for Our People to Go,'" pp. 9–10; Brown, *In the Midst of All That Makes Life Worth Living*, pp. 199, 226–228; interview with Charlie McNeill, February 26, 2002; Charlie McNeill, "Were They Pioneers, Too?" *Polk County Historical Quarterly* 26 (September 1999): 9–11.

51. Sherman Sweet interview, February 27, 2002; Sanborn Map Company, *Fire Insurance Map of Bartow, Florida* (New York: Sanborn Map Company, 1917).

52. Sherman Sweet telephone interview, January 11, 2002; Sherman Sweet interview, February 27, 2002; Charlie McNeill interview, February 26, 2002.

53. Sherman Sweet interview, February 27, 2002; "A Tribute to the Sweet Family"; Sweet family plot, Evergreen Cemetery; 1910 U.S. census manuscript, Bartow Town, Polk County, Florida.

54. Sherman Sweet interview, February 27, 2002; *Directory of Polk County, Florida, 1913* (Bartow [?]: Polk Company Abstract Company, 1913), p. 72, copy available in Polk County Historical Library. In 1906, Henry Sweet bought three lots adjoining his land for a total of $45. See land deed November 20, 1906, deed record, v. 73, p. 90.

55. Sherman Sweet interview, February 27, 2002; "Race Psychology Told in Sweet's Testimony," *Detroit Free Press*, November 19, 1925.

56. Sherman Sweet interviews, January 11, 2002, and February 27, 2002.

57. Ibid.

58. H. K. Oliphant, "Thoughts on the Race Question," *Bartow Courier-Informant*, August 2, 1899, p. 2; Brown, "'Bartow Is the Place for Our People to Go,'" pp. 13, 15; Brown, *In the Midst of All That Makes Life Worth Living*, p. 199; "A Historical Sketch of Union Academy," July–August 1997, copy in author's possession; minutes of the town council, January 6 and March 6, 1896.

59. "Annual Report of County Superintendent of Public Instruction," *Bartow Courier-Informant*, October 25, 1899; "List of Polk County Teachers," *Bartow Courier-Informant*, October 11, 1899; "School Term Reduced," *Bartow Courier-Informant*, July 15, 1903; Sherman Sweet interview, January 11, 2002.

60. "New School Building," *Bartow Courier-Informant*, August 20, 1902.

61. Philip Dray, *At the Hands of Persons Unknown: The Lynching of Black America* (New York: Random House, 2002), particularly chapter 2; John Dollard, *Caste and Class in a Southern Town* (1937; repr. Madison: University of Wisconsin Press, 1988), pp. 335–343; Litwack, *Trouble in Mind*, chapter 6.

62. Ayers, *Promise of the New South*, chapters 10 and 11; Williamson, *The Crucible of Race*, part 2; Glenda Gilmore, *Gender and Jim Crow: Women and the Politics of White Supremacy in North Carolina, 1896–1920* (Chapel Hill: University of North Carolina Press, 1996), chapter 4. Tillman quoted in Litwack, *Trouble in Mind*, p. 303.

63. Ayers, *Promise of the New South*, p. 110; Brown, *In the Midst of All That Makes Life Worth Living*, pp. 200–202; Zora Neale Hurston, *Mules and Men* (1935; repr. New York: Harper and Row, 1990), p. 59.

64. "The Wickedest Town in Florida," *The Illustrated American*, July 20, 1895, pp. 78–79, copy in the "African Americans" vertical file, Polk County Historical Library, Bartow, Fla.

65. "The Negro Died Last Week," *Bartow Courier-Informant*, January 11, 1899; "Bloody Scene at Kingsford," *Bartow Courier-Informant*, January 27, 1900.

66. "General Presentments," *Bartow Courier-Informant*, October 21, 1903.

67. See, for example, minutes of the town council, January 3, 1893; "Sabbath Is Violated," *Bartow Courier-Informant*, July 15, 1903.

68. The story of Fred Rochelle's lynching is recounted in "Black Brute's Heinous Crime!" *Bartow Courier-Informant*, May 29, 1901, and "Burned at the Stake," and "To the World," *Bartow Courier-Informant*, June 5, 1901. There is no census entry for Fred Rochelle. But a Henry Rochelle appears in e.d. 130, sheet 6, 1900 U.S. census manuscript, Polk County, Fla. He is a nineteen-year-old working in the phosphate pits. Serena Rochelle was married to Bartow's baker, a Manx immigrant.

69. "Our Sheriff Was Game," *Bartow Courier-Informant*, December 30, 1903; Brown, *In the Midst of All That Makes Life Worth Living*, pp. 225–226.

70. Marcet Haldeman-Julius, *Clarence Darrow's Two Great Trials* (Girard, Kan.: Haldeman-Julius Publishing Company, 1927), p. 33.

71. Sherman Sweet interview, February 27, 2002.

72. Charles Sumner Long to James Weldon Johnson, December 14, 1925, frame 870, reel 23, part 5, NAACP Papers.

Chapter Three: Migration

1. U.S. Bureau of the Census, *Thirteenth Census of the United States, 1910: Population by Counties and Minor Civil Divisions, 1910, 1900, 1890* (Washington, D.C.: Government

Printing Office, 1912), p. 417; Raymond Boryczka and Lorin Lee Cary, *No Strength Without Union: An Illustrated History of Ohio Workers, 1803–1980* (Columbus: Ohio Historical Society, 1982), pp. 112–113; Helen Hooven Santmyer, *Ohio Town* (Columbus: Ohio State University Press, 1962).

2. Wilberforce University catalogue, 1912–1913, Wilberforce University Archives, Xenia, Ohio; Annetta Louise Gomez-Jefferson, *In Darkness with God: The Life of Joseph Gomez, a Bishop in the African Methodist Episcopal Church* (Kent, Ohio: Kent State University Press, 1998), p. 32.

3. Edward Ayers, *The Promise of the New South: Life After Reconstruction* (New York: Oxford University Press, 1992), chapter 1; Leon Litwack, *Trouble in Mind: Black Southerners in the Age of Jim Crow* (New York: Random House, 1998), pp. 482–489; Emmett J. Scott, *Negro Migration During the War* (New York: Oxford University Press, 1920), pp. 8–12; Stewart Tolnay and E. M. Beck, "Rethinking the Role of Racial Violence in the Great Migration," in Alferdteen Harrison, ed., *Black Exodus: The Great Migration from the American South* (Jackson: University Press of Mississippi, 1991), p. 22; U.S. Bureau of the Census, *Twelfth Census of the United States*, part 2 (Washington, D.C.: Government Printing Office, 1901), p. cxi.

4. Eric Foner, *Reconstruction: America's Unfinished Revolution, 1863–1877* (New York: Harper and Row, 1988), pp. 470–472; Litwack, *Trouble in Mind*, p. 488.

5. Kevin Boyle, "Work Places: The Economy and the Changing Landscape of Labor, 1900–2000," in Harvard Sitkoff, ed., *Perspectives on Modern America: Making Sense of the Twentieth Century* (New York: Oxford University Press, 2001), pp. 102–104; Kenneth Kusmer, *A Ghetto Takes Shape: Black Cleveland, 1870–1930* (Urbana: University of Illinois Press, 1976), pp. 85–89; John Bodnar, Roger Simon, and Michael P. Weber, *Lives of Their Own: Blacks, Italians, and Poles in Pittsburgh, 1900–1960* (Urbana: University of Illinois Press, 1982), pp. 59–62; James Grossman, *Land of Hope: Chicago, Black Southerners, and the Great Migration* (Chicago: University of Chicago Press, 1989), pp. 187–189.

6. W. E. B. Du Bois, "Negro Education" (1918), reprinted in David Levering Lewis, ed., *W. E. B. Du Bois: A Reader* (New York: Henry Holt, 1995), p. 262; oral history interview with Sherman Sweet, February 27, 2002, Bartow, Fla., transcript in author's possession.

7. W. E. B. Du Bois diary entry, n.d. [1896], frame 520, reel 87, W. E. B. Du Bois Papers, W. E. B. Du Bois Library, University of Massachusetts, Amherst.

8. Wilberforce University catalogue, 1908–1909, Wilberforce University Archives; Arthur Garfield Hays opening statement to the jury, *People v. Ossian Sweet et al.*, November 16, 1925, frames 920–938, reel 3, part 5, NAACP Papers. There was a direct connection between Wilberforce and Bartow's St. James AME, the Sweets' home church. One of the church's early members also served on the university's board of trustees. See Canter Brown, Jr., "'Bartow Is the Place for Our People to Go': Race and the Course of Life in Southern Polk County" (unpublished paper in author's possession), p. 13.

9. David Levering Lewis, *W. E. B. Du Bois: Biography of a Race* (New York: Henry Holt, 1993), pp. 151–152.

10. Wilberforce University catalogue, 1909–1910, Wilberforce University Archives; Santmyer, *Ohio Town*, p. 90; forty-seventh annual report of the president, June 14, 1910, Wilberforce Archives. For views of Wilberforce, see Hallie Q. Brown, *Pen Pictures of Pioneers of Wilberforce* (New York: G. K. Hall, 1997). A standard institutional history is Frederick A. McGinnis, *A History and Interpretation of Wilberforce University* (Blanchester, Ohio: Brown Publishing Company, 1941).

11. Hays opening statement, November 16, 1925; Marcet Haldeman-Julius, *Clarence Darrow's Two Great Trials* (Girard, Kan.: Haldeman-Julius Publishing Company, 1927), p. 35.

12. Lewis, *W. E. B. Du Bois*, p. 288.

13. Foner, *Reconstruction*, pp. 144–148; Adam Fairclough, *Better Day Coming: Blacks and Equality, 1890–2000* (New York: Viking, 2001), pp. 47–48.

14. Matthew Frye Jacobson, *Whiteness of a Different Color: European Immigrants and the Alchemy of Race* (Cambridge, Mass.: Harvard University Press, 1998), chapter 2; Roosevelt quoted in Lewis, *W. E. B. Du Bois*, p. 276.

15. The standard study of Washington is Louis Harlan, *Booker T. Washington: The*

Making of a Black Leader, 1856–1901 (New York: Oxford University Press, 1972), and Louis Harlan, *Booker T. Washington: The Wizard of Tuskeegee, 1901–1915* (New York: Oxford University Press, 1983). On Wilberforce's deal with the state of Ohio, see David Gerber, *Black Ohio and the Colored Line, 1860–1915* (Urbana: University of Illinois Press, 1976), p. 331; on the role of the manual training school, see Wilberforce University bulletin, June 1925, Wilberforce University Archives; Scarborough lays out his distinction between educated and working classes in W. S. Scarborough, "The Educated Negro and Menial Pursuits," *The Forum* 26 (December 1898): 434–440.

16. Francis P. Weisenburger, "Scarborough, William Sanders," in Rayford Logan and Michael R. Winston, eds., *Dictionary of American Negro Biography* (New York: W. W. Norton, 1982), pp. 545–546; David A. Gerber, *Black Ohio and the Color Line, 1860–1915*, p. 55.

17. Wilberforce University catalogue, 1912–1913.

18. Minutes of the faculty meeting, October 21, 1913, box 17, Wilberforce University Papers, Wilberforce Archives; Wilberforce University catalogue, 1908–1909; minutes of the faculty meeting, November 2, 1909, box 16, Wilberforce University Papers; W. E. B. Du Bois notes, February 1896, frame 536, reel 87, Du Bois Papers.

19. Wilberforce University catalogues, 1908–1909 and 1912–1913; minutes of the faculty meeting, October 21, 1913, box 17, Wilberforce University Papers; Lewis, *Du Bois*, p. 176; Fifty-fourth Annual Report of the President, June 21, 1917, Wilberforce Archives; David Kennedy, *Freedom from Fear: The American People in Depression and War, 1929–1945* (New York: Oxford University Press, 1999), p. 771.

20. Gerber, *Black Ohio and the Color Line*, pp. 234–235, 257–258.

21. Gail Bederman, *Manliness and Civilization: A Cultural History of Gender and Race in the United States, 1880–1917* (Chicago: University of Chicago Press, 1995); Stephen Kantrowitz, *Ben Tillman and the Reconstruction of White Supremacy* (Chapel Hill: University of North Carolina Press, 2000), pp. 268–286.

22. Gerber, *Black Ohio and the Color Line*, pp. 65–66, 257–263; W. S. Scarborough, "The Subsidized North," *The Voice of the Negro* 4 (January–February 1907): 32.

23. Lewis, *W. E. B. Du Bois*, p. 330.

24. Fairclough, *Better Day Coming*, p. 67; Lewis, *Du Bois*, pp. 387–388.

25. Lewis, *Du Bois*, pp. 388–391; Charles Kellogg, *NAACP: A History of the National Association for the Advancement of Colored People* (Baltimore: Johns Hopkins University Press, 1967), pp. 9–19.

26. Lewis, *Du Bois*, pp. 391–407; Kellogg, *NAACP*, pp. 19–26.

27. Wilberforce University catalogue, 1909–1910; *The Tawawa Remembrancer* 1914 (no publisher available), Wilberforce University Archives; minutes of the faculty meeting, April 7, 1914, box 17, Wilberforce University Papers; minutes of the faculty meeting, February 28, 1911, box 16, Wilberforce University Papers.

28. Wilberforce University catalogue, 1912–1913; *The Tawawa Remembrancer* 1914; minutes of the faculty meeting, May 20, 1913, box 16, Wilberforce University Papers; minutes of the May 17, 1917, faculty meeting, no box number.

29. Minutes of the faculty meeting, May 12, 1914, box 17, Wilberforce University Papers.

30. Ibid.

31. Arthur Garfield Hays opening statement, November 16, 1925; Gavin Wright, *Old South, New South: Revolutions in the Southern Economy Since the Civil War* (New York: Basic Books, 1987), p. 202, for relative wage rates in Detroit and the South.

32. Olivier Zunz, *The Changing Face of Inequality: Urbanization, Industrial Development, and Immigrants in Detroit, 1880–1920* (Chicago: University of Chicago Press, 1982), pp. 219–224; Joyce Shaw Peterson, *American Automobile Workers, 1900–1933* (Albany: SUNY Press, 1987), pp. 11–14; David Katzman, *Before the Ghetto: Black Detroit in the Nineteenth Century* (Urbana: University of Illinois Press, 1973), pp. 104–123.

33. Arthur Garfield Hays opening statement, November 16, 1925; Haldeman-Julius, *Clarence Darrow's Two Great Trials*, p. 35.

34. Hays opening statement, November 16, 1925; Haldeman-Julius, *Clarence Darrow's Two Great Trials*, pp. 35–36.

35. Haldeman-Julius, *Clarence Darrow's Two Great Trials*, p. 35.

36. Paul Starr, *The Social Transformation of American Medicine* (New York: Basic Books, 1982), chapters 1, 3; Mr. Hopkins to the secretary of the interior, June 17, 1920, box 2069, RG 48, Department of Interior, Central Classified Files, 1907–1936, National Archives, Washington, D.C.

37. Starr, *Social Transformation of American Medicine*, p. 124; Martha Tracy to Hubert work, January 16, 1924, box 2064, RG 48, Department of Interior Central Classified Files, 1907–1936.

38. Arthur Link, *Woodrow Wilson and the Progressive Era, 1910–1917* (New York: Harper and Row, 1954), p. 282.

39. Lewis, *Du Bois*, pp. 529–531; Fairclough, *Better Day Coming*, pp. 92–93.

40. Fifty-fourth annual report of the president, June 21, 1917, no box number, Wilberforce University Papers; Lewis, *Du Bois*, p. 532; Hays opening statement, November 16, 1925.

41. David Kennedy, *Over Here: The First World War and American Society* (New York: Oxford University Press, 1980); Joseph McCartin, *Labor's Great War: The Struggle for Industrial Democracy and the Origins of Modern American Labor Relations, 1912–1921* (Chapel Hill: University of North Carolina Press, 1997); William Preston, Jr., *Aliens and Dissenters: Federal Suppression of Radicals, 1903–1933* (New York: Harper and Row, 1963), chapter 4.

42. Constance McLaughlin Green, *The Secret City: A History of Race Relations in the Nation's Capital* (Princeton, N.J.: Princeton University Press, 1967), pp. 171–176; Lewis, *W. E. B. Du Bois: Portrait of a Race*, pp. 532–533.

43. James Grossman, *Land of Hope: Chicago, Black Southerners, and the Great Migration* (Chicago: University of Chicago Press, 1989), pp. 13–15; Carol Marks, *Farewell— We're Good and Gone: The Great Black Migration* (Bloomington: Indiana University Press, 1989), chapter 4.

44. Elliot M. Rudwick, *Race Riot at East St. Louis, July 2, 1917* (Carbondale: Southern Illinois University Press, 1964), chapters 2–5; Eugene Levy, *James Weldon Johnson: Black Leader, Black Voice* (Chicago: University of Chicago Press, 1973), pp. 183–189; Ann Douglas, *Terrible Honesty: Mongrel Manhattan in the 1920s* (New York: Farrar, Straus and Giroux, 1995), pp. 325–326.

45. Lewis, *W. E. B. Du Bois*, pp. 539–540; Green, *The Secret City*, pp. 185, 198; Stephen Grant Meyer, *As Long as They Don't Move Next Door: Segregation and Racial Conflict in American Neighborhoods* (Lanham, Md.: Rowman and Littlefield, 2000), pp. 20–26.

46. Rayford Logan, *Howard University: The First Hundred Years, 1867–1967* (New York: New York University Press, 1969), chapters 1 and 2; James Borchert, *Alley Life in Washington: Family, Community, Religion, and Folklife in the City, 1850–1970* (Urbana: University of Illinois Press, 1980); David Levering Lewis, *District of Columbia: A Bicentennial History* (New York: W. W. Norton, 1976), pp. 152–153; William B. Gatewood, *Aristocrats of Color: The Black Elite, 1880–1920* (Bloomington: Indiana University Press, 1990), chapter 2; David Levering Lewis, *When Harlem Was in Vogue* (New York: Alfred A. Knopf, 1979), pp. 149–151; "A Service of Commemoration for Frank D. Reeves and James A. Cobb," October 19, 1976, box 2, James Cobb Papers, Moorland-Spingarn Collection, Howard University, Washington, D.C.

47. Starr, *Social Transformation of American Medicine*, pp. 117–123; Logan, *Howard University*, pp. 160–164. Gradually the AMA strengthened educational requirements so that incoming medical school students had to have some college education.

48. Howard University catalogue, 1917–1918, p. 168, copy available in Moorland-Spingarn Collection; agreement between the assistant secretary of the interior and the District of Columbia board of charities, July 1909, entry 309, box 2, Patents and Miscellaneous Division, Department of Interior, RG 48, National Archives, Washington, D.C.; AMA's report quoted in Logan, *Howard University*, p. 162.

49. Howard University catalogue, 1917–1918; Howard University *Enopron* 1920–1921, copy available in Moorland-Spingarn Collection; Howard University *Bulletin* 1, no. 4 (1921–1922): 284–285; Charles West photograph, box 1, Charles West Collection, Moorland-

Spingarn Collection; report of Freedman's Hospital, year ending June 30, 1914, box 130-13, Louis Wright Collection, Moorland-Spingarn Collection.

50. Logan, *Howard University*, p. 161; Howard University catalogue, 1917, p. 173, copy available in Moorland-Spingarn Collection; Arthur Garfield Hays opening statement, November 16, 1925.

51. Howard University *Enopron*, 1920–1921; Logan, *Howard University*, p. 160.

52. Starr, *The Social Transformation of American Medicine*, pp. 85–88; Howard University *Enopron*, 1920–1921; *Regulations of the Freedman's Hospital, 1909* (Washington, D.C.: Government Printing Office, 1909), pp. 8–17, box 3, entry 311, RG 48, Department of Interior, Patents and Misc. Division, National Archives.

53. "A Tribute to the Sweet Family," July–August 1997, copy in author's possession; Haldeman-Julius, *Clarence Darrow's Two Great Trials*, pp. 35–36.

54. Haldeman-Julius, *Clarence Darrow's Two Great Trials*, p. 36; Starr, *Social Transformation of American Medicine*, pp. 167–168.

55. Logan, *Howard University*, pp. 181–183; Arthur Garfield Hays closing statement, November 16, 1925; Kennedy, *Over Here*, pp. 191–201.

56. Madison Grant quoted in John Higham, *Strangers in the Land: Patterns of American Nativism, 1860–1925* (New York: Atheneum, 1971), p. 306.

57. Mark Robert Schneider, *"We Return Fighting": The Civil Rights Movement in the Jazz Age* (Boston: Northeastern University Press, 2002), p. 13; Stewart E. Tolnay and E. M. Beck, *A Festival of Violence: An Analysis of Southern Lynchings, 1882–1930* (Urbana: University of Illinois Press, 1995), p. 272; Lewis, *Du Bois*, p. 579; Fairclough, *Better Day Coming*, pp. 102–106.

58. Elizabeth Clark-Lewis, *Living In, Living Out: African American Domestics in Washington, D.C., 1910–1940* (Washington D.C.: Smithsonian Institution Press, 1994), p. 73; Green, *The Secret City*, pp. 190–191; "Negroes Attack Girl," *Washington Post*, July 19, 1919.

59. "Attack on Woman Leads to Race Riot," *Washington Post*, July 20, 1919; "Scores Are Injured in More Race Riots," *Washington Post*, July 21, 1919; John Shillady to A. Mitchell Palmer, July 25, 1919, frame 479, reel 5, part 12A, NAACP Papers.

60. "Police Officer, Two Negroes and One White Killed; Others Are Fatally Hurt as Races Battle in the Streets of Washington," *Washington Post*, July 22, 1919; "One Dead and Another Dying; 2000 Regular Troops Guard Capital Streets," *Washington Post*, July 23, 1919.

61. "One Riot Victim Dies; Troops Quiet Capital; Crowds Quit Streets," *Washington Post*, July 24, 1919; James Weldon Johnson, "The Washington Riots," September 1919, box 30, Clarence Darrow Collection, Library of Congress.

62. R. L. Polk and Company, *Boyd's Directory of the District of Columbia* (Washington, D.C.: R. L. Polk and Company, 1920).

63. Mark Robert Schneider, *"We Return Fighting,"* p. 301. For other personal experiences of mob attacks in Washington, see James Scott statement, August 14, 1919, frame 481, reel 5, part 12A, NAACP Papers, and Francis Thomas statement, n.d., frames 482–484, reel 5, part 12A, NAACP Papers.

64. William Tuttle, *Race Riot: Chicago in the Red Summer of 1919* (New York: Atheneum, 1970); Lewis, *Du Bois*, p. 579; Mark Robert Schneider, *"We Return Fighting,"* pp. 33–34 and chapter 5.

65. Stoddard quoted in Jacobson, *Whiteness of a Different Color*, p. 96; Higham, *Strangers in the Land*, pp. 289–296.

66. Terrell quoted in Lewis, *District of Columbia*, pp. 75–76; Allan H. Spear, *Black Chicago and the Making of a Negro Ghetto, 1890–1920* (Chicago: University of Chicago Press, 1967), pp. 219–220; Tolnay and Beck, *A Festival of Violence*, p. 272.

67. Thomas Holt, Cassandra Smith-Parker, and Rosalyn Terborg-Penn, *A Special Mission: The Story of Freedman's Hospital, 1862–1962* (Washington D.C.: Howard University Academic Affairs Division, 1975), pp. 47–48; July 1909 agreement, assistant secretary of interior and D.C. board of charities; Borchert, *Alley Life in Washington*, pp. 183–184.

68. Howard University *Bulletin* 1, no. 4 (1921–1922). Description of Ossian comes from his graduation photo, copy in author's possession.

69. Vanessa Northington Gamble, *Making a Place for Ourselves: The Black Hospital Movement, 1920–1945* (New York: Oxford University Press, 1995), pp. 30–31; Memorandum for assistant secretary, April 8, 1909, entry 311, box 32, RG 48, Department of Interior, Patents and Misc. Division.

70. W. A. Warfield to secretary of the interior, March 28, 1913; R. L. Owen to Warfield, July 21, 1921; Thomas Martin to secretary of interior, June 2, 1921; Warfield to secretary of interior, June 11, 1921; Warfield to secretary of interior, September 8, 1921, all in box 2070, RG 48, Central Classified Files.

Chapter Four: Uplift Me, Pride

1. Arthur Garfield Hays opening statement, *People v. Ossian Sweet et al.*, November 16, 1925, frames 920–938, reel 3, part 5, NAACP Papers.

2. Olivier Zunz, *The Changing Face of Inequality: Urbanization, Industrial Development, and Immigrants in Detroit, 1880–1920* (Chicago: University of Chicago Press, 1982), parts 2 and 4; Robert Conot, *American Odyssey* (Detroit: Wayne State University, 1986), pp. 241–244; "Dodge's $8,000,000 Addition Under Way," *Detroit News*, September 20, 1925; Douglas Brinkley, *Wheels for the World: Henry Ford, His Company, and a Century of Progress* (New York: Viking, 2003), pp. 275–292.

3. Zunz, *The Changing Face of Inequality*, p. 376; Reinhold Niebuhr, *Leaves from the Notebook of a Tamed Cynic* (1929; repr. New York: Harper and Row, 1980), p. 143.

4. Stephen Meyer III, *The Five Dollar Day: Labor, Management, and Social Control in the Ford Motor Company, 1908–1921* (Albany: SUNY Press, 1981), chapters 6–7; Zunz, *The Changing Face of Inequality*, pp. 313–319; David Allan Levine, *Internal Combustion: The Races in Detroit, 1915–1926* (Westport, Conn.: Greenwood Press, 1976), pp. 6–7, 24–31; Raymond Fragnoli, *The Transformation of Detroit: Progressivism in Detroit—and After, 1912–1933* (New York: Garland, 1982), particularly chapter 4; Conot, *American Odyssey*, p. 197.

5. Sunnie Wilson with John Cohassey, *Toast of the Town: The Life and Times of Sunnie Wilson* (Detroit: Wayne State University Press, 1998), p. 51; William Barlow, *"Looking Up At Down": The Emergence of a Blues Culture* (Philadelphia: Temple University Press, 1989), p. 284; Lars Bjorn with Jim Gallert, *Before Motown: A History of Jazz in Detroit, 1920–1960* (Ann Arbor: University of Michigan Press, 2001), chapters 1 and 2; "Vice Rampant, Says Holsaple," *Detroit News*, November 4, 1925.

6. Allan Nevins and Frank Ernest Hill, *Ford: Expansion and Challenge, 1915–1933* (New York: Charles Scribner's Sons, 1957), pp. 311–316.

7. Robert Dunn research notes, n.d. [1926?], box 1, Robert Dunn Collection, Archives of Labor and Urban Affairs, Walter P. Reuther Library, Wayne State University, Detroit, Mich.; Peter Gavrilovich and Bill McGraw, eds., *The Detroit Almanac* (Detroit: Detroit Free Press, 2001), p. 485; Roaldus Richmond, "Open All Night," *American Life Histories: Manuscripts from the Federal Writers' Project, 1936–1940* available at http://memory.loc.gov, last accessed December 11, 2003.

8. Record of Ossian Sweet's state medical exam, November 14, 1921, Wayne County Physicians Register, v. 10, RG 85-38, Michigan State Archives, Lansing; R. L. Polk and Company, *Detroit City Directory, 1922–1923* (Detroit: R. L. Polk and Company, 1923); Forrester Washington, "The Negro in Detroit" (Detroit: Associated Charities of Detroit, 1920), no pagination; Zunz, *The Changing Face of Inequality*, pp. 352–353.

9. R. L. Polk and Company, *Detroit City Directory, 1917* (Detroit: R. L. Polk and Company, 1917); David M. Katzman, *Before the Ghetto: Black Detroit in the Nineteenth Century* (Urbana: University of Illinois Press, 1973), p. 67; Zunz, *The Changing Face of Inequality*, pp. 137–141.

10. George Haynes, *Negro New-Comers in Detroit: A Challenge to Christian Statesmanship* (1918; repr. New York: Arno Press, 1969), pp. 8–9, 12–20; Levine, *Internal Combustion*, pp. 54–61; lyrics quoted in Lars Bjorn, "From Hastings Street to the Bluebird: The Blues and Jazz Tradition in Detroit," *Michigan Quarterly Review* 25 (spring 1986): 258.

11. Richard W. Thomas, *Life for Us Is What We Make It: Building Black Community in Detroit, 1915–1945* (Bloomington: Indiana University Press, 1992), pp. 26, 30.

12. Robert W. Adams, "Detroit's Negro Population Is Now 53,000," *The Detroiter*, July 30, 1923, p. 13, clipping in E and M Files, Negroes in Detroit, Social Surveys, Miscellaneous Materials, Burton Historical Collection, Detroit Public Library, Detroit, Mich.; Levine, *Internal Combustion*, p. 59.

13. Katzman, *Before the Ghetto*, pp. 91, 93–94; R. L. Bradby to Velma McDonald, September 25, 1926, reel 3, Second Baptist Church Collection, Michigan Historical Collection, Bentley Library, University of Michigan, Ann Arbor; minutes of the Human Resources Association of Greater Detroit, April 8, 1920, box 1, Human Resources Association of Greater Detroit Papers, Michigan Historical Collection; Sam Griggs statement, November 25, 1928, box G-95, group I, NAACP Papers, Library of Congress, Washington, D.C.

14. Joyce Shaw Peterson, *American Automobile Workers, 1900–1930* (Albany: SUNY Press, 1979), pp. 47–58; Thomas, *Life for Us Is What We Make It*, p. 107; August Meier and Elliot Rudwick, *Black Detroit and the Rise of the UAW* (New York: Oxford University Press, 1979), pp. 5–9; Robert Mansfield notes and Marcus [?] notes, n.d. [c. 1925], box 1, Robert Dunn Collection, Archives of Labor and Urban Affairs, Wayne State University, Detroit, Mich.; minutes of Human Resources Association of Greater Detroit meeting, November 11, 1920, box 1, Papers of the Human Resources Association of Greater Detroit, Michigan Historical Collections, Bentley Library, University of Michigan, Ann Arbor.

15. Washington, "The Negro in Detroit," chapter 7; Victoria W. Walcott, *Remaking Respectability: African American Women in Interwar Detroit* (Chapel Hill: University of North Carolina Press, 2001), pp. 29–30, 80–81.

16. Thomas Lee Philpot, *The Slum and the Ghetto: Immigrants, Blacks, and Reformers in Chicago, 1880–1930* (New York: Oxford University Press, 1978), chapters 6 and 8; Washington, "The Negro in Detroit," no pagination; Levine, *Internal Combustion*, pp. 130–132; Haynes, "Negro New-Comers in Detroit," p. 10.

17. Levine, *Internal Combustion*, p. 45.

18. Forrester B. Washington report, August 25, 1917, box 1, Detroit Urban League Papers, Michigan Historical Collection.

19. Polk, *Polk's City Directory*, 1922–1923, for Clinton Street; Elaine Latzman Moon, *Untold Tales, Unsung Heroes: An Oral History of Detroit's African American Community, 1918–1967* (Detroit: Wayne State University Press, 1994), p. 49; Mayor's Inter-Racial Committee, *The Negro in Detroit* (Detroit: Detroit Bureau of Governmental Research, 1926), section 2, p. 10.

20. Thomas, *Life for Us Is What We Make It*, p. 91.

21. "Conditions Among Newcomers in Detroit," spring 1918, and Detroit Urban League rental survey, October 1921, both in box 1, Detroit Urban League Papers; Washington, "The Negro in Detroit," no pagination; John Ihlder, "Booming Detroit," *The Survey* (July 29, 1916): 449; Mayor's Inter-Racial Committee, *The Negro in Detroit*, section 5; Haynes, "Negro New-Comers in Detroit," pp. 21–24.

22. Washington, "The Negro in Detroit," no pagination; Mayor's Inter-Racial Committee, *The Negro in Detroit*, section 5, p. 21.

23. Washington, "Negro in Detroit," no pagination; Mayor's Inter-Racial Committee, *The Negro in Detroit*, section 5, pp. 21–22.

24. Zunz, *The Changing Face of Inequality*, pp. 113–128, 377; Detroit Urban League Report, n.d. [spring 1918], box 1, Detroit Urban League Collection; Mayor's Inter-Racial Committee, *The Negro in Detroit*, section 5, pp. 1–2, 20–22.

25. John Dancy to James Inches, November 27, 1920; minutes of meeting, October 24, 1923, both in box 1, Detroit Urban League Collection; George E. Worthington, "Prostitution in Detroit," summer 1926, p. 6, box 14, Detroit Citizens' League, Additional Material Collection, Burton Historical Collection, Walcott, *Remaking Respectability*, pp. 106–107; F. H. Croul to Frank Doremus, December 20, 1923, Mayor's Papers, 1924, Burton Historical Collection.

26. Washington, "The Negro in Detroit," no pagination; Mayor's Inter-Racial Commit-

tee, *The Negro in Detroit,* section 6, pp. 3–6; G. Arthur Blakeslee to John Dancy, March 11, 1926, box 1, Detroit Urban League Collection.

27. Mayor's Inter-Racial Committee, *The Negro in Detroit,* section 6, pp. 8–16; Washington, "The Negro in Detroit," no pagination.

28. Washington, "The Negro in Detroit," no pagination; Mayor's Inter-Racial Committee, *The Negro in Detroit,* section 6, pp. 18–19; "Where Hygiene Is Ousting Voodooism," *Detroit Free Press,* August 26, 1923.

29. Marcet Haldeman-Julius, *Clarence Darrow's Two Great Trials* (Gerard, Kan.: Haldeman-Julius Publishing Company, 1927), p. 35; Polk, *Detroit City Directory 1922–1923;* Register of Licensed Pharmacies, v. 4, p. 398, RG 84-105, Michigan State Archives; e.d. 222, p. 2, 1920 U.S. census manuscript, Detroit, Michigan; Sanborn Map Company, *Fire Insurance Map of Detroit, Michigan* (New York: Sanborn Map Company, 1922), available at http://sanborn.umi.com.

30. Polk, *Detroit City Directory,* 1921–22, p. 1701; e.d. 223, p. 21, 1920 U.S. census manuscript, Detroit, Michigan; Arthur Garfield Hays opening statement, November 16, 1925; Farokh Erach Udwadia, *Tetanus* (Bombay: Oxford University Press, 1994), pp. 2–3, 68–71.

31. Arthur Garfield Hays opening statement, November 16, 1925; Ossian Sweet statement to police, September 9, 1925, police department file, *People v. Ossian Sweet et al.,* copy in author's possession.

32. The best source for information for the black business class is Arthur Turner and Earl Moses, eds., *Colored Detroit* (Detroit: n.p., 1924), from which the list of businessmen is drawn. On Ossian's memberships, see Walter White to Roscoe Bruce, January 20, 1926, frames 453–454, reel 9, part 2, NAACP Papers, and on his church membership, Haldeman-Julius, *Clarence Darrow's Two Great Trials.* Haldeman-Julius asserts that Ossian wasn't a religious man—that he joined his church simply for the business connections it afforded—but other evidence suggests Ossian was a devout member of the AME Church, like his parents before him. See Ossian Sweet information for Committee on Candidates, August 8, 1932, and July 12, 1950, candidate files, 1950, Civic Searchlight Collection, Burton Historical Collection.

33. Carrie Curtis, "A Tribute to Our Attorneys in the Sweet Case," *Detroit Independent,* n.d. [November 1925], clipping in Ossian Sweet biographical file, Burton Historical Collection.

34. "Doctor Edward Carter," in Joseph Boris, ed., *Who's Who in Colored America, 1928–1929* (New York: Who's Who in Colored America Corp., 1929), p. 71.

35. Information for this and the preceding paragraph comes from David Katzman, *Before the Ghetto,* chapter 5; Arthur Burns and Earl Moses, éds., *Colored Detroit,* pp. 14, 29, 121; Moon, *Untold Tales, Unsung Heroes,* pp. 37–38.

36. John Dancy to L. Mayer, June 19, 1936, box 9, Detroit Urban League Papers; http://www.cr.nps.gov/nr/travel/detroit/d28htm, last accessed March 15, 2004; Mayor's Inter-Racial Committee, *The Negro in Detroit,* section 6, pp. 16–17; Turner and Moses, *Colored Detroit,* p. 38; oral history interview of Waldo Cain, June 11, 1998, box 2, Kellogg African-American Health Care Project, Walter Reuther Library; Thomas, *Life for Us Is What We Make It,* pp. 180–184; Vanessa Northington Gamble, *Making a Place for Ourselves: The Black Hospital Movement, 1920–1945* (New York: Oxford University Press, 1995), chapters 1–2; for context.

37. Arthur Garfield Hays opening statement, November 16, 1925; Turner and Moses, *Colored Detroit,* pp. 24, 38; Katzman, *Before the Ghetto,* p. 22; H. Payton Johnson biographical sketch, Johnson Reading Room File, Burton Historical Collection.

38. David Levering Lewis, *W. E. B. Du Bois: Biography of a Race, 1868–1919* (New York: Henry Holt, 1993), p. 501; Adam Fairclough, *Better Day Coming: Blacks and Equality, 1890–2000* (New York: Viking, 2001), pp. 117–119.

39. Mark Robert Schneider, *"We Return Fighting": The Civil Rights Movement in the Jazz Age* (Boston: Northeastern University Press, 2002), pp. 12–13; "How to Stop Lynching," *The Messenger* 2 (August 1919): 8–9; David Levering Lewis, *When Harlem Was in Vogue* (New York: Oxford University Press, 1979), pp. 23–24.

40. Thomas, *Life for Us Is What We Make It,* pp. 194–201.

41. Levine, *Internal Combustion*, pp. 85, 88.

42. Ibid., pp. 65–90; Turner and Moses, *Colored Detroit*, p. 23; "Health Week Time Extended," n.d. [possibly 1925], box 1, Detroit Urban League Collection.

43. Thomas, *Life for Us Is What We Make It*, p. 230; "NAACP Secures Ending of Jim Crow Cars in Detroit," n.d. [1920], frame 705, reel 11, part 12C, NAACP Papers; Walter White to James Weldon Johnson, October 13, 1920, frames 733–734, reel 2, part 8A, NAACP Papers; Schneider, *"We Return Fighting,"* pp. 197–198.

44. Eugene Levy, James Weldon Johnson, *Black Leader, Black Voice* (Chicago: University of Chicago Press, 1973), pp. 223–226; Robert Bagnall to Walter White, December 17, 1920; clipping, *Michigan State News*, February 8, 1921, both in reel 3, part 12C, NAACP Papers.

45. Schneider, *"We Return Fighting,"* pp. 305–306.

46. M. Louise Hood to W. D. Sterns, August 3, 1925, and minutes of meeting, October 24, 1923, both in box 1, Detroit Urban League Papers; Mayor's Inter-Racial Committee, *The Negro in Detroit*, section 9, p. 22.

47. Gladys Sweet to Walter White, n.d. [October 1925], frames 353–360, reel 3, part 5, NAACP Papers; Haldeman-Julius, *Clarence Darrow's Two Great Trials*, p. 35; Robert Toms closing statement in *People v. Henry Sweet*, May 12, 1926, Michigan Historical Collection; Health Week roster of participating doctors, 1922, box 1, Detroit Urban League Papers.

48. Charles C. Alexander, *Ty Cobb* (New York: Oxford University Press, 1984), pp. 67–68; Al Stump, *Cobb: A Biography* (Chapel Hill, N.C.: Algonquin Books of Chapel Hill, 1994), pp. vii, 141, 160–161, 170.

49. Arthur Garfield Hays opening statement, November 16, 1925.

50. Lynchings figures from http://memory.loc.gov/ammem/aap/timelin3.html, last accessed March 17, 2004; Philip Dray, *At the Hands of Persons Unknown: The Lynching of Black Americans* (New York: Random House, 2002), p. 268; Tim Madigan, *The Burning: Massacre, Destruction, and the Tulsa Race Riots of 1921* (New York: St. Martin's Press, 2001), pp. 179–182; "Dr. Sweet Is Cross-Examined," *Detroit News*, November 19, 1925, frames 64–66, reel 4, part 5, NAACP Papers.

51. Schneider, *"We Return Fighting,"* pp. 354–356; Toms closing statement, May 12, 1926.

52. Arthur Garfield Hays opening statement, November 16, 1925; Haldeman-Julius, *Clarence Darrow's Two Great Trials*, p. 28.

53. Haldeman-Julius, *Clarence Darrow's Two Great Trials*, p. 28.

54. On the Mitchell family, see sheet 4, enumeration district 600, 1920 U.S. census manuscript, Detroit, Mich. There is no trace of Rosella in the Pittsburgh census. But Benjamin Mitchell appears in e.d. 138, p. 2, 1900 U.S. census manuscript, Alleghany County, Penn. Mitchell's musical career—already begun before coming to Detroit—is mentioned in Haldeman-Julius, *Clarence Darrow's Two Great Trials*, p. 28, and in Walter White handwritten notes, n.d. [September 1925], frames 374–396, reel 3, part 5, NAACP Papers; Levine, *Internal Combustion*, p. 160.

55. Mitchell entry, 1920 census; Sanborn Map Company, *Fire Insurance Map of Detroit, Michigan* (New York: Sanborn Map Company, 1915); Walter White to James Weldon Johnson, September 16, 1925, frames 943–946, reel 2, part 5, NAACP Papers.

56. Mitchell entry, 1920 census; Haldeman-Julius, *Clarence Darrow's Two Great Trials*, pp. 28, 30–31.

57. Gladys Sweet to Walter White, n.d. [October 1925]; Haldeman-Julius, *Clarence Darrow's Two Great Trials*, pp. 28–30; Mitchell entry, 1920 U.S. census manuscript.

58. Arthur Garfield Hays opening statement, November 16, 1925; Haldeman-Julius, *Clarence Darrow's Two Great Trials*, p. 28; Levine, *Internal Combustion*, p. 160.

59. Returns of marriages recorded in the County of Wayne, 1922, reel 166, Library of Michigan, Lansing; death certificate 8694, Baby Sweet, July 21, 1923, Vital Records Division, Wayne County, Mich.

60. Ossian and Gladys reported their home as Cairney Street on a variety of documents in the year after their marriage. See, for example, Baby Sweet death certificate, July 21, 1923.

61. Turner and Moses, *Colored Detroit*, p. 74; Levine, *Internal Combustion*, p. 61; Du Bois quoted in David Levering Lewis, *W. E. B. Du Bois: Biography of a Race, 1868–1919* (New York: Henry Holt, 1993), p. 566.

62. Arthur Garfield Hays opening statement, November 16, 1925.

63. John Walton, Paul Beeson, and Ronald Bodley Scott, *Oxford Companion to Medicine* v. 1 (New York: Oxford University Press, 1986), p. 332; Rosalynd Pflaum, *Grand Obsession: Madame Curie and Her World* (New York: Doubleday, 1989), p. 224.

64. Death certificate #8694, Baby Sweet.

65. Ossian Sweet passport application, August 20, 1923, reel 2353, 10Wi M-1490, RG 59, National Archives, Washington, D.C.

66. "Winter Tourists Sailing to Europe," *New York Times*, October 6, 1923; Haldeman-Julius, *Clarence Darrow's Two Great Trials*, pp. 28–29.

67. "Winter Tourists Sailing to Europe"; R. F. Foster, *Modern Ireland, 1600–1972* (London: Penguin Press, 1988), pp. 508–515; A. J. P. Taylor, *English History, 1914–1945* (New York: Oxford University Press, 1965), pp. 194–202; James Hinton, *The First Shop Stewards' Movement* (London: George Allen and Unwin, 1973); Helmut Gruber, *Red Vienna: Experiment in Working-Class Culture, 1919–1934* (New York: Oxford University Press, 1991), p. 15.

68. U.S. Department of Labor Immigration Service, List of U.S. Citizens, S.S. *Paris*, New York, June 28, 1924, p. 5, copy available at http://www.ellisisland.org.

69. Quinn, *Marie Curie*, pp. 388–389; oral history interview with Sherman Sweet, February 27, 2002, notes in author's possession; Sweet information for Committee of Candidates, July 12, 1950.

70. Brigitte Hamann, *Hitler's Vienna: A Dictator's Apprenticeship* (New York: Oxford University Press, 1999); Tyler Stovall, *Paris Noir: African Americans in the City of Light* (Boston: Houghton-Mifflin, 1996), chapter 1; Michel Fabre, *From Harlem to Paris: Black American Writers in France, 1840–1980* (Urbana: University of Illinois Press, 1993), particularly chapters 5 and 6.

71. Arthur Garfield Hays opening statement, November 16, 1925; Haldeman-Julius, *Clarence Darrow's Two Great Trials*, p. 29.

72. Ibid.

73. List of U.S. Citizens, S.S. *Paris*, New York, June 28, 1924, p. 5 lists the baby's name as Marguerite. Every other account of the family refers to her as Iva.

Chapter Five: White Houses

1. Fred Benoit testimony, *People v. Ossian Sweet et al.*, November 10, 1925, Michigan Historical Collection, Bentley Library, University of Michigan, Ann Arbor; trial testimony of Eban Draper, November 7, 1925; John Getke testimony at preliminary hearing, *People v. Ossian Sweet et al.*, September 17, 1925, box 1, Ossian Sweet Collection, Burton Historical Collection, Detroit Public Library, Detroit, Mich.

2. David Allan Levine, *Internal Combustion: The Races in Detroit, 1915–1926* (Westport, Conn.: Greenwood Press, 1976), p. 158.

3. Ray Dove Testimony, November 6, 1925; George Suppus trial testimony, November 10, 1925; Ulric Arthur trial testimony, November 10, 1925; telephone interview with Bill McGraw, November 1999.

4. "Darrow Scores Point in Sweet Murder Trial," *Detroit Free Press*, May 2, 1926; Otto Eberhardt trial testimony, November 7, 1925; articles of association, Waterworks Park Improvement Association, February 13, 1926, Michigan Department of Consumer and Industry Services, Bureau of Commercial Services, Corporation Division, Lansing, Mich.

5. Marcet Haldeman-Julius, "Clarence Darrow's Defense of a Negro," *Haldeman-Julius Monthly* 4 (July 1926): 23–24; "Stop Rioting, Smith Pleads with Citizens," *Detroit Free Press*, July 12, 1925.

6. Haldeman-Julius, "Clarence Darrow's Defense of a Negro," p. 24.

7. Marcet Haldeman-Julius, *Clarence Darrow's Two Great Trials* (Girard, Kan.: Haldeman-Julius Publishing Company, 1927), p. 32.

8. Arthur Garfield Hays opening statement, *People v. Ossian Sweet et al.*, November 16, 1925; Haldeman-Julius, *Clarence Darrow's Two Great Trials*, p. 29. Over the years, Ossian would come to claim that he'd received advanced degrees abroad, though the brief time he spent studying makes it all but impossible. See Ossian Sweet Information on Committee for Candidates, July 12, 1950, candidate files, Civic Searchlight Collection, Burton Historical Collection.

9. R. L. Polk and Company, *Detroit City Directory*, 1925–1926 (Detroit: R. L. Polk and Company, 1926).

10. Dentist registration book, 1923, p. 65, reel 1947, RG 76-2, Michigan Department of Licensing and Registration, Michigan State Archives, Lansing; R. L. Polk, *Detroit City Directory*, 1923–1924 (Detroit: R. L. Polk and Company, 1924); Arthur Turner and Earl Moses, *Colored Detroit* (Detroit: n.p., 1924), p. 55; Haldeman-Julius, *Clarence Darrow's Two Great Trials*, pp. 35–36; Lars Bjorn with Jim Gallert, *Before Motown: A History of Jazz in Detroit* (Ann Arbor: University of Michigan Press, 2001), pp. 7–10.

11. For details on Henry's college activities, see Wilberforce's yearbook, *The Forcean*, for 1925, and Wilberforce University bulletin (June 1924), both in Wilberforce University Archives, Xenia, Ohio. Also see "Doctor Sweet to Tell of Fears," *Detroit Times*, May 7, 1926; Haldeman-Julius, *Clarence Darrow's Two Great Trials*, pp. 27–28; Lester Moll closing statement, *People v. Henry Sweet*, May 10, 1926, Michigan Historical Collection.

12. "Posse Chases Man Believed to Be One of Four Who Threatened Colored Farmer," *Xenia (Ohio) Gazette*, October 13, 1924; "Martin Gets Rest While Armed Men Guard Premises," *Xenia (Ohio) Gazette*, October 15, 1924; Moll closing statement, May 10, 1926.

13. Richard W. Thomas, *Life for Us Is What We Make It: Building Black Community in Detroit, 1915–1945* (Bloomington: Indiana University Press, 1992), p. 27; "City 1,242,044 Census Shows," *Detroit Free Press*, September 27, 1924; "Cites Home Benefits of City's East Side" and "Buy Land and Hold It, Is Advice of Veteran," both in *Detroit Free Press*, October 25, 1925; Walter Clyde, *A Million Dollar Secret* (Detroit: Walter Schulte Corporation, 1927).

14. Raymond Fragnoli, *The Transformation of Detroit: Progressivism in Detroit—and After, 1912–1933* (New York: Garland, 1982), chapter 5; Sidney Fine, *Frank Murphy: The Detroit Years* (Ann Arbor: University of Michigan Press, 1957), pp. 91–102.

15. Fine, *Frank Murphy*, pp. 102–107.

16. Fine, *Frank Murphy*—the first volume in Fine's monumental biography—details Murphy's background. On Murphy's religious devotion, also see oral history interview of Robert Toms, November 28, 1959, Alex Baskin Collection, Michigan Historical Collection; oral history interview with Hilmer Gellein, n.d. [early 1970s], box 1, Ossian Sweet Collection. On Murphy's relation to women, see Josephine Gomon notes, n.d., box 9, Josephine Gomon Papers, Michigan Historical Collection. Murphy quotes from Fine, *Frank Murphy*, pp. 109, 114.

17. Fine, *Frank Murphy*, pp. 111–112; Fragnoli, *The Transformation of Reform*, pp. 263–274, quote on p. 273.

18. Fine, *Murphy*, pp. 112, 114–116, quote on p. 117. Also see Fragnoli, *The Transformation of Reform*, pp. 273–277.

19. Kenneth T. Jackson, *The Ku Klux Klan in the City, 1915–1930* (New York: Oxford University Press, 1967), pp. 118–132.

20. Jackson, *The Ku Klux Klan in the City*, p. 134.

21. "A New Al Smith—But This Time a Republican," *Literary Digest*, November 28, 1925, clipping in box 3, Mayor's Papers 1923, Burton Historical Collection; "Long Fight Is Ended for Civic Leader," *Detroit Free Press*, June 18, 1942, copy in "Smith, John W." file, Detroit Free Press Clipping Morgue, Detroit, Mich.; John Smith career summary, n.d. [c. 1930]; "John W. Smith," *Detroit Saturday Night*, September 16, 1922; "John Smith Dies, Head of Council," *Detroit News*, June 18, 1942; untitled *Detroit Times*, August 31, 1924, profile, all in "John Smith" file, Detroit News Clipping Morgue, Detroit, Mich.; Fragnoli, *The Transformation of Reform*, pp. 308–309, 313–314.

22. Jackson, *The Ku Klux Klan in the City*, pp. 133–136; Levine, *Internal Combustion*, pp. 138–141; untitled clipping, *Detroit Mirror*, December 4, 1931, clipping in "Smith, John W." file, Detroit Free Press Clipping Morgue.

23. Thomas Lloyd Jones, "Labor and Politics: The Detroit Municipal Election of 1937," (Ph.D. dissertation: University of Michigan, 1998), pp. 72, 160; Reinhold Niebuhr, *Leaves from the Notebook of a Trained Cynic* (San Francisco: Harper and Row, 1929), p. 144; Reinhold Niebuhr, "Detroit in the Twenties," unpublished typescript, n.d. [1950s], box 47, Reinhold Niebuhr Papers, Library of Congress, Washington, D.C.

24. Jackson, *The Ku Klux Klan in the City,* pp. 135–137; Levine, *Internal Combustion,* p. 140, for the vote in Black Bottom.

25. Jackson, *The Ku Klux Klan in the City,* pp. 137–139; Levine, *Internal Combustion,* p. 141.

26. Jackson, *The Ku Klux Klan in the City,* p. 141; "Klan Out to Elect Bowles," *Detroit Times,* September 23, 1925; "Bares Klan Scheming to Rule City Council," *Detroit Free Press,* October 31, 1925.

27. Haldeman-Julius, *Clarence Darrow's Two Great Trials,* pp. 29–30; Mayor's Inter-Racial Committee, *The Negro in Detroit* (Detroit: Detroit Bureau of Governmental Research, 1926), section 9, pp. 34–35.

28. Committee on Negro Housing, *Negro Housing* (1932; repr. New York: Negro Universities Press, 1969), pp. 40–42; "Restrictions for B. E. Taylor's Properties," E and M, Detroit Real Estate, Burton Historical Collection, Detroit Public Library, Detroit, Mich.; Harold Black, "Restrictive Covenants in Relation to Segregated Negro Housing in Detroit," M.A. thesis, Wayne State University, 1947, p. 6; advertisement for the Brownell Corporation, *Detroit News,* September 6, 1925; "Rigid Restrictions Urged for New Plats," *Detroit Free Press,* September 20, 1925.

29. Committee on Negro Housing, *Negro Housing,* pp. 93–104; Detroit Real Estate Board, *By-Laws* (1921), has no such prohibition. Real Estate Board, *By-Laws* (1926), part III, section 37, contains the restriction, along with a notation that the change was adopted in 1924. Both copies available in Burton Historical Collection; remarks of Ira Jayne, annual business meeting of the NAACP, January 4, 1926, frame 711, reel 13, NAACP Papers [microfilm edition].

30. "Open $150,000 Damage Suit," *Chicago Defender,* April 18, 1931; Hays opening statement, November 16, 1925.

31. Hays opening statement, November 16, 1925; "Darrow Calls Sweet to Stand," *Detroit Times,* May 6, 1925.

32. Haldeman-Julius, *Clarence Darrow's Two Great Trials,* p. 30; "Dr. Sweet Wanted Home for His Baby," *Chicago Defender,* December 5, 1925.

33. Walter White to James Weldon Johnson, September 16, 1925, frames 943–946, reel 2, part 5, NAACP Papers; White handwritten notes, n.d. [September 1925], frames 374–396, reel 3, part 5, NAACP Papers; Peter Gavrilovich and Bill McGraw, eds., *The Detroit Almanac: 300 Years of Life in the Motor City* (Detroit: Detroit Free Press, 2001), p. 485.

34. On neighborhood house prices, see classified ads, *Detroit News,* September 4, 5, 8, 17, 1925. The terms of the deal are detailed in Walter White to James Weldon Johnson, September 16, 1925; Sweet Defense Fund disbursements, n.d. [December 11, 1925], frames 811–814, reel 3, part 5, NAACP Papers; "Darrow Calls Sweet to Stand," May 6, 1926; plat book entry, 2905 Garland Avenue, Wayne County Registrar of Deeds.

35. Walter White to James Weldon Johnson, September 16, 1925.

36. "Darrow to Rest Riot Defense," *Detroit Times,* November 19, 1925; "Detroit Riot Case Trial Near Close," n.d. [November 1925], Associated Negro Press story, clipping at frame 142, reel 4, part 5, NAACP Papers.

37. Levine, *Internal Combustion,* p. 158; Ray Dove trial testimony, November 6, 1925; e.d. 629, pp. 4–9, 1920 U.S. census manuscript, Detroit, Michigan; Harry Monet trial testimony, November 10, 1925.

38. Oliver Zunz, *The Changing Face of Inequality: Urbanization, Industrial Development, and Immigrants in Detroit, 1880–1920* (Chicago: University of Chicago Press, 1982), chapter 6; Hannah Real Estate Exchange, "Real Estate Obtained Without Use of Coin or Greenbacks," 1895 pamphlet available at E and M, Detroit Real Estate, Burton Historical Collection. On sacrificing children's education in exchange for home ownership, see

Stephan Thernstrom, *Poverty and Progress: Social Mobility in a Nineteenth Century City* (Cambridge, Mass.: Harvard University Press, 1964), pp. 117–122, 155–157.

39. The development of Garland Avenue can be traced through building permit index, v. 3, Detroit Building and Safety Department Records, 1909–1924, Burton Historical Collection. Property restrictions are spelled out in deed for 2960 Garland Avenue, November 9, 1915, Wayne county Registrar of Deeds; plat books for Garland Avenue for information on Getkes' and Smiths' loans. On the transformation of the real estate market more generally, see Alexander Von Hoffman, "Weaving the Urban Fabric: Nineteenth-Century Patters of Residential Real Estate in Outer Boston," *Journal of Urban History* 22 (January 1996): 191–230.

40. E.d. 629, pp. 4–9, 1920 U.S. census manuscript, Detroit, Michigan. Polk, *Detroit City Directory*, 1925–1926; Robert Dunn research notes, n.d. [mid-1920s], box 1, Robert Dunn Collection, Archives of Labor and Urban Affairs, Wayne State University, Detroit, Mich.; e.d. 24, p. 2A, 1910 U.S. census manuscript, Mauch Shunk Township, Carbon County, Pennsylvania.

41. The President's Conference on Home Building and Home Ownership, *Tentative Report of the Committee on Finance* (Washington, D.C.: Government Printing Office, 1931), pp. 7–24; G. Walter Woodworth, *The Detroit Money Market* (Ann Arbor: University of Michigan School of Business Administration, 1932), pp. 125–130. On ubiquity of secondary mortgage market, see classified ads, *Detroit Free Press*, October 26, 1925.

42. President's Conference, *Tentative Report of the Committee on Finance*, pp. 18–21; e.d. 629, pp. 4–9, 1920 U.S. census manuscript, Detroit, Michigan; Ray Dove testimony, November 6, 1925; George Suppus testimony and Ulric Arthur testimony, November 10, 1925; Peter Gavrilovich and Bill McGraw, eds., *The Detroit Almanac: 300 Years of Life in the Motor City* (Detroit: Detroit Free Press, 2001). p. 77.

43. Mayor's Inter-Racial Committee, *The Negro in Detroit*, section 1, p. 10; R. L. Polk and Company, *City of Detroit Directory*, 1919–1920 (Detroit: R. L. Polk and Company, 1920); Levine, *Internal Combustion*, p. 155. For an intimate view of the west-side community, see The Westsiders, *Remembering Detroit's Old West Side, 1920–1950: A Pictorial History of the Westsiders* (Detroit: self-published, 1997).

44. "Beautiful Mrs. Mathies Shoots After Bricks Were Hurled," *The Detroit Independent*, April 17, 1925, clipping in box 30, Clarence Darrow Collection, Library of Congress, Washington, D.C.; case report, *People v. Fleta Mathies*, n.d. [spring 1925], box G-95, group I, NAACP Papers, Library of Congress.

45. "Beautiful Mrs. Mathies Shoots After Bricks Were Hurled," April 17, 1925.

46. Sanborn Map Company, *Fire Insurance Map of Detroit, Michigan* (New York: Sanborn Map Company, 1926); oral history interview with Cecil Rowlette, August 1, 1960, Baskin Collection.

47. "House Stoned, Negro Quits It," *Detroit News*, June 24, 1925; "Mob of 5,000 Forces Negro to Quit Home," *Detroit Free Press*, June 24, 1925; Levine, *Internal Combustion*, pp. 154–155; data regarding the Detroit cases, n.d. [October 1925?], frame 352, reel 3, part 5, NAACP Papers; oral history interview with Cecil Rowlette, August 1, 1926. Contrary to common perception, the mob was not made up exclusively of the working class. Among the leaders of the Tireman Avenue Improvement Association were the Turners' next-door neighbor, Christian Schollenberger, a building contractor, and a man who lived down the block, Ruel Caldwell, an executive in an engineering firm.

48. "Row Over Homes Brings Bullets," *Detroit News*, July 8, 1925; "Throng Wields Pistols, Guns at Negro Home," *Detroit Free Press*, July 8, 1925; "Police Rout 2,000 as Tenants' Quarrel Breaks Anew," *Detroit Free Press*, July 9, 1925; "Police Again Disburse Mob," *Detroit Free Press*, July 10, 1925; Vollington Bristol statement, November 15, 1925, box 5, Darrow Collection; Levine, *Internal Combustion*, pp. 155–157.

49. "Negroes Shoot White Youth in New Home Row," *Detroit Free Press*, July 11, 1925; John Fletcher statement, November 15, 1925, box 5, Darrow Collection; Levine, *Internal Combustion*, p. 157.

50. Gladys Sweet to Walter White, n.d. [October 1925], frames 353–360, reel 3, part 5, NAACP Papers.

51. Mark Robert Schneider, *"We Return Fighting": The Civil Rights Movement in the Jazz Age* (Boston: Northeastern University Press, 2002), pp. 305–306; R. L. Bradby to Walter White, December 14, 1925, frame 277, reel 3, part 5, NAACP Papers, for list of branch officers.

52. Lester Moll's closing statement, May 10, 1926; D. F. Moore to William Pickens, n.d. [September 1925?], frames 1106–1107, reel 2, part 5, NAACP Papers.

53. "Negroes Shoot White Youth in New Home Row," July 11, 1925; Levine, *Internal Combustion*, pp. 157–158.

54. John Smith quoted in "Argument of Clarence Darrow in the Case of Henry Sweet" (NAACP pamphlet, 1927), p. 31, box 5, Darrow Collection.

55. Oral history interview with Cecil Rowlette, August 1, 1960; Polk, *Detroit City Directory*, 1925–1926, for Sims's office; "Sweet to Describe Riot Fear," *Detroit Times*, November 18, 1925; "Darrow to Rest Riot Defense," *Detroit Times*, November 19, 1925; Walter White to James Weldon Johnson, September 15, 1925; "Darrow to Rest Riot Defense," *Detroit Times*, November 19, 1925.

56. Harry Monet trial testimony, November 10, 1925; Eban Draper trial testimony, November 7, 1925; Waterworks Park Improvement Association, articles of association, February 13, 1926; e.d. 629, p. 9, 1920 U.S. census manuscript, Detroit, Michigan.

57. E.d. 629, p. 1, 1920 U.S. census manuscript, Detroit, Michigan; Raymond Alf trial testimony, November 11, 1925; Waterworks Park Improvement Association, articles of association, February 13, 1926.

58. Association by-laws are reprinted in the trial testimony, November 10, 1925.

59. "The Weather," *Detroit Free Press*, July 14 and 15, 1925; "Free Doctor Sweet and Ten Others," *Chicago Defender*, April 25, 1931; "Darrow Scores Point in Sweet Murder Trial," May 2, 1926; Ray Dove trial testimony, November 6, 1925; John Getke trial testimony, November 9, 1925.

60. Norton Schuknecht trial testimony, November 5, 1925; R. L. Polk and Company, *Detroit City Directory*, 1910 (Detroit: R. L. Polk and Company, 1910); Polk, *Detroit City Directory*, 1925–1926; e.d. 94, p. 2, 1900 U.S. census manuscript, Detroit, Michigan, for Schuknecht's birth family; e.d. 603, p. 6, 1920 U.S. census manuscript, Detroit, Michigan, for Schuknecht's wife and children.

61. Detroit Police Department, *Sixteenth Annual Report* (Detroit: Police Press, 1925), pp. 2–3, copy available in the Library of Congress; Leslie Woodcock Tentler, *Seasons of Grace: A History of the Catholic Archdiocese of Detroit* (Detroit: Wayne State University Press, 1990), pp. 268–269; "Heart Attack Fatal," *Detroit News*, July 18, 1939; Rebecca Reed, "Regulating the Regulators: Ideology and Practice in the Policing of Detroit, 1880–1918," Ph.D. dissertation, University of Michigan, 1991, p. 152; sheet 6, e.d. 603, 1920 U.S. census manuscript, Detroit, Michigan.

62. Norton Schuknecht trial testimony, November 5, 1925; "Mayor Traces Riot to Klan" and "Letter Still in Mails, Croul Is Reserved," both in *Detroit News*, September 13, 1925, on tensions between mayor and police department.

63. Walter White to James Weldon Johnson, September 16, 1925. There were rumors that Schuknecht himself was a klansman, though there is no evidence to support the assertion. See White to Johnson, September 17, 1925, frames 1031–1032, reel 2, part 5, NAACP Papers.

64. Oral history interview with William Osby, Sr., July 27, 1960, Alex Baskin Collection; Vollington Bristol statement, November 15, 1925.

65. "Sweet Says He Provided Guns," *Detroit Free Press*, May 8, 1926; "Opens $150,000 Damage Suit," *Chicago Defender*, April 18, 1931.

66. "Other Race Troubles Figure in Sweet Trial," *Detroit Free Press*, November 18, 1925.

67. "Negroes Break Up Two Meetings of Realty Men," *Detroit Free Press*, July 17, 1925.

68. James Weldon Johnson letter to the editor, August 3, 1925, frame 964, reel 2, part 5, NAACP Papers [microfilm edition]; William Pickens to R. L. Bradby, July 31, 1925, frame 941, reel 2, part 5, NAACP Papers.

69. "Sweet Says He Provided Guns," May 8, 1926; "Opens $150,000 Damage Suit,"

April 18, 1931; "Darrow to Rest Riot Defense," November 19, 1925; Arthur Garfield Hays opening statement, November 16, 1925; Ossian Sweet, William Davis, Joe Mack, and Norris Murray statements to police, September 9, 1925, Detroit Police Department File, *People v. Ossian Sweet et al.*, copy in the author's possession.

70. Vollington Bristol statement, November 15, 1925; John Hayes trial testimony, November 9, 1925.

71. "Court Darkens KKK Sign," *Detroit Times*, October 10, 1925; Norton Schuknecht trial testimony, November 5, 1925.

72. "Free Dr. Ossian Sweet," April 25, 1931; Black, "Restrictive Covenants in Relation to Segregated Negro Housing in Detroit," p. 26.

73. "200 Police Guard Scene as 1 Is Slain and 1 Shot by Negroes," *Detroit Free Press*, September 10, 1925; "Other Race Troubles Figure in Sweet Trial," November 18, 1925.

74. Robert McPherson service record, July 12, 1929, copy in clipping morgue, *Detroit News*, Detroit, Mich.; Norton Schuknecht trial testimony, November 4, 1925; John Hayes trial testimony, November 1925.

75. "Officer Slain, Partner Kills His Assailant," *Detroit Free Press*, September 8, 1925; oral history interview with Robert Toms, November 28, 1959, Alex Baskin Collection, Michigan Historical Collection; "Fear of Riot Told at Trial," *Detroit News*, November 5, 1925; Schuknecht trial testimony, November 5, 1925.

76. Kathleen Dove statement to police, September 10, 1925; Della Getke trial testimony, November 9, 1925.

77. Clarence Darrow, *The Story of My Life* (New York: Charles Scribner's Sons, 1934), p. 305; "200 Police Guard Scene as 1 Is Slain and 1 Shot by Negroes."

78. Arthur Garfield Hays opening statement, November 16, 1925; Gladys Sweet statement to police, September 9, 1925; Kathleen Dove statement to police, September 10, 1925.

79. "Other Race Troubles Figure in Sweet Trial," November 18, 1925; Mack statement to police, September 9, 1925.

80. John Getke statement to police, September 10, 1925; Ray Dove trial testimony, November 6, 1925; Eric Houghburg statement to police, September 10, 1925; George Suppus trial testimony, Ulric Arthur trial testimony, November 10, 1925.

81. George Suppus trial testimony, Ulric Arthur trial testimony, November 10, 1925; Otis Sweet statement to police, September 9, 1925; oral history interview with Otis Sweet, August 1, 1960, Baskin Collection; "Race Psychology Told in Sweet's Testimony," *Detroit Free Press*, November 19, 1925.

Chapter Six: The Letter of Your Law

1. Norton Schuknecht to superintendent, September 9 [actually September 10], 1925, Detroit Police Department case file, copy in author's possession; "Slaying Leads to Night Riot," *Detroit News*, September 10, 1925; "Police Fear Riot Reprisals," *Detroit Times*, September 10, 1925; "200 Police Guard Scene as 1 Is Slain and 1 Shot by Negroes," *Detroit Free Press*, September 10, 1925.

2. Wayne Andrews, *Architecture, Ambition, and Americans: A Social History of American Architecture* (New York: Free Press, 1978), pp. 252–254; W. Hawkins Ferry, *The Buildings of Detroit: A History*, rev. ed. (Detroit: Wayne State University Press, 1980), pp. 214–215.

3. Fred Williams to Frank Doremus, October 4, 1923, box 3, Detroit Mayor's Papers, 1923, Burton Historical Collection, Detroit Public Library, Detroit, Mich.; minutes of meeting, October 24, 1923, box 1, Detroit Urban League Collection, Michigan Historical Collection, Bentley Library, University of Michigan, Ann Arbor; Cosmopolitan League circular, n.d. [1925], frame 947, reel 2, part 5, NAACP Papers; Mayor's Inter-Racial Committee, *The Negro in Detroit* (Detroit: Detroit Bureau of Governmental Research, 1926), section 9, pp. 5, 33–34; Sidney Fine, *Frank Murphy: The Detroit Years* (Ann Arbor: University of Michigan Press, 1975), p. 127.

4. "Sweet Verdict Due This Week," *Detroit Free Press*, May 6, 1926; Robert Toms opening

statement, *People v. Ossian Sweet et al.*, November 5, 1925, Michigan Historical Collection.

5. Transcript of William Davis statement to police, September 10, 1925, Detroit Police Department file; transcript of Ossian Sweet statement to police, September 9, 1925.

6. Oral history interview with Charles Mahoney, August 1960, Alex Baskin Collection, Michigan Historical Collection; oral history interview with Cecil Rowlette, August 1, 1960, Baskin Collection; Davis statement to police, September 10, 1925.

7. Transcript of Ossian Sweet statement to police, September 9, 1925.

8. Ibid.

9. Charles Washington, Leonard Morse, William Davis, John Latting, and Joe Mack statements to police, September 9, 1925.

10. Norris Murray, William Davis, John Latting, Charles Washington, Leonard Morse, Hewitt Watson, and Joe Mack statements to police, September 9, 1925.

11. John Latting, Hewitt Watson, and Charles Washington statements to police, September 9, 1925.

12. Joe Mack statement to police, September 9, 1925.

13. John Latting, Leonard Morse, William Davis, Joe Mack, Norris Murray, Otis Sweet, and Hewitt Watson statements to police, September 9, 1925.

14. Gladys Sweet statement to police, September 9, 1925.

15. Henry Sweet statement to police, September 9, 1925.

16. "200 Police Guard Scene as 1 Is Slain and 1 Shot by Negroes"; Ferry, *The Buildings of Detroit*, p. 230. The jailhouse was built in 1897; untitled newspaper clipping, *Detroit Free Press*, June 24, 1928, clipping in "County Jail" file, Detroit Free Press Clipping Morgue, Detroit, Mich.

17. "A Tribute to Our Attorneys in the Sweet Case," *Detroit Independent*, no date, clipping in Ossian Sweet biographical file, Burton Historical Collection, Detroit Public Library, Detroit, Mich.; "Career of Slave's Son Inspires College Drive," *Detroit Times*, May 14, 1947; "An Era Has Begun Since They Parted," *Detroit Free Press*, June 28, 1957; oral history interview with Cecil Rowlette, August 1, 1960, Alex Baskin Collection, Bentley Historical Library; Walter White to James Weldon Johnson, September 16, 1925, frames 943–946, reel 2, part 5, NAACP Papers.

18. Oral history interview with William Osby, Sr., July 27, 1960, Baskin Papers; David Alan Levine, *Internal Combustion: The Races in Detroit, 1915–1926* (Westport, Conn.: Greenwood Press, 1976), pp. 82–83; "Mahoney Scores a Double First," *Detroit Free Press*, August 1, 1954; "Charles Henry Mahoney," n.d., copy available in Detroit Free Press Clipping Morgue, Detroit, Mich.

19. William M. Beany, *The Right to Counsel in American Courts* (Ann Arbor: University of Michigan Press, 1955), p. 127; "Officer's Shot Slew Breiner, Is New Claim," *Detroit Free Press*, November 22, 1925; "Dr. Sweet Goes on Stand," *Chicago Defender*, November 28, 1925.

20. Walter White to James Weldon Johnson, September 16, 1925, frames 943–946, reel 2, part 5, NAACP Papers; W. Hays McKinney to James Weldon Johnson, frames 931–932, reel 2, part 5, NAACP Papers; "Murphy Raps Police Raiders," *Detroit Free Press*, July 14, 1925.

21. White to E. P. Lovett, October 26, 1925, frames 20–21, reel 3, part 5, NAACP Papers; oral history interview with Rowlette; White to Johnson, September 16, 1925.

22. McKinney to Johnson, September 12, 1925; Mark Robert Schneider, *"We Return Fighting": The Civil Rights Movement in the Jazz Age* (Boston: Northeastern University Press, 2002), pp. 197–199.

23. "200 Police Guard Scene as 1 Is Slain and 1 Shot by Negores"; R. L. Polk and Company, *City of Detroit Directory*, 1925–1926 (Detroit: R. L. Polk and Company, 1926).

24. Norton Schuknecht testimony, November 5, 1925, *People v. Ossian Sweet et al.*, trial transcript, Bentley Historical Library; "Police Fear Riot Reprisals"; "Slaying Leads to Night Riot"; "200 Police Guard Scene as 1 Is Slain and 1 Shot by Negroes."

25. "200 Police Guard Scene as 1 is Slain and 1 Shot by Negroes."

26. Ibid.

27. Bill McGraw, "Race, Journalism, and the Civil War: *The Detroit Free Press* and the

Riot of 1863," unpublished paper in author's possession; Frank Angelo, *On Guard: A History of the Detroit Free Press* (Detroit: Detroit Free Press, 1981), pp. 119–143; Peter Gavrilovich and Bill McGraw, eds., *The Detroit Almanac: 300 Years of Life in the Motor City* (Detroit: Detroit Free Press, 2001), p. 450; Sidney Fine, *Frank Murphy: The Detroit Years* (Ann Arbor: University of Michigan Press, 1975), pp. 96–97, 104–105, 110–113.

28. "Police Fear Riot Reprisals."

29. Josephine Gomon, draft of Frank Murphy biography, box 9, Josephine Gomon Collection, Michigan Historical Collection, "Dr. Sweet Goes on Stand"; "Officer's Shot Slew Breiner, Is New Claim."

30. Josephine Gomon book drafts; "Slaying Leads to Night Riot."

31. "Robert Morrell Toms," biographical file, Burton Historical Collection, E. A. Batchelor, "Personal and Confidential: Robert M. Toms," *Detroit Saturday Night*, January 10, 1925.

32. Toms biographical file; "Toms Named to 33rd Degree," *Detroit News*, September 27, 1945, and "Toms Denies He's Klansman," *Detroit News*, September 9, 1924, copies in Detroit News Clipping Morgue, Detroit, Mich.; Felix Holt to Walter White, March 22, 1926, frame 621, reel 9, part 2, NAACP Papers.

33. An excellent summary of the right to self-defense, both as a general principle and in Michigan law, is available in Frank Murphy's charge to the court, May 13, 1925, frames 822–854, reel 3, part 5, NAACP Papers. Also see Arthur Garfield Hays opening statement, November 16, 1925, frames 920–938, reel 3, part 5, NAACP Papers. On Toms's counterargument, see Toms opening statement, November 5, 1925, trial transcript.

34. Cover sheet for police department case file, n.d. [September 1925]; Norton Schuknecht statement to police, September 10, 1925; "Moll Demands Slayers in Riot Case Pay Penalty," *Detroit Times*, November 24, 1925.

35. Norton Schuknecht statement to police, September 10, 1925; Schuknecht to superintendent, September 9, 1925; "Put Guard at Home of Negroes"; "200 Police Guard Scene As 1 Is Slain and 1 Shot by Negroes"; "Slaying Leads to Night Riot."

36. Schuknecht statement to police, September 10, 1925.

37. Otto Lemhagen statement to police, September 10, 1926.

38. William Johnson and [?] Hoffman to Edward Fox, n.d. [September 1925?], Detroit Police Department case file, copy in author's possession; Kathleen Dove statement to police, September 10, 1925.

39. Ray and Kathleen Dove statements to police, September 10, 1925. On Ray Dove's place of birth, see the transcript of his testimony in *The People v. Ossian Sweet et al.*, November 6, 1925.

40. George Strauser, William Arthur, George Getke, and Della Getke statements to police, September 10, 1925.

41. John Getke statement to police, September 10, 1925.

42. For a sense of prison conditions, see untitled *Detroit Free Press* clipping, June 24, 1928; G. A. Thomas to Commissioner of Police, December 10, 1923, Mayor's Papers 1923, Burton Historical Collection; R. H. Ferris to Frank Murphy, April 22, 1926, reel 92, Frank Murphy Papers [microfilm edition], Bentley Library; and Detroit House of Corrections, *68th Annual Report* (Detroit: n.p., 1928), copy at Library of Congress, Washington, D.C.

43. Marcet Haldeman-Julius, *Clarence Darrow's Two Great Trials* (Girard, Kan.: Haldeman-Julius Publishing Company, 1927), p. 42; oral history interview with Otis Sweet, August 1, 1960, Baskin Collection; Otis Sweet et al. to W. E. B. Du Bois, September 29, 1925, frame 1088, reel 2, part 5, NAACP Papers.

44. William Davis statement to police, September 10, 1925.

45. Fine, *Frank Murphy*, p. 103; Gomon untitled book draft, box 9, Gomon Papers; "Ten Are Held for Murder in Race Conflict," *Detroit Free Press*, September 11, 1925; warrants against Ossian Sweet et al., September 10, 1925, box 1, Ossian Sweet Collection, Burton Historical Collection.

46. Fine, *Frank Murphy*, pp. 106, 134, 140; Sidney Fine interview with Hilmer Gellein, n.d., box 1, Sweet Collection; John Bugas to J. Edgar Hoover, January 6, 1939, Frank Murphy File, Federal Bureau of Investigation, Washington D.C.; "Warrants Issued After Death Riots," *Detroit News*, September 11, 1925.

47. R. L. Polk and Company, *Detroit City Directory*, 1923–1924 (Detroit: R. L. Polk and Company, 1924); "Property Owners Talk Plans to Sustain Values," *Detroit Free Press*, September 11, 1925; "Callahan Still Dodges Klan Questions Asked by Times," *Detroit Times*, October 30, 1925; "Mistrial Hint in Sweet Case," *Detroit News*, April 29, 1926; "Klan Answers Smith Attack," *Detroit News*, September 14, 1925.

48. "Warrants Issued After Death Riots," *Detroit Times*, September 11, 1925.

49. W. Hayes McKinney to James Weldon Johnson, September 12, 1925, frame 931, reel 2, part 4, NAACP Papers. Haldeman-Julius, *Clarence Darrow's Two Great Trials*, p. 42, says the lawyers saw their clients late Friday afternoon, not Saturday, but there is no evidence to support that claim.

50. O. H. Sweet statement, September 12, 1925, frame 924, reel 2, part 5, NAACP Papers.

51. "Citizens Back Smith on Rioting," *Detroit Times*, September 14, 1925; McKinney to James Weldon Johnson, September 12, 1925.

52. "Riot Curb Demanded by Mayor," *Detroit Times*, September 13, 1925.

Chapter Seven: Freedmen, Sons of God, Americans

1. "Seek Ten Arrests in Race War," *New York World*, September 11, 1925, clipping on frame 968, reel 2, part 5, NAACP Papers [microfilm edition], Library of Congress, Washington, D.C.

2. Robert Bagnall report, September 9, 1925, frame 992, reel 28, part 11B, NAACP Papers; James Weldon Johnson report to the NAACP board of directors, September 1925, reel 4, part 1, NAACP Papers; B. P. Young to Walter White, September 9, 1925, and copy of Norfolk, Va., city ordinance, frames 989–990, reel 28, part 11b, NAACP Papers.

3. Arthur Spingarn profile of James Weldon Johnson, n.d. [1938], box 11, Arthur Spingarn Papers, Moorland-Spingarn Collection, Howard University, Washington, D.C.

4. David Levering Lewis, *When Harlem Was in Vogue* (New York: Oxford University Press, 1979), pp. 143–144; James Weldon Johnson, *Along This Way: The Autobiography of James Weldon Johnson* (1933; repr. New York: Viking, 1968), p. 11.

5. David Levering Lewis, *W. E. B. Du Bois: Biography of a Race* (New York: Henry Holt, 1993), p. 213; Johnson, *Along This Way*, pp. 11, 65, 84–86; Eugene Levy, *James Weldon Johnson: Black Leader, Black Voice* (Chicago: University of Chicago Press, 1973), chapters 2 and 3.

6. Levy, *James Weldon Johnson*, pp. 75–98; Lewis, *When Harlem Was in Vogue*, pp. 146–149; Sondra Kathryn Wilson, *James Weldon Johnson: Complete Poems* (New York: Penguin Books, 2000), pp. 117–121; Sondra Kathryn Wilson, *The Crisis Reader: Stories, Poems, and Essays from the NAACP's Crisis Magazine* (New York: Modern Library, 1999), p. 33.

7. Levy, *James Weldon Johnson*, chapters 5 and 7; Mark Robert Schneider, *"We Return Fighting": The Civil Rights Movement in the Jazz Age* (Boston: Northeastern University Press, 2002), pp. 42–44; Lewis, *W. E. B. Du Bois*, pp. 25–27, 283; Ann Douglas, *Terrible Honesty: Mongrel Manhattan in the 1920s* (New York: Farrar, Straus and Giroux, 1995), pp. 326–327; Lewis, *When Harlem Was in Vogue*, pp. 143, 147–149.

8. James Weldon Johnson to Rev. R. L. Bradby, September 11, 1925, frame 929, reel 2, part 5, NAACP Papers.

9. W. Hayes McKinney to James Weldon Johnson, September 12, 1925, frame 931, reel 2, part 5, NAACP Papers; Johnson to McKinney, September 12, 1925, frame 956, reel 2, part 5, NAACP Papers; Johnson, *Along This Way*, pp. 383–384; handwritten notes, n.d. [September 12, 1925], frame 926, reel 2, part 5, NAACP Papers.

10. James Weldon Johnson, "Harlem: The Cultural Capital," in Alain Locke, ed., *The New Negro* (1925; repr. New York: Atheneum, 1974), pp. 301–311.

11. Kenneth T. Jackson, *The Ku Klux Klan in the City, 1915–1930* (1967; repr. Chicago: Ivan Dee, 1992), pp. 175–177; Walter White, "The Paradox of Color," in Locke, *The New Negro*, p. 363; "Residential Segregation," (Philadelphia) *Public Journal*, October 10, 1925,

frame 985, part 5, NAACP Papers. See also W. E. B. Du Bois, "The Shape of Fear," *North American* 23 (June 1926): p. 292.

12. Gilbert Osofsky, *Harlem: The Making of a Ghetto* (New York: Harper and Row, 1963); Johnson, "Harlem," pp. 302–308.

13. Oscar Handlin, "Introduction," in Charles Reznikoff, ed., *Louis Marshall: Champion of Liberty*, v. I (Philadelphia: Jewish Publication Society of America, 1957), pp. ix–xliii; Morton Rosenstock, "Louis Marshall," in John A. Garraty and Mark C. Carnes, eds., *American National Biography* v. 14 (New York: Oxford University Press, 1999), pp. 571–573; Stephen Grant Meyer, *As Long as They Don't Move Next Door: Segregation and Racial Conflict in American Neighborhoods* (Lanham, Md.: Rowman and Littlefield, 2000), pp. 15–28.

14. Clement E. Vose, *Caucasians Only: The Supreme Court, the NAACP, and the Restrictive Covenant Cases* (Berkeley: University of California Press, 1959), pp. 9–13, 17; Joseph Boris, ed., *Who's Who in Colored America, 1928–1929* (New York: Who's Who in Colored America Corporation, 1929), p. 94; Shelby Davidson to James Weldon Johnson, January 28, 1924, frame 9, reel 6, part 12A, NAACP Papers, Davidson to James Weldon Johnson, January 28, 1924, frames 956–961, reel 1, part 1, NAACP papers.

15. "A Service of Commemoration for Frank D. Reeves and James A. Cobb," October 10, 1975, box 2, James Cobb Papers, Moorland-Spingarn Collection, Howard University, Washington, D.C.; NAACP press release, n.d. [late 1925], frames 960–961, reel 28, part 11B, NAACP Papers; Vose, *Caucasians Only*, pp. 17–18; Schneider, "*We Return Fighting,*" p. 287.

16. NAACP press release, December 23, 1924, frame 636, reel 13, part 1, NAACP Papers; NAACP press release, September 12, 1924, frames 936–937, reel 28, part 11B, NAACP Papers; Levy, *James Weldon Johnson*, p. 229.

17. W. E. B. Du Bois, "Americanization," *Crisis* (August 1922): 154–155; Lewis, *W. E. B. Du Bois*, pp. 95–96.

18. David Levering Lewis, ed., *W. E. B. Du Bois: A Reader* (New York: Henry Holt, 1995), pp. 464, 555. The literature on racial divisions between African-American and white immigrant workers—and within the working class more generally—is growing exponentially. Particularly valuable are James R. Barrett and David Roediger, "In-between Peoples: Race, Nationality, and the New Working Class," in Rick Halpern and Jonathan Morris, eds., *American Exceptionalism? U.S. Working-Class Formation in an International Context* (New York: St. Martin's Press, 1997); Bruce Nelson, *Divided We Stand: American Workers and the Struggle for Black Equality* (Princeton, N.J.: Princeton University Press, 2001), chapters 1 and 4; and David Roediger's path-breaking, *The Wages of Whiteness: Race and the Making of the American Working Class* (London: Verso, 1991), particularly chapters 1 and 7. A thorough overview of the literature is Eric Arnesen, "Up from Exclusion: Black and White Workers, Race, and the State of Labor History," *Reviews in American History* 26 (March 1998): 146–174.

19. NAACP typescript, September 19, 1924, frame 940, reel 28, part 11B, NAACP Papers; NAACP press release, n.d. [late 1925], frames 960–961, reel 28, part 11B, NAACP Papers; NAACP press release, October 20, 1925, frames 1015–1017, reel 28, part 11B, NAACP Papers. See also NAACP press release, September 12, 1924, reel 28, part 11B, NAACP Papers, and Louis Marshall to William Borah, April 19, 1926, reprinted in Reznikoff, *Louis Marshall*, p. 464.

20. NAACP press release, September 18, 1925, frames 998–999, reel 28, part 11B, NAACP Papers; "Segregation Grows Bitter in California," *St. Louis Argus*, April 19, 1925, clipping at frame 1068, reel 28, part 11B, NAACP Papers; William Pickens to James Weldon Johnson, May 18, 1925, frame 965, reel 28, part 11B, NAACP Papers; Johnson report to the NAACP board, August 1925, reel 4, part 1, NAACP Papers; Pickens to Robert Bradby, July 31, 1925, frame 941, reel 2, part 5, NAACP Papers; Robert Bagnall to Robert Bradby, July 30, 1925, box G-95, group I, NAACP Papers, Library of Congress, Washington, D.C.

21. Gloria Garrett Sampson, *The American Fund for Public Service: Charles Garland and Radical Philanthropy, 1922–1941* (Westport, Conn.: Greenwood Press, 1996), pp. 1–3; Mark V. Tushnet, *The NAACP's Legal Strategy Against Segregated Education, 1925–1950*

(Chapel Hill: University of North Carolina Press, 1987), p. 4; James Weldon Johnson to Moorfield Storey, September 12, 1925, frames 586–587, reel 17, part 1, NAACP Papers.

22. Johnson to Storey, September 12, 1925.

23. Walter White to Claude McKay, August 28, 1925, frame 178, reel 9, part 2, NAACP Papers; White to L. M. Hussey, September 5, 1925, frame 193, reel 9, part 2, NAACP Papers; White to Julius Bledsoe, September 14, 1925, frame 213, reel 9, part 2, NAACP Papers; James Weldon Johnson to W. Hayes McKinney, September 13, 1925, frame 934, reel 2, part 5, NAACP Papers.

24. Kenneth Janken, *White: The Biography of Walter White, Mr. NAACP* (New York: New Press, 2003), pp. 3–27; Walter White, *A Man Called White: The Autobiography of Walter White* (New York: Viking, 1948), p. 3.

25. White, *A Man Called White*, pp. 5–12. White's biographer casts some doubt on the veracity of the story. Though the family was trapped inside its home, he concludes, Walter never took up arms to protect his family. See Janken, *White*, pp. 14–18.

26. Joel Spingarn to Amy Spingarn, November 22, 1926, box 15, Joel Spingarn Collection, Moorland-Spingarn Collection; Janken, *White*, pp. 190–191.

27. Janken, *White*, pp. 29–32.

28. Ibid., chapter 2; White, *A Man Called White*, pp. 50–51.

29. Levy, *James Weldon Johnson*, p. 224; Janken, *White*, pp. 64–68, 90–95.

30. Ann Douglas, *Terrible Honesty: Mongrel Manhattan in the 1920s* (New York: Farrar, Straus and Giroux, 1995), p. 354; Lewis, *When Harlem Was in Vogue*, pp. 93–94.

31. Lewis, *When Harlem Was in Vogue*, pp. 137–140; Janken, *White*, pp. 95–103.

32. Lewis, *When Harlem Was in Vogue*, p. 142; Janken, *White*, pp. 104–110; Walter White, *The Fire in the Flint* (New York: Alfred A. Knopf, 1924), pp. 140–141.

33. White, *A Man Called White*, p. 68; Edward E. Waldron, *Walter White and the Harlem Renaissance* (Port Washington, N.Y.: Kennikat Press, 1978), pp. 63–78; Lewis, *When Harlem Was in Vogue*, p. 136; Janken, *White*, pp. 108–111; *New York Tribune*, September 28, 1924; *The Nation* (October 8, 1924): 386; Lewis, *W. E. B. Du Bois: Fight for Equality*, p. 175.

34. James Weldon Johnson to W. Hayes McKinney, September 14, 1925, frame 936, reel 2, part 5, NAACP Papers; McKinney to Johnson, September 12, 1925, frame 932, reel 2, part 5, NAACP Papers.

35. Walter White to L. M. Hussey, September 14, 1925, frame 212, reel 9, part 2, NAACP Papers; White to Johnson, September 16, 1925, frames 943–946, reel 2, part 5, NAACP Papers.

36. "Jayne to Retire from Active Role," *Detroit News*, December 9, 1956.

37. Knights of the Ku Klux Klan to the Citizens of Detroit, September 12, 1925, Detroit Organizations—Ku Klux Klan File, Burton Historical Collection, Detroit Public Library, Detroit, Mich.; "Klan Attacks Mayor by Mail," *Detroit Times*, September 17, 1925; "Victim of Racial Battle Is Buried," *Detroit Free Press*, September 15, 1925; White to Johnson, September 16, 1925, frames 943–946, reel 2, part 5, NAACP Papers; Walter White handwritten notes, n.d. [September 1925], frames 374–396, reel 2, part 5, NAACP Papers.

38. White to Johnson, September 16, 1925; Sweet Defense Fund statement of cash receipts, n.d. [December 11, 1925], frames 811–814, reel 3, part 5, NAACP Papers.

39. White to Johnson, September 16, 1925.

40. "Tells of Home Row Shooting," *Detroit Free Press*, September 17, 1925. In his memoir, White says on the day of his arrival he went directly from the train station to the jail, where he met with all eleven of the accused. "One of the defendants," he wrote, "half sobbed and exclaimed, 'Thank God! We can now rest easy and get some sleep!'" White, *A Man Called White*, p. 74. White's notes from his time in Detroit indicate, however, that he didn't speak to the defendants at all and therefore only saw them at the preliminary hearing. See handwritten notes, n.d. [September 1925].

41. "Rioters Trial Is Opened," *Detroit Times*, September 17, 1925; transcript of preliminary hearing, September 16–17, 1925, box 1, Ossian Sweet Collection, Burton Historical Collection, Detroit Public Library, Detroit, Mich.; Walter White to James Weldon Johnson, September 17, 1925, frames 1031–1032, reel 2, part 5, NAACP Papers.

42. Norton Schuknecht testimony at the preliminary hearing, September 16, 1925, and Ray Dove testimony, September 17, 1925.

43. John Getke testimony at the preliminary hearing, September 17, 1925.

44. Norton Schuknecht testimony, September 16, 1925. Rowlette's handling of Schuknecht was tough enough to earn even the grudging admiration of White. See White to Johnson, September 17, 1925.

45. Ray Dove testimony, September 17, 1925.

46. John Getke testimony, September 17, 1925.

47. Walter White to James Johnson, September 18, 1925, frame 1046, reel 2, part 5, NAACP Papers. On Faust as a member of the court's liberal bloc, see Raymond Fragnoli, *The Transformation of Detroit: Progressivism in Detroit—and After* (New York: Garland, 1982), pp. 259–267.

48. White to Johnson, September 17, 1925; White handwritten notes, n.d. [September 1925]; draft agreement between NAACP and defendants, September 17, 1925, frames 1037–1038, reel 2, part 5, NAACP Papers.

49. Walter White to Ira Jayne, September 21, 1925, frames 1056–1057, reel 2, part 5, NAACP Papers; Walter White to Mose Walker, September 21, 1925, frame 1055, reel 2, part 5, NAACP Papers; Walker to White, September 22, 1926, frames 1060–1061, reel 2, part 5, NAACP Papers; White to Oscar Baker, October 5, 1925, frames 1115–1118, reel 2, part 5, NAAP Papers.

50. Walter White to R. L. Bradby, September 19, 1925, frame 1053, reel 2, part 5, NAACP Papers.

51. "[unreadable] Detroit Citizens," *Dallas Express*, September 19, 1925, clipping at frame 973, reel 2, part 5, NAACP Papers; "[unreadable] Test Up in Detroit," *St. Louis Argus*, September 18, 1925, copy at frame 972, reel 2, part 5, NAACP Papers; "Racial Clash Seems Near: Blame KKK," *Houston Informer*, September 26, 1925, copy at frame 975, reel 2, part 5, NAACP Papers; "Quell Detroit Race Clash," and "What's Wrong in Detroit?" *Chicago Defender*, September 19, 1925; James Grossman, *Land of Hope: Chicago, Black Southerners, and the Great Migration* (Chicago: University of Chicago Press, 1989), pp. 74–82.

52. NAACP press release, September 18, 1925, frames 998–999, reel 28, part 11B, NAACP Papers; NAACP press release, September 25, 1925, frame 1000, reel 28, part 11B, NAACP Papers; minutes of the NAACP board of directors, September 14, 1925, frames 42–43, reel 2, part 1, NAACP Papers; "Citizens Plan Strong Defense for Doctor," (Jacksonville) *Florida Sentinel*, September 26, 1925, clipping in frame 976, reel 2, part 5, NAACP Papers.

53. NAACP press release, September 18, 1925.

54. "Plans Completed for Sweet Defense," *Detroit Independent*, September 18, 1925, copy at frames 970–971, reel 2, part 5, NAACP Papers; "NAACP Holds Another Successful Meeting for Sweet Fund at St. John's CME Church," *Detroit Independent*, October 2, 1925, frame 981, reel 2, part 5, NAACP Papers; James Weldon Johnson report to the NAACP board, October 1925, frame 647–651, reel 4, part 1, NAACP Papers; report of the Department of Branches, October 1925, frame 652–654, reel 4, part 1, NAACP Papers; Walter White to James Weldon Johnson, September 26, 1925, frame 1002, reel 28, part 11B, NAACP Papers.

55. Sweet Defense Fund statement of receipts and disbursements, n.d. [December 11, 1925]; "Residential Segregation," (Philadelphia) *Public Journal*, October 10, 1925, copy at frame 985, reel 2, part 5, NAACP Papers.

56. Henry Strong Huntington to Charles [*sic*] Weldon Johnson, September 24, 1925, frames 1072–1073, reel 2, part 5, NAACP Papers. For Johnson's reply, see his letter to Huntington, September 29, 1925, frame 1085, reel 2, part 5, NAACP Papers.

57. Walter White to Oswald Garrison Villard, September 22, 1925, frame 1062, reel 2, part 5, NAACP Papers; typescript, "Segregation Comes North," n.d. [September 1925], frames 1047–1054, reel 28, part 11B, NAACP Papers.

58. Walter White to Ira Jayne, September 21, 1925, frames 1056–1057, reel 2, part 5, NAACP Papers; White to M. L. Walker, September 21, 1925, frame 1055, reel 2, part 5,

NAACP Papers; memorandum of telephone conversation, September 25, 1925, frame 1079, reel 2, part 5, NAACP Papers.

59. "City Wide Committee for Sweet Fund Is Organized," *Detroit Independent*, October 2, 1925, clipping at frame 980, reel 2, part 5, NAACP Papers; William Pickens to Arthur Spingarn, November 2, 1925, frame 56, reel 5, Arthur Spingarn Papers, Library of Congress; William Pickens to James Weldon Johnson and Walter White, October 25, 1925, frame 29, reel 3, part 5, NAACP Papers. Pickens claimed that Gomez defied the NAACP because, among other things, "he hates Du Bois."

60. Mose Walker to Walter White, n.d. [September 27, 1925], frame 1040, reel 2, part 5, NAACP Papers; "NAACP Holds Another Successful Meeting for Sweet Fund at St. John's CME Church."

61. Sweet defense fund, statement of receipts and disbursements, n.d. [December 11, 1925]; oral history interview with Otis Sweet, August 1, 1960, Alex Baskin Collection, Michigan Historical Collection, Bentley Library, University of Michigan, Ann Arbor.

62. I have dated Henry Sweet's visit to Detroit through "NAACP Holds Another Successful Meeting for Sweet Fund at St. John's CME Church." Sweet appeared at the September 27 mass rally, the story recounts.

63. Oral history interview with Sherman Sweet, February 27, 2002, notes in author's possession.

64. Otis Sweet, William Davis, Leonard Morse, and Charles Washington to W. Hayes McKinney, September 29, 1925; and Sweet, Davis, Morse, and Washington to W. E. B. Du Bois, September 29, 1925, frames 1086 and 1088, reel 2, part 5, NAACP Papers. The evidence indicates that Otis, Davis, Washington, and Morse asked the other defendants to sign the letter, but they refused.

65. Ibid.; Sweet, Davis, Morse, and Washington to Du Bois, October 1, 1925, frame 1108, reel 2, part 5, NAACP Papers.

66. Walter White to Ira Jayne, October 1, 1925, frame 1103, reel 2, part 5, NAACP Papers; memorandum of telephone conversation, Walter White and Arthur Spingarn, October 1, 1925, frame 1097, reel 2, part 5, NAACP Papers; White to Spingarn, October 2, 1925, frame 1111, reel 2, part 5, NAACP Papers.

67. Ira Jayne to Walter White, September 30, 1925, frame 1095, reel 2, part 5, NAACP Papers; White to Oscar Baker, October 5, 1925; "Klan Out to Elect Bowles," *Detroit Times*, September 23, 1925; "Klan Prepares for Election," *Detroit Free Press*, September 30, 1925.

68. Motion to quash, *The People of Michigan vs. Otis Sweet et al.*, September 3, 1925, box 5, Clarence Darrow Papers, Library of Congress.

69. Memorandum of telephone conversation, Walter White and Mose Walker, October 8, 1925, frames 1152–1153, reel 2, part 5, NAACP Papers; Walter White to Mr. Seligman, October 22, 1925, frames 3–4, reel 3, part 5, NAACP Papers; "Klan Sweeps Primary" and "Backers of Bowles Jubilant," *Detroit Times*, October 7 and 8, 1925.

70. N. K. McGill to Walter White, October 2, 1925, frame 1114, reel 2, part 5, NAACP Papers.

Chapter Eight: The Prodigal Son

1. James Weldon Johnson to Clarence Darrow, October 7, 1925, and Johnson to Darrow, October 8, 1925, frames 1137 and 1151, reel 2, part 5, NAACP Papers; Cora Arons to Johnson, October 7, 1925, frame 1135, reel 2, NAACP Papers; Walter White to Johnson, October 8, 1925, frame 1150, reel 2, part 5, NAACP Papers.

2. R. L. Polk and Company, *General Directory of New York City* (New York: R. L. Polk and Company, 1925), p. 1008; Irving Stone, *Clarence Darrow for the Defense* (Garden City, N.Y.: Doubleday, 1941), pp. 469–470.

3. Stone, *Clarence Darrow for the Defense*, p. 470; Clarence Darrow, *The Story of My Life* (New York: Charles Scribner's Sons, 1934), p. 302.

4. The story had had various tellings. See, for instance, Arthur Garfield Hays, *Let Freedom Ring* (New York: Liveright, 1937), pp. 196–197; Stone, *Clarence Darrow for the Defense*,

pp. 469–470, for Spingarn's account; Walter White, *A Man Called White: The Autobiography of Walter White* (New York: Viking, 1948), pp. 75–76.

5. Frank Walsh quoted in Stone, *Clarence Darrow for the Defense*, p. 171; Masters quoted in J. Anthony Lukas, *Big Trouble: A Murder in a Small Western Town Sets Off a Struggle for the Soul of America* (New York: Simon and Schuster, 1997), p. 327.

6. Christine Stansell, *American Moderns: Bohemian New York and the Creation of a New Century* (New York: Henry Holt, 2000), pp. 45–46.

7. Darrow, *The Story of My Life*, p. 14; Kevin Tierney, *Darrow: A Biography* (New York: Thomas Y. Crowell, 1934), chapters 1 and 2; Lukas, *Big Trouble*, p. 305.

8. William Cronon, *Nature's Metropolis: Chicago and the Great West* (New York: W. W. Norton, 1991), pp. 354–355; Thomas Lee Philpot, *The Slum and the Ghetto: Immigrants, Blacks, and Reformers in Chicago, 1880–1930* (1978; repr. Belmont, Calif.: Wadsworth, 1997), p. 6. On Darrow's multiple political commitments, see John Livingston, *Clarence Darrow: The Mind of a Sentimental Rebel* (New York: Garland, 1988), though Livingston's analysis of Darrow's core beliefs is very different from mine.

9. Stansell, *American Moderns*, pp. 50–55; Dale Kramer, *Chicago Renaissance: The Literary Life in the Midwest, 1900–1930* (New York: Appleton-Century, 1966), for a glimpse of Chicago's avant-garde; Gerald W. McFarland, *Inside Greenwich Village: A New York City Neighborhood, 1898–1918* (Amherst: University of Massachusetts Press, 2001); Lukas, *Big Trouble*, p. 316.

10. Clarence Darrow, *Farmington* (Chicago: A. C. McClurg, 1904); Darrow, *An Eye for an Eye* (New York: Fox Duffield, 1905); Tierney, *Darrow*, p. 144; Stone, *Clarence Darrow for the Defense*, chapter 2; Nick Salvatore, *Eugene V. Debs: Citizen and Socialist* (Urbana: University of Illinois Press, 1982), pp. 126–138; Miriam Gurko, *Clarence Darrow* (New York: Thomas Y. Crowell, 1965), p. 75.

11. For details on Darrow's labor cases, see Tierney, *Darrow*, chapters 13, 17, 20, and 22; Stone, *Clarence Darrow for the Defense;* Geoffrey Cowan, *The People v. Clarence Darrow: The Bribery Trial of America's Greatest Lawyer* (New York: Times Books, 1993). Lukas, *Big Trouble*, p. 315 for quote.

12. Darrow, "Attorney for the Defense," *Esquire,* (May 1936): 36; Lukas, *Big Trouble*, p. 314; Darrow, *The Story of My Life*, p. 76.

13. Stone, *Clarence Darrow for the Defense*, pp. 165–166; Tierney, *Darrow*, pp. 106–108, 220–226; Arthur Weinberg, ed., *Attorney for the Damned* (New York: Simon and Schuster, 1957), pp. 486–487; Lukas, *Big Trouble*, pp. 707–712, 721–723.

14. Tierney, *Darrow*, p. 182; Stone, *Clarence Darrow for the Defense*, chapters 8 and 9; Cowan, *The People v. Clarence Darrow.*

15. Tierney, *Darrow*, pp. 306–310, 317; Weinberg, *Attorney for the Damned*, p. 172; Darrow, *The Story of My Life*, pp. 226–243; Hal Higdon, *The Crime of the Century: The Leopold and Loeb Case* (New York: Putnam, 1975). Paula Fass, "Making and Remaking an Event: The Leopold and Loeb Case in American Culture," *Journal of American History* 80 (December 1993): 919–940.

16. Edward J. Larson, *Summer for the Gods: The Scopes Trial and America's Continuing Debate over Science and Religion* (Cambridge, Mass.: Harvard University Press, 1998), chapters 2–4; Arthur Garfield Hays, *City Lawyer: The Autobiography of a Law Practice* (New York: Simon and Schuster, 1942).

17. Larson, *Summer for the Gods*, pp. 140–143; Weinberg, *Attorney for the Damned,* p. 188.

18. Larson, *Summer for the Gods*, pp. 187–190; Stone, *Clarence Darrow for the Defense,* p. 458.

19. Tierney, *Darrow,* pp. 8–9; H. L. Mencken, "Aftermath," *Baltimore Evening Sun,* September 14, 1925; Darrow, *The Story of My Life*, p. 282.

20. Tierney, *Darrow*, p. 8; Darrow, *The Story of My Life*, p. 302; Clarence Darrow, "John Brown," *Crisis* (May 1926): 16; Clarence Darrow's address to the 1910 Annual Conference, Part 1, Reel 8, Part 1, NAACP Papers. I am grateful to Patricia Sullivan for providing me with the latter document.

21. Darrow, *The Story of My Life*, p. 302; Hays, *Let Freedom Ring*, p. 195.

22. Salvatore, *Eugene V. Debs*, p. 138; Tierney, *Darrow*, pp. 244–250; Stone, *Clarence Darrow for the Defense*, pp. 418–419; Larson, *Summer for the Gods*, pp. 200–201; Darrow address, 1910; "Advises Negroes to Stop Working," undated clipping [1910], box 30, Darrow Papers; David L. Lewis, *W. E. B. Du Bois: Biography of a Race* (New York: Henry Holt, 1993), p. 425; Glenda Elizabeth Gilmore, *Gender and Jim Crow: Women and the Politics of White Supremacy in North Carolina, 1896–1920* (Chapel Hill: University of North Carolina Press, 1996), chapter 4.

23. Memorandum of expenses, November 30, 1925, frames 174–175, reel 3, part 5, NAACP Papers; James Weldon Johnson to Clarence Darrow, October 14, 1925, frame 1188, reel 2, part 5, NAACP Papers; James Weldon Johnson to Walter White, October 14, 1925, frame 1182, reel 2, part 5.

24. Walter White to James Weldon Johnson, October 8, 1925, frame 1150, reel 2, part 5, NAACP Papers; Walter White to Cecil Rowlette, Julian Perry, and Charles Mahoney, October 12, 1925, frames 1155 and 1174, reel 2, part 5, NAACP Papers; Walter White to James Weldon Johnson, October 8, 1925, frame 1150, reel 2, part 5, NAACP Papers.

25. Walter White to Ira Jayne, October 22, 1925, frame 2, reel 3, part 5, NAACP Papers; White to James Weldon Johnson, October 8, 1925.

26. Louis Marshall to Moorfield Storey, September 24, 1925, in Charles Reznikoff, ed., *Louis Marshall: Champion of Liberty* (Philadelphia: Jewish Publication Society of America, 1957), p. 461; James Weldon Johnson to Walter White, October 7, 1925, frame 1006, reel 28, part 11B, NAACP Papers; minutes of the NAACP board of directors meeting, November 9, 1925, frames 52–54, reel 2, part 1, NAACP; Johnson to Moorfield Storey, October 20, 1925, frame 589, reel 17, part 1, NAACP Papers.

27. NAACP press release, October 15, 1925, frame 1189, reel 2, part 5, NAACP Papers.

28. "Darrow to Defend 11 Negroes in Detroit Mob Shooting," *New York Post*, October 14, 1925, clipping at frame 987, reel 2, part 5, NAACP Papers; "Darrow Defends Negroes," *New York World*, October 16, 1925, frame 989, reel 2, part 5, NAACP Papers; "Negro Murder Trial Inflames Detroit," *Chicago Daily News*, October 17, 1925, clipping at frame 997, reel 2, part 5, NAACP Papers; "Race Riots in Northern Cities," *Chicago Daily News*, reprinted in *Chicago Defender*, October 24, 1925; "Law for Whites and Negroes," *New York World*, reprinted in *Chicago Defender*, October 31, 1925.

29. Walter White to Wilson Midgley, October 23, 1925, frame 288, reel 9, part 2, NAACP Papers; "Darrow Delays," *Detroit Times*, October 16, 1925; "Darrow Gets Riot Case Stay," *Detroit News*, October 16, 1925; White to Mr. Seligman, October 22, 1925, frames 3–4, reel 3, part 5, NAACP Papers.

30. Leonard Mose [*sic*], William Davis, Hewitt Watson, and Charles Washington to Walter White, October 8, 1925, frame 1142, reel 2, part 5, NAACP Papers. Unlike the previous messages, this plea was not signed by Otis Sweet. Perhaps he thought better of defying his brother a second time.

31. Memorandum of telephone conversation, Mose Walker and Walter White, October 8, 1925, frames 1152–1153, reel 2, part 5, NAACP Papers; Walter White to O. H. Sweet, October 9, 1925, frame 1155, reel 2, part 5, NAACP Papers; Alex Baskin oral history interview with Otis Sweet, August 1, 1960, Alex Baskin Collection, Bentley Library.

32. Darrow, *Story of My Life*, p. 303; Walter White to James Weldon Johnson, October 14, 1925, frame 1183, reel 2, part 5, NAACP Papers. Arthur Garfield Hays vividly recalled the jailhouse visit in his memoirs. "Up two flights of steps, steel doors were unlocked to permit passage, then closed. We were ushered into a small room, dimly lighted by a dirty window, furnished with a table and a few broken chairs." See Hays, *Let Freedom Ring*, p. 198. Unfortunately, Hays wasn't there that day. See James Weldon Johnson to Arthur Garfield Hays, October 16, 1925, frame 1205, reel 2, part 5, NAACP Papers.

33. White, *A Man Called White*, pp. 76–77.

34. Walter White to Mr. Seligman, October 22, 1925, frames 3–4, reel 3, part 5, NAACP Papers; oral history interview with Otis Sweet, August 1, 1960.

35. Otis Sweet oral history, August 1, 1960.

36. James Goodman, *Stories of Scottsboro* (New York: Random House, 1994), pp. 62–64; "Clarence Darrow and American Rights, *Houston* [unreadable], November 5,

1925, frame 1126, reel 3, part 5, NAACP Papers; "Dr. Sweet," *Florida Sentinel*, November 14, 1925, frame 1126, reel 3, part 5, NAACP Papers; "Dr. Sweet," *Florida Sentinel*, November 14, 1925, frame 34, reel 4, part 5, NAACP Papers; (Little Rock) *Mosaic Guide*, November 28, 1925, frame 138, reel 4, part 5, NAACP Papers.

37. "What's Wrong in Detroit?" *Chicago Defender*, September 19, 1925.

38. "The Retention of Clarence Darrow," *Washington Daily American*, October 19, 1925, clipping at frame 1000, reel 2, part 5, NAACP Papers; "We Must Fight if We Would Survive," (New York) *Amsterdam News*, November 18, 1925, frame 57, reel 4, part 5, NAACP Papers.

39. Sweet defense fund, statement of cash receipts and disbursements, December 11, 1925, frames 811–814, reel 3, part 5, NAACP Papers; William Pickens to office, October 25, 1925, frame 19, reel 3, part 5, NAACP Papers; report of the department of branches, November 1925 and December 1925, frames 656–659, reel 4, part 1, NAACP Papers; Edward Lovett to NAACP, October 22, 1925, frame 5, reel 3, part 5, NAACP Papers; "Howard Students Rally to Support of Dr. Sweet," *Washington Daily American*, October 30, 1925; minutes of the general faculty meeting, November 3, 1925, box 17, Wilberforce University Papers, Wilberforce Archives, Xenia, Ohio.

40. Walter White to Gladys Sweet, October 27, 1925, frame 23, reel 3, part 5, NAACP Papers; R. L. Polk and Company, *Detroit City Directory*, 1925–1926 (Detroit: R. L. Polk and Company, 1926); Gladys Sweet to Walter White, October 23, 1925, frames 11–13, reel 3, part 5, NAACP Papers.

41. Gladys Sweet to Walter White, n.d. [late October 1925], frames 353–360, reel 3, part 5, NAACP Papers; W. E. B. Du Bois, "The Challenge of Detroit," *Crisis* (November 1925): 7–10; David Levering Lewis, *W. E. B. Du Bois: The Fight for Equality and the American Century* (New York: Henry Holt, 2000), pp. 154–155.

42. Marcet Haldeman-Julius, *Clarence Darrow's Two Great Trials* (Girard, Kan.: Haldeman-Julius Publishing Company, 1927), pp. 37–39; Ossian Sweet to Ruby Darrow, n.d. [1930], box 5, Darrow Papers.

43. Walter White to Wilson Midgley, October 23, 1925, frame 288, reel 9, part 2, NAACP Papers; White to Clarence Darrow, October 24, 1925, frame 18, reel 3, part 5, NAACP Papers; White to Darrow, October 20, 1925, frame 1210, reel 2, part 5, NAACP Papers; Darrow to White, October 22, 1925, frame 7, reel 3, part 5, NAACP Papers; James Cobb to Arthur Spingarn, October 24, 1925, frame 44, reel 5, Arthur Spingarn Papers, Library of Congress, Washington, D.C.; Oscar Baker to White, frames 1219–1210, reel 2, part 5, NAACP Papers; Langston Hughes to White, October 29, 1925, frame 352, reel 9, part 2 NAACP Papers.

44. Walter White to James Weldon Johnson, October 8, 1925; White to Ira Jayne, October 22, 1925; Mose Walker to White, n.d. [October 26[?], 1925], frame 26, reel 3, part 5, NAACP Papers.

45. Frank Murphy to Marguerite Murphy, November 6, 1925, box 1, Frank Murphy Papers, Bentley Historical Library, University of Michigan, Ann Arbor; Sidney Fine, *Frank Murphy: The Detroit Years* (Ann Arbor: University of Michigan Press, 1975), p. 179; Walter White to Frank Murphy, October 14, 1925, reel 3, Murphy papers.

46. "Four Throngs Acclaim Mayor," *Detroit Times*, October 13, 1925; "East Side Gives Smith Ovation," *Detroit Free Press*, October 15, 1925; "Vets Cheer Mayor at Reunion," *Detroit Times*, October 17, 1925; "Five Crowds Applaud Mayor," *Detroit Times*, October 17, 1925; "K of C Affair to Open Tonight," *Detroit Times*, October 23, 1925; "Foes Are Routed by Mayor Smith," *Detroit times*, October 24, 1925; "Where to Hear the Candidates," *Detroit News*, November 2, 1925; "Principles Scored as Disgrace," *Detroit Times*, October 15, 1925.

47. "Mayor 'Sorry' for His Foe," *Detroit News*, November 2, 1925.

48. Kerby Miller, *Emigrants and Exiles: Ireland and the Irish Exodus to North America* (New York: Oxford University Press, 1985), pp. 378–380; Charters Wynn, *Workers, Strikes, and Pogroms: The Donbass-Dnepr Bend in Late Imperial Russia, 1870–1905* (Princeton, N.J.: Princeton University Press, 1992), pp. 60–62; Jacquelyn Dowd Hall et al, *Like a Family: The Making of a Southern Cotton Mill World* (Chapel Hill: University of North Carolina Press, 1987), pp. 66–67; John Higham, *Strangers in the Land: Patterns of American Nativism,*

1860–1925 (New Brunswick, N.J.: Rutgers University Press, 1955), chapter 10; Lynn Dumeniel, *The Modern Temper: American Culture and Society in the 1920s* (New York: Hill and Wang, 1995), chapters 5–6.

49. "Attorney Raps Klan as Political Influence," *Detroit Times,* October 13, 1925; "Women Canvass Homes to Aid Mayor Smith," *Detroit Times,* October 22, 1925; "Progressives Back Mayor," *Detroit Times,* September 25, 1925; "Ku Klux Klan Assailed by Detroit Ministers," Detroit Times, November 2, 1925.

50. "Ku Klux Klan Assailed by Detroit Ministers"; Richard Wightman Fox, *Reinhold Niebuhr: A Biography* (New York: Pantheon, 1985), p. 91.

51. "Bowles No Klansman, He Says," *Detroit Times,* October 16, 1925; "Bowles Denies He's Klansman," *Detroit Free Press,* October 16, 1925; "Klan Issue Is Dodged by Bowles," *Detroit Free Press,* October 26, 1925; "Klan's Aid Disdained by Bowles," *Detroit Times,* October 27, 1925; Ku Klux Klan pamphlet, n.d. [October 1925], E and M Files—Ku Klux Klan, Burton Historical Collection, Detroit Public Library, Detroit, Mich.

52. "Pastor's Wife Would Tar All Smith Voters," *Detroit Free Press,* October 23, 1925; "Forsythe Raps 'Rome,' Smith," *Detroit Free Press,* October 26, 1925; "Bares Klan Scheming to Rule City Council," *Detroit Free Press,* October 31, 1925; "Threat Is Laid to Candidate," *Detroit Times,* November 3, 1925.

53. "Bowles Called Myth Picked Up on Crest of Crowd Movement," *Detroit Free Press,* October 26, 1925.

54. "Five Crowds Applaud Mayor," *Detroit Times,* October 17, 1925; "Mayor in District of Rival," *Detroit Times,* October 21, 1925.

55. "Detroit Police Saved Mob," *Detroit Independent,* April 17, 1925, box 30, Clarence Darrow Papers; Vollington Bristol statement, n.d., box 5, Darrow Papers; "Darrow Delays," *Detroit Times,* October 16, 1925; Walter White to Mr. Seligman, October 22, 1925.

56. Arthur Garfield Hays to NAACP, October 19, 1925, frame 1208, reel 2, part 5, NAACP Papers; Ronald Steel, *Walter Lippmann and the American Century* (New York: Random House, 1980), p. 9; theory of defense, n.d. [October 1925], and summary of precedents, n.d. [October 1925], both in box 5, Darrow Papers.

57. *Pond v. People of Michigan,* 8 Mich 150 (Mich. Supreme Crt. 1860); summary of precedents, n.d. [October 1925], motion to dismiss, n.d. [October 1925], and "Theory of the Defense," n.d. [October 1925], all in box 5, Darrow Papers.

58. Arthur Garfield Hays to NAACP, October 19, 1925, frame 1208, reel 2, part 5, NAACP Papers; "Race Question" clipping file, box 30, Darrow Papers; Walter White to Clarence Darrow, October 20, 1925, frame 1210, reel 2, part 5, NAACP Papers; White to Arthur Garfield Hays, October 21, 1925, frame 1214, reel 2, part 5, NAACP Papers; White to Darrow, October 22, 1925, frame 8, reel 3, part 5, NAACP Papers.

59. Louis Marshall to Moorfield Storey, December 12, 1924, in Reznikoff, *Louis Marshall,* pp. 460–461; Clement Vose, *Caucasians Only: The Supreme Court, the NAACP, and the Restrictive Covenants Cases* (Berkeley: University of California Press, 1959), pp. 13–19; Du Bois, "Challenge of Detroit," p. 12.

60. Darrow, *The Story of My Life,* pp. 426–428; Tierney, *Darrow,* pp. 154–155; Stone, *Clarence Darrow for the Defense,* pp. 165–166.

61. Walter White to Frank Murphy, October 28, 1925, frame 32, reel 3, part 5, NAACP Papers.

62. NAACP press release, October 30, 1925, frame 37, reel 3, part 5 NAACP Papers.

63. Josephine Gomon diary entry, October 30, 1925, box 6, Josephine Gomon Collection, Bentley Library; "Jurors Shun Sweet Trial," *Detroit Free Press,* October 31, 1925.

64. Larson, *Summer for the Gods,* pp. 147, 151–152; Marcet Haldeman-Julius, "Clarence Darrow's Defense of a Negro," *Haldeman-Julius Monthly* (July 1926): 4; "Breiner Widow and Other Principles in East Side Riot Trial," *Detroit Times,* April 28, 1926.

65. "Jurors Shun Sweet Trial." The description of Darrow as "champion of the poor" comes from his friend Judge William Holly quoted in Stone, *Clarence Darrow for the Defense,* p. 518.

66. Walter White to James Weldon Johnson, n.d. [October 31, 1925], frames 54–55, reel 3, part 5, NAACP Papers; "May Seek to Justify Slaying," *New York Herald-Tribune*, n.d. [October 31, 1925], clipping at frame 326, reel 3, part 5, NAACP Papers; "Darrow Hints Right to Shoot," *Detroit Times*, October 31, 1925; "Jurors Shun Sweet Trial"; "Darrow Wary in Riot Trial," *Detroit News*, October 31, 1925.

67. "Darrow Wary in Riot Trial"; White to Johnson, n.d. [October, 31, 1925]; e.d. 304, sheet 15A, 1920 U.S. census manuscript, Detroit, Michigan, for details on Buell; "Darrow Hints Right to Shoot."

Chapter Nine: Prejudice

1. "Jurors Shun Sweet Trial," *Detroit Free Press*, October 31, 1925; "Darrow Wary in Riot Trial" and "Court Rebukes Riot Hecklers," both in *Detroit News*, October 31, 1925 [early and late editions]; "Intimidation Charged in Sweet Case," *Detroit Free Press*, November 1, 1925; Walter White to James Weldon Johnson, n.d. [October 31, 1925], frames 54–55, reel 3, part 5, NAACP Papers [microfilm edition], Library of Congress, Washington, D.C.

2. J. Anthony Lukas, *Big Trouble: A Murder in a Small Western Town Sets Off a Struggle for the Soul of America* (New York: Simon and Schuster, 1997), pp. 525–553.

3. Clarence Darrow, *The Story of My Life* (New York: Charles Scribner's Sons, 1934), pp. 306–307; Oscar Baker to Walter White, October 21, 1925, frames 1219–1220, reel 2, part 5, NAACP Papers.

4. Clarence Darrow, "Attorney for the Defense," *Esquire*, May 1936, pp. 36, 211. Also see Darrow, *Story of My Life*, pp. 307–308.

5. Christine Stansell, *American Moderns: Bohemian New York and the Creation of a New Century* (New York: Henry Holt, 2000), pp. 23–26; Ann Douglas, *Terrible Honesty: Mongrel Manhattan in the 1920s* (New York: Farrar, Straus and Giroux, 1995), particularly chapters 2 and 7.

6. "Mayor Given Ovations at Meetings" and "Vets Rally to Aid of Smith," *Detroit Times*, October 31, 1925; "Crushing of Klan Urged," *Detroit Times*, November 2, 1925; "Negro Gatherings Hear Bowles and Smith Talk," *Detroit News*, November 2, 1925; "Mayor Smith, in Final Talk, Urges All Citizens to Vote," *Detroit Times*, November 3, 1925.

7. "Klan Settles Who's American," *Detroit Free Press*, November 3, 1925.

8. "Record Vote in Klan Fight," *Detroit Free Press*, November 3, 1925; "Pastor Pleads for Ten Judges," *Detroit News*, November 2, 1925; "Prelates of Three Faiths Urge Duty to Vote," *Detroit Times*, November 1, 1925; Leslie Tentler, *Seasons of Grace: A History of the Catholic Archdiocese of Detroit* (Detroit: Wayne State University Press, 1990), p. 301.

9. "Detroit Puts Record of Smith Up to Race," *Chicago Defender*, October 31, 1925; "Clamor Marks Bowles Meet," *Detroit Free Press*, October 27, 1925; Josephine Gomon draft biography of Frank Murphy, n.d., box 9, Josephine Gomon Papers, Michigan Historical Collections, Bentley Library, University of Michigan, Ann Arbor. For pure shock value, nothing could match the weekend's most widely publicized attack. When a reporter asked Henry Ford what he thought of the KKK, he answered with a heartfelt, if typically idiosyncratic, condemnation of an organization whose hatreds he seemed to share. "I know nothing of the Ku Klux Klan, but I will say this," he replied. "Most of these movements are ordered by Wall Street. . . . They are comprised of harebrained people who only lose the fee they pay for membership. I don't care which side of the question you're on, they have no place in America. The same goes for unions." See "Ford Endorses Mayor," *Detroit Times*, October 31, 1925.

10. "Town Talk," *Detroit News*, November 2, 1925; "Smith Re-Elected by 31,000," *Detroit Times*, November 4, 1925. In the Tireman Avenue area that had seen the worst of the summer's violence, for instance, Bowles beat Smith by a mere eight votes.

11. "Police Halt Anti-Klan Melee," *Detroit Times*, November 4, 1925.

12. Walter White to James Weldon Johnson, n.d. [October 31, 1925], frames 54–55, reel 3, part 5, NAACP Papers.

13. "Expect to Fill Riot Case Jury," *Detroit News*, November 3, 1925; "Sweet Jury Still Unfilled," *Detroit Free Press*, November 3, 1925; White to James Weldon Johnson, n.d. [October 31, 1925].

14. "3 Women Out of Riot Jury," *Detroit News*, November 4, 1925; "Call First Riot Witness Today," *Detroit News*, November 5, 1925, clipping at frame 1110, reel 3, part 5, NAACP Papers; R. L. Polk and Company, *Detroit City Directory*, 1920–1921 (Detroit: R. L. Polk and Company, 1921).

15. The jury list is available at frame 38, reel 3, part 5, NAACP Papers, and the jurors' professions are available in "Will Try to Force Tom's Hand," *Detroit Times*, November 4, 1925. To create as comprehensive a description of the jurors as possible, I reviewed their entries in either the 1920 or 1930 U.S. census manuscript for Detroit and, where possible, in both censuses. The information available there—age, marital status, children at home, race, country of origin, parents' country of origin, profession, and home ownership—was supplemented by the Detroit city directories for the mid-1920s, which provided the jurors' exact professions in the middle of the decade.

16. Irving Stone, *Clarence Darrow for the Defense* (Garden City, N.Y.: Doubleday, 1941), p. 478.

17. "Sweet Trial Presents Dramatic Court Scene," *Detroit Free Press*, November 22, 1925.

18. Detroit Police Department witness list, October 2, 1925, box 1, Ossian Sweet Collection, Burton Historical Collection, Detroit Public Library, Detroit, Mich.; "Free Doctor Sweet and Ten Others," *Chicago Defender*, April 25, 1931; Articles of Incorporation, Waterworks Park Improvement Association, May 26, 1926, Bureau of Commercial Services, Corporation Division, Michigan Department of Consumer and Industry Services, Lansing.

19. Lukas, *Big Trouble*, pp. 290–293 and chapter 14; Edward J. Larson, *Summer for the Gods: The Scopes Trial and America's Continuing Debate over Science and Religion* (Cambridge, Mass.: Harvard University Press, 1997), pp. 157–158; oral history interview with Robert Toms, November 28, 1959, Alex Baskin Collection, Bentley Historical Library.

20. Walter White to James Weldon Johnson, November 15, 1925, frame 92, reel 3, part 5, NAACP Papers; Robert Toms opening statement, November 5, 1925, trial transcript, *People v. Ossian Sweet et al.*, Michigan Historical Collection, Bentley Library, University of Michigan, Ann Arbor; testimony of Herman Craft and William D. Ryan, both on November 5, 1925, trial transcript.

21. Testimony of Norton Schuknecht, November 5, 1925, trial transcript.

22. Testimony of Bert McPherson, November 13, 1925, trial transcript.

23. Testimony of Clayton Williams, November 9, 1925; testimony of James Sprott, November 13, 1925; testimony of Paul Schellenberger, November 5, 1925, testimony of Joseph Neighbauer, November 9, 1925, testimony of Frank Lee Gill, November 6, 1925, all in trial transcript; "Sprott to Give Riot Evidence," *Detroit News*, November 12, 1925, frame 11, reel 4, part 5, NAACP Papers.

24. Testimony of George Fairbairn, Almarion Wolfe, and Marvin Leach, all November 9, 1925, trial transcript.

25. Testimony of Joseph Grohm, November 9, 1925, trial transcript; "Darrow Hints at Demand for Another Jury," *Detroit Free Press*, November 19, 1925, clipping at frame 1150, reel 3, part 5, NAACP Papers.

26. Testimony of Dwight Hubbard, November 11, 1925; testimony of Otto Lemhagen, November 11, 1925; testimony of Edward Wettlaufer, November 7, 1925; testimony of John Getke, November 9, 1925; testimony of Della Getke, November 9, 1925; testimony of Ray Dove November 6, 1925; testimony of George Suppus, November 10, 1925; testimony of Ulric Arthur, November 10, 1925; testimony of Eric Houghburg, November 11, 1925, testimony of Bruce Stout, November 10, 1925.

27. Getke testimony, November 9, 1925.

28. Hubbard testimony, November 11, 1925.

29. R. L. Polk and Company, *Detroit City Directory*, 1925–1926 (Detroit: R. L. Polk and Company, 1926); Wettlaufer testimony, November 7, 1925.

30. On the pronunciation of Goethe Street, see, for example, testimony of Otto Eberhardt, November 7, 1925, trial transcript.

31. Testimony of Edward Belcher, November 10, 1925, trial transcirpt.

32. Testimony of Mary Henley, testimony of Fred Benoit, testimony of Harry Short, all on November 10, 1925; testimony of Eber Draper, November 7, 1925; Houghburg testimony, November 11, 1925; Eberhardt testimony, November 7, 1925.

33. Walter White to James Weldon Johnson, November 13, 1925, frames 82–84, reel 3, part 5, NAACP Papers; trial transcript, pp. 194–195, 588–601; "Sweet Plans Mistrial Plea," *Detroit News*, November 10, 1925; "Darrow Hints at Demand for Another Jury," *Detroit Free Press*, November 10, 1925; oral history interview with Otis Sweet, August 1, 1960, Alex Baskin Collection, Bentley Historical Library; "Sweet Trial Presents Dramatic Court Scene."

34. Darrow, *Story of My Life*, pp. 427–428.

35. "Sweet Trial Develops into Battle of Wits," *Detroit Free Press*, November 9, 1925, clipping at frame 1141, reel 3, part 5, NAACP Papers; Houghberg testimony, November 11, 1925.

36. "Sweet Trial Develops into Battle of Wits"; "Darrow Makes Sweet Trial Great 'Human Show,'" *Baltimore Afro-American*, November 14, 1925, frame 32, reel 4, part 5, NAACP Papers.

37. Schuknecht testimony, November 5, 1925; "Darrow, Grilling State's Witnesses, Batters Holes in Case Against Dr. Sweet," *Chicago Defender*, November 14, 1925.

38. Schuknecht testimony, November 5, 1925; "Darrow Quizzes Officer," *Detroit Times*, November 6, 1925.

39. Ray Dove testimony, November 6, 1925.

40. "Sweet Counsel Attacks Clubs," *Detroit Free Press*, November 8, 1925; testimony of Russell Burns, November 7, 1925; testimony of Raymond Alf, November 11, 1925; Della Getke testimony, November 9, 1925.

41. "'Man's House His Castle,' Argues Counsel for Sweet," *Chicago Defender*, November 21, 1925; Neighbauer testimony, November 9, 1925; testimony of Ernest Stanke, November 13, 1925; testimony of Ray Schaldernbrand, November 13, 1925; Sprott testimony, November 13, 1925.

42. Testimony of Harry Monet, November 10, 1925; Eberhardt testimony, November 7, 1925; Draper testimony, November 7, 1925; "Darrow Hits Riot Silence," *Detroit Times*, November 8, 1925; "Darrow Wins Point in Trial," *Detroit News*, November 13, 1925; "Darrow Aroused," *Detroit Times*, November 12, 1925, clipping at frames 8–9, reel 4, part 5, NAACP Papers; Darrow, *Story of My Life*, p. 308.

43. Hubbard testimony, November 11, 1925.

44. E.d. 629, sheet 9b, 1920 U.S. census manuscript, Detroit, Michigan; "Darrow Aroused"; "21 More to Be Called by State," *Detroit Times*, November 13, 1925.

45. Suppus testimony and Arthur testimony, both November 10, 1925; "Boycott Is Charged," *Detroit Times*, November 10, 1925, frames 1147–1148, reel 3, part 5, NAACP Papers; "Saw Stones Hurled at Sweet Home, Claim," *Detroit Free Press*, November 11, 1925.

46. Report of the secretary, December 1925, frames 661–664, reel 4, part 1, NAACP Papers; Walter White to James Weldon Johnson, November 15, 1925, frame 92, reel 3, part 5, NAACP Papers; Report of the Department of Branches, December 1925, frames 665–671, reel 4, part 1, NAACP Papers; White to Johnson, November 7, 1925, frames 65–66, reel 3, part 5, NAACP Papers.

47. Frank Murphy to Marguerite Murphy, November 6 and 7, 1925, box 1, Marguerite Murphy Papers, Michigan Historical Collections; "Crowd Waits in Line for Sensational Sweet Trial," *Chicago Defender*, November 14, 1925; "Another Myth Breaker," *Detroit News*, November 3, 1925; Sidney Fine, *Frank Murphy: The Detroit Years* (Ann Arbor: University of Michigan Press, 1975), pp. 86–87.

48. "Darrow Explains Evolution," *Detroit Times*, November 10, 1925; "Darrow Sees Crime Aided by Punishment," *Detroit Free Press*, November 16, 1925; report of the Department of Branches, December 1925; "1,500 Negroes Hear Darrow at Detroit," *Chicago Daily News*, November 9, 1925, clipping at frame 1135, reel 3, part 5, NAACP Papers.

49. Reinhold Niebuhr, *Leaves from the Notebook of a Tamed Cynic* (1929; repr. New York: Harper and Row, 1980), p. 88; Josephine Gomon diary entries, November 15, 1925, and undated, both in box 6, Gomon Papers.

50. Gomon diary entry, n.d. [November 1925], box 6, Gomon Papers.

51. "Darrow Tells Racial Aims," *Detroit Times*, November 9, 1925; "Darrow Says Dry Act Hasn't Killed 'Appetite,'" *Detroit Free Press*, November 9, 1925; "1,500 Negroes Hear Darrow at Detroit," *Chicago Daily News*, November 9, 1925.

52. Statement of O. H. Sweet Defense Fund, n.d. [mid-November 1925], frames 802–804, reel 3, part 5, NAACP Papers. White did send NAACP headquarters several newspaper clippings reporting Darrow's remarks, which were duly filed away.

53. Walter White to James Weldon Johnson, November 13, 1925; White to Johnson, November 15, 1925.

54. White to Johnson, November 13, 1925.

55. In fact, Darrow and Hays floated the idea in court, though the effort was half-hearted. See "Officer's Shot Killed Breiner, Is New Claim," *Detroit Free Press*, November 22, 1925. The argument certainly ran counter to Darrow's advice to criminal lawyers not to make an argument jurors would find unbelievable. See Darrow, *Story of My Life*, p. 427.

56. Walter White to James Weldon Johnson, November 15, 1925, frame 92, reel 3, part 5, NAACP Papers. Filing a motion to dismiss was standard practice for Darrow. See Lukas, *Big Trouble*, pp. 565–567. For the motion itself, see motion to dismiss, box 5, Clarence Darrow Collection, Library of Congress, Washington, D.C.

57. "Defense Asks Dismissal of Sweet Trial," *Detroit Free Press*, November 15, 1925; "'Man's Home His Castle,' Argues Counsel for Sweet"; "Defense Asks 11 Be Freed," *Detroit Times*, November 15, 1925; Arthur Garfield Hays, *Let Freedom Ring* (New York: Liveright, 1937), p. 214; Arthur Garfield Hays, *City Lawyer: The Autobiography of a Law Practice* (New York: Simon and Schuster, 1942), p. 209.

58. "Defense Asks 11 Be Freed." Also see "'Man's Home His Castle,' Argues Counsel for Sweet."

59. White to Johnson, November 15, 1925.

60. "Riot Case Plea Ruling Awaited," *Detroit News*, November 14, 1925; "Case Unproved, Declares Hays," *Detroit News*, November 14, 1925; "'Man's Home His Castle,' Argues Counsel for Sweet"; "Moll Demands Slayer in Riot Case Pay Penalty," *Detroit Times*, November 24, 1925; "Judge Murphy Denies Motion in Sweet Trial," *Pittsburgh Courier*, November 21, 1925, frame 78, reel 4, part 5, NAACP Papers.

61. Fine, *Frank Murphy*, p. 159; "New Move by Sweet Attorney," *Detroit Times*, November 17, 1925.

62. Arthur Garfield Hays opening address to the jury, November 16, 1925, frames 920–938, reel 3, part 5, NAACP Papers.

63. For this and previous paragraph, see "Other Race Troubles Figure in Sweet Trial," *Detroit Free Press*, November 18, 1925; "Dr. Sweet Goes on Stand," *Chicago Defender*, November 28, 1925; "Witness Tells of Sweet 'Mob,'" *Detroit News*, November 17, 1925.

64. The details of Sweet's testimony are recounted in Walter White to James Weldon Johnson, November 20, 1925, frames 143–145, reel 3, part 5, NAACP Papers; NAACP press release, November 20, 1925, frame 181, reel 3, part 5, NAACP Papers; "Race Psychology Told in Sweet's Testimony," *Detroit Free Press*, November 19, 1925; "Sweet Depicts Fear in Court," *Detroit Free Press*, November 20, 1925; "Darrow to Rest Riot Defense," *Detroit Times*, November 19, 1925; "Detroit Riot Case Near Close," *Arizona Times*, November 28, 1925 (Associated Negro Press story), frame 142, reel 4, part 5, NAACP Papers; "Influence of Race Wars Part of Sweet Defense," *New York Herald-Tribune*, November 18, 1925, frame 60, reel 4, part 5, NAACP Papers; "Dr. Sweet Goes on Stand," *Chicago Defender*, December 5, 1925; David Lilienthal, "Has the Negro the Right of Self-Defense?" *Nation* (December 23, 1925): 72.

65. "Dr. Sweet Is Cross-Examined," *Detroit News*, November 19, 1925; "Sweet Depicts Fear in Court"; "Witness Hurts Sweet Defense," *Detroit Free Press*, November 21, 1925; "Moll Demands Slayers in Riot Case Pay Penalty"; "Darrow Employs Sarcasm," *Detroit*

News, November 22, 1925; "Both Sides in Riot Trial to Rest Cases," *Detroit Times*, November 21, 1925.

66. Walter White to James Weldon Johnson, November 18, 1925, frame 137, reel 3, part 5, NAACP Papers; "Darrow, Hays Charge Police with Perjury," *Detroit Free Press*, November 25, 1925, clipping at frames 30–32, reel 4, part 5, NAACP Papers.

67. "Darrow, Hays Charge Police with Perjury"; "Highlights in Sweet Trial Argument," *Detroit Free Press*, November 25, 1925, frame 104, reel 4, part 5, NAACP Papers.

68. Arthur Garfield Hays closing statement, November 24–25, 1925, Bentley Library.

69. "[Unreadable] Plea Brings Tears," *Detroit Times*, November 25, 1925; Lilienthal, "Has the Negro the Right of Self-Defense?" p. 725; Clarence Darrow closing statement, November 24, 1925, Michigan Historical Collection.

70. Toms interview, November 28, 1959.

71. Darrow closing statement, November 24–25, 1925.

72. Lilienthal, "Has the Negro the Right of Self-Defense?" p. 725.

73. Ibid.; oral history interview with Charles Mahoney, August [?], 1960, Alex Baskin Collection; Josephine Gomon diary entry, n.d., box 6, Gomon collection.

74. "Tom's Closing Plea to the Jury," *Detroit News*, November 26, 1926.

75. "Sweet Jurors Still Debating," *Detroit News*, November 26, 1925.

76. Walter White to James Weldon Johnson, November 25, 1925, frame 151, reel 3, part 5, NAACP Papers; "Sweet Jurors Still Debating."

77. "Sweet Jurors Still Debating"; "Deadlock Report Is Refused," *Detroit Times*, November 26, 1925.

78. "Sweet Jurors in a Deadlock," *Detroit News*, November 27, 1925; Hays, *Let Freedom Ring*, p. 232; Walter White, *A Man Called White: The Autobiography of Walter White* (New York: Viking, 1948), p. 78.

79. "Sweet Jurors in a Deadlock"; "Darrow Asks Bail for 11 Clients in Move for New Trial," *Detroit Times*, November 27, 1925.

80. Josephine Gomon diary entry, n.d. [November 26, 1925], box 6, Gomon Papers; "Riot Jury Returns to Task," *Detroit Times*, November 27, 1925.

81. "Sweet Jurors in a Deadlock." Charles Naas's age is taken from e.d. 531, sheet 18A, the 1920 U.S. census manuscript, Detroit, Michigan.

82. "Sweet Jurors in a Deadlock."

83. NAACP press release, November 28, 1926, frame 164, reel 3, part 5, NAACP Papers; Oscar Baker to Walter White, November 30, 1925, frame 186, reel 3, part 5, NAACP Papers; White draft statement, December 8, 1925, frame 244, reel 3, part 5, NAACP Papers; "Darrow Asks Quick Retrial," *Detroit Times*, November 28, 1925.

84. "Darrow Asks Bail for 11 Clients in Move for New Trial"; "Darrow Asks Quick Retrial."

Chapter Ten: Judgment Day

1. "Darrow Asks Quick Retrial," *Detroit Times*, November 28, 1925; Arthur Garfield Hays to James Weldon Johnson, December 8, 1925, frame 251, reel 3, part 5, NAACP Papers.

2. Walter White to Roland Hayes, frame 318, reel 9, part 2, NAACP Papers; White to Russell Jelliffe, December 10, 1925, frame 333, reel 9, part 2, NAACP Papers.

3. Mose Walker to Walter White, December 16, 1925, frame 282, reel 3, part 5, NAACP Papers; Hays to Johnson, December 8, 1925; David Lilienthal, "Has the Negro the Right of Self-Defense?" *Nation*, December 23, 1925, pp. 724–725; "Noble Nordic Darrow," *Dearborn Independent*, January 9, 1926; "Detroit Sentiment Favorable to Sweets," (New York) *Amsterdam News*, December 30, 1925; Oscar Baker to White, November 30, 1925, frame 186, reel 3, part 5, NAACP Papers; Arthur Garfield Hays to gentlemen, December 31, 1925, frame 325, reel 3, part 5, NAACP Papers.

4. Walter White to Arthur Garfield Hays, December 4, 1925, and December 17, 1925, frames 356 and 357, reel 9, part 2, NAACP Papers; Ann Douglas, *Terrible Honesty: Mongrel*

Manhattan in the 1920s (New York: Farrar, Straus and Giroux, 1995), p. 125; Walter White to Frank Murphy, December 4, 1925, frames 230–231, reel 3, part 5, NAACP Papers; Frank Murphy to "Unc" [Walter White], December 31, 1925, frames 389–390, reel 9, part 2, NAACP Papers; White to Robert Toms, December 2, 1925, frame 206, reel 3, part 5, NAACP Papers.

5. Present status of the Legal Defense Fund, December 11 [1925], frame 794, reel 3, part 5, NAACP Papers; expenses to the national office, n.d. [December 1925], frame 816, reel 3, part 5, NAACP Papers; William Sears to James Weldon Johnson, November 25, 1925, frame 709, reel 22, part 1, NAACP Papers.

6. James Weldon Johnson to Henry Sachs, December 29, 1925, and Johnson to William Graves, January 23, 1926, frames 767 and 950, reel 23, part 5, NAACP Papers; David Levering Lewis, *W. E. B. Du Bois: The Fight for Equality and the American Century, 1919–1963* (New York: Henry Holt, 2000), p. 98; Walter White to Johnson, December 29, 1925, frame 321, reel 3, part 5, NAACP Papers; "Defends Negro's Right to Invade White Districts," *New York World,* December 20, 1925; "Women Make Great Progress in Aiding Defense Fund Drive," *Washington Daily American,* December 19, 1925, clipping at frame 397, reel 4, part 5, NAACP Papers; White to H. L. Mencken, December 9, 1925, frame 329, reel 9, part 2, NAACP Papers; White to Blanche Knopf, December 1, 1925, frame 321, reel 3, part 2, NAACP Papers; White to Sinclair Lewis, January 29, 1926, frame 490, reel 9, part 2, NAACP Papers.

7. Walter White to Clarence Darrow, December 8, 1925, frame 239, reel 3, part 5, NAACP Paper; Ruby Darrow to Irving Stòne, n.d. [1940?], box 34, Clarence Darrow Collection, Library of Congress, Washington, D.C.; "Sing Negro Spirituals," *New York Times,* December 18, 1925; mass meeting program, December 13, 1925, frame 321, reel 13, part 11b, NAACP Papers; "Two Negro Audiences Applaud Darrow," *New York World,* December 14, 1925; "Darrow Jeers 'Noble Nordics' Before Negroes," *New York Herald-Tribune,* December 14, 1925, clipping at frame 334, reel 13, part 11b, NAACP Papers; report of field work meetings, December 1925, frames 665–671, reel 4, part 1, NAACP Papers.

8. Walter White to Gladys Sweet, November 28, 1925, frame 166, reel 3, part 5, NAACP Papers; Walter White memorandum of phone conversation, December 1, 1925, frame 194, reel 3, part 5, NAACP Papers; Walter Nelson to NAACP, December 2, 1925, frame 198, reel 3, part 5, NAACP Papers.

9. Bond postings, November–December 1925, box 1, Ossian Sweet Collection, Burton Historical Collection, Detroit Public Library, Detroit, Mich.; "Doctor Sweet Goes on Stand," *Chicago Defender,* November 28, 1925; Mose Walker to Walter White, December 9, 1925, frame 255, reel 3, part 5, NAACP Papers; R. L. Polk and Company, *Detroit City Directory,* 1925–1926 (Detroit: R. L. Polk and Company, 1926), pp. 1808, 2087. Darrow thought it would be a mistake for the Sweets to move into the bungalow until the case was settled. Clarence Darrow to White, December 26 [1925], frame 809, reel 3, part 5, NAACP Papers.

10. Alex Baskin interview with Otis Sweet, August 1, 1960, Alex Baskin Collection, Michigan Historical Collection, Bentley Library, University of Michigan, Ann Arbor; "Give Us Civil Rights," *The Arizona Times,* December 5, 1925; "Thank God for the Men and Women of New England," *The Cleveland Call,* December 5, 1925; "Dr. O. H. Sweet Thrills Big Audience," *Detroit Independent,* December 11, 1925, clipping at frame 185, reel 4, part 5, NAACP Papers; James Weldon Johnson to Ossian Sweet, December 15, 1925, frame 283, reel 3, part 5, NAACP Papers.

11. Minutes of the fifteenth annual meeting, January 4, 1926, frame 715, reel 13, part 1, NAACP Papers; advertisement, (New York) *Amsterdam News,* December 30, 1925, frame 205, reel 4, part 5, NAACP Papers; "Flay Segregation of Negroes in Cities," *New York World,* January 4, 1925; Robert Bagnall to L. F. Dyer, frame 844, reel 13, part 1, NAACP Papers; address of Arthur Garfield Hays, January 3, 1926, frames 400–407, reel 3, part 5, NAACP Papers.

12. NAACP press release, January 15, 1926, frame 415, reel 3, part 5, NAACP Papers; Robert Bagnall to James Weldon Johnson, n.d. [January 11, 1926], frames 357–358, reel

15, part 1, NAACP Papers; "Dr. Sweet Flays Detroit Police in Speech Here," *Chicago Defender*, January 16, 1926.

13. Robert Bagnall to James Weldon Johnson, n.d. [January 10, 1926], frames 356–357, reel 15, part 1, NAACP Papers; Robert Bagnall to Johnson, n.d. [January 11, 1926]; "Sweet, Wife Will Tell of Detroit Case," *Chicago Defender*, January 9, 1926.

14. Secretary's report to the board of directors, February 1926, frames 684–687, reel 4, part 1, NAACP Papers.

15. Secretary's report to the board of directors, November 9, 1925, frames 52–54, reel 2, part 1, NAACP; Stephen Grant Meyer, *As Long as They Don't Move Next Door: Segregation and Racial Conflict in American Neighborhoods* (Lanham, Md.: Rowman and Littlefield, 2000), pp. 24–31; James Cobb to Arthur Spingarn, December 16, 1925, frame 85, reel 5, Arthur Spingarn Collection, Library of Congress, Washington, D.C.

16. Moorfield Storey to James Weldon Johnson, January 12, 1926, frame 283, reel 24, part 1, NAACP Papers.

17. James Cobb to James Weldon Johnson, January 13, 1926, frames 466–467, reel 4, part 5, NAACP Papers; NAACP press release, January 1926, frames 960–961, reel 28, part 11B, NAACP Papers.

18. NAACP press release, January 1926; Clement E. Vose, *Caucasians Only: The Supreme Court, the NAACP, and the Restrictive Covenant Cases* (Berkeley: University of California Press, 1959), p. 53.

19. Louis Johnson to Moorfield Storey, May 28, 1926, reel 27, Spingarn Papers; Mark Robert Schneider, *"We Return Fighting": The Civil Rights Movement in the Jazz Age* (Boston: Northeastern University Press, 2002), p. 288; Storey to James Weldon Johnson, January 12, 1926; James Cobb to Arthur Spingarn, January 9, 1926, frame 103, reel 4, Spingarn Papers.

20. Typescript, "The Sweet Trial in Detroit," December 8, 1925, frame 244, reel 3, part 5, NAACP Papers; Clarence Darrow to Walter White, January 12, 1926, frame 414, reel 3, part 5, NAACP Papers; White to Darrow, March 9, 1926, frame 465, reel 3, part 5, NAACP Papers; Walter White report, March 21–24, 1926, frames 423–426, reel 3, part 5, NAACP Papers.

21. White report, March 21–24, 1926; license 2337, records of drugstores, v. 8, RG 87-106, Licensing and Registration, Michigan State Archives, Lansing. Sanborn Map Company, *Fire Insurance Map of Detroit, Michigan* (New York: Sanborn Map Company, 1922), provides a description of Garafalo Drugs, and e.d. 82–235, p. 19B, 1930 U.S. census manuscript, Detroit, Michigan, offers a picture of the surrounding neighborhood. For details on the Sweets' apartment building at 526 E. Hancock, see Marcet Haldeman-Julius, *Clarence Darrow's Two Great Trials* (Girard, Kan.: Haldeman-Julius Publishing Company, 1927), p. 27, and R. L. Polk and Company, *Detroit City Directory, 1927–1928* (Detroit: R. L. Polk and Company, 1928).

22. Ossian Sweet to William Pickens, December 20, 1930, reel 26, Spingarn Papers; White report, March 21–24, 1926; Haldeman-Julius, *Clarence Darrow's Two Great Trials*, pp. 30–31, 34–40, 43–44.

23. Alex Baskin interview with Cecil Rowlette, August 1, 1960, Baskin Collection; Walter White to Clarence Darrow, December 23, 1925, and Darrow to White, January 2, 1926, frames 318 and 413, reel 3, part 5, NAACP Papers; Mose Walker to White, March 18, 1926, frame 473, reel 3, part 5, NAACP Papers.

24. Walter White memorandum of conversation, February 2, 1926, frame 439, reel 3, part 5, NAACP Papers; James Weldon Johnson to Ira Jayne, April 9, 1926, frames 519–520, reel 3, part 5, NAACP Papers; White report, March 21–24, 1926.

25. Clarence Darrow to Walter White, January 2, 1926; Herbert Friedman to White, December 4, 1925, frame 250, reel 3, part 5, NAACP Papers; William Pickens to James Weldon Johnson and Legal Committee, December 19, 1925, frame 90, reel 5, Spingarn Papers; memorandum of conversation, Clarence Darrow, Walter White, and James Weldon Johnson, February 2, 1926, frame 439, reel 3, part 5, NAACP Papers.

26. Raymond R. Fragnoli, *The Transformation of Reform: Progressivism in Detroit—*

And After, 1912–1933 (New York: Garland, 1982), pp. 321–322; Richard Fox, *Reinhold Niebuhr: A Biography* (New York: Pantheon, 1985), pp. 91–92; Mayor's Inter-Racial Committee, *The Negro in Detroit* (Detroit: Detroit Bureau of Governmental Research, 1926); William P. Lovett, "Sketches of American Mayors: John W. Smith of Detroit," *National Municipal Review* 15 (April 1926): 205–207; "Stout Ousted as Klan Dictator," "Strife-Torn Klan Showdown Due," and "Warring Kluxers to Meet Tuesday," *Detroit Times,* December 19, 20, and 22, 1925; Felix Holt to Walter White, March 22, 1926, frame 621, reel 9, part 2, NAACP Papers.

27. James Weldon Johnson to Moorfield Storey, December 30, 1925, frames 607–608, reel 17, part 1, NAACP Papers.

28. Arthur Garfield Hays, *City Lawyer: The Autobiography of a Law Practice* (New York: Simon and Schuster, 1942), pp. 203–205; Walter White to Clarence Darrow, March 13, 1926, frame 470, reel 3, part 5, NAACP Papers. Hays was also scheduled for an early April appearance on the Boston Common, where he planned to join H. L. Mencken in selling copies of the recently banned *American Mercury.* See Arthur Garfield Hays, *Let Freedom Ring* (New York: Livright, 1937), pp. 160–185.

29. White report, March 21–24, 1926. Darrow had his first contact with Chawke on Thanksgiving Day 1925, as the deliberations in the first Sweet trial dragged on. Darrow called Chawke that evening for advice on whether to accept a hung jury or insist that the deliberations continue. See Alex Baskin interview with Thomas Chawke, August 4, 1960, Baskin Collection.

30. Oscar Baker to Walter White, March 8, 1926, frames 462–464, reel 3, part 5, NAACP Papers; Walter White report, March 21–24, 1926; White to Baker, October 5, 1925, frames 1115–1118, reel 2, part 5, NAACP Papers; memorandum of telephone conversation, October 7, 1960, frames 1152–1153, reel 2, part 5, NAACP Papers; *Centennial of the Diocese of Detroit, 1833–1933* (Detroit: Michigan Catholic, 1933), p. 78; "Defense Attorney Thomas Chawke Dies," *Detroit News,* December 26, 1974, copy in "Chawke" reading room file, Burton Historical Collection.

31. White report, March 21–24, 1926; James Weldon Johnson to Ira Jayne, April 5, 1926; Thomas Chawke to Walter White, April 6, 1926; and James Weldon Johnson to Chawke, April 7, 1926, frames 503–505, reel 3, part 5, NAACP Papers.

32. "The Weather," *Detroit News,* April 19, 1926; "Darrow in Quiz for Jurors," undated clipping [*Chicago Defender*], Detroit Free Press Clipping Morgue, Detroit, Mich.; Josephine Gomon diary entry, April 20, 1926, box 6, Josephine Gomon Collection, Bentley Library; Frank Murphy to Marguerite Murphy, n.d. [April 1926], box 1, Marguerite Murphy Collection, Bentley Library; "Henry Sweet to Face Trial," *Detroit Free Press,* April 13, 1926; Clarence Darrow, *The Story of My Life* (New York: Charles Scribner's Sons, 1934), p. 311; "Jurors Are Selected for New Sweet Trial," *Detroit Free Press,* April 20, 1926.

33. "Darrow in Quiz for Jurors"; Marcet Haldeman-Julius, "Clarence Darrow's Defense of a Negro," *Haldeman-Julius Monthly* (July 1926): 12, copy in box 16, Clarence Darrow Collection, Library of Congress, Washington, D.C.; "Sweet Trial Delay Is Seen," *Detroit Free Press,* April 22, 1926; "Toms to Continue Quiz," *Detroit Times,* April 22, 1926; "Jurors Are Selected for New Sweet Trial," *Detroit Free Press,* April 20, 1926.

34. "Riot Trial Lawyers Clash," *Detroit Times,* April 21, 1926; "Sweet Trial Is Race Issue, Darrow Insists," *Detroit Free Press,* April 21, 1926.

35. Haldeman-Julius, "Clarence Darrow's Defense of a Negro," pp. 12–13; Hilmer Gellein article draft, "The Sweet Trials, 1925–26," n.d. [c. 1973], box 1, Ossian Sweet Collection, Burton Historical Collection; e.d. 221, 1930 U.S. census manuscript, Detroit, Michigan, 221 for George Small, e.d. 158 for Ralph Feulling; e.d. 723, 1920 U.S. census manuscript, Detroit, Michigan, for Edward Birnie; "Sweet Jury Slowed by Darrow," *Detroit Times,* April 20, 1926; "Sweet Trial Delay Is Seen"; "Sweet Jurors Hard to Find," *Detroit News,* April 21, 1926; "Sweet Jury Selected; Trial to Begin Monday," *Detroit Free Press,* April 25, 1926; "Court Is Surprised by Darrow," *Detroit Times,* April 25, 1926.

36. "Darrow Defends Riot Slaying," *Detroit Times,* April 26, 1926; "Police Grilled in Sweet Case," *Detroit Free Press,* April 27, 1926; transcript of Henry Sweet interrogation, September 9, 1926, copy in author's possession; Chawke interview.

37. Haldeman-Julius, "Clarence Darrow's Defense of a Negro," pp. 14–16; "Darrow Defends Riot Slaying"; Josephine Gomon draft of Frank Murphy biography, n.d., box 9, Gomon Collection; Irving Stone, *Clarence Darrow for the Defense* (New York: Doubleday, 1941), pp. 483–484. According to Chawke, Darrow had planned to delay his opening statement as he'd done in the first trial, but when he saw that Toms had brought the guns into the courtroom he decided that the impression they created had to be countered immediately.

38. Haldeman-Julius, "Clarence Darrow's Defense of a Negro," pp. 7–9; Chawke interview; "Darrow Plans Motion to Dismiss Sweet Case," *Detroit Free Press*, May 5, 1926; "Breiner Widow and Other Principals in East Side Riot Trial," *Detroit Times*, April 28, 1926.

39. "Police Hit by Darrow at Trial," *Detroit Times*, April 27, 1926; "Police Grilled in Sweet Case"; Haldeman-Julius, "Clarence Darrow's Defense of a Negro," p. 18. Emphasis is mine.

40. "Police Hit by Darrow at Trial"; Haldeman-Julius, "Clarence Darrow's Defense of a Negro," pp. 16–18.

41. "Juror May Stop Riot Hearing," *Detroit Times*, April 28, 1926; "Juror Illegal, Claim; Sweet Mistrial Seen," *Detroit Free Press*, April 29, 1926; Haldeman-Julius, "Clarence Darrow Defends a Negro," pp. 20–21.

42. "Hedging Stirs Sweet Lawyer," *Detroit News*, May 3, 1926.

43. "Darrow Plans Motion to Dismiss Sweet Case"; Kevin Tierney, *Darrow: A Biography* (New York: Thomas Y. Crowell, 1979), p. 383; "Blame Society in Sweet Trial," *Detroit Free Press*, May 4, 1926; "Darrow in Clash with Teacher," *Detroit Times*, May 4, 1926.

44. "Blame Society in Sweet Trial"; "Darrow Fights Riot Re-Trial," *Detroit Times*, April 29, 1926.

45. Haldeman-Julius, "Clarence Darrow's Defense of a Negro," pp. 21–22; "Darrow Scores Point in Sweet Murder Trial," *Detroit Free Press*, May 2, 1926; "Darrow Digs at Association," *Detroit News*, May 1, 1926; James Weldon Johnson, "Detroit," *Crisis* (July 1926): 117.

46. Haldeman-Julius, "Clarence Darrow's Defense of a Negro," pp. 22–24; "Darrow Scores Points in Sweet Murder Trial"; "Defense Ready in Sweet Trial," *Detroit News*, May 2, 1926.

47. "Surprise Given in Sweet Case," *Detroit News*, May 5, 1926; "Doctor Sweet to Tell of Fears," *Detroit Times*, May 7, 1926, clipping at frame 262, reel 4, part 5, NAACP Papers; Haldeman-Julius, "Clarence Darrow's Defense of a Negro," p. 26; John Dancy to E. K. Jones, May 12, 1926, box 1, Detroit Urban League Collection, Bentley Library. The defense opened its case on May 5.

48. "Darrow Calls Sweet to Stand," *Detroit Times*, May 6, 1926; "Defense Opens in Sweet Case," *Detroit Free Press*, May 6, 1926; "Surprise Given in Sweet Case."

49. Haldeman-Julius, "Clarence Darrow Defends a Negro," p. 28; "Sweet Verdict Due This Week," *Detroit Free Press*, May 9, 1926.

50. Haldeman-Julius, "Clarence Darrow's Defense of a Negro," p. 28; Walter White, *Rope and Faggot: A Biography of Judge Lynch* (New York: Alfred A. Knopf, 1929), p. 256; "Sweet's Fate to Jury Soon," *Detroit Times*, May 9, 1926; "Sweet Says He Provided Guns," *Detroit Free Press*, May 8, 1926, copy at frame 265, reel 4, part 5, NAACP Papers.

51. "Sweet Says He Provided Guns"; "Sweet's Fate to Jury Soon."

52. W. E. B. Du Bois, "The Sweet Trial," *Crisis* (July 1926): 114.

53. David Allan Levine, *Internal Combustion: The Races in Detroit, 1915–1926* (Westport, Conn.: Greenwood Press, 1976), p. 187.

54. Transcript of Lester Moll's closing statement, pp. 17, 54–55, 60, Michigan Historical Collection.

55. Transcript of Thomas Chawke's closing statement, pp. 4, 13, 52–55, Michigan Historical Collection.

56. "Darrow in Final Plea," *Detroit Times*, May 11, 1926; "You're All Prejudiced, Darrow Tells Jurors," *Detroit Free Press*, May 12, 1926; Johnson, "Detroit," p. 118; Haldeman-Julius, "Clarence Darrow's Defense of a Negro," p. 28.

57. Darrow's plea is reprinted in "Argument of Clarence Darrow in the Case of Henry

Sweet," NAACP pamphlet, 1927. All quotations are from the pamphlet. Details of his performance are taken from Haldeman-Julius, "Clarence Darrow's Defense of a Negro," pp. 28–32; Josephine Gomon diary entry, n.d., box 6, Gomon Papers; Johnson, "Detroit," pp. 118–119; "You're All Prejudiced, Darrow Tells Jurors," *Detroit Free Press*, May 12, 1926; "Darrow in Final Plea"; Stone, *Clarence Darrow for the Defense*, pp. 484–485. James Weldon Johnson to Walter White, May 14, 1926, frames 651–652, reel 3, part 5, NAACP Papers. Darrow later claimed that "my long sympathy for the colored people conspired to help me make one of the strongest and most satisfactory arguments that I ever delivered." Darrow, *The Story of My Life*, p. 311.

58. Johnson, "Detroit," p. 119. Others were just as moved by Darrow's plea. "As Judge Murphy left the bench I met him just inside the door of his office," Josephine Gomon recalled. "He took my hand and said, 'This is the greatest experience of my life. That was Clarence Darrow at his best. I will never hear anything like it again. He is the most Christlike man I have ever known." Stone, *Clarence Darrow for the Defense*, p. 484.

59. Transcript of Robert Toms closing statement, May 12, 1926, pp. 99–100, Michigan Historical Collection; Felix Holt to Walter White, May 12, 1926, frame 34, reel 10, part 2, NAACP Papers; "Court to Rule Today in Mistrial in Riot Case," *Detroit Times*, May 13, 1926; "Sweet Denied Mistrial Move," *Detroit Free Press*, May 13, 1926; Haldeman-Julius, "Clarence Darrow's Defense of a Negro," p. 32.

60. Transcript of Frank Murphy charge of the court, May 13, 1926, pp. 30–31, Michigan Historical Collection.

61. Chawke interview; Gomon diary entry, n.d. [May 13, 1926]; Gomon draft, "The Sweet Trial," p. 43; "Henry Sweet Acquitted in Murder Trial," *Detroit Free Press*, May 14, 1926.

62. Johnson, "Detroit," pp. 119–120; "Toms May Drop Riot Cases," *Detroit Times*, May 14, 1926.

63. Haldeman-Julius, "Clarence Darrow's Defense of a Negro," p. 32; Gomon draft, "Judge of the Recorders Court," p. 43; Stone, *Clarence Darrow for the Defense*, p. 486; "Toms May Drop Riot Cases."

64. Haldeman-Julius, "Clarence Darrow's Defense of a Negro," p. 32; Johnson, "Detroit," p. 120.

65. Gomon Diary entry, n.d.; Gomon draft, p. 43; Johnson to White, May 14, 1926; "Toms May Drop Riot Case." Gomon claims that when the verdict was read Darrow slumped in his chair. A worried Toms reached out to him. "Are you all right, Mr. Darrow?" the prosecutor asked. "Oh yes," he replied. "I've heard that verdict before." Gomon draft, "The Sweet Trial," p. 44.

Epilogue: Requiescam

1. "Crowd Mass Meetings of NAACP," *Chicago Defender*, July 3, 1926; David Levering Lewis, *W. E. B. Du Bois: The Fight for Equality and the American Century, 1919–1963* (New York: Henry Holt, 2000), pp. 175–176; Kenneth Robert Janken, *White: The Biography of Walter White, Mr. NAACP* (New York: New Press, 2003), pp. 113–115; "To Fight 'Jim Crow' Laws," *New York Times*, June 28, 1926.

2. Elazar Barkan, *The Retreat of Scientific Racism: Changing Concepts of Race in Britain and the United States Between the World Wars* (Cambridge, England: Cambridge University Press, 1992); Stephan Thernstrom and Abigail Thernstrom, *America in Black and White: One Nation, Indivisible* (New York: Simon and Schuster, 1997), p. 103; Stephen Grant Meyer, *As Long as They Don't Move Next Door: Segregation and Racial Conflict in American Neighborhoods* (Lanham, Md.: Rowan and Littlefield, 2000), p. 136.

3. Kevin Tierney, *Darrow: A Biography* (New York: Thomas Y. Crowell, 1979), pp. 386–425; James Goodman, *Stories of Scottsboro* (New York: Random House, 1994), pp. 37–38; Irving Stone, *Clarence Darrow for the Defense* (Garden City, N.Y.: Doubleday, 1941), p. 518.

4. "Defense Attorney Thomas Chawke Dies," *Detroit News*, December 26, 1974;

Raymond Fragnoli, *The Transformation of Detroit: Progressivism in Detroit—and After, 1912–1933* (New York: Garland, 1982), pp. 320–328; Reinhold Niebuhr, *Leaves from the Notebook of a Tamed Cynic* (1929; repr. New York: Harper and Row, 1980), p. 144; "Long Fight Is Ended for Civil Leader," *Detroit Free Press*, June 18, 1942.

5. Arthur Garfield Hays, *City Lawyer: The Autobiography of a Law Practice* (New York: Simon and Schuster, 1942). Darrow is quoted on p. 461.

6. Niebuhr, *Leaves from the Notebook of a Tamed Cynic*, p. 143; Mayor's Inter-Racial Committee, *The Negro in Detroit* (Detroit: Detroit Bureau of Governmental Research, 1926); "Report of the Mayor's Committee on Race Relations," *Public Business* 4 (March 10, 1927), copy in box G-95, NAACP Papers, Library of Congress, Washington, D.C.; Richard Fox, *Reinhold Niebuhr: A Biography* (New York: Pantheon, 1985), chapters 5–7; Taylor Branch, *Parting the Waters: America in the King Years, 1954–63* (New York: Simon and Schuster, 1988), pp. 81–87.

7. "Ex-Judge Toms Dies at Age 73," *Detroit Free Press*, April 7, 1960; "300 Judges, Lawyers, Attend Toms' Funeral," *Detroit News*, April 10, 1960; NAACP Detroit branch membership list, June 8, 1937, frame 1090, reel 13, part 12, NAACP Papers; "Luminary of the Week," *[Detroit?] Legal Chronicle*, May 22, 1964, copy in Detroit Free Press clipping morgue, Detroit, Mich.

8. Sidney Fine, *Frank Murphy: The Detroit Years* (Ann Arbor: University of Michigan Press, 1975), pp. 215–223, 442–451.

9. Sidney Fine, *Frank Murphy: The Washington Years* (Ann Arbor: University of Michigan Press, 1984), pp. 130–131, 168–177, 381–383, 393–393, 412–424, 448, 565.

10. Eugene Levy, *James Weldon Johnson: Black Leader, Black Voice* (Chicago: University of Chicago Press, 1973), pp. 287–292; Janken, *White*, chapters 5–12; Patricia Sullivan, *Days of Hope: Race and Democracy in the New Deal Era* (Chapel Hill: University of North Carolina Press, 1996); Genna Rae McNeil, *Groundwork: Charles Hamilton Houston and the Struggle for Civil Rights* (Philadelphia: University of Pennsylvania Press, 1983); Mark V. Tushnet, *Making Civil Rights Law: Thurgood Marshall and the Supreme Court, 1936–1961* (New York: Oxford University Press, 1994); Richard Kluger, *Simple Justice: The History of Brown v. Board of Education and Black America's Struggle for Equality* (New York: Vintage, 1975); and, for an insider's account, Jack Greenberg, *Crusaders in the Court: How a Dedicated Band of Lawyers Fought for the Civil Rights Revolution* (New York: Basic Books, 1994).

11. James Weldon Johnson to Clarence Darrow, May 28, 1926, frame 681, reel 3, part 5, NAACP Papers; Harold Black, "Restrictive Covenants in Relation to Segregated Negro Housing in Detroit," (unpublished M.A. thesis, Wayne State University, 1947), pp. 6, 10, 24, 37–38; Kenneth Jackson, *Crabgrass Frontier: The Suburbanization of the United States* (New York: Oxford University Press, 1985); Douglas Massey and Nancy Denton, *American Apartheid: Segregation and the Making of the Underclass* (Cambridge, Mass.: Harvard University Press, 1993), chapter 2. Also see Arnold Hirsch, *Making the Second Ghetto: Race and Housing in Chicago, 1940–1960* (Cambridge, England: Cambridge University Press, 1983).

12. On white liberals and neighborhood segregation in Detroit, see Thomas Sugrue, *The Origins of the Urban Crisis: Race and Inequality in Postwar Detroit* (Princeton, N.J.: Princeton University Press, 1996), pp. 190–194, chapters 8–9; and Sidney Fine, *"Expanding the Frontiers of Civil Rights": Michigan, 1948–1968* (Detroit: Wayne State University Press, 2000), chapter 5. The beginning point for understanding mid-twentieth-century racial liberalism is Gunnar Myrdal, *An American Dilemma* (New York: Harper and Row, 1944). For an insightful recent treatment, see Gary Gerstle, *American Crucible: Race and Nation in the Twentieth Century* (Princeton, N.J.: Princeton University Press, 2001).

13. Clement Vose, *Caucasians Only: The Supreme Court, the NAACP, and the Restrictive Covenant Cases* (Berkeley: University of California Press, 1959), chapters 6–8; Hugh Davis Graham, *The Civil Rights Era: Origins and Development of a National Policy* (New York: Oxford University Press, 1990), chapter 10; Meyer, *As Long as They Don't Live Next Door*, pp. 212–221; Sugrue, *The Origins of the Urban Crisis;* Massey & Denton, *American Apartheid*, chapters 3–4; Reynolds Farley, Sheldon Danzinger, and Harry Holzer, *Detroit Divided* (New York: Russell Sage Foundation, 2000), chapters 7–8; http://www.census.gov/hhes/www/housing/resseg/tab5-4.html, last accessed February 7, 2004.

14. Minutes of the NAACP board of directors' meeting, September 13, 1926, frame 98, reel 2, part 1, NAACP Papers; "Baby of Dr. Sweet Dies in Arizona," *Chicago Defender,* August 28, 1926; Elaine Latzman Moon, *Untold Tales, Unsung Heroes: An Oral History of Detroit's African American Community, 1918–1967* (Detroit: Wayne State University Press, 1994), p. 83.

15. R. L. Polk and Company, *Detroit City Directory,* 1927–1928 (Detroit: R. L. Polk and Company, 1928); NAACP press release, n.d. [June 1928], frame 169, reel 29, part 11B, NAACP Papers; death certificate 14568, November 10, 1928, Department of Health Records, Detroit, Mich.

16. "Little Is Changed Since '25 Trial," *Detroit Free Press,* November 3, 1975, copy available in Biographical Files/Negroes, "Sweet, Dr. Ossian H.," Biographical Files/ Negroes, Burton Historical Collection, Detroit Public Library, Detroit, Mich.; "Home of Mercy," *Michigan Chronicle,* June 4, 1955, clipping in box 2, Kellogg African-American Health Care Project, Archives of Labor and Urban Affairs, Wayne State University, Detroit, Mich.; Polk County, Fla., Registry of Deeds, *Index,* 1927–1956, p. 110, Polk County Building, Bartow, Fla; oral history interview with Claude Woodruff, Bartow, Fla., February 25, 2002, notes in author's possession.

17. "Wife Accuses Doctor in Suit," *Detroit Free Press,* September 30, 1947, copy available in envelope 11, "Sweet, Dr. Ossian H.," Detroit Free Press Clipping Morgue; personal correspondence with Pat Crews, February 15, 2003, copy in author's possession; "Words of Wisdom," *Detroit Free Press,* February 1, 2004; Ossian Sweet to William Pickens, December 20, 1930, reel 26, Arthur Spingarn Collection, Library of Congress, Washington, D.C.; O. H. Sweet file, July 1950, Civic Searchlight Collection, Burton Historical Collection; H. W. Sweet to Thurgood Marshall, August 27, 1937, frames 969–970, reel 13, part 12, NAACP Papers; "Negro Lawyer, Sweet, Is Dead," *Detroit Free Press,* January 21, 1940.

18. Entries for 2905 Garland, December 22, 1950–April 28, 1958, plat book, Wayne County Registrar of Deed, Detroit, Mich.; oral history interview with William Baxter, October 20, 2001, Detroit, Mich.

19. Oral history interview with Claude Woodruff; Alex Baskin interview with Robert Toms, November 28, 1959, Alex Baskin Collection, Michigan Historical Collection, Bentley Library, University of Michigan, Ann Arbor; "Bullet Is Fatal to Negro Doctor, Slay-Case Figure," *Detroit Free Press,* March 20, 1960; "Dr. Sweet's Death Recalls Infamous Housing Case Here," *Michigan Chronicle,* March 26, 1960, copy in Sweet biographical file, Burton.

ACKNOWLEDGMENTS

When I set out to tell the story of Ossian Sweet, I knew the work was going to be different than anything I'd done before. But I never guessed how far I'd travel beyond the comfort of my office or how many people would guide me along the way. Every author says his or her book wouldn't have been possible without assistance. In my case, it's true.

Like every historian, I owe an irredeemable debt to archivists and librarians. Thanks to the staffs of the Polk County (Florida) Historical Society, the Florida State Archives, the Wilberforce University Archives, the Moorland-Spingarn Center at Howard University, the Library of Congress Manuscript Reading Room, the National Archives (and its branch at Pittsfield, Massachusetts), the Western Reserve Historical Society, the Ohio Historical Society, the University of Michigan's Harlan Hatcher Library, the University of Massachusetts's W. E. B. Du Bois Library, Ohio State University's William Oxley Library, and the State Library of Michigan. As always, I relied on the patience and expertise of my friends at Wayne State University's Walter P. Reuther Library, who are too polite to say they're tired of seeing me. Imperturbable Tom Featherstone again tracked down many of the photos that appear in the book. I am particularly grateful to the librarians of the Detroit Public Library's Burton Historical Collection, who helped me wander through the collection's vast holdings, and to the extraordinary professionals at the Michigan Historical Collection at the University of Michigan's

Bentley Library, where my research began. Thanks especially to Assistant Director Bill Wallach, who not only helped me gain access to several important collections but also gave my family a place to stay for two weeks.

As important as archives were, the Sweets' story wasn't the sort that could be told straight from library shelves. I went to Bartow, Florida, not knowing a soul. Two marvelous gentlemen, Claude Woodruff and Clifton Lewis, took me under their wings, showing me through the streets of East Bartow, introducing me to its rich history and fascinating people. While in Florida, I also benefited from the kindness of Vickie Sweet, Charlie McNeill, Mike Denham, Canter Brown, and the pastor of St. James AME Church. Then there was the magical moment when Mr. Woodruff took me to meet Ossian Sweet's baby brother, Sherman Sweet, who lives in a house he built on the lot his father bought a century ago. I will never forget sitting with Mr. Sweet in his living room, listening as he talked of the past. For his time and his memories, I am forever grateful.

In Detroit, too, history opened up in unexpected ways. Daniel Baxter invited me into the bungalow on the corner of Garland and Charlevoix, which his parents, William and Ruby Baxter, bought from Ossian Sweet in 1958. To stand at the bedroom window, seeing the street as Ossian would have seen it on the night of the shooting, transformed the book, as did the opportunity to talk to the Baxters about the doctor. Brilliantly talented Arthur Beer of the University of Detroit Mercy gave me what I believe is the only existing copy of the interrogation transcripts made on the night the Sweets and their friends were arrested. Professor Alex Baskin granted me permission to use the interviews he conducted with most of the principals in the case more than forty years ago. My friend and fellow east-sider Bill McGraw made it possible for me to use the clipping morgues at both the *Detroit Free Press* and the *Detroit News*, without which it would have been impossible to trace the Sweets' story beyond 1926. Thanks as well to the *Detroit News'* editor, Tarek Hamada, and librarian Patricia Zacharias. Around the nation, Detroit has the reputation of being a tough town. But you won't find more big-hearted people no matter where you look.

Financial support for the initial research came from a University of Massachusetts Faculty Research Grant and a Bentley Library Bordin/ Gilette Research Travel Fellowship. Should they read *Arc of Justice*, I hope Fred Byron and Fran Blouin will feel their confidence in the project was well-founded. When it came time to write, I had the great luck to receive fellowships from the National Endowment for the Humanities, the American Council of Learned Societies, and the John Simon Guggenhiem Foundation. What a dream it was to have the support needed to devote myself to the book full-time. There aren't words sufficient to express my appreciation.

Arc of Justice bears the imprint of the University of Massachusetts's history department, my academic home for eight terrific years. I received great personal support from chairs Mary Wilson, Kathy Peiss, and David Glassberg. The devoted members of the AbbyandNan forum—Marla Miller, Alice Nash, Carl Nightingale, Brian Ogilvie, Max Page, and Kate Weigand—gave lots of advice, direction, and dessert. UMass also taught me to think of history as belonging not only to historians but to the public, a lesson that shaped every page of this book. My new colleagues at Ohio State University welcomed me into a stimulating atmosphere. Dean Michael Hogan and chairs Leila Rupp and Ken Andrien granted me a year's leave to work on the manuscript; Judy Wu and Steve Conn took time out from their frantic schedules to read early drafts; and Gail Summerhill provided a wonderful reading of a later version. Their comments were invaluable in helping me figure out what I was doing and how it might be made better. Jane Berger also read drafts, talked me through perplexing problems, commiserated over the challenges of transitions, and watched my daughters' impromptu performances with inspiring enthusiasm. Thank you, Jane. At the last minute, Ron McLean of Ohio State's TELR office stepped in to rescue photos from the obscurity of microfilm.

Over the years, I have leaned heavily on colleagues, friends, family, and a few folks I don't even know. Sidney Fine taught me to be a historian. With their great generosity, Patricia Sullivan and Waldo Martin made it possible for me to imagine contributing in some small way to the study of civil rights. The new generation of Detroit historians—Tom Klug, Suzanne Smith, Tom Sugrue, Heather Thompson, and Victoria Wolcott—taught me a great deal about the city, and in one short conversation, John Staudenmeier, S. J., helped me think about the complexity of Sweet's experience, much as he made me think about being an academic when I was an undergraduate. I've been fortunate to work with many extraordinarily talented students. The undergraduates at University College Dublin and the University of Massachusetts who took my civil rights courses gave me so much to think about. And the graduate students who've come my way—Grace Abarca, Babette Faehmel, Julie Gallagher, Peter Lau, Lincoln Lounsbury, Leo Maley, Marian Mollin,

Kathleen Nutter, Bob Surbrug, and so many others—taught me more than I ever taught them. To those who attended presentations at the University of Connecticut, the University of Michigan-Dearborn, Wayne State University, the University of Detroit Mercy, and Harvard University's NEH Summer Seminar on civil rights history, thank you for your suggestions and criticisms. And to three authors I never met—Taylor Branch, David Levering Lewis, and the late Anthony Lukas—I offer my deepest appreciation. Whenever I needed inspiration, which was more often that I ought to admit, I turned to their books to see how history should be written. God, how I wish I could write like that.

If I have moved a little closer to that standard, it is due to my editor, George Hodgman. Since taking on the book, George has patiently weaned me from academic prose, taught me new ways to write, made me think hard about the structure of storytelling, understood when I stumbled, and championed my work even when it didn't deserve to be championed. Scouring the Web one day, I read an article that referred to George as a "much beloved" editor. I know why. My thanks as well to Supurna Banerjee, who pushed the manuscript—and me—through the publication process, and to Henry Holt's superb production staff, which made *Arc of Justice* such a handsome book.

No one could ask for better friends than Marty Hershock, Terry and Cindy Hopman, Kevin Hurst, Bil and Katie Kerrigan, Barry Levy and Jackie Wolf, David and Camela Moskin, Mike Smith, Joe and Nancy Tolkacz, and Joe and Paula Zehetmeier, all of whom at one time or another sat and talked about the Sweets, about work, about kids, about politics, about just anything worth talking about. Our neighbors in Bexley, Ohio, have enveloped our new home in midwestern friendliness. Thanks to Terry Kemp for explaining the law to me; to Angie Mally, Tim and Lynn Johnson, and Deneece Kemp for making us feel so welcome; and to Terri Ghitman and Laura Jones for regularly asking whether I'd finished that book yet. That's really what kept me working this past year and a half.

Art and Judy Getis have made me a member of their family, a precious gift for in-laws to bestow. It's always a great pleasure to spend time with them and the rest of the Getis clan: Hilary, Jamal, Sophie, and Christina Tarazi, and Annie, Tony, Darby, Trevor, and Matty Tibbetts.

My parents, Kevin and Anne Boyle, put me up whenever I came to Detroit, read and commented on the entire manuscript, sent me bits of news, encouraged me to keep going, and sympathized with me when I needed them to. The only thing I can offer in return is my love.

Finally, there are the greatest debts.

I knew things were getting out of hand when my family went on a long-promised vacation to Disney World and instead of spending another day at the Magic Kingdom, I hustled us off for a drive through Bartow. But Abby and Nan accepted the imposition with good grace, just as they accepted all the impositions I've made in pursuit of the Sweets' story. They're the greatest kids imaginable and I am honored—absolutely honored—to be their daddy. For Vicky, thanks seem so insufficient. It was her encouragement that got me to start the book and led me to apply for the fellowships that set me to writing. Then the demands really escalated. Time and again, she talked me through trouble spots, outlined sections, read chapters, listened to doubts and complaints, cajoled, encouraged, and commiserated. As invaluable as all that has been, though, it pales in comparison to the ways in which Vicky has filled our lives with her boundless love. She has said a few times that this book is a family project, and so it is. That's why *The Arc of Justice* is dedicated to Abby, Nan, and Vicky together, my coauthors and my joys.

INDEX

ABOUT THE AUTHOR

Born and raised in Detroit, KEVIN BOYLE is an associate professor of history at Ohio State University. He is the author of *The UAW and the Heyday of American Liberalism, 1945–1968* and the coauthor (with Victoria Getis) of *Muddy Boots and Ragged Aprons: Images of Working-Class Detroit, 1900–1930*. He lives in Bexley, Ohio, with his wife, their two daughters, and an aging border collie.

2011–12 GREAT MICHIGAN READ

The Michigan Humanities Council's Great Michigan Read is a book club for the entire state. Each year, it features a new book by a Michigan author about a Michigan topic. With a statewide focus on a single book, Michiganians are encouraged to learn more about our state, our society, and our history, sharing ideas with others in their community who are also reading the book.

The 2011–12 selection is *Arc of Justice: A Saga of Race, Civil Rights, and Murder in the Jazz Age.* Written by Detroit native Kevin Boyle, it is a masterful recounting of a landmark historical event, culminating in an epic legal battle that helped lay the foundation of the civil rights movement.

In 1925, African American physician Ossian Sweet purchased a home in a white neighborhood in Detroit. Determined to protect his family and property, Sweet chose to defend himself from the mob organized to drive him out.

Arc of Justice provides essential historical background as Americans continue to confront issues of tolerance and equality.

This special edition of the book is intended for free distribution to Great Michigan Read partners for use in discussion groups and classrooms.

The official reader's guide, with additional historical background, photos, and a map of Sweet trial landmarks, is available in print from Great Michigan Read partners (libraries, schools, Meijer stores, and others) and online at www.michiganhumanities.org.

Visit the Web site for additional details, including a calendar of events, additional resources, and to register your organization for free support materials. Join the Michigan Humanities Council Facebook group or follow @mihumanities (#greatMIread) on Twitter.

The Great Michigan Read is presented by the Michigan Humanities Council with support from Meijer and the National Endowment for the Humanities.

DISCUSSION QUESTIONS

1. How does Ossian Sweet's journey to the North differ from that of the hundreds of thousands of other African Americans who left the South during that time period?

2. How did life for African Americans in Northern cities compare with the conditions they faced in the South?

3. Before Black Bottom became known as a primarily African American district, it was home to many white immigrants. How and why do neighborhoods change composition over time?

4. What are the consequences of the fact that many American cities continue to exhibit segregated housing patterns?

5. Imagine living in 1920s Detroit. If you were committed to racial justice, how would you work to achieve this goal?

6. Why would the Sweets decide to move to the Garland Street residence despite the threat of racial violence?

7. How did the defense team manage to turn the trial from a murder case to a broader consideration of race, prejudice, and discrimination in 1920s America?

8. Are you aware of any similar historical events that occurred in your community? How are issues of discrimination, segregation, bullying, and/or intolerance still relevant in your community, Michigan, and America today?

Q & A WITH THE AUTHOR

How did you find out about the story of Ossian Sweet?

Sweet's story is a part of Detroit lore. I'd heard about it growing up in the city—not everything, of course, but enough to pique my interest.

Why were you compelled to write Arc of Justice?

I really wanted to write about the struggle of civil rights. But I wanted to look at civil rights in a place and time that didn't fit the standard story of the movement, a story that took place in the North, not in the South, and in the 1920s, not the 1950s and 1960s. And I desperately wanted to write about Detroit.

What is the story's most compelling lesson for today?

Arc of Justice captures the moment when the Northern system of segregation was created, a system that divides the nation's great cities into different neighborhoods—separate and unequal. We still live with that system today. I like to think that Sweet's story makes us look around us—and wonder why we continue to accept such injustice.

ABOUT THE MICHIGAN HUMANITIES COUNCIL

The Michigan Humanities Council connects people and communities by supporting quality cultural programs. It is Michigan's nonprofit affiliate of the National Endowment for the Humanities. Since 1974, the Michigan Humanities Council has supported communities through family literacy programs, special cultural and historical exhibits, book discussions, author tours, scholarly lectures and mentors, films, cultural celebrations, and school programs and performances that have reached millions of Michiganians.

Michigan Humanities Council
119 Pere Marquette Dr., #3B
Lansing, MI 48912
ph: 517-372-7770
www.michiganhumanities.org

THE MINISTER'S MANUAL
2011 EDITION

EIGHTY-SIXTH
ANNUAL ISSUE

Edited by Lee McGlone

JOSSEY-BASS
A Wiley Imprint
www.josseybass.com

EDITORS OF THE MINISTER'S MANUAL
G.B.F. Hallock, D.D., 1926–1958
M.K.W. Heicher, Ph.D., 1943–1968
Charles L. Wallis, M.A., M.Div., 1969–1983
James W. Cox, M.Div., Ph.D., 1984–2007
Lee McGlone, Ph.D.

Translations of the Bible referred to and quoted from in this book may be indicated by their standard abbreviations, such as NRSV (New Revised Standard Version) and NIV (New International Version). In addition, some contributors have made their own translations and others have used a mixed text.

Published by Jossey-Bass
A Wiley Imprint
989 Market Street, San Francisco, CA 94103–1741   www.josseybass.com

Library of Congress Cataloging Card Number
25-21658
ISSN 0738-5323
ISBN 978-0-470-58786-7

Printed in the United States of America
FIRST EDITION
PB Printing
10 9 8 7 6 5 4 3 2 1

CONTENTS

PREFACE

Pastors and other church ministers will find in the *The Minister's Manual, 2011 Edition*, a variety of aids in preparation for worship. The material included is not intended to replace the rigorous mental labor that is required of a congregational leader. It is intended, however, to serve as a stimulus that will fan our creative, intellectual, and spiritual flames. I pray this edition will be encouragement to us all.

The different sections of the *Manual* are useful to different individuals. Some pastors indicate that the prayers are especially important, others the children's sermons, others the hymn suggestions, others the illustrations, and others the special articles. But the sermons seem to be the most useful of the resources. The fifty-two lectionary sermons are offered as a way to help "prime the pump" for faithful preachers who go to the pulpit weekly declaring the unsearchable riches of the Gospel of Jesus Christ.

Again this year, I express my thanks to Marcia Thompson, friend and teacher from Sioux Falls, South Dakota, who secured and edited the lectionary children's sermons for each week. I also express appreciation to Dr. Charles Fuller, former dean of the School of Fine Arts at Ouachita Baptist University, Arkadelphia, Arkansas, who chose the suggested hymns and musical selections. Dr. Mark McKim, senior minister of the First Baptist Church, Regina, Saskatchewan, Canada, provided a challenging Lenten preaching series from the days of "exile." Dr. William P. Tuck, former pastor and professor, faced a number of the "difficult sayings of Jesus" with wisdom and insight. Lisa Hill, a writer and lay-leader in my congregation, provided a short series of Advent devotions. Also this year I have included a number of prayers written by upper level students at Ouachita Baptist University, Arkadelphia, Arkansas. The names of these students are provided in the Contributors listing.

I also wish to express appreciation to the editorial staff at Jossey-Bass Publishers for the fine attention to detail given to this volume—and especially to Alison Knowles for her kindness and proficiency.

I pray that this volume will provide encouragement, inspiration, and challenge to the sacred work of preaching.

Lee McGlone, Ph.D.
Pastor, First Baptist Church
Arkadelphia, Arkansas

GENERAL AIDS
AND
RESOURCES

Civil Year Calendars for 2011 and 2012

2011

January
S	M	T	W	T	F	S
						1
2	3	4	5	6	7	8
9	10	11	12	13	14	15
16	17	18	19	20	21	22
23	24	25	26	27	28	29
30	31					

February
S	M	T	W	T	F	S
		1	2	3	4	5
6	7	8	9	10	11	12
13	14	15	16	17	18	19
20	21	22	23	24	25	26
27	28					

March
S	M	T	W	T	F	S
		1	2	3	4	5
6	7	8	9	10	11	12
13	14	15	16	17	18	19
20	21	22	23	24	25	26
27	28	29	30	31		

April
S	M	T	W	T	F	S
					1	2
3	4	5	6	7	8	9
10	11	12	13	14	15	16
17	18	19	20	21	22	23
24	25	26	27	28	29	30

May
S	M	T	W	T	F	S
1	2	3	4	5	6	7
8	9	10	11	12	13	14
15	16	17	18	19	20	21
22	23	24	25	26	27	28
29	30	31				

June
S	M	T	W	T	F	S
			1	2	3	4
5	6	7	8	9	10	11
12	13	14	15	16	17	18
19	20	21	22	23	24	25
26	27	28	29	30		

July
S	M	T	W	T	F	S
					1	2
3	4	5	6	7	8	9
10	11	12	13	14	15	16
17	18	19	20	21	22	23
24	25	26	27	28	29	30
31						

August
S	M	T	W	T	F	S
	1	2	3	4	5	6
7	8	9	10	11	12	13
14	15	16	17	18	19	20
21	22	23	24	25	26	27
28	29	30	31			

September
S	M	T	W	T	F	S
				1	2	3
4	5	6	7	8	9	10
11	12	13	14	15	16	17
18	19	20	21	22	23	24
25	26	27	28	29	30	

October
S	M	T	W	T	F	S
						1
2	3	4	5	6	7	8
9	10	11	12	13	14	15
16	17	18	19	20	21	22
23	24	25	26	27	28	29
30	31					

November
S	M	T	W	T	F	S
		1	2	3	4	5
6	7	8	9	10	11	12
13	14	15	16	17	18	19
20	21	22	23	24	25	26
27	28	29	30			

December
S	M	T	W	T	F	S
				1	2	3
4	5	6	7	8	9	10
11	12	13	14	15	16	17
18	19	20	21	22	23	24
25	26	27	28	29	30	31

2012

January
S	M	T	W	T	F	S
1	2	3	4	5	6	7
8	9	10	11	12	13	14
15	16	17	18	19	20	21
22	23	24	25	26	27	28
29	30	31				

February
S	M	T	W	T	F	S
			1	2	3	4
5	6	7	8	9	10	11
12	13	14	15	16	17	18
19	20	21	22	23	24	25
26	27	28	29			

March
S	M	T	W	T	F	S
				1	2	3
4	5	6	7	8	9	10
11	12	13	14	15	16	17
18	19	20	21	22	23	24
25	26	27	28	29	30	31

April
S	M	T	W	T	F	S
1	2	3	4	5	6	7
8	9	10	11	12	13	14
15	16	17	18	19	20	21
22	23	24	25	26	27	28
29	30					

May
S	M	T	W	T	F	S
		1	2	3	4	5
6	7	8	9	10	11	12
13	14	15	16	17	18	19
20	21	22	23	24	25	26
27	28	29	30	31		

June
S	M	T	W	T	F	S
					1	2
3	4	5	6	7	8	9
10	11	12	13	14	15	16
17	18	19	20	21	22	23
24	25	26	27	28	29	30

July
S	M	T	W	T	F	S
1	2	3	4	5	6	7
8	9	10	11	12	13	14
15	16	17	18	19	20	21
22	23	24	25	26	27	28
29	30	31				

August
S	M	T	W	T	F	S
			1	2	3	4
5	6	7	8	9	10	11
12	13	14	15	16	17	18
19	20	21	22	23	24	25
26	27	28	29	30	31	

September
S	M	T	W	T	F	S
						1
2	3	4	5	6	7	8
9	10	11	12	13	14	15
16	17	18	19	20	21	22
23	24	25	26	27	28	29
30						

October
S	M	T	W	T	F	S
	1	2	3	4	5	6
7	8	9	10	11	12	13
14	15	16	17	18	19	20
21	22	23	24	25	26	27
28	29	30	31			

November
S	M	T	W	T	F	S
				1	2	3
4	5	6	7	8	9	10
11	12	13	14	15	16	17
18	19	20	21	22	23	24
25	26	27	28	29	30	

December
S	M	T	W	T	F	S
						1
2	3	4	5	6	7	8
9	10	11	12	13	14	15
16	17	18	19	20	21	22
23	24	25	26	27	28	29
30	31					

Church and Civic Calendar for 2011

January

1	New Year's Day
6	Epiphany
7	Orthodox Christmas
14	Orthodox New Year
17	Martin Luther King Jr. Day

February

2	Groundhog Day
14	Valentine's Day
20	World Day of Social Justice
21	Presidents Day

March

8	Mardi Gras (Shrove Tuesday)
9	Ash Wednesday
13	Daylight Saving Time Begins
17	St. Patrick's Day
20	Purim
20	Vernal Equinox

April

15	Tax Day
17	Palm Sunday
19	First Day of Passover
21	Maundy Thursday
22	Good Friday
22	Earth Day
24	Easter
26	Last Day of Passover
29	Arbor Day

May

5	National Day of Prayer
5	Cinco de Mayo
8	Mother's Day
30	Memorial Day

June

2	Ascension Day
12	Pentecost
14	Flag Day
19	Trinity Sunday
19	Father's Day
23	Corpus Christi

July

4	Independence Day
24	Parent's Day

August

1	Ramadan Begins
9	Tisha B'Av
12	International Youth Day

September

5	Labor Day
10	National Grandparents Day
17	Citizenship Day
21	International Day of Peace
23	Autumn Equinox
29–30	Rosh Hashanah (Jewish)

October

2   World Communion Sunday

8   Yom Kippur

10   Columbus Day

13   First Day of Sukkot

16   World Food Day

19   Last Day of Sukkot

30   Reformation Day

31   All Hallows' Eve (Halloween)

November

1   All Saints' Day

2   All Souls' Day

6   Daylight Saving Time Ends

11   Veterans Day

24   Thanksgiving Day

27   First Sunday of Advent

December

4   Second Sunday of Advent

7   Pearl Harbor Remembrance Day

10   Human Rights Day

11   Third Sunday of Advent

18   Fourth Sunday of Advent

21   First Day of Chanukah

22   Winter Solstice

24   Christmas Eve

25   Christmas Day

26   Kwanzaa (until January 1)

28   Last Day of Chanukah

31   New Year's Eve

The Revised Common Lectionary for 2011

The following scriptures are commended for use by various Protestant churches and the Roman Catholic Church and include first, second, and gospel readings, and psalms for 2011.

Season of Epiphany

Jan. 2: Isa. 60:1–6; Ps. 72:1–7, 10–14; Eph. 3:1–12; Matt. 2:1–12

Jan. 9: Isa. 42:1–9; Ps. 29; Acts 10:34–43; Matt. 3:13–17

Jan. 16: Isa. 49:1–7; Ps. 40:1–11; 1 Cor. 1:1–9; John 1:29–42

Jan. 23: Isa. 9:1–4; Ps. 27:1, 4–9; 1 Cor. 1:10–18; Matt. 4:12–23

Jan. 30: Mic. 6:1–8; Ps. 15; 1 Cor. 1:18–31; Matt. 5:1–12

Feb. 6: Isa. 58:1–9a (9b–12); Ps. 112:1–9 (10); 1 Cor. 2:1–12 (13–16); Matt. 5:13–20

Feb. 13: Deut. 30:15–20; Ps. 119:1–8; 1 Cor. 3:1–9; Matt. 5:21–37

Feb. 20: Lev. 19:1–2, 9–18; Ps. 119:33–40; 1 Cor. 3:10–11, 16–23; Matt. 5:38–48

Feb. 27: Isa. 49:8–16a; Ps. 131 or Ps. 62:5–12; 1 Cor. 4:1–5; Matt. 6:24–34

Mar. 6: Exod. 24:12–18; Ps. 99; 2 Pet. 1:16–21; Matt. 17:1–9

Season of Lent

Mar. 13: Gen. 2:15–17; 3:1–7; Ps. 32; Rom. 5:12–19; Matt. 4:1–11

Mar. 20: Gen. 12:1–4a; Ps. 121; Rom. 4:1–5, 13–17; John 3:1–17

Mar. 27: Exod. 17:1–7; Ps. 95; Rom. 5:1–11; John 4:5–42

Apr. 3: 1 Sam. 16:1–13; Ps. 23; Eph. 5:8–14; John 9:1–41

Apr. 10: Ezek. 37:1–14; Ps. 130; Rom. 8:6–11; John 11:1–45

Holy Week and Easter Season

Apr. 17 (Palm Sunday): Liturgy of the Palms: Ps. 118:1–2, 19–29; Matt. 21:1–11; or Liturgy of the Passion: Isa. 50:4–9a; Ps. 31:9–16; Phil. 2:5–11; Matt. 26:14–27:66 or Matt. 27:11–54

Apr. 24 (Easter Day): Acts 10:34–43; Ps. 118:1–2, 14–24; Col. 3:1–4; John 20:1–18 or Matt. 28:1–10

May 1: Acts 2:14a, 22–32; Ps. 16; 1 Pet. 1:3–9; John 20:19–31

May 8: Acts 2:14a, 36–41; Ps. 116:1–4, 12–19; 1 Pet. 1:17–23; Luke 24:13–35

May 15: Acts 2:42–47; Ps. 23; 1 Pet. 2:19–25; John 10:1–10

May 22: Acts 7:55–60; Ps. 31:1–5, 15–16; 1 Pet. 2:2–10; John 14:1–14

May 29: Acts 17:22–31; Ps. 66:8–20; 1 Pet. 3:13–22; John 14:15–21

June 5 (Ascension Sunday): Acts 1:1–11; Ps. 47; Eph. 1:15–23; Luke 24:44–53; or (if not celebrating the day as Ascension Sunday): Acts 1:6–14; Ps. 68:1–10, 32–35; 1 Pet. 4:12–14, 5:6–11; John 17:1–11

June 12 (Pentecost Sunday): Acts 2:1–21; Ps. 104:24–34, 35b; 1 Cor. 12:3b–13; John 7:37–39

June 19 (Trinity Sunday): Gen. 1:1–2:4a; Ps. 8; 2 Cor. 13:11–13; Matt. 28:16–20

June 26: Gen. 22:1–14; Ps. 13; Rom. 6:12–23; Matt. 10:40–42

July 3: Gen. 24:34–38, 42–49, 58–67; Ps. 45:10–17 or Ps. 72; Rom. 7:15–25a; Matt. 11:16–19, 25–30

July 10: Gen. 25:19–34; Ps. 119:105–112 or Ps. 25; Rom. 8:1–11; Matt. 13:1–9, 18–23

July 17: Gen. 28:10–19a; Ps. 139:1–12, 23–24; Rom. 8:12–25; Matt. 13:24–30, 36–43

July 24: Gen. 29:15–28; Ps. 105:1–11, 45b; Rom. 8:26–39; Matt. 13:31–33, 44–52

July 31: Gen. 32:22–31; Ps. 17:1–7, 15; Rom. 9:1–5; Matt. 14:13–21

Aug. 7: Gen. 37:1–4, 12–28; Ps. 105:1–6, 16–22, 45b; Rom. 10:5–15; Matt. 14:22–33

Aug. 14: Gen. 45:1–15; Ps. 133; Rom. 11:1–2a, 29–32; Matt. 15:(10–20), 21–28

Aug. 21: Exod. 1:8–2:10; Ps. 124; Rom. 12:1–8; Matt. 16:13–20

Aug. 28: Exod. 3:1–15; Ps. 105:1–6, 23–26, 45c; Rom. 12:9–21; Matt. 16:21–28

Sept. 4: Exod. 12:1–14; Ps. 148 or Ps. 149; Rom. 13:8–14; Matt. 18:15–20

Sept. 11: Exod. 14:19–31; Exod. 15:1b–11, 20–21; Rom. 14:1–12; Matt. 18:21–35

Sept. 18: Exod. 16:2–15; Ps. 105:1–6, 37–45 or Ps. 78; Phil. 1:21–30; Matt. 20:1–16

Sept. 25: Exod. 17:1–7; Ps. 78:1–4, 12–16; Phil. 2:1–13; Matt. 21:23–32

Oct. 2: Exod. 20:1–4, 7–9, 12–20; Ps. 19; Phil. 3:4b–14; Matt. 21:33–46

Oct. 9: Exod. 32:1–14; Ps. 106:1–6, 19–23; Phil. 4:1–9; Matt. 22:1–14

Oct. 16: Exod. 33:12–23; Ps. 99; 1 Thess. 1:1–10; Matt. 22:15–22

Oct. 23: Deut. 34:1–12; Ps. 90:1–6, 13–17; 1 Thess. 2:1–8; Matt. 22:34–46

Oct. 30 (Reformation Sunday): Josh. 3:7–17; Ps. 107:1–7, 33–37; 1 Thess. 2:9–13; Matt. 23:1–12

Nov. 6 (All Saints' Day): Rev. 7:9–17; Ps. 34:1–10, 22; 1 John 3:1–3; Matt. 5:1–12; or (if not celebrating the day as All Saints' Sunday): Josh. 24:1–3a, 14–25; Ps. 78:1–7; 1 Thess. 4:13–18; Matt. 25:1–13

Nov. 13: Judg. 4:1–7; Ps. 123 or Ps. 76; 1 Thess. 5:1–11; Matt. 25:14–30

Nov. 20 (Christ the King Sunday): Ezek. 34:11–16, 20–24; Ps. 100; Eph. 1:15–23; Matt. 25:31–46

Advent and Christmas

> Nov. 27 (First Sunday in Advent): Isa. 64:1–9; Ps. 80:1–7, 17–19; 1 Cor. 1:3–9; Mark 13:24–37

> Dec. 4 (Second Sunday in Advent): Isa. 40:1–11; Ps. 85:1–2, 8–13; 2 Pet. 3:8–15a; Mark 1:1–8

> Dec. 11 (Third Sunday in Advent): Isa. 61:1–4, 8–11; Ps. 126; 1 Thess. 5:16–24; John 1:6–8, 19–28

> Dec. 18 (Fourth Sunday in Advent): 2 Sam. 7:1–11, 16; Luke 1:46b–55; Rom. 16:25–27; Luke 1:26–38

> Dec. 25 (Christmas Day): Isa. 52:7–10; Ps. 98; Heb. 1:1–4 (5–12); John 1:1–14

Four-Year Church Calendar

	2011	*2012*	*2013*	*2014*
Ash Wednesday	Mar. 9	Feb. 22	Feb. 13	Mar. 5
Palm Sunday	Apr. 17	Apr. 1	Mar. 24	Apr. 13
Good Friday	Apr. 22	Apr. 6	Mar. 29	Apr. 18
Easter	Apr. 24	Apr. 8	Mar. 31	Apr. 20
Ascension Day	June 2	May 17	May 9	May 29
Pentecost	June 12	May 27	May 19	June 8
Trinity Sunday	June 19	June 3	May 26	June 15
Thanksgiving	Nov. 24	Nov. 22	Nov. 28	Nov. 27
Advent Sunday	Nov. 27	Dec. 2	Dec. 1	Nov. 30

Forty-Year Easter Calendar

2011 April 24	2021 April 4	2031 April 13	2041 April 2
2012 April 8	2022 April 17	2032 March 28	2042 April 6
2013 March 31	2023 April 9	2033 April 17	2043 March 29
2014 April 20	2024 March 31	2034 April 9	2044 April 17
2015 April 5	2025 April 20	2035 March 25	2045 April 9
2016 March 27	2026 April 5	2036 April 13	2046 March 25
2017 April 16	2027 March 28	2037 April 5	2047 April 14
2018 April 1	2028 April 16	2038 April 25	2048 April 5
2019 April 21	2029 April 1	2039 April 10	2049 April 18
2020 April 12	2030 April 21	2040 April 1	2050 April 10

Traditional Wedding Anniversary Identifications

1	Paper	7	Wool	13	Lace	35	Coral
2	Cotton	8	Bronze	14	Ivory	40	Ruby
3	Leather	9	Pottery	15	Crystal	45	Sapphire
4	Linen	10	Tin	20	China	50	Gold
5	Wood	11	Steel	25	Silver	55	Emerald
6	Iron	12	Silk	30	Pearl	60	Diamond

Colors Appropriate for Days and Seasons

White.   Symbolizes purity, perfection, and joy and identifies festivals marking events in the life of Jesus, except Good Friday: Christmas, Epiphany, Easter, Eastertide, Ascension Day; also Trinity Sunday, All Saints' Day, weddings, funerals. Gold may also be used.

Red.   Symbolizes the Holy Spirit, martyrdom, and the love of God: Good Friday, Pentecost, and Sundays following.

Violet.   Symbolizes penitence: Advent, Lent.

Green.   Symbolizes mission to the world, hope, regeneration, nurture, and growth: Epiphany season, Kingdomtide, Rural Life Sunday, Labor Sunday, Thanksgiving Sunday.

Blue.   Advent, in some churches.

Flowers in Season Appropriate for Church Use

January: carnation or snowdrop

February: violet or primrose

March: jonquil or daffodil

April: lily, sweet pea, or daisy

May: lily of the valley or hawthorn

June: rose or honeysuckle

July: larkspur or water lily

August: gladiolus or poppy

September: aster or morning star

October: calendula or cosmos

November: chrysanthemum

December: narcissus, holly, or poinsettia

Quotable Quotations

1. In my stars I am above thee; but be not afraid of greatness: some are born great, some achieve greatness, and some have greatness thrust upon them.—Shakespeare, *Twelfth Night*

2. I do not know with what weapons World War III will be fought, but World War IV will be fought with sticks and stones.—Albert Einstein

3. The Bible is like a telescope. If a man looks *through* his telescope, then he sees worlds beyond; but if he looks *at* his telescope, then he does not see anything but that.—Phillips Brooks

4. Cowards die many times before their deaths; The valiant never taste of death but once.—Shakespeare, *Julius Caesar*

5. Always aim at complete harmony of thought and word and deed. Always aim at purifying your thoughts and everything will be well.—Mahatma Gandhi

6. Home is the place where, when you have to go there, They have to take you in.—Robert Frost

7. I claim credit for nothing. Everything is determined, the beginning as well as the end, by forces over which we have no control.— Albert Einstein

8. No tears in the writer, no tears in the reader. No surprise in the writer, no surprise in the reader.—Robert Frost

9. A pessimist sees the difficulty in every opportunity; an optimist sees the opportunity in every difficulty.—Winston Churchill

10. From now on, ending a sentence with a preposition is something up with which I will not put.—Winston Churchill

11. Anybody can sympathize with the sufferings of a friend, but it requires a very fine nature to sympathize with a friend's success.—Oscar Wilde

12. If the devil does not exist, and man has therefore created him, he has created him in his own image and likeness.—Dostoevsky

13. When I think of God, my heart is so filled with joy that the notes fly off as from a spindle.—Joseph Haydn

14. What is hell? I maintain that it is the suffering of being unable to love.—Dostoevsky

15. Anger is an acid that can do more harm to the vessel in which it is stored than to anything on which it is poured.—Mark Twain

16. "Classic." A book which people praise and don't read.—Mark Twain

17. Fanaticism consists of redoubling your effort when you have forgotten your aim.—George Santayana

18. I suppose that I shall have to die beyond my means.—Oscar Wilde
19. The word Christianity is already a misunderstanding—in reality there has been only one Christian, and he died on the Cross.—Friedrich Nietzsche
20. After all is said and done, more is said than done.—Aesop
21. Anyone who has the power to make you believe absurdities has the power to make you commit injustices.—Voltaire
22. Everything that is done in the world is done by hope.—Martin Luther
23. Religion is the basis of civil society, and the source of all good and of all comfort.—Edmund Burke
24. The worst moment for the atheist is when he is really thankful and has nobody to thank.—Gabriel Rossetti
25. The chief end of man is to glorify God, and to enjoy him forever. —Westminster Catechism
26. Every person has his own road to follow, and we cannot know what it is beforehand. What counts in the end of the day is what God does, not what we do.—Paul Tournier
27. The pain you know, God knows. The fears you feel, God shares. Your tears are God's sorrow. Your laughter is echoed in eternal mirth. In Jesus Christ, God enters life and lives.—David Buttrick
28. All evil, all sin, suffering and damnation is "in God." They have been endured by him, abolished in him, transformed by him. These are "the benefits of his passion" for us.—Jürgen Moltmann
29. God does not foreordain that evil and disastrous things happen to us. Rather, he works *after the fact* of tragedy through our powers of perception to reveal to us new avenues of growth, hope, opportunity, and realization.—Wayne E. Oates
30. Character is that which can do without success.—Ralph Waldo Emerson

Questions of Life and Religion

1. What is the meaning of true community?
2. Are we all truly equal?
3. Why is envy bad?
4. What ethical issues are involved in abortion?

5. What is faith?
6. Can contemplating death add meaning to life?
7. What is the role of confession in Christian life and worship?
8. Are there better alternatives to capital punishment?
9. What are the positives and negatives of our aging?
10. How can we deal with the apparent absence of God in certain times and circumstances?
11. Are there appropriate legal ways of dealing with all harmful addictions?
12. How can we think of salvation as blessing?
13. In what ways are children related to purposes of God?
14. What is the church?
15. What is the proper relationship of church and state?
16. Is conscience always a safe guide?
17. What do we mean by conversion?
18. Does scientific research have important contributions to our understanding of creation?
19. What is the most significant aspect of Jesus' Crucifixion?
20. What steps will aid our decision making?
21. How can depression be brought under control?
22. What are the essential ingredients of Christian discipline?
23. Is illness some kind of punishment?
24. Is divorce an option for Christians?
25. What are the pluses and minuses of doubt?
26. What duties does the need for education place upon us?
27. In what way can we best understand the doctrine of election biblically?
28. How can we deal with the confusing interpretation of "the end times"?
29. What are our responsibilities toward our human environment?
30. When does eternal life begin?
31. How do faith and ethics connect?
32. Why is the Eucharist (Communion, the Lord's Supper) important in worship?
33. How is evangelism necessary in fulfilling the mission of the church?
34. How can we explain evil in relation to God?
35. How can we define family?

Biblical Benedictions and Blessings

The Lord watch between me and thee, when we are absent from one another.—Gen. 31:49

The Lord bless thee and keep thee: the Lord make his face to shine upon thee, and be gracious unto thee; the Lord lift up his countenance upon thee, and give thee peace.—Num. 6:24–26

The Lord our God be with us, as he was with our fathers; let him not leave us, nor forsake us; that he may incline our hearts unto him, to walk in all his ways, and to keep his commandments, and his statutes, and his judgments, which he commanded our fathers.—1 Kings 8:57–58

Now the God of patience and consolation grant you to be likeminded one toward another according to Christ Jesus; that ye may with one mind and one mouth glorify Christ. Now the God of hope fill you with all joy and peace in believing, that ye may abound in hope, through the power of the Holy Ghost. Now the God of peace be with you all.—Rom. 15:5–6, 13, 33

Now to him that is of power to establish you according to my gospel, and the preaching of Jesus Christ, according to the revelation of the mystery, which was kept secret since the beginning of the world, but now is manifest, and by the scriptures of the prophets according to the commandment of the everlasting God, made known to all nations for the obedience of faith: to God only wise, be glory through Jesus Christ for ever.—Rom. 16:25–27

Grace be unto you, and peace, from God our Father, and from the Lord Jesus Christ.—1 Cor. 1:3

The grace of the Lord Jesus Christ and the love of God, and the communion of the Holy Spirit, be with you all.—2 Cor. 13:14

Peace be to the brethren, and love with faith, from God the Father and the Lord Jesus Christ. Grace be with all them that love our Lord Jesus Christ in sincerity.—Eph. 6:23–24

And the peace of God, which passes all understanding, shall keep your hearts and minds through Christ Jesus. Finally, brethren, whatsoever things are true, whatsoever things are honest, whatsoever things are just, whatsoever things are pure, whatsoever things are lovely, whatsoever things are of God report; if there be any virtue, and if there be any praise, think on these things. Those things, which you have both learned, and received, and heard, and seen in me, do; and the God of peace shall be with you.—Phil. 4:7–9

Wherefore also we pray always for you, that our God would count you worthy of this calling, and fulfill all the good pleasure of his goodness, and the work of faith with power, that the name of our Lord Jesus Christ may be glorified in you, and you in him, according to the grace of our God and the Lord Jesus Christ.—2 Thess. 1:11–12

Now may the Lord of peace himself give you peace always by all means. The Lord be with you all. The grace of our Lord Jesus Christ be with you all. —2 Thess. 3:16–18

Grace, mercy, and peace, from God our Father and Jesus Christ our Lord. —1 Tim. 1:2

Now the God of peace, that brought again from the dead our Lord Jesus, that great shepherd of the sheep, through the blood of the everlasting covenant, make you perfect in every good work to do his will, working in you that which is well-pleasing in his sight, through Jesus Christ, to whom be glory for ever and ever.—Heb. 13:20–21

The God of all grace, who has called us unto his eternal glory by Christ Jesus, after that you have suffered a while, make you perfect, establish, strengthen, settle you. To him be glory and dominion forever and ever. Greet one another with a kiss of charity. Peace be with you all that are in Christ Jesus.—1 Pet. 5:10–11, 14

Grace be with you, mercy, and peace, from God the Father, and from the Lord Jesus Christ, the Son of the Father, in truth and love.—2 John:3

Now unto him who is able to keep you from falling, and to present you as faultless before the presence of his glory with exceeding joy, to the only wise

God our Savior, be glory and majesty, dominion and power, both now and forever.—Jude:24–25

Grace be unto you, and peace, from him which was, and which is to come; and from the seven Spirits which are before his throne; and from Jesus Christ, who is the faithful witness, and the first begotten of the dead, and the prince of the kings of the earth. Unto him that loved us, and washed us from our sins in his own blood, and has made us kings and priests unto God and his Father; to him be glory and dominion for ever and ever.—Rev. 1:4–6

SECTION II

LECTIONARY RESOURCES FOR FIFTY-TWO SUNDAYS

*Sermons, Illustrations,
Congregational Music,
Children's Sermons,
Worship Aids*

SUNDAY, JANUARY 2, 2011
Epiphany

LECTIONARY SERMON TOPIC: "Arise and Shine, Your Light Has Come!"

TEXT: Isa. 60:1–6

OTHER READINGS: Ps. 72:1–7, 10–14; Eph. 3:1–12; Matt. 2:1–12

Epiphany—an unexpected revelation. Sometimes an epiphany reinforces a decision we once made or reaffirms an action that we are following. Then there are those times when an epiphany dictates that we take an entirely different path than the one we are following. The Bible gives countless illustrations of epiphanies that changed lives and, in some instances, the very course of history. The Wise Men's instruction to take a different way home as told in Matt. 2 saved the life of the Christ child. Paul's call to come over into Macedonia was his epiphany that turned him from an eastward journey that would have taken him to the steppes of Russia to a westward journey that brought the gospel to Europe and ultimately to America. Just a small change that altered the course of history.

I. **"Arise! Shine! Your light has come" is the cry of the ancient prophet Isaiah to a distraught and downhearted people who had lost their sense of purpose.** Exile, strange customs, and distance from familiar practices and places had caused a darkness to settle over the Israelites, snuffing out their hope for a better day. Then comes Isaiah's revelation, his epiphany, letting the distressed and lost people know that they have not been abandoned, that the Lord they thought had forgotten them was still with them, shining through their darkness in all his resplendent glory. These people of slavery would once again be restored, become a beacon of light guiding nations to a higher destiny. Restoration of their land would draw Israelites from the corners of the earth. Once again riches would flow into their midst, and their light of influence would grow ever stronger. Such was Isaiah's epiphany that gave heart, hope, and determination to God's people who walked in darkness (Isa. 60:1–6).

The fulfillment of Isaiah's epiphany found its complete expression in the coming of the Lord Christ. In him the Wise Men discover the lasting light of eternal hope in all its brightness. The revelation of Jesus to these seeking Gentiles is the epiphany of the waiting world struggling in its darkness and at last hearing clearly those ancient words, "Arise, Shine! Your light has come!"

II. **Our world is not so different from that of Isaiah's time or the world of the Wise Men.** There is a darkness that consumes many people and many areas of the world today. Cries from desperate hearts can be heard everywhere. The darkness of the times, like that of past ages, finds its origin in the sins of greed, lust for power, abandonment of faith, and a host of other related causes. While the physical sun continues to rise and set, abandonment of God's wisdom, guidance, love, forgiveness, and chastisement has caused the presence of the Son of God to be dimmed. In some areas the light of the Son has been not only dimmed but even snuffed out like a candle blown out by strong winds.

Like the Israelites of another era, people of this age cry into the frightening darkness that blackens their life, "Watchman, what of the night?" (Isa. 21:11–12). With these ancient kinsmen, people today peer into the darkness looking for the dawn of hope. In that other time, the watchman on the wall turned his eyes to the east and cried that the night was passing and the dawn was rising faintly. Surely it would reveal the glory of a new day.

Who are the watchmen on the wall of our time? Who is shouting into the darkness of our day, "Arise! Shine! Your light has come"? Who are the bearers of good news who declare that the Son of Righteousness has risen with healing in his wings?

Are not the followers of Jesus the watchmen? Are not his modern-day disciples the bearers of the good news that the dawn has come, and with it the darkness is shattered and is passing? If this is true, and it is true, how do individual followers as well as the corporate body of believers make this good news known to our darkened world?

It must begin with we who are believers in Christ recognizing that we are not the source of the light that scatters the darkness of sin and evil and shows life and love and hope to people walking in darkness; we only *reflect* the greater light generated by Jesus who is the light of the world (John 8:12). Each follower of Jesus must be brave enough to reflect Christ's light and to join with other determined followers so that together they reflect the glory of God.

Then we are to shine in the midst of darkness. We are told by Jesus that we are to "let your light so shine that men may see your good works and glorify your Father in heaven" (Matt. 5:14). Good works and shining light must go together for our works to testify to the eternal glory of God.

We illuminate the darkness when we stoop to another's lowliest need, bend to someone's faintest cry, and reach to support the falling wounded in Christ's spirit of caring and love. The reflected light that we cast on the shadow world can and does give hope and freedom. It opens the door that leads out of the darkness into his glorious light.

III. **The other truth of which we must be aware is that we attract others to the light we reflect against the darkness.** As an outdoor light draws the attention of night insects, so light shining into the dark night of someone's life draws that person's attention and usually his or her presence. That is especially true if at the source of light, the person finds comfort, acceptance, forgiveness, healing, and love. Are not these attributes of his grace the proof of salvation from the devastating darkness in which so many have found themselves and from which they have been set free in Christ? If you and I simply accept the joyous responsibility of reaching out to others in their need, no matter how small or great, we will send out light that will attract them to the light of the world.

"Arise, shine! Your light has come and the glory of the Lord has shined upon you." Now go, "let your light so shine before men that they may see your good works and glorify your Father which is in heaven." Go out, be someone's epiphany today!—Henry Fields

ILLUSTRATIONS

Broken mirrors. Perhaps the saddest thing about Christians and among Christians is that there is more division than togetherness. Between denominations and, sadly, within denominations, division is rampant. We are to be mirrors of the truth and light that Christ brought to the world, offering a clear vision of who he is and all he can bring to every life that will make it whole. Yet we are too often more like cracked or shattered looking glasses offering a distorted picture of him that is more repulsive than appealing. Could that be the basic reason the church finds itself conforming to the ways of society instead of being a change agent in society? Could the distorted, broken picture people see when they are seeking a steady, clear vision offering wholeness be what is driving many people into other avenues seeking what the church has, but fails to deliver?

Only as each of us and all of us together commit to knowing Christ, letting him shine in us and through us, can the "light of the world" ably be seen in all his beauty and love for every person coming into the world.—Henry Fields

Light. In *Nine O'clock in the Morning*, Dennis Bennett tells of his wife's comment after meeting several Christians who had experienced God in a new and powerful way.[1] There was something about them that made her want to be like them. Christianity at its best has an attractiveness that can't be denied. Like the Magi of old, we are drawn to the light!—Lee McGlone

Musical Selections Appropriate to the Day

Isa. 60:1–6	*Come, Thou Almighty King*
Ps. 72:1–7, 10–14	*Jesus Shall Reign*
Eph. 3:1–12	*Make Me a Servant*
Matt. 2:1–12	*We Three Kings of Orient Are*

✺ Children's Lectionary Sermon

TITLE: A New Year's Resolution
SCRIPTURE: Ps. 72:1–7

---

[1]Dennis Bennett, *Nine O'clock in the Morning* (Gainesville, FL: Bridge-Logos, 1970).

KEY VERSES: *Please help the king be honest and fair just like you, our God. . . . Let the king defend the poor, rescue the homeless, and crush everyone who hurts them.* (Ps. 72:1–2, 4, CEV)

KEY CONCEPT: God's people should pray for their leaders.

MATERIALS: Bible

PREPARATION: Perhaps there is a current event, local or global, that may be an example of a leader's need for prayer to make wise decisions. Be aware of the current events that could be used with this sermon.

Happy New Year! Many people think of the new year as a time to make changes, to do things differently. They make New Year's resolutions or promises to themselves, promises like exercising more or eating healthier food or watching less television or making better grades in math. Have you made a New Year's resolution? Even if you have, here's one more I hope you will consider making.

I wonder what our world would be like on December 31, 2011, if every believer made and kept the same New Year's resolution: to pray daily for our leaders and decision makers. James 5:16 tells us that a believer's prayer has power and can help. Who are some leaders for whom we can pray? (*Accept suggestions from the group and add, as needed, to be sure the list includes church, community, national, and world leaders.*)

How should we pray? Certainly we'd ask God to bless our leaders with good health, energy, and strength. We'd ask God to keep them safe. We'd pray that leaders will feel God's presence and will trust God to guide their decisions.

(*Open Bible.*) Thousands of years ago, a Hebrew psalmist wrote a prayer for the king, the leader. *Please help the king be honest and fair just like you, our God,* wrote the psalmist. *Let the king defend the poor, rescue the homeless, and crush everyone who hurts them,* the psalmist continues. Using this example, we should pray that our leaders' decisions will be fair to everyone, especially poor people and people who are unable to speak up for themselves. We can pray that our leaders will ask God for guidance.

How do you think your school principal and our state governor and our president would feel knowing that your New Year's resolution is to pray for them every day? (*Pray with the children.*)—Sandra Canipe

❧ WORSHIP AIDS ❧

Call to Worship: "I am Alpha and Omega," says the Lord God, "who is, and who was, and who is to come, the Almighty" (Rev. 1:8, NIV).

Invocation: Father, Lord of creation, we thank you and honor you for what we know of you through the world of our senses. Yet we realize that your creation speaks clearly to us only as we have first known you through your Son, Jesus Christ our Lord. We trust you and offer ourselves to you as we worship. May our voices speak clearly our devotion to you as they blend with the music of the spheres. Father, we pray for your perfect will to be done among us. Amen.

Offertory Sentence: "From what you have, take an offering for the Lord. Everyone who is willing, bring to the Lord an offering of gold, silver, and bronze" (Exod. 35:5, NIV).

Offertory Prayer: Lord, your generosity is made known to us each day. You bless us beyond our deserving. Now we joyfully return to you our gifts of tithes and offerings and ask that they be multiplied for the building of your Kingdom. We joyfully bless your Holy Name. Amen.

Morning Prayer: (Prayer for New Beginnings) Sovereign and holy Creator God, Master Jesus, Comforter Spirit, you are the source of all things, the fountain of all wisdom, the poet-author of all knowledge, the illuminator of all understanding, the architect of reality. You are the Word of truth—the resolution to all eternal questions and the refining fire for our own overly self-confident imaginations.

We who preach find ourselves here again, facing streams of thought given shape, through the stain of ink on page, the order of line on screen, word spoken and heard. These bundles of word-images make us glad to be alive, cause us to question and speculate, doubt and believe. They give us strength for the day and joy for the night. We ask for discernment in separating wheat from chaff, vision to distinguish truth from less-than-truth, the ability to listen so that beauty and dignity and wonder make more sense to us than unrepentant anger or arrogant pretensions.

Teach us to measure our words as you have measured your own—that which you say is that which you will do. Father of all lights, may the pursuit of knowledge cause us to choose servanthood over mere information, choose gratitude over recognition, and prefer your soon-to-be-fulfilled Kingdom rather than our own. Like Jesus—your Son, our Savior—may we be gracious and patient, yet radically courageous and unwilling to acquiesce to any offer that is not the Father's divine will. By Holy Spirit weave us, threadlike, into the fabric of your Church, joining those who have gone before us in the faith, faithfully blazing the path for those who will come after us.

Above, underneath, and surrounding it all, you have called us to worship you in spirit and truth—so we join as one to offer all our hearts, all our souls, and all our strength to honor the one who is, and who was, and who is to come, even the Lord God Almighty. Yours is the glory, yours and yours alone. We long for the coming again of your Christ, and make these petitions before you today through him. Amen.—Rob Hewell

Benediction: We praise you, our God, whom we have served this past year and whom we will serve and praise this year, and whom we will serve and praise all our days, in the name of Jesus. Amen.—E. Lee Phillips

SUNDAY, JANUARY 9, 2011
First Sunday after Epiphany

LECTIONARY SERMON TOPIC: "Peter, Cornelius, and Us"
TEXT: Acts 10:34–43
OTHER READINGS: Isa. 42:1–9; Ps. 29; Matt. 3:13–17

He had grown up in a strong religious atmosphere. All of his life he had likely obeyed the legalities of the Jewish faith to the best of his ability. There were likely times when he ignored the rules. Don't we all? Yet the laws and customs of his people were so ingrained in him that he would never willingly and permanently abandon their keeping. That is, until the Apostle Peter runs head-on into an encounter with God described in chapter 10 of the Acts.

Dietary laws had been drilled into him from his earliest years. Who knows how many times he had heard a parent chasten him for playing with an unclean creature or perhaps entering the house of an unclean Gentile friend. When such things happened, only rigorous, special cleansing could restore the sinner to ceremonial acceptance and rightful worship. You just didn't eat legally unclean food as prescribed by Levitical law or associate with the unclean Gentiles who lived outside the law.

That Peter lives in us today. We reject much of the food that foreigners eat because it is not accepted in our culture. We place people of races, languages, colors, and education levels different from us in the unacceptable category. Peter, your pre-Acts chapter 10 spirit is alive and well in our religious world and culture of today.

I. **Peter was about to have an epiphany, and for him, change was on the way.** Hungry during his prayer time, which he observed on a flat rooftop where he could find privacy, Peter, in a trance, experienced God showing and telling him that what he has made, every rejected beast and creepy crawly thing, is clean, acceptable as food. Surely this blows Peter's mind. What does it mean? He is about to find out.

While he ponders this vision, he hears a knock at the gate. (Gentiles did not cross Jewish thresholds either.) When Peter answers the knock at the gate, he discovers a delegation of Gentiles waiting for him with a request that he accompany them to the house of their master, Cornelius. Peter begins to understand his housetop vision—namely, that Gentiles are as good as Jews and are acceptable as equals in God's sight (Acts 10:17–22).

II. **Cornelius, to whose home Peter is summoned or invited, was a Roman army officer in charge of one hundred troops.** He feared God and was highly respected by his troops and local civilians alike. Although he had what we might call the good life, he did not feel complete. Something was missing. There was a God-shaped blank in his life. Having heard of Jesus' grace and promise of salvation, he wondered if Peter, who proclaimed this message, could have the answer Cornelius sought. So, crossing the Jew-Gentile racial barrier, having seen for the first time the equality of all of God's children, Peter took the final step of faith resulting from his house-top vision. Crossing the threshold into Cornelius's house, Peter the Jew shared the good news, the gospel, with Cornelius the Gentile and welcomed him as the first Gentile convert into the movement of Christ, the Church.

III. **What did Peter say to Cornelius that changed Cornelius's life?** After accepting Cornelius's gracious invitation as issued by his servants sent to escort Peter to Cornelius's home, Peter began his speech by acknowledging that he now accepted the truth that to God every person is the same in his sight and that God accepts anyone who worships him and does what is right. It makes no difference what country or culture a person comes from; that is not important. The important thing is that all people hear and understand the message of good news that God sent to the people of Israel. That message is the good news that peace, forgiveness, and salvation have come through Jesus Christ. Such good news is for all people. The Jews who first received it are simply the vehicles through whom it is to be proclaimed to everyone everywhere.

Then, in a few words, Peter reminded Cornelius and his household of the things they had heard about Jesus. He spoke of how it all began in Galilee when Jesus, seen as the deliverer of the people, filled with the Holy Spirit went everywhere doing what is good and right for all people. He healed people by driving out the demons that claimed them, by cleansing them of their running sores and crippling diseases, by calling them from their sinful actions and forgiving them of their sins, and by restoring them to wholeness with God and themselves and loved ones and community. He did all these things because God was with him and in him. Peter went on to declare that those who followed Jesus saw all of this personally as they followed him through Judea and into Jerusalem.

They also were there and saw how he was arrested, tried in mockery, and crucified by those who opposed him. But they also were there when on the third day he arose from the dead, raised from the grave by the power of the same God who had been with him all during his journey through earth life and was still with him when earth life was ended. Although he was not seen by all the people, those whom God had chosen ate and drank with him, talked and walked with him after he was raised from the dead. The ones who did this became the witnesses to all that happened. They were the ones who have been commissioned to declare what they had heard, what they had seen, and what they had experienced so that others might believe and join the company of the committed through forgiveness, salvation, and the grace given by God through Christ Jesus. The witnesses of Jesus' Resurrection were to tell that Jesus is the one chosen by God to be the judge of the living and the dead. All those who believe in Jesus, choose to follow him, and receive his salvation will be forgiven of their sins, for God will forgive them through Jesus (Acts 10:34–43). That day Cornelius and his household experienced the coming of the Holy Spirit, were baptized, and became the first Gentiles to enter the body of believers.

IV. **What does this ancient story say to twenty-first-century people like us?** It says that in our emptiness, our clamor for things that do not satisfy, our sinfulness, our spiritual brokenness, our loneliness, and our wandering about in despair and hopelessness, we would do well to listen to the witness of Peter. The good news he brought to Cornelius and his people is still relevant in our day and age. For we too need the healing, the deliverance, the forgiveness, the salvation that only God in Christ can bring to us. We need life with meaning today and life that is eternal, not passing. Only as we possess such life can we live solidly in this time and all the time. Pray like Cornelius that we will be humble enough to seek the one who alone can fill the God-shaped blank in our lives and be brave enough to act on the truth Peter shared that changed Cornelius and his household forever.—Henry Fields

---

ILLUSTRATIONS

Freedom. It is a rich prescription for a rich man, designed to melt the lump in his throat and the knot in his stomach by dissolving the burden on his back, the hump that keeps banging into the lintel on the doorway to God. It is an invitation to become smaller and more agile by closing his accounts on earth and opening one in heaven so that his treasure is drawing interest inside that tiny gate instead of keeping him outside of it. It is a dare to him to become a new creature, defined in a new way, to trade in all the words that have described him up to now—wealthy, committed, cultured, responsible, educated, powerful, obedient—to trade them all in on one radically different word, which is free.—Barbara Brown Taylor[2]

Change. Thomas Wolfe wrote that you can't go back home again. In some ways he's right. We can't stay where our hearts have always been. Life is forever changing, and we are a part of the change. But perhaps we can do what Carlyle Marney suggested, that we can go back *through* home and accept all the stuff of our past, bad and good, which God has at his disposal for the shaping of our lives. God doesn't erase our past, but he gives us time, and grace, to receive it and be thankful for it, and the courage to rise high on the tiptoes of faith and to anticipate God at work in what is to come.—Lee McGlone

Musical Selections Appropriate to the Day

Isa. 42:1–9	*Open My Eyes*
Ps. 29	*O for a Thousand Tongues to Sing*
Acts 10:34–43	*Jesus Is Lord of All*
Matt. 3:13–17	*Come, Holy Spirit, Dove Divine*

✒ Children's Lectionary Sermon

TITLE: God's Power

SCRIPTURE: Ps. 29

KEY VERSE: *. . . honor the glory and power of the Lord!* (Ps. 29:1, CEV)

---

[2]Barbara Brown Taylor, *The Preaching Life* (Cambridge, MA: Cowley, 1992), pp. 121–126.

KEY CONCEPT: Now, as in ancient times, weather phenomena demonstrate God's power.

MATERIALS: Bible

PREPARATION: Be sensitive to the topic presented if you live in an area where children have been affected by destructive storms during which loss may have occurred.

Do you watch the Weather Channel? You can see some amazing things: wild lightning strikes, funnel clouds touching down as tornadoes, high hurricane winds. Using weather satellites, computers, and other instruments, meteorologists—the people who study weather—have an idea several days in advance of what kind of weather is coming our way. They tell us what to expect, and we make plans in response: a quick trip to the grocery store for milk and bread when a winter storm is expected, or planning a hike when warm, sunny days are forecast for the weekend. Although meteorologists can predict weather, only God controls weather. Only God controls blinding snowstorms, hurricanes with wind and drenching rain, fast-moving tornadoes. God is powerful; no one can do what God does.

(*Open Bible.*) Psalm 29, written thousands of years ago, is a poem praising God's power shown in weather. The psalmist writes, *The glorious Lord God thunders above the roar of the raging sea, and his voice is mighty and marvelous.* Could the psalmist be describing thunder? *The voice of the Lord destroys the cedar trees.* Is the psalmist saying that powerful lightning, which goes with thunder, can break even huge cedar trees? *Forests are stripped of leaves*, the psalmist says. Did a mighty wind twist and bend the trees? *God makes Mount Lebanon skip like a calf and Mount Hermon jump like a wild ox*, writes the psalmist. Are these words describing an earthquake?

The long-ago writer of Psalm 29 heard, saw, and felt God's power in the weather God sent. Thousands of years later, God sends weather to show us, too, that nothing is more powerful than God. "Wow, awesome!" we say, shielding our eyes from sunlight off high banks of new snow. "Wow" and "awesome" in the psalmist's words mean *honor the glory and power of the Lord!*—Sandra Canipe

☙ WORSHIP AIDS ☙

Call to Worship: "I sought the Lord, and he answered me; he delivered me from all my fears" (Ps. 34:4, NIV).

Invocation: Lord, we recognize your presence among us as we worship. You are in the singing and the prayers, the sermon and the offering, the silence and the sounds, in the fellowship we share, and in the joys and the burdens we bring. Bless this hour together. May we experience you again as our mighty God—and dearest friend. Amen.

Offertory Sentence: "The King will reply, 'I tell you the truth, whatever you did for one of the least of these brothers of mine, you did for me'" (Matt. 25:40, NIV).

Offertory Prayer: Dearest Father, open our eyes that we may see the impact for good our gifts will bring. Use these tithes and offerings to minister to the hidden Christ in each of us. And may spirits be enriched in the giving. Amen.

Morning Prayer: Father, today we bring to you our hopes and needs. We want to walk more closely in your way, but confess our sins and inadequacies. Give us grace to be strong in faith. Breathe your spirit upon us. Let us sense your guidance all along the way. Enable us to see the hurts and needs of others around us. Breathe within us the breath of your joy. Free us from the chains that bind us to the past. Open our eyes today to what we can become through Jesus Christ, who suffered and died for us and lives again. We offer this prayer in his name. Amen.—Lee McGlone

Benediction: As we celebrate the beginning of a new year, let us go forth determined to make the most of it. And may God be praised!—Lee McGlone

SUNDAY, JANUARY 16, 2011
Second Sunday after Epiphany

LECTIONARY SERMON TOPIC: "John the Baptist: Epiphany Concerning Jesus"
TEXT: John 1:29–42
OTHER READINGS: Isa. 49:1–7; Ps. 40:1–11; 1 Cor. 1:1–9

Everything has a beginning. Some beginnings are spectacular. Others are so low key that a gifted observer is required to interpret events so that others will know that a significant movement has begun. Such is what happened when Jesus moved from private citizen to spiritual, social, and life changer for all people through the ages.

John the gospel writer records for us how John the Baptist becomes the interpreter of the beginning of the new age inaugurated by Jesus. The Baptist likely knew his cousin Jesus long before Jesus came to him for baptism. Although the Baptist knew him as a part of his extended family, he did not fully recognize who Jesus actually was until through God's revelation he understood that Jesus was the promised one of God, the Messiah. The gospel writer tells of John the Baptist preaching repentance and baptizing those who came to hear this prophetic preacher and to be a part of the growing "back to God" movement. Jesus was among them. At first, the Baptist does not single out Jesus for public recognition. Divine revelation allows John to identify Jesus as the long-awaited promised Messiah. It seems that the first day of the Baptist's evangelistic crusade at the Jordan was spent letting religious leaders know that John himself was not the Messiah but only the forerunner setting the stage for the coming redeemer.

I. Perhaps it is after Jesus' baptism and temptation in the wilderness, just when Jesus is ready to begin his destined work in the world, that John introduces Jesus as none other than the Lamb of God (v. 29). This identification can be interpreted several ways. Some would interpret John's introduction of Jesus as the sacrificial Passover lamb whose shed blood protected God's people from the terror of the death angel down in Egyptian captivity. In truth Jesus does take the sting out of death, removes the fear of death, and replaces that fear with the promise of eternal life. In a very real sense, his shed blood does protect every Christian from death's grip and fear.

Others would see the Lamb of God in relation to the sacrifice of a lamb every morning and evening at the temple altar to deliver the people from their sins. Jesus is the sacrifice made for the sins of the people. But his sacrifice never needs repeating. It is a once-for-all-time sacrifice that makes null and void the necessity of a constant twice daily sacrifice to cover the sins of the people. Still others would see the Lamb of God as a fulfillment of prophetic utterances by Isaiah and others as being the one who by his suffering and sacrifice would redeem God's people (Isa. 53:7).

II. **John the Baptist next turns his witness to an explanation as to how he knew that Jesus is the Lamb of God who takes away the sin of the world.** By God's instruction, John was to look for the one on whom the Spirit comes and remains. This one will baptize not with water but with the Holy Spirit. John declared that he saw the Spirit come like a descending dove upon Jesus to identify him as the Son of God (vv. 32–34). Doves held an important place in Jewish religion. They have been called "the sacred bird." They are the only member of the avian family to be designated for sacrificial use. They were not to be used for food. Through the years, I have listened to the soft, haunting call of the mourning dove and have watched as it comes to the bird feeder. It does not fly to the feeder and land as other birds do. Instead it flies in, hovers over the perch, and with a gentle flapping of its wings, settles on the perch.

John the Baptist indicates that the Spirit did not at his baptism strike Jesus like a lightning bolt. Rather, like a dove gently settling on its perch, the Spirit came to Jesus. It did not come upon Jesus as it did to so many prophets and leaders of the Old Testament. For them the Spirit seems to have come and inspired them for a special message or empowered them for a special act. Then the Spirit left them until another task of God was theirs to perform. The Spirit came and dwelt in Jesus. The gospel writer goes out of his way to twice declare the permanence of the Spirit in Jesus. He plainly says the Spirit stayed, abided, dwelt in Jesus (vv. 32–33). In other words, it is as if the Spirit were a permanent resident in Jesus.

The Spirit of God coming upon Jesus indicates three great truths that made Jesus known as uniquely the Son of God. The Spirit, like the wind that the Hebrews called *ruach*, declares power. All of us know of the power of the wind. We have seen its path of destruction when harnessed in a tornado or hurricane. John says that power of untapped proportions dwelt in Jesus, who was filled with the Spirit of God.

The Spirit is the source of life. We preach and believe that Jesus is the source of life and brings life to all mankind. In the prologue to his gospel, John the writer clearly says, "In Him was life and that life was the light for all people" (John 1:4). It would be by the Spirit John the Baptist saw settling upon Jesus that men and women would know that Jesus is life. The Spirit is God. When the Spirit descended upon Jesus, it was to clearly declare that "here is God in your midst." The Spirit meant this for John: "God has come among you. He abides in this man you know as Jesus. Through Jesus you will see the power of God revealed. You will discover life as you have never known it. You will find God fully revealed as he is." The baptism of Jesus was certainly not just a traditional Jewish ceremony of cleansing. It was the proclamation that the Spirit and power of God had fully come to the world in his Son, Jesus.

III. **When we, like those who first heard John the Baptist, choose to follow Jesus, we experience the power of God's Spirit in Jesus to forgive our sins, save us, cleanse us of all unrighteousness, and set us free from the burden of guilt that sin brings.** We are given the power to live triumphantly in Christ's fashion and to serve in his spirit. We are filled with his courage, understand his truth, and are empowered to share that truth with others using our God-endowed talents and abilities. When we allow Jesus Christ to be Lord of all that we do, his spirit fills us, guides us, and makes us into new creations fit for his Kingdom and service. And all this revelation began when Jesus came to John to be baptized! —Henry Fields

ILLUSTRATIONS

Lamb of God. Then there would be those who would remember the remote idea that a horned lamb was a symbol of a mighty conqueror. This idea arose in the period between the Old and New Testaments when the Macabees ruled Israel. In that interbiblical period, Judas Maccabeus, Samuel, David, and Solomon are described as horned lambs, mighty conquerors. This view of the Lamb of God does not represent a weak, helpless animal destined for sacrifice, but rather a conquering champion who defeats the enemy by God's power. Jesus could readily fit this picture, as he is the one who conquered the enemy of sin that brings death. John the Baptist's succinct introduction of Jesus as the "Lamb of God who takes away the sin of the world" quite ably describes all aspects of God's Lamb, no matter what the hearers heard.—Henry Fields

Incarnation. Profound thought sometimes comes from unlikely places. While discussing the baptism of Jesus with a college class, one student suddenly seemed to get the idea of the subject. He said, "God, the Spirit, and Jesus are one, right? So God was in Jesus to show the world what God is really like, and Jesus reveals the Spirit person of the trinity to us so we can become what God wants us to be. God couldn't do it without Jesus and the Spirit. That's awesome!" Perhaps there are a lot of theological holes in that thinking, but in a way a profound thought had begun its work in the life of one young man. He was much closer to the meaning of Jesus' incarnation than he had been at the beginning of the class!—Henry Fields

Musical Selections Appropriate to the Day

Isa. 49:1–7	*Great Is Thy Faithfulness*
Ps. 40:1–11	*Blessed Assurance, Jesus Is Mine*
1 Cor. 1:1–9	*Amazing Grace*
John 1:29–42	*The Summons*

ᔕ Children's Lectionary Sermon

TITLE: A Prayer Answered

SCRIPTURE: Ps. 40:1–11

KEY VERSE: *I waited patiently, Lord, for you to hear my prayer. You listened.* (Ps. 40:1, CEV)

KEY CONCEPT: God hears us when we pray.

MATERIALS: Bible

Susan has two children: Will, age five; and Kayla, age three. She is a nurse at the local hospital. Since Will started kindergarten in September, Susan has just enough time after Will's bus comes to get Kayla to child care and herself to the hospital before her shift begins.

Susan's supervisor, noticing her good work, has offered Susan a new position with more hours, more responsibility, and more money. Susan is thankful for this opportunity. As a single mom, she really needs the extra pay. But working more hours means she will need to be at the hospital by seven in the morning, an hour before Will's bus comes to their house. Susan has a week to decide about accepting the new position.

"Dear God," Susan prays, "thank you for this job opportunity. I know this is your way of providing for our family. If I take the job, what shall I do about Will? I can't leave him at home alone until his bus comes." Susan prays this prayer often as she struggles toward a decision. On Sunday, the phone rings as Susan and the children are leaving for church. Mrs. Tate, who lives on the corner, needs a ride. Her car won't start. Driving to church, Susan tells Mrs. Tate about her job offer and about the early-morning scheduling problem with Will's bus.

"Susan, bring Will to me. He can wait for the bus at my house," Mrs. Tate says. "I'm an early riser who'd love company in the morning." "Thank you, Mrs. Tate. You are an answer to prayer," Susan replies. "And thank you, God, for giving me the answer," Susan says silently.

Susan prayed to God, and God heard her prayer. God answered her prayer (Open Bible.) *I patiently waited, Lord, for you to hear my prayer. You listened . . . and you gave me a new song, a song of praise to you,* writes the psalmist. We can be sure God hears our prayers, and we can be thankful.—Sandra Canipe

❧ WORSHIP AIDS ❧

Call to Worship: "All of you, clothe yourselves with humility toward one another, because God opposes the proud but gives grace to the humble" (1 Pet. 5:5b, NIV).

Invocation: Dearest God, only you are worthy of worship. To you all praise is due. Your holiness calls us to be holy. We praise you for your glorious redemption, that which comes through Jesus Christ. Let now your Holy Spirit breathe on us that we may worship in spirit and in truth. Amen.

Offertory Sentence: "Ascribe to the Lord, O families of nations, ascribe to the Lord glory and strength. Ascribe to the Lord the glory due his name; bring an offering and come into his courts" (Ps. 96:7–8, NIV).

Offertory Prayer: Creator God, all that is exists because of you. You are the owner of all the earth. The cattle on a thousand hills are yours—and too the hills. May the offerings we bring praise you here in this place and wherever your word is loved, taught, and preached. Amen.

Morning Prayer: Father, we thank you for being our Good Shepherd, our protector, our defender. Help us daily to grow in grace so that we may have a greater appreciation of who you are and how you love all of humankind. Encourage us to love all people—just as you do. Grant your help to the oppressed of the earth, those who hunger, those who suffer racial discrimination, and those who live under unjust political regimes. Make us more sensitive to you and to one another. Bring us to humility and boldness. Give us the courage to be merciful, the endurance to be faithful, and the readiness to speak boldly for you. It is in the name of the one true and everlasting God, Father, Son, and Holy Spirit that we pray. Amen.—Lee McGlone

Benediction: Now may our God, whom we know as Father, Son, and Holy Spirit, walk with us in the days of this week. And may we heed his direction and the opportunities for service placed daily before us. Amen.

SUNDAY, JANUARY 23, 2011
Third Sunday after Epiphany

LECTIONARY SERMON TOPIC: "To Whom Do You Belong?"
TEXT: 1 Cor. 1:10–18
OTHER READINGS: Isa. 9:1–4; Ps. 27:1, 4–9; Matt. 4:12–23

Corinth had long been a great city, the world crossroads of the Mediterranean. For Greece, its original builder, it was a port providing a safe route from north to south for travel and trade. Not long after its establishment it became one of the greatest trading centers of the ancient world. Whereas the north-south traffic of Greece passed through Corinth of necessity, the greater part of Mediterranean east-west traffic chose to take the Corinth route to bypass the deadly Cape Males.

Corinth acquired a dual personality and thus a dual reputation. Commerce spurred wealth, culture, and business opportunity that turned the city and surrounding area into a highly prosperous region that became a mecca for different cultures and races of people.

The dark, immoral side was fostered by the presence of pagan temples, especially the temple of Aphrodite sitting in its splendor overlooking the harbor and city from its perch on the Acropolis. Each night the one thousand priestesses, who were sacred prostitutes, descended into the city to ply their trade. Other vices followed, enhancing Corinth's reputation for corruption.

In 146 BC, the Romans invaded Greece and, to isolate the country, destroyed Corinth. One hundred years later, Julius Caesar rebuilt the city as a Roman colony. Prosperity and corruption returned. Again the population became cosmopolitan, including a large contingent of Jews, retired Roman soldiers and their families, people from the east with exotic customs, Greek adventurers, and others.

Corinth was not a place you would expect a Christian church to begin and thrive, yet in all the hodgepodge that was Corinth, one was established and seemed to flourish. The Apostle Paul seems to have personally spent about eighteen months with this church helping build a foundation for its continuing effectiveness. About 55 AD, while in Ephesus, he learned of deep trouble in the Corinthian church. Through a visit by servants from the house of Chole, a leading lady in the church, Paul learned the root of the problems and wrote what we know as 1 Corinthians to help solve the disturbing and divisive issues.

In our current church situation, when it seems that we emphasize more our differences than our commonalities, we need to hear Paul's strong words of advice and direction. Like those plaguing the church in Corinth, the differences we create around our limited understanding and interpretations can destroy us.

I. **1 Corinthians 1:10–17 is for us.** It deals with favoritism and misunderstanding among the various groups making up the fellowship of that early church congregation. Paul writes to them not as a schoolmaster who breathes punishment, but as an agent of reconciliation. He calls the members "brothers"—family members. He writes as one of them, not as an outsider who is ignorant of their situation. Thus he softens his rebuke while at the same time showing how wrong and painful their divisions really are. Love words rather than condemnatory phrases can change attitudes and practices faster than harshness and threats.

Paul urges the Corinthian Christians to solve their differences, knit their lives and the life of the fellowship back together, and, in a hostile environmental setting, present a united front by serving together in unity and love.

II. **What divisions does Paul address?** He names four groups that are exalting certain preachers rather than the Lord. Factions have formed around certain former leaders in the church, with each group being named after their favorite messenger, though the messengers did not start or encourage any factions or groups.

There is the Pauline group who follow Paul himself. These would likely be those who were converted under Paul's preaching and therefore feel a love and loyalty for him because of what he brought to them and how his message changed their lives.

Others committed their loyalty to Apollos, the eloquent, learned graduate of the University of Alexandria in Egypt, whose logic and golden-tongued speech enthralled many listeners. In the cosmopolitan culture of Corinth there would be many of Greek background in the infant Christian church. They, along with other Gentiles in the congregation, would be swayed by Apollos's eloquence and rhetorical style. Coming into the faith under his preaching, their loyalty would be to the gifted Apollos. Such eloquent and gifted preachers still do noble work among us. Like Apollos, they enthrall their listeners even as they proclaim the unsearchable riches of Christ. A bond of fierce loyalty binds listener and preacher almost to the exclusion of anyone else. Therein lies the danger.

Peter had his following in the Corinthian church. He was seen as the leader of the twelve apostles. Unlike Paul, he was not seen as simply an apostle to the Gentiles. It would not be uncommon for the Jewish members to cling to Peter because of the perception that he retained more of the true Jewish spirit than did Paul. Thus his preaching in Corinth had fostered a following loyal to him.

Then there was a seemingly super-pious group who arrogantly said in effect, "We are the real Christ party." Perhaps in their understanding of the Lord they had outdistanced all other groups in the church. But rather than seeking to help their fellow Christian family members understand the need to exalt Jesus as Lord, they looked down on all who gave loyalty to others as their hero leaders. Such a super-pious attitude has no place in Christ's church. It becomes a point of separation rather than a path to unity. Even to this day there are groups of Christ's followers who pityingly look down on other groups of followers. This happens when any person or any group sees itself as more loved by and attached to Christ than anyone else.

III. **So where does all of this leave us today?** What does Paul's message to the ancient church say to us? Misplaced loyalty, then as now, leads to division. Where there are cliques or groups that exist within the church, more effort is spent nurturing the clique than in building the church as a whole. The longer such activity and emphasis go on, the wider the divisions, until unity is lost.

Division leads to an arrogant attitude. The more we emphasize how right we are, the more wrong we see others as being. Continuing to follow such a spirit leads to seeing those outside our clique as inferior and unworthy of our concern and love. In such an atmosphere, the church body begins to crumble, and walls of separation are erected rather than torn down.

In such a setting, Christ cannot be glorified. His body, the church, is painfully divided, and he is not Lord at all. The appeal of the church is ignored by outsiders, and the preaching of the cross becomes even more foolish to them who perish. In such a condition, the church is unable to be the power of God unto salvation for all people. Such power comes only when there is congregational unity and Christ is Lord of *all*.—Henry Fields

---

ILLUSTRATIONS

Attachments. Such attachments as Paul wrote of here are still relevant today. More than fifty years separate me from the point of my conversion to Christ. Yet I still remember with great fondness and appreciation the fine minister who singled me out as a young boy to help me understand the need for the Savior. His gentle, kind preaching approach set the foundation for the remainder of my life, work, and practice. Many of us who were a part of the First Baptist Church of Augusta, Georgia, will forever retain a thankful and close connection and loyalty to that church and especially to the pastor of our conversion, Dr. Warren Huyck. So it was with some in Corinth who saw Paul as the one who claimed their loyalty.—Henry Fields

Memory. There is a French proverb that says, "Gratitude is the heart's memory." It suggests that as we recall the past, we are moved to thanksgiving. I realize I run the risk of being tuned out by many who believe that anything that happened more than twenty-five years ago is unimportant. But I'll take the risk. Memory is too important to take lightly. It has within it the ability to bless or to curse. One can just as easily grow cynical or bitter. So we must then *choose* how to handle our memories. And the best choice is to allow them to be for us the basis for gratitude.—Lee McGlone

Musical Selections Appropriate to the Day

Isa. 9:1–4	*Here I Am, Lord*
Ps. 27:1, 4–9	*Jesus, What a Friend for Sinners*
1 Cor. 1:10–18	*I Am Thine, O Lord*
Matt. 4:12–23	*Jesus Calls Us o'er the Tumult*

☙ Children's Lectionary Sermon

TITLE: He Has Called Us, Too

SCRIPTURE: Matt. 4:12–23

KEY VERSE: *Jesus said to them, "Come with me! I will teach you how to bring in people instead of fish."* (Matt. 4:19, CEV)

KEY CONCEPT: We are Jesus' disciples who can bring others to Jesus.

MATERIALS: Bible, map of Palestine during Jesus' ministry, words to song on poster board

PREPARATION: Print these words on poster board, folding up the bottom of the sheet to cover the refrain until the point indicated in the sermon. This listing of disciples is from Matthew 10:1–4:

> There were twelve disciples Jesus called to help him:
> Simon Peter, Andrew, James, his brother, John,
> Philip, Thomas, Matthew, James, the son of Alphaeus,
> Thaddaeus, Simon, Judas, and Bartholomew
> *Refrain* (*No need to print "Refrain," just leave a space.*)
> He has called us, too; he has called us, too.
> We are his disciples; I am one, and you. (*Sing refrain twice.*)

Matthew's gospel tells us that Jesus went to Galilee after John baptized him in the Jordan River. (*Show the Jordan River and Galilee on the map.*) Instead of going to Nazareth, his hometown, Jesus moved to Capernaum. (*Show these two towns.*) Capernaum is beside the Sea of Galilee. In Capernaum, Jesus began his ministry of telling people who God is and what God wants. (*Open Bible.*)

Matthew writes, *Then Jesus started preaching, "Turn back to God! The kingdom of heaven will soon be here."* Jesus needed to get this word to everyone.

What could Jesus do, since newspapers, telephone, television, e-mail—none of these ways to communicate were available to him? He found friends to help him spread the word. Walking beside the Sea of Galilee, Jesus saw Simon and Andrew, two fishing brothers. *"Come with me!"* Jesus invited. *"I will teach you how to bring in people instead of fish."* Farther along the shore, Jesus invited brothers James and John, also fishermen. They, too, went with Jesus. When Jesus finished his inviting, twelve men had left their usual work to come with Jesus.

What did Jesus do then? He went all over Galilee teaching, preaching about the Kingdom, and healing people who had all kinds of diseases and sickness. As the twelve men saw Jesus do these wonderful things, they must have wanted to know more about him. Jesus was glad to teach them.

What about us? The answer is in a song sung to "Bringing in the Sheaves," an old gospel song. Listen first and then I will let you sing with me. (*Display poster board with bottom folded up to cover refrain.*) The most important part is the refrain. (*Reveal the refrain.*) Let's sing this together. We are disciples, too. We can spread the news of God's Kingdom, too.—Sandra Canipe

❧ WORSHIP AIDS ❧

Call to Worship: "I know your deeds. See, I have placed before you an open door that no one can shut. I know that you have little strength, yet you have kept my word and have not denied my name" (Rev. 3:8, NIV).

Invocation: Lord, we gather to worship. We come as your children, sons and daughters every one, seeking to practice your presence, to know your will. Your Son, Jesus, promised, "Seek and you will find." We claim now that promise. Amen.

Offertory Sentence: "Tell the Israelites to bring me an offering. You are to receive the offering for me from each man whose heart prompts him to give" (Exod. 25:2, NIV).

Offertory Prayer: We come to you, Lord, as your children and bring these gifts as acts of devotion. May your name be praised. Bless these tithes and offerings that they will enhance the work of the gospel here and around the world. Amen.

Morning Prayer: As we gather before you today, Lord, we ask that you grant us faith like that of the disciples—that which called them to abandon everything and follow Christ. O, Lord, make us fishers of men. For our family and friends who are not believers, make us powerful witnesses to your glory. Let others see Jesus in us. O, Lord, make us fishers of men. For the lost in our communities, grant us your Spirit's boldness to proclaim the gospel so they may be added to your Kingdom. O, Lord, make us fishers of men. To the unbelievers of every tribe, tongue, and nation, send us out to spread the Word of life so that persons of all cultures will know and worship the Creator. O, Lord, make us fishers of men. Amen.—Nick Dawson

Benediction: Lord God, whom we know as Father, Son, and Holy Spirit, guide your people as we go out to serve in the days of this week. May our ways reflect the nature of Jesus Christ who lives within us. And fill our lives with your peace. Amen.

SUNDAY, JANUARY 30, 2011
Fourth Sunday after Epiphany

LECTIONARY SERMON TOPIC: "The Cross: Stumbling Block, Foolishness, or What?"
TEXT: 1 Cor. 1:18–31
OTHER READINGS: Mic. 6:1–8; Ps. 15; Matt. 5:1–12

In that first-century troublesome Corinthian church, Paul ran head-on into a church problem. Jews had come in, and evidently a goodly group wanted to incorporate their Jewish understanding of salvation and thereby greatly water down the meaning of the cross. Greeks arrived with their patterns of thought and sometimes convoluted philosophies, and wanted to impose their thoughts and ways on the church, thus again diluting the power of the cross. Others were content, like many today, just to drift with the currents of the moment, never question anything, and get mired in a thin meaning of the cross.

In 1 Corinthians 1:18–25, Paul hits these attitudes fast and hard. He plainly declares to the Corinthian church and thereby the Church of the ages that man's wisdom and understanding can never figure out the truth of God's intent. The world is seeking God through various avenues and always has been. But despite man's effort and wisdom, God has never been found. Such a search declares man's helplessness. Only God can design a way through which he is fully revealed. That way points everyone to Christ on the cross. Paul interprets plainly and simply the meaning of the cross.

I. **He begins with the Jews. For Paul, the learned Jew is a natural starting place.** He knew from experience that the idea of God dying on a cross to reveal himself was to a devout Jew totally unacceptable. It still is unacceptable to folks who think they know a better way to discover God. Even with all the preaching in Paul's time that proclaimed that God's appointed time had come, the way of the cross was questioned. Early preaching certainly proclaimed that Jesus was the Son of God; that he was born, lived, and died to reveal God and fulfill Jewish prophecy; that Jesus will come again; and that you can know the God of Jesus by repenting and receiving the gift of the Holy Spirit. Still, Jews and others rejected the truth about the cross.

There were basically two reasons for this rejection. (1) Because Jesus ended up on a cross, he could not be the one chosen by God to reveal God to men. After all, they had the revealed law that said, "Cursed is the man who hangs on a tree" (Deut. 21:23). Not even Isaiah 53, the suffering servant chapter, could convince a Jew that Jesus was the chosen of God. (2) Signs were sought by the Jews as a revelation that God had chosen a person to reveal himself. They wanted startling and even shattering happenings.

Jesus didn't fill the bill here either. He was not flamboyant. In fact, the Jews looked on him as meek and lowly. Again and again at their challenge he rejected the spectacular, even when he was dying on the cross. He did not expect people to serve him as if he were a king. Instead he served others like a lowly slave, a stance the Jews could not accept as revelation of God. His challenge of Jewish ways, thoughts, and laws brought him death on the cross at their hands. All of this painted for the Jews an unacceptable picture of God's chosen one. To the Jews, the cross was a stumbling block.

II. **Paul further tells the Corinthian church that to the Greeks the cross is foolishness.** Maybe he was teaching a Sunday school class for Greeks and heard one voice that opinion. This idea of the cross as foolishness was born amid two views held by the Greeks, and sadly they are still held by many folks in our midst today.

The Greeks saw their gods as completely apathetic—unfeeling. They reasoned that if their gods could feel, then mankind was in control. Such control would make mankind greater than the gods. So they argued that the gods could not have feelings. You can see the dilemma for the Christian Church: the cross meant that God felt suffering. This was an unacceptable concept for the Greek.

Sadly, such an attitude abounds in our world today and has caused havoc even as it distorts truth. Hitler was a master at the craft of making the horrible into an acceptable norm. To a lesser but perhaps just as deadly degree, such happens in the church. Too many Christians have become intoxicated with fine words and intriguing but false interpretations of God's Word. Perhaps what we need is a resurgence of the strong, blunt message delivered by the unlettered preachers of Paul's time. To the Greek, the cross was foolishness. But God's foolishness is still wiser than the wisest man or woman, and God's weakness is stronger than all our combined strength.

III. **If the cross is not to be seen by present-day folks as a stumbling block or foolishness, what is its meaning for us?** First Corinthians 1:18–25 gives us the answer. Paul tells the Corinthian church that "the teaching of the cross seems foolish to those who are lost. But to those who are being saved it is the power of God" (v. 18). The wise were not chosen by God as the bearers of his good news. That privilege was reserved for lowly shepherds, smelly fishermen, and common folk. Because of their haughty intellectualism, the worldly wise would not grasp the simple and saving and transforming truth about the cross. Although some truly wise and learned people gladly accepted the message of God's love and salvation as exhibited by Christ's death on the cross, most followers were not powerful, highborn folks. They may seem foolish to the wise, but God chose the foolish things of the world, like a cross and lowly people, to put to shame those who were wise. As Paul puts it, "He chose the weak, despised things that have no importance to the world to bring to nothing the things that the world thinks important" (1 Cor. 1:25).

Through the foolishness of the cross, God made us part of Jesus Christ. It is because of Christ that we are right with God, freed from sin's grip and made different (holy) from those who do not know and accept Jesus as Savior and Lord. It is still the humble who, accepting the cross, confound the wise. It is still from the ranks of the worldly weak that God calls his messengers to overcome the strong. It is still the persons with open minds and receptive hearts who go out to change the world for the better as they yield themselves to the way and power of the cross. May we be included in their number.—Henry Fields

---

ILLUSTRATIONS

Church. Church people have a way of getting all mixed up about the reason for the Church. This usually happens because the central theme of the Church's message becomes lost among the various ideas of what is important to various groups. The Church of our day seems to have lost the central reason for its being. More energy, resources, and time are spent trying to turn the Church and its ministries into what we want them to be than is spent in the central focus of the Church, which is the cross. In recent times, I have heard more and more people asking in some form or fashion, "What can the Church do for me?" Wrong question! The real question is, "What can I do for the Church to help it proclaim to the world the unsearchable riches of Christ and the power of his cross for every person?"—Henry Fields

Wisdom and Foolishness. From the beginning, the Greeks sought wisdom. Gathered in the shadow of the Athenian Acropolis, those first Greek thinkers generated philosophies and argued ideas that still exist among us today. From those giant thinkers came the beginnings of our science, literature, government, art, culture, and the basic foundation of civilization as we know it. Those ancient Greek searchers after truth and meaning were wise and learned. They were described as "sophists": wise men. However, with the passing of time, wise men became those with the ability to be mental acrobats who used clever rhetoric to make what was bad seem good. A nimble, cunning brain and a golden tongue could and did sway multitudes, many times away from truth and honest searching. Whatever pleased the crowd became the message.—Henry Fields

Musical Selections Appropriate to the Day

Mic. 6:1–8	*What Does the Lord Require?*
Ps. 15	*Step by Step*
1 Cor. 1:18–31	*Be Thou My Vision*
Matt. 5:1–12	*Purer in Heart, O God*

ᕙ Children's Lectionary Sermon

TITLE: Remember and Do

SCRIPTURE: Ps. 15, Mic. 6:6–8, Matt. 5:1–12

KEY VERSE: *See that justice is done, let mercy be your first concern, and humbly obey your God.* (Mic. 6:8b, CEV)

KEY CONCEPT: In the Bible, God tells us many times what we should remember and do.

MATERIALS: Bible, chart tablet with blank paper, felt-tip marker, poster board

PREPARATION: Print these three directives, one below the other on the poster board: Obey God. Treat others fairly. Be kind to others.

When you are learning to spell a new word, you look at the word, say it aloud, spell it aloud, and write it several times. If you study piano, flute, violin, or another instrument, you play the same piece again and again until you learn it.

Our brains need to have new information repeated several times before we can remember it. Repetition helps us learn. Have you noticed that your parents repeat the things they really want you to learn and remember? Use your manners. Wash your hands. Buckle your seatbelt.

God knows that we need to hear the important things again and again if we are to remember them. (*Open Bible.*) Here's what God says in Psalm 15:1–3: *Who may stay in God's temple or live on the holy mountain of the Lord? Only those who obey God and do as they should. They speak the truth and don't spread gossip; they treat others fairly and don't say cruel things.* What does God want us to remember and do? (*Accept answers and record on chart paper.*)

The prophet Micah tells us what God wants us to remember and do. *See that justice is done, let mercy be your first concern, and humbly obey your God* (Mic. 6:8b). What is God saying in Micah that God said in Psalm 15? (*Accept answers and record on chart paper.*)

In Matthew 5:6–7, Jesus tells us what God wants us to remember and do. *God blesses those people who want to obey him. . . . God blesses those people who are merciful.* Are any of these ideas in Psalm 15 and in Micah's words?

A psalmist, a prophet, and Jesus—all three tell what God wants us to remember and do. Let's read together. (*Display prepared poster board and read with children.*)

Obey God.

Treat others fairly.

Be kind to others.—Sandra Canipe

❧ WORSHIP AIDS ❧

Call to Worship: "Blessed are those who wash their robes, that they may have the right to the tree of life and may go through the gates into the city" (Rev. 22:14, NIV).

Invocation: Father, we cannot worship you unless you put within us your praise. We cannot obey you unless the love of Christ constrains us. We confess that we are often cold in heart and ask that you kindle within us the flame of sacred love—that we may glorify your name. Amen.

Offertory Sentence: "Then he said to them all: 'If anyone would come after me, he must deny himself and take up his cross daily and follow me'" (Luke 9:23, NIV).

Offertory Prayer: Eternal God, ever living and ever giving, we rejoice that you have called us to partner with you in the work of redemption. Herein we find our purpose for living. May these offerings become extensions of our strength, may they enter into your purpose, and may they bring blessing wherever they are used. Amen.

Morning Prayer: God of grace, we worship in your presence this morning. How often would we practice brutality and do damage beyond repair to one another if we were not aware of the wonder of God's grace alive in life and abroad in the world? How unforgiving we would be toward one another if we forgot the power of forgiveness imbedded in your grace! How quickly the compassion needed among us would die, and the unmerited love necessary to create social sensibleness would disappear. Grace has touched our hearts and remolded them in godlike fashion. How could we but worship the God of grace and God of glory?

God of inward strength, we come to you this morning. Inner weakness so many times is the culprit causing outward wrongs to be done by us. We need the renewing of the inner person, the acquiring of a brave spirit, the power of godlike courage so that your strength will find its outlet to the world through us. This morning we ask for the indwelling power of your Spirit so that strength from beyond ourselves may flow into us and make us truly usable in doing truth and right in all circumstances we meet. In a world needing high moral, ethical, and spiritual strength, how could we not come to you, the giver of such strength?

So we are here in your presence this morning, seeking to offer praise, adoration, and worship fit for your glory. Pray, Father, take our time before you and give us the blessing you want us to have, even as we renew our commitments to follow him whom you gave to save the world and all of us. Amen.—Henry Fields

Benediction: May hearts gladdened with the good news of Jesus Christ lead us from this place. May the nature of our Lord, all loving and all good, be reflected in our choices. As we go, we surrender again to the one who lives and reigns forever. Amen.

SUNDAY, FEBRUARY 6, 2011
Fifth Sunday after Epiphany

LECTIONARY SERMON TOPIC: "Making Sure the Light Shines On"
TEXT: Matt. 5:13–20
OTHER READINGS: Isa. 58:1–9a (9b–12); Ps. 112:1–9 (10); 1 Cor. 2:1–12 (13–16)

In his book, *Behold I Do a New Thing,* C. Kirk Hadaway speaks of "*goal displacement*—a process by which the primary mission of an organization is replaced by operative goals that have little, if anything, to do with the organization's original reason for being. . . . It often happens that what an organization does has little to do with its purpose."[1]

I. **The point is illustrated by the story of the lighthouse that forgot what its purpose was.** In a quaint little seaside village, a lighthouse was built to be a lifesaving station. Its purpose was to warn sailors at sea and, in the unfortunate event of a shipwreck when ships didn't heed or could not see its warning because of dense fog, to help rescue those who crashed upon the rocks. Well, as time went by, there weren't many ships that needed its

---

[1]C. Kirk Hadaway, *Behold I Do a New Thing* (Cleveland: Pilgrim Press, 2001), pp. 7, 10.

lifesaving services, so the lighthouse devoted less and less energy to lighthouse activities. It soon became nothing more than a social gathering place for the village. Villagers would drop by to chat with the lighthouse keeper. On Friday and Saturday nights they would play Rook, or maybe strike up a band and have a dance, and on occasion hold an ugliest-dog-in-the-village contest. Before long, everyone had forgotten what the lighthouse's initial purpose really was—to be a lifesaving station to sailors at sea. And so, the light in the tower that gave the lighthouse its identity was allowed to burn out. Then when a ship crashed upon the rocks for lack of a warning light, the villagers were not prepared for the rescue. The lighthouse had become a place to have fun. But we all know that having fun is not what lighthouses are built for. And strictly speaking, neither are churches. Although we often have fun at churches, and *should* have fun at churches, we know deep in our hearts that having fun is not the primary purpose for which the church is built. Like the lighthouse, the church has a high purpose and calling. And every now and then it is good to take time to revisit what our real purpose is, for it is sometimes easy for churches to forget.

II. **It was the Hebrew prophet Isaiah who first instilled the vision that a primary purpose of God's people should be as "a light to the nations" (Isa. 42:1–9).** In fact, Eugene Peterson, in his contemporary translation of the Bible, *The Message*, renders verse 6 in Isaiah 42, "I have provided you as a lighthouse to the nations." Isaiah was speaking to God's people at a critical time in their history. There were political uncertainty, changes occurring in the world as they knew it, and spiritual soul-searching. It sort of sounds like what is going on in our world today, doesn't it? But all these changes also presented a wonderful opportunity for Israel to be a light to the nations by sharing the message of God, working for justice, and ministering to the oppressed. Israel had an unprecedented opportunity to provide much-needed instruction, be a religious guide, shed some light in the darkness, and give hope to a searching, wandering, suffering humanity.

III. **It is not surprising that Jesus drew from Isaiah's "light to the nations" imagery when he exhorted his followers to be "the light of the world."** Through personal and collective witness in the community; good works with the hungry, homeless, poor, and oppressed; and celebrative, transformative worship, the light of Christ can indeed shine forth from us.

I am reminded of the sign that is said to have been on a lamp outside Albert Schweitzer's jungle hospital in Africa. The sign said, "Here in whatever hour you come, you will find light and help and human kindness." So it should be with the church, a light to the community. And as put by Puritan preacher John Winthrop, in his sermon titled "A Model of Christian Charity," which he delivered to a group of Puritans as they crossed the Atlantic Ocean on their way to the Massachusetts Bay, "we must consider that we shall be as a city upon a hill." In other words, a light to the world.

As you know, for decades Hatteras Lighthouse on North Carolina's Outer Banks has served as a beacon of light, warning all passing ships of the treacherous shoreline that has been nicknamed "Graveyard of the Atlantic." But a few years ago, Hatteras Lighthouse reached a critical juncture in its history. Over time the ocean had eroded the shoreline so that the waves were lapping at the very base of the lighthouse itself, threatening to destroy it. But through a long, complicated, precision maneuver, Hatteras Lighthouse was actually moved inland, intact, about a half mile away from the shore. It is a fascinating story. Now firmly established again, Hatteras Lighthouse is poised to be a much-needed beacon of light for another hundred years or so.

IV. **Well, could all of this be a parable of sorts for the church we know and love?** In the past few years, I have come to realize that being the church in today's world is much more difficult than it was twenty years ago. Many congregations are declining in membership; others are closing their doors. The costs of keeping the church doors open are more than many small congregations can afford to bear. And for many people in America, the traditional church has become irrelevant. So there is a fair amount of weight riding on the decisions church leaders make. It is important that our churches have leadership that can help us navigate the challenges of the future. As with Hatteras Lighthouse, decisions that are made now can help ensure that our beloved church will continue to be a beacon of light—a city upon a hill—for decades to come. May the church we know and love continue strong as a lighthouse upon the shore and as a bright city upon the hill, if I may mix metaphors. As we consider our God-given purpose, seek discernment, and chart the course of the future, may the light of our church continue to shine brightly and never, never grow dim.—Randy Hammer

...

ILLUSTRATIONS

Christian Joy. The true joy of the Christian life belongs to the poor who have no security, no possessions to call their own, not even a foot of earth to call their home. No earthly society can claim their allegiance.—Dietrich Bonhoeffer[2]

Justice. Archbishop Desmond Tutu, during one of his encounters with the governmental defenders of South Africa's apartheid policies, reminded them that tyrants end up "on the flotsam and jetsam of history," that "the resurrection of our Lord and Savior declares for all to know that light will triumph over darkness, that goodness will triumph over evil, that justice will triumph over injustice, that freedom will triumph over tyranny. I stand before you as one who believes fervently what Paul wrote when he said, 'If God be for us, who can be against us?'"—Randy Hammer[3]

Musical Selections Appropriate to the Day

Isa. 58:1–9a (9b–12)	Guide Me, O Thou Great Jehovah
Ps. 112:1–10	Immortal, Invisible, God Only Wise
1 Cor. 2:1–12 (13–16)	I Worship You, Almighty God
Matt. 5:13–20	Firm Foundation

Children's Lectionary Sermon

TITLE: Let Your Light Shine
SCRIPTURE: Matt. 5:13–20
KEY VERSE: *"Make your light shine, so that others will see the good that you do and will praise your Father in heaven."* (Matt. 5:16, CEV)

---

[2]Dietrich Bonhoeffer, *The Cost of Discipleship* (New York: Macmillan, 1963), p. 120.
[3]Desmond Tutu, *Hope and Suffering* (Grand Rapids, MI: Eerdmans, 1984), p. 158.

KEY CONCEPT: "Making your light shine" means doing what Jesus would do.
MATERIALS: Bible, rubber band WWJD bracelet or other rubber band bracelets, nine- by twelve-inch poster board
PREPARATION: Print WWJD in large letters on the poster board.

Have you seen anyone wear a rubber band bracelet? Perhaps you have one. (*Display the bracelet.*) People wear these bracelets to show support for various good causes: cancer research, animal protection, and stopping world hunger, for example.

One type of rubber band bracelet is yellow with the letters WWJD pressed into the rubber. (*Display the WWJD poster board.*) "WWJD" are the first letters of "What Would Jesus Do?" Those letters on a bracelet remind the wearer to think of what Jesus would do in every situation and then to do likewise.

(*Open Bible.*) In Matthew 5, Jesus is teaching his disciples how to live God's way. *"You are like a light for the whole world. . . . A lamp is placed on a lampstand, where it can give light to everyone in the house,"* Jesus told them. *"Make your light shine, so that others will see the good that you do and will praise your Father in heaven"* (Matt. 5:14, 15b–16, CEV).

Do you think there is a connection between WWJD and "making your light shine"? When we do what is right and good, we are doing what Jesus would do. We are living God's way, making our lights shine.—Sandra Canipe

◈ WORSHIP AIDS ◈

Call to Worship: "He who was seated on the throne said, 'I am making everything new'" (Rev. 21:5, NIV).

Invocation: Holy God, as we pause to sing and pray in worship today, cause us to listen deeply, ponder thoughtfully, and commit wholeheartedly to the cause of our Lord Jesus Christ. Amen.—E. Lee Phillips

Offertory Sentence: "You will be my witnesses in Jerusalem, and in all Judea and Samaria, and to the ends of the earth" (Acts 1:8, NIV).

Offertory Prayer: Before you this morning we bring the symbols of our dedication to you, our steadfastness in following you, and our devotion to doing your work in the present world. Use these tithes and offerings to your glory even as we give them gladly in your name. Amen.—Henry Fields

Morning Prayer: God, you are bigger than anything in the universe! You reign over everything! You are the creator of all. You made the heavens and the earth. Lord, may we never replace you with worldly things, things that will not last. You are the true everlasting God, and your love goes on and on! We are amazed by your attributes, O Lord. You are love and you are wrath at the same time. You are beauty and simultaneously strength! We can never understand your glory and holiness. You are far more than we can comprehend. In this, we know that you are infinitely big enough, God, big enough to sustain, big enough to love, and big enough to save! Thank you, Lord, for saving us. It is through your son, Jesus Christ, who sits at your right hand, that we pray. Amen.—Tyler Burleson

Benediction: Because of our worship here, may the power of God embolden and empower you, deepen and expand you, enrich and energize you for all God has for you, until we meet again. Amen.—E. Lee Phillips

SUNDAY, FEBRUARY 13, 2011
Sixth Sunday after Epiphany

LECTIONARY SERMON TOPIC: "You Must Be Kidding, Lord!"
TEXT: Matt. 5:21–37
OTHER READINGS: Deut. 30:15–20; Ps. 119:1–8; 1 Cor. 3:1–9

Today's gospel reading possibly is one of the most difficult and trouble-some passages in the entire Bible for those who seek to take Christian living seriously. Within these seventeen verses are contained at least four "stumbling blocks" that conspire to keep us from living an exemplary life. All of us have most assuredly wrestled with one of more of them in the course of our lives.

I. **Take, for instance, anger.** Who of us doesn't get angry with our friends and relatives every now and then? And what about that person who cuts you off on the freeway? Or the high school teacher or even a teenage boyfriend who is inappropriate for your teenage daughter? Or the next-door neighbor who throws his grass clippings and tree trimmings across the fence onto your lawn? Not to mention how our government officials sometimes disappoint us, how they are sometimes accused of gross moral failure or make decisions that adversely affect our futures. How can one not get angry every once in a while? Yet "If you are angry with a brother or sister you will be liable to judgment," Jesus is reported to have stated (Matt. 5:22, NRSV). Wow! That is a pretty stern and sobering warning, isn't it? Now, we do gain a little reprieve when we read the translation footnotes that tell us that some ancient authorities add "without cause." Then it would read, "If you are angry with a brother or sister *without cause*." Does that mean it is okay to get angry with my brother or sister, *if I have good cause to do so*? I am not so sure, since most of the translations do not include "without cause" in the body of the text, seeming to indicate that the most authoritative sources imply that it is dangerous to get angry—period. It even goes so far as to suggest that anyone who gets angry with another is guilty of murder.

II. **And then what about lust?** "Everyone who looks at a woman with lust has already committed adultery with her in his heart" (Matt. 5:28). Any and every healthy male stands condemned, for it is virtually impossible to look at a beautiful woman and not have fleeting (and sometimes inappropriate) thoughts. Such is why one serious Christian who took the Bible literally, including the subsequent verse that states it is better to pluck out one's eyes and be blind than to look and lust and be liable for judgment, took a pair of scissors and actually poked out his own eyes in ancient Oedipus Rex fashion. Did Jesus *really* say what it says he said about looking and lusting, and if so, did he *really* mean it?

III. **Closely related is the warning against divorce.** Anyone who divorces a spouse, except for the cause of unfaithfulness, and takes up with another commits adultery and also causes the former partner to commit adultery if he or she finds another. Such is the way the teaching goes. But it is now a fact of life and common knowledge that at least 50 percent of marriages end in divorce, and most of those who end up in divorce court go on to form relationships with others. Does that mean that at least half of American adults are living in unforgivable sin? In my years of ministry, I have observed that getting divorced and finding another was often the best thing that could have happened to some people. I have seen a number of mismatched marriages (perhaps the couple was far too young) that should never have taken place that ended in divorce, and the divorced partners went on to find their perfect soul mates. What do we make of that? Who is to say that such unions cannot be divinely blessed? Are the words about divorce attributed to Jesus to be taken literally, no exceptions?

IV. **And a fourth challenge in this passage has to do with oaths and swearing.** Because of this passage, at least in part no doubt, some faith groups refuse to swear in a court of law. But couldn't the injunction against swearing also include frivolous exclamations like "I swear to God!" or "God d--n"? There are a few people who never ever let any kind of swear word or inappropriate language slide across their lips. But I suspect that they are few and far between. Most of us occasionally let loose a few choice words that would be better off kept inside. Perhaps you are washing a glass in the sink and it shatters, slicing open your hand. Or you slam your finger in the car door. Or you just realize that someone has stolen and had a field day with your credit card number. Is it always a gross sin to use language that should never be used in public? Is this really what you mean, Lord? So as we study these seventeen verses, we may be inclined to say, "You must be kidding, Lord!" Who in the world can live every day without failing in some way?

I think that the teachings given in this chapter represent the ideal, that high road of morality and faithfulness to which each believer should be aspiring. At the same time, when we fail, we need to remember that "grace prevails." When we slip and think something we shouldn't think or say something we shouldn't say, we are not abandoned by God and condemned for all eternity. Perhaps a proper response to these demanding verses, in place of "You must be kidding, Lord!" would be, "Please bear with me and help me, Lord; remember, you are not finished with me yet."—Randy Hammer

ILLUSTRATIONS

Courage. In *Ethics and Other Liabilities*, Harry Stein titled one essay "The Curse of Right and Wrong."[4] He points to numerous persons throughout history who sought the courageous best over the expedient good, from Nathan Hale to those portrayed in JFK's *Profiles in Courage*—and who paid for it. Why is it, we often ask, that so many truly bad people prosper? Must we be amoral to succeed? "The answer," says Stein, "is that it helps a lot. . . . In the real world, the meek generally earn $15,000 a year and never get their names in the paper."—Lee McGlone

Victory.

> Leave no unguarded place, No weakness of the soul,
>
> Take every virtue, every grace, and fortify the whole.
>
> From strength to strength go on; Wrestle and fight and pray
>
> Tread all the powers of evil down And win the well fought day.
>
> —Charles Wesley[5]

Musical Selections Appropriate to the Day

Deut. 30:15–20	*Blessed Be the God of Israel*
Ps. 119:1–8	*In the Presence of the Lord*
1 Cor. 3:1–9	*Purer in Heart, O God*
Matt. 5:21–37	*Let It Be Said of Us*

☙ Children's Lectionary Sermon

TITLE: The Choice Is Yours
SCRIPTURE: Deut. 30:15–20

---

[4]Harry Stein, *Ethics and Other Liabilities* (New York: St. Martin's Press, 1982), p. 78.
[5]Charles Wesley, "Soldiers of Christ Arise," *The Pilgrim Hymnal* (Boston: Pilgrim Press, 1958), hymn 384.

KEY VERSES: *Choose life! Be completely faithful to the Lord your God, love him, and do whatever he tells you.* (Deut. 30:19b–20a, CEV)

KEY CONCEPT: We should obey God in the choices we make.

MATERIALS: Bible; enough unsharpened pencils in two colors for each child to have one

You may have heard the saying, "You can't have your cake and eat it, too." What do you think that means? (*Accept answers, restate, and clarify.*)

Here are some (*state color*) pencils and some (*state color*) pencils. Each of you may choose one. (*Pass the pencils to the children.*)

Saving your piece of cake for later or eating it now is making a choice. Deciding to take a (*color*) pencil or a (*color*) pencil is making a choice. Some choices are easy to make; others are harder. But easy or hard, every choice has a consequence. If you eat your cake now, the consequence is that you will have none to eat later. If you choose a (*color*) pencil, you can't have a (*color*) pencil.

Our lives are filled with choices and consequences. If you choose to stay up past your bedtime, you will be tired the next day. If you choose to practice piano every day, you will do well at your next lesson. If you choose to save your allowance for several weeks, you will have money to buy a treat. If you choose not to put on sunscreen when you go to the pool, you will get sunburned.

Our Bible has much to say about choices and their consequences. (*Open Bible.*) In Deuteronomy we read the story of God's people, the Israelites, getting ready to cross the Jordan River into the land God had prepared for them. Moses, their leader, reminded them again of what God wanted them to do: *Choose life. Be completely faithful to the Lord your God, love him, and do whatever he tells you.* When we choose to obey God, the consequence is life filled with God's blessings! Let's thank God for the life God has given us.—Sandra Canipe

❧ WORSHIP AIDS ❧

Call to Worship: "In the morning, O Lord, you hear my voice; in the morning I lay my requests before you and wait in expectation" (Ps. 5:3, NIV).

Invocation: Almighty God, may the quiet and serenity of this hour issue into the strong resolve and moral strength of people of faith who stand firm in the storms of life and faint not. In Jesus' name. Amen.—E. Lee Phillips

Offertory Sentence: "Now it is required that those who have been given a trust must prove faithful" (1 Cor. 4:2, NIV).

Offertory Prayer: Lord, may we in times of need give cheerfully, not withholding, to help another in need of the savior. Amen.—E. Lee Phillips

Morning Prayer: Remind us, O Lord, of the wonders of your steadfast mercy. You created us in your own image, you walked with us throughout the days of old, you entered into your creation and became one of us through your only Son, and you have walked by our sides all the days of life. We bow in reverence and obedience and seek to honor you in the choices we make and the paths we follow. Teach us to honor all things good and noble and to involve ourselves in pursuits that have eternal purposes. Let us not grow weary in well-doing, but instead be faithful to you in every endeavor to which you call us. May your name be praised forever and ever.—Lee McGlone

Benediction: Now we go from worship to translate to the world the spiritual realities experienced here, the biblical truths reaffirmed here, the Christ encountered here, and God's will made known from here. Amen.—E. Lee Phillips

SUNDAY, FEBRUARY 20, 2011
Seventh Sunday after Epiphany

LECTIONARY SERMON TOPIC: "The Ancient Gospel"
TEXT: Lev. 19:1–2, 9–18
OTHER READINGS: Ps. 119:33–40; 1 Cor. 3:10–11, 16–23; Matt. 5:38–48

Our text is one of the most beautiful passages in the Hebrew Bible. (I say "Hebrew Bible" because the thirty-nine books Christians generally call the Old Testament came to us from the Hebrew [Jewish] people. Those books constituted the "Bible" of the Jews long before they became the Bible of Christians. So to use the term "Hebrew Bible" is to show respect for the origin of the books as well as for the Hebrews who gave birth to and cherished them.) Indeed, this passage might aptly be called the ancient Hebrew gospel. The words represent the pinnacle of ancient ethical teaching and quite advanced thinking for the time from which they came. The passage opens by calling on God's people to "be holy" (19:2). To "be holy" is to be different from base, carnal, animal-like behavior whose only motive is to look out for number one. It is to be godlike in thought, motivation, and action. To be holy is to be motivated by love and care for all creation of which we are all a part.

I. **Leviticus 19 seeks to show us how to get along with one another in the world.** "No man is an island," the poet rightly observed. And as the Apostle Paul put it, "we do not live to ourselves alone and we do not die to ourselves alone" (Rom. 14:7). We must learn to live together in unity; we must learn, as Martin Luther King Jr. put it, to live together as brothers and sisters or perish together as fools. So Leviticus 19 calls for consideration of one another. We are urged to be considerate of others as we would want them to be considerate of us. But special consideration is implored on behalf of the poor and the foreign, travelers or transients. When fruits and vegetables were harvested, the fields, trees, and vines were not to be picked totally clean. It was okay and commendable that some be left for the poor or those passing through.

II. **In large measure, this passage in Leviticus is about compassion.** Compassion for one's neighbors, the poor, travelers, and, shall we add, immigrants. If true religion is about anything at all in the world, I contend that it is about compassion in action. True religion is not really about right beliefs or right doctrine. We can say we believe and can have all our intellectual and doctrinal ducks in a row all day long. But if we are lacking in compassion, we are lacking in true religion, and the religion of Jesus, as we shall soon see. Compassion leads to fairness, or justice. It has to do with respecting the rights, property, and life of others. It is about respecting others' good names. The summary of the passage is to "love your neighbor as yourself" (19:18). As Christians we have heard that somewhere else before, haven't we? It is quoted by Jesus as one of the two most important commandments in the Hebrew scriptures (Matt. 22:39). As a pious Hebrew, Jesus knew well the Hebrew scriptures, and he knew what was important—compassion in action, which stems from true love.

III. **These teachings in Leviticus 19 might also be considered a summary of the so-called Golden Rule**, the Jewish teaching that said, "Do not do to others what you do not want others to do to you" and the injunction of Jesus to "Do to others as you would have them do to you" (Luke 6:31). What a wonderful foundation the ancient Hebrew writer left us in this nineteenth chapter of Leviticus. It surely presents a challenge to each of us to lead more dedicated and holy lives. But in the principles enjoined here also lies the potential of a better, more compassionate and just world. —Randy Hammer

---

ILLUSTRATIONS

Compassion. We are reminded of one of the many moving scenes in the old black-and-white movie based on John Steinbeck's great epic novel, *The Grapes of Wrath*, where the Joad family comes upon fruit trees where the fruit is falling to the ground and decaying. Yet they are forbidden from gathering any in spite of the fact that they are on the verge of starvation. Such destitution is something that ought not occur in a world where everyone seeks to live by the instructions in Leviticus. Some years ago, an organization called Traveler's Aid was established to provide aid for travelers and transients down on their luck. But often Traveler's Aid does not have the financial resources to help everyone who needs help. And it often is a challenge for ministers, churches, and other organizations to determine who really needs aid and who is just seeking to work the system. Perhaps the best course of action is to be as considerate as we can possibly be and err on the side of compassion.—Randy Hammer

Neighbor Love. Many years ago, I was sitting in a barbershop waiting to get my hair cut. There happened to be a "Christian" businessman in the shop who was talking to the owner and just shooting the breeze, as they say. This man was talking all kinds of loud, pious Christian talk. Just to have heard his "testimony," you would have thought he was a saint. Pretty soon a mentally challenged man whom everyone in town recognized came into the shop. Tom, as I shall call the mentally challenged man, had a reputation of making a round through town every day asking anyone he met for a quarter. "Hey, Buddy, you got a quarter?" Tom would say. Well, when Tom came in the shop asking for a quarter, the "Christian" businessman cut loose on him, yelling, calling him names, and demanding that he get out of there and never come back. *What has happened to the Christian spirit in this man?* I thought to myself. *My God, if that is a Christian, then I want no part of it!* There was in this man no godlike behavior, no consideration or compassion, no loving his neighbor as himself, and no doing to others as he would have them do to him.—Randy Hammer

Musical Selections Appropriate to the Day

Lev. 19:1–2, 9–18	*Living for Jesus*
Ps. 119:33–40	*Trust and Obey*
1 Cor. 3:10–11, 16–23	*The Church's One Foundation*
Matt. 5:38–48	*As the Deer*

 Children's Lectionary Sermon

TITLE: Forgive!

SCRIPTURE: Matt. 5:38–48

KEY VERSE: *"But I tell you to love your enemies and pray for anyone who mistreats you."* (Matt. 5:44, CEV)

KEY CONCEPT: Jesus wants us to forgive others.

MATERIALS: Bible

Nancy was thirty-five when her world began to turn gray; objects and people became blurred. She was not surprised when the doctor said she had an incurable eye disease that causes blindness. The disease is inherited; Nancy's grandmother, cousin, and an aunt were blind because of the disease. At age forty-five, Nancy, too, was blind.

Without sight, Nancy relied on her four other senses to remain involved in church and community. She learned Braille to continue reading her Bible and teaching a Sunday school class. She learned to use a lap loom and taught weaving at the community center. She joined the rose-growers society, learning distinct fragrances of roses well enough to judge rose shows.

One day Nancy and a friend had been to lunch. The friend drove her home. Nancy, who could do almost anything by feeling her way, unlocked the back door and went inside. Immediately she sensed someone's presence. "Hello? Who's there?" she called. A figure rushed past her, shoved her to the floor, and ran out. The fall broke Nancy's arm. She phoned her husband, who phoned the police. Within two hours, the police caught the intruder still carrying the camera and cell phone he had stolen from Nancy's house.

Nancy wanted to meet the man who had shoved her and had stolen from her. She went to visit him in jail. "I don't know why you stole from me," Nancy told him, "but I forgive you. I will pray every day that you can know God's forgiveness and love." After the man was tried and sent to prison, Nancy mailed a Bible and other books, wrote to him often, and continued to pray.

Why? Nancy remembered a teaching from Jesus about forgiveness. (*Open Bible.*) *"But I tell you to love your enemies and pray for anyone who mistreats you."*

When we are mistreated or hurt, it can sometimes be hard to forgive. When we hurt or mistreat others and realize it, we want to be forgiven. Jesus taught us to be forgiving. Let's ask God to help us be people who forgive.—Sandra Canipe

❧ WORSHIP AIDS ❧

Call to Worship: "I will give thanks to the Lord because of his righteousness and will sing praise to the name of the Lord Most High" (Ps. 7:17, NIV).

Invocation: Lord, we would not walk away from this hour of worship the same as we came; therefore, shape and mold us after the pattern of our

Savior, who prayed without ceasing and finished the task to which he was called. Amen.—E. Lee Phillips

Offertory Sentence: "Each one should use whatever gift he has received to serve others, faithfully administering God's grace in its various forms" (1 Pet. 4:10, NIV).

Offertory Prayer: Father, these offerings we bring to be used in Kingdom enterprises. Inspire us not to give the residue of our wealth, but the first fruits as a sign of our deeper devotion to the Lord in whose name we pray. Amen.—Henry Fields

Morning Prayer: Most Gracious Heavenly Father, once again we rejoice in this opportunity that is ours to worship, to have our hearts lifted by music that stirs our souls, and to have our minds opened by the hearing of your Word. May the experience of this hour carry over into our attitudes and actions in the days that lie ahead. In our prayers we would think not only of ourselves but of others. We would lift up to you those who are suffering in mind or in body that through you their pain may be eased. Some of these are hungry, some are filled with anxiety, some are lonely and just need to be loved and appreciated. May they hear you saying to them in a very personal way, "Come unto me and I will give you rest." And then there are others who appear to be managing very well, who give of themselves in service to others and in an effort to make this a better community, a better society, a better world. They, too, need your guiding hand and words of encouragement. We would offer a special prayer for all those men and women who serve their country. May we see them as preservers of the peace, a peace that allows freedom and justice for all. We pray, "Thy kingdom come."—Lee McGlone

Benediction: Part now with God's blessings, live in God's mercy, and return in God's grace, God's love to make known. Amen.—E. Lee Phillips

SUNDAY, FEBRUARY 27, 2011
Eighth Sunday after Epiphany

LECTIONARY SERMON TOPIC: "A Lesson on Life"

TEXT: Matt. 6:24–34

OTHER READINGS: Isa. 49:8–16a; Ps. 131 or 62:5–12; 1 Cor. 4:1–5

In *Groundhog Day*, a movie that has now become a classic, the character Phil Connors, played by Bill Murray, gets the chance to change his life and make something good of it. He is given the opportunity to learn how to live. Phil is a weatherman who has no joy in living. He has become oblivious to life. Life has become a chore for him. There is no enthusiasm, no meaning in it all. Phil is self-centered, conceited, and pompous. He is sarcastic and pessimistic. He has little regard for other people, except when he can manipulate and use them for his own gratification. The television station that Phil works for sends him and his crew to a little town in Pennsylvania on Groundhog Day to do the traditional story on the town groundhog coming out of his hole to predict the next six weeks of weather. But something strange happens. Phil Connors gets caught in a time warp. For days, weeks, months when he wakes up at 6:00 AM it is the same day—Groundhog Day. It is as though God or fate is saying to Phil Connors, "You are going to repeat this day until you get it right, until you learn how to live." This is precisely what Jesus is talking about in the scripture that we heard read from Matthew, in the Sermon on the Mount—learning how to live. Jesus tells us:

I. **Life is meant to be lived free of worry.** "Do not worry about your life," Jesus tells us. My children always used to tell me, "Dad, you worry too much." "It's a Daddy's job to worry," I would reply. It is natural for us to worry a little bit about our children's safety and other family matters. Statistics show that "The people most likely to feel stressed are college graduates, those with the highest income, and persons forty to forty-nine years of age."[6] Two out of three of those made me a pretty good candidate for stress and worry when my children were at home. But worry should not be the dominating force in our lives. We should not live to worry. We should not get up in the morning to worry and still be worrying when we go to bed at night. It has been said that people spend the most time worrying about things that never happen anyway. And worrying about something doesn't change it a bit. We can't add a single day to our span of life by worrying about it. Our generation may be killing itself with stress, hypertension, and unnecessary worry. Jesus is encouraging us to relax and trust in God. One of the rides that I enjoyed at Opryland theme park before it closed some years ago was Chaos, the indoor roller coaster that spiraled up and back down through the darkness. When I first starting riding Chaos, it made my neck hurt. I finally realized that when I rode Chaos I tensed up the muscles in my back and neck. I finally said to myself, "Hey, you've ridden this thing several times before. You haven't gotten thrown off yet. Why don't you just relax and enjoy the ride?" So I learned to relax, sit back, and enjoy the ride. You know, some people go through life like that—all tensed up, stressed out, and worried about everything. A good relaxing exercise for us would be reading Psalm 131 whenever we begin to feel stressed or feel worry or anxiety coming on. The psalmist says, "I do not occupy myself with things too great and too marvelous for me. But I have calmed and quieted my soul." I think this is the kind of thing Jesus had in mind—relaxing, and calming and quieting our soul.

II. **We should aim to live our lives to their fullest.** Some people learn late in life how to live. Others never learn how to live at all. I wish I had learned how to relax, enjoy life, and live life to its fullest much earlier than I did. Jesus encourages us to take time to look at the birds of the air and consider the beautiful lilies of the field. We need to learn how to stop and smell life's roses. Such is what Phil Connors learns in *Groundhog Day*. He learns how to live life to its fullest. Phil learns how to play the piano; he learns how to produce beautiful ice sculptures; he learns to read and appreciate French poetry; he learns the true meaning of friendship and what it takes to really

[6]Herb Miller, *The Vital Congregation* (Nashville: Abingdon Press, 1990), p. 107.

be a friend; he learns how to be humble and really listen to other people. But most important, Phil learns how to love other people, and he learns that the true joy of life comes in serving others: fixing the flat tire of little old ladies, catching a little boy who falls out of a tree, keeping a man from choking to death on a piece of steak, and doing a host of other things that bring joy to other people with no thought of himself and his own needs. And when Phil learns to love and serve other people unselfishly, he finds happiness and comes out of the time warp a changed man.

To really live life to its fullest and to find true happiness is to come follow Christ and the way he has laid out for us in the Sermon on the Mount (Matt. 5–7). For in the Sermon on the Mount, Jesus teaches us of love, forgiveness, patience, prayer, faithfulness, service, and trust. Life gives us one day at a time—that is what we have to work with. God gives us life in one-hour segments. Taking care of the present is what should concern us, not the mistakes of the past and not what might happen in the future. "Do not worry about tomorrow," Jesus says; today's concerns are enough for today. Phil Connors asks, "If you only had one day to live, what would you do with it?" Such is a good philosophy and approach to life. This is a way to learn how to live: relax and trust the goodness of God, live life to its fullest by loving and serving others, and take life one day at a time.
—Randy Hammer

ILLUSTRATIONS

Life Questions. We would do well to ask ourselves three questions each morning: (1) What can I do this day to better myself? (2) What can I do this day to show my love for my family? (3) What can I do this day in my job to improve my productivity and give my employer his money's worth?—Randy Hammer

"Just for Today."

Lord, for tomorrow and its needs I do not pray;
Keep me, my God, from stain of sin just for today.
Let me both diligently work and duly pray,

Let me be kind in word and deed just for today.
Let me be slow to do my will, prompt to obey,
Help me to mortify my flesh just for today.
Let me no wrong or idle word unthinking say:
Set Thou a seal upon my lips just for today.
Let me in season, Lord, be grave, in season gay,
Let me be faithful to Thy grace, just for today.
And if today my tide of life should ebb away,
Give me Thy sacraments divine, sweet Lord, today.
So for tomorrow and its needs I do not pray;
But keep me, guide me, love me, Lord, just for today.
—Samuel Wilberforce

Musical Selections Appropriate to the Day

Isa. 49:8–16a	*He's Got the Whole World in His Hands*
Ps. 131 or Ps. 62:5–12	*We Bow Down*
1 Cor. 4:1–5	*The Servant Song*
Matt. 6:24–34	*Seek Ye First*

◈ Children's Lectionary Sermon

TITLE: Forget Something?

SCRIPTURE: Isa. 49:8–16a

KEY VERSE: *"Jerusalem, I can never forget you! I have written your name on the palms of my hands."* (Isa. 49:16, TEV)

KEY CONCEPT: God always remembers us.

MATERIALS: Bible, six- by eighteen-inch poster board

PREPARATION: Print the word "mnemonics" in large letters on the poster board.

Have you ever forgotten to return a school library book on time? Forgotten to get the DVD or game back to the rental store on time? Or, worse yet, have you ever forgotten your mother's or father's birthday? We all forget things now and then.

Here's a word for you: mnemonics. (*Display the word.*) Mnemonics are methods or little tricks that help you remember something. You are using mnemonics when you put your library book beside the door where you can see it and pick it up as you leave for school. And when you really, really, must remember something . . . like an important phone number . . . you can write that important something on the palm of your hand with a pen. Forgetful people like us need mnemonics; God doesn't.

The prophet Isaiah tells of a time when God's people, the Israelites, disobeyed God, ignoring God's laws. Because of their disobedience, the Israelites were defeated by the Babylonians, who took many of them to live in Babylon, far from Jerusalem and the Temple, where the Israelites believed God lived. The Israelites were homesick and discouraged, and they felt forgotten by God. (*Open Bible.*) In Isaiah 49:14 it says, *The Lord has abandoned us! He has forgotten us.* But God had not forgotten. Isaiah told them in verses 8 and 16, *The Lord says to his people, "When the time comes to save you, I will show you favor and answer your cries for help. . . . I will let you settle once again in your land that is now laid waste, . . . I can never forget you! I have written your name on the palms of my hands."*

What a wonderful word picture: the names of God's people written on the palms of God's hands. God knows you the same way. God will never forget you and never leave you. Let's thank God because of God's amazing love for us.—Sandra Canipe

☙ WORSHIP AIDS ☙

Call to Worship: "I will praise you, O Lord, with all my heart; I will tell of all your wonders" (Ps. 9:1, NIV).

Invocation: Holy God, our temptation is to stray. Call us back. Our minds wander and resolve weakens. Speak to us and leave us not the same. Amen.—E. Lee Phillips

Offertory Sentence: "So then, each of us will give an account of himself to God" (Rom. 14:12, NIV).

Offertory Prayer: Father, help us understand that what we are is the result of your grace and that what we have is a gift from your hand. This morning we bring back some of the material blessing we have received. Pray do your gracious work in others through the gifts we bring. Amen.—Henry Fields

Morning Prayer: Lord, we come to you in prayer and seek the still waters. Restore our souls. We have known your guidance in paths of righteousness, and we have felt your presence in the valley of the shadow. For the ways you have overflowed our lives with goodness and mercy, we are forever thankful. Forgive us, Father, when we take for granted your grace, and help us to be good stewards. We pray for those bruised in spirit, victims of someone else's inconsideration, betrayed or exploited; for those who look fine on the outside, but who inside hurt and cry. Help us do what we can to help those who stagger under burdens too heavy to carry alone. We ask today for our community, our nation, and our world. Bless our leaders with strength to know and do what is right. May your voice be heard on high. We ask in Christ's name. Amen.—Lee McGlone

Benediction: Live richly this week. Pray fervently. Reach out to the needy. Comfort the grieving. Encourage the discouraged. Aid the seekers. For as you give you will receive—for heaven touches the compassionate. Amen.—E. Lee Phillips

SUNDAY, MARCH 6, 2011
Ninth Sunday after Epiphany/Transfiguration Sunday

LECTIONARY SERMON TOPIC: "The Fellowship of Jesus Only"
TEXT: Matt. 17:1–9
OTHER READINGS: Exod. 24:12–18; Ps. 99; 2 Pet. 1:16–21

Today is Transfiguration Sunday, the day on which we remember and reflect on that event in which Peter, James, and John witnessed Jesus being transformed before their eyes—we are probably meant to understand this as a prefiguring of the glory that would be his in his Resurrection—and having a conversation with Elijah and Moses, the content of which neither Mark nor Matthew tell us but of which Luke says they "spoke of his departure, which he was to accomplish at Jerusalem" (Luke 9:31).

Upon witnessing the Transfiguration, Simon Peter stammered out something about putting up some dwellings for Jesus, Elijah, and Moses to dwell in; perhaps Peter was just trying to be hospitable, maybe he had the Feast of Booths in mind, or maybe he thought that they could all just settle down there and wait for the end of things to roll around.

When Peter finished spitting out his words, a cloud enveloped the scene, and a voice from the cloud said, "This is my Son, the Beloved One; with him I am well pleased; listen to him!" (v. 5). And when the three disciples looked around, they saw no one "save Jesus only" (KJV). God told the disciples that it was Jesus to whom they were to listen and that for them there was no one to listen to except Jesus. They were to be, in other words, the Fellowship of Jesus Only.

We who are disciples of Jesus in these days are members of that same fellowship; Jesus, the beloved Son of God, the culmination and epitome of God's plan of salvation, the Incarnate Word of God, is our Lord, and we are to listen to him and to him only when it comes to ultimate issues, to the matters of life and death.

I. **What kinds of things did and does Jesus say that they needed to heed and that we need to heed?** Well, the only thing that Jesus said in close proximity to the Transfiguration event was his instruction to the three disciples not to tell anyone what they had seen until after Jesus had risen from the dead (v. 9). After Jesus was raised, they could and did tell it all; and all of us live on this side of the Resurrection, so we know and can tell and should tell the whole story—with our words and with our lives.

Indeed, as the current members of the Fellowship of Jesus Only, we are also members of the Fellowship of the Resurrected Jesus, and that makes a huge difference. In light of the fact of the Resurrected Christ whom we have experienced and do experience for ourselves, we know that we should listen to him in all things. His Resurrection has validated his life and his teachings; we have no doubt of his ultimate and utter authority.

II. **So I ask again: What did he say to which they were to listen and to which we should listen?** He said that the way of grace that shows itself in a life of service and sacrifice is God's way for his people. That's what Jesus said just before the Transfiguration, and that's what he said not long after it. Just six days before the Transfiguration (and just a few sentences before it in Matthew's telling), Peter had made his great confession that Jesus was the Messiah (16:16) and then Jesus had explained what that meant, "that he must go to Jerusalem and undergo great suffering . . . and be killed, and on the third day be raised" (16:21). When Peter rebuked Jesus for saying such a thing, Jesus in turn rebuked Peter and then said about all of us who would follow him, "If any want to become my followers, let them deny themselves and take up their cross and follow me. For those who want to save their life will lose it, and those who lose their life for my sake shall save it."

III. **There it is again: we are to listen to what Jesus says, and what Jesus says is that the Christian life is all about giving yourself away (16:24–25).** Yes, there is resurrection at the end, but the path to resurrection goes through love and grace and mercy and service and selflessness and sacrifice. Then Jesus led his disciples down from the mountain on which Peter had wanted to park and stay—we can't stay on the mountain, can we?—down into the valley where human beings with all their needs dwelled and where human beings with all their needs still dwell—and for now that's where we belong, isn't it? To be members of the Fellowship of Jesus Only means to be members of the Fellowship of the Crucifixion. Inspired by and filled with Jesus, we give of ourselves to meet the needs of people, to heal their hurts, to feed their hunger, to touch their lives, to show them the one who can forgive their sins.

IV. **And then, to hammer the point home, Jesus told them (and us) again: "The Son of Man is going to be betrayed into human hands, and they will kill him, and on the third day he will be raised" (17:22b–23a).** "And they were greatly distressed," Matthew tells us (17:23b); remember, though, that after his Crucifixion and Resurrection they got past their distress and moved on to living out the Crucifixion and Resurrection in their lives.

So it must be with us. If we are going to be the Fellowship of Jesus Only—the people who listen to him; if we are going to be the Fellowship of the Resurrection—the people who have encountered the Resurrected

Lord and who know that he must be listened to; if we are going to be the Fellowship of the Crucifixion—the people who know that the way to glory, the way to eternity, the way to God, is the way of grace that shows itself in service and selflessness and sacrifice—then we will be the people who put that way first in our lives.

So let us ask ourselves some questions. When we have the opportunity to forgive this week, will we? When we have the chance to give something up for the Lord and for someone else, will we? When we have privilege to go out of our way and to break our routine to help someone, will we? When we get the chance to break the cycle of sin that escalates when we hold grudges and take vengeance by instead practicing radical grace and mercy, will we? When we have the opportunity to love someone who is hard to love, will we?

We are members of the Fellowship of Jesus Only. Let's listen to him. Let's not be ashamed of his words. And let's show it with our lives.—Michael Ruffin

---

ILLUSTRATIONS

Life. In the movie *Gladiator* there's a powerful scene just prior to the opening battle. Battle lines were drawn. The enemy was in sight. Both sides were ready for a fight. Then the Roman general, Maximus, rode his horse in front of his elite cavalry, preparing them for the battle and rousing their emotions. Everyone knew that many were about to die. Then the general shouted this challenge: "What we do in this life echoes in eternity!" You know, there's a lot of Bible written all over that. We live with one eye on eternity and another on the world in which we live. It was said that Paul Tillich, the American theologian, lived out his faith with the Bible in one hand and the newspaper in the other. That's good advice. What we do in life echoes in eternity.—Lee McGlone

Faith. A deepening faith yields a heart of compassion . . . a heart that reaches out beyond itself. While Jesus and the three disciples were engaged in a mountaintop experience, the other disciples were down below dealing with the heartache of a loving father with a woefully ill son. True faith arrives at both places—and with ready spirits. D. T. Niles, Methodist missionary to India, spoke of two conversions: one to Christ and the other to the world. It is far too easy to assume concern only for those around us. True faith sees beyond itself.—Lee McGlone

Musical Selections Appropriate to the Day

Exod. 24:12–18	*Guide Me, O Thou Great Jehovah*
Ps. 99	*We Bow Down*
2 Pet. 1:16–21	*Name of All Majesty*
Matt. 17:1–9	*Holy Ground*

❧ Children's Lectionary Sermon

TITLE: God's Own Dear Son

SCRIPTURE: Matt. 17:1–9, 2 Pet. 1:16–21

KEY VERSE: *"This is my own dear Son, and I am pleased with him. Listen to what he says!"* (Matt. 17:5b, CEV)

KEY CONCEPT: God's Holy Spirit helps us know that Jesus is God's Son.

MATERIALS: Bible, Transformer toy

PREPARATION: Learn how to transform the figure or get a child to demonstrate.

Today is Transfiguration Sunday. To understand what this day means to Christians, we must know what "transfigure" means. Another word for "transfigure" is "transform."

Raise your hand if you have played with a Transformer. (*Display the toy and "transform" it while speaking, or have a child fix it for you.*) This toy has one appearance, but with twists and turns, you make it look entirely different. It's transformed, or transfigured, into something else. When something is transformed or transfigured, its appearance is changed.

(*Open Bible.*) Chapter 17 of Matthew tells of Jesus taking Peter, James, and John with him for time alone on a mountain. While they were there, Jesus' face began to glow, and his clothes became bright white. Jesus appeared different; he was transfigured. Then from a shining cloud, a voice said, *"This is my own dear Son, and I am pleased with him. Listen to what he says!"* Afraid, Peter, James, and John fell flat on the ground. Jesus touched them, told them to get up, and told them not to be afraid. Jesus looked again like the Jesus they'd known before, but now they knew more about him: Jesus was God's Son. As the four of them walked down the mountain, Jesus warned them to tell no one what they had seen and heard. Who would believe they'd heard God's voice saying Jesus was God's own Son?

Years later, Peter wrote about that day on the mountain, the day he came to believe that Jesus is God's Son. He wanted the early Christians firmly to believe, too. Peter also wrote that the Old Testament prophets were not just making up stories about Jesus' coming. The Spirit of God guided them to know this truth.

God's Holy Spirit also helps each of us know the truth: Jesus is the Son of God. The Holy Spirit can speak to us and help us each day.—Sandra Canipe

WORSHIP AIDS

Call to Worship: "The Lord is in his holy temple; the Lord is on his heavenly throne. He observes the sons of men; his eyes examine them" (Ps. 11:4, NIV).

Invocation: Loving Lord, mediate to us by your Holy Spirit that which most we need for worship—and for lives renewed to serve God in the need of others, for Jesus' sake. Amen.—E. Lee Phillips

Offertory Sentence: "The earth is the Lord's, and everything in it, the world, and all who live in it" (Ps. 24:1, NIV).

Offertory Prayer: It is such a small amount we bring when compared to the vast blessings we experience and the huge need abroad in the world. By itself it can accomplish very little. But connected with the small gifts of others, it can make a difference. This morning we give what we have brought, laying it on the altar with love, asking that it be divinely invested in Kingdom efforts, we pray in Jesus' name. Amen.—Henry Fields

Morning Prayer: Sovereign God, you alone are the Creator to whom we ascribe worship. As mortal women and men, we cannot fathom your ingenuity. We cannot understand the thoughts that governed the establishment of the heavens, the earth, the seas, and light. We do not know the brilliance with which you created celestial beings. Yet we praise you constantly. Our lack of knowledge only gives us more reason to worship you. In our ignorance, we trust your infinite knowledge. Because of our unawareness, we marvel even more at your abilities. By what privilege do we have the ability to know you? Your people stand in further awe that you choose to have relationship with us. God, we give thanks that you gave to us a portion of your artistic abilities. In our worship, we will strive to offer praise in truly creative ways—with creative thoughts that you alone have allowed us to think. Father, as we make an effort, please increase our sensitivity to you that we may discover vital and creative approaches to honor you. For the life you created in us, we are truly thankful. For the privilege of knowing you in our lives, we are even more obliged. Creator God, you are beautiful, and you alone deserve our praise. Amen. —Sarah Casey

Benediction: Lord, dismiss us with your blessing, guide us by your grace, keep us safe in your love, in the name of Jesus, whom we serve. Amen. —E. Lee Phillips

SUNDAY, MARCH 13, 2011
First Sunday in Lent

LECTIONARY SERMON TOPIC: "What's Ruling Your Life?"
TEXT: Gen. 2:15–17, 3:1–7
OTHER READINGS: Ps. 32; Rom. 5:12–19; Matt. 4:1–11

Life is a gift. Our role is to accept the gift and to celebrate the gift and to live the gift. See our universal representatives Adam and Eve in the Garden. They have productive and uncomplicated work to do; they belong together and are drawn together and share together, unencumbered by fear and shame; they live in the love and grace of God and of each other.

They even have the guidance of God's Word; God said, "You can eat of all the trees in the Garden except this one," which they should have heard with celebration, but which they instead heard with resentment.

All of humanity has fallen prey to that temptation. We are prone to do so because we are human and because that's what humans do, but we also choose to do so when we get the opportunity.

I. **How differently Jesus acted in the face of temptation!** Adam and Eve approached their temptation well fed; yet when confronted with the fruit, which they did not need, they ate. Jesus approached his temptation famished after a forty-day fast; yet when confronted with the temptation to turn the stones into bread that he did need, he refused.

Adam and Eve participated with the serpent in questioning the Word of God. When the serpent asked, "Did God say, 'You shall not eat from any tree in the garden'?" Eve entered into dialogue with the serpent and thereby entered into questioning God's motivation behind God's injunction; it was born out of love, but Eve let the serpent turn it into an unjust stricture. So they questioned God's Word. Jesus, in contrast, when confronted with temptation, relied on and took refuge in the Word of God. Because Jesus resisted and stayed true to who he was under God until his obedience finally led him to the cross, we can be saved. And because of Jesus, things can be different for us.

Consider, then, another contrast. Adam and Eve were God's children who had God's care and protection. When confronted by the serpent, they chose to believe that there was something better for them than being the beloved children of God. Maybe they got some of what they wanted, but along with it, they found anxiety and despair. Jesus, in contrast, had just heard the voice of God at his baptism affirm, "This is my beloved Son, with whom I am well pleased." Immediately came the tempter who said, "*If* you are the Son of God . . ." The devil tried to raise doubts in Jesus' mind as to whether or not he was really the Son of God. Maybe, the devil wanted Jesus to consider, he needed something more than being the beloved Son of God if he was going to make it. The road ahead of him, the one required of him by his Father, would be a hard one, and maybe he needed to choose a way other than the Father's way. But Jesus would have none of it. He chose rather to rest in the fact that he was God's beloved Son.

We have a choice as to how we will live. We have all made Adam and Eve's choice. We have all chosen to believe that we are less than God's beloved children and that we thus need to seize something more for ourselves. Even we Christians can choose to keep living as the children of Adam and Eve rather than as the beloved children of God—but we don't have to do so.

Jesus Christ has made new and real and abundant and eternal life a reality for us; we really can live in that life. Why would we not choose grace over guilt, assurance over doubt, life over death, joy over fear, belonging over longing, and peace over anxiety?

II. **But all too often we do not.** Understand this, too: the serpent and Adam and Eve were wrong. Life is not expanded by going a way other than God's way. Life is limited and truncated and drained by going a way other than God's way. We can make a case that the testing that comes to us is a part of God's plan; the forbidden tree and the serpent were both put in the Garden by God, and the Holy Spirit compelled Jesus to go out into the wilderness. Perhaps Jesus had learned from experience that we need to pray "lead us not into temptation." It may be that we can't become fully who we are supposed to be without such testing. What I want to guard against, though, is the notion that somehow we need to make our own way apart from God if we are going to be who we are supposed to be.

Sometimes the Church—the real Church in our real world, now—does stand in the way because sometimes we inappropriately try to limit inquiry and to inhibit science; worst of all, the Church sometimes stands in the way of people reaching their full potential by fostering the very things that Adam and Eve chose and by which God does not want us to be encumbered: guilt, shame, and anxiety. Such should not be, because God wants us to have life and have it more abundantly. God wants our lives to be ruled by grace rather than guilt; God wants our lives to be ruled by God's Word rather than by the limits of our own wisdom.

III. **Real life is not found when we live in fear and guilt and anxiety, which are the ways of death.** Real life is found when we rest in God's grace, when we rest in the fact that we are God's beloved children. Real life is not found when we try to be our own god and try to go our own way apart from God. Real life is found when we rest in God's Word, when we rest in the fact that God is always there for us, showing us the way.

So what's ruling your life? Is it guilt and shame and death, or is it grace and love and life?—Michael Ruffin

---

ILLUSTRATIONS

Church Mission. In Philip Pullman's *His Dark Materials* trilogy, a "God" whom you would not recognize as God is killed and his "Church" is an institution that the heroes want to destroy because the Church stands in the way of real advance, of real inquiry, and of real life. In ways that are too complicated to get into here, Pullman's "Church" keeps people from having the life they are meant to have; real life can be found only by going your own way and living this life for all it is worth through study and kindness and love.—Michael Ruffin

Sin. So when they heard, "When you eat, your eyes will be opened and you will be like God," they ate, and when their eyes were opened they realized that they were naked and tried to cover themselves up because they realized the other possibilities implied by their realization of their nakedness—the possibility that there could be guilt instead of grace, conflict instead of peace, brokenness instead of wholeness. They knew that once they had crossed that Rubicon—or maybe that Tigris—there was no going back; they knew that now they and all those who came after them, when left to their own devices and their own choices, would choose as they had.—Michael Ruffin

Musical Selections Appropriate to the Day

Gen. 2:15–17; 3:1–7	*I Sing the Mighty Power of God*
Ps. 32	*Forgiven*
Rom. 5:12–19	*Name of All Majesty*
Matt. 4:1–11	*How Firm a Foundation*

Children's Lectionary Sermon

TITLE: God's Way Is Best

SCRIPTURE: Genesis 3:1–7

KEY VERSES: *"You will not surely die," the serpent said to the woman. "God knows that your eyes will be opened as soon as you eat it, and you will be like God, knowing both good and evil."* (Gen. 3:4–5, NIV)

KEY CONCEPT: God's will is best for us.

MATERIALS: Bible; sock puppet, with eyes if possible; bag in which to put puppet

Who were the very first people God made? (*Let the children respond.*) That's right, Adam and Eve. Now Adam and Eve lived in a beautiful garden, and they could just pick fruit off the trees and eat it. Life was good. God gave them only one rule to follow. He told them they could eat anything, except the fruit from one tree in the middle of the garden.

Well, a sneaky snake (*pull out sock puppet*) came along and asked Eve about God's rules. She explained that they were not supposed to eat from that one tree. If they did, they would die. The snake lied to Eve (*make the puppet talk saying the key verses*): *"You will not surely die," the serpent said to the woman. "God knows that your eyes will be opened as soon as you eat it, and you will be like God, knowing both good and evil."*

So what did Eve do? She ate the fruit, even though she knew that was not God's way for her. And she gave some to Adam, and he ate it too, even though he knew that was not what God wanted them to do. Because they disobeyed God, they had to leave the beautiful garden, and they weren't going to live forever anymore, but would have to die.

Sometimes we know what God wants us to do, and we also get to thinking another way might be better. But choosing another way always leads to trouble. It's better to obey God's way for our life.—Dawn Burnett

₰ WORSHIP AIDS ₰

Call to Worship: "I will sing unto the Lord, for he has been good to me" (Ps. 13:6, NIV).

Invocation: May the Lord fill you with all peace and power, that your worship this day may be God-honoring, soul-stirring, and life-changing, for Jesus' sake. Amen.—E. Lee Phillips

Offertory Sentence: "For every animal of the forest is mine, and the cattle on a thousand hills" (Ps. 50:10, NIV).

Offertory Prayer: Lord, accept these gifts we bring, dedicated to the work of the church, the spread of the gospel, and to your everlasting glory. Amen. —E. Lee Phillips

Morning Prayer: Thank you, Father, for the privilege to worship. It allows us to discover who we are in you. As we worship you, Lord, you give us our true identity. We are your saints. As we worship, we are drawn closer to

Christ. Here we connect with Christ and feel his power. Lord, you change our identity as we enter your presence: we are changed into the image for which Christ has designed us. Lord, enable us to live as true believers. May we experience worship in such a powerful way that our very nature is changed. God, show us more of ourselves and what we are to be. Connect us with you through your Son. Thank you, Father, for the privilege to worship. It allows us to discover who we are in you. Amen.—Kendall Summons

Benediction: We have gathered to worship and now part to serve. Honor God as you go and live in God's will—which to know is the joy of the soul. Amen.—E. Lee Phillips

SUNDAY, MARCH 20, 2011
Second Sunday in Lent

LECTIONARY SERMON TOPIC: "The Struggle to Believe"
TEXT: John 3:1–17
OTHER READINGS: Gen. 12:1–4a; Ps. 121; Rom. 4:1–5, 13–17

In his struggle to believe, Nicodemus consistently misses the point that Jesus is trying to make. When Nicodemus asks, "Can one enter a second time into the mother's womb and be born?" he is saying that Jesus has stated a physical, literal impossibility. In one way, Nicodemus's thinking was wrong; he was bound by his limitations, so he could think only of the physical. In another way, though, Nicodemus's thinking was right; what has to take place for a person to come into eternal life is not physically possible—it comes from beyond us.

Where the NRSV has Jesus say, "You must be born from above," other translations say, "You must be born again." The Greek word can mean either; it seems best to read the text this way: Jesus meant "born from above," and Nicodemus heard "born again."

I. **The imagery of being born guards us against two misunderstandings.** One is the notion that we do something to bring about our own salvation. Sometimes we hear Jesus' words "You must be born from above," and we think in terms of something that we must do—but being born is not something that we *do*; it is something that happens *to* us. Jesus said that we must be born from above, from heaven, from the Spirit. We don't do it; God does it.

The other misunderstanding against which the imagery of being born guards us is the one that says that being "born from above" must be an instantaneous experience. Now, it is true that a moment came when you and I made our appearance in the world; it is also true that a moment came when we were born into new life. But an awful lot had to happen before we arrived on the scene. Somebody married somebody and had a child; that child married somebody and had a child; and so on. If any one of those events had not happened—if someone had married someone else or if someone had not had a child—then you would not be here.

II. **Similarly, a lot has to happen before you can be "born from above."** All those events that happened and all the thoughts you have thought and all the sins you have committed and all the love you have shared and all the hurt you have inflicted and all the achievements you have had and all the failures you have suffered—all of that goes into your experience of rebirth.

We move toward Jesus lugging our limitations along with us. Nicodemus brought whoever and whatever he was with him—he brought his smarts, his standing, his reputation. He also brought that hole in his soul that he couldn't reason or will away. He came to Jesus because it seemed that Jesus might have something that he needed; the Spirit spoke into his emptiness to cause him to move toward Jesus.

III. **What do you bring as you come out of the darkness?** You certainly bring your sin, your background, all of the experiences that have formed you. You bring the steps and missteps, the successes and failures, the joys and sorrows. Perhaps you bring your pedigree, your security blankets, your opinions, your reputation, and your value system. But something is nagging at you. You've never quite been able to believe in Jesus, but something is nagging at you. Or maybe you've been professing belief in Jesus for a long time, but something is nagging at you.

Something may be drawing you toward Jesus. If so, that's a good thing, because only the Spirit of God can do that. That's what Jesus meant when he said, "Do not be astonished that I said to you, 'You must be born from above.' The wind blows where it chooses, and you hear the sound of it, but you do not know where it comes from or where it goes. So it is with everyone who is born of the Spirit." The wind goes where it will and blows on whom it will; so does the Spirit. That's what God does—God happens to you, and it's wondrous and mysterious and fantastic. You have to believe, it's true. But you can only believe because God has first come to you. You can only follow because God summons. You may be struggling to believe because you think you have to understand or because you can't break out of your box or because it all sounds so outlandish. Well, let me tell you— you won't understand, and you do have to break out of your box, and, quite frankly, it is all outlandish.

Maybe—just maybe—the Spirit of God is pursuing you. Maybe—just maybe—the Spirit is driving you toward Jesus. Maybe—just maybe— the Spirit is trying to get you to throw your life open to the miracle that he is trying to do in you. Nicodemus just couldn't get it. Don't you see, though—that's the point. You don't get it—it gets you! You don't get God— God gets you! Amen. And so may it be for all of us.

Jesus Christ is God's only begotten Son, and whosoever believes in him will not perish but will have everlasting life. Is he pursuing you? Is the Spirit prompting you? Is his love making the stakes feel rather desperate to you? Be glad. Be very glad. And stop struggling.—Michael Ruffin

ILLUSTRATIONS

Born Again. A story told by Donald Miller helps us here. His friend Laura was depressed. Don asked her what was wrong with her, and it wasn't any of the usual things. So Don asked her, "Is it God?" She said, "I feel like he is after me." When Don asked who was after her, Laura answered, "God." Don told her that he thought that was a beautiful thing. She answered, "I can't do this." When he asked her was it was she couldn't do, Laura replied, "Be a Christian."

She said, "My family believes. . . . I feel as though I need to believe. Like I'm going to die if I don't believe. But it is all so stupid." They talked a while,

Don encouraging her to confess, which was something she had said she felt a need to do. Then she said, "I can't Don. It isn't a decision. It isn't something you decide." When he asked her what she meant, Laura replied, "I can't get there. I can't just say it without meaning it. I can't do it. It would be like, say, trying to fall in love with somebody, or trying to convince yourself that your favorite food is pancakes. You don't decide those things, they just happen to you. If God is real, He needs to happen to me."

Later, Don received an e-mail from his friend Laura. It said, simply: "Dearest friend Don, I read through the Gospel of Matthew this evening. I was up all night. I couldn't stop reading so I read through Mark. This Jesus of yours is either a madman or the Son of God. Somewhere in the middle of Mark I realized He was the Son of God. I suppose this makes me a Christian. I feel much better now. Come to campus tonight and let's get coffee. Much love, Laura."[1]—Michael Ruffin

Spiritual Formation. Someone in my house was recently sent home from school with a book titled *Hands Are Not for Hitting*.[2] It seems that this particular family member has not yet learned how to respond when he or she does not get what he or she wants. It's a wonderful little book that tells us what our hands are made for and the hurt that is caused when we use them inappropriately. I recommend its purchase for anyone in your family who is unsure about what to do with his or her hands. And it seems to have the power of scripture to transform, because after one evening of reading the book, this person was no longer hitting people, and was repeating the refrain, "Hands are not for hitting."

However, we had to give the book back, and a week later, the hitting had started up again. You know why? Because for any change to last, spiritual formation is required. Our actions always stem from who we are on the inside, and to change requires that we be shaped spiritually. And there are no quick fixes in the realm of spiritual formation. But spiritual formation in the way of Jesus is the primary purpose of the church.—Greg Pope

[1]Donald Miller, *Blue Like Jazz: Non-Religious Thoughts on Christian Spirituality* (Nashville: Thomas Nelson, 2003), pp. 52–58.
[2]Agassi Martine, *Hands Are Not for Hitting* (Minneapolis: Free Spirit, 2000).

Musical Selections Appropriate to the Day

Gen. 12:1–4a	*Have Faith in God*
Ps. 121	*Sing Praise to God Who Reigns Above*
Rom. 4:1–5, 13–17	*Before the Throne of God Above*
John 3:1–17	*Immortal Love, Forever Full*

ᴥ Children's Lectionary Sermon

TITLE: Trusting Without a Map
SCRIPTURE: Genesis 12:1–4a
KEY VERSE: *The Lord had said to Abraham, "Leave your country, your people and your father's household and go to the land I will show you."* (Gen. 12:1, NIV)
KEY CONCEPT: Abraham trusted God.
MATERIALS: Bible, map of your city
PREPARATION: Mark your home and the church on the map.

This is a map of our city, _____. Here's where my house is. Here's where the church is. When I'm going somewhere, I really like to have a map. Why do you think that is? How would a map help me? (*Let the children respond.*) Well, I don't want to get lost, and I want to make sure I get to the right place.

In the Bible, there's a story about a man named Abraham. One day, God told Abraham to pack up his family and all the stuff he owned and go to a new place God would show him. (*Open Bible.*) In Genesis 12, *The Lord had said to Abraham, "Leave your country, your people and your father's household and go to the land I will show you."* Abraham didn't know what this new place would be like, and he didn't have a map to get there. He just had to trust that God loved him, so God would guide him to a good place, and God would help him go in the right direction so that he wouldn't get lost.

Do you think you could trust God that much? I hope I could, but that would be really hard, to just get up and move without knowing anything about where you're headed. But sometimes, God wants us to do things, and we don't really know how it will turn out. We just have to trust that God loves us and that what he wants us to do will turn out to be the best for us.—Dawn Burnett

❧ WORSHIP AIDS ❧

Call to Worship: "Lord, who may dwell in your sanctuary? Who may live on your holy hill? He whose walk is blameless and who does what is righteous, who speaks the truth from his heart" (Ps. 15:1–2, NIV).

Invocation: Stir us in worship, Lord. Move us and prod us to be open to your Holy Spirit and committed to your perfect will. Amen.—E. Lee Phillips

Offertory Sentence: "The silver is mine, and the gold is mine, says the Lord of Hosts" (Hag. 2:8, NIV).

Offertory Prayer: Keep us faithful, Lord, that what we do in this hour may eventuate into mighty acts that magnify our Lord Jesus Christ. Amen. —E. Lee Phillips

Morning Prayer: (Prayer on John 3:14–21) Father, your love for us is greater than we could ever imagine. And it is your love that caused you to send your Son to die on our behalf. Because of Christ's love, we participate in eternal life with you—life that is everlasting and full of joy, and that assures the hope of glory. You sent Jesus not to condemn us but, rather, that through him we might be saved. In him we find no condemnation—for his righteousness is given to us. And our sin is given to the cross. Father, you have sent your light into the world. Help us when we love darkness more than light. Help us draw others to your light despite their love for darkness. Help us when we feel as though we still live in darkness to know that you have delivered us from it—that indeed we are free to walk with you in the light. The gift of your Son on the cross is more than we could ever deserve. May we praise you forever for this incredible gift! Amen.—Amy Crecink

Benediction: The grace, peace, and love of the triune God guide, protect, and defend you, that in all ways you might stand strong in the faith by which you are kept . . . forever. Amen.—E. Lee Phillips

SUNDAY, MARCH 27, 2011
Third Sunday in Lent

LECTIONARY SERMON TOPIC: "Trying to Get to 20/20"

TEXT: Exod. 17:1–7

OTHER READINGS: Ps. 95; Rom. 5:1–11; John 4:5–42

Sometimes we get in the habit of seeing things the wrong way. Sometimes we see things in a false way for so long that we become unable to see things in a true way. Sometimes we talk so much about our skewed way of experiencing and seeing life that when we do gain some clarity, neither we nor anyone listening to us quite believes it. Too often the people of God choose to see life with flawed vision, with the result that we don't grow in our faith and in our witness.

I. **Consider the lie that the Hebrews insisted on living.** When they found themselves trapped at the sea, they cried out in panic to Moses, saying that it would have been better had they stayed in bondage in Egypt. God parted the sea so they could cross. They found themselves in need of food. They complained again, saying that they would have been better off back in Egypt. God sent them bread from heaven. Then, as our text tells us, they found themselves in need of water. They complained yet again, saying that they would have been better off back in Egypt. God gave them water from a rock.

Now it's understandable that anyone, including God's people, would express concern when trapped between the devil and the deep blue sea, when hungry with no source of food, and when thirsty with no supply of water. You would think, though, that by the time the water crisis arose, the Hebrews would have begun to understand the way things work when God is in your midst. Of course, you would also think that by the time your latest crisis or my latest crisis arose, we too would have learned a lot about the way things work when God is with us.

The real problem with the Hebrews' attitude is revealed in their question "Is the Lord among us or not?" The Lord had already shown them many times that he was in fact among them. The Lord has already shown us many times that he is in fact among us. The Hebrews needed to rehearse, believe, and live that truth, and so do we. To do otherwise is to believe and live the lie that God is not with us.

II. **We need to learn the truth that the times of testing and trial that come to us are opportunities for us to grow toward our ultimate salvation in Christ.** That is the truth in which we need to live.

I've been getting my vision checked and adjusted for all my life. You know how the process works. You sit in that chair and put your chin in that little depression. The doctor swings that big contraption in front of you and clicks a lens down in front of each eye and asks you to read those ridiculously small letters. Then she starts clicking lenses of differing strengths down before your eyes. "Which one is clearer? Is it this one? Or this one?" The doctor is trying to get your vision as close to 20/20 as possible. Finally satisfied that it is as clear as it is going to get, she leans back and says, "There, read it now." And she will write your new prescription based on that information.

But what if you lie about what you see? What if, although you can see clearly through that final pair of lenses that the sixth line from the top says "AZ3PS," you choose to say that it says "4X8RB"? You will have chosen to claim that what you see is not what you see, and the doctor will end up prescribing glasses that will cause you to see your world in a warped way.

We all have trials and tribulations; we all have pain and suffering. Some of us deal with very severe situations, which I will not minimize by saying something trite like "You just need to have faith, and it'll be all right," because some of us have struggles that may endure until the day we die.

I will say, though, that all the experiences of our lives work like the lenses on the eye doctor's machine—they can bring the truth into greater and greater clarity. Here is a death, here is a rebellious child, here is a serious illness, here is a vocational struggle—God sees us through. And each crisis can and should cause us to be more aware and more convinced of the truth that God is indeed among us and with us. We live, practice, believe, and tell that truth.

III. **How different the Hebrews' experience could have been!** Had they said, when trapped at the sea, when in need of food, and when in need of water, "Well, this is bad. But God got us out of Egypt, and God will get us through this," things could have been different.

I'm not saying that they should have looked at their world through rose-colored glasses, but they surely should not have looked at it through the blinders of fear and disbelief and mistrust. They should have let their progressive experiences with God as he brought them through trial after trial lead them closer and closer to 20/20 vision, to a way of looking at the world in the way that God intended.

That's what needs to be happening in our lives. When that is happening, we can say with Paul, "We . . . boast in our sufferings, knowing that suffering produces endurance, and endurance produces character, and character produces hope, and hope does not disappoint us, because God's love has been poured into our hearts through the Holy Spirit that has been given to us" (Rom. 5:3–5). In other words, our sufferings and trials move us closer and closer to God's 20/20 vision, because our experience with them moves us closer and closer to living in hope.—Michael Ruffin

---

ILLUSTRATIONS

Living a Lie. The movie *The Hoax* (2006) is a fictionalized account of the true story of the attempt by Clifford Irving in 1971 to publish a fake autobiography of Howard Hughes. Irving spent months living a lie—actually, living several lies at once. As he produced the fake autobiography, he spent so much time imagining that he was inside Hughes's head that he began to think that there was some real connection between them. As he was being unfaithful to his wife, he was able to tell her that it wasn't true and even to believe that it wasn't. He began to see things in such an untrue way that the untruth became reality for him. The film teaches us that if we persist in living a lie, we will come to believe the lie.—Michael Ruffin

Credibility. In the movie *The Window* (1949), nine-year-old Tommy has a penchant for telling tall tales. His family is going to move from their New York City apartment to his father's ranch as soon as they can kill all the Indians; he saw a truck strike and kill a large group of people. But such things are going on only in his head. One night, though, he really sees a neighbor couple kill a man. But Tommy has lived in lies for so long that no one will believe him when he tells the truth. If we persist in telling lies, no one will believe us when we try to tell the truth.—Michael Ruffin

Musical Selections Appropriate to the Day

Exod. 17:1–7	*Lead Me, Guide Me*
Ps. 95	*O Worship the King*
Rom. 5:1–11	*Grace Greater Than Our Sin*
John 4:5–42	*O Master, Let Me Walk with Thee*

⌦ Children's Lectionary Sermon

TITLE: God Loves Whiners, Too

SCRIPTURE: Exod. 17:1–7

KEY VERSE: *"I will stand there before you by the rock. . . . Water will come out of it for the people to drink."* (Exod. 17:6, NIV)

KEY CONCEPT: God loves us no matter what.

MATERIALS: Bible

Do any of you ever whine? (*Listen to their answers and react accordingly.*) You know, sometimes I get kind of whiny and crabby. It happens to everyone sometimes—even grown-ups.

The Bible tells us how Moses led the Israelite people out of Egypt. They had to walk around in the desert for a long, long time before they could go into the good land God promised to give them. What's a desert like? (*Let the children answer and then reflect back their answers.*) Well, it's hot, and there's very little water there.

One day, after a long day of marching, the people set up camp, but there was no water in that place, not one little river. So the people started complaining and whining about Moses, who was their leader, and about God, because God was the one who brought them out of Egypt. "Why did you bring us out here to die of thirst!?!" they said.

Moses talked to God about the situation, and God told him to walk on ahead and strike a certain rock with his walking stick. (*Open Bible.*) God said to Moses, *"I will stand there before you by the rock. . . . Water will come out of it for the people to drink."* When Moses struck the rock, water gushed out for all the people to drink. They were very happy.

So even though they were whining and grumpy, God still loved them and took care of them, didn't he?

It's nice to know God still loves us, even when we're feeling crabby. Let's thank God for loving us even when we aren't very fun to be with.—Dawn Burnett

❧ WORSHIP AIDS ❧

Call to Worship: "In my distress I called to the Lord; I cried to my God for help. From his temple he heard my voice; my cry came before him, into his ears" (Ps. 18:6, NIV).

Invocation: May each of us in our silent ways listen for the still, small voice of God, and quietly pray, seek, and obey—mountains to move. Amen. —E. Lee Phillips

Offertory Sentence: "If we live, we live to the Lord; and if we die, we die to the Lord. So whether we live or die, we belong to the Lord" (Rom. 15:8, NIV).

Offertory Prayer: Loving Lord, may we be wise stewards of all you have given us, ever ready to share and sacrifice for the victorious cause of Christ. Amen.—E. Lee Phillips

Morning Prayer: This gathered congregation waits before you, Father. We really do not know fully how to address you and express what needs to be said. Sometimes we wonder why we need to say anything, because our faith teaches us that you already know all there is to know about us. Yet we feel the need to be met by you. Such meeting gives us a sense of assurance; helps us understand our smallness, our limitations; and grants us a fleeting glimpse of majesty and glory. Through a hymn, a scripture, a prayer, an anthem, we seem to be brought closer to ultimate reality so that in moments like these we can better understand ourselves in the presence of our loving Father.

Here today in this sacred place, show us how to manage our personal struggles. So strike us with your consuming presence that we will see ourselves as we are and, understanding our need, cast our very souls on your mercy, forgiveness, love, and redemption.

We need to be here, Father. Only in your presence can we find our way and not stumble in the dark. Let the light come upon us even now, we pray in Jesus' name. Amen.—Henry Fields

Benediction: Give God thanks for a new week. Relish opportunities to share God's love. Stay close to the word and devout in prayer. And the eternal love of God keep you till we meet again. Amen.—E. Lee Phillips

SUNDAY, APRIL 3, 2011
Fourth Sunday in Lent

LECTIONARY SERMON TOPIC: "Blind Spots"
TEXT: John 9:1–41
OTHER READINGS: 1 Sam. 16:1–13; Ps. 23; Eph. 5:8–14

So this guy comes up to me last week, and without so much as a "Here's mud in your eye," he spits into the dirt—a pretty healthy spit, it must have been, because he makes enough mud to rub over my eyes. "Go wash yourself off in the pool down the road," he says, and I'm thinking it's a dirty trick to play on a blind man. But what else am I going to do? I won't get anything begging looking like I've been bobbing for mud pies. So off I go, and when I wash off the mud, I can see. Downright amazing, I say, but when I look for the mud-maker to say thanks, he's gone.

I. **Nobody believed it.** In fact, some people who have known me all my life refused to accept what they saw. "Yeah, he sounds the same, and he looks the same, but he can't be the same, because he can see." As if blindness was, all along, the thing that really defined me—talk about blind! And the Pharisees—good, godly people, all of them, but more than a little stubborn about new ideas—suspected some kind of trick. It was last Sabbath when it happened, see? And you know how strict they are about not working on God's holy day. "How did he do it?" they wanted to know, so I told them—he put mud on my eyes, and when I washed it off, I could see. "But it's Sabbath," they said. "You know the law: no work, and if this man is a healer, that's his work, and so he deliberately broke the law. He treated God's holy day as if it were an ordinary weekday when he did that—he's a sinner." "But wait, Yakov," said another expert on God's holiness, "you gotta admit that this man can see. If his eyes were healed, God did it; would God do that for a sinner?"

Good point, I thought—the mud-maker must be a prophet like Elijah or Moses if he can get God to answer his prayers. God knows, I prayed for healing for years until I gave up on it. This man must be somebody special, so when the Pharisees stopped arguing long enough to ask me what I thought, that's what I told them—that God worked a miracle through him, so therefore he's a prophet.

II. **"Hold on, not so fast," says a skeptic.** "This could all be a set-up. How do we know you were really blind? There are plenty of con artists out there pretending to be blind or lame who are really just too lazy to work."

Can you blame the skeptics? What they say is true—you can't just go around believing every crazy thing that some religious nut tells you. Lots of people make lots of money by pretending to speak for God. So I didn't blame them when they wanted to make sure I had truly been blind—if you want to pretend that nothing is an illusion, then you're blinder than I was.

But when they had questioned my parents: Is this truly your son? Was he actually born blind? And after my folks told them yes, that's our boy, and he was born blind, and we have no idea how he got his vision—after all that, they still didn't believe. Or more precisely, despite all the evidence, they refused to believe, because they already knew who my mud-maker was, and they had already decided he was a bad guy. So they questioned me one more time: "Look, you—we know the man who did this to you is a sinner. Tell the truth before God—don't you agree?" "I'm no theologian," I said. "All I know is that yesterday I was blind, and today I can see." "But how did it happen?" they said. "Maybe he did something wicked; maybe he used Satan's power rather than God's. What did he do?"

III. **Blind spots—how else can we explain how long it took for good, godly, Christian people to agree that slavery was evil?** Or the quasi-slavery of the Jim Crow segregation laws? How else can we explain Christian racism? Yes, Jesus loves the little children of the world, but they flood our hospitals and take our jobs and overcrowd our schools, and we need the government to send them packing—with Jesus' blessing, I guess. We know the Pharisees in this story are the bad guys, because they give priority to Sabbath over healing. But we put all sorts of things ahead of feeding and healing the poor, don't we? It's too expensive, we say—meaning that we won't be in favor of a plan that changes what we have. They should get a job like I did, we say—I haven't gotten any handouts.

The Pharisees tried that with me, too. I wouldn't agree that Jesus was a sinner, so they decided that I was one, too—"you were born in sin," they said. Insults are always the last resort of the willfully blind.—Richard Vinson

ILLUSTRATIONS

Blind Spots. You know how a teenager can walk past an overflowing garbage can and never notice it? Or how a teen can say, "Mom, I don't have any clean socks!" when you've just put a stack of them on top of the dresser? More seriously, you know how people can walk by the same blind man every day on their way home and never really look at him? I sure do—all those people with perfectly good eyes who never paid any attention to me, or at least not enough to be able to recognize me when I wasn't sitting in my spot begging. More seriously still, do you know how people who are convinced of the rightness or wrongness of something can keep refusing to see evidence that could make them change their minds? Blind spots, I call them.—Richard Vinson

Clear Vision. Annie Dillard, in *Pilgrim at Tinker Creek*, writes about how hard it is to see.[1] You stare at a stream, hoping to see a muskrat, and it's like the minnows and water-striders are in your way. Or you're admiring how beautiful the leaves are on a tree, and suddenly a hundred birds fly out of it. Even when we're trying really hard, we can miss so much—the needs of those closest to us, the biases through which we interpret the world, the categories we plug people into. Today, as we near the end of our Lenten journey, can we pray that Jesus will put mud in our eyes so we'll have to go wash and maybe see more clearly?—Richard Vinson

Musical Selections Appropriate to the Day

1 Sam. 16:1–13	*Rise Up, O Men of God*
Ps. 23	*Praise to the Lord, the Almighty*
Eph. 5:8–14	*City of God*
John 9:1–41	*On Jordan's Stormy Banks I Stand*

---

[1]Annie Dillard, *Pilgrim at Tinker Creek* (New York: HarperCollins, 1974), pp. 14–25.

🐚 Children's Lectionary Sermon

TITLE: God Looks at the Heart

SCRIPTURE: 1 Sam. 16:1–13

KEY VERSE: *Man looks at the outward appearance, but the Lord looks at the heart.* (1 Sam. 16:7, NIV)

KEY CONCEPT: It's not so important that you are big or strong, but that you love God.

MATERIALS: Bible, anointing oil

The Bible tells us about a time when God was ready to choose a new king to lead his people, the Israelites. He told the prophet Samuel to go to a certain town and be ready to put oil on the person he had chosen.

This is anointing oil. (*Show them flask.*) In those days, when you wanted to show that someone was really, really important, you would put oil on their head. And when God had a special job for someone, he would have oil put onto the person's head before he started. Might seem kind of strange to us, but that's what they did.

Anyway, the prophet Samuel went, and God directed him to look at some sons of a man named Jesse. Jesse had his sons come one by one in front of Samuel, but God kept telling him "No, that's not the right person to be king." Samuel was surprised because he thought the first son really looked like a king. He was tall and handsome. But God said no, I'm not looking at the outside, I'm looking at the inside. (*Open Bible.*) In 1 Samuel it says, *Man looks at the outward appearance, but the Lord looks at the heart.* It's not so important how tall or good looking they are, the important thing is—do they really love me?

Finally, Jesse brought in his youngest son, who had been out watching the sheep. His name was David. And God told Samuel, that's the one, because David really loved God. And Samuel anointed David with oil. He later became the king.—Dawn Burnett

☙ WORSHIP AIDS ❧

Call to Worship: "The heavens declare the glory of God; the skies proclaim the work of his hands. Day after day they pour forth speech; night after night they display knowledge. There is no speech or language where their voice is not heard" (Ps. 19:1–3, NIV).

Invocation: In this sacred hour, on this holy day, we come into your presence, Father, with praise and thanksgiving in our hearts and on our lips. Meet us in the majesty of your power that we might realize how finite we really are. Open before us the expanse of eternity that we might come to know the boundaries of earth time. Show us the depths of your love that we might see the shallowness of our own. Reveal to us again the wonder of Christ's redemption that we might in him find our true salvation.—Henry Fields

Offertory Sentence: "But seek first his kingdom and his righteousness, and all these things will be given to you as well" (Matt. 6:33, NIV).

Offertory Prayer: Lord, accept these gifts we bring, dedicated to the work of the church, the spread of the gospel, and given to your everlasting glory. Amen.—E. Lee Phillips

Morning Prayer: Lord, you are awesome, and your creation testifies to the awe that you are due. You are the one and only Savior and hope for the people of all the world—now and forever. You, the most high God, spoke all of creation into existence. All creation is at your beckoning call. For who can say, "It is I that formed the mountains!"? There is not one! For who could claim to embody the power of your majesty? There is not one!

For who can calm the raging seas and settle their waves? There is not one! For who can impede the turmoil of the nations of the earth? There is not one! The whole earth fears your power and marvels at your acts of righteousness. The earth sings your praise no matter the time of day—morning or night. It is evident to all, Almighty God, that you are sufficient to exceed every need we could possibly encounter, and there is no need to be concerned with the things of this earth, for you will tend to the earth's needs. For you water the crops when the land is infertile, you overflow the fields with bountiful harvests, you provide grasslands and meadows that tell of your mercy, and through it all we begin to understand that you are omnipotent and sovereign over all creation! Amen.—Tim Statton

Benediction: In the Spirit of the living Lord Jesus Christ, we go forth. May his presence and power direct our way—and multiply our service in his name. Amen.—Lee McGlone

SUNDAY, APRIL 10, 2011
Fifth Sunday in Lent

LECTIONARY SERMON TOPIC: "Can These Bones Live?"
TEXT: Ezek. 37:1–14
OTHER READINGS: Ps. 130; Rom. 8:6–11; John 11:1–45

The valley was full of bones, lots and lots of them, and they were very dry. And God says to the prophet, "Mortal, can these bones live?" In our experience, mostly not. Isn't that so? We don't know what happens beyond that last breath. We believe, or so many of us say we believe when we recite the creed, in "the resurrection of the dead and the life everlasting." But on some days, the reality of what we see and experience is so strong that it's hard to believe that those dry bones can ever live.

I. **We sit by the bedside, listening to how hard it is for our loved one to breathe, until the moment comes when all sound stops.** We sit by the graveside to see the place where those bones will be lowered. We may never be whole again, but we know the road toward something approaching wholeness has to begin with facing the loss and admitting that it's real. "Mortal, can these bones live?" Not so that I can hold him, not so that I can touch her, they can't. "Mortal, can these bones live?" What a cruel question—of course they can't.

Look on the Habitat for Humanity Web site sometime at the Faces and Places tab—story after story of restoration. A single woman, homeless, with no goals except to find enough to eat and a warm, dry place to sleep, feels as though she has been resurrected—the prospect of owning a home led to employment opportunities that gave her a chance to start over. A family, having lost their home to unemployment and high mortgage rates, splits up because they can't support each other any longer. The Habitat house reunited them, resurrecting their common life. Can these bones live? Sometimes not—not every Habitat story is a success. Some folks default and go back to the streets. But sometimes, yes, people's lives are restored, because enough people are convinced it's possible.

II. **Or take Ezekiel himself, trying to minister to a congregation wrenched from its homeland by a powerful enemy and taken into exile.** Thousands died at the hands of the Babylonians; tens of thousands lost their families, their homes, their possessions, their country, their Temple; many assumed that they'd lost their God as well. Can these bones live? It doesn't seem possible. How will we ever get back home? And even if we did, how could we ever rebuild what was torn down?

"Mortal, can these bones live?" God asks the question, but Ezekiel can't answer, nor can we; God alone knows. But on that day, God tells the prophet to do what he does best: "Prophesy to these bones," says God, "and tell them, 'Hear the word of the Lord, O dry bones!'" Surely Ezekiel felt more than foolish; quite possibly he was angry as he thought about the death of his own wife, or the deaths of those who perished in the siege of Jerusalem. But he does what God commands. And you know, it doesn't happen all at once. The bones come together with a creepy rattling sound, and flesh covers them, but they still aren't alive. God tells him then, "Prophesy to the Ruach—the great wind that blows around the earth, the breath in your body, and the Spirit of God that ties all things together— prophesy to that Ruach, mortal, and tell it to breathe on the dead" (Ezek. 37:13). He does, and they live.

III. **We know why we have this text in our lectionary.** We're almost at the end of Lent, almost to Palm Sunday and Holy Week, and we're hearing one of the great Hebrew Bible texts that at least float the notion of a resurrection. Much of the Old Testament says, like the psalm, that the dead lie forgotten in Sheol. They are dead, like poor old Marley in *A Christmas Carol*, dead as a doornail; or as the hymn says, "They fly, forgotten, as a dream dies at the opening day." That's our experience, too. Things wear out; people die; hopes fade; the world rolls on, but there's an end for every living thing, and beyond that end, there are only dry, dry bones.

That's our experience. But . . . but we've also experienced better things. Broken hearts that find love once again. The first easy breath you take, after a long grief that has felt like an iron band wrapped around your chest. The first sight of home for the exiles returning from Babylon; the first Passover they celebrated back in Israel; the way the old folks wept when the new Temple was dedicated, grieving what was lost, but celebrating what was beginning. Yes, mortal things perish, but then God's Spirit breathes, and things live.

Mortal, can these bones live? Can we believe that a man who suffered under Pontius Pilate, was crucified, dead and buried—can we believe that he lives? And if he does—can we believe that has anything to do with us? We say we believe that he is alive, and that because God raised him from the dead, God will raise us as well. Deep into Lent, surrounded by dry bones, it's hard to believe. So prophesy, brothers and sisters. Tell the gospel to each other. Let me see the spirit and image of the Risen Christ in you, and I'll pray that you'll see him in me.—Richard Vinson

---

ILLUSTRATIONS

Hope. You may have heard of Jane Goodall's book *Hope for Animals and Their World*, which recounts stories of animal species all but extinct that have been brought back from the brink.[2] A little bird, native only to New Zealand, the black robin, was down to only five members, including only one fertile female.

---

[2] Jane Goodall, Gail Hudson, and Thane Maynard, *Hope for Animals and Their World* (New York: Grand Central, 2009).

A man named Don Merton intervened, and after twenty-five years there are 250 of the little birds. Goodall tells story after story like this, of endangered species recovering. Can these bones live? Sometimes, if enough people are convinced it's possible.—Richard Vinson

Optimism. Margaret Odell's recent treatment of this passage suggests that God's question to Ezekiel is "cruel and the reply all too polite."[3] She thinks it unlikely that Ezekiel, having faced the death of his wife, the destruction of his people, and the desolation of the religion of which he was a priest, would have had any optimism about this valley of dry bones. But, surprise, he did.—Richard Vinson

Musical Selections Appropriate to the Day

Ezek. 37:1–14	*Redeemed*
Ps. 130	*Out of My Bondage, Sorrow, and Night*
Rom. 8:6–11	*Holy Spirit, Rain Down*
John 11:1–45	*Breathe on Me, Breath of God*

Children's Lectionary Sermon

TITLE: Jesus Doesn't Give Up

SCRIPTURE: John 11:1–45

KEY VERSE: *Then Jesus said, "Did I not tell you that if you believed, you would see the glory of God?"* (John 11:40, NIV)

KEY CONCEPT: Although we might give up hope, God continues to work to bring life.

MATERIALS: Bible

---

[3]Margaret S. O'Dell, *Ezekiel* (Macon, GA: Smyth & Helwys, 2005), p. 460.

Have you ever given up trying something? (*Let the children respond.*) Like maybe you wanted to open up a jar of jelly or a bottle of pop, and you really, really tried, but you just had to give up. Sometimes things are just hard, and it is easier to give up.

There were some friends of Jesus who really gave up one day. They gave up believing that Jesus could even help them. In this family there were two sisters, Mary and Martha, and a brother named Lazarus. Well one day, Lazarus got sick, and the sisters sent word asking Jesus to come and help him, because they knew that Jesus could heal sick people. Jesus didn't come right away, and Lazarus died before he got to their house.

Mary and Martha were crying and so sad. When Jesus came, they were still so very sad, because they thought there was nothing anyone could do. Lazarus was dead, so they gave up. But Jesus didn't give up. (*Open Bible.*) In the gospel of John, *Jesus said, "Did I not tell you that if you believed, you would see the glory of God?"* He went to the grave where Lazarus's body was. It was like a cave. And he told them to open it up, to take away the big stone that was in front of the cave. Then he prayed to God and called out, "Lazarus, come out!" And out Lazarus came—alive again!

There are times when things seem so difficult that we know no matter hard we try, it will not be enough. But with Jesus, nothing is beyond his power, and we need to go to him when we are in need of help.—Dawn Burnett

೫ WORSHIP AIDS ೫

Call to Worship: "Be exalted, O Lord, in your strength; we will sing and praise your might" (Ps. 21:13, NIV).

Invocation: Gathered before you this morning, Father, we wait for the opportunity to encounter you in all the ways that you come to seeking souls. Each brings separate circumstances to this hour for your consideration. All bring the need for divine intervention in our lives as we try to understand and manage the events surrounding us. Our wisdom is so meager. Our knowledge, even at its best, is so small. Our abilities to function in our own strength and foresight are far too insignificant. We know that without you we will fall and fail and flounder. So today, meet us in this sacred place, we pray, and lead us to do your will in all things even as was done for those first followers whom Christ taught to pray: (Lord's Prayer).—Henry Fields

Offertory Sentence: "But just as you excel in everything—in faith, in speech, in knowledge, in complete earnestness and in your love for us—see that you also excel in this grace of giving" (2 Cor. 8:7, NIV).

Offertory Prayer: Lord, here is our monetary offering. It is but seed to be planted in your service. May there be sufficient seed to bring forth a good harvest as it is broadcast in the fertile soil of your purpose to germinate and blossom and produce fruit fit for your Kingdom. Amen.—Henry Fields

Morning Prayer: Lord, teach us to pray. How do we pray for one another as we should? In the course of the day, we hear of another's need, but our knowledge of that person is limited, and we do not seem able to pray for him or her from the depths of our hearts. Lead us by your Spirit as we seek to become more adept in praying for others. Stir compassion within us that we may feel their anguish and pain. Ignite pity in our souls for them that we might be stirred to action on their behalf. Magnify love in our hearts that we might see all others in the light of the redeeming love of Christ. Remind us that praying is more than words, more than feelings; it is acting in Christ's name on behalf of another. Call us to you this morning and teach us to pray.

Lead us out to service in Christ's name. Keep us faithful to the commitments we have made to the church, to teaching, leading, empowering. But inspire us to serve Christ beyond the doors of the gathered church as we go out into the world where need and lostness meet us everywhere. Wherever we go, make us aware of the call we have accepted to be servants of the Lord, for it is in his name that we pray. Amen.—Henry Fields

Benediction: People of God, go forth in the joy of the Lord. And may that joy increase as we pour ourselves out in behalf of others in the days of this week. Amen.—Lee McGlone

SUNDAY, APRIL 17, 2011
Palm Sunday

LECTIONARY SERMON TOPIC: "Who Is This?"

TEXT: Matt. 21:1–11

OTHER READINGS: Liturgy of the Palms: Ps. 118:1–2, 19–29; Matt. 21:1–11; or Liturgy of the Passion: Isa. 50:4–9a; Ps. 31:9–16; Phil. 2:5–11; Matt. 26:14–27:66 or Matt. 27:11–54

Who is this? That's not a bad question for Palm Sunday, as we round the last turn and head into Holy Week, the home stretch for our Lenten journey. Who is this man, precariously balanced on mama burro and her colt, riding into the city surrounded by a shouting mob? The people of Jerusalem wanted to know "What's all the hubbub, bub? Who is this guy anyway?"

I. **Begin by asking those closest to him: they have been making some progress in their understanding of Jesus.** Early on in this gospel, when they watch him calm a storm, they are simply amazed: "What sort of person is this, that the wind and sea obey him?" But after the second storm-stilling, especially after seeing him walk the waves, they worship him as Son of God. They may not be the quickest mice in the maze, but they get to the cheese eventually. And later, when Jesus asks them who they think he is, Peter speaks for all of them: You are the Messiah, the Son of God. "Bingo!" says Jesus. "No human told you this, Peter; this was a message from God." Pretty high praise. So, presumably, if the people of Jerusalem had asked Peter or John or one of the other twelve, they could have told them who he was: the Messiah, the Son of God.

Had the Jerusalemites asked his adversaries, the Pharisees, they'd have heard a different answer. Early in the gospel, they also come to a firm conclusion about him. He's a sinner who breaks the Sabbath. He's a magician who does miracles only by Satan's power. He is a troublemaker who has no legitimate authority. "Show us a sign," they say, but he won't. "Why don't you obey God's law just as we do?" they ask, and he calls them hypocrites. He is dangerous, and they want him dead. Who is he? Ask a Pharisee, and you'd hear, "He's a quack, he's a heretic, and he needs to be silenced."

II. **The swing votes, so to speak, are the crowds.** To this point, they have followed Jesus, thronged him, pressed him, praised him. They have been amazed by his miracles ("Never before has this happened in Israel!") and by his words ("He teaches with authority, not like our other teachers"). They seem generally favorable, but they don't all say the same thing. When Jesus asks the twelve who the crowds say he is, they report that some say he's a prophet, like Elijah; others say he has taken up the mantle of the late, great John the Baptist, and is a preacher of the coming end of time. But on this day, the crowds come close to giving the official party line, the A-plus answer. When they shout, "Hosanna to the Son of David!" that's a confession that he is the Messiah, the descendant of King David who would retake the throne of Israel. And when the folks in the city ask the folks who walked into Jerusalem with Jesus who he is, they say "Jesus of Nazareth, a prophet." "Prophet" means that God has sent him and has given him his message—that explains the authority of his words; and some prophets, like Moses and Elijah, could do amazing miracles to back up their words.

There you have it, right? Surely the disciples and the crowds can't both be wrong. Jesus is Son of David, the future king; is a prophet, sent from God; is even Son of God, God's uniquely chosen messenger. They roll out the red carpet for him, as they might do for a king. They wave palms in the air and sing the old lines from the Psalms that celebrate the coming of that long-awaited deliverer sent from God.

III. **Here's the problem, the sticking point on this gloriously celebrative morning: Jesus has said that he must die.** He tells the twelve disciples straight out, "Look, when we get to Jerusalem, I will be handed over to the Temple leaders, and they will condemn me to death; they will give me to the Romans, and the Romans will nail me to a cross." Somehow that part hasn't sunk in yet, and on this day of applause and adulation, the twelve won't get any closer to comprehension. "No, Jesus, that can't be," Peter said, and Jesus says "Get out of my way, Satan!" This is not up for debate or vote, no matter what the twelve and the crowds think Jesus ought to do.

IV. **So who is this guy? He looks really peaceful sitting there on the donkey, but the man in the Temple is a little scary.** Do you think he wants to die—that he is deliberately getting them riled up so that he can be crucified? No, I don't think Jesus had a death wish. But here's what he said: you gain your life by giving it away. You want to be number one? Be a servant, not a king. You want to enter God's ideal realm someday? Then pick up your cross.

If he's a king, then he intends to rule from the cross. If he's a prophet, then he's going to be like Amos, standing up for the helpless and standing up to the powerful. If he's the Son of God, then he's going to demonstrate his power, not by calling on the mob to storm the Temple with him, but by trusting that God's power will prevail.

Who is this guy? He's your master and mine. But sometimes he makes me really nervous. What if he asked me to follow him, to step off the edge with him, to go all the way to Good Friday with him and then to whatever lies beyond? Do I really want to know him as well as I say I do? God grant me the courage to follow my master all the way to his cross and mine.—Richard Vinson

ILLUSTRATIONS

Confrontation. And so, according to Matthew, on that day of palms and hallelujahs, Jesus went into the Temple and raised holy hell. He chased out people trying to buy animals to make sacrifices to God. The folks who swapped the Roman coins with the emperor's face on them for coins that were not idolatrous—he tipped over their tables and ran them out, too. In other words, Jesus deliberately angered the folks in charge. Early in the gospel, when his enemies were the Pharisees? That's something like angering the Methodists—unpleasant, but it won't get you killed. But making the Temple leaders his enemies? That was a seriously dangerous provocation.—Richard Vinson

Sacred Moments. The sacred moments are often the everyday moments, the moments that, if we do not look with more than our eyes or listen with more than our ears, reveal only the gardener, a stranger coming down the road behind us, a meal like any other meal. But if we look and listen with the eyes and ears of our hearts, open to the sacred and holy, what we might see is Jesus himself, what we may hear is the faint sound of a voice somewhere deep within us saying that there is a purpose in this life, in our lives, whether we can understand it completely or not. We might come to a moment where we realize we are not alone after all; hope is not lost. We are in the hands of God, one of whose names is forgiveness; another, love. That is what the stories about Jesus' coming back to life mean: Jesus was the love of God, alive among us; and not all the cruelty and blindness of the world could kill him.[4]—Greg Pope

Musical Selections Appropriate to the Day

Liturgy of the Palms:

| Matt. 21:1–11 | All Glory, Laud, and Honor |
| Ps. 118:1–2, 19–29 | This Is the Day the Lord Has Made |

Liturgy of the Passion:

Isa. 50:4–9a	Beneath the Cross of Jesus
Ps. 31:9–16	Cares Chorus
Phil. 2:5–11	At the Name of Jesus
Matt. 26:14–27:66 or	Alas, and Did My Savior Bleed
Matt. 27:11–54	

⟨⟩ Children's Lectionary Sermon

TITLE: The Welcome Mat
SCRIPTURE: Matt. 21:1–11

---

[4]This paragraph is based on the words of Frederick Buechner, *The Magnificent Defeat* (New York: HarperCollins, 1966), pp. 87–88.

KEY VERSE: *"Hosanna to the Son of David! Blessed is he who comes in the name of the Lord! Hosanna in the highest!"* (Matt. 21:9b, NIV)

KEY CONCEPT: Welcoming Christ

MATERIALS: Bible, doormat with the word "Welcome"

PREPARATION: Prior to the service, place the welcome mat in front of the entrance to the sanctuary; or place it on the floor where the children will gather, and then invite them up so that they notice the mat as they walk over it to sit down at the front.

(*Point to the welcome mat.*) Do you have one of these at your house? What do your welcome mats look like? (*Let the children answer.*) Why do you think your parents put those welcome mats by your front door at home? (*Let the children respond.*) That's right! I have one of these at home too . . . in fact, this is *my* welcome mat! You see, when people come to my house I want them to feel right at home. I want them to feel welcome before they even step one foot in the door!

(*Open Bible.*) In our scripture for today, we read about how Jesus and his disciples arrived in Jerusalem after a very long journey. And do you know what? There were huge crowds of people there to welcome them! And as Jesus and his friends the disciples got close to the city, the people began shouting, *"Hosanna to the Son of David! Blessed is he who comes in the name of the Lord! Hosanna in the highest!"*

These people were welcoming Jesus and his disciples to the city. And the words they shouted come from the book of Psalms in the Old Testament.

And do you know what else they did? They took their own coats and soft leaves from palm trees and spread them out on the ground—just like a great big welcome mat!

This next couple of weeks we are going to celebrate the great gift of Jesus, how he died and rose again so that we can be with God forever. Because of Jesus, we can each put our own "welcome mats" out for God—we can welcome God into our hearts and our lives, to help us love others and be who God has created us to be. So this week, think about how you can welcome Jesus into your heart, just as the crowds welcomed him into Jerusalem.

(*Pray with the children.*) Lord, thank you for sending Jesus to us, to die for our sins and rise from the dead so that we can be with you forever. Help us welcome you into our hearts just like those crowds welcomed Jesus into Jerusalem. Amen.—Krista Mournet

WORSHIP AIDS

Call to Worship: "Lift up your heads, O you gates; lift them up, you ancient doors, that the King of glory may come in. Who is he, this King of glory? The Lord Almighty—he is the King of glory" (Ps. 24:9–10, NIV).

Invocation: This morning awaken us to the need to follow the leadership of your Holy Spirit. Soften our souls that we may be open to doing the highest with renewed strength guided by eternal wisdom. Let our vision be clear, our purpose steadfast, and our love genuine as we walk among those to whom you lead us for the ministry each of us can perform. May the presence of the Lord accompany us even as he accompanied those first followers whom he taught to pray: (Lord's Prayer).—Henry Fields

Offertory Sentence: "For you know the grace of our Lord Jesus Christ, that though he was rich, yet for your sakes he became poor, so that you through his poverty might become rich" (2 Cor. 8:9, NIV).

Offertory Prayer: Gracious God, receive these gifts of tithes and offerings as expressions of our love, and multiply them for the cause of the gospel here and to the ends of the earth. We pray in Jesus' name. Amen.

Morning Prayer: Our Lord and Savior, Jesus Christ, as we come before you today in worship, focus our minds and hearts on you alone. We acknowledge that all true worship is both by and to you. It is our deepest desire that our praise be just that. May the message of this holy season cause each of us to give you the preeminence in all things. Wrap our lives around who you are and rain down your endless grace into our lives. Keep us from falling into any form of vain ritualism and instead give us a living and inspired spirit of worship. As we enter this wonderful season of Easter, allow your glorious Resurrection to be constantly on our minds that it may be our joyful song through all of life's journeys. Your unspeakable gift of salvation has eternally altered who we are, and we will forever exalt your name and obey your word. Open our minds to your truth in this time that we may worship in spirit and in truth. Amen.—Nick Dawson

Benediction: May the God of all creation, whom we know as Father, Son, and Holy Spirit, guide your ways in the days of this week—and may we find in him the security that makes for joy. Amen.

SUNDAY, APRIL 24, 2011
Easter Sunday

LECTIONARY SERMON TOPIC: "Going to See the Tomb"

TEXT: Matt. 28:1–10

OTHER READINGS: Acts 10:34–43; Ps. 118:1–2, 14–24; Col. 3:1–4; John 20:1–18

Sometimes the hardest thing about interpreting a New Testament text is that we have bits and pieces of other texts rolling around in our heads. We look at the one in front of us, but we hear echoes of the others, and in our minds we blend them together. On this blessed Easter Sunday, let's try hard to listen only to Matthew, shall we? Let's try to experience that first Easter as he pictured it, and imagine ourselves at the scene as he describes it.

I. **The Sabbath is past.** God's holy day, when you are to do no work, is the seventh day of the week, and it goes from Friday sundown until Saturday sundown. The first day of the week is just dawning. The two women are up early. Maybe that wasn't so unusual for them, but whether or not they were normally early risers, they are this day. Grief can do that to you, can't it? You wish you could sleep and make things go away, but sometimes you just can't. So they're up, and they head out of town "to see the tomb." Mark and Luke say they went because Jesus died so close to the start of Sabbath that his body could not be properly washed and anointed, so they were going back to do what Jews normally did to give their loved ones an honorable burial. Matthew just says, "to see the tomb," and I want us to imagine it that way this morning. Some of you know precisely what that means—you've lost someone, and you feel so empty, and you just need to go and be at the grave for a while. Did Mary Magdalene and the other Mary want to pray, or share stories with each other, or talk to their departed loved one, or just sit quietly?

II. **Then the morning erupts.** The earth shakes. An angel comes out of heaven right in front of their eyes. It's so frightening that the Temple soldiers standing guard over the tomb faint dead away. The angel rolls back the stone while the women watch, and sits on it. OK—now, *we* know that it's Easter, and that the news will be good, but can you imagine what that must have been like the first time it happened? What I mean is that we celebrate this day annually; we've been slogging through Lent to get to Easter, and we're impatient to get to the "He isn't here; he has been raised!" But pause a minute, while the angel adjusts his robe and crosses his legs; what might these grieving women be feeling? The armed guards have collapsed with fear; what keeps these women on their feet? Are they grief-numbed, operating on autopilot, while the world shakes around them?

If that's true, there's no blame involved. Many of you have been there, when sadness sucks the color from the world and leaves you in a gray funk; you can't hear the birds sing, you can't smell the roses, and you have no clue what would make you smile. Grief can do it, but so can other things—too much stress, too little sleep, job loss, money pressures, ongoing conflicts with your spouse, betrayals. Life's hard edges can cut you up bit by bit or clobber you all at once and knock you senseless. Many of you have been there; maybe most of us have been there at some time; maybe some of you are there now.

The earth rumbles, the angel descends, the guards collapse, and the women wait. And then, the voice of the angel: "Stop being afraid. I know you're looking for Jesus the crucified, but he isn't here, because he was raised, just as he said." He invites them to look in the tomb to see that Jesus' body is missing. The text doesn't say whether they did or not, but if I had to guess how Matthew imagined it, I'd say they did—usually Matthew's characters do what angels tell them to do. So maybe they confirm that part of the angel's news, that Jesus' body is no longer in the tomb. But the "he is raised" part—that much they can't confirm, and as Matthew's gospel points out, there are other possible explanations for why his body is gone—perhaps somebody took it. Again, the angel: "He has been raised from the dead, and he is going ahead of you to Galilee, and you'll see him there"—they can't see or touch or feel anything in that tomb that will prove that what the angel says is true.

III. **So what will they do?** Would you have blamed them had they just sat down at the entrance to the tomb and wept? They've been through an awful ordeal, and now this; maybe the shock of it all could have stunned them. Instead, they turn around to hurry back into Jerusalem, to do what the angel commanded: "Go tell his disciples just what I told you." They leave the tomb quickly and run with fear and great joy to tell his disciples. And as they are going, Jesus meets them, to tell them once again to let go of their fear and to tell the good news to those who need to hear it.

Come with your fears, your griefs, all the things that make your world go gray; come to the tomb. Your hurts aren't imaginary, and we aren't going to tell you so. But we believe that God raised Jesus, and we believe that God will raise you, too, if you will open yourself to God's presence. That's the good news, brothers and sisters.—Richard Vinson

ILLUSTRATIONS

Resurrections. As Matthew tells it, there are two resurrections that day. The first one, the one we celebrate every year at this time, happens off-stage, off-camera. There is no description of the moment when Jesus was raised. His Resurrection moment goes unrecorded, and so we wonder when it happened—during the earthquake? Just before the stone rolled back? Sometime even earlier, before the women arrived? Jesus' Resurrection isn't described—it's simply reported. Matthew focuses instead on the Resurrection that happens in these two women, and how their faith and life is restored. They go that morning to see the tomb, but then God's messenger challenges them to lay aside their fear, their grief, their sense of loss—all that has paralyzed them. He challenges them to spread the world-shaking news that Jesus has been raised. They turn, in fear and joy—grief takes time, after all—but they turn and run, and as they go, Jesus meets them.—Richard Vison

Church. Anne Lamott came to faith as an adult through a faith community that was for her a safe place. In her marvelous memoir, *Traveling Mercies*, she explains why she makes her son go to church: "The main reason is that I want to give him what I found in the world, which is to say a path and a little light to see by. Most of the people I know who have what I want—which is to say, purpose, heart, balance, gratitude, joy—are people with a deep sense of spirituality. They are people in community, who pray, or practice their faith; they are Buddhists, Jews, Christians—people banding together to work on themselves and for human rights. They follow a brighter light than the glimmer of their own candle; they are part of something beautiful." She describes her church like this. She says: "When I was at the end of my rope, the people at St. Andrew tied a knot in it for me and helped me hold on. The church became my home in the old meaning of home—that it's where, when you show up, they have to let you in. They let me in. They even said, 'You come back now.'"[5] That's the kind of church I want to be a part of.—Greg Pope

Musical Selections Appropriate to the Day

Acts 10:34 –43	*Jesus Is Lord of All*
Ps. 118:1–2, 14–24	*The Wonderful Cross*
Col. 3:1–4	*Christ the Lord Is Risen Today*
John 20:1–18	
or Matt. 28:1–10	*Low in the Grave He Lay*

❧ Children's Lectionary Sermon

TITLE: The Wonderful Secret
SCRIPTURE: Matt. 28:1–10

---

[5]Anne Lamott, *Traveling Mercies* (New York: Pantheon Books, 1999), p.100.

KEY VERSE: *Then Jesus said to them, "Don't be afraid! Go tell my brothers to leave for Galilee and they will see me there."* (Matt. 28:10, NLT)

KEY CONCEPT: Resurrection

MATERIALS: Bible, gifts for the children

PREPARATION: Get small gifts, enough for all the children. Gifts may include fresh Easter lilies or flowers (one for each child), a piece of candy, an inexpensive book, a page to color with an Easter picture. Hide the gifts close to where you are giving the sermon.

Hey kids, I have a really great secret. I'd love to tell it to you, but I can't! Oh, it's so hard! Have you ever had to keep a REALLY WONDERFUL SECRET? I have. (*Tell a story from your life about having to keep a really wonderful secret.*) It was so hard to keep that secret; I just wanted to tell everybody!

In today's scripture text, Mary Magdalene and another Mary, both close friends of Jesus, were terribly sad, because just a few days before, the Lord Jesus had been crucified. In fact, in this story we read that they are on their way to visit the tomb. Imagine how sad they must have been! But when they got there, they saw an angel at the tomb, who told them wonderful news. Jesus had risen from the dead! The women were so excited; they ran quickly to get back to the disciples to tell them—but then something even more wonderful happened! While they were on the way, Jesus himself came to them! They fell at his feet and worshipped him. Then Jesus gave them a message—to tell the disciples to go to Galilee, where they would meet him too. What wonderful news!

They must have been ready to burst with excitement with such wonderful news! Today we celebrate the Resurrection of Jesus Christ, who died for our sins so that we can be with God forever. This is wonderful news! And guess what? We don't have to keep it a secret! We can tell everyone the good news of Jesus!

(*Pray with children.*) Dear God, thank you for the gift of Jesus. Thank you for the wonderful story of how Jesus died and rose again so that we can be with God forever. Help us to tell others about your love and about Jesus. Amen.

Remember how I told you that I had a really great secret? I brought a present for each of you! (*Get the gifts from their hiding place and give each child one.*) When you go to your seat, take one of these to help you remember the good news of Jesus!—Krista Mournet

⚘ WORSHIP AIDS ⚘

Call to Worship: "O Lord, open my lips, and my mouth will declare your praise" (Ps. 51:15, NIV).

Invocation: Almighty God, we rejoice in our Risen Savior. Let Christ Jesus, whom no tomb could hold, nor death vanquish, renew in us faith everlasting. Amen.—E. Lee Phillips

Offertory Sentence: "For if the willingness is there, the gift is acceptable according to what one has, not according to what he does not have" (2 Cor. 8:12, NIV).

Offertory Prayer: Eternal God, may these gifts represent our inner commitment to love you above all else in the world . . . and to love all the people in your world, all those in every age and in every place, for whom your dear Son died. Amen.

Morning Prayer: We express today thanksgiving for the children, young people, young couples, singles, and adults in our church and for the varieties of ways they serve you now and the possibilities that are within them for future service. We thank you for the yearnings we have to know you and your way better. Help us as a church to grow in our faith and serve you better. Give us as adults, youth, and children the strength to love and serve you more faithfully. May the joy, wonder, grace, and mystery of our faith be real to us. In this hour of prayer, may we be open, honest, and real. We know you see us as we really are. Thank you for loving us and accepting us, even as you know us.

Thank you, O God, for opening your loving arms to us. Teach us how to open our arms and love others who are hurting. Through Christ, who gave his life out of love for us, we pray. Amen.—William Powell Tuck

Benediction: May we be challenged by the Risen Christ to walk expectantly into the new week, living triumphantly because Jesus lives. Amen.—E. Lee Phillips

SUNDAY, MAY 1, 2011
Second Sunday of Easter

LECTIONARY SERMON TOPIC: "Making Room for Questions"
TEXT: John 20:19–31
OTHER READINGS: Acts 2:14a, 22–32; Ps. 16; 1 Pet. 1:3–9

On the evening of that first Easter Day, the disciples locked themselves in a room, afraid for their lives. You've been in that room before, haven't you? Someone you love has died, and the thought of facing the future without that person has you paralyzed. You've lost your job, and at your age you're wondering what you will do with your life. Your parents have picked you up and moved you to a new city where nothing is familiar and the new seems so scary. You're divorced, and the thought of loving again makes you so afraid, you want to lock your heart away.

Or life's just not going the way you planned, and depression has you locked away behind closed doors. Or something is finally going right in your life, and you're scared it's all going to fall apart. Yes, most of us have spent time with the disciples locked in a room somewhere, afraid of something. Maybe you're there now. And you need to know more than anything that Jesus stands in your midst and offers you the blessing of peace. There is no room too dark, there is no lock too tight, that the Risen Christ cannot enter and bring to your heart a word of peace.

And who knows—like the disciples, you too might find joy in his presence. He is risen! You need not be afraid. The worst that can happen to you cannot keep Christ from you. Death he has conquered. No longer bound by physicality, the abiding spirit of Christ goes with you always, bringing joy and peace to your sad and troubled heart.

I. **Thomas did not receive the blessing of peace on Easter evening.** For some reason he was not there. When the disciples told him they had seen Jesus, he said "No way! I've got to see it for myself. Until I see the nail marks in his hands and side and touch them for myself, I will not believe."

We all sometimes struggle to believe something, don't we? I can't believe my wife turned thirty-eight yesterday. She looks so young and beautiful! I really can't believe we're having another baby. But unlike Thomas when he first heard the news of the Resurrection, I have heard the heartbeat, and in six months will place my hand in his (or hers) and see for myself at two in the morning and truly believe.

Our struggles and questions and doubts are deeper than that and have us locked behind closed doors. Sometime they run to the very core of our faith in God. And what we need to know is that doubt and questions are a vital part of faith. Doubt is not the opposite of faith. Certainty is the opposite of faith. Certainty does not require faith because no risk is involved. And faith in God is risky if it is anything.

Questions come to us all, even to those, perhaps especially to those, of a mature faith. Doubt and questions can lead us to despair when we do not see them as a part of honest faith. But faith should always stand in tension with doubt. Doubt will always challenge faith to move to a deeper and more honest level. We need doubt and faith, questions and answers. We need both within us. We need both among us.

II. **Thomas would not let his questions go unanswered, his doubts unaddressed.** We've often called him Doubting Thomas, which is unfortunate. I think we should call him Honest Thomas because he would not ignore the questioning within his heart. He would not say he believed when he didn't believe.

We have in this gospel story the Great Commission according to John. Jesus says to the disciples, "As the Father has sent me, so I send you." And he breathes on them and says, "Receive the Holy Spirit." I find it interesting that Jesus said these words to the disciples in the absence of Thomas. Could it be that part of our mission is to go to those who are not here, who have doubts and questions, and listen to them, listen and not condemn?

It has been my experience in reading and in conversation with those on the margins of the church or outside the church altogether that they do not stay away out of disdain for Jesus and the church, God and the gospel. For many, they have questions that they do not feel they can ask in church without being condemned. They are questions you've probably heard before. You may even have asked some of them yourself. They're not easy to answer, but they do merit conversation.

III. **Given the time and space and experience, Thomas came to faith.** His confession marks the great claim of scripture. In the presence of the Risen Christ he proclaims, "My Lord and my God!" Great faith requires that you ask and live into all of your questions. You probably won't receive all the answers you're looking for. But the honesty and courage of your questions may allow you to live with the mystery of it all. And who knows, even the Church might tie a knot at the end of your rope and help you hang on.

This world is not a place for blind faith or easy answers. Jesus has a word for those who struggle with faith, those in whose mind and heart big questions abound: "Blessed are those who have not seen and yet believe."—Greg Pope

ILLUSTRATIONS

Questions. Jayber Crow is one of my favorite citizens of Port William, Kentucky, a fictitious town created by Wendell Berry. Raised at the Good Shepherd home for boys, at the age of fourteen J., as he was called, began to suspect that he might be called to preach, a notion he disliked with all his heart. He was uncertain of the call, but decided he had better accept the call that had not come, just in case it had come and he missed it. He became a pre-ministerial student at Pigeonville College, where, he says, "I believe I felt the influence of my unthought questions, but I continued not to think them. . . . But finally, the questions I had not thought of caught up with me, and had to be thought of, and had to be asked." Questions about God and scripture and prayer and war. He reached a point where he wasn't just asking questions, but was being changed by them: "Lying awake at night, I could feel myself being changed—into what, I had no idea. It was worse than wondering if I had received the call. I wasn't just a student or a going-to-be preacher anymore. I was a lost traveler wandering in the woods, needing to be on my way somewhere but not knowing where."

Doubt and questions, though essential to the life of faith, can leave us feeling lost. Jayber said: "I went to my professors with my questions. . . . They were decent enough men, according to their lights. The problem was that they'd had no doubts. They had not asked the questions that I was asking and so of course they could not answer them. They told me I needed to have more faith; I needed to believe; I needed to pray; I needed to give up my questioning, which was a sign of weakness of faith. That I should give up my questioning was good enough advice, which I would have been glad enough to take, except that my questioning would not give me up."

Finally he went to the professor he was afraid to go to because he knew he would tell him the truth. So he poured out his questions. The dialogue concludes this way. The professor says, "You have been given questions to which you cannot be given answers. You will have to live them out—perhaps a little at a time."

"And how long is that going to take?" asks Jayber.

"I don't know. As long as you live, perhaps."

"That could be a long time."

"I will tell you a further mystery," he said. "It may take longer."

So Jayber, believing he cannot be a preacher if he has no answers, eventually returns to Port William to live out his calling as the town barber.[1]—Greg Pope

Answers. Difficult questions are often asked about faith. And there are no easy answers. And the people who ask them, I don't think they're necessarily looking for easy answers. *They just want a safe place where they can ask the questions.* That is the only place true faith can flourish.—Greg Pope

Musical Selections Appropriate to the Day

Acts 2:14a, 22–32	*There Is a Balm in Gilead*
Ps. 16	*Shout to the Lord*
1 Pet. 1:3–9	*Refiner's Fire*
John 20:19–31	*So Send I You*

---

[1]Wendell Berry, *Jayber Crow* (Washington, DC: Counterpoint, 2000), pp. 42–54.

Children's Lectionary Sermon

TITLE: Living God's Way

SCRIPTURE: Ps. 16

KEY VERSE: *You have made known to me the path of life.* (Ps. 16:11, NIV)

KEY CONCEPT: God's Word

MATERIALS: Bible, flashlight, volunteer

PREPARATION: Before the sermon, put a flashlight where you can get it. Get a volunteer to stand by the light switches in the sanctuary while you share the children's sermon.

Last week we celebrated Easter—the Resurrection of Jesus from the dead. We talked about how because of Jesus, we can be with God forever, and we can learn to live the way God created us to live.

But have you ever wondered what that means? I mean, have you ever wondered what it means for us to live God's way? Well, our scripture for today can help us. (*Open Bible.*) In Psalm 16, it says *You have made known to me the path of life*. The Bible says that God tells us the right way to live our lives.

It's kind of like this. Suppose these lights all turned off. (*At this moment, the volunteer shuts off all the lights.*) Oh no! All the lights are off! How are we going to know how to get back to our seats?! Wait! I think I have something that will help us. (*Pull out the flashlight and turn it on.*) We could use this flashlight to help us, couldn't we? I don't think we'll have to do that this morning, though. (*Volunteer turns the lights back on.*)

You see, like we said last week, God sent Jesus so that we could be forgiven of our sins and be with God forever. And do you know what else? God sent us the Bible, so that we could learn how to live God's way! The Bible is like God's flashlight! It lights our way so that we can see the right way to live.

Let's pray: Dear God, thank you for sending Jesus to us. And thank you for giving us your Word, the Bible, so that we can learn how to live your way. Help us learn from the Bible. Amen.—Krista Mournet

☙ WORSHIP AIDS ☙

Call to Worship: "Show me your ways, O Lord, teach me your paths; guide me in your truth and teach me, for you are God my savior and my hope is in you all day long" (Ps. 25:4–5, NIV).

Invocation: Lord, we who seek longingly and listen expectantly, now bow humbly and pray fervently, that the words of our mouths, and the meditations of our hearts, may be acceptable in your sight, O Lord, our strength and our redeemer. Amen.—E. Lee Phillips

Offertory Sentence: "Remember this: Whoever sows sparingly will also reap sparingly, and whoever sows generously will also reap generously" (2 Cor. 9:6, NIV).

Offertory Prayer: These are the gifts we bring, O Lord: simple faith, humble offerings, and abiding prayers, the church of Christ to embolden. Amen. —E. Lee Phillips

Morning Prayer: Ever-faithful God, we know that you never leave or forsake us. We know that you have been faithful throughout the ages to your people. And we know that you are faithful to the covenant that you have made with us. For your faithfulness we celebrate. Together as your people, we celebrate your faithfulness.

Ever-gracious God, we know that through the death of your son we have received grace, the pardon of our sin. We know your grace is freely given, that your grace comes to us as unmerited favor and love. For your grace we celebrate. Together, we celebrate your grace.

Forever-good God, we know that you are good and that you use what we intend for evil for your good. We know that you work all things together for the good of those who love you. Together, we celebrate your goodness.

Great God, not only are you always good, but you are forever great. You're the creator of the heavens and earth and all that touches our senses. We stand in awe of you and your greatness. Together, we celebrate your greatness.

Father, we enter this time acknowledging that it is a time of celebration. Together, we celebrate you and all that you are. Amen.—Amy Crecink

Benediction: We go out now with hearts gladdened by the good news we believe and share. May our lives in the days of this week be reflections of the nature of God our Savior, Father, Son, and Holy Spirit, who lives and reigns through us. Amen.

SUNDAY, MAY 8, 2011
Third Sunday of Easter

LECTIONARY SERMON TOPIC: "Burning Hearts, Broken Bread"
TEXT: Luke 24:13–35
OTHER READINGS: Acts 2:14a, 36–41; Ps. 116:1–4, 12–19; 1 Pet. 1:17–23

Cleopas and Annas, two lesser known people from the extended group of Jesus' followers, are taking a walk toward Emmaus on Easter Sunday afternoon. They are still in grief over the death of their hope that this prophet, Jesus of Nazareth, was the one who would save them. They saw him die. And while there were rumors of resurrection, well, the witnesses were women, and who can trust that? It was simply a rumor too good to be true. I wonder why it is that we are quick to believe rumors of scandal and tragedy, but cannot believe good news when we hear it?

I. **Here we have these two followers of Jesus, walking down the road together, talking, wondering what they will do with their lives now that hope is gone.** You've had those conversations before, haven't you? Walking with a friend, talking about a troubled relationship or a marriage that has failed. Or you've been laid off from work. Or your best friend in the whole world has died. Or you've lost faith in God. These are holy conversations.

If we only had the eyes and ears and hearts to recognize it, we would often find Jesus walking with us. Sometimes the presence and voice of

Jesus come in the presence and voice of a friend or stranger. Jesus comes as a stranger to these pilgrims on the road to Emmaus. He becomes present in the midst of their conversation, but they are unaware of who he is.

His appearance has obviously changed in some way so that seeing him is now a matter of spiritual vision rather than physical proof. We never know in whose face we might encounter the Risen Christ. Incognito, Jesus joins the Emmaus conversation. He asks them what they are talking about. They can't believe he doesn't know what has happened. It was on CNN, in all the newspapers, talk of the town. Alan Culpepper points to the irony in this conversation. These two pilgrims on the road believe that Jesus is the only one who doesn't know what has happened, when in reality he is the only one who knows the meaning of all that has happened.[2] A reminder that just when we think Jesus is blind to our troubles, the truth is that he knows all about our troubles.

II. **They tell Jesus what has happened, how their hopes had died, but that there were rumors of resurrection.** Jesus tells them that if they had known the scriptures, they would not be so surprised. When they arrive at the village, they're not ready for Jesus to go. They're not sure who he is, but they know they want him to stay. Something about the way he spoke, something about his presence with them on the road, makes them urge Jesus to stay. There's just something about him. So he stays. And at the table, turning an ordinary meal into a Eucharistic moment, Jesus takes the bread, blesses and breaks it and gives it to them, and their eyes are opened, and they recognize in their midst the one in whom they had placed their hopes. But as soon as they recognize him, he vanishes from their sight. Then as they think back on the day, they recall how during their time with him on the road, their hearts burned within them.

It takes special eyes and ears to embrace his presence. Scripture has to be heard as more than words on a page. The bread and cup have to be experienced as more than a once-a-month ritual. Educated, intellectually oriented congregations tend to make the study of scripture a complex exercise that leaves our heads aching. We need to read and study scripture

---

[2]Alan Culpepper, "Luke," *New Interpreter's Bible* (Nashville: Abingdon Press, 1995), p. 477.

rigorously with all of our minds. But sometimes we need the kind of Bible study that causes our hearts to burn within us.

I think the Methodists are on to something with their quadrilateral understanding of the source of truth: scripture, tradition, reason, and experience. It was a deeply religious experience, some would even call it the conversion, of Methodist founder John Wesley that changed him so profoundly. After years of training and ministry, one lonely night, May 24, 1738, he walked into a Moravian meeting house on Aldersgate Street and heard a reading of Luther's preface to the Book of Romans. At about a quarter before nine, he felt his heart "strangely warmed." He was then sure of his salvation. Wesley went on to become the founder of Methodism and an influential spiritual leader in the history of Christendom, because he moved from an intellectual appropriation of his religion to an engagement with the living Christ who had seized his heart.

III. **When was the last time your heart burned within you?** When have you allowed your mind to descend into your heart and feel the burning flame of God's Spirit within you? Believing, you know, is a matter not of the mind but of the heart.

When was the last time you gave your heart the chance to believe in hope and to burn within you a holy fire? What road were you traveling? Was it at a youth camp or a retreat a year ago, twenty years ago, even longer, when shared experience, enlightened by the scriptures, became a transcendent moment? Was it a moment in this sacred room, amid the rustling waters of baptism, in the dedication of a child, at a memorial for a loved one? How long has it been since your heart burned within you?—Greg Pope

---

ILLUSTRATIONS

Easter Quiet. Frederick Buechner reminds us that when the gospel writers come to the most important part of the story, they tell it in whispers. It appears they are not trying to tell it as convincingly as they can, but as truthfully as they can. Buechner suggests that whispering of resurrection might be more true to the gospels than all the fanfare we usually associate with Easter worship. He says, "All the wonderful things that are going on around us on Easter Sunday can sometimes make us more conscious than usual that nothing even close to all that wonderful is going on inside ourselves. And that is why the Sundays after Easter are so precious, because they are closer to the reality of the resurrection as you and I are apt to experience it."[3]—Greg Pope

God's Presence. Andrew Greeley tells the story of a husband and wife who lived with much conflict between themselves. They fought over money. They fought over the time they spent with their family. They fought over where they would go on vacations. They fought over their children. And, of course, they fought over what the fights were about. Once the man and woman had been deeply in love with one another. They thought that they were still in love with one another. Only there were so many things to do in life that the conflicts had filled up the time that used to be devoted to love. Finally the man suggested one night that they get a babysitter and go out for dinner. The woman said they didn't have time for that anymore, but the man insisted. Well, the meal was wonderful, and they relaxed and had a good time and a great conversation. They saw how silly their quarrels had been and how easy it would be to avoid them, especially if they broke bread together more often. "You know," the wife said on the way home, "it was almost as though God were with us while we were eating, opening our eyes us to how foolish we've been." "Maybe," her husband replied, "God was present."[4]—Greg Pope

Musical Selections Appropriate to the Day

Acts 2:14a, 36–41	*There's a Wideness in God's Mercy*
Ps. 116:1–4, 12–19	*My Tribute*
1 Pet. 1:17–23	*Blessed Redeemer*
Luke 24:13–35	*Christ Beside Me*

---

[3]Frederick Buechner, *The Longing for Home* (New York: HarperCollins, 1996), pp. 142–144.
[4]Andrew Greeley, "April 21," http://www.agreeley.com/homilies96/apr2196.html.

Children's Lectionary Sermon

TITLE: Trust Me!

SCRIPTURE: 1 Pet. 1:17–23

KEY VERSE: *Through Christ you have come to trust in God. And you have placed your faith and hope in God because he raised Christ from the dead and gave him great glory.* (1 Pet. 1:21, NLV)

KEY CONCEPT: Trust

MATERIALS: Bible

Often when we come to worship we sing or talk about "faith" or "trust." How would you describe "trust"? (*Let the children respond—guide them if they get off track.*) When we trust, we have confidence, hope, belief, and dependence on whomever we trust. We count on those we trust. Do you have someone special you trust? (*Let the children respond.*)

(*Open Bible.*) Peter wrote a letter to Christians who were living all over the world. He wanted to encourage them, to remind them whom they should trust. In 1 Peter 1:21, Peter wrote, *Through Christ you have come to trust in God. And you have placed your faith and hope in God because he raised Christ from the dead and gave him great glory.* The Christians Peter wrote to were reminded that their trust was to be in God and that the Easter story was the reason for their faith and their hope.

We have special people in our lives we trust to share secrets or special things in our lives. But how wonderful it is that we have a God who was made known through Jesus. As we continue to celebrate this Easter season, we have faith and hope because of the Easter story too. We know we can live with God forever.—Marcia Thompson

◈ WORSHIP AIDS ◈

Call to Worship: "This is the day the Lord has made; let us rejoice and be glad in it" (Ps. 118:24, NIV).

Invocation: How would we function, Father, but for your presence and guidance with us? In our own strength and wisdom we stumble and fail. This morning as we contemplate the importance of family, we desperately need your guidance. Invade our minds, come to our souls, and visit our congregation as we expectantly wait in this gathering of believers, praying as followers who through the ages have prayed: (Lord's Prayer).—Henry Fields

Offertory Sentence: "Each man should give what he has decided in his heart to give, not reluctantly or under compulsion, for God loves a cheerful giver" (2 Cor. 9:7, NIV).

Offertory Prayer: Kind Father, accept these gifts as our effort to return to you a portion of the bounty that you have poured out on us. Multiply these gifts for the building of your Kingdom. Give us wisdom and compassion in our giving and receiving. Amen.

Morning Prayer: Today is a day in which we ponder relationships, Father. We do not do this enough, for if we did, it is probable that we would manage these close family relationships in a better manner. Yet we could not live well without them, and we are thankful for them.

Especially today are we thankful for mothers, who have been our chief caregivers through the years as well as the source of much of the wisdom and truth that we have received. Thank you for the endless hours they spent with us as we grew into maturity and for the honor that they have bestowed upon us in our adult years. Bless them with your presence as they continue their journey, some keeping busy at the task of raising little children, others fretting over the near-grown child, and still others basking in the freedom from constant responsibility for doing the best and right thing for children. For others who have fulfilled their earthly tasks, may our memories of them and their influence on our lives be the blessing we receive on this special day.

Especially this morning do we ask that you call us to a closer walk with you, Father. Only in that relationship can we find peace, act right, do good, accomplish high purpose, and add significantly to the welfare of others. And as we hear the whisper of your call, pray that we will not turn a deaf ear to you, but bravely and boldly and gladly turn aside to follow after him who is indeed Lord and Savior of us all. So in this hour let Holy Spirit meet with our spirit for our renewal and commitment, we pray in Jesus' name. Amen— Henry Fields

Benediction: Let us depart in the joy of Christ's spirit, and go forth into the days of this week, in our times of labor and leisure, to speak lovingly his Holy Name and to live in his power. May his peace be yours. Amen.

SUNDAY, MAY 15, 2011
Fourth Sunday of Easter

LECTIONARY SERMON TOPIC: "Carpe Diem".
TEXT: John 10:1–10
OTHER READINGS: Acts 2:42–47; Ps. 23; 1 Pet. 2:19–25

Jesus said, "I have come that you might have life and have it abundantly. I have come that you might have life that overflows." Did these words really come from the man of Gethsemane and Golgotha, the man who knew poverty and rejection and suffering? Did he really speak these words?

Jesus experienced life in all of its fullness. He knows what life is like in our kind of world. Life in our world has its beautiful moments. The birth of a healthy child. Finding love. Accomplishing some task that means a great deal to us and has an impact in the lives of others. Seeing spring bud in the world of nature and in our very hearts. Life has its great moments. Life also has its seasons of pain and violence, of suffering and grief.

  I. **Tony Campolo has written an inspiring book, *Carpe Diem.*** It tells of the abundant life and the search for life's meaning and purpose. In the preface of that book he writes, "It was time for me to write a book. I'm 58 years old, and I'm wondering where my life has gone. It seems to me that just as soon as my pimples cleared up, my hair fell out. All at once I feel like my life is on the final run, and I want to be sure that I get all that life has to offer out of what's left. That is why I decided to stop and reflect on what life is all about and what makes it worth living."[5]

He goes on to say, "I want life to be fun. . . . I want it to be rich and gratifying . . . , and I want to know if Jesus can help make that happen. I've always preached about Jesus and what he can do for those who embrace the life he offers. . . . I have declared how living in intimate fellowship with [Jesus] creates an aliveness . . . that makes people talk of experiencing eternal life right here and now. But there are times when I stop and ask myself if all of this is true."[6]

Campolo taught sociology at Eastern College in Pennsylvania. On the first day of a seminar he was leading, he posed a question to the class: "How long have you lived?" he asked. No one answered. So he picked out one of the students, and instinctively the student answered, "Twenty-four years." Campolo responded, "No! No! I didn't ask you how long you have existed as a breathing, functioning member of the human race. I want you to tell me how long you have been really alive!" By the end of class that day, the young man said, "When I stop and think about it, most of my life has been the meaningless passage of time between all too few moments when I have been really alive."[7]

II. **If the truth be known, after years of life on earth, most people die without really having lived at all.** There are those who never reflect with any degree of seriousness on the meaning and purpose of their lives. They eat and sleep, they work and reproduce, they study and forget. They play it safe and tiptoe through life with no aspiration other than to get all the pleasure they can out of life and arrive at death safely.

In the *Dead Poets Society*, the teacher John Keating gathers his class in the center of the room and quotes a line from Walt Whitman (Uncle Walt, as he calls him). It is a line about life that reads, "The powerful play goes on and you may contribute a verse." Have you ever thought about

---

[5]Tony Campolo, *Carpe Diem* (Nashville: Thomas Nelson, 1994), p. 9.
[6]Ibid.
[7]Ibid., pp. 13–15.

what your verse will be? When I think of people who have contributed a significant verse to the powerful play, I think of people like Jimmy Carter. Whatever you may think of his presidency or his politics, his humanitarian impact on our world as peacemaker and advocate for the poor is unmatched.

And there are law students who defend the poor and their rights. And social workers improving the lives of the disadvantaged. And teachers making a difference in the lives of children, even when they can't always see it. And parents investing their lives in their children.

III. **Jesus said, I have come that you might have life and have it more abundantly.** I have come that you might not live a life of quiet desperation. I have come that you might live deeply and find meaning. I have come so that you may not arrive at the end of your life and discover that you've not really lived. I have come to empower you to the seize the day, every day, to risk something big for something good, to make the most of the only life you have to live.

"The powerful play goes on and you may contribute a verse." What will your verse be?—Greg Pope

---

ILLUSTRATIONS

Life's Meaning. John Keating called his students to avoid a meaningless life. In the film *Dead Poets Society*, Robin Williams plays John Keating, an English teacher at an all-boys preparatory school set in 1959. The school was strict, very conservative, and rich in tradition. Part of its tradition sought to make the students carbon copies of each other and their parents, teaching them to live life just like everybody else, simply fulfilling their purpose in life (which was, of course, whatever their parents determined that purpose to be). John Keating set out to go against that tradition because it failed to allow the students to think for themselves and to express their own uniqueness. On the first day of class, Keating invited his students out into the hallway. He chose one of them to read the opening lines of a John Herrick poem:

Gather ye rosebuds while ye may:
Old time is still a-flying,
And this same flower that smiles today
Tomorrow will be dying.

He asked them about that opening line: "Gather ye rosebuds while ye may." He told them of a Latin phrase for that sentiment, *Carpe diem*, which means "Seize the day!" Then he led the students before a large glass case. Through the glass you could see pictures of former students from a hundred years back. Keating says to his class, "Boys, look into their eyes. They're just like you. Same haircut. Invincible, just like you feel. The world is their oyster. They believe they are destined for great things, just like many of you. Their eyes are full of hope just like you. But now, they're fertilizing daffodils. Did they wait until it was too late to make from their lives even one iota of what they were capable? Lean closer, boys, and you can hear them as they whisper their legacy of dreams to you."

As they lean toward the glass case, Keating stands behind them and whispers: "Carpe. Carpe. Carpe diem. Seize the day, boys. Make your lives extraordinary." Throughout the film, Keating attempts to teach those boys and to teach all of us that we have only one life on this earth, and we have the opportunity to do something extraordinary with that life. One life. A life that, no doubt, will have its regrets. But the size and degree of those regrets will be determined, in large part, by what we choose to do with our lives.
—Greg Pope

Difference Makers. I think of people like Abraham Lincoln and Martin Luther King Jr., who have exposed racism as the ugly demonic sin that it is, and died trying to make this world a better place. I think of Mitch Snider, who left his comfortable middle-class lifestyle and went to live among the homeless in the inner city of Chicago and died there trying to improve their lives. And there are others who graduate from medical school and, instead of setting up a practice in a nice suburban community, go into inner cities or poor rural communities or Third World countries and serve as doctors and nurses, making a life-saving difference for those who cannot afford health care.

Some of you may think you're too young to make a difference. But the other night at Volunteer Jacksonville, Christy Brookins, sixteen years old, received an award for working with young girls at a safe house, volunteering over six hundred hours of her time, making a difference. Others of you may think you're too old. Another Volunteer Jacksonville award recipient was eighty-five-year-old Mary Morris, who just last year made numerous quilts for the homeless, literally saving lives in the process. For others of you, it may not be your age that keeps you back. It may be some failure in your past that keeps you from taking any risks with your life, or makes you think you can't be used by God. The past can have a strong hold on us. But the Resurrection offers us a future, a future where grace frees us from the past and empowers us to live courageously, to seize the day.—Greg Pope

Musical Selections Appropriate to the Day

Acts 2:42–47	*We Are the Body of Christ*
Ps. 23	*He Leadeth Me*
1 Pet. 2:19–25	*Day by Day*
John 10:1–10	*Where He Leads Me*

Children's Lectionary Sermon

TITLE: Jesus, Our Guardian

SCRIPTURE: 1 Pet. 2:19–25

KEY VERSE: *But now you have turned to your Shepherd, the Guardian of our souls.* (1 Pet. 2:25b, NLT)

KEY CONCEPT: Jesus guides us each day.

MATERIALS: Bible, shepherd's staff cutout with verse written on it

PREPARATION: Find a clipart image of a shepherd staff, make it large enough that you can write the verse on it so it can be seen, and cut it out.

Our scripture passages we are reading today all talk about how Jesus is our Shepherd. In biblical times, many people raised sheep, so this was a picture that writers used to help people understand Jesus and their relationship to Jesus. The shepherd's job was to watch the sheep and keep them safe. What do you think a shepherd would do for the sheep? (*Let the children respond, and reflect back their answers.*) The shepherd would lead the sheep, feed the sheep, and protect the sheep.

(*Open Bible.*) One of our Bible readings today comes from 1 Peter:2, and I have it written here for you to see. (*Show the verse and invite the children to read it with you.*) *But now you have turned to your Shepherd, the Guardian of our souls.* Peter is telling the Christians that they have made the right choice to turn and follow Jesus. Jesus was the guardian. What do you think that means? (*Let the children answer. Depending on the children's age and depth of knowledge, you may get a variety of answers; explain if you have to using the words provided.*) Other words we could use for guardian are *protector, guard, keeper, defender*, and *shield*. Jesus is the protector of your very spirit—your very being forever. We can celebrate Jesus today and forever, because as we turn to Jesus our Shepherd, he will lead us to make right choices, he will feed us and help us to grow, and we will live with him forever.—Marcia Thompson

WORSHIP AIDS

Call to Worship: "The Lord is my light and my salvation—whom shall I fear? The Lord is the stronghold of my life—of whom shall I be afraid?" (Ps. 27:1, NIV).

Invocation: Father of all life, who spared not your own Son for our salvation, grant that today our worship will reflect the true devotion of our hearts. Encourage us to pray, to praise, to confess our sin, to hear your Word, and to surrender life to you. Reveal to us the presence of your dear Son, Jesus, who is the Christ. Amen.

Offertory Sentence: "And God is able to make all grace abound to you, so that in all things at all times, having all that you need, you will abound in every good work" (2 Cor. 9:8, NIV).

Offertory Prayer: Father, receive these gifts as expressions of our faith and of our readiness to partner with you in the work of grace. Multiply our offerings for the building of your Kingdom. Amen.

Morning Prayer: Father, there are times when I don't understand what it is you are wanting from my life. I know that my main purpose is to glorify you in all things. However, when I think of my weakness, I am intimidated by your plans. I have heard that I should follow your love letter to me, and my questions will be answered. If this is true, why do I still have questions? Why do I struggle to understand your nature? Why am I unsure of precisely what the Bible teaches about the difficult matters of right and wrong? Lord, I ask one thing. Give me ears that are quick to listen, but lips that are slow to speak. Let me grow into a discerning heart so that I will be attentive and sensitive to others around me. I may never understand you, and I may never have all the right or wrong answers, but if you would give me a sensitive heart for all people around me, I will seek never to be a stumbling block. Make my sins evident to me. Lord, in all your ways guide me and make me a man after your own heart. Amen.—Jarrett Davis

Benediction: We now depart in the joy of Christ and go forth into the days of this week, in our times of labor and leisure, to speak lovingly his Holy Name and to live in his power. May his peace be yours. Amen.

SUNDAY, MAY 22, 2011
Fifth Sunday of Easter

LECTIONARY SERMON TOPIC: "Who Will You Be When You Grow Up?"
TEXT: Acts 7:55–60; 1 Pet. 2:2–10
OTHER READINGS: Ps. 31:1–5, 15–16; John 14:1–14

In various ways throughout the Bible, we are encouraged to grow spiritually, to be transformed, to become more like Jesus. Our epistle reading for today calls us to grow into salvation, into wholeness, into the person God created us to be.

Dallas Willard is a professor of philosophy at the University of Southern California. He is also a prolific writer on the spiritual life, and on discipleship in particular. For our help in spiritual formation he offers the acronym VIM. The *V* stands for *Vision*: Who are we are, and who are we called to be? The *I* stands for *Intention*: Do we intend to live and become this kind of person? The *M* stands for *Method and Means*: What are we going to do in order to become this person?[8]

I. **Vision.** We must have a vision of who we are and who we are called to become. Peter tells us, "Once you were not a people, but now you are God's people." That's who we are. We belong to God; we are created in God's image, of infinite worth to God, made to live in love with God and one another. Our biblical texts this morning describe the kind of people God wants us to become.

We will be people filled with the Holy Spirit. It was said of Stephen, the first Christian martyr, that he was filled with the Holy Spirit (Acts 7:55). And when we are filled with Holy Spirit on the inside, we will put away, as Peter said, all malice and guile and insincerity and envy and slander, and we will produce in our lives what the Bible calls fruit of the Spirit: love, joy, peace, patience, kindness, goodness, generosity, faithfulness, gentleness, self-control. That is the kind of person the Holy Spirit shapes into being. And if that is not who we are becoming, then something is wrong. If you want to know whether or not you are growing, ask the members of your family. That should make for a pleasant ride home. But they know us better than anyone. The role of the Holy Spirit is crucial in our spiritual growth, because simply *trying* to act more lovingly will only lead to despair. It is the work of God's Spirit in the depths of our being that enables us to grow in Christlikeness.

Scripture reminds us that we are all God's people and that the whole world is made up of God's children. Peter says that as the Church, we must let ourselves be built into a spiritual house and a holy priesthood, for we

---

[8]Dallas Willard, *Renovation of the Heart* (Colorado Springs, CO: NavPress, 2002), pp. 85–91.

are a chosen race, a royal priesthood, a holy nation, God's own people (1 Pet. 2:5, 9). A sign of growing up spiritually is to be able to live in community with others, some of whom we may not like. And in the midst of community grow in Christlikeness. That is the vision of who God wants us to be as we grow up: filled with the Holy Spirit, producing fruit of the Spirit, forgiving those who hurt us, trusting God more and more to lead and guide us, and to do so living in community with one another. In essence, we are to be people who embody the Kingdom of God, the kingdom of justice and joy and righteousness.

II. **Intention.** The question we each must ask ourselves is whether or not this is our intention. Do you intend to grow and change and be transformed into Christlikeness? Have you ever decided, *This is the kind of person I am going to become. I'm going to bring every element of my being, working from the inside out, into harmony with the will of God and the character of Jesus.* We must intend the vision if it is to be realized.

A man meets a woman at a party, and he is stunned by her beauty. He thinks to himself, "I cannot let this women get away. I've got to figure out some way to create a connection." So he says to her, "You know, I may not look like much, but my father is a very wealthy man, and he's in bad health. He's an old guy. He's not going to live more than two years at the most. And when he dies, I will be worth fifty million dollars." Well, you can tell the woman is impressed. She asks for his business card. Three days later he gets a note from her informing him that she is now his stepmother. This woman caught a vision. Then she set her intentions upon obtaining that vision. Then she discovered the means and method by which to make that vision a reality.

III. **Method and means.** There are methods and means by which you make your vision a reality. To grow, to change, to be more loving, forgiving, trusting, requires more than intention. It requires, one, a reliance on the Spirit of God to work within us; and, two, an effort on our part through spiritual disciplines and practices through which God can shape us inwardly.

It's what Peter was talking about when he said we must long for pure spiritual milk so that we might grow into salvation (1 Pet. 2:2). We long for this, Peter says, because we have "tasted the kindness of the Lord." He's talking about nourishing our souls on the basics of spiritual formation: prayer, scripture, worship, reflecting on God's goodness, meditating on the person and teachings of Jesus, setting aside the time where we can be filled with God's Spirit.

Our actions spring from who we are inside. Our inner being has to change. The process of spiritual formation is a renovation of the mind, the emotions, the heart, the will, the spirit, the body, and the soul to the point where the entire self is organized around God and fully integrated under God.—Greg Pope

---

ILLUSTRATIONS

Christlikeness. Writer and pastor John Ortberg tells of a man in his church he calls Hank. Hank had attended church since he was a boy, and now was in his sixties. He was known by everyone—but no one really liked him. He had difficulty loving his wife. His children could not speak freely with him and felt no affection from him. He was not concerned for the poor, had little tolerance for those outside the church, and tended to judge harshly those who were inside.

One day someone in the church asked him, "Hank, are you happy?" Without smiling, he responded, "Yes." "Well, then," the person replied, "tell your face." Hank's outward demeanor mirrored a deeper and much more tragic reality: Hank was not changing. He was not being transformed. He was not growing toward Christlikeness. But here's what is most remarkable: nobody in the church was surprised by this. No one called an emergency meeting of the church leaders to consider this strange case of a person who wasn't changing. No one really expected Hank to change, so no one was surprised when he didn't. There were other expectations in the church. People expected that Hank would attend services, give money, and do church work. But no one expected that day by day, month by month, decade by decade, Hank would be transformed and grow more and more into the likeness of Jesus. People did not expect that he would become a progressively more loving, joyful, and winsome person. So they were not shocked when it did not happen.[9]—Greg Pope

---

[9]John Ortberg, Laurie Pederson, and Judson Poling, *Fully Devoted: Living Each Day in Jesus' Name* (Grand Rapids, MI: Zondervan, 2000), pp. 15–16.

Vision. Two weeks ago in the Karen worship service, someone told the story about his mother being mistreated at work. His mother was told that in essence the Karen people were zeroes. This of course broke his heart. So he went home that night and prayed. He heard nothing from God. The next morning he woke up and God spoke to him. God said, "I am one. And when you put a one in front of a zero, you have ten. And when you put another zero after that, you have a hundred and then a thousand. With me," God said, "the Karen are never zeroes!" With God no one is a zero. Not even the ignorant person who has no idea to whom he was speaking. We are all of us God's people. God's children. God's beloved. We must hold before us that vision of ourselves, along with the vision of the kind of people God is creating us to be.—Greg Pope

Musical Selections Appropriate to the Day

Acts 7:55–60   *My Faith Looks Up to Thee*
Ps. 31:1–5, 15–16   *A Mighty Fortress Is Our God*
1 Pet. 2:2–10   *Called as Partners*
John 14:1–14   *On Jordan's Stormy Banks*

Children's Lectionary Sermon

TITLE: "God's People"
SCRIPTURE: 1 Pet. 2:2–10
KEY VERSE: *Once you had no identity as a people; now you are God's people.* (1 Pet. 2:10a, NLV)
KEY CONCEPT: Living as God's people
MATERIALS: Bible, ID tags from different people in the congregation, ID badges with "God's people" written on them to give to the children and the congregation

PREPARATION: Contact various people in the congregation who wear ID badges to work. Get a pack of ID badges and write or type "God's people" on them.

I want to show you some different ID badges I borrowed from some of our church family. (*Show the different ID badges, talking about what each person does who wears the particular badge. Talk about how the identity badge is used both for security and to show the person's job, whether it be doctor, teacher, lawyer, and so on.*) ID badges show people our name and the job we do. These badges don't tell everything about a person, do they?

(*Open Bible.*) In 1 Peter 2:2–10, Peter wrote to some Christians about their identity. Peter wrote, *Once you had no identity as a people; now you are God's people.* He was sharing with these believers that God had chosen them to become a part of God's Kingdom. We too are God's people and a part of God's Kingdom. I want each of you to come up and get an ID badge. It says "God's people." Then I want you to take some and give them to our church family. This ID badge is a reminder that we are God's people all the time and everywhere we go. We want to share and invite others to be a part of "God's people" too. (*Have a prayer and then send the children out with the badges.*) —Marcia Thompson

◈ WORSHIP AIDS ◈

Call to Worship: "One thing I ask of the Lord, this is what I seek: that I may dwell in the house of the Lord all the days of my life, to gaze upon the beauty of the Lord and to seek him in his temple" (Ps. 27:4, NIV).

Invocation: Father of life, grant that today our worship will reflect the true devotion of our hearts. Encourage us to pray, to praise, to confess, to hear your Word, and to surrender life to you. Reveal to us the presence of your dear Son, Jesus, who is the Christ. Amen.

Offertory Sentence: "As it is written, 'He has scattered abroad his gifts to the poor; his righteousness endures forever'" (2 Cor. 9:9, NIV).

Offertory Prayer: Bless what we give, O Lord, and shape it after your will that it may benefit many and honor the Christ. Amen.—E. Lee Phillips

Morning Prayer: (Prayer on Ps. 22:23–31) Holy God, I come before you with a fearful spirit, fearful of your power, fearful of losing your grace and love that cannot be fully repaid. Yet you listen to me in my time of darkness. You lead me through my suffering. Lord, you shine the light in a dark place. You prove yourself time and time again to your people. Show me the ways to live. Give me ears to listen. Give me eyes to witness as you wish.

All peoples of the world belong to you, O God. The believers are yours. The seekers are yours. The nonbelievers are yours. You rule them all with mercy. O God, people will remember you forever. Amen.—Ben Reeves

Benediction: As we depart, let us go in the knowledge and power of the gracious God we know as Father, Son, and Holy Spirit. And may we gather again next Lord's day as God's children full of joy and hope. God's peace be with you. Amen.

SUNDAY, MAY 29, 2011
Sixth Sunday of Easter

LECTIONARY SERMON TOPIC: "How Do We Talk About Our Faith in a Pluralistic World?"

TEXT: Acts 17:22–31; 1 Pet. 3:13–22

OTHER READINGS: Ps. 66:8–20; John 14:15–21

We live in a whole new world. We call it "postmodern" and "pluralistic," even "post-Christian." Pluralism is the recognition of other voices of religious authority and the diversity of cultures living together in one place. Postmodernism is a rejection of the idea that the only truth we can know is that which can be proven by the modern scientific method. In some of its forms, postmodernism denies the reality of absolute truth altogether. Many postmoderns do not believe there is a such thing as absolute truth: whatever is true for me may not be true for you.

This morning I want us to think together about what it means to share our faith in this new world. How do we go about fulfilling the Great Commission to go into all the world sharing the gospel and making disciples?

I. **Let me begin by saying that I think those Christian communities best suited for a postmodern world are those with an emphasis on individual freedom.** The last thing our postmodern, pluralistic world is going to listen to is the church telling them how wrong their beliefs are and forcing down their throats what we think are the right beliefs. People are not led to change their minds or to understand something in a new way when they are told their beliefs are stupid and that they must see things our way because we alone possess the truth about God. For us to be able to say that we respect every person's right to believe as he or she feels led to believe will go a long way in gaining an audience with whom we can share our faith. There is a fascinating conversation going on these days among those who call themselves part of the Emergent Church. Some within this group believe that the church is in the midst of such a seismic shift that it is not an understatement to call it a reformation, equivalent to the changes that came with the Protestant Reformation five hundred years ago.

II. **In our epistle lesson for today, Peter tells us to be prepared to give an account of the hope that is within us, to be ready to talk about our faith, but to do so with gentleness and reverence.** It is crucial, I think, to look at the world and realize why many of us hold to the particular faith that we do. If the truth be told, many of us are Christian simply because of the home in which we are raised. This is not the case with all Christians, but it is true about most of us. For most of us, our parents or grandparents were Christian, and they made sure we were in a Christian church. And if our home was not Christian, chances were very strong that if we were going to adopt any religion, it would be Christian simply because of the country in which we live.

We learn to respect one another's religious beliefs by entering into conversation with those of other faiths. Recent books on evangelism are saying we should "count conversations, not conversions." I believe it is a biblical model of evangelism, exemplified by Jesus and Paul. You don't have to share a person's belief system to respect his or her faith. And we do not need to relinquish our beliefs and our convictions to the point of relativity whereby we say it doesn't matter what one believes. It does matter. It matters to the Jew, to the Buddhist, the Hindu, and the Muslim, and they expect our beliefs to matter to us.

III. **But in talking about my faith with others, I must realize that my Buddhist, Hindu, Jewish, and Muslim sisters and brothers believe as wholeheartedly in their faith as I do in mine.** Looking at the story from Acts we read earlier, the Athenians' situation looks similar to ours today. They are described as those who would spend their time in nothing but telling or hearing something new—which sounds a lot like postmodernism. As Paul talks with them, he compliments them on how extremely religious they are. He is respectful of their objects of worship. And then he points to their altar that bears the inscription, "to an unknown god." There appears to be an openness on the part of the Athenians to learn more about an unknown god.

And notice how respectful Paul is in speaking with them. Meeting them where they are in their own faith journeys, he says, "Let me share with you what I believe about this unknown God." And he shares the story of his faith. He tells them that this God who made the earth and all that is within it is very near to each one of us. That it is this one in whom we live and move and have our being. And quoting from their own poets, seeking to draw from their religious traditions, he agrees with them that we are all God's offspring.

Paul shared his faith by engaging the world and culture of his hearers. So can we with the music, movies, literature, and arts of our culture. And they listened to him, the text says. Some scoffed at him. But others said, "We will hear you again about this." Because of his respectful conversation with them about their own religion, Paul gained a hearing.

IV. **Jesus calls us to be witnesses.** To be a witness is to enter into a respectful, open conversation with others about our faith. It is to say, "I'm not here to tell you how wrong you are. I'm here to learn what your faith tradition has to teach me, as well as share with you what my faith means to me." Evangelism is a two-way conversation, not a one-way presentation. And let us never forget that it is the work of the Holy Spirit to change people. When John the gospel writer talks about the Holy Spirit, he speaks of the Spirit as one who leads us into truth, who convicts us, who abides with us always, and who provides us with the words to say at the appropriate time.—Greg Pope

ILLUSTRATIONS

Religious Respect. Other religions and those who practice them deserve our respect. Several years ago, I was part of a series of interfaith conversations, and one Jewish man shared how rare it is to find a Jewish child who has not been told by some Christian that they and their family are going to hell. To tell a child that is not in the least bit Christian. It makes me think of a Southern Baptist evangelist's words on the platform of the Southern Baptist Convention when he proclaimed to a standing ovation, "God Almighty does not hear the prayers of a Jew." Who are we to say whom God will or will not listen to! I believe that God Almighty hears the prayers of every Jew and the prayers of every human being created in God's image. And every person, no matter what his or her religion, deserves our respect for the beliefs he or she holds dear, as long as those beliefs do not bring harm to others.—Greg Pope

Faith-Quake. A couple of weeks ago, the city of Louisville awoke to the ground shifting beneath our feet. Tremors from a real, live earthquake. For the past couple of decades, the religious landscape has also been shifting beneath our feet, tremors from a real live faith-quake. If you fell asleep in 1950 and woke up today, you would perhaps feel as though you had traveled to another planet, religiously speaking. It is a very different world than the one in which most us grew up. In the 1950s, cutting-edge interfaith conversations would have taken place between Baptists and Catholics. Today the conversations take place between Christians and Jews and Buddhists and Muslims.

Back in 1950, many Christians did not even know someone of another religion. Today Buddhists and Jews and Muslims and Christians are neighbors. Fifty years ago, the Bible was the only holy book most of us knew existed.

Now we are aware of the Koran, the Bhagavad Gita, and the Tao Te Ching. In this new world, there is no longer just one holy book embraced by all as the authority on religious truth. In this new world, there are voices from various other religions calling for the freedom to express their faith and not be forced to practice Christianity by praying the Lord's Prayer at a high school football game or going to court to find the Ten Commandments hanging there.—Greg Pope

Musical Selections Appropriate to the Day

Acts 17:22–31	*The Solid Rock*
Ps. 66:8–20	*You're Worthy of My Praise*
1 Pet. 3:13–22	*Ask Ye What Great Thing I Know*
John 14:15–21	*Because He Lives*

Children's Lectionary Sermon

TITLE: Explain Yourself

SCRIPTURE: 1 Pet. 3:13–22

KEY VERSE: *Instead, you must worship Christ as Lord of your life. And if someone asks about your Christian hope, always be ready to explain it.* (1 Pet. 3:15, NLV)

KEY CONCEPT: Sharing life in Christ

MATERIALS: Bible, complex cell phone with all the extra gadgets

PREPARATION: If you don't have a cell phone with lots of extras such as Internet, music, and GPS, find someone in your congregation who has one who would not mind showing and explaining all the different things about it.

I want to show you my cool phone. It can do all different types of things. (*Go on to show the children some of the different features of your phone, such as*

Internet or GPS. Explain in good detail how it works. You might even have a few techies in the group of children who can add to your information. Encourage any children who have some knowledge to share it too.)

It was real easy for me to explain to you all about my phone. I bet most of you can work a computer, and some of you might even be able to explain how it works. Things we know about are easy to share or explain to other people. We like to tell them about the things we know or are good at.

There is something else very important we should be able to explain. (*Open Bible.*) In 1 Peter 3:15, Peter writes, *Instead, you must worship Christ as Lord of your life. And if someone asks about your Christian hope, always be ready to explain it.* It is so important that we are ready to tell others about Christ in our lives. (*Here use your own story of Christ in your life to model for the children. Make it simple, but include ways God uses other people, events, and so on to make Christ known to you in tangible ways.*)—Marcia Thompson

❧ WORSHIP AIDS ❧

Call to Worship: "Hear my voice when I call, O Lord, be merciful to me and answer me" (Ps. 27:7, NIV).

Invocation: Lord, we delight in meeting you here today. In this hour, may your Word be heard and heeded. Speak to our hearts from your kind affection and draw us near to you. Grant that we may know the fullness of your grace. Amen.

Offertory Sentence: "Now he who supplies seed to the sower and bread for food will also supply and increase your store of seed and will enlarge the harvest of your righteousness" (2 Cor. 9:10, NIV).

Offertory Prayer: Bless, O Lord, these offerings we bring. These tithes and gifts are given in honor of your Holy Name . . . and from them we pray the increase of your Kingdom. Multiply our giving in the ways that please you best. Help us to be sensitive to your Holy Spirit as you guide us each day. May your name be forever praised! Amen.—Lee McGlone

Morning Prayer: Great are the works of the Lord. Each day you surprise us as you work things together for your glory. Glorious and majestic are your deeds. There is none like you. You caused the wonders to be remembered. May we never lose sight of the ways you have worked in us. You provide food for those who fear you. You take care of your people, who are living to glorify you. You have shown your people the power of your works. Help us always to give due credit to you as you act in our lives. The works of your hands are faithful and just. They are steadfast forever. As you are faithful to us, may we be faithful to you. Though we are flowers quickly fading, your glory will never fade. You provide redemption for your people and call us to be your people forever. The fear of the Lord is the beginning of wisdom. Help us recognize our follies so that we may find wisdom in you. All of God's people join in saying, Amen.—Sarah Johnson

Benediction: We go forth today full of confidence and hope knowing that God goes before us. God's presence will guide you, keep you, and strengthen you for the living of these days. May you be a powerful presence in the world, bringing peace to those whose lives you touch. Amen.

SUNDAY, JUNE 5, 2011
Seventh Sunday of Easter/Ascension Sunday

LECTIONARY SERMON TOPIC: "Raised to New Heights"
TEXT: Acts 1:1–11
OTHER READINGS: Ps. 47; Eph. 1:15–23; Luke 24:44–33

There is something wonderful about seamless transitions. We see far too few of them in life and in ministry, yet it is the very thing that occurs in the opening sentences of Acts. The writer, whom we presume to be Luke, picks up the discourse to the Christian known as Theophilus (1:1) by giving a thumbnail sketch of the ministry of Jesus. His words ring clear "about all that Jesus did and taught from the beginning until the day when he was taken up to heaven" (1:1–2). It was Luke's way of saying, "You remember that I wrote previously of these things, and now I am finishing the story."

I. **Luke's reminders are all predicated upon the power of resurrection.** The Resurrection was the theological theme that linked the church to the immutable power of God. If God can do *that*, then God can do anything. For the earliest followers, that fact that Jesus presented himself "alive" (v. 3) was all the reality and proof they needed to validate the power of this God. But this resurrection reality was couched in the language of Kingdom waiting. The forty days of postresurrection reality was a true reminder to the followers of Jesus. They were to remain in Jerusalem until the Father's promise was fulfilled in their midst.

Some perhaps think that following the resurrection reality of Jesus, the followers would eventually sink into a somewhat normal routine. But on the heels of something as out of bounds as a resurrection, nothing could ever be the same. Frankly, this resurrection business was heady stuff, and it was almost too much to bear. When it really sunk in, the matter was incomprehensible; hence, the wait. God inserted some waiting time into their lives in order for the reality to sink in and for the real power of resurrection to grip them. This was no ordinary event; death was overcome by life. None of us, quite frankly, is equipped to handle that kind of reality.

Something that big and that momentous is not processed by the human mind. We need help. We need God-size help to comprehend that. And that is exactly what God gave us. He gave us God-size help in the form of the Spirit.

II. **To comprehend God's global vision for the Kingdom, we need the power of the Spirit.** Some of the initial reviews of the Resurrection and the Kingdom were met with less than a global view. Evidently there were still those who were more concerned with the kingdom of Israel than with the Kingdom of God (1:6). In addition, many were fixated on the moment when these things would happen.

There must be a place deep in the recesses of the human spirit that needs to know specific things. I remain amazed at the number of people who are absolutely spellbound by the preaching and teaching that sets Kingdom timetables. Evidently it doesn't matter how many times Jesus says that no one knows the hour (Mark 13:32ff), there are still those who espouse that they have mysteriously decoded the workings of the Kingdom clock. Even more perplexing than those who advocate this knowledge are the vast numbers of people who actually believe specific predictions.

For Jesus such specificity was perilous. Calendars and clocks are of no value in the Kingdom. Rather, the Kingdom imperative is to work diligently to bear witness to the resurrection reality (1:8). When we focus on the task at hand, there is no time to bog down in peripheral things.

Jesus likewise reminded his followers that when the power of the Spirit was upon them, they would bear witness at home, in their region, to the stranger, and ultimately to the whole world (1:8). These last, poignant words of Jesus provide the impetus for the ministry of the church. The church has sacred responsibility to perpetuate the story of Jesus. And the power comes from all that surrounds the story: it comes from the Spirit that God promised to send, and it comes, too, from the ethos that accompanies last words.

III. **Whereas the followers needed clarity about their purpose and their waiting, in these parting words Jesus gave them (and us!) all the clarity we need.** There is work to be done. And with that, Jesus ascended back to the Father in heaven.

What is there about last words? In my life and ministry, I have encountered the power of last words. Two of the most poignant moments in my life were when I heard the death whispers of my beloved grandfather and my own father. Those tender moments will never escape me, and I can dial them up in my memory anytime I want. Likewise, I have stood with others as they uttered their last words. Last words, I have discovered, weigh more than ordinary words!

Which validates all the more the power of that holy moment when having charged his followers to spread the gospel everywhere, Jesus ascended back to the Father. He said what needed to be said and then he left. But in so doing, he left for us his last words, and he left for us the Kingdom charge: go tell everyone what God has done for you.—Danny West

ILLUSTRATIONS

Focus. During the 2009 National Championship run of the University of North Carolina basketball team, coach Roy Williams implored his players not to look at the score or the clock. Instead they were to remain focused at all times by fiercely guarding the opposition, making good decisions with the ball, and playing as a team. Indeed, Williams himself quipped that during the National Championship game against Michigan State, he did not look at the scoreboard until late in the first half of play.—Danny West

Waiting. One of the truly remarkable and frustrating aspects of our faith is this messy little notion of waiting. Frankly, most of us are lousy at waiting. In part we wait ever so impatiently because most of us are instinctive, impulsive people. We believe that our time is more valuable than other people's and that waiting is unproductive and unredemptive. Nothing could be further from the truth. God's strange timepiece has always accommodated periods of waiting. The forty-day postresurrection wait was hauntingly reminiscent of that other "forty-something" wait—the waiting and wandering of the Israelites in the wilderness. Don't tell me God doesn't ask us to wait!—Danny West

Musical Selections Appropriate to the Day

Acts 1:1–11	*Spirit of the Living God*
Ps. 47	*Clap Your Hands*
Eph. 1:15–23	*Open the Eyes of My Heart*
Luke 24:44–53	*I Will Sing of My Redeemer*

Children's Lectionary Sermon

TITLE: Eyewitness

SCRIPTURE: Luke 24:44–53

KEY VERSE: *You are witnesses of these things.* (Luke 24:48, NRSV)

KEY CONCEPT: Witnesses of God's love

MATERIALS: Bible, real microphone or pretend one (a bullhorn would work as well)

Have you ever seen an eyewitness reporting what he or she saw happen on the news? What does it mean to be an eyewitness? (*Let the children respond, and take all answers; do not emphasize right or wrong answers, but lead toward the idea of "seeing with your own eyes."*)

The disciples of Jesus were eyewitnesses. They had seen with their own eyes how he was treated. They watched him die on the cross. They actually got to talk to him and spend time with him after God raised him from the dead. (*Open Bible.*) In the gospel of Luke we read, *You are witnesses of these things*. Jesus is about to be taken to be with God right before their very eyes. How amazing would that be?

We may not be eyewitnesses to what Jesus did for us. We weren't actually there to see it. Jesus did all of that for us because he loved us so much and wanted us to be forgiven for our sins. Sins are the not-so-good choices that we make sometimes. We feel God's love when we say we are sorry to our family and friends when we have done something that hurts their feelings. We feel God's love because of what Jesus did for us.

I don't know about you, but that makes me want to tell everyone. I can use this (*hold up microphone or bullhorn*) to tell the people in this room how much God loves them. (*Speak loudly.*) GOD LOVES YOU SO MUCH HE SENT JESUS. I am pretty sure that someone in this room needed to hear that this morning. There are a lot of people who need to hear how much God loves them. We can be witnesses. We can tell our friends and our families how God makes us feel and how much God loves them.—Sherrie Harmon

❧ WORSHIP AIDS ❧

Call to Worship: "I am still confident of this: I will see the goodness of the Lord in the land of the living. Wait before the Lord; be strong and take heart and wait for the Lord" (Ps. 27:13–14, NIV).

Invocation: God of peace, you have taught us that in coming to you we shall be saved and that in quiet confidence we shall know strength. In this hour, and by your Spirit, be present to us. Help us to be still and to know that you are God. Amen.

Offertory Sentence: "Thanks be unto God for his indescribable gift" (2 Cor. 9:15, NIV).

Offertory Prayer: Father, whose loving hand has provided all that we possess, grant us grace that we may honor you in our giving. Remembering the account that we will one day give, may we be faithful stewards of your bounty. Amen.

Morning Prayer: (Prayer on Rev. 19:5–7) "Hallelujah! For our Lord God Almighty reigns! Let us rejoice and be glad and give him glory! For the wedding of the Lamb has come. His bride has made herself ready. Fine linen, bright and clean was given her to wear."

Lord, the time is coming for the church to stand spotless before you. O, how great the day will be when we can peer into the shining eyes of Jesus. May our righteous acts prepare for us glorious clothing. God, we choose to be devoted to you. We live our lives in view of eternity.—Megan Williams

Benediction: As we go out, may we know that the God of grace, Father, Son, and Holy Spirit, will guide our way. We walk not alone—but in the strength of God. In joy and peace, we depart to serve and to live at peace with all mankind. Amen.

SUNDAY, JUNE 12, 2011
Pentecost Sunday

LECTIONARY SERMON TOPIC: "When the Spirit Comes"

TEXT: Acts 2:1–21

OTHER READINGS: Ps. 104:24–34, 35b; 1 Cor. 12:3b–13; John 7:37–39

What a scene it must have been! The apostles did their best to wait and watch for the promises of God, just as Jesus had instructed. But the kind of waiting they were asked to do was no ordinary waiting. They were waiting on God. That kind of waiting is not easily done. But is it not true that often our best work is done in moments of inactivity and waiting? We need look no further than the Christ followers in Acts 2 to validate the inherent power of waiting.

 I. **On the day of Pentecost, the Christ followers were assembled together in the same room.** I suspect that for them it was a room quite like all the other rooms in their lives. The room was filled with potential and hope, but it was also the waiting room of all waiting rooms. They were waiting on God. What followed was beyond anything they could imagine in their wildest dreams. God showed up with a power that all but blew the roof off. More than that, what occurred in that room blew the lid off the whole wide world.

   It was the very thing Jesus spoke of in his ministry (John 14:15ff; Acts 1:8), and now the fulfillment had come. As a result of the coming of the Spirit, everything about the followers was changed. Most profound was the change of speech. They now spoke a "Kingdom" language, a language empowered by the Spirit. It does not appear to have been a "secret language," as some in the modern world espouse. Rather, this new language was simply a spiritual paradigm shift for the followers of Jesus. It was God's way of empowering them to begin to translate the gospel message for the whole world. No longer was the gospel a proprietary element of Judaism; this new language "spoke" to the need to proclaim the good news to the whole world . . . to be the witnesses that Jesus referenced in Acts 1:8. In order to speak to a new constituency, they would need a new vocabulary and tongue.

 II. **Naturally, the religionists so accustomed to order and stability were "bewildered" by the stirrings in Jerusalem (2:6).** For the Spirit not only empowered a new dialect but also blessed a new listening. The followers "heard" something new as well. It is an exciting picture of what the power of the Spirit of God does for our speech and our listening. We speak and we hear in altogether different ways. They began to hear the message of God in their native tongue. "Are those speaking not Galileans? And how is it that we hear, each of us, in our native tongue?" they asked (2:7–8).

As the emotions stirred and as tongues were unleashed for the hearing, Peter attempts to bring clarity and calm to the moment. One can only imagine the furor that this outpouring caused. So confusing was the miracle that evidently many believed the Christ followers to be drunk with wine (2:15).

What an intriguing indictment. Typically those who are intoxicated make very little sense. Their speech is slurred, their eyes are dimmed; most inebriated folks ramble on, speaking and acting foolishly. As Luke describes the outpouring of the Spirit upon the Christian community, the event is in no way an act of confusion. Out of the ordinary? Yes! Something different? Without question! But what happened at Pentecost was God's way of bringing clarity, not confusion. Remember: they spoke and were understood in different languages. To claim they were intoxicated was absurd, and Peter spoke to that.

III. **And in clarity Peter reminded the Christ followers then as he does us today that when the Spirit comes, all of creation comes under his power.** "Young men and women will prophesy, young men will dream, and the old men will have visions" (Acts 2:18). Those in bondage and those who are free are all under the power of this Spirit (2:17–20). The Spirit is not bound by human prejudice and social more; the Spirit empowers all to proclaim the good news.

This outpouring was simply and powerfully about one thing: it was about bringing all persons within earshot of the gospel. When they get that close, no matter what ethnicity they bear and with what tongue they speak, none has an excuse. Because of God's great Spirit, "All that call upon the name of the Lord shall be saved!" (2:20). And the people of God say in every tongue "Amen" and "Amen."—Danny West

---

ILLUSTRATIONS

Pentecost. In biblical imagery what happens at Pentecost is the undoing of the Tower of Babel (Gen. 11). There God confused the language of the earth like a game of Scrabble gone mad. The people's tongues were twisted and tangled so that nothing they said made any sense. Here God unravels the cultural and linguistic differences present in creation so that there would be no mistaking the message: God is clearing up anything that would hinder the power of the gospel. That is the point. Some bog down in the passage and waste great effort and time arguing the nuances of the text. Whether the miracle of Pentecost is a miracle of speaking or one of listening is really not the point. What God is doing is unbinding humanity—unleashing all tongues to do what they were created to do: to speak to and honor God.—Danny West

Possibility. The truth is that we often fail, but God never fails. "Impossible" is a word that does not belong to us. It is God's word. It declares that God plus one is enough. Someone has said, "I am only one, but I am still one. I cannot do everything, but still I can do something; and because I cannot do everything, I will not refuse to do something that I can do." And with God all things are possible.—Lee McGlone

Musical Selections Appropriate to the Day

Acts 2:1–21	*Spirit of God, Descend Upon My Heart*
Ps. 104:24–34, 35b	*Great Is the Lord*
1 Cor. 12:3b–13	*Come, Holy Spirit*
John 7:37–39	*Like a River Glorious*

ᓚ Children's Lectionary Sermon

TITLE: Help!

SCRIPTURE: Acts 2:1–21

KEY VERSE: *All of them were filled with the Holy Spirit.* (Acts 2:4a, NRSV)

KEY CONCEPT: Holy Spirit helps us.

MATERIALS: Bible

Today we are celebrating Pentecost. When Jesus and his disciples were alive, the Jewish people celebrated Pentecost fifty days after Passover. Christians celebrate Pentecost for a different reason. We celebrate God's sending the Holy Spirit to help us.

Last week, we read and talked about Jesus' disciples being eyewitnesses to Jesus' death, his being raised from the dead and going to be with God. Jesus told the disciples right before he went up into the heavens that help would come if they just waited. They were going out into the world to tell people about a man who had been raised from the dead. Do you think everyone they told believed them? (*Let the children respond.*)

If you tell someone the truth about something that happened and that person doesn't believe you, how do you feel? (*Let the children respond.*) The disciples probably felt the same way. They were just trying to tell people that Jesus came into this world because God loves us. They were just trying to tell people that Jesus was raised from the dead and is now in heaven with God, to show us that God will take us to heaven too someday.

(*Open Bible.*) God knew the disciples needed help. They needed help to find the right words to tell people about God's love. They needed help in knowing just what to do to help the people around them. So when the disciples were all gathered celebrating Pentecost together, God sent a helper. He sent it in a loud rushing wind. *All of them were filled with the Holy Spirit . . .* They couldn't see it, but they could feel it.

We celebrate Pentecost in our church to remember that God sent a helper to the disciples and to us. The Holy Spirit helps us find the right words to tell people how much God loves them. The Holy Spirit helps us help other people feel God's love when we show love to them. The Holy Spirit never leaves us and can help us whenever we need it, just like the disciples a long time ago.—Sherrie Harmon

❧ WORSHIP AIDS ❧

Call to Worship: "Sing to the Lord, you saints of his; praise his holy name" (Ps. 30:4, NIV).

Invocation: Loving Lord, just as long ago many nations and tongues understood clearly the message of Christ, repeat that same evangelistic reality today . . . beginning with us. Amen.—E. Lee Phillips

Offertory Sentence: "Blessed are the poor in spirit, for theirs is the kingdom of heaven" (Matt. 5:3, NIV).

Offertory Prayer: Lord, accept these gifts we offer in the name of your Son, Jesus Christ, who is our Savior. Empower us through faith in the living Christ to utilize these resources for the proclamation of the gospel and the healing of the nations. Amen.

Morning Prayer: Father, thank you for your Holy Spirit, which you left for your people here on earth. The Holy Spirit serves as our comforter, keeper, and guide. He brings us comfort to live in the world but not of the world. Being people of God, we must have the Holy Spirit to fuel our passion for Christ and give us confidence to continue seeking him during hard times. Father, your Holy Spirit also serves as an encourager. You knew when you created man that we would need your Holy Spirit to build us up where we are torn down. Then, Father, the Holy Spirit directs us. He shows us as your people the path we need to take on earth to fulfill the purpose you've given every Christian. Thank you for the Holy Spirit, Father. He comes from you, and gives your people what they need.—Kendall Summons

Benediction: Lord, just as the Holy Spirit came unlimited, unbound, and free at Pentecost, dismiss us with the indwelling power of that day, with changes to make, for Jesus' sake, throughout the world. Amen.—E. Lee Phillips

SUNDAY, JUNE 19, 2011
First Sunday after Pentecost/Trinity Sunday

LECTIONARY SERMON TOPIC: "The Intimate Power of God"
TEXT: Ps. 8
OTHER READINGS: Gen. 1:1–2:4a; 2 Cor. 13:11–13; Matt. 28:16–20

Apart from Psalm 51, this particular psalm is perhaps the most intimate and revealing of the writings of David. It has the feel of one who is taking stock of things one day. Certainly David had much to ponder in his life. There was his remarkable call into service as the youngest son of Jesse, which was quickly followed by the astonishing defeat of Goliath, the Philistine giant. David's notoriety and his fall are well documented in biblical lore. But as in all of our lives, for both the mighty and the meek, there come those defining moments in our journey where in quiet reflection we check the shelves of our lives to see what we have stored and hidden there.

I. **This psalm appears to describe one of those life-defining moments for David.** One can almost imagine that the images presented within this poem are those captured in David's mind and personality while he was tending the sheep on the hills of Bethlehem. Shepherds were star gazers. It is clear that David was a star gazer, too. In those quiet moments of tending the sheep at night, he would no doubt gaze into the heavens and ponder the larger realities of life and of God.

For David the conversation begins with God (8:1). When rightly considered, this God balances the larger questions of life. Those very questions flooded the mind of David. He takes stock of the creative prowess of God. He scans the heavens and discovers there the very glory of God. But God's majesty is not confined to the firmament, for when we drop our heads from looking up at the heavens, we discover an equally remarkable God who has revealed himself "out of the mouths of babes and infants" (8:2).

II. **Somewhere in this process of adoration and intense reflection, David has an "aha" moment.** It dawns on him that the same God who flung the stars into their respective orbits and who has masterfully decorated all of creation is the very same God who created him; indeed, God is the one who creates us all. It was an awe-inspiring moment for the king.

All of us are created to come to that moment of reckoning. We are called to recognize our role in God's world. That statement calls for deep reflection. We are to find and accept our place, but that place is ultimately God's. This is God's world, and we are God's creation. Although humanity is indeed the centerpiece of God's good creation, God, not humanity, is at the heart. Sometimes we forget that important biblical and theological premise. In the midst of David's contemplative process, this recognition comes to him.

It is almost as if we can hear him reasoning to himself. As he scans the heavens and takes into account the fullness of God's power, the light begins to slowly turn on in his spirit. The God who creates the big things of this world is the same God who creates the little things too. It is in that mind-set that David begins to recognize the order of creation and the place that humans serve in that created order. God actually invested greatly in the human race, placing us just a notch below the angels of heaven. That significance was not lost on David. With that ranking comes enormous blessing and abounding responsibility.

III. **David offers up one more powerful lesson.** He begins this reflective moment with an affirmation of God's immutable power and sovereignty; he closes the discourse in the identical manner. As David processed the wonders of life and creation, he saw that it started and ended with God. What an insightful recognition: begin with God and end with God. It is a lofty concept. For David, as for all of us, all of life—indeed all of creation—begins and ends with God. Is that not the heart of biblical revelation? Genesis begins with the creative realities of our God, and Revelation closes with the consummative reality of God. Everything rises and falls with God. What a riveting reminder.

Think of the ramification for our lives. What if we *really* started and ended with God? What if we took that notion as radically and as literally as it sounds? What would happen in between? What would our lives look like? What would our families look like? What would our vocation look like? What would God's church look like? It is a startling reminder that all of life is God's. It begins with him, and it ends with him. For those who have the courage to live it out, the results are beyond anything we can imagine.—Danny West

---

ILLUSTRATIONS

Power of God. On occasion, most of us have experienced moments when the gyroscope of life was teetering and crying out for balance, and just then we discovered the power of the stars. There is something calming and mystical about staring long and deep into God's heaven. It has a remarkable way of putting life back together again. The calmness, the majesty . . . they cry out "Look at the power of God." That is what happened for David.—Danny West

Ecology. As humans we have a holy assignment from God to tend to his creation. Dominion is more than mere dominance; dominion is inherently about responsibility. Many among us deny that reality. Sadly, some of the most passionate voices against creation care are within the Christian community. The voice of scripture, however, trumps them all. David helps us recognize our God-given responsibility.—Danny West

Musical Selections Appropriate to the Day

Gen. 1:1–2:4a	*This Is My Father's World*
Ps. 8	*Majesty*
2 Cor. 13:11–13	*Grace to You*
Matt. 28:16–20	*Lord, Speak to Me That I May Speak*

⤴ Children's Lectionary Sermon

TITLE: God's Voice in the World

SCRIPTURE: Matt. 28:16–20

KEY VERSES: *"Therefore, go and make disciples of all the nations, baptizing them in the name of the Father and the Son and the Holy Spirit. Teach these new disciples to obey all the commands I have given you. And be sure of this: I am with you always, even to the end of the age."* (Matt. 28:19–20, NLT)

KEY CONCEPT: Witness

MATERIALS: Bible, party hats and gadgets (optional)

Today we celebrate God! What do you normally do when you celebrate something? (*Let the children respond. They may give answers like "tell somebody," "have a party," and so on.*) When we celebrate, we often want to shout out and tell the world about why we are so happy. We might have a party and invite all our friends. There is a bubbly feeling of excitement when we celebrate.

(*Open Bible.*) In Matthew 28, the disciples were extremely happy. After the Resurrection, Jesus had told them to go to a mountain. There they saw him. Can you imagine how excited they must have been? I bet some couldn't believe what they were seeing. They celebrated Jesus' appearance by worshipping him.

Then Jesus gave them a message to take to the world. He wanted them to share the celebration of knowing God, by telling the world about God's love for them. Jesus told them this: *"Therefore, go and make disciples of all the nations, baptizing them in the name of the Father and the Son and the Holy Spirit. Teach these new disciples to obey all the commands I have given you. And be sure of this: I am with you always, even to the end of the age."* I think Jesus knew that the disciples would be excited and scared. Jesus had given them a mission to do, but Jesus also told he would always be with them.

The mission he gave to the first disciples is also the mission Jesus gives each of us who know him. We are to tell the good news of Jesus so that others can become Jesus' followers too. And we too have the promise that Jesus is with us always. Let's pray together that Jesus will help us as we grow to be his disciples and to share what we know and learn with others.—Marcia Thompson

❧ WORSHIP AIDS ❧

Call to Worship: "Be strong and take heart, all you who hope in the Lord" (Ps. 31:24, NIV).

Invocation: Hear our prayers and bless our worship today, O Lord, that growing in grace we might become children of light and faith as you intended. Amen.—E. Lee Phillips

Offertory Sentence: "In the same way, let your light shine before men that they may see your good deeds and praise your Father in heaven" (Matt. 5:16, NIV).

Offertory Prayer: O God, as we bring our gifts of tithes and offerings to you, grant that we may be mindful of the greater gift you have given to us—that of your Son and our Savior, the Lord Jesus Christ. And may our giving reflect true devotion as Jesus' disciples, and may we walk in his ways. —Lee McGlone

Morning Prayer: (Prayer for Trinity Sunday worship) Almighty God, we come to you, for you are our Creator. Who can ever surpass you? Your works speak for themselves. They speak of your omnipotence and your divine creativity. They speak of your might. We come to you aware of our position of privilege. What other people can communicate directly with you? To what other people do you speak directly and give direction?

Almighty God, we come to you, for you are our Father. Who else can love us as you do? You did not create us to live in fear. We were not made to be servants or to be slaves. You restored us to relationship. We come to you grateful to be considered sons and daughters. Abba, Father, who can love us better than you? Almighty God, we come to you, for you are our defender. Who can ever defeat you? You encourage us to stand firm, but we never have to rely on our own strength; you fight for us. We come to you trusting, confident that you will always be with us. For who can eliminate obstacles better than you?

Almighty God, you are Creator, Father, defender. There is none like you. All who agree, join me in saying, Amen.—Sarah Johnson

Benediction: As we go, we are led by the presence of Almighty God, Father, Son, and Holy Spirit. May our lives this week be useful for the Kingdom and, as we gather next Lord's day, may it be with testimonies of praise to you. Amen.

SUNDAY, JUNE 26, 2011
Second Sunday after Pentecost

LECTIONARY SERMON TOPIC: "A Mystifying Faith"
TEXT: Gen. 22:1–14
OTHER READINGS: Ps. 13; Rom. 6:12–23; Matt. 10:40–42

Frankly, I don't get it! I don't quite fathom what God was asking of Abraham in the strange moment that our text refers to. And even more perplexing for me is the preposterous faith that Abraham exhibited in taking that little boy, Isaac, up the hill of sacrifice. It is a mystifying faith.

 I. **It is a strange request by all counts.** "Take your son, your only son Isaac, whom you love, and go to the land of Moriah, and offer him there as a burnt offering" (22:2). It is not only a strange request; Abraham offers an even stranger reply: he is as quiet as a mouse. He doesn't argue with God, nor does he question God. He stands there and takes it.

  Instead of asking questions, Abraham faithfully begins the process of starting the journey. Early the next day, as if in a strange way there was eager anticipation for this, Abraham makes very careful preparation for the journey that awaits him. There is a sneaky insertion that accompanies the biblical text. Abraham, says the scripture, was to take the boy to a mountain that God would show him (22:2). Those words are strangely reminiscent of those spoken by God so many years earlier when he called Abraham to go to the land that he would show him (12:1). Likewise, in this defining moment of great faith and even greater courage, Abraham planned for the journey that from all indications would end with the death of his only son, Isaac.

 II. **Upon arriving at the designated place (evidently revealed to Abraham in advance), Abraham stopped the caravan and ordered them to stay in their place, for he and his son had something they had to do.** There is intrigue in his words: "the boy and I will go over there; we will worship, and then we will come home" (22:5). Remember, God had ordered him to take the boy and offer him as a sacrifice, yet Abraham confidently believed that the two of them would return. That was certainly not in the command of God. There was no hint that the boy would be spared. In fact, the words of God are crystal clear: "offer him there as burnt offering" (22:2).

  Believing they would return did not diminish Abraham's faith capacity to allow the charge of God to run its full course. He loaded up the wood for the fire on the shoulders of his son, and the knife for the killing and the fire for the offering on his own person. With everything present for the sacrifice, the two toddled together up the hill. Young Isaac was astute enough to know that something in the sacrificial equation did not add up. They had the wood, the fire, the knife, but . . . where was the sacrificial lamb?

He mustered what little manhood he possessed and asked his father, "Where is the lamb?" Abraham replied, "God himself will provide it" (22:7–8), and the two of them proceeded upward.

The little guy still must have wondered what awaited him when they reached the pinnacle of the mountain, for this is where the story takes on incredible meaning.

III. **The questions asked by little Isaac were soon to be answered.** Arriving at the designated spot, Abraham dropped the wood, built an altar, and in one of the most horrifying scenes in all of human history, binds up his little boy and "laid him on the altar, on top of the wood" (22:9).

Whew! What a story. But if truth be told, I still don't get it. Oh, I know what happened, and I thank God for what didn't. There is still this haunting, frightening image of old Abraham and little Isaac about to cross beyond the norm into a world none of us can quite imagine.

At the heart of the story lies one distinctive feature; indeed, it is the singular thread of Abraham's life. He trusted God. Inherently and without reservation, he trusted God. He trusted God to lead him to the land of the unfamiliar, to become a father when he was nearly one hundred, and to potentially offer up his beloved son as a sacrifice. Faith was a radical reality in Abraham's life. It was no mere concept or theological premise; it was the very nuts and bolts of his life. He did not smuggle faith into situations as do many in a puny attempt to redeem the moment; no, faith led him into situations, and therein lies the redemption for him. Faith didn't bail him out of predicaments . . . it led him into them.

And I can see him now, can't you? Old Abraham toddling along in faith; holding on to little Isaac with one hand and God with the other. What a remarkable picture. What a man. What a God.—Danny West

---

ILLUSTRATIONS

Quandary. As a parent I cannot comprehend this story at all. Believing that God would ask for the sacrifice of a child is bigger than my mind can conceive and much larger than my faith can embrace. How in the world does a loving parent allow himself to become an accomplice to this kind of faith act? This would be particularly true, one would suspect, for an ancient relic like Abraham and his octogenarian wife, Sarah. These two had outlived their youth, but they evidently had not outlived their life! God still had work for them to do in their old age. And after years of wondering and waiting, praying and waiting, confusion and waiting, the long-awaited son, Isaac, was born to them. After all of that God then commands a rather strange thing of old Abraham. That for which he longed, the promised son, was to be sacrificed back to God.—Danny West

Alternate Sacrifice. To be honest, my heart pounds every time I read this story. The drama and passion of the moment are beyond mortal words. Everything that Abraham does in this event is done so calmly and rationally. If there were bitter tears, the biblical writer offers us no clues to that effect; if there was a fist-shaking negotiation scene between the created and the Creator, it is not recorded for us. Rather, with calm demeanor and even calmer faith, Abraham systematically proceeds to offer up his son as a sacrifice. He even goes as far as gripping the knife of death, preparing to plunge it into the chest of his little boy, when he hears the familiar voice of God that stops the proceedings, offers a fitting tribute to Abraham's faith, and provides an alternate sacrifice to be offered (Gen. 22:9–14).—Danny West

Musical Selections Appropriate to the Day

Gen. 22:1–14	*Speak, O Lord*
Ps. 13	*How Deep the Father's Love for Us*
Rom. 6:12–23	*Speak to My Heart*
Matt.10:40–42	*O Jesus, I Have Promised*

Children's Lectionary Sermon

TITLE: Welcome!
SCRIPTURE: Matt. 10:40–42

KEY VERSE: *"Whoever welcomes you welcomes me."* (Matt. 10:40a, NRSV)
KEY CONCEPT: Hospitality
MATERIALS: Bible

What makes you feel welcome when you visit a friend or family member? (*Let the children respond.*) If you felt welcome, do want to go back to visit them again? (*Let the children respond.*)

In today's Bible reading, Jesus is talking to the disciples, and he is telling them that whoever makes them feel welcome, actually makes Jesus feel welcome too. (*Open Bible.*) In Matthew, as Jesus taught the disciples he was sending out, he said, *"Whoever welcomes you welcomes me."*

How do we make other people feel welcome here at church? (*Let the children answer. If there is some particular ministry you do for visitors, include it as you talk with the children.*) We want to show people who come to worship with us that we care. By showing we care, we can help people know of Jesus' love for them by our acts of kindness.

(*Pray with the children.*) Jesus, help us make people feel welcome so they can know your amazing love. Help us make people feel welcome by showing them your love so they might want to come back again and learn more about you.—Sherrie Harmon

WORSHIP AIDS

Call to Worship: "I will extol the Lord at all times; his praise will always be on my lips" (Ps. 34:1, NIV).

Invocation: Father, as we gather to worship, may we experience a deepening love for you. Open our hearts to receive a full measure of your indwelling Spirit; and may we then in turn share with the world the joy of faith—which is the good news of your salvation. Amen.

Offertory Sentence: "But store up for yourselves treasures in heaven, where moth and rust do not destroy, and where thieves do not break in and steal" (Matt. 6:20, NIV).

Offertory Prayer: Father, the gifts we bring are reflections of our love for you and expressions of our responsible stewardship. May every aspect of our living, our working, our leisure, our saving, our planning, be lived mindful of your grand intentions for us—and may our giving be multiplied for the building of the Kingdom. Amen.

Morning Prayer: Dear Lord, as we gather to worship, help us to ask the right questions. Help us not to ask, "What am I getting out of this?" Instead, help us to ask, "Is this pleasing to you?" We confess that often we focus on the wrong things and don't see you. Likewise, we forget that the only thing in the universe worthy of praise is you—our Lord, Savior, and Creator. Give us, we pray, a sense of focus. Give us the ability to focus on you and your will. Help us to listen, to learn of you, and to invite into our lives whatever changes you intend. So prepare our hearts, Lord. Open us to the things that you are trying to teach. Help us to hear you. Help us to know your perfect plan and to live it out joyfully each day. Amen.—Taylor Post

Benediction: May we go forth today fully assured that life lived according to the high priorities of faith matters forever. Guided by the faithful one, Father, Son, and Holy Spirit, live this week in confidence—and power. Amen.

SUNDAY, JULY 3, 2011
Third Sunday after Pentecost

LECTIONARY SERMON TOPIC: "A Double Reminder"
TEXT: Gen. 24:34–38, 42–49, 58–67
OTHER READINGS: Ps. 45:10–17 or Ps. 72; Rom. 7:15–25a; Matt. 11:16–19, 25–30

If we read Genesis 24 straight through from beginning to end, we might do a double take when we get to verse 34, which is where this scripture passage begins. As we continue reading, we might scratch our heads wondering if we fell asleep while reading or accidentally skipped ahead. Didn't we just hear this story just a few paragraphs earlier? Yes, we did. And *twice* encountering the story of how Rebekah came to be Isaac's wife should indicate to us that something in this narrative must be doubly significant.

I. **The first telling of the story occurs just after Sarah's death and burial.** Abraham calls to one of his servants to ask him to swear that he will find a wife for his son, Isaac, from his home country and not from among the Canaanite people with whom he is living. All we know about this servant is that he is the "oldest of his house" and that he is "in charge of all that Abraham had." Abraham obviously trusted this servant greatly, but as readers we never even learn his name. The unnamed servant prays for a specific way to recognize the woman that he should bring back to be the wife of Isaac. He prays that the woman he seeks would be the one who offers water to his camels after he asks for a drink of water—if nothing else, this would at least be a good indication of the woman's generosity, a trait to be desired in any relationship. Before the servant even finishes his prayer to God, Rebekah shows up. The servant asks her for a drink of water, and as if Rebekah had read his mind, she also offers to water his camels. Because of her response, the servant knows that Rebekah is the right woman for Isaac. He gives her jewelry to pay the bride price, and she offers him a place to spend the night. Then the narrator proceeds to tell the same story again detail by detail as Abraham's servant explains to Rebekah's brother and father the reason for his visit. This second telling is where we pick up.

For a book that begins "in the beginning" and contains extraordinary stories, such as that of Noah and the Ark, the birth of Isaac to Sarah and Abraham in their old age, and Joseph being sold into slavery to then become second in command in Egypt, the events surrounding this story seem slightly ordinary to justify the amount of effort and space devoted to telling it twice in detail. We would not have given it any thought if the narrator had simply said, "and the servant told the story again to Rebekah's family." As readers, we already know how the story progresses the second time around, but something in this text is important, and the narrator wants to make sure we don't miss it. As the narrator recounts the servant's story a second time, he emphasizes the prayers that the servant prayed before and after Rebekah arrived, thereby ensuring that we know that his happening upon a woman drawing water for her family at just the right time, as well as her generosity, were not matters of luck or chance—God was there all along in the midst of it all.

II. **God works through ordinary situations and ordinary people.** In many of the stories we read in Genesis, God speaks directly to people, but not in this story. As Walter Brueggemann notes, except for the prayer the servant offers to God as he arrives at the spring, this story seems rather "secular."[1] It sounds like an ordinary report of how Rebekah was chosen to be Isaac's wife to continue Abraham's lineage. God does not tell the servant where he will find a woman or how he will know if the woman he chooses is the right one. God does not even guarantee that the servant will find a woman. And as for Rebekah, when I read this story I have to wonder how many times she had made that trip to the spring to draw water for her family. This was part of her daily routine to aid in the chores necessary to ensure the survival of her family. She could not have guessed that this trip to the spring would be unlike the trip she took earlier that day or the trip she took the day before or the week before. God does not tell Rebekah that on this day a stranger would approach her with a marriage proposal and that she and her family should say yes. God is there, answering the servant's prayers in the midst of the ordinary tasks of life.

III. **The manner in which this story unfolds is not unlike our own lives: God's presence is revealed in and through the ordinary parts of our lives.** One commentator reminds us that "The servant illustrates what life is like for many servants of God. They enter into the service of their master and proceed faithfully in quite ordinary situations remaining anonymous in the overall scheme of things, but they are crucial vehicles for the leading and blessing work of God in daily affairs."[2] If God is intimately involved in the life of this servant wandering around with camels and looking for an unknown woman, and if God is intimately involved in the life of Rebekah as she makes one more trip to the spring to draw water, then surely God is also intimately involved in our lives as we go about our daily, often

---

[1]Walter Brueggemann, *Interpretation: Genesis* (Atlanta: John Knox, 1982), p. 200.
[2]Terence E. Fretheim, "The Book of Genesis," *The New Interpreter's Bible*, Vol. 1 (Nashville: Abingdon Press, 1994), p. 512.

mundane routines and tasks. We may not be on our way to draw water from a spring or sent to find a spouse for someone, but we are often on our way to another meeting, on our way to the grocery store or to pick up the kids from school, and in situations in which we come in contact with people we may have never met before. Maybe this story reveals how God approaches us and works in our lives—in ordinary places, in the often subtle situations that might be unnoticeable if we are not paying attention. We do not have to wait for the presence of God to arrive in some spectacular way. This story confirms not once but twice that God is present and at work in the very things we are doing right now, however routine they may seem. And for this we can be thankful.—Brittany Riddle

---

ILLUSTRATIONS

Stamina. One of our great problems is giving up too soon. Marriages too soon end in divorce, church members too soon drop out, pastors too soon move on. Giving up too soon ends the chance for God to work. Copernicus worked thirty-six years on his theory of the universe before anyone would publish it. Wilma Rudolph was a U.S. Olympic champion but had to overcome polio, pneumonia, scarlet fever, braces, and poverty on her way to success. Madame Curie worked through over ten thousand failed experiments before she isolated the radium atom. These individuals could have given up any time, but determination proved the victor. God uses people who refuse to give up easily.—Lee McGlone

Patience. Some years ago, I heard the most remarkable declarations of faith from a woman who was a member of our congregation. On Friday afternoon, I preached her husband's funeral. On Sunday afternoon, a call came that the lady's teenage son had been seriously injured in an automobile accident. My wife and I sat with the mother most of the night. The sorrow of her husband's death was still fresh on her soul. Then there was the double sorrow of her son's impending death. He did die before the night was over. During the night, she talked softly and slowly about her feelings. I listened without saying much. What caught my attention was her clear insight into faith. "You know, pastor," she said, "I don't understand this, but I know God is here—somewhere. I don't reckon we have the right to know until God's through with it."—Lee McGlone

Musical Selections Appropriate to the Day

Gen. 24:34–38, 42–49, 58–67	*Ancient Words*
Ps. 45:10–17 or Ps. 72	*Holy God, We Praise Your Name*
Rom. 7:15–25a	*Holiness*
Matt. 11:16–19, 25–30	*Near to the Heart of God*

☙ Children's Lectionary Sermon

TITLE: It's Tough Being Good

SCRIPTURE: Rom. 7:15–25a

KEY VERSE: *For what I do is not the good I want to do; no, the evil I do not want to do—this I keep on doing.* (Rom. 7:19, NIV)

KEY CONCEPTS: Sin, human nature

MATERIALS: Bible

Once there was a boy who bit his fingernails. He would chew on them all the time. In fact, you could hardly ever catch him not chewing on his nails. One day, the boy's mother told the boy that he needed to stop chewing on his fingernails and explained the reasons why it was not good for him. The boy really wanted to obey his mother, so he tried really, really hard to stop. But it seemed that no matter how hard the boy tried, he always found himself with his hands in his mouth chewing his fingernails.

(*Open Bible.*) In today's passage from Romans, Paul tells us, *For what I do is not the good I want to do; no, the evil I do not want to do—this I keep on doing.* Now chewing on your fingernails is not evil, but the point of the story is that the boy had problems trying to quit doing something that he was told not to do. Today's passage points out that there is something about us that makes it hard for us to stop doing things that we know we should not do. God has given us some rules for our own safety because God wants what is best for us, but we have a tendency to want to break these guidelines that God has given us. No matter how hard we try to keep them, we will mess up every now and then. This is why we need to ask God for help so that we can live the way God wants us to.—Seth A. Michael

◈ WORSHIP AIDS ◈

Call to Worship: "Glorify the Lord with me; let us exalt his name together" (Ps. 34:3, NIV).

Invocation: Father of life and light, you declare that you do love us all, that you forgive our sins, and that you welcome us into your presence. Grant that today we may admit our human plight, our sins and inadequacies, and reach out to you for mercy and strength. Amen.

Offertory Sentence: "For where your treasure is, there will be your heart also" (Matt. 6:21, NIV).

Offertory Prayer: Lord God, take what we share this day and multiply it by the Holy Spirit to do great deeds the worth of which only heaven can fully measure. Amen.—E. Lee Phillips

Morning Prayer: O God, our Father, Creator, sustainer, we thank you for your steadfast love, for being the everlasting God! We thank you for being able to gather to worship you, O God. We thank you for initiating worship with us. We realize that everything we have today comes from you. Thank you for sending your Spirit upon us that we may be empowered to do your work.

Go with us, Father, in the days ahead. May our lives be a reflection of you and your glory. May we shine as beams of hope and love to a lost and dying world. May our sacrifices of praise today be acceptable in your sight. We honor you, O God, giving you all of our attention, praise, and adoration. May your Spirit continue to comfort us in our times of need and guide us throughout our lives. In the name of Jesus Christ, who paid the debt of sin on our behalf, and who intercedes for us now. Amen.—Tyler Burleson

Benediction: Today we worshipped in a land of liberty and conscience. May our coming days be filled with missionary zeal, for we are ambassadors for Christ in a free land. Amen.—E. Lee Phillips

SUNDAY, JULY 10, 2011
Fourth Sunday after Pentecost

LECTIONARY SERMON TOPIC: "Remembering the Words"

TEXT: Ps. 25

OTHER READINGS: Gen. 25:19–34; Ps. 119:105–112; Rom. 8:1–11; Matt. 13:1–9, 18–23

Think of all of the material we learned through songs, rhymes, and other mnemonic devices when we were children. How many of us can alphabetize without singing through the alphabet song? Or remember how many days are in each month without the rhyme, "Thirty days hath September, April, June, and November?" Or name the colors of the rainbow in order of their hue on the visible spectrum without first thinking about Roy G. Biv? Our minds like patterns, and these mnemonic devices aid our memory and help us recall information by finding associations between new information to be learned and information we already know. The effectiveness of mnemonic devices is not a recent discovery, and we know that ancient writers used similar techniques to make their words memorable for those who would hear them.

Psalm 25 is one example of the use of a mnemonic device by an author of an ancient text. Although it may not be evident to us at first glance in English, this psalm is one of the few psalms in the Bible that is written as an acrostic poem. Read in its original Hebrew, each verse begins with a successive letter of the Hebrew alphabet, which at the time it was written would have allowed listeners who knew the Hebrew alphabet to more easily recall what came next in each line of the psalm. For us, this would like saying, "A is for apple, and B is for bat . . . ," though the words of the psalmist are much more thoughtful and significant. This psalm encourages us to remember its words and teachings.

I. **When we remember the words of this psalm, we remember that we are students of God's ways and that God cares about us enough to teach** us and lead us. Whereas many psalms seem to appeal directly to our hearts, this psalm speaks to our minds as well. Psalm 25 is packed with the language and imagery of learning and leading. Words such as "teach," "instruct," "lead," and "know" are sprinkled throughout this psalm as the author pleads with God to deliver him from the "troubles of his heart." We do not know the specifics of what the psalmist was facing as he wrote the words of this psalm, but we do know that he believed that God's instruction could help deliver him from his pain.

II. **When we remember the words of Psalm 25, we remember that God can handle all our anxieties and confessions.** Three times in Psalm 25 the psalmist appeals to God's *hesed*. Entire books have been written on the meaning of this Hebrew word, but in essence the psalmist is appealing to God's mercy, steadfast love, and faithfulness. In a rather bold request, the psalmist pleads with God to remember him according to God's *hesed* and to forget the sins of his youth. Although it may seem risky to approach God to ask God to forget something from the past, I am reassured by the psalmist's request. Sometimes we hold back our questions and are afraid to make a request to God to be generous with love and mercy. Sometimes we water down our prayers and laments in order not to sound as though we are challenging God. We are afraid of what might happen if we are honest about our questions, doubts, and anxieties. This psalm reminds and reassures us that God can handle all of our weaknesses, inadequacies, and sin. If we are willing learners, God will instruct us so that we can better learn to walk in the paths of God's steadfast love and faithfulness.

III. **When we remember the words of this psalm, we remember that they are part of our own stories.** We have made mistakes in our pasts. We have hurt other people with our words and actions. We have done harm through our inaction. We have ignored those in need. We have not taken care of ourselves as well as we should. We have sinned against others. We have sinned against ourselves. We have sinned against God, more times than we would like to remember. Psalm 25 gives us hope that despite all of this, we can appeal to God with humble hearts to take away our shame. Being taught in the ways of the Lord may not immediately eliminate our pain. Even the psalmist realized this as he wrote "for you I wait all day long." The shame may not go away today. The mistakes of the past may not be resolved today. The process of learning will surely last a lifetime. But we know that our instruction comes from a merciful and loving God, which gives us the hope to keep learning.

Knowing that we lead similar lives of sin, Psalm 25 is worth keeping where we can always access it. The psalmist made it easier for people hearing the words to memorize the acrostic poem, because he knew the significance of the words in the lives of everyone who desires to learn from God. It is in the act of studying, rehearsing, memorizing, and learning that these words can become a part of who we are. One author tells of "a lovely Hasidic story of a rabbi who always told his people that if they studied the Torah, it would put Scripture on their hearts. One of them asked, 'Why *on* our hearts, and not *in* them?' The rabbi answered, 'Only God can put Scripture inside. But reading sacred text can put it on your hearts, and then when your hearts break, the holy words will fall inside.'"[3]

IV. **When our hearts break, when we have no idea which way is God's path, when our lives seem directionless, may these words be our prayer:** "Make me to know your ways, O Lord; teach me your paths. Lead me in your truth, and teach me, for you are the God of my salvation; for you I wait all day long" (Ps. 25:4–5, NRSV). And as we continue to pray these words and learn from God, may these words fall inside our hearts: "Good and upright is the Lord; therefore he instructs sinners in the way. He leads the humble in what is right, and teaches the humble his way" (Ps. 25:8–9, NRSV).—Brittany Riddle

---

ILLUSTRATIONS

Memory. Memory is a powerful reflector. My earliest job was hauling hay. I then went to pumping gas. Then there was college and the call as pastor to a small rural church . . . and then to working in a plywood mill at night while going to college in the daytime. And serving as a pastor. Later there was teaching

---

[3]Anne Lamott, *Plan B: Further Thoughts on Faith* (New York: Penguin Group, 2005), p. 73.

math in a middle school . . . and pastoring. And then the seminary and two master's degrees and the Ph.D. degree . . . and pastoring. Then teaching at the seminary . . . and pastoring. And continuing in that pastoral role for a total of forty-one years now. As I look back on it all, I can't in any way say that any one part of that has been more especially holy than any other. In fact, it was all holy. God, I believe, was in it all. As we look back, if we gaze close enough, we'll see God there all along the way!—Lee McGlone

Humility. Although George Whitefield disagreed with John Wesley on some theological matters, he was careful not to create problems in public that could be used to hinder the preaching of the gospel. When someone asked Whitefield if he thought he would see Wesley in heaven, Whitefield replied, "I fear not, for he will be so near the eternal throne and we at such a distance, we shall hardly get sight of him."—Warren W. Wiersbe[4]

Musical Selections Appropriate to the Day

Gen. 25:19–34	*Children of the Heavenly Father*
Ps. 119:105–112 or Ps. 25	*Thy Word*
Rom. 8:1–11	*Greater Is He That Is in Me*
Matt. 13:1–9, 18–23	*Send Forth Your Word, O God*

⚛ Children's Lectionary Sermon

TITLE: Who Is Your Teacher?

SCRIPTURE: Ps. 25

KEY VERSES: *Show me your ways, O Lord, teach me your paths; guide me in your truth and teach me.* (Ps. 25:4–5a, NIV)

---

[4]Warren W. Wiersbe, *Wycliffe Handbook of Preaching and Preachers* (Chicago: Moody Press, 1984), p. 255.

KEY CONCEPTS: Discipleship, learning the ways of God
MATERIALS: Bible

How many of you are in school or preschool or day care? (*Let the children respond.*) What is the name of your teacher, and what kind of things does he or she teach you? (*Call on individual children to share.*) Did you know that learning your ABCs will help you learn how to read? As you learn to read, you can learn about all kinds of things. As you get older, you will grow and learn more and more.

Have you ever thought about how God is your teacher? What kind of things do you think God would want to teach you? (*Let the children respond, and reflect back their answers.*) (*Open Bible.*) In Psalm 25, the psalmist asked God to be his teacher. It says, *Show me your ways, O Lord, teach me your paths; guide me in your truth and teach me.* The psalmist wants God to teach him how to live out his life according to God's plan. This is something that can only be done if we ask God to teach us what God's will is for our lives. God desires very much to teach each and every one of us, and what God teaches us can help us out throughout our whole life.—Seth A. Michael

❧ WORSHIP AIDS ❧

Call to Worship: "Taste and see that the Lord is good; blessed is the man who takes refuge in him" (Ps. 34:8, NIV).

Invocation: Our Lord's words declare the spirit in which we gather: "The hour comes, and now is, when the true worshippers shall worship the Father in spirit and in truth: for the Father seeks such to worship him" (John 4:23).

Offertory Sentence: "No one can serve two masters. Either he will hate the one and love the other, or he will be devoted to the one and despise the other. You cannot serve both God and money" (Matt. 6:24, NIV).

Offertory Prayer: Father, in our day many have truly been given much. Yet often we are untrusting stewards of that bounty. Increase our faith, remove the fears of calamity, open our hearts that they may be springs of refreshment—and may we discover the joy of giving. Amen.

Morning Prayer: How we need to be here this morning, Father. In recent days we have walked the ways of the world, experienced the joys and pains of life, struggled with achievements and temptations, and known both success and failure. We have tried to manage all things with our limited wisdom, power, and knowledge. We have stubbornly held to ideas that only hinder rather than help. We have neglected higher callings that we might avoid the struggle of mental and spiritual growth. In a word, Father, we have done with our days just about what we determined best.—Henry Fields

Benediction: We go out with the words of the psalmist declaring our way: "Glory in His holy name; let the hearts of those rejoice who seek the Lord! Seek the Lord and His strength; seek His face forevermore" (Ps. 105:3–4). Amen.

SUNDAY, JULY 17, 2011
Fifth Sunday after Pentecost

LECTIONARY SERMON TOPIC: "Who Knows Us?"
TEXT: Ps. 139:1–12, 23–24
OTHER READINGS: Gen. 28:10–19a; Rom. 8:12–25; Matt. 13:24–30, 36–43

How well are we known? How well do we want to be known? Psalm 139 wonderfully describes the tension I often feel in relationship with God. I am comforted by the thought, in the words of the psalmist, that God has "searched me and known me." At the same time, this terrifies me. I am encouraged that God knows my thoughts and my ways, but do I really want someone, even God, to know that much about me? Psalm 139 challenges our twenty-first-century notions of independence and desire for privacy, while at the same time presenting us with a reassuring sense that we are intimately cared for by God.

I. **God is a personal God.** The psalmist who wrote Psalm 139 clearly experienced God's presence deeply. He describes God not as a distant and abstract being but as a God with whom he has had personal encounters. God has searched and known him. God knows when he comes and when he goes, when he rests and when he wanders, when he thinks and when he speaks. God knows him backwards and forwards, inside and out.

If we read this psalm carefully, we will notice that almost every line has both first-person and second-person language. *You* (God) have searched *me* and known *me. You* know when *I* sit down and when *I* rise up. If *I* ascend to heaven, *you* are there. This language reinforces the deeply personal nature of our relationship with God. We are created in the image of God. God does not just want to know "us" in a general sense. God wants to know *you* through and through, and God wants to know *me* through and through. Frederick Buechner gets to the heart of the significance of this personal language when he writes, "In the book of Genesis the first word God speaks to a human being is 'You' (2:15), and in the book of Revelation the last word a human being speaks in effect to God is 'Come, Lord Jesus!' which is to say 'Come, you!' (22:20). It is possible that the whole miracle of creation is to bridge the immeasurable distance between Creator and creature with that one small word."[5]

II. **We find ourselves in a long-existing human paradox.** Psalm 139 speaks to our deepest longings and our deepest fears. We desperately want to be known and understood for who we truly are, but we aren't sure we want to let ourselves be that vulnerable. We don't want to be lonely, but we are acutely aware that being fully known means we might be rejected. The psalmist was dealing with the same tension. We can hear it in the questions he poses in verse 7 and in the answers he provides in verses 8 through 12. "Where can I go from your Spirit? Or where can I flee from your presence?" That word "flee" implies a running away from something. When we flee, we aren't just casually jogging or playing a game—we are running for our lives. Running for our lives as we know them, afraid of what our lives might hold, what we might be called to do, or where we might be called to go—if we let our guard down and allow ourselves to be truly and fully known.

---

[5]Frederick Buechner, *Beyond Words: Daily Readings in the ABC's of Faith* (New York: HarperCollins, 2004), p. 422.

III. **Many of us spend a lot of time running.** We do not know if the psalmist was simply asking a rhetorical question in order to reassure himself of the nearness of God or if he really wanted to flee from the presence of God, but the idea of fleeing had at least entered his mind. We can relate to the tension the psalmist presents. We know what it is like to desperately want something and need something—to be known in the presence of God—but at the same time to want to run away to a place where we feel less vulnerable and less exposed. The psalmist concludes that running would be futile. That whether we are in the farthest limits of the sea or in the darkness where we cannot find the light, God is with us, leading us and guiding us. And with this knowledge, some of our fears of abandonment and rejection are alleviated.

IV. **Many of us also spend a lot of time hiding.** Have you ever played hide-and-seek with a young child? If so, you know that children love to hide, but not for too long. And though we play along, they are rarely hard to find. Often, after a few minutes of hiding, the child will come searching for you if you haven't already found him or her. And then the child wants to hide again. This is how I sometimes feel it is with God. We run and hide (or think we are hiding) from God, all the while knowing that God knows exactly where we are. And that God can see through to our deepest desires and needs.

We hide our true selves. We cheerfully smile and tell everyone we are "fine" when things are falling apart in our personal lives. We try to hide the things that make us and other people uncomfortable. We try to hide the parts of ourselves that we think others will not like or will not approve of—our mistakes, addictions, weaknesses, and fears. We cannot acknowledge the difficulties we face at work, at school, and in our families. What would other people think if they knew *this* or *that* about us? And maybe we also try to hide all of these things from God.

V. **Psalm 139 reminds us that we do not need to (and cannot) hide our lives from God.** Psalm 139 brings us a word of grace—we are free to be ourselves and to live transparent lives before God. God knows us entirely, and God loves us because of and in spite of what God knows about us. This psalm says to us, *even when you don't know who you are, God knows who you are. Even when you don't know where you are, God knows where you are. Even if you aren't sure if anyone else is with you, God is there, leading you in the way everlasting.*—Brittany Riddle

ILLUSTRATIONS

Omnipresence. A thousand years ago, our world was still in the dark ages. Nothing much good was happening—or at least it so seemed. Yet God was at work! Changes were at work that would alter the world: the printing press, Protestant Reformation, discovery of America, making of the United States, and all that has happened since then. What will God do among us in the future? We surely don't know, but we do want to be a part of it. We are reminded of the response of the disciples before whom the father of a demon-possessed boy came, seeking their help. Alone they couldn't help. The father turned to Jesus and declared, "I besought your disciples to cast him out, but they could not." Jesus turned to the disciples and asked, "Do you believe?" Their response: "Yea, Lord, we believe. Help thou our unbelief." God is at work everywhere . . . all the time.—Lee McGlone

Humility. The famous inventor Samuel Morse was once asked if he ever encountered situations where he didn't know what to do. Morse responded, "More than once, and whenever I could not see my way clearly, I knelt down and prayed to God for light and understanding." Morse received many honors for his invention of the telegraph, but felt undeserving: "I have made a valuable application of electricity not because I was superior to other men but solely because God, who meant it for mankind, must reveal it to someone and He was pleased to reveal it to me."—Tim Hansel[6]

Musical Selections Appropriate to the Day

Gen. 28:10–19a	*Shout to the North*
Ps. 139:1–12, 23–24	*Search Me, O God, and Know My Heart*
Rom. 8:12–25	*A Child of the King*
Matt. 13:24–30, 36–43	*We'll Work till Jesus Comes*

[6]Tim Hansel, *Eating Problems for Breakfast* (Dallas: Word, 1988), pp. 33–34.

❧ Children's Lectionary Sermon

TITLE: Faraway Places

SCRIPTURE: Ps. 139:1–12, 23–24

KEY VERSE: *Where can I go from your Spirit? Where can I flee from your presence?* (Ps. 139:7, NIV)

KEY CONCEPT: God is with you everywhere.

MATERIALS: Bible, map of world or a globe, picture of outer space

PREPARATION: (Optional) Mark the location of your church on the map or globe.

This is a map of the world. What is the blue on the map? (*Let the children respond.*) That's right, water. And this is the United States. Can anybody show me on this map where we live? (*Call on a child to find it on the map or globe.*) Good job! We live in _____, which is right here on the map.

Did you know that I've been to _____? (*Tell the children about a "faraway" place that you have traveled, be it another country, another state, or another town. Just emphasize that it is a distance away from where you currently are. Show the children this location on the map.*) Have any of you been on a trip to a different place? Where have you been? (*Call on several children to share. Show children on the map some of the places they tell you they have traveled to.*)

(*Open Bible.*) In Psalm 139, the psalmist asked, *Where can I go from your Spirit? Where can I flee from your presence?* The psalmist knew there was no place he could go to get away from God's presence. Did you know you can go anywhere on this map, and God will be there with you? You can go (*point to various locations on the map*) here, and here, and here, and here. God is with you all the time—everywhere. God would even be with you if you went all the way to outer space! (*Show the picture of space.*)

Dear God, thank you that we can never go so far that we are away from you. Thank you that your love is always with us. We love you too. Amen.—Stacia Michael

❧ WORSHIP AIDS ❧

Call to Worship: "The Lord is close to the brokenhearted and saves those who are crushed in spirit" (Ps. 34:18, NIV).

Invocation: Father, encourage us today with such spiritual insight that the life and labor of our Lord Jesus will be remembered. Not something from long ago, buried in history, but living and vital among us now. Stir within our hearts the same Spirit who in Christ showed us the glory of your love—and who on Calvary's cross declared it forever. Amen.

Offertory Sentence: "But seek first his kingdom and his righteousness, and all these things will be given to you as well" (Matt. 6:33, NIV).

Offertory Prayer: Father, guide us today to determine the priories of life that matter most, to distinguish first things—and having distinguished them, help us keep first things first. Amen.

Morning Prayer: Lord, we thank you today for worship—for the ability that you have given us as humans to worship you. It is nothing short of amazing that you would allow sinners who fail you on a daily basis to enter into your presence. And yet you not only allow our worship but accept it. You are pleased by our worship. This is amazing, yet it is something that we take for granted.

Grant that we as worship leaders will remember that we are not mediators. Help us be flexible and open to how your Spirit is moving. Give us ears to listen to you as we worship. I give thanks that you have gifted and called individuals to be worship leaders. Thank you for giving us this opportunity, for trusting us to lead your people and do your will. Thank you for calling me. Amen.—Taylor Post

Benediction: As we go out into the week, may we so live that our words, and our deeds, will proclaim the joy that resides within. May the splendor of our calling be matched by the fervor of our living. May God forever be praised! Amen.

SUNDAY, JULY 24, 2011
Sixth Sunday after Pentecost

LECTIONARY SERMON TOPIC: "Do We Understand?"

TEXT: Matt. 13:31–33, 44–52

OTHER READINGS: Gen. 29:15–28; Ps. 105:1–11, 45b; Rom. 8:26–39

What is heaven like? A curious child might ask this question after hearing a Sunday school lesson about heaven or after hearing someone use the phrase "for heaven's sake." In the midst of grief, a person might ask this as she or he reflects on the loss of a loved one. Whatever the context, I imagine most of us have asked or been asked this question at some point in our lives. The parables in Matthew 13 suggest that Jesus' followers asked the same question, though the answer he gives is not what we expect and maybe not what we would like to hear. We want specifics of what the kingdom of heaven looks and sounds and smells like, but instead of providing us with concrete details or even giving us a clue as to the whereabouts of the kingdom of heaven, Jesus presents us with these parables and confronts our search for easy and concrete answers.

I. **The parables in Matthew 13 put our minds and imaginations to the test.** Just when we think we begin to understand how the kingdom of heaven is like a mustard seed, which grows into a great shrub, Jesus goes on to say that the kingdom of heaven is also like yeast a woman uses to leaven bread. And then a treasure in a field or a pearl that is so valuable someone is willing to sell all he has to buy it. And in case we were still confused, maybe we can understand the kingdom of heaven in comparison to a net that caught every kind of fish. I can understand each of the elements of these parables out of context, but I have a harder time connecting them to the kingdom of heaven. The elements that seem simple at first become more and more complex as I try to make sense of the peculiar comparisons Jesus makes. That, of course, is the point of a parable. Parables draw on our imagination, leave much room for interpretation, and, as one scholar suggests, function by "arresting the hearer by its vividness or strangeness, and leaving the mind in sufficient doubt about its application to tease it into active thought."[7] If teasing minds and stirring imaginations are what Jesus intended to do with his parables, he sure was successful.

After hearing all these parables and amidst all the questions that must have been running through the minds of those listening, Jesus simply asked his disciples, "Have you understood all this?" And they boldly answered yes. Jesus accepts their answer without question. Maybe the disciples really did understand the meaning of Jesus' words. Maybe they were only half-listening. Maybe "yes" is the only word they could manage to get out of their mouths as their heads were spinning and their eyes were glazed over from Jesus' rapid-fire parable telling. How else were they supposed to respond? They were listening to the man who healed blind people, cast out demons, and brought a woman back to life before their very eyes. Not too many people would be so bold as to ask Jesus to repeat himself or to clarify a point after he just explained the kingdom of heaven five different ways.

And then the question comes a little closer to home. Do *we* understand all of this? Unlike in some of Jesus' parables, such as the parable of the sower and the parable of the weeds where he provides the interpretation, Jesus does not give us an explanation for the parables in today's reading. These parables would be a lot easier to digest if Jesus had followed them with "and what I meant when I said the kingdom of heaven is like a mustard seed is this . . ." But from these parables we can glean a few ideas about the kingdom of heaven.

II. **The kingdom of heaven is not easy to define.** The kingdom of heaven is complex and simple. It is hidden in the ground, mixed in with the flour, and among the abundance of fish of every kind caught in a net. It is revealed like a treasure found in a field and a great shrub in which birds nest in its branches. It is something we search for and something that finds us. It is in yeast, a fungus that causes the bread to rise, and also in priceless pearls. We seek the kingdom of heaven, we find the kingdom

---

[7]Peter Rhea Jones, "Parable," *Mercer Dictionary on the Bible*, ed. by Watson E. Mills (Macon, GA: Mercer University Press, 1991), p. 644.

of heaven, we grow the kingdom of heaven, and we catch the kingdom of heaven. It starts out as the smallest of seeds, but is valuable enough to cause us to sell everything that we own to obtain it.

III. **Jesus tells us that the kingdom of heaven will change our lives.** Frederick Buechner suggests that instead of giving us specific information to appease our senses, when talking abstractly about the kingdom of heaven, "Jesus is maybe at his best in describing the feeling you get when you glimpse the Thing Itself."[8] The surprise and mystery of the formerly flat bread rising as it bakes. The joy and suspense of finding a treasure in a field. The transformation can begin now, Jesus says. We do not have to wait to experience the kingdom of heaven in some grandiose way in the future. It may start with the smallest of seeds and the smallest of actions, and it may be difficult to see a change occurring, but we know from these parables that its impact will ultimately be large. We will be surprised, and we cannot help but be transformed.

IV. **When we try to limit the kingdom of heaven, we miss opportunities to see and experience God at work.** I have to wonder if Jesus was not purposely trying to overwhelm his listeners with his quick, unexplained, seemingly abstract comparisons in order to challenge us to think more broadly about the kingdom of heaven. The kingdom of heaven is like all of these things and like so many others. The kingdom of heaven is all around us, offering opportunities for us to see, touch, hear, and experience God at work. If we want to know what the kingdom of heaven is like, Jesus tells us to pay attention to the world in which we live. All of those small, hardly noticeable, but valuable things will give us a glimpse of the kingdom of heaven and call us to participate in its beginning right now with the very things around us.—Brittany Riddle

ILLUSTRATIONS

God at Work. We may well see God at work in many places and miss the fact that God is work in us. Some feel that life has passed on by. A young person

[8]Buechner, *Beyond Words*, p. 214.

was heard to say, "Life met me face to face on a busy street. When it saw me coming, it crossed to the other side." Or there is the classic case of lovable Charlie Brown, the *Peanuts* character, who exemplifies many of us. In one episode, Lucy declares, "Life is like a grocery cart! Each of us has a grocery cart and the world is our supermarket. The world is filled with wonderful things. Push your cart down the aisles, Charlie Brown! That grocery cart is your life. Push it, Charlie Brown! Push it right up to the check-out counter." Charlie laments, "Which one? I think I have six items or less."—Lee McGlone

Incarnation. The Word of the Father, by whom all time was created, was made flesh and was born in time for us. He, without whose divine permission no day completes its course, wished to have one day for His human birth. In the bosom of His Father He existed before all the cycles of ages; born of an earthly mother, He entered upon the course of the years on this day. The Maker of man became man that He, Ruler of the stars, might be nourished at the breast; that He, the Bread, might be hungry; that He, the Fountain, might thirst; that He, the Light, might sleep; that He, the Way, might be wearied by the journey; that He, the Truth, might be accused by false witnesses; that He, the Judge of the living and the dead, might be brought to trial by a mortal judge; that He, Justice, might be condemned by the unjust; that He, Discipline, might be scourged with whips; that He, the Foundation, might be suspended upon a cross; that Courage might be weakened; that Security might be wounded; that Life might die.—St. Augustine[9]

Musical Selections Appropriate to the Day

Gen. 29:15–28	*All the Way My Savior Leads Me*
Ps. 105:1–11, 45b	*Let All Things Now Living*
Rom. 8:26–39	*I Am Thine, O Lord*
Matt. 13:31–33, 44–52	*Hear the Call of the Kingdom*

---

[9]St. Augustine, *Sermons on the Liturgical Seasons*, trans. by Sister Mary Sarah Muldowney (New York: Fathers of the Church, 1959), p. 28.

₰ Children's Lectionary Sermon

TITLE: Knowing the Good Stuff

SCRIPTURE: Matt. 13:31–33, 44–52

KEY VERSES: *"Again, the kingdom of heaven is like a merchant looking for fine pearls. When he found one of great value, he went away and sold everything he had and bought it."* (Matt. 13:45–46, NIV)

KEY CONCEPT: The Kingdom of Heaven

MATERIALS: Bible

I want to tell you a story today about a dog named Dakota. Dakota was a very smart and very sweet dog. She had a favorite toy: a tug rope. Dakota carried her tug rope with her everywhere she went. She would trot around inside and outside, in cold weather and warm, always with her tug rope in her mouth. She liked to play catch with it, to sleep with it; she did everything with her tug rope. So it was dirty and fraying, just about ready to fall apart.

There was only one thing that could make Dakota drop her tug rope. A treat. You see, even though Dakota loved her toy, she knew something even better when she smelled it. As soon as she saw the treat, she would leave her tug rope right where it was and come running.

Sometimes we have some favorite things that we hold on to really, really tightly. Like maybe your favorite toy or your special blanket or your Nintendo DS or anything that is really, really special to you. But guess what? There is something even better! Jesus taught that the Kingdom of Heaven is the best treasure in the world. (*Open Bible.*) Jesus told his disciples, *"Again, the kingdom of heaven is like a merchant looking for fine pearls. When he found one of great value, he went away and sold everything he had and bought it."* Knowing Jesus is even better, better than our favorite toy. It is like finding the best treasure ever!—Stacia Michael

₰ WORSHIP AIDS ₰

Call to Worship: "Then my soul will rejoice in the Lord and delight in his salvation" (Ps. 35:9, NIV).

Invocation: Lord, let us this day lay down every encumbrance that holds us back from the worship of our Savior, that with palms of delight and shouts of hosanna we proclaim the King of the Jews, Lord of our hearts. Amen.—E. Lee Phillips

Offertory Sentence: "And anyone who does not take up his cross and follow me is not worthy of me" (Matt. 10:38, NIV).

Offertory Prayer: Father, grant that we may lay our offerings joyfully before you without reservations or doubt. Help us remember your gift to us, that which came in Christ Jesus, the Lord. May any reluctance in giving perish as we recall the magnitude of your loving sacrifice. Amen.

Morning Prayer: God, your power is majestic. You show yourself to all who fervently seek you. To the ones who call out for your glory, you are always faithful to answer. No one can comprehend your worth. O Lord, you fill all of heaven and earth. Holy and great are you, O God. How honored we are that you choose us as your children. You are unashamed to hold us close to your heart. We constantly do things that don't deserve your love, but you see us through the eyes of your grace and forgive us. Praise be to you! May we always have praise on our lips and in our thoughts. Use us for your glory. Here we are, Lord, ready to do your will. In the name of Jesus. Amen.—Megan Williams

Benediction: We have worshipped in the presence of Christ. Now we go forth in his strength that fills our lives. May our efforts for the Kingdom bring to Christ glory and honor, now and forever, world without end. Amen.

SUNDAY, JULY 31, 2011
Seventh Sunday after Pentecost

LECTIONARY SERMON TOPIC: "You Give Them Something to Eat"
TEXT: Matt. 14:13–21
OTHER READINGS: Gen. 32:22–31; Ps. 17:1–7, 15; Rom. 9:1–5

"And now you know the rest of the story." These famous words ended Paul Harvey's radio broadcast, *The Rest of the Story*, each weekday for over seventy years. In his radio program, Harvey told stories about a variety of subjects that always ended with a surprise or twist, something unexpected that gave listeners a new outlook on a story of interest. What about the rest of the story? We ask this question a lot in our society in response to those things we cannot fully comprehend—surely there is something there that explains it all, something we missed because we did not see or hear or experience it. And the feeding of the five thousand? What about the rest of *this* story? We want answers. We want to know if it happened. We want to know how it happened. We want to know how Jesus managed to feed five thousand men, plus all of the women and children who were with them, with only five loaves of bread and two fish.

We want a footnote at the end of the text explaining what happened behind the scenes to enable these events to occur. But all we have is a few verses in all four gospels describing the same miracle. The details are similar in each of the gospels: five loaves, two fish, thousands of hungry people, skeptical disciples, and a calm, compassionate, hospitable Jesus. Evening came, and the thousands of people following Jesus were hungry. They needed to be fed, so the disciples offered Jesus a seemingly reasonable plan of action. "Send the crowds away so that they may go into the villages and buy food for themselves," they advised. They were tired and probably wanted some peace and quiet, but instead of following their recommendation, Jesus responded, "They need not go away; you give them something to eat."

I. **You give them something to eat.** "We have nothing," the disciples told Jesus. "Nothing but five loaves and two fish. How will we feed them?" A valid question as they took inventory of their meager food supply. It hardly appeared that they had enough food to feed themselves, much less the thousands who followed them. But Jesus knew they could not send the people in the crowd away hungry. Regardless of their doubt and hesitation, Jesus told them to bring the loaves and fish to him. He would bless them, and they would be enough. Just as it was enough when God provided manna for the Israelites as they traveled to the Promised Land (Exod. 16). And just as it was enough when Elisha had only twenty loaves of barley and fresh ears of grain, and God provided enough food for one hundred men to eat and have some left over (2 Kings 4:42–44).

II. **You give them something to eat.** Eating a meal in the first century was about hospitality and sharing, not about how quickly one could stuff oneself to go on to the next activity on the to-do list. As I read verse 20, the abundance of leftover food is obviously noteworthy, but I find the previous statement to be just as striking: "all ate and were filled [or satisfied]." Bread and fish were the ingredients of a basic meal in Jesus' day. The meal the people were fed was certainly not like that of the banquets we see in some of the other gospel stories, but the people still went away filled, with their hunger satisfied. Imagine the amazement the disciples must have experienced as they passed around the small amount of food that Jesus had blessed. Imagine how the disciples felt as they collected the leftover loaves and fish. They saw that the "nothing" they had given to Jesus was enough to feed thousands of people.

III. **You give them something to eat.** Who me? Jesus didn't initially say to the disciples, "Don't worry about our lack of food; I will perform a miracle and feed them." He said, "*You* give them something to eat." At least in the beginning, Jesus put the responsibility on the disciples to come up with some possible solutions to feed this large, hungry crowd. We sometimes assume that because this was a miracle performed by Jesus, we can't replicate it today. Will we be able to do exactly what Jesus did in the same way that Jesus did it? Probably not. But sometimes we try to make the needs of others God's problem when in reality we have exactly what they need. A cup of cold water. A hot meal. A listening ear. A shoulder to cry on. A word of encouragement. We are discouraged from sharing our food, providing hospitality, and giving of ourselves because we think we don't have enough. We don't think we can make a difference.

IV. **So what about the rest of this story?** We will never know exactly what took place that day. We will never fully understand how Jesus took five loaves of bread and two fish and fed thousands of people. We do know what comes next for Jesus and the disciples, but we have yet to hear the whole story. The rest of the story depends on us. One person, taking a leap of faith, steps up to take action. One person is willing to trust Jesus. One person believes that what he or she has is enough. And suddenly, a miracle happens and a crowd is fed. Are we waiting for someone else to do something about the needs of those we encounter? How will we respond when Jesus calls to us and says, "*You* give them something to eat"?—Brittany Riddle

---

ILLUSTRATIONS

Sharing. In describing how her Catholic Worker Movement began, Dorothy Day writes, "We were just sitting there talking when lines of people began to form, saying, 'We need bread.' We could not say, 'Go be thou filled.' If there were six small loaves and a few fishes, we had to divide them. There was always bread. We were just sitting there talking and people moved in on us. Let those who can take it, take it. Some moved out and that made room for more. And somehow the walls expanded."[10] Willingness to share—to bring what we have before Jesus and others—and faith that what we have is enough can make all the difference.—Brittany Riddle

Hope. I am not a connoisseur of great art, but from time to time a painting or picture will really speak a clear, strong message to me. Some time ago, I saw a picture of an old burned-out mountain shack. All that remained was the chimney . . . the charred debris of what had been that family's sole possession. In front of this destroyed home stood an old, grandfatherly man dressed only in his underclothes, with a small boy clutching a pair of patched overalls. It was evident that the child was crying. Beneath the picture were the words that the artist felt the old man was speaking to the boy. They were simple words, yet they presented a profound theology and philosophy of life. Those words were, "Hush child, God ain't dead!"

That vivid picture of that burned-out mountain shack, that old man, the weeping child, and the words "God ain't dead" keep returning to my mind. Instead of it being a reminder of the despair of life, it has come to be a reminder of hope! I need reminders that there is hope in this world. In the midst of all of life's troubles and failures, I need mental pictures to remind me that all is not lost as long as God is alive and in control of His world.—James DeLoach[11]

---

[10]Dorothy Day, *The Long Loneliness* (New York: HarperCollins, 1952), pp. 285–286.
[11]James DeLoach, quoted in *When God Was Taken Captive*, ed. by Willard Aldrich (Sisters, OR: Multnomah Press, 1989), p. 24.

Musical Selections Appropriate to the Day

Gen. 32:22–31	*God, Our Father, You Have Led Us*
Ps. 17:1–7, 15	*'Tis So Sweet to Trust in Jesus*
Rom. 9:1–5	*We Are God's People*
Matt. 14:13–21	*Break Thou the Bread of Life*

⚘ Children's Lectionary Sermon

TITLE: A Little Goes a Long Way

SCRIPTURE: Matt. 14:13–21

KEY VERSES: *"We have here only five loaves of bread and two fish," they answered. "Bring them here to me," he said.* (Matt. 14:17–18, NIV)

KEY CONCEPT: Jesus can do great things.

MATERIALS: Bible, box of crayons, large piece of paper

PREPARATION: Set up the piece of paper on a surface that the children can write on. Also, choose colors from the box of crayons that will make up a rainbow (pull out white, brown, black, and so on). Save a red crayon for yourself.

(As the children come forward for the lesson, hand each one of them a crayon. Don't ask which color they want and don't allow them to pick their own colors. Just hand each child a crayon.) Here, take the crayon I give you. I know these crayons aren't very big, but I'm sure that we can use them today to make something really special.

(Open Bible.) Our Bible story today is about a time when Jesus took just five loaves of bread and two fish and used these little things to feed five thousand people! *(You can add as many details to the telling of the Bible story as you wish.)* Jesus can do a lot of wonderful things with the little things we offer up to him.

(Using your red crayon, draw an arc as the beginning of a rainbow.) I'm drawing a picture of a beautiful rainbow. But all I have is this little red crayon. My little crayon can't make something very special, can it? What should we do?

(Help the children to suggest that their crayons can be used to complete the rainbow. Invite them to add their color to the rainbow. Be careful not to allow any one

child to take over the coloring—allow each student a chance to make his or her contribution.) Wow! Each of us used the little crayon that we had to make a beautiful picture of a rainbow! It's kind of like in the story today. Jesus took a little bit and made it into something awesome. And he loves it when we give him what we have, even if we think it's too little for him to use, because he wants to do great things with what we give him.—Stacia Michael

WORSHIP AIDS

Call to Worship: "I will give thanks in the great assembly; among throngs of people I will praise you" (Ps. 35:18, NIV).

Invocation: From a hurried world with its endless demands, we come to this quiet sanctuary for renewal and strength, Father. We invoke your blessing on those who struggle to get by financially, emotionally, and spiritually. Let this hour of reflection, prayer, meditation, and praise truly restore our souls. Allow us to walk for a little while with the renewing presence of your Spirit, even as the first disciples walked with the Lord and from him learned to pray: (Lord's Prayer).—Henry Fields

Offertory Sentence: "For whoever wants to save his life will lose it, but whoever loses his life for me will find it" (Matt. 16:25, NIV).

Offertory Prayer: Thank you for the joy of giving. May both gift and giver be used to glorify your name we pray. Amen.—Henry Fields

Morning Prayer: Lord God, you are powerful. You look over us with your divine grace. You are full of splendor, and you gave your only Son for us—a people who are sinners. You are the Father, and Jesus Christ the Son. How great is your name? You are God in human form, our intercessor, and our highway to God. You are Holy Spirit—God in us. Live in us, and make us vessels to reveal you. Help us to be your temple and further your Kingdom through us. You are God in us, the Holy Spirit. Amen.—Ben Reeves

Benediction: By the power and grace of God, we go out today bearing the spirit of truth. In our homes and businesses and schools and neighborhoods we carry the heart of faith—made glad by the comradeship we share with God and with one another. Go in peace. Amen.

SUNDAY, AUGUST 7, 2011
Eighth Sunday after Pentecost

LECTIONARY SERMON TOPIC: "Jesus Is Lord"

TEXT: Rom. 10:5–15

OTHER READINGS: Gen. 37:1–4, 12–28; Ps. 105:1–6, 16–22, 45b; Matt. 14:22–33

What do we have to hold us together? I suppose every generation raises the same concerns; certainly Paul did in writing so much of the New Testament. In fact, his writings were each addressed to meet specific needs. To the Roman Christians, readying to face opportunity in the Imperial City as well as opposition in form of persecution, Paul said there was one thing most necessary. You must determine the faith you believe: "Jesus is Lord." Define it, confirm it, and stick to it. Now what did it mean?

I. **As our confession, it conveys the attitude of subservience.** The Greek word for "Lord" used here, *kurios*, describes the relationship of master to slave, king to subject, god to worshipper. The Jews of the New Testament era used the word when reading the Hebrew Old Testament. When they came to the name of God (the four-vowel tetragram YHWH), instead of trying to say the name of God, because it was too holy, they would say the Greek word "kurios." They understood its holiness . . . and so must we. Christians at the end of the first Christian century were called on in the Revelation never to confuse the lordship of Christ with that of the Caesar. Their declaration was always to be, "Jesus Christ is Lord" and never "Caesar is Lord."

One thing the word does not describe is the "take it or leave it" attitude of many modern Christians. Many will claim that Jesus is Lord and then act as if they were the kings who sit on the throne. The requirement for the Kingdom is the kind of humility, like that of a little child, that looks upward before it looks inward. When I die, at some later day, we're going to sing at my funeral these words: "My faith has found a resting place, not in device nor creed . . . It is enough that Jesus died and that he died for me." He is the Lord of all.

II. **As our proclamation, it conveys the attitude of unity.** What have we to say to this world of ours, if we are not clear on this matter? A Christianity that really is not sure who it is cannot say much to our world of sadness and confusion. Jesus prayed for his disciples in John 17 "that you may be one, even as the Father and I are one, so that the world may believe." Various branches of Christianity have never believed exactly the same thing. Even Paul and Barnabas had their different opinions in Acts 15. Some have said that where two or three Baptists are together, you have three to four opinions about almost anything. And that is okay for the most part . . . except when we differ on the lordship of Christ. Here is the "tie that binds our hearts in Christian love, the fellowship of kindred minds, like to that above." It is our confession that becomes our proclamation.

III. **As our inspiration, it conveys the attitude of devotion.** The confession "Jesus is Lord" was used as part of early baptismal liturgy. The candidates in baptism declared their devotion to the Lord. In essence, their baptism declared that Jesus died and that his death was for our sins, but that he did not stay dead. God raised him from the dead. He rose and is alive again. The thrill of the Christian life is that we can live each day as a renewal experience.

In the book of Romans, only two owners of life exist: either sin or God. To be sure, we don't identify sin as an owner in such terms much anymore. We'd rather substitute advertising slogans, such as "Have it your way," "Different strokes for different folks," "Looking out for number one," "The end justifies the means," "Go along to get along," "Everybody's doing it." Not much confession of faith there. These are marketing strategies whose only product is death.

But for the Church, our confession of Christ is the heart and soul of life. We serve but one Lord. Deep commitment to Christ, clear thinking, good decisions . . . these are the right road to the best that life has to offer. It all begins when Christ is Lord of life.

Christ's lordship doesn't stifle life; it opens life up. It brings purpose to life so that everything means more: marriage, roles as parents and children, school, vocation. Lordship invokes a new interpretation of life: a loving Creator, a worthy creature made in God's own image, a natural submission of creature to Creator. That's God's way. Life at its best is never found except as we bend our knee at the foot of the cross.—Lee McGlone

---

ILLUSTRATIONS

Cynicism. This seems to be the age of the cynic. Here is a short poem, author unknown, that I found in my folders recently. It tells the tale: "This is the age of the half-read page / the quick hash and the mad dash / the bright night with nerves tight / the plane hop and the brief stop / the lamp tan in a short span / the big shot in a good spot / the brain drain and the heart pain. And the cat naps till the spring snaps—and the fun's done."—Lee McGlone

Mixed Messages. Some years ago I visited a large hospital in a neighboring city. Locating a parking place was a chore. After driving around for some time, I noticed a vacant spot and pulled in before someone else beat me to it. I maneuvered carefully into the narrow opening . . . and was quite pleased at my driving acumen. Just as I prepared to exit the car, I looked up and saw a street sign, the kind with red letters against a white background. In rather bold letters across the top were these words: NO PARKING. Once I saw it, I got the message. But then I saw several lines of smaller letters beneath the larger. They read, I think, "Monday–Friday, noon–5 PM, except on Sundays." By the time I finished reading the sign, I wasn't sure if I could park there or not. Conditions placed under bold themes are a sure way to confusion.—Lee McGlone

Musical Selections Appropriate to the Day

Gen. 37:1–4, 12–28	*Word of God, Across the Ages*
Ps. 105:1–6, 16–22, 45b	*Hear Our Praises*
Rom. 10:5–15	*How Beautiful*
Matt. 14:22–33	*Be Not Afraid*

ᢒᢡ᠍᠍ Children's Lectionary Sermon

TITLE: Beautiful Feet

SCRIPTURE: Rom. 10:5–15

KEY VERSES: *And how can they hear about him unless someone tells them? And how will anyone go and tell them without being sent? That is why the Scriptures say, "How beautiful are the feet of messengers who bring good news."* (Rom. 10:14b–15, NLT)

KEY CONCEPT: Sharing the story of Jesus

MATERIALS: Bible

PREPARATION: If possible, you could wear sandals or shoes that would be easy to slip off.

(*Look around and see if any children are wearing sandals where you can see their feet. Tell them they have beautiful feet.*) What do your feet do? (*Let the children respond, and reflect back their answers.*) Our feet hold us up; they help us move from one place to another; sometimes they cause us to trip; sometimes they can just dangle in a lake or a stream and help us feel good.

(*Open Bible.*) In Romans, Paul tells the Christians in the church about sharing the story of Jesus. Back in Bible times, they didn't have telephones or e-mail. They would send important messages by a messenger—a man who would run from one place to another to tell an important message to people who needed to hear it. In Romans 10:14b–15, Paul writes, *And how can they hear about him unless someone tells them? And how will anyone go and tell them without being sent? That is why the Scriptures say, "How beautiful are the feet of messengers who bring good news."* Now back in those days, the roads were dusty, and when someone arrived at your home, their feet would be dirty. Would you call their feet beautiful if they were all dirty and crusted with gunk? You don't mind how dirty a person's feet are if they are bringing you good news. The beauty was in the message of Jesus—the good news.

We can be the messengers who bring the good news of Jesus. We can tell and show others how much Jesus loves them. What are some ways you can think of that you could be a messenger for Christ so others will know him? (*Let the children respond, and reflect back their answers.*) Each of you can have the beautiful feet Paul talked about by sharing the message of Jesus with others.—Marcia Thompson

◈ WORSHIP AIDS ◈

Call to Worship: "How priceless is your unfailing love! Both high and low among men find refuge in the shadow of your wings" (Ps. 36:7, NIV).

Invocation: Father, grant that this day our joy shall be that of the Risen Christ. May we now seek the things that are above, where Christ reigns, seated at the right hand of the Father. Amen.

Offertory Sentence: "What good will it be for a man if he gains the whole world, yet forfeits his soul? Or what can a man give in exchange for his soul?" (Matt. 16:26, NIV).

Offertory Prayer: We give both because we have been instructed to and because we want to, Father. Call us to honest giving this morning that we may not only tithe as you called your followers to do long ago, but also give as an expression of appreciation for all our blessings. Then let distribution of our gifts be so made that your work may be accomplished in our community and around the world, we pray in Jesus' name. Amen.—Henry Fields

Morning Prayer: In this sacred place, show us how to honor, acknowledge, and glorify you, Father. Reveal to us your presence and power. Help us in our quest to worship and say what needs saying in your name. Let this meeting of your people help us to do better what we need to do in relationship with you. Call us to long-term, heartfelt commitment to Christ so that little by little as we experience his presence, we might more and more magnify his name, even as we pray with followers through the ages: (Lord's Prayer).—Henry Fields

Benediction: Go now in the power and under the guiding hand of the God who created us, sustained us, redeemed us—and now walks by our sides day by day. Father, Son, and Holy Spirit, three in one, lead us into the days of this week and bring us back together next Lord's Day. Amen.

SUNDAY, AUGUST 14, 2011
Ninth Sunday after Pentecost

LECTIONARY SERMON TOPIC: "Tenacious Faith"
TEXT: Matt. 15:(10–20), 21–28
OTHER READINGS: Gen. 45:1–15; Ps. 133; Rom. 11:1–2a, 29–32

How is your faith today? Please let the question sink deeply—and do not answer quickly or glibly. How is it this morning in the inner recesses of your soul? It's not enough to say "I have faith" or even "I don't have faith." In truth, we all have faith and live in it every day. Putting our lives into the hands of another—that is the gist of saving faith. Some see faith as propositional. *If* all goes well, *if* I am happy and prosperous, *if* I am healthy and hopeful, then I am a person of faith. *If* God does good for me, then I will believe. Biblical faith doesn't say "if." It says "though." Though all the forces of evil come against me, I will believe all the more; though everything goes wrong for me, though Gethsemane and the cross loom before me, I will believe and trust.

I. **Matthew's gospel paints Jesus as the faithful fulfillment of God's plan.** From birth, through life, and soon through death, Jesus was faithful—full of faith. And those around him? What of them? At times they were faithful, at other times unfaithful. Look at the flowers and the grass. Nothing even in Solomon's splendor could match their glory—yet they don't worry: O ye of little faith. There was a centurion whose servant was ill. "Lord help me. You don't have to come. Only speak the word." And Jesus replied, "No one in all Israel has such great faith."

The disciples were in a boat with Christ. "We're going to sink," they cried. Jesus spoke: "Why are you so afraid? Why so little faith? Peace, be still." Later the disciples were in another boat, and Jesus walked to them on the water. Peter cried out, "Lord save me." Jesus said, "O ye of little faith." An unnamed woman was ill for twelve years, but reached out to touch the hem of Jesus' garment. "Your faith has made you whole," the Lord summarized. And this: "Faith, even like the mustard seed, will move the mountains." But in our text is another story—unlike all the others. Let's look at it.

II. **Here is the story of a woman who loves her daughter dearly and comes to find a cure.** She was from the area of Tyre and Sidon. For some, this was unfamiliar and hostile territory. She was a Canaanite woman—not a Jew. Her request was simple: "Help my little girl." The Lord's response was silence. Let's not be surprised. He was often silent. In silence he watched the treasury and saw a woman with two mites. His silence broke Peter's heart on the night of denial. He stood silent before Herod and Pilate. On the cross he hurled no abuse. In silence he still watches over us.

The disciples' response was predictable: "Send her away. She's whining." There is no surprise here. They similarly desired to turn the little children away. So to both the children and to this woman, they said, "Go away. Don't bother the Master."

But what follows is a surprise. Twice Jesus answered negatively. "I was sent only to the lost sheep of Israel." And she cries, "Lord help me." And again, he spoke, "It is not right to take the children's bread [bread of the children of God] and toss it to the dogs [to the Gentiles]. This does surprise us—because we know this isn't the nature of Jesus. He's not out to harm anyone. He doesn't exclude anyone. He's open to everyone. And yet here it is. So we know there is more here than is on the surface.

There is another great surprise: the woman's response. Look closely. She is not overwhelmed! "Yes Lord, but even the dogs eat the crumbs from the Master's table." What a spirit she had. This is a woman you wouldn't want to joust with. Hers was a spirited, quick response that said much about who she was. Finally, Jesus brought closure to the matter: "What faith!" And then: "Your daughter is healed." I admire this woman and her unwillingness to give up.

III. **She wasn't willing to allow the common prejudice to damage her self-image.** A Canaanite was a nobody. So said the culture. But this woman said the culture was wrong. "It just doesn't make sense," I hear her say, "that just because one person is born in one place and another in another place, that one has value and another doesn't." And she is right. So what that one is born to wealth and another to poverty? Or that one is American and another from Botswana? Or that one is white, another black? My children reminded me the other day that in truth we are all part of one family, for we all share the same ancestral parents: Adam and Eve. While discussing this story with them, my children concluded, "There is one race—the human race. There is one earth. And we all are a part of it." This woman knew that. And she refused to give in to a lesser description of herself. Paul said it this way: "There is one Lord, one faith, one baptism. There are no Jews and no Gentiles. There are no rich no poor, no male and no female. Instead we are one in Jesus Christ."

IV. **She wasn't going to give up on her daughter.** There is pain and agony in her voice. Any parent can understand. We can identify with her at this point. Not a one of us would easily give up on gaining for our children the best we could provide. We stand adamantly on the side of our children!

But at another point, I don't identify at all. Her persistence provided the remedy she sought. What about those of us who persist and yet still lose? I've thought often of the account of Abraham and Isaac and their sacrificial moment on Mount Moriah. Abraham seemed ready to sacrifice his son. Only at the last split second, God intervened and altered the circumstance: "Do not do it. Take the ram caught in the bushes instead." And with that, Abraham came down the mountain joyously carrying his precious son, the heir of promise. What I can't help but think is this: "What of us who come down the mountain alone? What of us for whom no altering of circumstances came our way, even though we were caring and persistent?" I go away from this account with questions still unanswered.

V. **Jesus' conversation with the Canaanite woman also leaves us with unanswered questions.** But in the end, Jesus shows the way. I'm not sure why Jesus went about this the way he did. Did he know something about this woman's character already and know how she would respond? Did he do it for the disciples as a way of caricature? Was it shock therapy for them? I don't know. What I do know is that in the end, Jesus applauds her faith. He declared her to be one of God's precious daughters. "What great faith," he declared.

Perhaps today we need such affirmation—for we too are God's children, sons and daughters everyone. We are believers! Listen and you may hear the powerful voice of eternity say, "Great is your faith. You've not given up. You've stood the test." Or perhaps our need is a renewed experience of faith. It's only one prayer away: "Lord, help me." It's only one step: a step toward Christ. It's only one verse: "I surrender all."—Lee McGlone

ILLUSTRATIONS

Christian Loyalty. In a letter to the Roman emperor Trajan, Pliny, the governor of Bithnia (112 AD), draws conclusions after watching the early Christians. They were an unusual group, doing such unheard of things as caring for widows and orphans, loving one another, sharing food from house to house . . . and gathering regularly to worship in the midst of talk about eating flesh and drinking blood. In fact, he said, they shared everything they had—except their wives. They had an undying loyalty to one they called "Chrestus."—Lee McGlone

Faith. We all live by faith—even if we deny it. You get sick and go to a doctor, a doctor you don't know and whose name you can't pronounce. He gives you a prescription you can't read. You take it to a pharmacist you've never seen. He gives you medicine you can't understand. Yet you do it. You do it all in faith, trusting your life in the hands of others.—Lee McGlone

Musical Selections Appropriate to the Day

Gen. 45:1–15	*Leaning on the Everlasting Arms*
Ps. 133	*Sweet, Sweet Spirit*
Rom. 11:1–2a, 29–32	*Depth of Mercy*
Matt. 15:(10–20), 21–28	*I Will Trust in the Lord*

⌛ Children's Lectionary Sermon

TITLE: Harmony

SCRIPTURE: Ps. 133

KEY VERSE: *How wonderful and pleasant it is when [we] live together in harmony!* (Ps. 133:1, NLT)

KEY CONCEPT: Harmony

MATERIALS: Bible

PREPARATION: If you would like to extend the metaphors for how beautiful harmony can be, you could invite the choir or a group of people to sing a short song, both out of tune and in harmony. This would be a way to help children understand the difference in a unique way. You could get a picture of a mountain scene with dew to show the children as you talk about the metaphors used to describe harmony.

Do you always get along with your brother or sisters? How about your friends in the neighborhood, church, or school? (*Let the children respond. Make sure to keep control.*) I know it can be hard to get along all the time, but it sure is nice when we do. We can call that harmony—which can mean agreement, unity, or even peace.

(*Open Bible.*) In Psalm 133, there was a song written about harmony. The first verse says, *How wonderful and pleasant it is when [we] live together in harmony!* In the song, the writer used showy, expensive, extreme things to compare with harmony. It was as precious as anointing oil. This would be very expensive and not used very often because of the cost. It was also compared to the refreshing dew on a mountain. (*If you have one, show the children the picture of a mountain scene with fresh dew.*) It looks so peaceful and beautiful, and it is the way God wants our relationships to be with each other. When we have times we are in harmony, what does it feel like to you? (*Let the children respond, and reflect back their answers.*)

When we live in harmony with our family and our friends, we feel good and enjoy each other. We can thank God for the times we have together, because we don't often think about how beautiful it is to live in harmony. Let's thank God for the gift of harmony in our family and friendships.—Marcia Thompson

❧ WORSHIP AIDS ❧

Call to Worship: "I waited patiently for the Lord; he turned to me and heard my cry. He lifted me out of the slimy pit, out of the mud and mire; he set my feet on a rock and gave me a firm place to stand. He put a new song in my mouth, a hymn of praise to our God. Many will see and fear and put their trust in the Lord" (Ps. 40:1–3, NIV).

Invocation: Father, we give thanks for the fellowship of the gospel in which we share, for your work among us in which we so joyfully labor, and for the promise of its fulfillment according to your purpose. May this hour of worship encourage and strengthen our hearts that we may so serve you that your will shall be done among us on earth as it is in heaven. Amen.

Offertory Sentence: "The King will reply, 'I tell you the truth, whatever you did for one of the least of these brothers of mine, you did for me'" (Matt. 25:40, NIV).

Offertory Prayer: Even our best giving is small when compared to what you have given to us, Father. Yet we offer our tithes and gifts today knowing that you will multiply them as you always have and through them bless multitudes. So in faith we give in Jesus' name. Amen.—Henry Fields

Morning Prayer: (Prayer on Ps. 147:1–11, 20c) Praise God—the Lord—the Creator! It is an excellent thing to sing to you, God, and to know that it is pleasing to you! And even as it is pleasing to you, Lord, it is also pleasing to us. There is great joy in us, the created beings, singing to you our Creator!

You, Lord God, heal the brokenhearted. You are the healer of every wound with which your people are afflicted. You understand the pain, and you bring healing. For it is you, Lord God, who calls the stars by name. Your power never ends. Boundaries to you, Lord, do not exist. You care for our every need. So we sing our songs to you with thanksgiving from our hearts.

Remind us today that you are Lord of all. You sustain the humble and cast down the wicked. You delight most in us when we humbly surrender before you—and thereby gain for ourselves the peace of your unfailing love. So we thank you, gracious God, for the blessings you pour on us as your people! Amen.—Tim Statton

Benediction: By the power and in the Spirit of our Lord we go forth to honor his Holy Name, Father, Son, and Holy Spirit—and to declare in the days of this week the reign of truth under which we live. Go in peace. Amen.

SUNDAY, AUGUST 21, 2011
Tenth Sunday after Pentecost

LECTIONARY SERMON TOPIC: "Exercising Our Spiritual Gifts"
TEXT: Rom. 12:1–8
OTHER READINGS: Exod. 1:8–2:10; Ps. 124; Matt. 16:13–20

How we think about a thing determines to some extent how we value it, how interested we are in it, and how committed we are to it. My wife, Brenda, thinks of shopping as a way to relax and a source of great enjoyment. For me, it's one of those necessary evils that must be done but can be better done by someone else. For me, fishing is a way to relax, to enjoy God's creation, and to clear my mind. For Brenda, fishing is boring and hot and a waste of time. Whatever the task of life is, how we think about it determines to some extent how we will be involved in it.

That's so with the Christian life, too. "As boring as life can be," some may say. This note was from a friend's church newsletter: "The traditional meeting of the usual group will gather in the same place at the accustomed time when we will discuss our normal business if all this proves to be convenient and the way we have always done things." That is church to many. Others, however, find following Christ to be exhilarating and fulfilling. The difference can be seen in a football game. Are we one of many who sit in the stands applauding when things go well or jeering when things don't go well? Or are we the twenty-two players on the field energized and excited about the opportunity the next play brings? I'll admit to being one who wants to be on the field playing the game.

I. **That's what Paul had in mind when he gave us this image of the church:** you are like a body. Every part of the body is significant. Not a single part is insignificant. And every body part plays its role in the body's total health. Here now is where we come to the central concern of today's text: each person is unique, essential to the fulfillment of God's work in the world, "called" to the task of ministry, and "gifted" to fulfill that task. Let's look today to the New Testament teaching about spiritual giftedness and what that means to each of us—and to our church.

II. **There are at least a few reasons we have trouble with this idea.** First, there is among us as Baptists a concern about anything "spiritual." Almost as though if something is spiritual it is somehow beyond the realm of normal. Similarly, we have been told never to think of ourselves more highly than we ought. To see ourselves as unique, gifted, is to be guilty of human pride. And again, if we did admit we had special gifts, to accomplish unique tasks for God, we would then be accountable. It's easier just to deny our uniqueness and then not be responsible.

This whole conversation is tied to our belief in the mission of God in the world and our place in that mission. There is something here larger than ourselves. Victor Frankl, Swiss psychologist and prisoner in a Nazi death camp during World War II, concluded from his research that those who survived the horrors of the camps were those who had something for which to live—that is, something beyond themselves that gave them strength each day and drew out of them stamina to live. Frankl concluded that we are empowered by great thoughts that capture us.

This great thought is that we really are essential movers in what God is doing. It is an exciting adventure to discover our unique place in God's plan—that is, where we are called and how we are gifted. When these are discovered, we may declare, as Gordon Cosby suggested, a shout of "Eureka." We may dream great dreams and believe that nothing is impossible. Probably we will talk about the dream constantly . . . as others may grow weary of it. It perhaps needs also to be said that callings and giftedness are not always so exciting. They can become agony. Just ask Jesus.

III. **In Paul, the only criteria for using a gift is having it.** Gifts are not controlled by the church. They don't require ordination or selection to a committee. "If you have a gift, use it." Look at the list given in our text. Some of these, such as teaching and preaching, have found their way into institutional life. But it is not so for others. Where on the list of church ministries is the gift of encouragement? And what does the church need more of than encouragement? Paul even lists liberality in financial contributions as a spiritual gift. Are the gifts of "giving aid" and "acts of mercy" relegated only to a few? Hardly! The New Testament elsewhere adds other gifts to the list, but no list is understood as exhaustive.

Discovering our giftedness and locating God's calling in which the gifts are directed will change all of life. Perhaps the greatest change is that service to God is not centered any longer around church on Sunday morning. The focus has changed. The point of our Christianity is "out there," in the world for which Jesus died. Do you know how many lives we are going to touch here this morning as we worship? The several hundred who are here? But how many lives will the several hundred touch as we go out into the world this next week, in homes, in offices, in schools, in neighborhoods? Literally thousands will be touched. We are not to be "conformed" to the images of the world, as Paul wrote elsewhere, but are to be "transformed" by the renewing of our mind-sets.

IV. **Callings and giftedness go hand in hand**. Whatever God intends, God provides resources necessary to accomplish his purpose. It is this purpose, God's purpose entrusted to us, that claims the whole of life. Why would we give life for such concerns? We give ourselves as response to an even greater gift given to us. "I beseech you brethren, by the mercies of God, to present your bodies as living sacrifices, acceptable unto God, which is your spiritual worship" (Rom. 12:1, KJV). Where this morning, in this holy place, is the call of God touching a human life? Maybe there in you, or you, or me.—Lee McGlone

ILLUSTRATIONS

Spiritual. I'll never forget crawling through a cornfield when I was sixteen to get a look at a group of worshippers. Word came to town that some "holy rollers" had an outdoor camp meeting going on with all kinds of strange things happening. Several of us teenagers made our way there. I had never seen anything like it. A single light bulb was suspended from an oak tree limb. There really was sawdust on the ground. One lady played a portable organ and another played an accordion. Folks stood and sang and preached while some danced about and others fell to the ground. We soon saw all we wanted, and returned to the car. While going back through the cornfield, I had two very clear perceptions I remember to this day. First, I knew then that I had no business being there. It was wrong. Gawking at another group of worshippers was an insult to us all. But the second perception was this. I knew even then that there was more to being controlled by the Holy Spirit than what I had just witnessed. I wasn't sure exactly what that meant, but believed God would show me. God's Holy Spirit is at work in each of us—for we are all "spiritual" creatures made in God's image.—Lee McGlone

Calling. My call to ministry was not attended by rebellion—as is often the testimony of others. Mine was, simply put, a matter of confusion. I wasn't turned off by the idea of being a preacher, but I just had to know for sure. You see, I had a problem with stuttering. I thought later how I could have been another Mel Tellis and made millions of dollars with a singing and comedy routine—if only I could sing. Because of my problem, I raised the query to God. Me preach? I can't even talk in front of the class. Yet when that March night came, the final service of a weekend revival, this high school senior walked forward compelled to declare this calling. Three weeks later, my pastor said, "I want you to preach for us next Sunday night." I knew it was then or never. As I walked to the pulpit, my heart was filled with fear. But the most amazing thing happened. The pulpit felt like home. I knew in my heart, "This is it."—Lee McGlone

Musical Selections Appropriate to the Day

Exod. 1:8–2:10	*He Is Able to Deliver Thee*
Ps. 124	*In the Name of the Lord*
Rom. 12:1–8	*What Gift Can We Bring*
Matt. 16:13–20	*Built on the Rock*

Children's Lectionary Sermon

TITLE: Don't Copy That

SCRIPTURE: Rom. 12:1–8

KEY VERSE: *Don't copy the behavior and customs of this world, but let God transform you into a new person by changing the way you think. Then you will learn to know God's will for you, which is good and pleasing and perfect.* (Rom. 12:2, NLT)

KEY CONCEPT: Living in ways that please God

MATERIALS: Bible

PREPARATION: Before it's time to give the sermon, think about things you could have the children do to copy you.

I want us to play a game this morning. I want you to copy everything I do. (*Have a list of things the children can easily copy. Do several things before you ask them to do something totally absurd, like jumping off something really high. Think of something appropriate for your group of children that they would not readily do and would protest.*) Well, come on so we can _____. You don't want to copy me anymore? How come? (*Let the children answer.*)

Paul wrote to the church in Rome about something similar. He told the Christians not to copy the people around them—they were to be different. (*Open Bible.*) In Romans, he wrote, Don't copy the behavior and customs of this world, but let God transform you into a new person by changing the way you think. Then you will learn to know God's will for you, which is good and pleasing and perfect. Paul was trying to tell the Christians they could become different people by letting God change them and how they thought. It wasn't easy to be different in Rome then, either. People who were Christians often were put in prison or had their business closed down. It wasn't an easy choice or an easy thing to do to let God change them, but many did and believed.

It is easy to want and do things the way everyone else does. Sometimes we need to ask ourselves if others really can see we are different because we follow Christ. It isn't always easy as a kid or for the adults out there to do this. But we can ask through prayer for God to change us each day so that we can know what God wants for us that is good and pleasing and perfect. Let's ask God to help us now.—Marcia Thompson

❧ WORSHIP AIDS ❧

Call to Worship: "As the deer pants for streams of water, so my soul pants for you, O God. My soul thirsts for God, for the living God. When can I go and meet with God?" (Ps. 42:1–2, NIV).

Invocation: Father, in worship we open ourselves to you. We open our collective praise, the joy of our lips, and the heart of our fellowship. Grant that the splendor of our communion with you will so transform us that we shall serve you faithfully. Amen.

Offertory Sentence: "Give and it will be given to you. A good measure, pressed down, shaken together and running over, will be poured out into your lap. For with the measure you use, it will be measured to you" (Luke 6:38, NIV).

Offertory Prayer: Lord, large or small, let our gifts this day reflect faithful hearts that give joyfully and point to our Lord Jesus Christ. Amen.—E. Lee Phillips

Morning Prayer: Jesus, you are holy. Thank you for your sacrificial love. You left your throne to come to earth for us. You took our sin, you took our sentence, and you took our penalty. You spoke for us. You reconciled us with the Father.

Jesus, you are holy. Thank you for breaking the bonds of sin. You set us free. You have taken away our guilt, our shame, our disgrace. You have freed us from the Law. You made the way for the Spirit.

Jesus, you are holy. Thank you for carrying our burdens. You give us rest, peace, and joy. You are the remedy. You have healed what was broken.

Jesus, you are holy. Amen.—Jenny Konvicka

Benediction: Now may the Holy and Gracious God guide us from this place and into the activities of the coming week. Be to us, O Lord, our hands, and feet, and voices—that we may speak and live the gospel. Amen.

SUNDAY, AUGUST 28, 2011
Eleventh Sunday after Pentecost

LECTIONARY SERMON TOPIC: "Developing Healthy Attitudes: Relationships"
TEXT: Rom. 12:9–21
OTHER READINGS: Exod. 3:1–15; Ps. 105:1–6, 23–26, 45c; Matt. 16:21–28

Some people have no idea what healthy relational attitudes look like. They have been surrounded by unhealthy attitudes for so long that they've come to think that they are normal. These are those who are easily offended, angry, unforgiving, upset, and self-centered. Healthy attitudes toward relationships seem strange to some of us. To adopt the attitudes of Jesus may appear to be impossible, but it is not.

One of the best statements of healthy attitudes toward relationships is found in Romans 12:9–21. Faced with tensions in their church, how were believers to live out Christ's command to love one another? And how are we? Some people are just hard to love.

I. **A healthy attitude toward relationships begins in reality.** That's where the text begins. Look at the words used here: *evil, affliction, revenge, enemy.* Struggles brewed in relationships even then. We often idealize the way relationships are supposed to work. Everyone is supposed to understand, to be nice, to get along, and to agree. When that doesn't happen, we are hurt, angry, or disappointed. A healthy attitude recognizes that people don't always get along. Reality tells us that some people will never behave the way we want them to behave and that we may never have the kind of relationships with them that we would like to have. Reality is that some of life's relationships are wonderful and some are not. The healthy attitude realizes that we can't force good behavior on other people—and we're not responsible for doing so. We are, however, responsible for ourselves.

II. **To reality, we add love.** "Love must be sincere. Hate what is evil; cling to what is good. Be devoted to one another in brotherly love. Honor one another above yourselves" (Rom. 12:9–10). The teaching here is about love being lived out—that is, about being authentic in daily life. The word used here, "sincere," means "without wax" or "sun-judged." In the ancient days, a potter could unscrupulously hide cracks and imperfections in his jars and bowls by filling them with wax. It could be done so effectively that unless someone looked at the vessel intently, holding it up to the sun, one would never discover the imperfection. One could buy the vessel and never know it was fraudulent until it was placed on the fire to cook a meal—when the wax would suddenly melt and the imperfection would be discovered. Thus the call for love to be sincere and genuine. A forgery, a cover-up, something fraudulent just isn't good enough. Sincere love doesn't change when relationships heat up. Under the heat of fire, a good relationship is welded even more strongly.

To this Paul adds the strong imperatives: "Hate what is evil; cling to what is good." Here is healthy advice. Look for the good in every relationship—for the whole of a person is always more than the hurt that comes out at you. Love never requires us to approve the inappropriate, but it does call us to know the difference between good and evil—and to hold to the good. "Be devoted to one another in brotherly love." Brotherly love calls us to commit to others as a family member. And so we are brothers and sisters in Christ, members of the household of faith; Christ is our elder brother, and God is our Father. "Honor one another above yourselves." This is the most practical advice of all. In a loving relationship, we can't focus on how the other person treats us; we focus on our own responsibility to treat others well. Perhaps Thumper in Bambi's forest had it right: "If you can't say something nice, don't say nothing at all."

Do you want to feel good about yourself? Try honoring someone else who doesn't deserve it. It's the best shot you have at a better relationship—and besides, it feels good.

III. **And to love, we add forgiveness.** "Do not take revenge, my friends, but leave room for God's wrath, for it is written: 'It is mine to avenge; I will repay,' says the Lord." On the contrary: "If your enemy is hungry, feed him; if he is thirsty, give him something to drink. In doing this, you will heap burning coals on his head" (Rom. 12:19–20). Here, forgiveness is letting go of revenge. It means that we are willing to move on even though we have been treated poorly. Forgiveness doesn't mean you caved in. It doesn't mean you were wrong. It doesn't mean you are weak. Forgiveness means that you have chosen to let it go. Most of all, forgiveness means that you're going to trust God to handle what you can't. You loan someone money, and he or she fails to pay you back. The first impulse is revenge. But you don't have to have the money back to have a good relationship with the person.

This has to be one of the strangest quotes in the Bible. It tells us that we have a choice in our attitude about getting even. Just forgive others and let God worry about revenge if it is needed. And when we are forgiving, "you will heap burning coals on his head." This is a figure of speech. It means that the person might end up feeling embarrassed and guilty because you are so nice when he or she has been so wrong, and this might help the person change for the better.

IV. **Then, we take the initiative.** "Never be lacking in zeal, but keep your spiritual fervor, serving the Lord. Be joyful in hope, patient in affliction, faithful in prayer. Share with God's people who are in need. Practice hospitality. Bless those who persecute you; bless and do not curse. Rejoice with those who rejoice; mourn with those who mourn. Live in harmony with one another. Do not be proud, but be willing to associate with people of low position. Do not be conceited. Do not repay anyone evil for evil. Be careful to do what is right in the eyes of everybody. If it is possible, as far as it depends on you, live at peace with everyone" (Rom. 12:11–18).

Take the first step. Be Christ to the other person. Live out Christ in daily events. Look at these words from the text: *joyful, sharing, hospitality, blessings, rejoicing, harmony, humility, peacefulness.* Gracious Christians give each other the benefit of the doubt. We can cut each other some slack.—Lee McGlone

---

ILLUSTRATIONS

Greatest Evangelism. Kindness is contagious. It's our greatest evangelism. One person reaches in friendship to another—and good things begin to happen. There was a Volkswagen commercial on TV not long ago. A number of people were standing on the street corner. A Volkswagen convertible drove by. The very sight of the car made one person feel good enough to be nice to the next person and then the next to the next. Suddenly, the entire group was laughing. That was for sure an advertising fantasy, but in the real world, it's not so far-fetched. It happens each time one person reaches out in a Christian act of compassion to others—a cup of water here, a gentle word spoken there, an invitation to church . . . —Lee McGlone

Strained Relationships. Strained relationships are a common human experience. Only a few weeks ago, a young man passing through needed help and came by the church. After providing overnight lodging and food, I asked him why he didn't seek help from his family. He replied that he couldn't go to his mother's house. He had been there already, and she refused to open the door. His mother refused contact. I've never had anyone in my life to whom I would not speak. It's hard for me to understand her behavior. But haven't we seen just such things? Former spouses often won't be civil to one another, even long after the divorce is settled. Business partners will argue about every tiny detail—out of simple mistrust. Some siblings can't sit next to each other without calling names—and they can be nine or ninety. Families can get crossways quickly. How sad!—Lee McGlone

Musical Selections Appropriate to the Day

Exod. 3:1–15	*Lift Every Voice and Sing*
Ps. 105:1–6, 23–26, 45c	*Across the Lands*
Rom. 12:9–21	*Rejoice, the Lord Is King*
Matt. 16:21–28	*Take Up Your Cross*

ᕬ Children's Lectionary Sermon

TITLE: Happy and Sad

SCRIPTURE: Rom. 2:9–21

KEY VERSE: *Be happy with those who are happy and weep with those who weep.* (Rom. 12:15, NLT)

KEY CONCEPT: Loving people by honoring their feelings

MATERIALS: Bible, yellow paper, marker

PREPARATION: Cut the yellow paper into enough circles that each child has one to hold. On one side of the circle, draw a happy face, and on the other side, draw a sad face.

I want each of you to take one of these circles. On the circles, you see that one side has a happy face and one side has a sad face. I am going to tell you something that could happen, and I want you to show the happy face if it is a happy thing or the sad face if it is a sad thing. (*Go through the following: my dog died; I got a new bike; I fell and broke my arm; I was given $20 as a gift; and so on. As you go through each example, talk about why it would be a happy or sad event.*)

In the New Testament, Paul wrote the Christians in Rome and gave them some instructions on how to treat other people. One of the things he wrote was, *Be happy with those who are happy and weep with those who weep.* Why do you suppose he told them to do this for each other? (*Let the children respond. Reflect back the children's answers and help redirect if they get off track.*)

Have you ever been with a friend when he or she was happy or excited about something? When you are with someone who is happy, it can be contagious. You can't help but be happy and excited with and for the other person. What about when someone is sad? What do we do when someone is sad? Sometimes we try our best to make the person happy when he or she really can't be happy, because the person just needs to be sad for a while. Paul wanted the Christians then to know it was good to celebrate the good things that happen together, but also to be sad with those who were sad. We can learn from Paul too. When we are sad inside, it is good to know that others understand and can be sad with us. It is part of how God made us and how we can show our love to each other by honoring the feelings, both happy and sad, that we all feel.—Marcia Thompson

❧ WORSHIP AIDS ❧

Call to Worship: "Be still and know that I am God; I will be exalted among the nations, I will be exalted in the earth" (Ps. 46:10, NIV).

Invocation: Stir our hearts in this sacred hour, Father. Lift us out of our boredom, our indifference, and our routine so that we can be true children of faith. Help us to see the possibilities for doing right and good and send us forth to touch the world with the power of the living God. Indeed, make us true to Christ in the fashion of those first followers whom the Lord taught to pray: (Lord's Prayer).—Henry Fields

Offertory Sentence: "The good man brings good things out of the good stored up in his heart" (Luke 6:45, NIV).

Offertory Prayer: Here are our gifts and offerings, Father. They speak loudly about our inner commitment. Let them be filled with faith and endowed with love for Christ in whose name we give. Amen.—Henry Fields

Morning Prayer: God of refuge, be a strong refuge for the strugglers of life who are battered and worn with the struggle. God of comfort, be the present comforter for those who face all the questions of the unknown and sense loss larger than they can comprehend. God of healing, in gentleness touch the ill folks suffering from the many maladies of life, spirit, soul, and heart so that wholeness may be realized and health may be real. God of salvation, let the searching light of your truth and presence penetrate the darkness of our lostness so that we may be guided into the brightness of redemption. God of hope, fill the crevices of hopelessness with the sunshine of hope. God of faith, remind us of your faith in us that we might hold faith in you and have faith in others. God of joy, visit the joyless places of life with the wonder of your presence, which to abide in is life's greatest joy. God of love, impart your love to us that we might love genuinely, helpfully, powerfully, and eternally all whom we are called to love. God of eternity, make transparent the eternal dimension of life so that we may meet life in all its different phases without fear or dread, but with assurance and great expectation.

Throughout this hour surprise us with your presence, reveal to us your truth, bathe us in your love, assure us of your salvation, and fit us for the living of life as it opens before us throughout all the days to come, we pray in Jesus' name. Amen.—Henry Fields

Benediction: Lord God, whom we know as Father, Son, and Holy Spirit, walk with us in the days ahead. Inspire us to noble living, in word and deed, and bring us back again next Lord's day. Amen.

SUNDAY, SEPTEMBER 4, 2011
Twelfth Sunday after Pentecost

LECTIONARY SERMON TOPIC: "Operating in the Red"

TEXT: Rom. 13:8–14

OTHER READINGS: Exod. 12:1–14; Ps. 148 or 149; Matt. 18:15–20

When the writer of Proverbs penned the aphorism "the borrower becomes the lender's slave" (Prov. 22:7, NASB), he could hardly have imagined America's current credit crisis. It appears that operating in the red has finally caught up with our society. The national debt stands at multiple trillions of dollars (12.2 trillion in 2010) and continues to grow. The digits on the real-time debt clock spin at a dizzying rate.[1] Even as California faces a $42 billion state budget deficit,[2] consumers pay with plastic to make ends meet, bringing the average total debt per card to over $5,700.[3] The borrower knows he is beholden to his creditor until he pays off every red cent.

   I. **Paul offers his readers some sound advice:** to "owe nothing to anyone" (13:8), to pay to all what is due to them, be that taxes, revenue, respect, or honor (13:7). Yet even while advocating fiscal and civic responsibility, he acknowledges a single exception. In the Kingdom's economy, Christians can never expect to live completely debt-free, for they are forever bound by their obligation to love (13:8). In Romans 1:14, Paul labels himself a "debtor" (*opheiletas*), under obligation to share the gospel with the world at large. Here he reminds believers of their debt of love, also universal in scope, which reaches out to embrace not only those in the church (12:3–13) but state authorities (13:1–7) and enemies as well (12:14–21). God's active love is to be extended without distinction to "the other" (*ton heteron*), as the Greek puts it (13:8), to those who are different, without regard to our estimate of their worthiness.

  II. **In his threefold reference to the love of neighbor (13:8, 9, 10), Paul links Christian ethics to the Jewish law (Lev. 19:18).** Rabbi Hillel had previously summed up the Torah in the negative form of the Golden Rule: "That which you hate do not do to your fellows; this is the whole law; the rest is commentary."[4] For Jesus, too, "loving one's neighbor as oneself" recapped in a single precept the second table of the Decalogue, which purposed to

---

[1]Treasury Direct, "The Debt to the Penny and Who Holds It," http://www.treasurydirect.gov/NP/BPDLogin?application=np; Ed Hall, "U.S. National Debt Clock," http://www.brillig.com/debt_clock/.

[2]"The World at a Glance," *The Week*, June 26, 2009, p. 5.

[3]"The Bottom Line," *The Week*, June 19, 2009, p. 38.

[4]James Dunn, *Word Biblical Commentary*, Vol. 38B (Dallas: Word Books, 1988), p. 778.

promote positive personal relationships (Matt. 22:36–40). Jesus redefines "neighbor" in the most inclusive terms possible, as in the parable of the Good Samaritan, where love crosses ethnic boundaries (Luke 10:30–37). The law is subsumed by love (13:9).

In fact, the law by itself is an inadequate basis for ethics. Morality cannot be legislated, for law provides neither a sustainable incentive nor the power to comply. The motivation for Christian ethics springs rather from God's prior acceptance of us in Christ: "We love because He first loved us" (1 John 4:19). In meeting the needs of those whom God places in our path, we respond to God's initiative, paying our love debt forward (5:8) as an expression of gratitude. The selfless, other-centered conduct characteristic of *agape* (1 Cor. 13:4–7) stands in stark contrast to the carnality of "night life"—"deeds of darkness" that treat people as objects to be used for personal gratification (13:13).

III. **Righteous living is empowered as well as motivated by love, which is "poured out in our hearts through the Holy Spirit" (5:5).** Acting in love and resisting the lustful living that looks out for number one offer evidence that we have "put on the Lord Jesus Christ" (13:14) and his armor of light. In Greek the idea of being clothed with a person meant assuming the interests and viewpoint of another with the purpose of imitating him completely. The term recalls a skilled actor who in preparing for a role immerses himself in the character he is to portray, attempting to capture his essence, to bring him to life for the spectators. Those baptized into Christ are enabled by his Spirit to embody his love without partiality in the extended neighborhood.

IV. **One senses a certain urgency to Paul's call to Christlike living.** Verses 11 and 12 are replete with eschatological allusions—sleeping and wakefulness, dark versus light, a night far spent with a new dawn approaching. The current age is *kairos* time, laden with eternal significance. "The between-time, between the already of commitment in conversion-initiation and the not-yet of salvation—is pregnant with the about-to-be of God's purpose coming to full term."[5] Steeped in apocalyptic expectation, the

---

[5]Dunn, *Word Biblical Commentary*, p. 786.

early believers anticipated Christ's imminent return. Centuries later, the ticking of the cosmic clock has brought us ever nearer to the consummation of salvation history. The delayed parousia prompts us to be about the Master's ministry with one eye fixed on the horizon, watching for the "sunrise that shoots Time dead with golden arrows."[6]

If teleological tensions form the backdrop for the Christian experience, there is also the matter of our mortality, brought into clearer focus with humanity's capacity for global destruction. This sobering truth challenges us to order our lives according to Kingdom priorities, remembering that we are not guaranteed tomorrow and praying that God will make us sensitive and responsive to the needs all around us.

A popular bumper sticker captures the concept of indebtedness in a nutshell: "I owe, I owe. It's off to work I go." For the Christian, the work is a labor of love carried out as we spend our time, talent, and treasure on behalf of our creditors—all those "others" to whom we can demonstrate the love of God. It is a debt carried willingly and paid forward in the eternal currency of the Kingdom. Let us live *this* day in the light of that red-letter day of the final accounting, in the hope that the debt service recorded in our ledger will meet the approval of the Auditor, with none of love's labor lost.—Karen Hatcher

---

ILLUSTRATIONS

Conversion. The final verses of today's text are well known as the trigger for Saint Augustine's conversion. Having rejected the teachings of Christianity during his youth, he dedicated himself to the pursuit of sensual pleasures. One day, while walking in his villa garden outside Milan, he heard children's voices chanting: "Take up and read!" When he picked up the Bible in response to what he considered a divine directive, it fell open to verses 13 and 14 of Romans 13. Donning Christ's protective armor of light as a defense against his

---

[6]C. S. Lewis, *The Great Divorce* (New York: Simon & Schuster, 1996), p. 125.

former "deeds of darkness," Augustine at last found in God peace for his restless soul.—Karen Hatcher

Mission. In the film *Pay It Forward*, a middle school social studies assignment produces dramatic changes for characters struggling with life's challenges. The 2000 film considers the positive impact we might have on society if we responded to acts of kindness not by repaying our benefactor but by doing a good deed for a third party. The ripple effect that takes place recalls the exponential growth of the early Church, which Hans Küng attributes to the radical ethic of the gospel demonstrated by those who professed the crucified and Resurrected Christ (1 Cor. 2:4).[7] Jesus urges his followers to forget "payback" and to break the cycle of mutual obligation: "If you do good to those who do good to you, what credit is that to you? For even sinners do the same. . . . But love your enemies, and do good, and lend, expecting nothing in return; . . . and you will be sons of the Most High" (Luke 6:33, 35). Such a countercultural principle has the potential to transform our world.—Karen Hatcher

Musical Selections Appropriate to the Day

Exod. 12:1–14	*We Praise You, O God, Our Redeemer*
Ps. 149 or Ps. 148	*We Fall Down*
Rom. 13:8–14	*Children of God*
Matt. 18:15–20	*There's a Quiet Understanding*

ℛ Children's Lectionary Sermon

TITLE: Christ Clothes

SCRIPTURE: Rom. 13:8–14

KEY VERSE: *Instead, clothe yourself with the presence of the Lord Jesus Christ.* (Rom. 13:14, NLT)

---

[7]Hans Küng, *Christianity: Essence, History, and Future*, trans. by John Bowden (New York: Continuum, 2008), p. 151.

KEY CONCEPT: Christ in our daily life

MATERIALS: Bible, bag with different articles of clothes that cover different parts of the body

(Ask one of the children to come and help by pulling out the different articles of clothing you have in the bag. Adjust the message according to what articles of clothing you have chosen.) Let's look at these different pieces of clothes. Here is a hat. What do you use a hat for? *(Let the children respond.)* Of course, you put it on to cover your head when it is cold outside. What about these jeans? *(Let the children respond.)* You wear these in the fall or winter to cover your legs and keep them warm.

Clothes cover our bodies, and some are used to protect us from the weather. Clothes surround us and can be used as a picture to describe how we can surround ourselves with Christ. *(Open Bible.)* That is why when Paul wrote to the church at Rome he told them, *Instead, clothe yourself with the presence of the Lord Jesus Christ.* Paul wanted the Christians to surround themselves with Christ's presence, and he tells them to get rid of those "dirty" clothes—those things in our lives that separate us from Christ and from each other. How do you think we can clothe or surround ourselves with Christ's presence? *(Let the children respond. If you have younger children, you may need to treat this as a rhetorical question.)*

Let's pray for Christ to be present with us each and every moment, just as our clothes are.—Marcia Thompson

ꙅ WORSHIP AIDS ꙅ

Call to Worship: "Praise the Lord. / Sing to the Lord a new song, / his praise in the assembly of the saints. . . . / For the Lord takes delight in his people; / he crowns the humble with salvation" (Ps. 149:1, 4, NIV).

Invocation: "O Lord and Savior, draw near to us in this time of worship. Empower us through your Spirit to work out our salvation in acts of kindness, spurring one another on toward love as we see the Day approaching" (Heb. 10:24–25).

Offertory Sentence: "For God so loved the world that he gave." "Be imitators of God, therefore, as dearly loved children" (John 3:16a; Eph. 5:1, NIV).

Offertory Prayer: Generous Lord, accept these offerings as tangible evidence of our devotion. Stir the hearts of your people to spiritual acts of worship as we offer ourselves as well to your service, loving in word and deed all those you bring within our sphere of influence.—Karen Hatcher

Morning Prayer: Lord of Love, visit . . . your people with your grace. Fill us with the confidence that comes from your presence so that in all things we may set the light of your compassion before people and carry on with the work of salvation. . . . Grant that none who is hungry may go without food at our hands, none who is naked without clothing, none who is thirsty without water, none who is lonely without companion, none who is frightened without encouragement, none who is bereaved without comfort, none who is oppressed without justice, none who walks in darkness apart from you without the kindly light of your gospel.—L. Nyam[8]

Benediction: May the peace and power of God's love surround you. May the Lord go before you to guide you, stand behind you to guard you, and walk beside you to counsel you, as you go forth to serve others in the name of Christ.—Karen Hatcher

SUNDAY, SEPTEMBER 11, 2011
Thirteenth Sunday after Pentecost

LECTIONARY SERMON TOPIC: "Bridge Burners and Builders"
TEXT: Matt. 18:21–35
OTHER READINGS: Exod. 14:19–31; Exod. 15:1b–11, 20–21; Rom. 14:1–12

---

[8]L. Nyam, in *Give Us Grace: An Anthology of Anglican Prayers*, ed. by Christopher L. Webber (New York: Morehouse, 2004), pp. 494–495.

Mainline Protestantism, steeped in the individualism of American culture, has perhaps understandably emphasized personal responsibility before God at the expense of Christianity's communal dimension. Howard Snyder notes, "Too often the Church has been seen more as a mere collection of saved souls than as a community of interactive personalities. Christian growth has been more a matter of individual soul culture than the building of the community of the Spirit."[9]

Yet much of Jesus' teaching involved preparing his followers to live harmoniously together, guided by Kingdom principles. The discourse in Matthew 18 addresses a number of issues certain to arise within the context of communal living: status seeking, concern for the weak and wayward, and the discreet and loving restoration of the errant. Given the human propensity to err, it is not surprising that the disciples revisit the question of forgiveness, which was broached earlier (Matt. 6:12, 14–15).

I. **Just how often, Peter wonders, should one extend forgiveness for offenses committed by a fellow believer?** In view of certain Hebrew scriptures and later rabbinical writings that imply a limit of three,[10] his suggestion of seven seems generous. Jesus' response, however, is essentially, "Put away the calculator, Peter; you won't be keeping track." The number seventy-seven recalls and reverses the seventy-seven-fold blood vengeance vowed by Cain's descendant Lamech in Genesis 4:24.[11] The people of God were to move beyond unbridled retaliation and the *lex talionis* of the Jewish law to become a community that "doesn't keep score of the sins of others" (1 Cor. 13:5, The Message). He who tallies up the points has missed the point.

II. **The parable that follows shifts the focus from a call for repeated forgiveness to its motivation and necessity for those operating within the parameters of the in-breaking kingdom of heaven.** The drama, which unfolds in three scenes, opens as a king decides to settle accounts with

[9]Howard A. Snyder, from *The Community of the King*, cited in Rueben P. Job and Norman Shawchuck, *A Guide to Prayer for Ministers and Other Servants* (Nashville: Upper Room Books, 1983), p. 186.
[10]Donald A. Hagner, *Word Biblical Commentary*, Vol. 33B (Dallas: Word Books, 1995), p. 537.
[11]M. Eugene Boring, *The New Interpreter's Bible*, Vol. 8 (Nashville: Abingdon Press, 1995), p. 380.

his servants, one of whom owes the astronomical sum of ten thousand talents. A single talent—20.4 kilograms (9.3 lbs.) of silver—would have been equivalent to fifteen years' wages for a manual laborer. Annual tax revenues for all of Herod the Great's territories only reached nine thousand talents.[12] Clearly, the servant's situation is hopeless, in spite of his pitiful promise to repay all. The sight of the pleading man, prostrate before him and utterly at his mercy, moves the monarch to the deep-seated compassion (*splagchnistheis*) characteristic of deity (Matt. 9:36, 14:14, 15:32, 20:34). The unexpected cancellation of the debt represents God's extravagant act of grace in "having canceled out the certificate of [unpayable sin] debt consisting of decrees against us, . . . having nailed it to the cross (Col. 2:14).

The good news of the servant's release quickly reaches his coworkers, who witness an instant replay with a disturbingly different dénouement. Resorting to physical violence to collect the equivalent of four months' wages from a fellow slave, he refuses the other's reasonable request for patience to repay what amounted to a pittance compared with his own canceled debt. Deaf to the same pleas he had voiced himself, he consigns his colleague to the custody of the jailers, his hard-heartedness contrasting sharply with the mercy of his master. Heavyhearted, the servants seek out the sovereign, understanding that "forgiveness not shown is forgiveness not known."[13] Receiving the king's grace brings with it the responsibility to act graciously toward others.

III. **It is the servant's double standard—mercy for me and justice for others—that leads to a second summons, this time resulting in unremitting punishment rather than a remitted debt.** The core of the parable lies in the master's rhetorical question: Was it not necessary (*edei*) for you to have had mercy on your fellow slave as I had mercy on you? (18:33). Forgiveness is an imperative of Kingdom living, a required response to the divine King's prior graciousness. The concluding warning (18:35) emphasizes the awful price of unforgiveness with echoes of Matthew 6:14–15.

As folk wisdom has it, those who will not forgive burn the bridge over which they themselves must pass. The language of debt forgiveness that

---

[12]Boring, *New Interpreter's Bible*, p. 382.
[13]Klyne Snodgrass, *Stories with Intent* (Grand Rapids, MI: Eerdmans, 2008), p. 75.

punctuates today's text links it to the familiar petition "Forgive us our debts as we forgive our debtors," which uses the same Greek words. This corporate prayer acknowledges forgiveness as an indispensable girder in building relational bridges with our spiritual siblings. As a people who have been forgiven much, we can afford to love lavishly, tenderheartedly forgiving one another as God in Christ has done for us (Eph. 4:32). By overlooking petty offenses and submitting more serious sins to gentle reproof (18:15–17), members of the faith community can maintain mutual accountability against a backdrop of compassion motivated by and patterned after God's example. Having experienced the promised release from debtor's prison proclaimed in Jesus' messianic mission statement (see Luke 4:18, where *aphasis*—meaning "forgiveness" in today's texts—is rendered "release"), let us be about the business of bridging gaps among Christ's followers for the purpose of building up his Body in love.—Karen Hatcher

---

ILLUSTRATIONS

Empowerment. Corrie ten Boom, sent to a Nazi concentration camp with her sister, Betsy, for helping the Dutch Jews during World War II, describes how one of her later speaking engagements brought her face-to-face with a former foe. "It was at a church service in Munich that I saw him, the former S.S. [guard from] the processing center at Ravensbruck. . . . And suddenly it was all there—the roomful of mocking men, the heaps of clothing, Betsy's pain-blanched face. He came up to me as the church was emptying, beaming and bowing. 'How grateful I am for your message, Fraulein. . . . To think that, as you say, He has washed my sins away!' His hand was thrust out to shake mine. And I, who had preached so often to the people in Bloemendaal the need to forgive, kept my hand at my side. Even as the angry, vengeful thoughts boiled through me, I saw the sin of them. Jesus Christ had died for this man; was I going to ask for more? . . . I tried to smile, I struggled to raise my hand. I could not. . . . 'Jesus, [I prayed] give me Your forgiveness.' As I took his hand . . . a current seemed to pass from me to him, while into my heart sprang a love for this stranger that almost overwhelmed me. And so I discovered that . . . when

He tells us to love our enemies, He gives, along with the command, the love itself."[14]—Karen Hatcher

Reconciliation. Neil Anderson tells of a relational crisis that threatened his ministry. After numerous unsuccessful attempts to defuse conflict with a board member determined to sabotage his leadership, he decided to resign his pastorate. Incapacitated by a sudden illness before he could announce his intentions, he reread the gospel story of a blind man who, having been partially healed by Jesus' touch, "saw men . . . like trees." "I got the message," he relates. "I was seeing 'Calvin' like a tree, an obstacle in my path. . . . 'Lord, I don't love that man, but you do and I want to.'" Having chosen to forgive Calvin completely, Anderson went to church the following Sunday—to preach. "I croaked out a message from Mark 8:22–26 about our tendency to be independent in the face of our great need for God and for each other. . . . At the end of the sermon . . . the people streamed forward . . . going across the aisles to ask forgiveness and to be forgiven. . . . To my knowledge Calvin never changed, but I did. . . . I thank God [for] put[ting] me flat on my back to make me the pastor He wanted me to be."[15]—Karen Hatcher

Musical Selections Appropriate to the Day

Exod. 14:19–31	*Since I Have Been Redeemed*
Exod. 15:1b–11, 20–21	*How Majestic Is Your Name*
Rom. 14:1–12	*All Hail the Power of Jesus' Name*
Matt. 18:21–35	*Wonderful Grace of Jesus*

Children's Lectionary Sermon

TITLE: How Many Times?
SCRIPTURE: Matt. 18:21–35

---

[14]Corrie ten Boom, *The Hiding Place* (New York: Bantam Books, 1971), pp. 237–238.
[15]Neil T. Anderson, *Victory over the Darkness* (Ventura, CA: Regal Books, 2000), pp. 195–197.

KEY VERSE: *"No, not seven times," Jesus replied, "but seventy times seven."* (Matt. 18:22, NLT)

KEY CONCEPT: Forgiving one another

MATERIALS: Bible

In church, we use a lot of special words to talk about our relationship to Christ and to each other. One of those special words is *forgiveness*. (*Open Bible.*) In our New Testament story today, Peter asked Jesus how many times he should forgive someone who hurt him or wronged him. Peter asked if seven times was enough. *"No, not seven times," Jesus replied, "but seventy times seven."*

Now that seems like a lot of times to forgive someone, doesn't it. Seventy times seven—that's 490 times. Could you keep count to that number? (*Let children respond.*) I think it would really be hard to keep count. I would have to carry a piece of paper around to keep a count. That would be kind of silly, don't you think?

I think Jesus told Peter this because we should always be forgiving. We all do things that don't please Jesus. We can ask for forgiveness, and we are forgiven. Jesus wanted us to have this same relationship with people around us. Jesus forgives us, and Jesus wants us to forgive others just like he forgives us. It is easy to ask for forgiveness, but sometimes it isn't so easy to forgive when others hurt us.

Let's pray together that we will be forgiving of others.—Marcia Thompson

WORSHIP AIDS

Call to Worship: "'I will sing to the Lord, / for he is highly exalted. . . . / The Lord is my strength and my song; / he has become my salvation. . . . / Who among the gods is like you, O Lord? / Who is like you— / majestic in holiness, / awesome in glory, / working wonders'" (Exod. 15:1–2, 11).

Invocation: Great God of Wonders, "who is a God like you, who pardons sin and forgives the transgression" of your people (Mic. 7:18)? Grant that we who have been forgiven much may reflect your love and mercy to those who offend us, so that the body of Christ may minister in the unity of the Holy Spirit.—Karen Hatcher

Offertory Sentence: "Freely you have received, freely give" (Matt. 10:8, NIV).

Offertory Prayer: "All things are thine; no gift have we, Lord of all gifts, to offer thee; and hence with grateful hearts today, thine own before thy feet we lay."[16] May these offerings bring glory to you as they are invested in the work of your Kingdom. — Karen Hatcher

Morning Prayer: Merciful Lord, grant that we might grow in grace toward others, "be[ing] kind and compassionate to one another, forgiving each another, just as in Christ God forgave [us]" (Eph. 4:32, NIV), for all of us have missed your mark. "The hatred, which divides nation from nation, race from race, class from class; Father, forgive. The greed, which exploits the labours of men and lays waste to earth; Father, forgive. Our envy of the welfare and happiness of others; Father, forgive. Our indifference to the plight of the homeless and refugee; Father, forgive. The lust, which uses for ignoble ends, the bodies of men and women; Father, forgive. The pride, which leads us to trust in ourselves and not in God; Father, forgive."[17] This we ask in the name of Jesus Christ, who calls us to his ministry of reconciliation.

Benediction: "May the God who gives endurance and encouragement give you a spirit of unity among yourselves as you follow Christ Jesus, so that with one heart and mouth you may glorify the God and Father of our Lord Jesus Christ" (Rom. 15:5–6, NIV).

SUNDAY, SEPTEMBER 18, 2011
Fourteenth Sunday after Pentecost

LECTIONARY SERMON TOPIC: "Food for Thought"
TEXT: Exod. 16:2–15

---

[16]John G. Whittier, "All Things Are Thine," in *Trinity Hymnal* (Atlanta: Great Commission, 1990), p. 729.
[17]Prayer at the altar of Coventry Cathedral, cited in Job and Shawchuck, *Guide to Prayer*, p. 280.

OTHER READINGS: Ps. 105:1–6, 37–45 or Ps. 78; Phil. 1:21–30; Matt. 20:1–16

In its thought-provoking portrayal of the U.S. prison system, the 1994 film *Shawshank Redemption* offers insight into the devastating effects of extended incarceration. Having spent most of their lives behind bars, Brooks Hatlen and Ellis Redding face their impending release with mixed emotions. Years of regimented living within predictable parameters have transformed them into distrustful, passive people who depend on the institution for their very survival. The anxiety-producing prospect of meeting even basic physical needs in a hostile world prompts the aging Brooks to wish for an extension of his sentence and later to commit suicide when overwhelmed by the difficulties of life on the outside. Redding is tempted to become one of the many inmates who through further criminal activity return to America's correctional facilities, where they are guaranteed "three hots and a cot."[18] Freedom can be a frightening experience.

I. **In today's text we read that the Israelites, just released after four hundred years of captivity to Pharaoh, reach a similar conclusion.** The ecstatic echoes of worship for their wonder-working liberator have hardly faded when the implications of the walkout and the reality of life in the inhospitable wilderness begin to set in. Stripped of their accustomed support system, these village dwellers find themselves in a context where none of the former rules apply. A month after departing Egypt, having left behind the oasis of Elim (Exod. 15:27), the Hebrews face a bona fide food crisis (16:3) that highlights their distorted perception. Gripped by panic and powerless to meet their own needs, they lash out at their leaders, ready to trade their future for the full bellies of their slave days in Goshen, much as a famished Esau was willing to exchange his birthright for a single meal.[19] Fear, irrational thinking, and selective memory convince them that they have been redeemed only to be abandoned to fend for themselves. Better to go back than to starve.

[18]*Instructor Presentation and Facilitation Training Manual* (Ashburn, VA: Prison Fellowship, 2005), pp. 5–11.
[19]Walter Brueggemann, "Exodus," *The New Interpreter's Bible*, Vol. 1 (Nashville: Abingdon Press, 1994), p. 812.

II. **Their Redeemer, however, has something else in mind—a covenant relationship with a mission (Gen. 12:3).** But before this ragtag congregation can begin such an undertaking, their prison mentality must be reprogrammed. Walter Brueggemann observes that "their first task is leaving: the second task is *believing*"[20]—believing that Yahweh is not only a Pharaoh-defeating protector that controls the sea but also a divine parent that will sustain them in the life-threatening wilderness. The desert trek is a relationship-building period in which Israel, delivered through the birth canal of the Red Sea, comes to know Yahweh as a reliable provider (16:12). As a loving caregiver (Hos. 11:3–4), Yahweh must train the newborn nation to trust, guiding Israel like a little child through this primary developmental task of infancy.[21]

God's attentiveness to the people's legitimate need is evident in God's promise to "rain bread from heaven" (16:4). In this marvelous gift of food, the people will know that the same deity who brought them out of Egypt will bring them through this predicament as well (16:6). At this early stage, Yahweh treats their complaints with patience and counters their doubts by appearing before their eyes in the cloud (16:10)—the present, responsive, faithful source of their physical nourishment.

III. **But the purpose of this supernatural bread supersedes sustenance.** The abundant "angel food" (Ps. 78:25) is also a vehicle for spiritual teaching, a feast for the soul as well as the body (Deut. 8:3). As the saying goes, "No bread, no torah." The miraculous "manna" comes complete with instructions and a self-checking test. What, indeed, is it, this plentiful unknown food that falls every day but the Sabbath, rots if stored, and satisfies every appetite without lack or excess? This wonder bread is not given in well-watered Egypt but only in the barren wilderness, where Yahweh is creating a community of faith operating in obedience and dependency on divine providence. The natural consequences of disobeying the directives that accompany the heavenly loaves soon prove that hoarding, competition, perpetual labor, and the oppressive practices of Pharaoh's consumeristic regime have no place in this new setting, where needs are liberally met.

---

[20]Walter Brueggemann, *The Covenanted Self* (Minneapolis: Fortress Press, 1999), pp. 114–115.
[21]Arlene F. Harder, "The Developmental Stages of Erik Erikson," 2002, http://www.learningplaceonline.com/stages/organize/Erikson.htm.

IV. **Subsequent events reveal the Israelites' struggle with the manna message, that the flip side of release is reliance, not on self, but on God.** When the context shifts and Yahweh shows up as commander in chief for the conquest of Canaan, the people are again ready to pack for Egypt (Num. 13–14). We must acknowledge, if we are honest, that the lesson is not all that easy to learn. In the throes of our own crises, high anxiety induces memory lapses, idealization of the past, hand wringing, and a return to familiar, culturally conditioned, self-protective practices.

Trust is foundational to our *dynamic* relationship with Yahweh. The Lord is always doing a new thing (Isa. 43:19), especially today, when the landscape is changing at warp speed. God springs the latch on the maximum security prisons that keep us trapped in the paradigms of the past, calling us to participation in God's creative work, which unfolds in surprising, sometimes scary ways. It is an invitation to reset our mind-set, revisit our assumptions, and rethink our approaches to ministry and evangelism. Let us embrace this great adventure, nourished with our daily bread that comes down from heaven, tasting the goodness of the Lord (Ps. 34:8).—Karen Hatcher

ILLUSTRATIONS

Provision. Another miraculous aspect of the manna was its abrupt cessation once the Israelites entered the Promised Land and ate its produce (Exod. 16:35; Josh. 5:12). Corrie ten Boom relates a similar experience of supernatural provision that occurred during her imprisonment in a Nazi concentration camp. "The Davitamon bottle [we had smuggled past the guards] was continuing to produce drops. It scarcely seemed possible, so small a bottle, so many doses a day. . . . My instinct was always to hoard it [for my sister] Betsy. But others were ill as well. . . . [T]hese soon numbered fifteen, twenty, twenty-five. . . . And still, every time I tilted the little bottle, a drop appeared at the tip of the glass stopper. It just couldn't be! . . . Wonderful things happened all through the Bible. It was one thing to believe that such things were possible thousands of years ago, another to have it happen now, to us. . . . [Yet day after day] an awed little group of spectators [watched] the drops fall onto the daily rations of bread." One day a woman assigned to the hospital managed to slip them some pilfered vitamins. Opening the Davitamon bottle to finish off its contents first, Corrie found that "no matter how long [she] held it upside down, or how hard [she] shook it, not another drop appeared."[22]—Karen Hatcher

Presence. When our city-slicker family relocated to the country, I felt as if I had been sent to a foreign land. The alien perspectives of the tightly knit rural community challenged my thinking, and the factious, stagnating congregation contrasted sharply with the nurturing, progressive church we had left. Negativity set in, for there was no going back. Where was God in this barren place, I wondered?

Over the next several months, I discovered to my amazement several spiritually vibrant women scattered throughout the area. They mitigated my isolation, guided me with godly counsel, and contributed immeasurably to my growth in faith during my sojourn there. "Advance toward the Lord, for He has heard your grumbling," Aaron told the Israelites, and turning *toward the wilderness*, they perceived the Presence in the cloud (Exod. 16:9–10, TJSB). The Lord is there, even in seemingly godforsaken places.—Karen Hatcher

Musical Selections Appropriate to the Day

Exod. 16:2–15	*There Shall Be Showers of Blessing*
Ps. 105:1–6, 37–45 or Ps. 78	*I Stand in Awe*
Phil. 1:21–30	*Be Strong in the Lord*
Matt. 20:1–16	*And Can It Be*

ꙮ Children's Lectionary Sermon

TITLE: Wonderful Things
SCRIPTURE: Ps. 105:1–6, 37–45

---

[22]ten Boom, *Hiding Place*, pp. 202–203.

KEY VERSE: *Give thanks to the Lord and proclaim his greatness. Let the whole world know what he has done.* (Ps. 105:1, NLT)

KEY CONCEPT: God's goodness

MATERIALS: Bible, large chart paper, markers

PREPARATION: If you have an artist in your church who can draw extemporaneously, invite him or her to draw the things the children say God has given or done for them.

When we come to worship each week as a church family, we get to celebrate all the wonderful things God has done for us. Think of some of the Bible stories you have heard. Isn't it awesome that in our Old Testament lesson, God provided quails and manna for the Israelites while they were in the desert? I can't imagine what it must have been like to just go out of your tent and there was your food for the day. There are so many ways God has shown us in the Bible and even in our life together now that we have an awesome and great God.

(*Open Bible.*) In Psalm 105:1, the psalmist knew the stories about the people of God. *Give thanks to the Lord and proclaim his greatness. Let the whole world know what he has done.* As I call on you, I want you to share either a story from the Bible or something you are thankful for that God has done or given you. We will (*write or draw*) it here on this paper. (*If you have an artist, then let him or her draw the children's responses.*) If you don't want to share, then just say pass.

We have come up with a lot of great things God has done in the past and is doing now. Let's have a prayer together thanking God for God's greatness—and then to declare our willingness to share this with everyone we know.—Marcia Thompson

❧ WORSHIP AIDS ❧

Call to Worship: "Give thanks to the Lord, call on his name; / make known among the nations what he has done. / Sing to him, sing praise to him; / tell of all his wonderful acts. / Glory in his holy name; / let the hearts of those who seek the Lord rejoice. / Look to the Lord and his strength; / seek his face always. / Remember the wonders he has done, / his miracles, and the judgments he pronounced. / O descendants of Abraham his servant, / O sons of Jacob, his chosen ones" (Ps. 105:1–6, NIV).

Invocation: Almighty God, your Son Jesus Christ fed the hungry with the bread of his life and the word of his kingdom. Renew your people with your heavenly grace, and in all our weakness sustain us by your true and living bread, who lives and reigns with you and the Holy Spirit, one God, now and for ever. Amen.—Paul Gibson[23]

Offertory Sentence: "Just as you excel in everything—in faith, in speech, in knowledge, in complete earnestness and in your love for [the saints]—see that you also excel in this grace of giving" (2 Cor. 8:7).

Offertory Prayer: Lord of plenty, who supplies seed to the sower and bread for food, multiply these offerings for the increase of your Kingdom, scattering abroad these gifts to the poor in body and spirit, to the praise of your name (after 2 Cor. 9:9–13).

Morning Prayer: Our God and guide, we confess that as we walk through the wastelands of our world, our faith sometimes falters in the face of our fear and doubt. Help our unbelief. Strengthen us with an awareness of your presence as you train us in trust. Release us from the grip of ungodly attachments that would weaken our commitment, and grant that we might respond to everything we encounter along the way with gratitude rather than grumbling. Replace our withered imaginations with your vision of a world set right, that following in your footsteps, we may come to know and serve you as the Lord our God (after Exod. 16:12).—Karen Hatcher

Benediction: May the Lord establish you in faith and strengthen you through the Holy Spirit to face the difficulties and unknowns of life's journey with trust and confidence in God's provision.—Karen Hatcher

---

[23]Paul Gibson, in *Give Us Grace: An Anthology of Anglican Prayers*, ed. by Christopher L. Webber (New York: Morehouse, 2004), p. 428.

SUNDAY, SEPTEMBER 25, 2011
Fifteenth Sunday after Pentecost

LECTIONARY SERMON TOPIC: "Masterstroke"

TEXT: Exod. 17:1–7

OTHER READINGS: Ps. 78:1–4, 12–16; Phil. 2:1–13; Matt. 21:23–32

Moses made his way toward Mount Horeb, wrapped in thought, his aching throat as parched as the desolate landscape that spread out defenseless against the searing heat of the sun, the eye of Hor. The Egyptians' great sky-falcon had been proved as false as the other gods they worshipped when Yahweh had contended with Pharaoh, making a laughingstock of their pantheon and orchestrating the Israelites' dramatic escape from slavery. Moses remembered his first encounter with this wonder-working deity. It was on the very mountain looming before him that Yahweh had appeared to him, calling him to leave his flocks and to shepherd the children of Israel instead.

His initial misgivings about leading these uncooperative people now seemed justified. It was the fourth time they had questioned his intentions and clamored to return to Egypt (Exod. 14:11–12, 15:24, 16:2–3, 17:3). This time it was a lack of water that had them asking, "Is Yahweh with us or not?" Did they doubt that the Lord who rained down a daily supply of bread would also slake their thirst from a cleft rock? Their accusations were taking on a more sinister tone lately, he mused, with a full-fledged mutiny in the making. *Would he have become a victim of mob violence if Yahweh had not sent him on ahead to obtain water?* Moses wondered. Even among the elders who accompanied him, a sense of isolation crept over him. Yet he was not alone. There was Yahweh, designating the place as promised. With the witnesses watching, Moses approached the site, raised his rod and struck the rock . . .

I. **It was a *coup de maître*—a masterstroke—that accomplished several aims with a single blow.** The life-giving stream gushing from the rock not only solved Israel's immediate crisis but further established Yahweh's divine power, for in Hebrew scriptures water is a potentially chaotic element controllable only by deity.[24] God's abundant provision, celebrated in song and story, gave rise to the Talmudic legend of Miriam's well, a moving rock said to have watered the desert as Israel passed through (1 Cor. 10:4).[25]

II. **The life-saving blow to the rock also addresses a growing leadership crisis and the spirit of rebellion that had brought the Israelites to the brink of a coup.** Moses recognizes in the people's attempt to hold him personally responsible for their situation a thinly veiled attack on Yahweh (17:2). Moses, after all, is not acting on his own auspices, nor meeting needs from his own resources. Rather he serves as an agent executing the divine will. Wielding the Old Testament symbol of authority, Moses mediates this miracle with the same rod that made the waters of the Nile undrinkable (8:17), splitting the rock to reveal water as he had split the sea waters to reveal terra firma (14:16). This sign, performed in the presence of the elders, reaffirms Moses publicly as Yahweh's appointed one.

III. **Most important, the stroke of the rod signals the end of the Israelites' latest test of their commitment to follow the Lord's instruction (16:4).** Not only had they failed the assessment miserably by their lack of trust, but they had also dared to pass judgment on the curriculum and testing conditions, demonstrating precious little progress in their primary objective of knowing the Lord (16:6, 14). In a presumptuous role reversal, they lodge a complaint (*rîb*) and call Yahweh to task for alleged negligence. Subscribing to the notion that those who forget the past are destined to repeat it, Moses fixes Israel's impertinence permanently in corporate memory in the place names Massah ("proving" or "temptation"[26]) and Meribah ("dissatisfaction"[27] or "contention"). The incident functions not only as a warning (Deut. 6:16) but also as a foil and backdrop for the wilderness

---

[24]William F. McInerny, "An Unresolved Question in the Gospel Called Mark: 'Who Is This Whom Even Wind and Sea Obey?'" *Perspectives in Religious Studies*, Fall 1996, 23(3), 255–269.
[25]Göran Larsson, *Bound for Freedom: The Book of Exodus in Jewish and Christian Traditions* (Peabody, MA: Hendrickson, 1999), p. 119.
[26]S. R. Driver, *The Book of Exodus: Cambridge Bible for Schools and Colleges* (Cambridge, England: Cambridge University Press, 1953), p. 158.
[27]John I. Durham, "Exodus," *Word Biblical Commentary*, Vol. 3 (Dallas: Word Books, 1987), p. 228.

temptation of Jesus, who avoids Israel's mistake by refusing to put God to the test (Luke 4:1–12). Testing God is a form of disbelief. Perhaps it is this nuance of *peirasmos* that is foremost in the familiar petition of the model prayer—lead us not into "testing" rather than "temptation." At issue is not so much enticement to sin or trials of faithfulness but the human tendency to demand that God deliver on God's promises, to call God to account. Lord, keep us from putting you to the test.[28]

IV. **Centuries later, the community of faith still suffers from M and M (Massah and Meribah) syndrome.** When the going gets tough, it is easy to forget that we are called to contentment, not contention, and that it is we, rather than God, who have something to prove. If our allegiance and sense of God's presence depend on having our needs met on our timetable in expected ways, perhaps a spiritual inventory is in order. "[Should] we desire a simple test of the quality of our spiritual life," notes Evelyn Underhill, "a consideration of the tranquility, gentleness and strength with which we deal with the circumstances of our outward life will serve us better than anything that is based on [lofty] religious notions. . . . It is a test that can be applied anywhere and at any time."[29] If we find ourselves in the place of testing and quarreling, challenging God's provision and authority, a retrospective glance at God's gracious interventions may help us catch a glimpse of God standing by on the rock.

While this story warns against faithlessness and the audacity of putting God on trial, it also depicts the faithfulness of a rock-solid God who responds to our failures with compassion rather than a rod of discipline. The blow to the rock represents a coup de grâce in its literal sense—a stroke of mercy from a God that sustains us physically, ordains pastors to guide us, and provides periodic progress reports on our spiritual condition. Even when we do not pass with flying colors, we can rest assured that the Lord is indeed among us (17:7), God-with-us on our journey. "Your rod and your staff, they comfort me" (Ps. 23:4).—Karen Hatcher

---

[28]See Cornelius B. Houk, "[*Peirasmos*], the Lord's Prayer and the Massah Tradition," *Scottish Journal of Theology*, June 1966, *19*(2), 216–225.

[29]Evelyn Underhill, from *The Spiritual Life*, cited in Job and Shawchuck, *Guide to Prayer*, p. 209.

ILLUSTRATIONS

Foolproof. Like the narrator of today's text, Eugene O'Neill paints an unflattering portrait of humanity in survival mode in his one-act play *Thirst*. On the brink of death after days without water, a shipwrecked gentleman, a dancer, and a sailor share a life raft drifting in shark-infested seas under a merciless sun described as the "great angry eye of God." Deprivation distorts clear thinking, as the desperate dancer, prompted by the erroneous belief that the sailor is withholding water, offers a diamond necklace and sexual favors in exchange for a drink; the gentleman, who "would sell [his] soul for a drop of water," contemplates homicide of the one person whose skills might help them. The dialogue recalls the thirsting Israelites' clouded judgment, murderous intentions, and rash willingness to barter away their valuable freedom. Like O'Neill's faithless characters, they dismiss this Yahweh as a pitiless, distant deity.—Karen Hatcher

Bringing H$_2$O (Hope 2 Others). Bob Nolan's memorable song "Cool Water" tells of a cowboy and his companion crossing the desert with "throats burned dry and souls that cry for water." Fighting mirages of azure skies reflected as pools in the sand, the languishing singer turns to the Lord for help in finding a stream. The sensory lyrics emphasize the fragility of the human condition and the physical needs shared by people everywhere. For those of us who need only turn on the faucet to enjoy "cool, clear water," these texts are sobering reminders of the many around the globe who lack this basic necessity, prompting us to consider how we might become God's agents in reviving parched spirits and bodies with the gift of living water.—Karen Hatcher

Musical Selections Appropriate to the Day

Exod. 17:1–7	*If You Will Only Let God Guide You*
Ps. 78:1–4, 12–16	*Fresh as the Morning*
Phil. 2:1–13	*To Worship, Work, and Witness*
Matt. 21:23–32	*Stir Your Church, O God, Our Father*

꧁ Children's Lectionary Sermon

TITLE: All Mine
SCRIPTURE: Phil. 2:1–12
KEY VERSE: *Don't be selfish; don't try to impress others.* (Phil. 2:3a, NLT)
KEY CONCEPT: Helping others
MATERIALS: Bible, candy or cookies of your choosing

(*As the children come forward, pull out your bag of candy or cookies and start eating. The children will probably think you are going to share. Play up how good your snack is and ignore their questions about sharing.*) I am so glad you are here today. Did you know this (*candy or cookie type*) is my favorite? It is the best, and I just can't seem to stop eating it. (*Continue to talk about how it tastes, until you have enough protest or at least strange looks.*) Oh, do you want some too? I don't know. This is my favorite, and I'm not sure I really want to share. Should I share this with you? (*At this point, children will probably tell you that sharing is what you are supposed to do.*)

You know, you are right. I do need to share this, and I will give you some in just a minute. (*Open Bible.*) But first I want you to hear a verse from Philippians 2:3. It says, *Don't be selfish; don't try to impress others.* Paul wrote the church in Philippi, and this is part of what he told them. Paul wanted the Christians to look out for each other and to help each other. As a church family we do this when we visit people who are sick or take food to someone who needs help. These are some ways we show we are thinking about others.

Sometimes it's hard not to be selfish, but with Jesus' help we can do it, and we will want to do it. What are some ways you can help others at home or at school? (*Let the children respond, and reflect back their answers.*) There are so many ways we can help others by the choices we make and the things we do out of love for our friends and family.

Let's pray together asking Jesus to make us less selfish and more ready to help others.—Marcia Thompson

❧ WORSHIP AIDS ❧

Call to Worship: "O my people, hear my teaching; / Listen to the words of my mouth. / I will open my mouth in parables; / I will utter hidden things, things from of old— / What we have heard and known, what our fathers have told us. / We will not hide them from their children; / we will tell the next generation the praiseworthy deeds of the Lord, / his power and the wonders he has done" (Ps. 78:1–4).

Invocation: Almighty God and fountain of living waters (Jer. 17:13), we come to drink deeply from the wellspring of eternal life. Refresh our world-weary souls and renew our strength that we may in the name of Christ lead those who thirst to the source of salvation.—Karen Hatcher

Offertory Sentence: Pour into our hearts the spirit of your abundant generosity and make us ready and eager to share with others what we ourselves have so richly and freely received from you.—Peter Adebiyi[30]

Offertory Prayer: Lord, bless these offerings given for the advancement of your Kingdom, that people at home and abroad may be touched with the transformative power of the gospel to the glory of your name.—Karen Hatcher

Morning Prayer: O God, we know our own weakness. Our minds are darkened, and by ourselves we cannot find and know the truth. Our wills are weak, and by ourselves we cannot resist temptation, or bring to its completion that which we resolve to do. Our hearts are fickle, and by ourselves we cannot give to you the loyalty which is your due. Our steps are faltering, and by ourselves we cannot walk in your straight way. So this day we ask you to enlighten us, to strengthen us, to guide us, that we may know you and love you and follow you all the days of our life.—William Barclay[31]

---

[30]Peter Adebiyi, in *Give Us Grace: An Anthology of Anglican Prayers*, ed. by Christopher L. Webber (New York: Morehouse, 2004), p. 496.
[31]William Barclay, from *Prayers for the Christian Year*, cited in Job and Shawchuck, *Guide to Prayer*, pp. 104–105.

Benediction: As you go forth to water the barren places of your world with the oasis God has placed in your heart, may the presence of the Lord encourage you; may the power of the Lord energize you; may the praises of the Lord be ever on your lips.—Karen Hatcher

SUNDAY, OCTOBER 2, 2011
Sixteenth Sunday after Pentecost

LECTIONARY SERMON TOPIC: "Journey into Forever"
TEXT: Phil. 3:4b–14
OTHER READINGS: Exod. 20:1–4, 7–9, 12–20; Ps. 19; Matt. 21:33–46

Recently someone asked me what ten books I would want with me if I were stranded on a desert island. As I thought about it later, I realized that this was a considerable task. There are so many—and it was especially difficult when I got to numbers 8, 9, and 10. But the first three were easy. I would want with me more than any other book the Holy Bible, God's Word, a lamp unto my feet, a light unto my path. My second book would be the older edition of the Baptist Hymnal. It is one of the greatest collection of devotional material ever gathered. I would want as my third choice the 1675 classic, John Bunyan's *The Pilgrim's Progress*. It has been a favorite of mine for years, probably because it is so true to our experience in faith and in life.

You can almost hear in Bunyan's classic tale the heartthrob of another of God's saints, the Apostle Paul, who declared as a testimony of his own faith, "I press on for the upward call of God in Christ Jesus." I press on. I journey with God from here to where God wants me to be. Let's talk about the journey—our journey of faith.

I. **There is a way to see the journey beginning at birth—or even before.** The earliest experiences of life, the psychologists tells us, have profound influence on the rest of our lives. In fact, the things most neglected in our developmental days have a way of coming back in midlife to demand attention—often in negative ways. It's important for us, and for our children, that a firm foundation rooted in love and self-worth be laid early in life. That's why family and church are so important! This certainly is God's intention from the beginning of Creation. God looked at all he had made and said, "Behold, it is good—very good." It is here, at least in a general sense, in the contention of our worth, that our journey into forever begins. It begins with grace and acceptance, with God's grace and God's acceptance.

In our Baptist tradition, we place more than a general emphasis on God's grace and acceptance. We believe that faith is an individual matter. So much that each person comes to a point in life when individually, uniquely, personally, he or she discovers a level of intimacy with God through Christ. When does the journey begin? It begins when we sense the profound notion that God's hand of favor has been laid on us—one person at a time.

That's what Paul meant when he cried, I've not obtained this . . . haven't yet arrived . . . but I press on, *"because Christ Jesus has made me his own."* No more profound, nor helpful, word may come to us today. It's what salvation is all about. *Christ Jesus has made me his own.* The older American Standard Version translates this verse as "I press on that I may lay hold of that which has already laid hold of me." Life is not lived in a valueless vacuum. The events of life, the decisions we make, the directions we choose to take, the kind of person we decide to be—all of life is surrounded, and influenced, by God. There is a hand laid on us. When we sense that, we have begun the journey.

II. **Once begun, there is the toil, and the excitement, of the journey itself.** Ah, the journey! It's the journey where the water hits the wheel, where the memories are made, where life is at its best. And so we press on.

For Paul, the matter of "pressing on" was not just a part of his theology. It was a part of his life. Pressing on meant "forgetting the bad things that lie behind." He had much to forget, some things that were obviously not good. But they had to be forgotten. There was the persecution of the church and the stoning of Stephen. I don't know how Paul could have lived with the memories. He couldn't, except that he could "press on forgetting the bad things that lay behind."

But there were some *good* things he also wanted to forget. Recall what he said elsewhere of his own religious past: "I am of the people of Israel, of the tribe of Benjamin, a Hebrew born of Hebrew parents . . . as to the law, a Pharisee, as to zeal a persecutor of the church, as to righteousness under the law, blameless . . . but whatever gain I had, I count as loss for the sake of knowing Christ." I suppose we could add that there were some *good things about his present life* that he also needed to forget. You see, Paul could not rest on his laurels. Neither can we. So what that he carried the gospel to Macedonia and started great churches there! That was in the past. So what that he made great missionary journeys around the Mediterranean area! It was in the past. So what that he had borne witness to Christ in the very center of the political establishment of the Roman world! All passed. Even Paul could not rest on his laurels.

III. **We press on to what? "To the prize which is the upward calling of God in Christ Jesus." Here is the goal: to be "in" Christ Jesus.** The goal is the constantly developing life with Christ, the deepening of commitment, the growing intimacy. It is our mark—Christ in us. It's also about being "in Christ" forever. "Resurrection" was Paul's way of describing eternal life: "that I may know him and the power of his resurrection, and may share in his sufferings, becoming like him in his death, that I may attain the resurrection of the body." Ours is a journey into forever.

The promise is that, finally and forever, God will bring this journey of ours into its right and proper ending. Then, and only then, will the great mysteries of life be solved. Then, in the great day of resurrection, our hope will finally be fulfilled. For the unbeliever, that day is filled with despair. It is good for the believer to look to the future, but what of the unbeliever? It has to be madness for those out of Christ to look on. Look on to what? You would do better to look back—for your better days are past, or are now passing. You have no future, no spring to follow the bleak winter of life, no blessed resurrection morn, no hope of glory sure beyond the ages. Yet eternity holds no threats for God's people. Instead, the very thought of it is a source of comfort. Our journey covers lots of territory. But some day, just as we go to sleep at night weary and wake refreshed at dawn, so the Christian goes to sleep in death and awakes in an expanded and blessed eternity.—Lee McGlone

ILLUSTRATIONS

Endurance. One of my favorite men was Mr. Gene Williams. Gene was the deacon in my first pastorate. Gene died of lung cancer in 1980. Not long before his death, I sat by his bed and talked about the Bible and life—as often we did. He had been a Sunday school teacher for fifty years, and though he could no longer get to church, he still prepared a lesson every Saturday. He just couldn't break the habit. On that Sunday, the text was Paul's word to Timothy where, near the end of his own days, he declared, "I have fought the good fight, I have kept the faith, I have finished the race." You know the verse. About the middle of our conversation, Gene said, "Son, do you know what this means?" I said, "I think so." "No you don't," he said, with a twinkle in his eye. "No, you can't; you're not old enough. What it says is that life is like a race; it has a beginning, a middle, and an ending. But the race is not the one-hundred-yard dash. It's more like the cross-country endurance contest where there are dangers around every corner and over every hill. Winning is really a matter of finishing the course." There is wisdom in that.—Lee McGlone

Faith's Goal. Some years ago, a lady who lived in the neighborhood called for an appointment. She needed to talk. Her life was difficult and generally miserable. I listened to her as she lay open her soul. She confessed to being a Christian, but had not felt close to God for many years. Somewhere in the midst of the conversation, I asked her, "How is your quiet time?" To which she responded, "Quiet time? What is that?" As we talked in subsequent sessions, I encouraged her to renew her walk of faith, to institute a regular cycle of prayer and Bible study every day, to confess her sins and to receive God's forgiveness. When she left that first day, I had no idea whether she would ever return. But she did. To make a long story shorter, her life did something of a reversal. Her faith became very real. But it's what she said one day that has stayed with me over the years: "I just never knew that God could be so real, that God could love me so—nor that I could love God." I've never understood why she was so surprised. It's the natural order of things: receiving God's love, returning love to God. What could be more natural? Pressing on to what? To a life lived in the very presence and power of God.—Lee McGlone

Musical Selections Appropriate to the Day

Exod. 20:1–4, 7–9, 12–20	*Take Time to Be Holy*
Ps. 19	*You Are Holy*
Phil. 3:4b–14	*Come, All Christians, Be Committed*
Matt. 21:33–46	*For the Fruit of All Creation*

ᕱᕲ Children's Lectionary Sermon

TITLE: Get Rid of the Garbage

SCRIPTURE: Phil. 3:4b–14

KEY VERSES: *Yes, everything else is worthless when compared with the infinite value of knowing Christ Jesus my Lord. For his sake I have discarded everything else, counting it all as garbage so that I can gain Christ and become one with him.* (Phil. 3:8–9a, NLT)

KEY CONCEPT: Knowing Christ

MATERIALS: Bible, garbage in a clear plastic bag

PREPARATION: Throughout the week, collect some garbage to use with this sermon. Even though it might be a bit messy, make a garbage combination that looks really disgusting, and put it in a bag so it can be seen.

I brought something I would like to show you. What do you think this is? (*Let the children respond. Your garbage collection should be disgusting enough that there will not be any question.*) This bag of garbage I collected this week is disgusting. What do we do with garbage? (*Let the children respond.*) Yes, we put it out so that it can be taken to the garbage dump. It is stuff we don't keep.

   (*Open Bible.*) In Philippians 3, Paul writes to the church at Philippi about knowing Christ. He uses the word "garbage" to describe what isn't important in his life. Paul wrote, *Yes, everything else is worthless when compared with the infinite value of knowing Christ Jesus my Lord. For his sake I have discarded everything else, counting it all as garbage so that I can gain Christ and become one with him.*

Paul realized that knowing Christ was the most valuable thing to him. Before he knew Christ, Paul was a leader in the Jewish tradition and mistreated people who were Christians. He was very smart about the Jewish laws and traditions, but once Jesus spoke to him and changed him, he realized that all the stuff he had learned was like garbage. He had to throw out those things he once thought were true. Jesus was now the one Paul followed.

From Paul's teaching, we need to realize how valuable it is to know Christ. As you continue to learn and grow in Christ, you will understand even more what Paul means in this passage.

Let's pray together, asking Christ to help us understand that knowing and trusting him are the most valuable things we could ever have.—Marcia Thompson

✥ WORSHIP AIDS ✥

Call to Worship: "But I call to God, and the Lord saves me" (Ps. 55:16, NIV).

Invocation: O Lord, speak to us that we may hear. Tell us of your loving judgment that comes like a tender parent's discipline, which makes life better for us all. Tell us of your unending love that rekindles the fire of faith within. And grant that we may carefully listen as you speak. Amen.

Offertory Sentence: "From everyone who has been given much, much will be demanded; and from the one who has been entrusted with much, much more will be asked" (Luke 12:48b, NIV).

Offertory Prayer: Father, bless these gifts as expression of our renewed dedication to your service. Multiply them in ways that declare your glory. Make steadfast our resolve to love you more deeply and to serve you more fervently—that we may live faithfully and bear much fruit. Amen.

Morning Prayer: (Prayer on Exod. 20:8–11) Sovereign Father, we humbly approach your throne. We are grateful, most high God, that you have provided an intercessor for us, your Son, the light of the world—Jesus. We are also honored that, in our nothingness, you desire relationship with us. Our unworthiness is blinding. But with the aid of your marvelous light, we are able to see.

Father, we confess that we have failed. Thousands of years ago, upon Mount Sinai, you gave ten ordinances to Moses. In our daily lives, we have failed to keep even the simplest of these commandments. You have given us seven days in every week, days with which we may do whatever we please. But, for the Sabbath of these days, you have asked that we keep it holy—that we do no work and simply rest. In our society, we have chosen capital over obedience. And as your people, we have chosen to follow the crowd—to join the throng that does not honor you with their seventh day. Though we may piously claim that we will not work on the Sabbath, we force others to work in order that they may serve us. After you have bestowed so much, how can we blatantly neglect to honor you? And as we complain about our levels of stress and lists of things to do, how do we so readily ignore the time of rest you have provided? Father, we ask that in our ignorance you would forgive us. Even more, we ask that you would illumine the error of our ways that we may strive for correction. Amen.—Sarah Casey

Benediction: Lord God, whom we know as Father, Son, and Holy Spirit, walk with us in the days ahead. Inspire us to noble living, in word and deed, and bring us back again next Lord's day. Amen.

SUNDAY, OCTOBER 9, 2011
Seventeenth Sunday after Pentecost

LECTIONARY SERMON TOPIC: "Finding Peace in a Troubled World"
TEXT: Phil. 4:1–9
OTHER READINGS: Exod. 32:1–14; Ps. 106:1–6, 19–23; Matt. 22:1–14

"And the peace of God, that which passes all understanding, will keep your hearts and minds in Christ Jesus." We should say thanks to the Apostle Paul for giving us this gem of scriptural assurance. From a jail cell, in the midst of circumstances beyond his control that would determine his fate, he wrote to a beloved yet troubled congregation this word of hope. "Despite," he said, "whatever the circumstances of life may be, there is available for us God's all sufficient grace." Notice the mood of the text. There is joy—and joy again— the exuberant gladness of heart that comes as a by-product of faith. There is gentleness—the kind expression of a relaxed spirit that comes to those who carry not only Christ's name but also Christ's attitude. But most of all there is peace, the kind that goes beyond our wildest imaginations.

It's one thing to envision a peaceful world in the promise of God's perfect eternity. It's another thing to know peace in the troubled world in which we live. We live in a different world today than ever before. We live post–September 11, 2001. Images of passenger jets exploding into the World Trade Center, the scenes of terrified masses fleeing the city under siege, terrorism, anthrax—these memories will forever be etched into our minds. Is there, in a world like this, a place for peace and rest? Indeed there is. Thanks be unto God!

I. **We're not strangers to this talk of peace.** Every survey I've seen of the dreams of the American people includes desire for peace: world peace, national peace, the ending of crime and lawlessness, and personal peace. The prophets of old declared it . . . and we are still looking for the lion to lay down with the lamb. Jesus came to fulfill the Old Testament promise as "prince of peace." At his birth, the angels sang, "peace on earth, good will to men." To his disciples, he said, "My peace I leave with you . . . let not your hearts be troubled, neither let them be afraid."

Here Paul describes the peace we have in military terms. God, he said, will keep you—that is, God will "garrison" you. God will surround you with his care. We never fight the battles of life alone. God is with us. He is forever our Emmanuel—our peace.

II. **One of the most profound images of a peaceful life is that undue worry is not allowed to dominate.** Peace and overwhelming worry have a hard time sharing the same territory. Paul gives us direction. "Have no anxiety about anything." Here Paul sounds a lot like Jesus: "Look to the birds of the air and the lilies of the field. They don't worry about what they will eat, or drink, or wear. Yet they are well supplied the needs of life. And you matter more than birds or lilies. Will not the Father above also take care of you?" And the implied answer is, "Indeed, God will supply our needs."

Now, not all worry is a bad thing. Some amount of tension, as a driving force, may well be healthy. In the cold of winter, I start my car a bit early and let the motor warm up a bit before I drive it. It just does better once it's warmed up. So do we. Some tension, some worry, helps encourage us on in tasks that lie before us. But some of us are chronic worriers, perhaps members of the "rusty lining society." If we don't have something of consequence to worry about, we'll invent it. There's a black hole out there in the universe, snatching up matter to fill its colossal void. I'm afraid I'll be next. There's a hole in the ozone layer—and I think it is right above my house.

When Paul penned the words "have no anxiety about anything," he warned us against unhealthy, damaging, destructive worry. The word he used actually means "to be pulled apart at the seams." It describes a warfare in the soul, a tugging within, that gives no rest. Abraham Lincoln spoke of this when, at the height of the War Between the States, he wrote of the greatest civil war he knew—the one being fought in his soul. Said Lincoln, "I think I shall split asunder and die." Worry that kills is what Paul taught against.

There is a practical concern here. Worry doesn't do anyone any good. That's what Jesus said: "Which of you, by your worry, can add one day to the length of your life?" The intended answer is, "No one can." In fact, all that worry does is take away energy that could be used for creative and positive solutions to the things that trouble us. So, excessive worry is not a good thing.

III. **As an alternative to worry, there is prayer.** "Have no anxiety about anything, but in everything by prayer and supplication, let your requests be made known to God." What worldview would we rather have—the frantic chaos of life out of control, or the calm resolve that this is God's world and we are a part of it? Prayer is the positive alternative to a world out of control.

It occurs to me that there are at least two modern views of prayer that are woefully inadequate. The first is the kind that makes God into a vending machine and our prayers into coins. We put them in, push the right button, and get what we want. These suggest we should "name it and claim it." And Jesus said, "Father, not my will, but thine be done." Then there are those who say, "There's nothing to it. I can get along quite well without God and without prayer." And you can. You can "get along" without God and prayer—if you are satisfied just to get along.

How do we define prayer? Is it the bowed head in public worship? Indeed, but more. Is it the family routine of prayer at table or private prayers before bedtime? Indeed, but more. Prayer is all of life lifted to God—the developing comradeship and intimacy with the Father—for all of life belongs to God. Prayer is the greatest work of the heart. Prayer then is an exercise of believing people, believing that God is approachable, interested, and involved in life with us.

Prayer is the alternative to worry. Instead of wringing our hands in a frenzy, we are to be busy at the great work of prayer. We are called to a life of peace. Not a peace based on the ending of hostilities, but a peace located amid life's turmoil. We believe in, proclaim, bear witness to a living Christ, who is with us in everything and always—just as he said, "till the end of the world." When we rest in the loving care of our Father, mounted up on wings like eagles, then we can truly run and not be weary, we can walk and not faint. Father, in our troubled world, hold us close. Please.—Lee McGlone

ILLUSTRATIONS

Shalom. The beautiful baptistery at First Baptist Church, Sioux Falls, South Dakota, displays the word "Shalom." It's the Hebrew greeting that declares the peace of God among us, a significant level of well-being that comes as lives are lived congruent to God above, to the world around, and within our own souls. In the New Testament, the word describes a restored relation. Because of our sin, we are alienated from God. We are enemies of God. Yet in Christ Jesus, this wrong relationship is set right. We are reconciled to God and forgiven. God has made peace through the blood of the cross. Jesus used this word when he said, "go in peace and sin no more." Shalom y'all.—Lee McGlone

Prayer. Have you read Mark Twain's little books about the wayfaring river rats Huck Finn and Tom Sawyer? There is a bit of tragic humor when Twain has Huck Finn talk about his faltering prayer life. Said Huck, "Miss Watson she took me in the closet and prayed, but nothing come of it. She told me to pray every day, and whatever I asked for I would get it. But it warn't so. I tried. Once I got a fish-line, but no hooks. It warn't no good to me without hooks. I tried for the hooks three or four times, but somehow I couldn't make it work. By and by, one day, I asked Miss Watson to try for me, but she said I was a fool. She never told me why, and I couldn't make it out no way. I set down one time back in the woods, and had a long think about it. I says to myself, if a body can get anything they pray for, why don't Deacon Winn get back the money he lost on pork? Why can't the widow get back her silver snuffbox what was stole? Why can't Miss Watson fat up? No, says I to myself, there ain't nothing to it." Perhaps we deserve such satire.—Lee McGlone

Prayer. How glad I was, only a couple of months ago, when our liturgical dance team traveled to New York City and shared a word of hope in and around Ground Zero. When I watched the videotape of our young ladies reaching out to share the love of God in downtown firehouses, on street corners, with people in need, I was overwhelmed. They proclaimed the God of all comfort who comforts us in our affliction—who stands by us faithfully when the earth shakes and the mountains are cast into the sea. The video ended with these words from Jeremiah 31:13, "The young women will dance for joy. I will turn their mourning into laughter. I will give comfort—and exchange their sorrow for rejoicing." As the video ended, I cried. I cried because what I saw wasn't about a performance; what I saw was a prayer. It was a bold declaration of grace and the all-sufficiency of God to heal our deepest wounds. And I thought, in a troubled world like this there really is hope—as long as there are young people like this who so boldly declare faith in God.—Lee McGlone

Musical Selections Appropriate to the Day

Exod. 32:1–14	*I Am His, and He Is Mine*
Ps. 106:1–6, 19–23	*Wonderful, Merciful Savior*
Phil. 4:1–9	*Rejoice in the Lord Always*
Matt. 22:1–14	*We Are Called to Be God's People*

ᘒ Children's Lectionary Sermon

TITLE: Pray and Be Thankful
SCRIPTURE: Phil. 4:1–9
KEY VERSE: *Don't worry about anything; instead, pray about everything. Tell God what you need, and thank him for all he has done.* (Phil. 4:6, NLT)
KEY CONCEPT: Thankfulness
MATERIALS: Bible

Do you know what it means to worry? (*Let the children respond.*) Worry is like being fearful, concerned—it's something that bothers us and we just can't stop thinking about it. I remember when I was in school and got a bad grade on a test. I worried all day about having to show it to my parents. There are lots of things we worry about. We worry about friends, about people who are sick, and even about the clothes we wear.

(*Open Bible.*) Paul wrote to the church at Philippi and ended his letter to the Philippians with this: *Don't worry about anything; instead, pray about everything. Tell God what you need, and thank him for all he has done.* Paul told the Christians not to worry about things, but to pray to God about everything, asking God for what they need. Sometimes when we pray, we don't have a hard time asking God for what we need, but we don't always remember to thank God for what God has already done.

God wants us to pray and ask for what we need instead of worrying so much. What are some things you want to ask God for? (*Let the children respond.*) We also need to remember to be thankful for the things God has already done for us. Can you think of things God has done that you are thankful for? (*Let the children respond.*) There are so many things we can be thankful for. (*Repeat some of the children's responses.*)

Let's pray, asking God to help us to pray about everything and thank God for the things God has already done for us.—Marcia Thompson

ᘒ WORSHIP AIDS ᘒ

Call to Worship: "Cast your cares on the Lord and he will sustain you; he will never let the righteous fall" (Ps. 55:22, NIV).

Invocation: Lord, God, we know the Risen Savior who ascended into glory will one day come again. Keep us ready, expectant and watchful, for in such an hour as we know not, the Christ of the universe returns, as triumphant as when he left. Hallelujah! Amen.—E. Lee Phillips

Offertory Sentence: "And Jesus went on to say, 'I tell you, use worldly wealth to gain friends for yourselves, so that when it is gone, you will be welcomed into eternal dwellings" (Luke 16:9, NIV).

Offertory Prayer: Lord, we expect much from you, and we are not disappointed. May we respond in our stewardship as you have taught us how to give and thus be a blessing to others. Take both gift and giver and use them for your glory across the world we pray. Amen.—Henry Fields

Morning Prayer: (Prayer on Jesus' Model Prayer) Hallowed be thy name. May your name be regarded with the utmost respect. I ask that we, your people, live in a way that pleases you. Let us react to your holiness by living holy lives marked by love and respect for others.

Thy Kingdom come, thy will be done. Let all things be on earth as they are in heaven. We wait patiently for the fulfillment of your promises when your Kingdom comes in fullness.

Give us this day our daily bread. We know that you always provide for us. You showed yourself faithful to the Israelites with manna. You have shown yourself faithful to us in our day. Thank you for always giving us what we need.

Forgive us our debts. Forgive us of all of the sins that we have committed—the lust, the greed, the pride, the selfishness. Help us also forgive those that have committed sins against us—because we have been forgiven by you.

Lead us not into temptation. Keep us far from evil, and please don't let us fall into sin. Help us on our journey toward holiness and give us the strength to flee temptation when we are confronted with it.

Yours is the Kingdom, the power, and the glory forever. You are worthy of all praise. Your rule is never-ending. Your Kingdom shall reign forever. We ascribe to you the glory, honor, and adoration your name deserves. Amen.
—Sky Howard

Benediction: People of God, go out today in the power and love of our gracious God. May we speak often, and lovingly, his Holy Name—and may our spirits be sensitive to arenas of witness placed before us this week. Amen.

SUNDAY, OCTOBER 16, 2011
Eighteenth Sunday after Pentecost

LECTIONARY SERMON TOPIC: "A Godly Imitation"

TEXT: 1 Thess. 1:1–10

OTHER READINGS: Exod. 33:12–23; Ps. 99; Matt. 22:15–22

I heard the story of a nine-year-old girl who returned from Sunday school with questions for her father. "Father, why did God make all the leaves green?" "I don't know," he said. "What did God do before he made the world?" Again he said, "I don't know." "Father, how did Noah catch the two snakes and put them in the ark?" With a bit of exasperation, he put down his newspaper and said, "I don't know." The little girl, sensing her father's restlessness, asked, "Do you mind if I ask you questions?" He replied, "Not at all. How are you going to learn anything if you don't ask questions?" Tough questions are hard to answer.

I. **Here is a tough question:** What is the reputation of our church? What image pops into people's minds when they hear or think about us? What reports sound forth about us? Think about it in two ways, as it refers to this church in which we worship and serve and as it refers to each of us as members of Christ's body. I served a very fine congregation once that was known for its huge pipe organ, for its quality choir, and for the quality of the fur coats and the fine cars that could be seen there on a Sunday morning. One church had a great reputation for its Christian social ministry, having established a number of local outreach ministries that reached to all parts of the city. Another had the reputation as a squabbling church—and rightly so. One of the ladies of the church, who came to each business meeting with a calculator in her hand, told me God had given her the gift of stirring up the church. She did a good job of it! Another was known for its quality youth ministry, the height of its steeple seen from the local high school football field, and the lovely and professional manicure of its landscape. Every church, you see, has a reputation. What is ours? What is yours? Are we a people who make a difference, a people known for our faith in the living God?

II. **Paul wrote to the church in Thessalonica:** "We always give thanks to God for all of you and mention you in our prayers. In spite of persecution, you received the Word with joy inspired by the Holy Spirit . . . so that you became an example to all the believers in Macedonia and in Achaia. . . . In every place your faith in God has become known." Now there is the declaration of a great reputation! And with that great reputation there came great influence—the ability to move the hearts and minds of many to give praise to God and to walk closely with God. Is not this the Church's calling? "We are a chosen race, a royal priesthood, a holy nation, God's own people, in order that we may proclaim the mighty acts of him who called us out of darkness into his marvelous light" (1 Pet. 2:9). It is not a bad thing to be known for our friendliness and warmth, our cozy community, our classic sanctuary. But is it not better to be known for our faith, and for what we do in faith to express our love for God and for one another? "You are the salt of the earth," said Jesus. "You are the light of the world. You are a city built on a hill—which cannot be hid" (Matt. 5:13–14). What a marvelous reputation!

Paul's letter to the Thessalonians suggests to us what a godly reputation looks like. It suggests to us that we can have a godly reputation like those in Thessalonica if like them we practice a godly imitation: "We know, brothers and sisters, beloved by God, that he has chosen you, because our message of the gospel came to you not in word only, but also in power and in the Holy Spirit and with full conviction; just as you know what kind of persons we proved to be among you for your sake. And you became imitators of us and of the Lord" (1 Thess. 1:4–6).

III. **It matters the persons and life themes we choose to imitate.** Imitation is indeed the most sincere form of flattery—and perhaps the most powerful form of influence. Paul with clear conscience was able to appeal to the Thessalonians, for he carried authentic credibility. I recall hearing my father speak of a day when business deals were sealed with nothing more than a handshake, "for a man's word was his bond." It is persons like that, persons of integrity and honesty, who carry the great weight of positive influence in the world. How I hope my life will be so lived!

IV. **Each person and church has a life purpose.** It is an intention and direction for life that gives to us uniqueness. But our life purpose is never separated from God's purpose or from the needs of the world around us. Perhaps our best shot at living out that purpose is to do so as imitators of what we see of God in the person of Jesus. Jesus showed to us perfectly the image of God. As faithful disciples of Jesus, we are at our best when living as Jesus lived, loving as he loved, and pouring out our lives for him as he poured out his for us. Jesus came to give us life and that abundantly, to seek the lost and save sinners, to bring good news to the poor, to proclaim release to the captives and recovery of sight to the blind, to let the oppressed go free, and to proclaim the year of the Lord's favor.

That was his great work . . . and he shone in it! People wanted to be near him, to be like him. By the power of the Holy Spirit, it is our work too. "Truly, truly, I tell you," said Jesus, "the one who believes in me will also do the works that I do and, in fact, will do greater works than these, because I am going to the Father" (John 14:12). And so we pray, "Lord, help us to be imitators of you—so that your great work of redemption, which has come to us, may also go through us to the uttermost parts of the world.—Lee McGlone

ILLUSTRATIONS

Word of God. I heard another pastor tell the story of a man who was fired from the Highway Department. He was hired to paint the lines down the middle of the highway. The first day he painted ten miles, the second day he painted five miles, and the third day he painted only one mile. Out of exasperation, his supervisor asked, "Why did you paint ten miles the first day, five miles the second day, and only one the third day?" "Well, to tell you the truth," the man replied, "I just kept getting farther and farther away from the paint can." Could it be that our lives often feel distant from God, empty and shallow, because we keep getting farther and farther away from the Word of God?—Lee McGlone

Purpose. This is the true joy in life, the being used for a purpose recognized by yourself as a mighty one: the being thoroughly worn out before you are thrown on the scrap heap, and being a force of nature instead of a feverish selfish little clod of ailments and grievances, complaining that the world will not devote itself to making you happy.—George Bernard Shaw[1]

Musical Selections Appropriate to the Day

Exod. 33:12–23	*He Hideth My Soul*
Ps. 99	*Holy, Holy, Holy*
1 Thess. 1:1–10	*God, Our Father, We Adore Thee*
Matt. 22:15–22	*Open Our Eyes, Lord*

Children's Lectionary Sermon

TITLE: Ringing out the Good News

SCRIPTURE: 1 Thess. 1:1–10

KEY VERSE: *And now the word of the Lord is ringing out from you to people everywhere, even beyond Macedonia and Achaia, for wherever we go we find people telling us about your faith in God.* (1 Thess. 1:8, NLT)

KEY CONCEPTS: Sharing your faith, telling the good news of Christ

MATERIALS: Bible; items that make a ringing sound, such as a bell, school bell, doorbell, and cell phone; bag

PREPARATION: If you use visual and sound presentations in church, you can find lots of different examples of bell sounds to use. Otherwise, place different items in a bag big enough that the children can't see the items.

---

[1]George Bernard Shaw, quoted in Jon Johnston, *Courage—You Can Stand Strong in the Face of Fear* (Delhi, India: SP Publications, 1990), p. 171.

I brought some items that make a sound, and I want to see if you can guess what the item is. (*Start making the various sounds and let the children guess what item makes the sound. Then show the children the item.*) You were very good guessers for the sounds I brought today. Each one of these items rings out to tell someone to answer the door or the telephone, to go out for recess, or to make pretty music. (*Adjust this wording according to the sounds you choose.*)

Paul wrote a letter to the church at Thessalonica about how their faith in Christ was ringing out everywhere and how people noticed they were Christians. (*Open Bible.*) In 1 Thessalonians 1:8, Paul wrote, *And now the word of the Lord is ringing out from you to people everywhere, even beyond Macedonia and Achaia, for wherever we go we find people telling us about your faith in God.* In Bible times, being a Christian was dangerous. Paul was happy to hear from people in other places about the faith of these Christians.

So here are the big questions for all of us. Do other people notice our faith in God? Do we tell our friends about our faith? Do we tell others about Jesus? Do we make choices that are pleasing to God? Those are big questions for you and for our whole church family. We need to think about whether we are "ringers" of the good news of Christ so that people notice our faith.

Let's ask God to help us share our faith in all the things we do and say so that others will recognize our love for God.—Marcia Thompson

WORSHIP AIDS

Call to Worship: "I will praise you, O Lord, among the nations; I will sing of you among the peoples. For great is your love, reaching to the heavens; your faithfulness reaches to the skies" (Ps. 57:9–10, NIV).

Invocation: Lord God, we know the Risen Savior who ascended into glory will one day come again. Keep us ready, expectant, and watchful, for in such an hour as we know not, the Christ of the universe returns, as triumphant as when he left. Hallelujah! Amen.—E. Lee Phillips

Offertory Sentence: "Whoever can be trusted with very little can also be trusted with much, and whoever is dishonest with very little will also be dishonest with much" (Luke 16:10, NIV).

Offertory Prayer: Father, recognizing that it is you who entrusts us with what we have, we give thanks. May we be good stewards of your gifts. Because you first loved us, help us now to love you, through Christ. Amen.

Morning Prayer: In the course of this past week, Father, we have seen health return to people who were sick, and we have seen illness invade once healthy lives. We have visited homes where joy was real and homes where sadness prevailed. We have walked with those who have traveled with the companion of accomplishment and as well as those who tasted the bitterness of failure. We have stood with those who were victims of yielding to degrading temptations and have watched as others resisted the temptations that would destroy them. We have visited the place of restoration of life, and we have slowly entered the valley of the shadow with folks in the throes of loss. We have seen how faith in Christ brought strength and how faith only in self brought weakness. Ours this week has been a view of life at its best as well as life at its worst. For some there have been moments of doubt; for others the same circumstances have strengthened faith. We have stood amid this mystery and, as best we know how, sought your presence. And we have not been disappointed.—Henry Fields

Benediction: As we go, may our obedience to Christ make clear our surrender. Eternal one, whom we name as Father, Son, and Holy Spirit, guide our steps, enrich our days, and lead us in the way everlasting. Amen.

SUNDAY, OCTOBER 23, 2011
Nineteenth Sunday after Pentecost

LECTIONARY SERMON TOPIC: "An Undivided Heart"
TEXT: Matt. 22:34–46
OTHER READINGS: Deut. 34:1–12; Ps. 90:1–6, 13–17; 1 Thess. 2:1–8

What is the greatest commandment? Is it a trick question or a search for the basic duties of life? Perhaps we can't know. Regardless, it is a most difficult question. Jesus could have designated a cultic regulation, like bathing in the waters of purification from the ashes of a red heifer (Deut. 19), from which there was believed to come atoning powers. Quick opposition would have said, "Cultic law is not enough." If life's motivation is to love our fellow man, the critics would have said, "all you care about is social justice, nothing any respectable atheist would not apply." But Jesus did not elevate a single commandment. He simply pointed to the truth that lay behind all the commandments. What is that truth? The truth is that we belong to God with all our heart, soul, mind, and strength.

I. **To love God is the basic affirmation of human life.** It is indeed the choice that makes all the difference. We choose love as the basic ingredient of life. And with good reason. Despite the various calls from unbelievers that life makes no sense, that the evil of the world dispels any notion of direction or meaning, there stands at the heart of faith the foundational belief that at the center of all things is divine love. At the heart of the universe is love. The created order as we know and experience it came out of God's eternal love—God's very nature.

Because we are Christians, this world-altering view propels us onward to a life that exemplifies God's nature as ultimate love. We love because God first loved us. So Jesus, when aroused by the stinging question about the greatest commandment, had no hesitation: life is founded on loving God and loving others. Here rest all the laws and prophets—the whole duty of life. Not duty in the sense of a "have to" in order to accomplish an outward motive, but duty in the sense of the joy of faith lived out! The elder prodigal was keen on duty, but he missed the joy of his disciplined life. He would have been a happier person had he worked as hard to develop a relationship with his wayward brother as he did to plow the fields. The clerk you see in the grocery store, the frustrated driver in the lane next to you, the teenager with music blaring . . . these are all persons God loves . . . and persons God loves through us.

II. **The call to love demands an undivided heart.** There is no wavering on the part of Jesus. The great command, quoting the Pharisee's own religious tradition, was an undivided heart. God, they knew, was a jealous God and would not share his glory with anyone. So Jesus strikes at the heart of their dilemma. The Pharisees attempted to trap Jesus into damaging testimony; instead, he trapped them: God is one, and the call to a life of faith is surrender of all we are to the rule of God.

Surely there are ample pleas from myriad directions clamoring for our attention and fealty. The world, with its multiple loyalties, wants to own us—and use us. We are bombarded daily with persuasive techniques that pull us in every way. We twist and spin like a weather vane, but at some point we must make a clear choice. You cannot stand everywhere all at once. You can't stand just anywhere, for the forces that clamor for attention are not of equal moral value. Just as surely, you can't stand nowhere. Before the day is over, we will choose who owns our heart. But, indeed, we must stand somewhere. Something will claim us!

The heart fully devoted to God remains committed despite circumstances. We often wonder where God is in times of disaster. The truth is that despite the changes in our circumstances that leave us bewildered, God has not moved. God is always there. Circumstances do indeed test our loyalty—and our fealty. But the prior established design of life, the deep of God calling out to the deep that is within us, is sufficient for the need of each new day. The sign of love, an undivided heart, is enough to secure tomorrow. You wonder where God is! Here's your answer. Look to the lilies of the field and to the birds of the air. God's love for them is sufficient. And God cares for you more than them!

III. **An undivided heart is best expressed in purposeful living.** When we are overwhelmed by the fretfulness of life, the disasters that occur to us, there is often a collapse of our strength and dismay for our future. In the 1929 economic collapse, scores of persons could not face the next day—and so ended their lives. Our hearts grieve for the greater population all around who struggle with circumstances larger than life. Ours is a post 9/11 world—different than before. Despair has a way of creeping up and choking away the joy of life. Worry seems rampant. In our day, we need a hope that propels faith beyond the present dilemmas. We find it here: an undivided heart bent on purpose.

Purpose is vitally important. Victor Frankl, psychologist and World War II prisoner of war, observed that those who survived the death camps were those with something to look forward to beyond the prison. They had a purpose to live that gave added strength. Abraham in the Old Testament knew such a thing. He moved forward to a promised land, not knowing where it was but assured that the destination existed. He went by faith to a land he knew not of.

Each life has purpose. God gave it in the very act of creation. We are God's precious sons and daughters, created in God's image; our purpose for now and forever is in the return to that one from which we came. Our fulfillment is God's love through Jesus Christ. The call of Jesus summons us there. Love of God and for others is the design. God is all—and is in all! And we are called to love with undivided hearts. Do we dare to try it? Will we love the Lord our God with all our being? He wants us to trust him at his word.—Lee McGlone

ILLUSTRATIONS

Trust. February 15, 1921. New York City. The operating room of the Kane Summit Hospital. A doctor is performing an appendectomy. In many ways the events leading to the surgery are uneventful. The patient had complained of severe abdominal pain. The diagnosis is clear: an inflamed appendix. Dr. Evan O'Neill Kane is performing the surgery. In his distinguished thirty-seven-year medical career, he has performed nearly four thousand appendectomies, so this surgery will be uneventful in all ways except two.

The first novelty of this operation? The use of local anesthesia in major surgery. Dr. Kane is a crusader against the hazards of general anesthesia. He contends that a local application is far safer. Many of his colleagues agree with him in principle, but in order for them to agree in practice, they will have to see the theory applied. The patient is prepped and wheeled into the operating room. A local anesthetic is applied. As he has done thousands of times, Dr. Kane dissects the superficial tissues and locates the appendix. He skillfully excises it and concludes the surgery. During the procedure, the patient complains of only minor discomfort. The volunteer is taken into post-op, then placed in a hospital ward. He recovers quickly and is dismissed two days later. Dr. Kane had proven his theory. Thanks to the willingness of a brave volunteer,

Kane demonstrated that local anesthesia was a viable, and even preferable, alternative.

But I said there were two facts that made the surgery unique. I've told you the first: the use of local anesthesia. The second is the patient. The courageous candidate for surgery by Dr. Kane was Dr. Kane. To prove his point, Dr. Kane operated on himself! A wise move. The doctor became a patient in order to convince the patients to trust the doctor.—Max Lucado[2]

Love. The Greek word agape (love) seems to have been virtually a Christian invention—a new word for a new thing (apart from about twenty occurrences in the Greek version of the Old Testament, it is almost non-existent before the New Testament). Agape draws its meaning directly from the revelation of God in Christ. It is not a form of natural affection, however, intense, but a supernatural fruit of the Spirit (Gal. 5:22). It is a matter of will rather than feeling (for Christians must love even those they dislike—Matt. 5:44–48). It is the basic element in Christ-likeness. Read 1 Corinthians 13 and note what these verses have to say about the primacy (vv. 1–3) and permanence (vv. 8–13) of love; note too the profile of love (vv. 4–7) which they give.—James Packer[3]

Musical Selections Appropriate to the Day

Deut. 34:1–12	*Faith of Our Fathers*
Ps. 90:1–6, 13–17	*To God Be the Glory*
1 Thess. 2:1–8	*Christian Hearts, in Love United*
Matt. 22:34–46	*My Jesus, I Love Thee*

Children's Lectionary Sermon

TITLE: The Commandments
SCRIPTURE: Matt. 22:34–46

---

[2]Max Lucado, *In the Eye of the Storm* (Dallas: Word, 1991), pp. 35–36.
[3]James Packer, *Your Father Loves You* (Colorado Springs, CO: Harold Shaw, 1986), pp. 81–82.

KEY VERSES: *Jesus replied, "'You must love the Lord your God with all your heart, all your soul, and all your mind.'" This is the first and greatest commandment. A second is equally important: 'Love your neighbor as yourself.'"* (Matt. 22:37–39, NLT)

KEY CONCEPT: Loving God and others

MATERIALS: Bible, puppet or another adult dressed in biblical garb as a Pharisee

PREPARATION: Get someone to use a puppet to do the monologue or ask an adult who can prepare this monologue.

Today we have a guest who is coming to tell us about what it was like when he met Jesus. (*Open Bible.*) We can read about this person's meeting with Jesus in Matthew 22. Here he comes now. Listen and find out what this Pharisee learned from Jesus.

Monologue: Hi, kids. I am a Pharisee who lived when Jesus was going all around Galilee and Judea. Now a Pharisee is a person who studies and knows all about the law of Moses. I am sure you have heard of the Ten Commandments. Now I was an expert at religious law. My other Pharisee friends and I had a meeting with Jesus, and we were trying to trick Jesus into saying something that wasn't correct. So I asked Jesus this question: *Which is the most important commandment in the law of Moses?* (v. 36). We thought we had a question he couldn't answer, but we were wrong. *Jesus replied, "'You must love the Lord your God with all your heart, all your soul, and all your mind.'" This is the first and greatest commandment. A second is equally important: 'Love your neighbor as yourself.'"* We were amazed at his answer. Loving God with all your heart, soul, and mind was the greatest commandment. But *"Love your neighbor as yourself"* was even more amazing because all the other laws and commandments I could think of are covered by this commandment to love. If we love others, we would do and want the best for them. I learned from Jesus that day. Thanks for letting me tell you about it. (*Exit puppet or adult.*)

What did the Pharisee learn from Jesus? (*Let the children answer. Help them as needed.*) If we remember to love God with our whole self and love others around us, we are doing what Jesus asks from us. It is not always easy, but Jesus will help us if we ask him.

Let's ask Jesus to help us love God with our whole self and to love others as he commanded.—Marcia Thompson

☙ WORSHIP AIDS ☙

Call to Worship: "O my Strength, I sing praise to you; you O God, are my fortress, my loving God" (Ps. 59:17, NIV).

Invocation: Lord God, we know the Risen Savior who ascended into glory will one day come again. Keep us ready, expectant, and watchful, for in such an hour as we know not, the Christ of the universe returns, as triumphant as when he left. Hallelujah! Amen—E. Lee Phillips

Offertory Sentence: "He said to them, 'Then give to Caesar what is Caesar's, and to God what is God's'" (Luke 20:25, NIV).

Offertory Prayer: Gracious Lord, we acknowledge your ownership over all the earth and we who live within it. With the Spirit's help, we confess our love and loyalty to you and, with the Spirit's help, dedicate these gifts to your eternal purpose. Through him who gave his life for us. Amen.

Morning Prayer: Lord Jesus, you are the Son. You were with God from the beginning. Through you he created all that we see. You possess the holiness and infinite nature of the Father. You are the exact imprint of his nature. Yet you humbled yourself and wrapped yourself inside our injured flesh. You were tried and tempted in every way that we were, but you remained holy and became a pleasing offering on our behalf.

You are the healer. You have shown your power since the beginning of time. Your hands formed the seas, and your mouth breathed life into all things. Your power continued when you came to earth and showed that the Kingdom of God had come. You healed the sick and raised the dead and motivated others to care for those that society looked down on.

You are the sacrifice. You were pierced for our transgressions and crushed for our iniquities. Although you possess all of the power, glory, and dominion of the Father, you made yourself a servant and lived a holy life, signifying that you were a pure and spotless offering to God. Your sacrifice made us clean, and your sacrifice continues to minister to us by the Holy Spirit who indwells us.

You are the priest. Now you are exalted at the right hand of God, making prayers and petitions on our behalf. You are the great high priest, and your ministry is powerful, greater than any other.

You are the warrior. One day you will return to judge the earth. You will not be the servant but a warrior king coming to judge the quick, the dead, and the entire creation. Your children wait eagerly for this day where all sin will be vanquished and victory will be yours forever. Amen.—Sky Howard

Benediction: Go forth today in the power of the Holy Spirit. May we be reminded that the church is the work of the Spirit—and that through God's Spirit we live and move and have our being. Holy Spirit, lead us. Amen.

SUNDAY, OCTOBER 30, 2011
Twentieth Sunday after Pentecost/Reformation Sunday

LECTIONARY SERMON TOPIC: "Accepting God's Challenge"

TEXT: Josh. 3:7–17

OTHER READINGS: Ps. 107:1–7, 33–37; 1 Thess. 2:9–13; Matt. 23:1–12

Twenty-five years ago, Wes Seeleger wrote a little book titled *Western Theology*.[4] Taking a clue from an earlier year of our country's history, he chose two contrasting images to help us clarify the issues: the settler spirit and the pioneer spirit. The settler spirit was quite satisfied with the conditions around him. He liked the lay of the land and the conditions of it. He was settled. The pioneer spirit, in contrast, was never quite settled. Adventure was his middle name. Without tending to judge the settler spirit in a negative way, it's not hard to see where the thrust of the biblical witness is. The book of Joshua is clear. God's people are a people on the move. They know that as they go, God goes with them—for God is on the move too. God is the great deity of the road.

---

[4]Wes Seeleger, *Western Theology* (Atlanta: Forum House, 1973).

I. **Their deepest desire was to enter the promised land.** It began as a glimmer of hope in Egypt. But now, after forty long years of wandering, their desire reached fever pitch. They stood on Jordan's stormy banks and cast a wishful eye into Canaan's fair and happy land. But standing between them and their desire was this river—one more time. They had fought the good fight, but had not yet finished the course. There was this river. By this time, the spring of the year, the snow cap of Mount Hermon had melted and caused the river to be at its highest. There were no bridges to cross, no ferries to ride, no shallow shoals to wade; only the deep and fear-laden waters of the Jordan. For a while, they surely believed they would never make it all the way home.

We have all been to that river, many times. Whenever one of the significant transitions of life comes, we feel all over what the ancient Hebrews felt. The river is there whenever we risk a new adventure. A marriage, a birth, a child on the way to school for the first time ever, a graduation, a career, a move, buying a home, aging, even death. Wherever fear is, there is that river.

II. **What then to do? How are we to cross the swollen river?** The Bible helps us here. Here is the word to God's pilgrim people. "When you see the ark of the covenant of the Lord your God, and the priests, the Levites, bearing it, then you shall set out from our place and go after it. Yet there shall be a space between you of about two thousand cubits. Do not come near it, that you may know the way by which you must go, for you have not passed this way before" (vv. 3–4).

The Ark of the Covenant was not an elaborate thing—only a simple wooden box, forty-five inches by twenty-seven inches. It got its significance for what it represented. Inside were a few of the relics from Israel's holy history: Moses' rod, some manna, but most of all the tablets of the Ten Commandments. The ark represented the presence of God among his people.

Then this: "When you see the ark being carried before you, set out and follow it." And in the end, beyond our reading, we learn how it ended. Verse 17 declares, "Then the priests who bore the ark of the covenant of the Lord stood firm on dry ground in the midst of the Jordan; and all Israel crossed over on dry ground, until all the people had crossed completely over the Jordan." Do you hear what it says? When God moves out ahead of us, we are to get up and go with God. That's how we face and cross the swollen rivers of life.

God is present with us. The Ark of the Covenant was the symbol of God's presence. It was built with rings along its sides into which poles were inserted for carrying it. It was ready at any moment to move. There was no static legalism here, as the Old Testament is often blamed with. The God of the covenant was on the move. It's a funny thing about the Ark of the Covenant. With as much significance put on it, you never hear about it after the Temple is built. Somehow the symbol of the times changed. Maybe that's why they were told to walk behind it two thousand cubits, almost a thousand yards. Don't get too attached to this thing. It's only going to be here for a while. When you enter the new land, a new faith will be required. The God you have known in the wilderness has something new and vital in store for you. Be ready for it.

III. **Where, then, is God moving among us?** All around us! In the renewed sense of commitment that so many of our people feel. In the vitality of our children. In the warmth of our fellowship. In the sense of "being" the family of faith. God is at work in the life of each Christian. If we stop long enough to listen, clear our minds of all the distractions, we'll find that God is near.

For us the journey extends in two directions. There is a journey inward. It is an intensely spiritual journey, not an easy journey, one that takes a long time (at least a lifetime), one that is not achieved without much prayer. It lays us bare before him with whom we have to do, so said the preacher in Hebrews. The inward journey provides depth of faith, strength of character, an inner resolve to be everything that God intends. There is also the journey outward. It is the life of service and ministry that flows out of the inward experience of grace. It is the natural overflow of abundant grace. Much like an artesian well, it flows freely from out of the depths, bubbling and effervescent. The journey inward provides depth; the journey outward provides fruitfulness. One may be theologically correct yet irrelevant to the world.

The first, the inward journey, defines who we are. The second, the journey outward, describes the work we accomplish. One without the other is a counterfeit Christianity. Our future is still open, available for God to develop and to bless. Tomorrow is not yet determined. "You've not passed this way before!" Opportunities for today will never come again.

IV. **A passion-driven faith is what it takes to claim the land beyond the river.** There is one other word in our text: Joshua said, "Sanctify yourselves, because tomorrow the Lord will do wonders among you" (v. 5). "Sanctify yourselves." What does that mean? For Israel, it may have meant certain ceremonial washing, certain sacrifices to be made on an altar. But, you know, outward expressions can have little to do with inward realities. And so today we talk about confessing of our sin, forgiveness, commitment, deciding within our heart of hearts, "I have decided to follow Jesus, no turning back, no turning back."

I wonder this morning, are we ready to move across the river? I think I hear the washing of many waters . . . and the shuffling of many feet. God, let it be so!—Lee McGlone

---

ILLUSTRATIONS

Passion. Someone wrote, "A wolf never attacks a painted sheep." A wolf is not fooled by fakery, even if it is good fakery. No one is fooled by counterfeit Christianity. Either we choose to be resolved in our work of mercy and redemption, service and ministry, journey inward, journey outward, or we don't.—Lee McGlone

Energy. One New Year's Day, in the Tournament of Roses parade, a beautiful float suddenly sputtered and quit. It was out of gas. The whole parade was held up until someone could get a can of gas. The amusing thing was this float represented the Standard Oil Company. With its vast oil resources, its truck was out of gas. Often, Christians neglect their spiritual maintenance, and though they are "clothed with power" (Luke 24:49) find themselves out of gas.—Steve Blankenship[5]

---

[5]Steve Blankenship, cited in Max Lucado, *God Came Near* (Portland, OR: Multnomah Press, 1987), p. 95.

Musical Selections Appropriate to the Day

Josh. 3:7–17	*Once to Every Man and Nation*
Ps. 107:1–7, 33–37	*Now Thank We All Our God*
1 Thess. 2:9–13	*Let It Be Said of Us*
Matt. 23:1–12	*In Christ Alone*

⮐ Children's Lectionary Sermon

TITLE: A Word That Works

SCRIPTURE: 1 Thess. 2:9–13

KEY VERSE: *You accepted what we said as the very word of God—which, of course, it is. And this word continues to work in you who believe.* (1 Thess. 2:13, NLT)

KEY CONCEPT: God's Word

MATERIALS: Bible

I want us to talk about work. Raise your hand if you want to tell me what your parent does when he or she goes to work. (*Call on several of the children. Talk about the action the job entails so that the children see that work is effort and action.*) You have shared some of the things your moms and dads do at work. They do actions, and those actions take effort. Work is something you do.

(*Open Bible.*) In 1 Thessalonians 2:13, Paul wrote, *You accepted what we said as the very word of God—which, of course, it is. And this word continues to work in you who believe.* The church this letter was written to had listened to Paul as he told them about Christ. They believed that the words he spoke were from God. Paul then tells them the Word of God was still working in them. These Christians suffered persecution from those around them. It took effort and action—work—to follow the Word of God.

So how and where do we hear the Word of God so that the Word can work in us? (*Let the children respond. Keep moving as necessary and treat it as a rhetorical question if the children are not responding.*) We hear God's Word as we read and listen to scripture. We might see the Word of God in the actions of others.

(*Give an example of something your church has done.*) The Word of God is action. We listen and we respond by doing loving actions in Jesus' name.

Let's pray that God's Word will work in us, leading us to listening and to doing loving actions.—Marcia Thompson

❧ WORSHIP AIDS ❧

Call to Worship: "Hear my cry, O God; listen to my prayer. From the ends of the earth I call to you, I call as my heart grows faint; lead me to the rock that is higher than I" (Ps. 61:1–2, NIV).

Invocation: Father, give us today a fresh experience of your grace. Help us express to you appropriate praise in psalms and hymns and spiritual songs, in the reading and preaching of your Word, and in the commitments of ourselves we make to you. Amen.

Offertory Sentence: "In everything I did I showed you that by this kind of hard work we must help the weak, remembering the words the Lord Jesus himself said: 'It is more blessed to give than to receive'" (Acts 20:35, NIV).

Offertory Prayer: Lord, teach us to serve you as you deserve. May we give cheerfully and without murmur. May our actions and attitudes reflect your grace alive with us. May we serve and give sacrificially and not expect reward—except in knowing that we are doing your will. Amen.

Morning Prayer: Our Father, we come before you again this day, grateful for your openness that welcomes us here. We need you, loving God, more than we need any other thing—more than the next breath of air, more than the next meal, more than rest, more than labor. Grant that as we come to you now, seeking you, that we shall find you.

Grant to each of your children the grace gifts you have planned for us today. You who own the cattle of a thousand hills, and the hills on which they stand, shower us with your care. Let your forgiveness wash over us and cleanse us of every sin. Where we are blinded by the care of this world, open our eyes that we may see. Where there is a troubled soul, give your gentle encouraging touch. If by chance there are some at the point of exhaustion, on the verge of despair, Lord place your strong hand upon their souls and help them through another day—and tomorrow—through another—and then through another . . . forever.

We love you, Lord, and we seek to do your will. Our love is not perfect—nor complete. We pray as did our Lord's disciples long ago, "Lord, increase our faith." May your hand of loving mercy guide us to seek you and your way for us. May your name be honored, and your people be strengthened. In Jesus' name. Amen.—Lee McGlone

Benediction: By the power and grace of God we go out with joy and with a decided intention to do God's will. May we allow his favor to rest upon us—and to be faithful in every opportunity for service that rises before us. Amen.

SUNDAY, NOVEMBER 6, 2011
Twenty-First Sunday after Pentecost/All Saints' Sunday

LECTIONARY SERMON TOPIC: "Being Children of God"
TEXT: 1 John 3:1–3
OTHER READINGS: (All Saints' Day) Rev. 7:9–17; Ps. 34:1–10, 22; Matt. 5:1–12; or (if not celebrating the day as All Saints' Sunday): Josh. 24:1–3a, 14–25; Ps. 78:1–7; 1 Thess. 4:13–18; Matt. 25:1–13

Phrenologists claim that they can tell what type of a person you are, or will be, by the bumps on your skull. Graphologists claim they can read your character through your handwriting. Physiognomists claim that they can read your character by the shape of your nose, the set of your jaw, the texture of your skin. These are complicated ways of judging a person's character. I suggest a quicker method. Find out the consuming passion of a person's life. What is his or her greatest love? Is it the love of money? Then no matter what the subject of the conversation, it will come back to money matters over and again. Or is it love of gossip? Then it will show on the face. Eyes will sparkle at some spicy comment that causes conflict for another. Truth is, everyone takes on something of the countenance of the thing he or she loves most. That is why faith is so important.

I. **Identity, personhood, being—these are central themes in the text that stands before us, and themes of great need in our world today.** Our identity, our true personhood all begins with God. God's love has made us who and what we are. John says, "See what love the Father has given us, that we should be called children of God; and that is what we are." For John there can be no greater status, no finer identity, than being named by God through his love as children of God. As the writer goes on to explain, our identity, our true personhood is inseparable from how we live as Christians.

Those of us who are parents know how the identities of our children grow out of our relationship with them. Children, especially when they are young, love to imitate their parents. They often try to talk and act the same way they see their parents talking and acting. As we all know, this can be a humbling as well as inspiring experience for us—for our children pick up both our bad and good habits.

II. **John says that the same is true for us.** Our identity, says John, is influenced by fixing our lives on Christ. As children of God, we become more Christlike by following or imitating Christ's words and actions. One of the words John uses in this passage to highlight the importance of our identity being rooted in Christ is the word *see.* In verse 1 he says, "*see* what love the Father has given us." Then in verse 2 he says, "What we do know is this: when he [that is Christ] is revealed, we will be like him, for we will *see* him as he is." And again, in verse 6 he says, "No one who abides in him sins; no one who sins has either *seen* him or known him." For John, how we Christians *see* Christ is very important. Why is this so? Well, many biblical scholars believe that one of the groups that were influencing John's faith community was the Gnostics. They were teaching something very different about Jesus than what John was teaching. The Gnostics believed that matter, and therefore the human body, was not important. The soul, however, was really important. Therefore, the way one lived in this world really was not relevant, since matter and the body had no influence on the soul. A person could do whatever he or she pleased; whether it was good or bad it made no difference. Therefore, for the Gnostics, Jesus really did not come as the Savior to suffer and die on a cross for our sins.

John responds to this Gnostic view by emphasizing that Jesus did come into the world to suffer and die for our sins, and that what we do with our physical bodies does matter. Therefore, John instructed his community not to follow the example of what they *see* in the Gnostics. Rather, follow the example they see in Christ. "You know that he [that is Christ] was revealed to take away sins, and in him there is no sin. No one who abides in him sins; no one who sins has either seen him or known him. Little children, let no one deceive you. Everyone who does what is right is righteous, just as he [that is Christ] is righteous."

III. **John is not saying that we no longer sin.** He is saying that everyone who is a child of God will be influenced by Christ's love and grace. Thus, that influence of Christ will change their hearts, minds, and lives. The influence of Christ alters one's will . . . so we are able to do what is right. Christ makes us aware of the harmfulness and destructiveness of our sin. We are then free to do what is right.

An image on film is latent. It requires development to draw out the picture. We too have potential as children of God. However, we need development and the proper process to make it plain and usable. We are, for as long as we live, works in progress. The work of the Holy Spirit in us and through us is always ongoing—so we continue to grow in our journey of faith as children of God. Discipleship is rooted in discipline.

So today, here is both a call to repentance and a word of grace. It is a call to repentance in that as followers of Christ we are to have an open attitude, a willingness to be corrected, and the courage to change our ways when we engage in destructive behaviors. It is a word of grace because it reminds us of the dignity and high status we're given as children of God. With the Holy Spirit's help, we are able to live out our true identity by following Christ's perfect example.—Lee McGlone

ILLUSTRATIONS

Perfection. While playing a piece for my piano teacher, I missed a note. She asked that I play it again. I missed the same note again. She chastised me and suggested that I kept playing the wrong note because that was the way I had practiced it all week. It was a sharp and not a flat, and I should mark it with a pencil. If I continued to play it wrong, she said, it would sound normal and would be difficult ever to change. I learned from that experience that what we do, even when it is wrong, if done repeatedly becomes normal . . . and is hard ever to change. There is an old saying that practice makes perfect. Practice only makes permanent.—Lee McGlone

Modeling. Parents often serve as role models for their children. I recall standing in our kitchen talking with my wife prior to an evening meal. I had leaned back against the counter, folded my arms across my chest, and informally crossed my legs. Somewhere in the course of our conversation, I noticed something. Our youngest son, perhaps three years old at the time, was standing at my side—laid back against the cabinet, arms folded and legs crossed. I was stunned. This little boy was imitating his dad. What a humbling thought! He wanted to be like me.—Lee McGlone

Musical Selections Appropriate to the Day

Revelation 7:9–17	*Be Still, My Soul*
Ps. 34:1–10, 22	*Stand Up and Bless the Lord*
1 John 3:1–3	*Children of the Heavenly Father*
Matt. 5:1–12	*Blest Are They*

❧ Children's Lectionary Sermon

TITLE: Working for Peace

SCRIPTURE: Matt. 5:1–12

KEY VERSE: *God blesses those who work for peace, for they will be called the children of God.* (Matt. 5:9, NLT)

KEY CONCEPT: Peace

MATERIALS: Bible, newspaper clippings that show both peaceful and nonpeaceful events

PREPARATION: During the week, check the newspaper for articles and pictures that show both peaceful and nonpeaceful events. You might even search in online papers for these.

Do you know what peace is like? (*Let the children respond, and help as needed.*) Peace can be described as calm, harmony, and freedom from war. I brought some news articles I want to show you. As we look at these, I want you to tell me if it represents peace or not peace. (*Show the children the various articles you have that represent peace and those that don't represent peace. Make sure to mix them up. Talk about why each represents a peaceful or nonpeaceful situation.*) There are so many ways people can help make peace, and there are many people who live without peace.

(*Open Bible.*) In our gospel lesson from Matthew 5, Jesus was teaching his disciples about God's blessings. In verse 9, it reads, *God blesses those who work for peace, for they will be called the children of God.* Peace is something we all like. People are at peace when they have calm and harmony in their lives. There are many places around the world where people don't have peace, and we can pray for this to change.

We can also work for peace right here where we live. What are some ways you can work for peace at home or at school? (*Let the children respond, and reflect back their answers.*) When we help others who might have less than us, we bring some calm into their lives. We bring peace. (*Give some examples of things your church family has done in the community and tie it into the peace idea.*)

Let's pray that God will help us be people who work for peace.—Marcia Thompson

WORSHIP AIDS

Call to Worship: "Because your love is better than life, my lips will glorify you" (Ps. 63:3, NIV).

Invocation: Father, teach us today that perfect peace is found in your will. Come to us in this hour that we may experience your presence again. Speak tenderly, yet clearly and powerfully, your word to us. Having heard your word, may we be not only attentive but also obedient. Amen.

Offertory Sentence: "The earth is the Lord's, and everything in it, the world and all who live in it" (Ps. 24:1, NIV).

Offertory Prayer: Father, giver of all things good and proper, source of peace and love, bless these tithes and offerings given in your name for the work of the gospel. Strengthen our resolves to more accurately reflect Jesus' love— to the end that our witness, by word and deed, will draw many into the family of faith. Amen.

Morning Prayer: (Prayer on Ps. 19) The law of the Lord is perfect. Righteous Judge, teach us to be a church that understands your calling. Righteous Judge, help us to daily follow in your path toward righteousness. Righteous Judge, allow your laws to be the catalyst for converting our souls.

The testimony of the Lord is sure. Lord, let us be a beacon of your love in such a dark world. Lord, allow us to be a church that is a safe haven for those who hurt. Lord, reveal your abounding glory to the meek and weary through our hands and feet.

The statutes of the Lord are right. King Jesus, give us the wisdom and courage to stand strong for what we believe. King Jesus, place your ambassadors in necessary governmental and national leadership positions. King Jesus, let our desire to follow your precepts be the delight of our hearts.

The commandment of the Lord is pure. Deliverer, reveal to our eyes the beauty in honoring your will. Deliverer, make us a church that unwaveringly sticks to your commandments even in the darkest times. Deliverer, raise up a new generation of believers knowledgeable of your death, burial, and Resurrection.

The fear of the Lord is clean. Master, make us a church full of reverent fear for your name. Master, show us your glory. Master, let our hands and feet be muddy for doing your work and clean with your righteousness. Amen.
—Jarrett Davis

Benediction: Let us go forth today strengthened in our resolve to be faithful followers of Jesus Christ. In the days of this new week, may we speak his name often and lovingly. And may our spiritual gifts be utilized in work of the Kingdom. Amen.

SUNDAY, NOVEMBER 13, 2011
Twenty-Second Sunday after Pentecost

LECTIONARY SERMON TOPIC: "God at Work in Human Affairs"

TEXT: Ps. 76

OTHER READINGS: Judg. 4:1–7; Ps. 123; 1 Thess. 5:1–11; Matt. 25:14–30

Do you wonder where life, and the world in general, are going? We live in what seems to be, at least occasionally, a terrifying age. We read the daily papers, hear the nightly news, join in barbershop conversation . . . and declare, "Oh my, how could they? Why did they do that? What is the world coming to?" And then we sense that such a declaration of despair stands squarely opposed to our worldview—that is, to our faith-view of the world. The psalmist, I think, felt the same quandary. We can learn from him.

I. **Here is a psalm by Asaph the Seer.** The heart of the psalm is in verse 10: "Surely the wrath of man shall praise you, the remainder of wrath you shall restrain." God uses the wrath of mankind, but the surplus or excess of it he restrains. God brings good out of our worst efforts, and then contains his radical judgment on what abides. Let's note how the psalmist approaches this theme. We are reassured that God moves among his people: "In Judah he is known." Judah, the most influential of the tribes, was the seat of political power for the entire nation. God was active where the decisions were made. But not only was God "known" in the nation, he was also "knowing" in the nation. Herein lies the assurance we so need. We may surely wonder, after endless hours of viewing C-Span's coverage of the U.S. Congress, if anyone knows what is going on. But faith's claim is sure: God knows.

II. **Here is the promise we need to hear: God dwells among his people.** God not only moves among his people but also dwells among them. He tabernacled with them as they passed through the Exodus wilderness. Jesus promised to be where two or three are gathered together in his name. Therein is our strength: gathered together in unity . . . and empowered by his presence in our midst. Catch this image: we are together moving forward in the enterprise of God's Kingdom, united in purpose, intent on fidelity, assured of victory, walking side by side with the Master, and glad to be a part of the great work God is doing. Someday when I die, one of the great hymns of the faith we will sing at my funeral is "We're Marching to Zion." It declares beautifully and clearly the hope we share.

God has promised to be present with his people in the land that is fairer than day, the one that by faith we shall see from afar, just beyond the river. But he is also with his gathered people now. Your lives are testimony to God's presence. In times of distress, in the hospital, in the cemetery, in those times of heartache, you have risen up to declare the presence of God with you. I've heard many of you declare it: "I don't know how we got through it all. Surely God gave us strength beyond our own. Surely God was with us!" Yes, you and the psalmist agree. God dwells among his people.

III. **But look further. The psalmist develops the theme:** "The stouthearted are spoiled, they have slept their sleep, and none of the men of might have found their hands." What we consider to be strength and prowess are useless when rendered so by God. So what of our high technology? What of our sophisticated weaponry? What of our advanced political agendas? All can one day be rendered useless—but God is still the abiding force in human affairs. Perhaps the day may hasten when we shall be surprised at what "technology" God has. He who set the universe in motion is still working in it.

Here is the psalmist's teaching: we struggle for our brief life and then go to sleep. The stout of heart are no longer stout. They simply "go to sleep"—the sleep of death. The men of might can no longer find their hands—that is, their strength—any more than the stouthearted can find their spirit. They have lost their influence in the world. The great men and mighty ideas are smoldering in the decay of some grave somewhere. But God is forever. And God is still at work in human affairs.

IV. **Note the prophetic language used in the song:** "You are more glorious and excellent than the 'Mountains of Prey.'" Invaders, from Assyria in particular, besieged the cities of Judah and became rich with mountains of spoil. But all the world, the psalmist assures us, will know when God rises to judge. Think about our world today and how rapidly things have happened in the past few years, which we could never have imagined only a few years ago. Slavery, an accepted economic and social essential only 150 years ago, is now understood as the evil that it was. Women have the right to vote. Laborers have unions. The Soviet Union no longer exists. The Berlin Wall came tumbling down. The nations are being confronted at every turn with a demand for human rights. We elected our nation's first African American president—and some thought it would never happen. The mountains of prey are still coming down. God is at work in his world.

God turned the evil actions of Joseph's brother into something good. Hatred in Pharaoh's heart made life hard for the Israelite captives, but God brought up Moses to bring them out under God's mighty hand. What looked like simply another Roman execution on the hill called Golgotha gave way to the mighty act of Easter—very early in the morning on the first day of the week—bringing salvation to all the nations. Hear it again: "Surely the wrath of mankind shall praise you, the remainder of wrath you shall restrain." Thank you, dearest God, for your gracious love that restrains us from the most hurtful of our intentions. Help us to know, way down deep, that you are still in control . . . and that your purposes for us and the world you will bring to pass.—Lee McGlone

ILLUSTRATIONS

Justice. Read the account in 2 Kings 10:35 where Sennacherib is approaching Jerusalem. It seemed that Israel was only history. Everybody seemed sure that Israel would be wiped out. But to the surprise of all, when Sennacherib gathered his armies around the city, the angel of the Lord went out at night and destroyed the camp. In the morning, 185,000 lay dead—and Israel's army had not picked up a sword. The angel of the Lord did it. I will not conjecture that this is a teaching about the sanctity of Israel. I will not suggest that Israel has liberty to disregard the sanctity of other nations and peoples around it. But we can rest assured, in looking at the larger picture of all things, that the psalmist is right. God cannot be ignored. God does move in the tide of human affairs— and as others have said, "like a great arc stretching out across eternity . . . bending toward justice." Amen!—Lee McGlone

Human Will. A young man meets a young woman. They are immediately attracted to one another. They both say to themselves, "Now there is someone I'd like to marry." At that point, if the emotions had their way, there would be a wedding. But the intellect intervenes, questioning the impulsive emotional response. Would we be compatible? What is she really like? Can I afford to support her? Both conclude it would be better to take some more time and answer a few questions before they proceed. So the two begin spending more time with each other. He eventually concludes that she is as beautiful on the inside as she is on the outside. Now his intellect has sided with the emotions on the idea of marriage. But the final and heaviest vote remains to be cast— that of the will. It stops the march toward the altar with the questions, "Am I willing to give up this lifestyle for another? What about my freedom—is it worth the trade? Am I willing to assume the added responsibility?" The marriage will occur only when the will finally agrees with the emotions and the intellect. And so it is in coming to Christ.—Jim Peterson[1]

Musical Selections Appropriate to the Day

Judges 4:1–7	*Faith Is the Victory*
Ps. 123 or Ps. 76	*Worthy of Worship*
1 Thess. 5:1–11	*Living Stones*
Matt. 25:14–30	*We Give Thee but Thine Own*

---

[1]Jim Peterson, *Living Proof* (Colorado Springs, CO: NavPress, 1989), p. 170.

❧ Children's Lectionary Sermon

TITLE: Cheering for One Another

SCRIPTURE: 1 Thess. 5:1–11

KEY VERSE: *So encourage each other and build each other up, just as you are already doing.* (1 Thess. 5:11, NLT)

KEY CONCEPT: Encouraging one another

MATERIALS: Bible, pom-poms, poster board

PREPARATION: On the poster board, write the cheer included in the sermon. You may want to practice the cheer in advance. If you have access to pom-poms, you can use them to make the cheer even more effective.

(*Come out very excited, shaking the pom-poms.*) I am so excited to be with each of you today. In fact, I am so excited, I want us to do a cheer together. I have it written here on this poster, and I want us to cheer for each other. (*Have the children stand. Place the poster where the children can see the words. Move around and place your hand on the head of the child you are cheering and keep it going until everyone has been cheered.*)

"Clap your hands (*clap three times*). Stomp your feet (*stomp three times*). [Insert name] can't be beat. Go [insert name]!" Now I would like you to sit down for a moment. Did you like being cheered? (*Let the children respond.*) It can make us feel good when others give us a cheer. (*Open Bible.*) In Thessalonians 5:11, Paul asked the Christians to encourage each other. He wrote, *So encourage each other and build each other up, just as you are already doing.* It is like cheering each other instead of saying things that are hurtful. It is cheering each other to do those things that please God.

Let's ask God to make us be encouragers of each other.—Marcia Thompson

❧ WORSHIP AIDS ❧

Call to Worship: "My soul finds rest in God alone; my salvation comes from him" (Ps. 62:1, NIV).

Invocation: Lord, you have called us to be your people—and we gladly are! We exist in order to bring honor and glory to your Holy Name. We are your witnesses in this world. Strengthen us today with your Spirit's power that we may be all that you intend us to be. Open our hearts to receive the fullness of your grace. Amen.

Offertory Sentence: "For none of us lives to himself alone and none of us dies to himself alone" (Rom. 14:7, NIV).

Offertory Prayer: Gracious Father, you have often delivered us from our troubles and shown us the path of light in a dark world. You have given to us material gifts that meet our needs—and far beyond our needs. We praise your goodness, not in words alone but also in the giving of tithes and offerings. Amen.

Morning Prayer: Our Father, we acknowledge with joy and steadfast faith that the earth is your creation, that we are your handiwork, that life is your gift. Grant, our Father, that we may so think of your loveliness that we may grow into your likeness. Teach us the meaning of grace—that it is to love in the presence of hatred, to forgive in the face of slander, to celebrate life even in death, to be bearers of light in a world often filled with darkness. We pray this morning for the fulfillment of your purposes in our lives. Encourage us never to yield to lesser goals. Keep our minds on the prize of the high calling of Christ among us. For our youth, encourage them in their high aspirations to make the world a better place. For our parents, grant increased faith and much wisdom that we may lovingly guide our sons and daughters. May in all things your will and way have the place of highest supremacy among us. Through Christ we pray. Amen.—Lee McGlone

Benediction: The world stands before us as an open door. Let us go out into it, and into all the opportunities that await us this week, energized by the presence of our God, Father, Son, and Holy Spirit. And may God's peace be with you. Amen.

SUNDAY, NOVEMBER 20, 2011
Christt the King Sunday

LECTIONARY SERMON TOPIC: "What Christ Offers the Faithful"
TEXT: Eph. 1:15–23
OTHER READINGS: Ezek. 34:11–16, 20–24; Ps. 100; Matt. 25:31–46

Paul opens his heart to the believers in Ephesus. He tells them how he will pray for them—that is, that which lay at the bottom of his heart. Listen to his tenderness: "I have heard of your faith in the Lord Jesus and your love toward all the saints, and for this reason I do not cease to give thanks for you as I remember you in my prayers" (vv. 15–16). And this: "I never stop giving thanks for you." And this: *"You are my joy and my crown."* A church alive in the Spirit and walking in the love of Christ is surely a joy to God. To such faithful folks, the apostle pointed to the assurances they possessed.

I. **Because of Christ, we are people of hope:** "I pray that the eyes of your heart may be enlightened, so that you may know what is the hope of His calling, what are the riches of the glory of His inheritance in the saints" (Eph. 1:17–18). "Enlightenment" is Paul's prayer for the church at Ephesus. This is surely not the same enlightenment defined by the Gnostic heresy but rather the authentic illumination of the believer's life through the experience of Christ. He prays for spiritual growth as foundational to the hope that stands before us.

Spiritual growth comes to believers as we come to know Jesus Christ and to walk with him in a personal way. Facts are important, but facts are not the full experience of God within us. There is a difference between *knowing about* and *knowing* God. It is the distinction between the two that serves to propel the believer to the "hope of his calling." Out of the daily experience of Christ, we face the future on tiptoe. We anticipate and joyfully celebrate what God is doing now . . . and what God will do in the tomorrows.

II. **Because of Christ, we are people of power.** "[A]nd what is the surpassing greatness of His power toward us who believe. These are in accordance with the working of the strength of His might which He brought about in Christ, when He raised Him from the dead, and seated Him at His right hand in the heavenly places" (vv. 19–20).

It is difficult to overstate the phrase "the surpassing greatness of His power." We might try, for example, "super mega power," but even that does not quite get it. This is the power, Paul says, that God used in raising Christ from the dead and that brought about the reality pointed to in the creed, when it is affirmed that Christ is "seated at the right hand of God the Father Almighty."

One of the great issues in our world today is the sense that people feel powerless. We have not really begun to understand what the real intent of faith for our lives and for our church is all about until we come together as a church in God's power to carry out our mission in the world around us. We are called to be salt and light, to give witness to God's mighty power to bring about justice, hope, and love. Yet it is more than clear that none of this can take place within our own strength. It is when we are in touch with and energized by the power of God that is intended to work within us that we begin to sense the possibility of changing the world around us.

In some ways, Paul points to the fact that this power of God that can work within us is not something ordinary. He prays for the Church continually that we will have the spiritual knowledge it takes to be the powerful church of God.

III. **Because of Christ, we are people of victory.** ". . . far above all rule and authority and power and dominion, and every name that is named, not only in this age, but also in the one to come. And He put all things in subjection under His feet, and gave Him as head over all things to the church" (vv. 21–22). These thoughts take us back to one of the central themes in all of scripture, namely, *God's people live under the power of a divine promise that no matter how long the road may seem or how dark the night may appear to be, God's victory over all unrighteousness is certain.*

We live under the promise of the Resurrection, the power of God within the community of faith, and the affirmation that "all things" have been put under the feet of Christ, who is "head over all [things] to the church." It is the certainty of God's victory in the long term that powers our life of faith in the short term.

IV. **Because of Christ, we are a people of fullness**. ". . . which is His body, the fullness of Him who fills all in all." We need to untangle this a bit, but the heart of this short verse of scripture is that Jesus Christ brings fullness—that is, completeness and full maturity—to our lives as God intended them to be. *But*—this is directed at the Church, the family of faith, the people of God. This is not a "Jesus and me" kind of individualistic fulfillment that would imply that God's greatest concern is that I live a happy and comfortable life.

The New Testament vision of a church that is healthy and whole, a church where people may discover the fullness of Christ, is a church that is self-consciously bound together as the Body of Christ. This is a church where Christ is the head—and not in name only. This is not something that comes about because we hang a mission statement in the halls of the church building or open with prayer at church board meetings. This is Christ as head of the church as evidenced by our openness to God, to each other, and to the cries of a broken world. It is something people know by experiencing our life together and not something they read in our newsletter.

One of the reasons we don't experience the fullness of Christ in the church these days is that we have too low a view of the church. It is seen by too many as just another social grouping. We will gain the power God has for us when we regain a very high sense of the Church as the Body of Christ and ourselves as intimately woven together in a fabric of faithful community. Perhaps it would help to recenter ourselves on Paul's words in Eph. 5:25: "Christ loved the church and gave himself up for her."

The Apostle Paul's prayer actually opens up God's design for the church. In Jesus Christ we have hope, in him we have power, in him we have victory, and in him we have fullness.—Lee McGlone

---

ILLUSTRATIONS

Heaven. We know very little about heaven, but I once heard a theologian describe it as "an unknown region with a well-known inhabitant," and there is not a better way to think of it than that. Richard Baxter expresses the thought in these lines:

> My knowledge of that life is small,
> The eye of faith is dim,
> But it's enough that Christ knows all,
> And I shall be with him.

To those who have learned to love and trust Jesus, the prospect of meeting him face to face and being with him forever is the hope that keeps us going, no matter what life may throw at us.—James Packer[2]

Grace. How does one define the goodness that is God's grace? The classic definition is "the unmerited favor of God." Philip Yancey says it more simply: "Grace means there is nothing we can do to make God love us more . . . and there is nothing we can do to make God love us less"[3] My own definition? "Grace is God's loving disposition toward all of us all the time."

Jesus did not just talk about grace; he lived it. When he healed a blind man or a man with a withered hand or a woman with a blood disease or a demon-possessed boy, he was demonstrating God's disposition toward people. When he spoke in public to a woman of questionable character, touched lepers, and hung out with publicans and sinners, he was showing God's disposition toward all of us all of the time. In the midst of his greatest act of grace, while he was suffering on the cross, he paused to pardon the thief—grace upon grace.—Lee McGlone

Musical Selections Appropriate to the Day

Ez. 34:11–16, 20–24	*Savior, Like a Shepherd Lead Us*
Ps. 100	*All People That on Earth Do Dwell*
Eph. 1:15–23	*Bless His Holy Name*
Matt. 25:31–46	*The Power of the Cross*

---

[2]James Packer, *Your Father Loves You* (Colorado Springs, CO: Harold Shaw, 1986), pp. 72–73.
[3]Philip Yancey, *What's So Amazing About Grace?* (Grand Rapids, MI: Zondervan, 1997), p. 57.

❧ Children's Lectionary Sermon

TITLE: Real Joy

SCRIPTURE: Ps. 100

KEY VERSES: *Shout with joy to the Lord, all the earth! Worship the Lord with gladness. Come before him, singing with joy.* (Ps. 100:1–2, NLT)

KEY CONCEPT: Joy

MATERIALS: Bible

PREPARATION: Choose a praise song that is familiar to your congregation to use at the end of the sermon.

I want us to start with a question this morning. What do you get really excited about? (*Let the children respond. You may get a variety of answers, such as Christmas, birthdays, or other special occasions. Talk about why these are so exciting.*) We get excited about lots of different things like birthdays, Christmas, parties, and being out of school. (*Adjust according to what the children share.*) Real excitement or something we are thrilled about can be called joy.

In our scripture lesson from the Psalms, the writer wrote a song about real joy. (*Open Bible.*) In Psalm 100:1–2 it says, *Shout with joy to the Lord, all the earth! Worship the Lord with gladness. Come before him, singing with joy.* The psalmist felt excitement, even thrill to come to worship God. It was an overwhelming gladness to come before God and to praise God. Worshipping God together should be just as exciting as all those special things we talked about earlier. I want us to sing a praise song with all the joy we have, because God loves us so much, and we have so much to be thankful for.

(*Sing praise song here.*) Let's ask God to help us always worship with a joyful spirit.—Marcia Thompson

❧ WORSHIP AIDS ❧

Call to Worship: "My salvation and my honor depend on God; he is my mighty rock, my refuge" (Ps. 62:7, NIV).

Invocation: Lord, you have called us to be your people. We exist in order to bring honor and glory to your Holy Name. Strengthen us today with your Spirit's power that we may be all that you intend us to be. Open our hearts to receive the fullness of your grace. Amen.

Offertory Sentence: "The Lord said to Moses, 'Tell the Israelites to bring me an offering. You are to receive the offering for me from each man whose heart prompts him to give'" (Exod. 25:1–2, NIV).

Offertory Prayer: Generous God, let our worship this day rise out of thanksgiving and praise that in the midst of our plenty we may give generously where need is fact, and faith in Christ is essential. Amen.—E. Lee Phillips

Morning Prayer: Because of the cross of Christ, we are called again to witness your love exemplified, and we cannot remain immune to such a mighty display of sacrifice for us. Thus we lift our voices in praise and adoration in the presence of your holiness, knowing that there is something in us that cries for the expression of awe and wonder and thanksgiving. In all about us we see the handiwork of your caring and grace. Only callousness on our part would refuse worship of the one who ever abides with us and creates for us and dies to express eternal love to us. As we bow here in prayer, help us try to pray. Please, kind sir, be responsive to the deep needs of our lives even as you are responsive to the cravings of our souls, which we cannot find words to express. Meet the restlessness in our lives that cannot be stilled until it finds solution in you. Search deeply our struggling questions and bring them to resolution through your truth. Hear our deepest weeping, stirred by life's losses and pains and problems, and soothe our aching hearts even as you turn weeping to joy, loss to gain, and problems to possibilities. In the quiet of these sacred moments, grant us the balm of your peace in our hearts even as you call us to come to the restoring fountain of your gracious salvation for our very lives and souls. Amen.—Henry Fields

Benediction: We know that to whom much is given, much is required; therefore may we take our many blessings and fashion from them gifts of generosity and sacrifice—to the honor of our Creator.—E. Lee Phillips

SUNDAY, NOVEMBER 27, 2011
First Sunday in Advent

LECTIONARY SERMON TOPIC: "Are You Getting Ready for Christmas?"
TEXT: Mark 13:24–37
OTHER READINGS: Isa. 64:1–9; Ps. 80:1–7, 17–19; 1 Cor. 1:3–9

Are you getting ready for Christmas? Surely our city prepares spectacularly. Wreathes hang on lampposts, lights blink in windows, a Salvation Army quartet sings "Joy to the World" at our four corners. And as we hear of newspapers struggling for ads, there appears even yet a ton of Christmas advertising spilling across our living room floors. I'm convinced some stores skipped Halloween and aimed directly at the Christmas jugular. No doubt, more than one person here finished Thanksgiving dinner, gulped and exclaimed, "Good grief, I've not given a thought to Christmas." This next month brings with it many moods: it triggers hopes, immerses us in memories, floods us with sentimentality. We spend much of these coming weeks getting ready for Christmas.

I. **Amid all this Christmas commerce and fantasy, the New Testament reminds us again of the hope at the root of all our frenzied activity.** In that striking passage we read a moment ago, Mark himself, writing amid violent, brutal, desperate circumstances, assures us we still live by the promise of a new age. Mark proclaims to us that though we may suffer the threats of war, economic dislocation; though we may undergo the grief of dreams gone awry, relationships turned sour, love gone down the drain, we still live by the confidence of a new world, a new human community rooted and grounded in healing, reconciliation, and peace. Indeed, the New Testament affirms that we not only look forward to a healed world but also that in the birth of Jesus Christ, the first taste, the "green shoots" of our anticipation, the whiff of what we might call God's Christmas world sneaks in among us.

II. **Do you believe that?** Do you trust the promise of the new world the anticipated Christ child bears? I suspect that some of us find it hard. These

Advent days can bring as much cynicism as hope among us. At this time of year, perhaps more so than at any other, we recognize the vast chasm between the way we run the world and the way God wants it. The faces of the poor and the hungry; the tragedy of dissolving families; the isolated elderly; the threats to our livelihood and future from a precarious economy; the terrible divisions and hatreds fueled by nationalism, greed, and religion; the specter of armies slaughtering one another in the Afghan mountains—all of this seems even more grotesquely depicted against the brilliant light thrown by the Advent-Christmas promise.

III. **And yet—and yet we gather here this morning not as a community of despair, not as a gang of cynics, nor as a company of the forlorn about the future.** We gather in Advent as a community of hope! Come war or recession, we know Christmas comes, too. We bet our lives finally on the deeper realities of joy, peace, and Christmas promises. So get ready, Mark insists. Get ready for that new age of grace and reconciliation by doing the deeds of the Christmas world right now. That new world will come, he promises; live every moment, every day as an opportunity for its final breakthrough.

IV. **Live every moment, every day as a chance for a Christmas world breakthrough?** Indeed, obeying Mark, how get ready for Christmas? At least two ways, I think.

The first lies inevitably in a decisive ethical tilt. Desmond Tutu offers us a reminder. "The heart of the Gospel," he writes, "is precisely that God, the all holy One, the all powerful One is also the One full of mercy and compassion. He is not a neutral God inhabiting some inaccessible Mount Olympus. He is a God who cares about his children, and cares enormously for the weak, the poor, the naked, the downtrodden, the despised. He takes their side not because they are good, since many of them are demonstrably not so. He takes their side because he is that kind of God, and they have no one else to champion them."[4] We get ready for Christmas by striving to live by that conviction.

---

[4]Desmond Tutu, quoted in Naomi Tutu, *The Words of Desmond Tutu* (New York: Newmarket Press, 1989), p. 26.

And second, on a more personal and immediate level, getting ready for Christmas means accepting and offering the surprises of love. It means opening ourselves and opening others to the oblique and joyful possibilities of life. Get ready, Mark insists, for a surprise. A surprise! Like the gifts in that wacky little song, "The Twelve Days of Christmas." Remember? On the first day of Christmas, my true love gave to me—a partridge in a pear tree." A PARTRIDGE IN A PEAR TREE! *That*, from our true love? Not so bad, says Halford Luccock in a marvelous little essay about the startling surprise packed in that bizarre gift. "People," Luccock writes, "have been singing about that partridge in a pear tree for seven hundred years; would they sing about a floor-mop from Tru-valu hardware, or wool socks from Filene's Basement? Not on your life. Our gift giving shows no imagination," he says.[5] On their twenty-fifth anniversary, a husband will give his wife a vacuum cleaner or a Mix-Master; she'll give him a lawnmower or hedge clippers. So friends, on this first Sunday in Advent, are you getting ready for Christmas? I hope so. Be prepared to stand for all the hope in God's creation. To hope and, yes, to serve as a messenger of loving surprise, allowing your kindness to ramble around as you wait, as you watch, as you make ready for the breaking in of God's Christmas world. Yea! O come, O come, Emmanuel!—James Crawford

---

ILLUSTRATIONS

Advent Surprise. Take a suggestion for your shopping list. Give your true love a surprising inappropriate gift. Don't get grandma another lace cap or pair of woolen mittens. She has plenty already, and besides she hates the things. Get her a little bottle of Chanel No. 5 or a set of lipsticks or a pair of dancing slippers. That will boost her morale, make her feel she is still alive. As you reach for that fine book for your beloved pastor, that learned tome, *Archaeology and the Bible*, stay your hand. Reach over to the next counter and get him the *New*

---

[5]Halford Luccock, *A Sprig of Holly* (New York: Pilgrim Press, 1978), p. 87.

Yorker Book of Cartoons. There will be several cartoons by Peter Arno, highly inappropriate for the clergy. . . . And for your true love—well that has me stumped as usual. How about a -er- ah—Oh well, how about a partridge in a pear tree? It would be a surprise. Indeed, like a babe in a Bethlehem manger.—Halford Luccock[6]

A Courageous Response. Having heard the call of God upon her life, Mary replied, "I am your servant. Let it be unto me according to your word." These are dangerous words, but absolutely necessary words for the searching disciple. When God speaks our names, "Mary," "Moses," "Samuel," "Paul," the situation is getting intensely personal. God surely knows who we are, far better than we know ourselves—and where we are. But the courageous response is always our choice to make. Mary declared, "Let it be unto me according to your word." Moses said, "Here am I." Samuel spoke, "Your servant hears." Paul cried out, "Lord, what will you have me do?" They made themselves available to God—and took the risk of faith. When we respond to God's voice, we are taking a chance.—Lee McGlone

Musical Selections Appropriate to the Day

Isa. 64:1–9	*As a Fire Is Meant for Burning*
Ps. 80:1–7, 17–19	*O Come, O Come, Emmanuel*
1 Cor. 1:3–9	*Come, Thou Long Expected Jesus*
Mark 13:24–37	*Wake, Awake, for Night Is Flying*

Children's Lectionary Sermon

TITLE: Worth the Wait

SCRIPTURE: 1 Cor. 1:3–9

---

[6]Halford Luccock, *A Sprig of Holly* (New York: Pilgrim Press, 1978), p. 9.

KEY VERSE: *Therefore you do not lack any spiritual gift as you eagerly wait for our Lord Jesus Christ to be revealed.* (1 Cor. 1:7, NIV).
KEY CONCEPT: Hope
MATERIALS: Bible, wrapped box with removable lid or a Christmas gift bag (box or bag will be used for all Advent sermons)
PREPARATION: Wrap a shoebox and lid separately.

Today is the first Sunday in Advent. Advent is a special time of waiting and hoping. Sometimes it can be very hard to wait during this Christmas season. We are so full of excitement and hope that we feel as though we are going to burst! We look forward to celebrating Jesus' birthday, and we just can't wait for all our special Christmas traditions. One thing we look forward to at Christmas is exchanging gifts. I brought a gift box with me today. (*Show wrapped box.*) If this box had your name on it, what would you hope was inside? (*Take time to listen to the children's answers.*) Those are some exciting things to wait and hope for.

At Christmas, we remember that Jesus came to us a baby. We look forward to giving and receiving gifts. But did you know that there is something even more that we are waiting and hoping for? (*Open Bible.*) The Bible says, *Therefore you do not lack any spiritual gift as you eagerly wait for our Lord Jesus Christ to be revealed.* Christians are eagerly waiting for Jesus to come again someday! God's own Son came to us long ago, and God's own Son is coming to us again. This Christmas season, let's remember that we have something worth waiting for. Better yet, let's remember that we have some*one* worth waiting for. Jesus is coming again, and Jesus is worth the wait!—Trudy Bender

◈ WORSHIP AIDS ◈

Call to Worship: "O God, you are my God, earnestly I seek you" (Ps. 63:1, NIV).

Invocation: Let us hear anew the words of comfort you uttered to your people long ago, Father. Amid our struggles, fears, failures, and losses we long for a comforting presence to abide with us. Let us hear again the good news that our warfare has ceased because of the coming of the Prince of Peace. Above all, at this Advent season remind us that you have come to say in person that our iniquity is pardoned and that we can live beyond our failures and our sins in the assurance of eternal forgiveness and love. With those who first discovered such mighty truth and from the giver of every good and perfect gift learned to pray, we too join in their prayer, saying: (Lord's Prayer)—Henry Fields

Offertory Sentence: "From what you have, take an offering for the Lord. Everyone who is willing is to bring to the Lord" (Exod. 35:5, NIV).

Offertory Prayer: Father, we admit that often our giving is the last thought of our busy and hectic weeks. Grant, O Lord, that every arena of Christian discipleship will come to bear on our lives. Make us faithful, cheerful, sacrificial givers—for the Kingdom's sake. Amen.

Morning Prayer: We come this morning journeying to Bethlehem, Father. This journey is an old experience for many, but for others it is a new adventure. Today help us all to experience the wonder of Christ's birth in a manner that will not only catch our interest but also transform our lives. Let the deeper meaning of Christmas be born in our hearts today.—Henry Fields

Benediction: We go now under the power and influence of our Lord Jesus to live as worthy followers. We are not perfect, far from it, but we are God's people. Let us go rejoicing in the good news of our salvation—and may we share it wherever we go. Amen.

SUNDAY, DECEMBER 4, 2011
Second Sunday in Advent

LECTIONARY SERMON TOPIC: "Amid Everything Else: Hope"

TEXT: Ps. 85:1–2, 8–13

OTHER READINGS: Isa. 40:1–11; 2 Pet. 3:8–15a; Mark 1:1–8

Our psalmist finds himself in a trying, frustrating, nearly hopeless situation. He and his people have made it back home from a terrible exile. All those years under the thumb of a cruel, bloodthirsty tyrant generated dreams of returning home, of nestling again in their dream city, Jerusalem. And now he's home. And what does he discover? Chaos reigns. The city lies in ruins, its houses a shambles, the streets ruled by thugs, muggers, bullies. The psalmist's hopes and dreams projected from the years in exile and slavery: null and void, the promises of God an apparent illusion. "Will you revive us again," he pleads, "that we may rejoice in you? Why do we, even as we arrive home, feel damned, rejected, isolated, cursed? When will you restore us?"

But wait just a minute. Our psalm is more than an exercise in despair, more than a lament arising from divine abandonment. Our psalmist opens with testimony to a past deliverance. He offers thanksgiving for intentions and activities of a Divine Savior who brought the psalmist's slavery to an end. He praises a God who defeats the oppressing empire. The psalmist and his people, for all their current troubles and frustration, for all the wreckage surrounding them—they remember one whose purpose operates to release them from bondage, directs them toward freedom, liberates them to return to their home, and enables them to consider the possibility of restoring their fragmented people and ruined city.

I. **And more! The psalmist evokes not only this memory of deliverance.** He includes also a creative and empowering hope. As the psalmist surveys the destruction about him, as he broods over the chaos and suffering afflicting his people, his city, and his nation, the *memory* of the God who initiated deliverance compels him to celebrate this God whose liberating promises will transform and ultimately overcome the current devastation tearing them apart. The psalmist envisions a community grounded, as a reverent observer once remarked, "in the very character of God." The psalmist's vision includes literal flesh-and-blood images: love and faithfulness meeting, righteousness and peace kissing. He depicts unblemished trust rising up from the earth to be greeted by the embrace and ebullient forgiveness and welcome of the God who wishes only our welfare and happiness. You see, amid these troubled and desolate circumstances, the psalmist trusts in one who saved him once before from oppression and despair and whose very character promises to do the same again.

II. **Friends, the psalmist's vision expresses the Advent promise.** Amid everything else getting us down, eating us up, stressing us out: hope against hope, as the psalmist asserts, is "at hand"! And the question lurking in our hearts is simple: Can we believe it? *Is* hope at hand? Amid the evidence in our world, where cynicism seems rampant and we label hope "denial," where our human condition, especially in light of the Advent promises, seems to be on the wrong side of a wide abyss, far distant from the content and radiance of those promises—Advent hope is hard to believe. Salvation? Love? Faithfulness? Peace? Healing? Goodness? Justice? Are you kidding? An Advent hope in a world like ours? Many of us feel ourselves closer to the psalmist as he laments his city's devastation.

III. **Well, God bless our psalmist!** For amid everything else, he remembers the goodness of God. Amid the tangle of life, he trusts the love of God. Amid everything denying it, he hopes for the future of God. Our psalmist speaks uniquely to us who wait for that healing, reconciling, compassionate world he describes from the ruins of his own city—a world we Christians, on the one hand, wait for and, on the other hand, confess to be borne among us by this man Jesus, compelling us to call him Christ. The psalmist's memory and hope we find embodied in the person of Jesus.

We do not worship this morning, as the psalmist did, in a ruined and devastated city. But we do gather under the cross! Talk about devastating, catastrophic circumstances. Like the psalmist amid his ruined city asking furious questions about the faithfulness of God, we might ask of the cross: If the forces of this world can mutilate and kill the likes of Jesus, then where is our hope? If goodness like that can be put on the gibbet by political and religious coalitions who think they do it for good, then where is our hope? You know where. For our faith, hope is right there amid the ruined city, at the foot of the cross all the time. Hope emerges not necessarily in the devastating circumstances but through them. Hope does not necessarily prevent or change tragic circumstances, but bears us through them. Hope may burst from a new vision of the future, radically changing our perception of the situation where we find ourselves. Like the psalmist's wasted city, the cross—if anything—can be understood as the final sign of cynicism and despair, the vivid signal that evil really does bear the last word, that goodness is up for grabs, that love is a fraud and hope a pathetic joke. The cross can be seen as the concentrated symbol of that abyss between our troubled everyday reality and our Advent hope.

IV. **But the cross is not a symbol of the abyss. Anything but!** We worship here this morning the very God who through the toughest, most unfair, troubled, and inhumane circumstances bears us hope. This empty cross at the head of our chancel represent a new reality, a new community, a new creation we might describe as the psalmist does, love and faithfulness meeting, grace and peace kissing each other, trust and forgiveness reaching toward one another from the ends of the universe—promises assured by a power able to take a bloody cross and turn it into the visible fact of love that never lets us go and a hope that will, in God's good time, re-create and transform us all. Hope, you see, from a ravaged city; hope through a ravaging cross. Hard to believe! Where hope is lost—hope at work! Where circumstances say no, the transforming power of God, even there, says yes to life and love.—James Crawford

---

ILLUSTRATIONS

Wishful Thinking. Those of us in the ministry are not immune to the world's condition. We, too, feel the distance between the broken character of our lives and the healed and reconciled character of the new era and community promised by our Advent psalm. Just a few examples.

Item: my son Benjamin called from New York on Tuesday. He described himself as shaking and reported that the father of a friend of his left a New Jersey Devils hockey game, walked across the street, and was killed by a truck. Item: I passed a bearded man dressed in army fatigues in the park by the merry-go-round; many of you have seen him too—kicking, screaming, violently defending himself against some demon threatening to assault him again, shredding his life and identity. Oh, that the "legion" could be exorcized, the man brought to his right mind! Item: I follow the news from Goma, a city in the Republic of the Congo, a city our family visited and stayed in several years ago—at that time stable, friendly, on the edge of one of the great natural forests and gorilla habitats in the world. And now? The site of genocide, tribal fury, family loss, and waves of refugees; the locus of intrigue, terror, national collapse.

You get the point and could make your own catalog of threatening and troubled circumstances—family dispersion, chronic illness, job catastrophe, financial wipeout, friends' betrayal, a loved one's protracted illness or sudden death—circumstances flying in the face of the Advent hope, which often seems like no more than wishful thinking.—James Crawford

God's Glory.

You come down, O Lord, with gladness,

in mercy and goodwill,

to bring an end to sadness

and bid our fears be still.

In patient expectation

we live for that great day

when a renewed creation

your glory shall display.[1]

Musical Selections Appropriate to the Day

Isa. 40:1–11	*Comfort, Comfort Now My People*
Ps. 85:1–2, 8–13	*Lift Up Your Heads, O Mighty Gates*
2 Pet. 3:8–15a	*Of the Father's Love Begotten*
Mark 1:1–8	*Comfort, Comfort Now My People*

✺ Children's Lectionary Sermon

TITLE: Get Ready

SCRIPTURE: Mark 1:1–8

KEY VERSE: *Prepare the way for the Lord, make straight paths for him.* (Mark 1:3b, NIV)

---

[1] *The Psalter Hymnal* (Grand Rapids, MI: CRC Publications, 1987), hymn 331.

KEY CONCEPTS: Salvation, humility
MATERIALS: Bible, gift box or bag, a sandal
PREPARATION: Place sandal in box or bag.

We do many things to get ready for Christmas. We put up special decorations, we send cards to family and friends, and we bake Christmas treats. Many of us are getting our homes ready for family and friends to stay. Will any of you have special visitors this Christmas? Or will you go to visit someone special? (*Listen to answers.*) Some lucky children have cousins to play with at Christmastime, but I'm pretty sure that no one here has a cousin quite like Jesus did.

Jesus had a cousin named John. When he was older, they called him "John the Baptist." (*Open gift box and take out the sandal.*) John lived in the desert and wore camel's hair for clothes. He ate locusts (bugs!) and wild honey. He was an unusual person! But people came from all over the land to hear John's message. John prepared the people to receive Jesus. He told them to be sorry for the wrong things they had done and to turn to God. He told them that their Savior was coming, someone so great that John was not even worthy to untie his sandal.

(*Open Bible.*) We can read the story of John the Baptist in the Bible. In Mark 1 there is a verse that tells about what John did. *Prepare the way for the Lord, make straight paths for him.* We get lots of things ready at Christmastime. Let's remember to get ourselves ready, too. Are you ready to receive Jesus? Are you prepared to give him your life? I hope you will follow John the Baptist's example and get ready for Jesus.—Trudy Bender

ᕗ WORSHIP AIDS ᕗ

Call to Worship: "The next day John saw Jesus coming toward him and said, 'Look, the Lamb of God, who takes away the sin of the world'" (John 1:29, NIV).

Invocation: Lord, we begin today our pilgrimage toward Christmas. As in years past, we rejoice in the good news of Jesus Christ, born in Bethlehem as the Savior of the world. Purify our hearts, O Lord, that we may welcome his coming with heart, mind, soul, and strength. We praise you for the gift of Christ, born in winter's darkness to be the light of the world. Amen.

Offertory Sentence: "A generous man will prosper; he who refreshes others will himself be refreshed" (Prov. 11:25, NIV).

Offertory Prayer: Our gifts this morning are not gold and frankincense and myrrh, Father. They are just the meager earnings of our hands. Still, we give them to the Lord that they may be used to glorify his life and name throughout the world, even as those first gifts declared his royalty. Amen.—Henry Fields

Morning Prayer: We are an expectant people, Lord. Indeed, at Christmas we are like little children who view the season with sparkling eyes as if they have seen the greatest gift in the world. Let us, like the children, become excited about the baby in the manger, born to show us your will, to share with us your love, and to tell us that your Kingdom has come to us and can be shared through us with the entire world. Thank you that Christ's coming is not just some distant event that took place in an obscure place long ago, but something that repeats itself again and again. How we rejoice that the living Spirit of the Lord guides us in faith every day; walks with us through every valley; stands with us in all upright living; whispers to us like a still, small voice; and abides in our hearts and minds with the vision and hope of things eternal.

Thank you that in this sacred season we are moved from carelessness to thoughtfulness, from selfishness to giving, from being hard and callous to being kind and gentle, from indifference to concern. Let such a Spirit abide with us not just in this season, but throughout the journey of life.

Now we ask that you make of our souls a manger wherein the Lord of life is born again, we pray in his Holy Name. Amen.—Henry Fields

Benediction: People of God, go forth today energized to serve faithfully and lovingly in the days of this week. May we live in the light of God's redemptive love—and share that love with others. May we speak the name of Jesus often—and lovingly! Amen.

SUNDAY, DECEMBER 11, 2011
Third Sunday in Advent

LECTIONARY SERMON TOPIC: "What Are We Waiting For?"
TEXT: Isa. 61:1–4, 8–11
OTHER READINGS: Ps. 126; 1 Thess. 5:16–24; John 1:6–8, 19–28

As Christmas creeps closer, just what is it we wait for? Some of us, of course, wait for family to arrive. We look forward to reunions with parents or children or grandchildren. Our family surely joins with you in this joyous anticipation.

Signs of the season, of course, surround us: lights in windows, shoppers galore, the Salvation Army clarinetist. One book catches the mood: "you hear people whistling *Jingle Bells*, and nobody cares if they whistle good."[2] And, naturally, there is the anticipation of presents, with all the complications of choice and cost, cash and credit. But just what is it we wait for?

I. **Well, we wait for the birth of a babe—that's for sure.** We stand on tiptoe waiting for a child. But it's more than that. This child signifies something greater than itself, far larger than any other human birth in our world. This birth signals the breaking into our broken and warring world of a new configuration of human relationships; it promises a human family living in peace with itself and with a vast and glorious universe. The birth of Jesus represent the birth of a new creation.

The prophet Isaiah, offers the classic vision of what it is we wait for . . . this new creation. There he stands, some twenty-four hundred years ago, finally home in Jerusalem after fifty years in an alien and enemy land, a hostage to the imperial dreams of a cruel tyrant, a half-century in a desert concentration camp. But now, he's home. He's back in Jerusalem. That's the good news. And the bad news? Jerusalem is a postwar wreck. What

---

[2]David Heller and Elizabeth Heller, *The Best Christmas Presents Are Wrapped in Heaven* (New York: Villard Books, 1993).

was once a city is now a pile of rubble. It wallows in weeds and is covered with trash. The Temple lies in shambles. The city crawls with marauders, thieves, and murderers. Poverty, hostility, rapaciousness stalk the streets.

And yet—yet—as he reviews this hopeless mess, Isaiah articulates a vision reflecting a quantum leap from the devastation surrounding him; he soars with an incredible promise for the ruined city: "The Spirit of the Lord is upon me," he cries, "because God has anointed—compelled me— to bring good tidings, a word of salvation, a releasing promise to this god-forsaken, war-ravaged, chaos-ridden people."

II. **And where lies this news?** What's so good about it? What promise emerges from this postwar urban desolation? The good news lies here: to bring healing to those hearts breaking from the wounds of grief, loss, and abandonment; to free those who find themselves prisoners of contempt or abuse, humiliation or political captivity; to offer comfort and hope to those who despair over the rift between what life could be and what it is; to reclothe in festive attire those whose lives have been torn apart grieving for loved ones who died in the death marches, massacres, and killing fields decimating his people; to change the songs and poems of his people from dirges and eulogies to songs of joy and hope; to re-create their identities from a defeated, crushed, and enslaved people to a new being: "oaks of salvation," "trees of righteousness," conveying compassion and justice to all the world; to rebuild, refashion, renew their demolished city and wasted countryside; and finally, most important, to affirm the dawning of a fresh era, the inauguration of a new age, a time immersed in the love of God, when a community embraced by peace born of justice, mutuality, and integrity might ground our life together.

Do you hear those promises? Can you imagine them spoken right here at our crossroads, in the subway station downtown, in the projects? Can you hear them in Islamabad, Gaza, Kinshasa? In these churning and troubled urban settings where life confronts challenge and threat—here we find the promise of Christmastide; in the places we see the baby Jesus inaugurating love's blessed community—right here, among us, right now on our troubled and beautiful planet.

III. **What a hope! What a promise!** Do you see what it means for us? It means that the child's birth in Bethlehem is no sentimental matter, no mawkish event. If this child bears any hope for our lives, if these hopes at all resemble the public promises reflected in Isaiah, then those of us who count ourselves faithful begin to realize that we embrace a faith bearing enormous social and ethical consequences. The Christian faith seeks not simply to produce new people; it seeks to seed new societies. The prophet's vision, the child's birth deal not only with individuals: they envision a new community.

IV. **Just one thing more:** Do you recall the young Galilean returning from the desert some four hundred years after Isaiah's words of hope? "What are you up to?" they asked. His answer: "The Spirit of the Lord is upon me, because he has anointed me to bring good news to the poor. He has sent me to proclaim release to the captives and recovering of sight to the blind, to let the oppressed go free, to proclaim the year of the Lord's favor" (Luke 4:18–21, NRSV). "Today," he asserted, "that scripture has been fulfilled in your hearing." Do you believe that? I pray you do. For ultimately, at that moment in Nazareth, we catch a glimpse of the one for whom, and yes, for what we wait.—James Crawford

---

ILLUSTRATIONS

Advent Waiting. Bill Veeck, that fabulous baseball impresario, tells of buying a Christmas hobbyhorse for his granddaughter. He describes his adventure this way. The hobbyhorse "came in a large box which said it contained 189 parts and could be put together in an hour. Sure it could—if you just graduated from MIT or have a machine shop in your basement. I didn't have to accept that kind of indignity. So, when I went to pay for it, I tore my check into 189 pieces and wrote them a little note telling that if they like to put things together let them work on *that*. One sad ending to my tale . . . they did."[3] Christmas is just around the corner. What is it we wait for?—James Crawford

---

[3]Bill Veeck, quoted in William Cole, *Bah, Humbug* (New York: St. Martin's Press, 1992), pp. 34–35.

Advent Responsibility. Perhaps Martin Luther King Jr. captures the Advent-Christmas public mission and responsibility as well as anyone. He reminds us, "A religion true to its nature must also be concerned about man's social conditions. Religion deals with both earth and heaven, time and eternity. Religion operates not only on the vertical plane but also on the horizontal. It seeks not only to integrate men with God but to integrate men with men and each man with himself. This means at bottom, that the Christian Gospel is a two-way road. On the one hand, it seeks to change the souls of men and thereby unite them with God; on the other hand, it seeks to change the environmental conditions of men so that the soul will have a chance after it is changed. Any religion that professes to be concerned with the souls of men and is not concerned about the slums that damn them, the economic conditions that strangle them, and the social conditions that cripple them is a dry-as-dust religion. Such a religion is what the Marxists (used to) call—an opiate of the people."[4]—James Crawford

Musical Selections Appropriate to the Day

Isa. 61:1–4, 8–11	*Arise, Your Light Is Come*
Ps. 126	*Of the Father's Love Forgotten*
1 Thess. 5:16–24	*It Came Upon the Midnight Clear*
John 1:6–8, 19–28	*Shine, Jesus, Shine*

Children's Lectionary Sermon

TITLE: Filled with Joy
SCRIPTURE: Ps. 126

---

[4]Martin Luther King Jr., quoted in Coretta Scott King, *The Words of Martin Luther King, Jr.* (New York: Newmarket Press, 1983), p. 66.

KEY VERSE: *The Lord has done great things for us, and we are filled with joy.* (Ps. 126:3, NIV)

KEY CONCEPT: Joy

MATERIALS: Bible, gift box or bag, Christmas ornament

PREPARATION: Place ornament in box or bag. Optional: arrange to sing "Joy to the World" before or after the children's sermon.

I love singing Christmas carols together with my church family, don't you? (*Optional: ask children to name some favorite Christmas carols.*) One of the most loved carols of all is "Joy to the World." People today and people long ago have loved to sing songs of joy to God. (*Open Bible.*) In fact, Psalm 126 is a song of joy. It says, *The Lord has done great things for us, and we are filled with joy.* Remembering what God has done fills us with joy!

Christmas is a time when we remember things that God has done for us. (*Open gift box.*) Today we have a Christmas tree ornament in our gift box. We love ornaments because they remind us of things. Some have pictures or shapes that remind us of the Christmas story, like angels and stars. Some ornaments are gifts from people who are special to us. Some ornaments remind us of wonderful places we've visited or things we like to do. Maybe you've made an ornament for your parents or grandparents. When they see it they are reminded of how much they love you.

When you look at Christmas ornaments this week, think about all of the good things God has done for you. Be thankful for the people who care for you and for the special times you share during this season. Most of all, remember that Jesus came to be our Savior. Be filled with joy!—Trudy Bender

❧ WORSHIP AIDS ❧

Call to Worship: "I will sing of the Lord's great love forever; with my mouth I will make your faithfulness known through all generations" (Ps. 89:1, NIV).

Invocation: Dear Lord, prepare us for the great things you intend to do in and through us today. May our journey through the Advent season awaken our slumbering souls and quicken us to a fresh and vital walk of faith. What we seek we cannot do alone—so we await your help. Amen.

Offertory Sentence: "For God so loved the world that he gave his one and only Son, that whoever believes in him shall not perish but have eternal life" (John 3:16, NIV).

Offertory Prayer: Father, we offer ourselves and our means as expressions of gratitude for your love and forgiveness. We ask that you bless these gifts for the Kingdom's purpose—for the purpose of reconciling all people everywhere to you. Amen.

Morning Prayer: Many among us cannot celebrate joyfully, Father. Life has dealt them severe blows, and faith has been shaken. Some have become so ill that Christmas celebration is more of a burden than a blessing. Others, walking in loneliness, feel like strangers standing outside the party looking in. Some even wonder if there will ever be a joyous Christmas for them again. Let the bright star of Bethlehem shine in their skies, we pray. Through the darkness of their night, let the angelic news be sung. Over the pathways leading to Christ's presence, may they journey and for themselves see this thing which has come to pass, which the Lord has made known unto us.

And may those of us more able to celebrate his coming seek out the ones needful of his presence and power and bring them to his consolation. Now we commit the hour into your hands. Overrule our agenda if necessary and have your way with us as we wait and worship before you, we pray in the name and power of Christ. Amen.—Henry Fields

Benediction: Go out today with hearts filled with joy. The days of Advent require us to think deeply, and lovingly, of God's great work of grace among us. This same God, whom we name as Father, Son, and Holy Spirit, walks with us along the way. Amen.

SUNDAY, DECEMBER 18, 2011

Fourth Sunday in Advent

LECTIONARY SERMON TOPIC: "Mary? In Stained Glass?"
TEXT: Luke 1:46b–55
OTHER READINGS: 2 Sam. 7:1–11, 16; Rom. 16:25–27; Luke 1:26–38

In many churches around the world, you will discover stained glass windows depicting the crèche. You will see oxen and sheep, shepherds and Wise Men, and, of course, Mary, Joseph, and the babe lying in a manger. We love those windows; they tell the story of our Lord's birth. And in many churches, certainly among our Roman Catholic brothers and sisters, Mary often becomes the centerpiece, or holds a window on her own.

I. **It's that "stained glass Mary" who shines from so many windows who shines also from our lesson this morning.** Remember? After hearing from an angel that she will bear a son, in surprise and awe Mary hustles over to the house of her cousin Elizabeth to share exuberantly this exciting news. Elizabeth rejoices with Mary. She too is pregnant, and the unborn child she carries, who grows up to be John the Baptist, leaps in her womb, recognizing the special one Mary bears. Elizabeth offers impassioned congratulations to Mary, and Mary—Mary sings this astounding song. We call it "Magnificat" because in Latin it begins, "Magnificat anima me Dominum": "My heart magnifies the Lord."

But while singing or while listening to or reading Mary's song, what do we discover? As we take a closer look at "Magnificat," what do we see? What do we hear? A Hebrew folk song? No. An Aramaic lullaby? Hardly! A classical aria? Perhaps. We will hear it sung as classical refrains and in orchestral and choral settings during this Christmas season. But these sublime versions of poetry and music, inspiring as they may be, while telling the story beautifully, do not tell all of it. Aesthetics blunt the point. We may miss the force of Mary's song by its ethereal recasting. To be sure, we celebrate here a resplendent psalm, but Mary's song bears a striking vision; it comes to us not so much as an anthem composed for a garland- and poinsettia-adorned sanctuary like this one, not by a long shot. It explodes! It's dynamite! Mary's song takes that CD rendering of John Eliot Gardner with the Monteverdi Choir and English Baroque soloists I listened to while writing this sermon and exposes its jagged edges. Her song sounds not so much like a choral motet, but rather like fingernails scratching across a blackboard. It is chilling, defiant, revolutionary. You see, Mary sings a freedom song. She speaks for God as she anticipates the birth of the one lodging in her womb—she expects a world turned upside down; she envisions our humanity turned around 180 degrees; she filters the promises of the prophets, insisting that for God's sake "let justice run down like waters, and righteousness like an ever-flowing stream" (Amos 5:24, NRSV). She anticipates in the life of the one she carries the embodiment of that promise. As we go about our various holiday routines, discovering that on the overbooked flight we're the "overbookee"; discovering that our eggnog is little more than a cup of cholesterol, that the bicycle comes with 125 nuts and bolts and widgets, with directions straight out of some demon's den—amid all this Christmas prep, we encounter this poetic bomb from the mother of the expected Messiah—she asserts that Christmas invokes a massive U-turn, an about-face. "Christmas," Mary insists, "turns our world upside down."

II. **And where do we find evidence for such a reading of Mary's song?** Think of *Mary*, the most popular name given at baptism; the most used of epithets, "Jesus, Mary, and Joseph"; and the "Ave Marias" repeated millions of times each day. How dare we suggest that this pillar of religious and profane culture, this radiant image glazed in stained glass windows, turns the world topsy-turvy! Well, let's hear from Mary again as she contemplates the meaning of the child she bears.

Do you recall? Mary speaks of "one who shows strength with his arm and scatters the proud in the thoughts of their hearts." Oh, oh, friends. Mary at Christmastime—Mary fails as a sentimental poet for Hallmark cards. Little of our holiday cheer for her. She takes a different tack. The "thoughts of the proud" that Mary sees scattered at Christmastime deal with lies, deception, fraud. She recognizes one who comes telling truth, tearing the veil from those who would deceive us for their own benefit, whose self-interest distorts their every word and action. She bridles at those who scapegoat others, who use every conceivable rationale to hide and justify their own tawdry ends. Mary knows well that deception in high places, the twisting of truth and substituting propaganda for candor lead to the erosion of trust, subvert the social contract, corrupt the law, poison institutions, lead to personal disintegration. "The proud scattered by the thoughts of their hearts." No stained glass Mary here!

III. **But Mary is not done.** She continues with the confidence that "our God lifts those of low degree and fills the hungry with good things, sending the rich empty away." Take those political and economic debates roiling our country regarding "redistribution of wealth" and creeping socialism. Well, the New Testament makes an economic statement in Mary's "Magnificat" that might compel those worried about such a future to think again.

Friends, a nation first in gross domestic product and in the number of millionaires and billionaires ought to commit itself to narrowing the chasms separating its citizens in education, health care, housing, income, and safety—"to fill the hungry with good things" and, for heaven's sake, persuade the rich to get on board for peace established through justice that we might all live in mutuality with fairness and equal opportunity, that no one be sent away empty.

So friends, those crèches in our stained glass windows, Mary alone gracing many of them, promise a new kind of world, where justice and peace, equity and truth, reconciliation and human solidarity become the order of the day. That's the promise of Advent. And the voice and commitment attributed to that woman we so frequently ensconce in stained glass compel us to ask, "Really? Mary? In stained glass? Don't you believe it."—James Crawford

---

ILLUSTRATIONS

Mary's Protest. Pursuing a glimpse of the resistance her child brings to the deceivers and corrupt of the age, Mary proceeds to throw a spotlight on those in high position possessing not only vast financial resources but military arsenals and political clout. "God has put down the mighty from their thrones." How dare she sing this song of revolt? Well, perhaps Mary reviews the history of her own people: she recalls Assyria, Egypt, Greece, Persia—poof! And yes, what do *we* see? We see Rome, Venice, and the Ottoman, the Austro-Hungarian, the British, the Russian empires sprawled on the scrapheap of history. Some of us recall the Thousand-Year Reich. Ah, Mary knows that empire builders, superpowers—nay, even hyperpowers—need be careful in their claims, their self-perception, their presumption to innocence in the exercise of their muscle. Careful, Mary protests. Great empires in God's world succor illusions marking them vulnerable.—James Crawford

Social Needs. Listen to how the Children's Defense Fund frames the matter in a recent report. The United States is first in Gross Domestic Product; first in number of billionaires; first in number of persons incarcerated; first in health expenditures; first in military technology; first in defense expenditures; first in military weapons exports; twenty-first in fifteen-year-olds' science scores; twenty-second in low birth weight rates; twenty-fifth in fifteen-year-olds' math scores; twenty-fifth in infant mortality rates; last in relative child poverty; last in the gap between the rich and the poor; last in protecting our children against gun violence.[5]—James Crawford

Musical Selections Appropriate to the Day

2 Sam. 7:1–11, 16	*Once in Royal David's City*
Luke 1:47–55	*Tell Out, My Soul, the Greatness*
Rom. 16:25–27	*He Is Born*
Luke 1:26–38	*The Angel Gabriel from Heaven Came*

---

[5]Children's Defense Fund, *The State of America's Children–2008* (Washington, DC: Children's Defense Fund, 2008), p. 1.

∽ Children's Lectionary Sermon

TITLE: Surprise!

SCRIPTURE: Luke 1:26–38

KEY VERSE: *"I am the Lord's servant,"* Mary answered. *"May it be to me as you have said."* (Luke 1:38, NIV)

KEY CONCEPT: Obedience

MATERIALS: Bible, gift box or bag, angel or picture of angel

PREPARATION: Place the angel in the box or bag.

Have you ever been really surprised? Do you like surprises? Two thousand years ago, a girl named Mary had a visitor that surprised her. (*Open gift box.*) That visitor was an angel named Gabriel. Gabriel brought Mary a message from God. He told Mary that she would have a son named Jesus who would be the savior of her people. The Bible tells us that Mary was afraid, but she listened to God's messenger. (*Open Bible.*) God called her to do a special job, and Mary was obedient to God. *"I am the Lord's servant,"* Mary answered. *"May it be to me as you have said."* Then the angel left her.

God has plans for you, the girls and boys sitting right here. God will call you to share the good news of Jesus with other people. He may call you to be a pastor or a missionary or to serve him in all kinds of different ways. When you hear God's Word at church and at home, when you read your Bible, when you pray, carefully listen to God's message. It can be surprising sometimes. We might even be afraid to do what God wants us to do. But we can remember Mary and follow her example. Be on the lookout for a surprise from God, and be ready to obey!—Trudy Bender

∽ WORSHIP AIDS ∽

Call to Worship: "The people walking in darkness have seen a great light; on those living in the land of the shadow of death a light has dawned. . . . For to us a child is born, to us a son is given, and the government will be on his shoulders. And he will be called Wonderful Counselor, Mighty God, Everlasting Father, Prince of Peace" (Isa. 9:2, 6–7, NIV).

Invocation: Dearest Lord, we rejoice that you are with us—that you have always been with us and will be with us forever—and that we will rejoice forever. Through your presence we are strengthened for the life of faith and duty. Grant that in this Advent season, we will be further strengthened to live in fullness all our days. Amen.

Offertory Sentence: "The shepherds said to one another, 'Let us go to Bethlehem and see this thing that has happened, which the Lord has told us about'" (Luke 2:15 NIV).

Offertory Prayer: Lord, let Jesus coming into the time of earth affect our giving this day so others may know the Incarnation heaven and earth cannot forget. Amen.—E. Lee Phillips

Morning Prayer: Loving Father, who long ago walked down the stairway of the stars and laid a baby in a manger so that the Word became flesh, come again, we pray, to renew us this Christmas week. Show us again the many ways in which you became incarnate. Let us see the Word again become flesh. Enable us to understand the mystery of your movements in the affairs of nations and peoples.

In the midst of changing times, let us not forget the source of every good and perfect gift. Let us not be deaf to a baby's soft cry, shepherds' wondering praises, and a mother's lullaby. Lead us from the cradle to Calvary and Easter that we may know with assurance that every tragedy has redemptive meaning when viewed through the love and purpose of Christ, whose message to us began so powerfully that night when angels sang and Christmas became a reality. Now as we worship in this holy season, we rejoice that you meet us here—once again. Amen.—Henry Fields.

Benediction: We go forth today assured of God's presence. As truly as God dwelt with his people in Christ long ago, he dwells with us today. May God, whom we know as Father, Son, and Holy Spirit, bring life and light to this holy season. Amen.

SUNDAY, DECEMBER 25, 2011
Christmas Day

LECTIONARY SERMON TOPIC: "Homeless"

TEXT: John 1:1–14

OTHER READINGS: Isa. 52:7–10; Ps. 98; Heb. 1:1–4 (5–12)

You receive, I suspect, scores of Christmas cards over the length of this season. Some of them are cute, others affectionate. Some show teddy bears, others candy canes, still others stockings crammed with toys. And yes, we receive some beautiful greetings with the Christmas story painted or etched out. On those cards, we see the dark inside of a stable, oxen and sheep, shepherds leaning on their crooks, three royal figures from the Orient, and angels hovering over the scene blowing golden trumpets. At the center, Mary, Joseph, and the manger-babe gather in golden, halo light. We cherish the story, and this panorama makes it vivid for us.

But I wonder—I wonder if those of us who encounter Christmas this way, year in and year out—I wonder if we see and hear the message afresh. Indeed, I wonder if we really open ourselves to receive the new world of Christ Jesus announced by our cards and our carols, and, on Christmas Eve, by our candlelight.

I ask these questions because John, that most profound of our evangelists, includes two striking allusions as he begins his reflection on the meaning of Jesus: "He was in the world, and the world came into being through him, but the world did not know him. He came to what was his own, but his own people did not accept him" (John 1:10–11, NRSV). The world did not know or accept him? Why not? I believe that the Christmas event, for all of our beautiful cards and lovely aesthetic decorations and gorgeous music, provokes a crisis of recognition. I believe that what most of us hope for in a savior is not what we get. I believe that what we look for, what we expect, what we want in a Christ frequently blinds us to the Christ who really comes. And I am persuaded that those of us in the Christian ministry are among the most sadly deceived. He came to what was his own, but his own people did not accept him! Why? I think it's because this "Word become flesh" comes to us as stranger, as outsider, as one with no place to lay his head. He seeks a home among us, but cannot find one.

I. **This strange, homeless Jesus pervades the New Testament perspective on all of our Lord's life.** The gospels illustrate it from the very beginning. No acceptance, no security, no home. Luke makes reference to it when he tells us bluntly that Jesus comes into the world in a stable because "there was no place for him at the inn" (Luke 2:7, NRSV). But Matthew offers an even more vivid account. That splendid narrative we read year after year about the three Magi—their following the star; their arrival at the manger; their offering of gold, frankincense, and myrrh—comes couched in a story telling of Herod's outright rejection. Herod sends those Magi as informers, as personal spies. No sooner is Jesus born in the outbuildings of a Bethlehem inn than his little family flees the country. Can you imagine it? Dodging border patrols, damping noise, wandering in circles in the bleak desert night, this husband with his wife and child: refugees. That's how Jesus spent the first years of his life—on the run, homeless. "He came to what was his own, but his own people did not accept him."

II. **And we find this crisis not only at our Lord's birth; his life and ministry engage us with one who seems uneasy among us.** His parables, for instance, confront us with a world so different from the one we support with our taxes; a world so different from the imperialism, militarism, and greed we nourish and encourage; a world so different as to be virtually unrecognizable. Jesus tells the parable of the Good Samaritan (Luke 10:25–37) to national chauvinists, ethnic elites, political and religious insiders who believe their closed circles to be special, who see no good coming from beyond their own tastes and class. "Who is my neighbor?" they ask, convinced he will look like them. What neighbor does Jesus give them? An enemy, an outsider, an alien, one whom they consider foreign to their own land—a Samaritan comes and saves that "insider" lying in the ditch, when those who look like that insider, think like him, speak like him, pray like him—pass right by. That parable falls on stunned and disbelieving ears unable to embrace saving truth outside themselves.

III. **And if our Lord's birth and his ministry illustrate his homelessness among us, what really lies behind his death?** Simply put, we were not able to fit him into the categories we believe to be appropriate—and thus rose up against him. He defies containment in orthodox dogma or institution. He refuses to indulge in our religious sentimentality. He made friends with what his compatriots considered social scum, extortionists, the disabled and mentally ill. As for his patriotism, he refused to surrender loyalty to the imperial designs of the oligarchs and the sellouts among his own people. Jesus' activity triggered a "Special Committee on Unorthodox and Anti-Roman Activities." The verdict? Death to the atheist; death to the traitor. "He came to what was his own" . . . was unrecognized, driven into a far country, refused a home.

IV. **Does John's observation strike a note with us?** Whom do we expect this Christmas Day? What do we want at Christmas? Do we want an "insider," someone who speaks our language, responds to our hopes, feeds our dreams? Someone we recognize as our own, a friend we'd invite over for mulled cider and Christmas cookies? Perhaps. But mark this well: the Christ who offers salvation through outsiders, who hangs around the ne'er-do-wells from nowhere; this Christ who began life headed across the border; this Christ who made heroic the hated, foreign Samaritan; this Christ hanging on that cross outside the city walls; this Christ born outside the inn—at Christmastide he comes to his own country, this world, this city, this church, your life and mine, and seeks a home.

And I worry. I worry because among us he may find himself homeless. In a world where power, money, guns, success, connections, credentials rule the roost—in such a world, weakness; poverty; bread; service; solidarity with the failed, the vulnerable, the prisoner become laughable, a joke, a mistake, unrecognizable as anything but a losing cause.

But is it? ". . . he has scattered the proud in the thoughts of their hearts. He has brought down the powerful from their thrones, and lifted up the lowly; he has filled the hungry with good things, and sent the rich empty away" (Luke 1:51b–53, NRSV). Luke puts those words in Mary's mouth as she anticipates Christmas. Are these words foolish when we witness the vulnerability and, from time to time, the collapse of high finance? Or again, in a society where we determine personal identities by grade-point average, office location, niche on the church hierarchy, income or fragrance, automobile logo—in such a society, can we find a home for identities rooted in love embracing the marginal, the failure, the fringe, the misfit, the lonely, the homeless? Can we, as Simone Weil asks, "remain in a sense anonymous, ever ready to be mixed into the common paste of humanity?"[6] That is where Jesus, whom we call Christ, finds himself—in the "common paste of humanity"—no place, no home for a *real* Christ—but in hope and in love, the only home.

V. **Oh friends, this world, this city, your heart and mine are more truly the home of this Christmas child.** He is not meant to be homeless, here. No one is meant to be homeless here. The great Christmas challenge before each of us is to create a world where Jesus Christ can be at home anywhere; a world secured not by class or income but by love and justice; a world sustained not by pecking orders and dog-eat-dog competition but by reconciliation and mutual service; a world bound by our solidarity with one another and our so-called enemies; a world grounded by faith that amid our chaos and broken dreams there throbs love, risking herself among us, ready to take whatever we dish out, and yes, never letting us go. The world where the Christ child may finally lay his head is the world where the wanderers in our alleys, the "wino" on the grates, the vagrant living his Vietnam or Iraq wounds, and yes, the child of Darfur or Gaza or Chechnya or Afghanistan have a place to lay their heads, to rest their feet, to live in joy, hope, and peace. The Bethlehem refugee invites us to design and build that kind of world. Can we accept the invitation? Can we work this Christmas for a true homecoming? God grant this day we may open our hearts to this, so far, derelict child and declare, "Welcome, friend, welcome home in your birth this Christmastide."—James Crawford

---

ILLUSTRATIONS

God's Love. I fled Him down the nights and down the days; / I fled Him, down the arches of the years; / I fled Him down the labyrinthine ways of my own mind; / And in the midst of tears I hid from Him, and under running laughter. /

---

[6]Simone Weil, *Waiting for God* (New York: Capricorn Books, 1959), p. 47.

Up vistaed hopes I sped; and shot, precipitated, adown Titanic glooms of chasmed fears. . . . Halts by me that footfall: Is my gloom, after all, / Shade of His hand, outstretched caressingly? / "Ah, fondest, blindest, weakest, I am He Whom thou seekest! / Thou dravest love from thee, / Who dravest Me.—Francis Thompson[7]

Faith. Understanding is the reward of faith. Therefore seek not to understand that thou mayest believe, but believe that thou mayest understand. —Augustine

Musical Selections Appropriate to the Day

Isa. 52:7–10	*Go, Tell It on the Mountain*
Ps. 98	*Joy to the World!*
Heb. 1:1–4 (5–12)	*The First Noel*
John 1:1–14	*Angels, from the Realms of Glory*

ᕀ Children's Lectionary Sermon

TITLE: The Message

SCRIPTURE: John 1:1–14

KEY VERSE: *The Word became flesh and made his dwelling among us.* (John 1:14a, NIV)

KEY CONCEPT: The coming of God's Son into the world

MATERIALS: Bible, gift box or bag, Christmas card(s)

PREPARATION: Place card(s) in the box or bag.

This is a very special day. I hope that you are not too tired to open another gift! Let's find out what is in our gift box this morning. (*Open gift box and*

---

[7]Francis Thompson, *The Hound of Heaven* (Mount Vernon, NY: Peter Pauper Press, 1908, 1940), pp. 5, 26.

show cards.) Christmas cards bring greetings and messages from loved ones all around the country and even the world. Many people hang Christmas cards up in their homes and enjoy reading the messages inside. Some cards bring news and family pictures. We send greetings to those we love.

Did you know that the most important Christmas message ever sent wasn't in a card? It wasn't even written on paper. No, the greatest message was sent as a person, Jesus. (*Open Bible.*) John 1:14 says, *The Word became flesh and made his dwelling among us.* The Word became flesh? That means that the Word of God, God's own Son, became a human person. Jesus is the Word; Jesus is the message! God became a person like you and me so that he could share his love in a way that we could understand. Jesus showed us how to live, how to die, how to love one another. He didn't just write it down; he lived it out for us to see. Jesus himself is the message of Christmas, the Word of God for us. God sent a message to those he loved. He sent Jesus, the best message we could ever receive. Merry Christmas!—Trudy Bender

❧ WORSHIP AIDS ❧

Call to Worship: "I will sing of the mercies of the Lord for ever: with my mouth will I make known thy faithfulness to all generations" (Ps. 89:1, NIV).

Invocation: God of Incarnation, make known your will this Christmas that as children of the new birth in Christ Jesus, we may reflect the nativity light of Bethlehem, even the Light of the world, Christ Jesus, that never dims. Amen.—E. Lee Phillips

Offertory Sentence: On coming to the house, they saw the child with his mother Mary, and they bowed down and worshipped him. Then they opened their treasures and presented him with gifts of gold and of incense and of myrrh" (Matt. 2:11, NIV).

Offertory Prayer: Gracious Lord, receive our gifts this day as expressions of our devotion to you. May the thoughts of Bethlehem and Calvary capture our minds today—and throughout the year. Bless these gifts for the work of ministry in Jesus' name here in our city and in the whole world. Amen.

Morning Prayer: Father, we come again to the manger of Bethlehem. And with all the tapestry of customs and culture, we pray that the good news of Christmas will come into our hearts and lives. Come to us today in some unexpected way. Surprise us with a transforming miracle in our hearts, so the joy and the spirit of Christmas may stay with us, now and forever. In the name of Jesus of Bethlehem, the Light of the world. Amen.—Henry Fields

Benediction: As we go, we celebrate the joy of this season. While the lights on our trees and in our streets may well dazzle us, may our faith be lived brightly that the warmth and joy of Christ will be revealed to our world. God, let it be so. Amen.

SECTION III

RESOURCES FOR PREACHING

CHAPTER ONE

Sermons from Exile: A Lenten Series

Dr. Mark McKim

Senior Minister, First Baptist Church,
Regina, Saskatchewan, Canada

Just as the exiled people of Judah were surrounded by the culture, values, and beliefs of Babylon (and later Persia), so also God's Church in the western world today is "in exile," surrounded by a culture that does not buy into our worldview. We have passed from a time when Christians and the Church dominated society to a time when being a person of faith is a minority choice. No longer in Christendom, we, like Judah, have to learn how to maintain, pass on, and live out our faith in Christ surrounded by an increasingly secular society that does not accept the picture of reality we find in scripture. These sermons from the exilic books (Isaiah, Jeremiah, Ezekiel, Daniel, and Esther) seek to allow the accounts from days of old to speak to our current needs. Notice that the final sermon moves to Holy Week and portrays Jesus as the "ultimate exile."

THE FIRST SUNDAY OF LENT

Living in Exile–I
TOPIC: The Exile's Job
SCRIPTURE LESSONS: Old Testament Lesson—Isa. 42:1–7, 53:1–11
 Responsorial Lesson—Ps. 74:1, 4, 7, 12, 16–17
 Gloria Patri
 The Epistle—Col. 1:24
 The Gospel—Matt. 25:1–13

HYMNS: "O Come, O Come, Emmanuel" (v. 1)
"Tell Out My Soul"
"Go, Labour On"

You may well have been puzzled by this morning's introit ("O Come, O Come, Emmanuel"). Maybe you wondered if the pastor had gotten a bit mixed up. Today is the first Sunday of Lent, the period of preparation leading to Easter. And yet we were singing a piece usually associated with Advent, the weeks leading up to Christmas. It is true that now and then I have a cog slip in my memory, but this *isn't* one of those occasions. The piece was chosen deliberately, because it refers to the people of God, in exile.

And exile is going to be our theme during Lent this year. Exile. It means being excluded from one's group or usual place. Twenty-five hundred years ago, God's ancient people, the Jews, experienced exile. In those days, God's people were not, as today, found as part of the church in every nation on earth. They took the form of an actual country—Judah. They were supposed to be God's own people, an example to the surrounding nations, showing what God was really like. Sadly, however, Judah did not live up to its calling. Neither the leaders nor the people listened when the prophets condemned injustice and corruption in what was supposed to be an exemplary society. Often, instead of the worship of Yahweh, there was a sort of buffet-style approach to faith. People tried to have a bit of worship of Yahweh but a side order of several other gods as well. In the end, the superpower of the day, the Babylonian Empire, became God's instrument of judgment. Judah was invaded. The capital city, Jerusalem, was sacked, the great Temple destroyed. Large numbers of people were forcibly deported to Babylon. Exile.

I. **We live, as Christians, surrounded by a culture that ignores or rejects the values and beliefs of our faith, centered on Jesus Christ.** In a very real sense, we too are in exile. True, the comparison of our situation and that of ancient Judah isn't exact. The Church has not been militarily conquered; we are not refugees.[1] But the similarities *are* there. We have passed from a time when Christians and the Church dominated society to a time when being

---

[1] Jon Derrick Marshall, *The Ethics of Exile* (master's thesis, St. Paul University, Ottawa, Ontario, 2008), p. 15.

a person of faith is a minority choice. For centuries Christians and the Church had a place of power and privilege, now lost.[2] Even though Jesus never even hinted that his followers should go about using pressure and force, that is what we did. We created a society that made it easy—for *us*. Supposedly public schools recited Christian prayers. Legislation enforced specifically Christian values. The Church was the center of social life—and there was social pressure to belong. We dominated the public square and excluded others. Yet not one hint of that do we see in the teachings of Jesus, who always pictured the Church, his followers, living as a minority within the wider society: his disciples would be as salt (small in quantity compared to the amount of food) and light (the modest oil lamp of a dark village) and yeast (small in amount compared to the whole loaf of bread).[3] Judah's fall was ultimately due not to Babylon but to its own moral and spiritual failures from within. Perhaps the Church's loss of position is a result of our failure—choosing a way that Jesus never taught.[4]

And now, in our own sort of exile, we too, like ancient Judah, must learn to live out our faith as a minority. We must learn to live in exile—as Jesus intended. We must walk a tightrope. On the one hand, we must be careful not to buy into everything our society says and does. That is the way to oblivion. On the other hand, we must not simply hide ourselves away in a Christian ghetto, reading only Christian books, watching only to Christian TV, having only Christian friends. That is isolation. That is not how we can influence our society and draw others to follow Jesus. We must walk between these extremes. We must embrace exile and live out our faith in exile—creatively, courageously, and thoughtfully. So we *can* learn a great deal from ancient Judah's experience in exile.

II. **The Book of Isaiah speaks to just that situation—of exile.** Scholars debate whether Isaiah was written by one or more persons, and precisely when. But what is important to us is that there is little doubt that much of Isaiah speaks to the experience of ancient Judah's exile. And therefore, it has something to say to us—to *our* exile. How do *we* live in exile, as a minority?

---

[2]Marshall, *Ethics of Exile.*
[3]Douglas John Hall, *Confessing the Faith: Christian Theology in a North American Context* (Minneapolis: Fortress, 1996), pp. 123–126.
[4]Marshall, *Ethics of Exile*, p. 16.

Today's Old Testament reading from Isaiah is one of the so-called songs of the suffering servant. There are several such poems or songs in Isaiah. They describe something of what it meant for ancient Judah—and I believe also for us—to live in exile, as God's people.

The suffering servant of Isaiah means us: the followers of Jesus today. When we hear Isaiah's words, we immediately think of Jesus: he was despised and rejected by others, a man of suffering and acquainted with infirmity . . . Surely he has borne our infirmities and carried our diseases . . . He was wounded for our transgressions, crushed for our iniquities; upon him was the punishment that made us whole . . . He was cut off from the land of the living . . . They made his grave with the wicked and his tomb with the rich . . . (Isa. 53:3a, 3b, 4a, 5a–5c, 8c, 9a, 9b, NRSV).

That we think immediately of Jesus isn't unusual. After all, we know his story, don't we? Jesus was rejected and despised. We believe he suffered for us, took on himself the punishment due to us; we know he was crucified between thieves and was put in the borrowed grave of a rich man. So naturally we think of Jesus when we hear these words. And without doubt, these words did refer, by way of prediction, to Jesus. But remember that when they were first written, Jesus hadn't been born. They were words, in the first instance, written for the people of Judah, exiles in Babylon. I suggest that they are words written also for God's people today—the Church—the successor of God's ancient people, for us.

The suffering servant of Isaiah does not suffer just for the sake of suffering, but for the sake of others. The picture we are given, the role of the exile, is suffering for the sake of others, to rescue them. This *is* the role of the exile. In the ultimate sense, of course, we know that only the suffering and death of Jesus are enough to rescue humanity, to set us free from sin. He, who was the ultimate exile, underwent the ultimate suffering, for the ultimate salvation of humanity.

But God's people are to follow that same path of suffering. And for the same reason. In some mysterious way, our suffering, our exile, is linked to that of Jesus. How that works, I cannot venture to guess. I do not know. I understand only that scripture says it does work.

We see exile and suffering in the Christian college student who suffers the ridicule of his peers because he isn't sleeping around, or who gets a lower grade on a paper that he actually wrote instead of bought from some Internet site. We see exile and suffering in the businessman, a person of quiet faith, who refuses the shady but profitable deal—and sees his competitor feted for his "success." We see it in the believer who writes a check to provide health care in a war zone, and lives a bit more simply so he can do so. We see it in the follower of Jesus who takes the risk of telling someone else about Jesus—in a society where there is all sorts of social pressure to keep that sort of thing to yourself. We see it in the writer, the poet, the preacher who refuses to accept the definitions of reality given by our society[5] and instead sets out the *real* picture given to us in scripture. "We are frightened nearly to death to run any risks, to stand out in the crowd, to go against [the dominant] opinion. Who knows? If one criticizes the [current] arrangements, one might lose a job or [one's] place in the university [or the company]."[6] And you may. But there are some Christians who find the courage to challenge what is wrong, to speak out, to risk—and sometimes to suffer the consequences. But it is not suffering just for suffering's sake. It is for the sake of others.

The suffering servant of Isaiah will, by his suffering, change the world. If all that Isaiah had to say to us about exile was that it involves suffering, what a depressing thing that would be! But the good news is this: the suffering servant—ultimately Jesus, but also God's ancient people, and God's people today, the Church—will change and transform the world. The servant songs of Isaiah speak into exile, speak of suffering, but they also speak of victory. The picture we are given is that God intends to set his world to rights.

The God who gives us to the world, to exile, to the job of being "a light to the nations" (Isa. 42:6d, NRSV), who calls us "to open the eyes that are blind" (42:7a, NRSV), and "to bring out the prisoners" (42:7b, NRSV) is the same God who promises that our exile will end, that the "former things" will finish, and wonderful "new things" will arrive (42.9a, 9b, NRSV). And on that day, God's will, his Kingdom, will come in full. In the meanwhile, *we* are the suffering servant. That *is* the exile's job.

---

[5]Walter Brueggemann, *Hopeful Imagination: Prophetic Voices in Exile* (Philadelphia: Fortress, 1986), p. 95.
[6]Ibid., p. 103.

THE SECOND SUNDAY IN LENT

Living in Exile–II

TOPIC: Letter to Exiles

SCRIPTURE LESSONS: Old Testament Lesson—Jer. 29:1, 4–7, 10–14

    Responsorial Psalm—Ps. 137:1–4

    The Epistle—Rom. 8:18–25

    The Gospel—Mark 14:53–62

HYMNS: "Sing to God Who Reigns Above"

    "This Is My Father's World"

    "Brethren, We Have Met to Worship"

    "Christ Is Coming"

SUGGESTED PRELUDE: "The Homecoming"—Hagood Hardy

SUGGESTED CHOIR ANTHEM: "By the Rivers of Babylon"—Brent Dowe, Trevor McNaughton

In many respects, the Book of Jeremiah was a "how to live in exile" book. How to, as the psalmist put it "sing the Lord's song in a strange land" (Ps. 137:4, Authorized Version). Exile. It means being excluded from one's group or usual place. There is scholarly debate about just when Jeremiah reached its final form and when it was composed. But regardless of those details and through what hands and editing the book passed, this is what we have today, which we believe to be God's Word to us. And certainly the book does speak to the situation of exile.

I. **Jeremiah lived in troubled times.** He felt inadequate when called to be God's spokesman, his prophet. "[Jeremiah] believed it was a time of dying. He envisioned [he foresaw] the death of a culture, a society, a tradition. He watched his world dying and he felt pain."[7] And just as he had long predicted, his country, Judah, was invaded by the superpower of the day, Babylon. In 586 BC, Jeremiah saw the city of Jerusalem fall and the great Temple looted. The leading citizens were carried off into exile. Deported. To Babylon. Exile.

---

[7]Walter Brueggemann, "Because No One Cares (Jeremiah 30:12–17)," in *Hopeful Imagination: Prophetic Voices in Exile* (Philadelphia: Fortress, 1986), p. 32.

II. **Our situation has similarities to the situation of those exiles to whom Jeremiah wrote.** We live in a society where "until quite recently it was the assumption . . . that [our] faith would dominate the public square . . . be the dominant cultural force, supported . . . by the structures of society."[8] We used words like "Christendom" and talked about "Christian nations." But this was a false reality. God's ancient people may have taken the form of a nation, Judah. But that was *not* to be the way for the Church, the followers of Jesus, the successor to God's ancient people. Nowhere did Jesus tell his followers to go and establish "Christian" nations. Nowhere did he ask his disciples to create whole societies in which there would be social pressure for people to attend church or follow him, or schools that required those who weren't his to pray Christian prayers. Jesus spoke instead about his followers living as a small minority, within the wider society. "Many of the images Jesus uses . . . have to do with little things—things that are invisible or hidden . . . vulnerable to rejection. . . . [The church] is about a little bit of yeast, a candle in the night, a pinch of salt, a little flock."[9]

Now, as that way of doing things ends, we must return to the way Jesus *actually* taught his followers to live: in exile, as a minority. Not expecting our schools, laws, culture, or neighbors to understand or support what we are about. So our situation is *very* much like those exiles to whom Jeremiah wrote. As John Calvin put it, "The Children of God *wherever* they have lived have always been strangers and foreigners in the world"[10] (emphasis added). Here the exiles to whom Jeremiah wrote were surrounded by people who didn't accept their beliefs. In a society where Jeremiah's "how to live in exile" letter might very well have been written yesterday—for us. And because we believe this is God's Word to us, that shouldn't be much of a surprise! So what advice *did* Jeremiah give? How *can* we live in exile?

III. **Jeremiah said, "Believe in God's sovereignty."** Jeremiah had what Walter Brueggemann calls "a robust view of God."[11] I like that phrase! Jeremiah

---

[8]Mark G. McKim, *Christian Theology for a Secular Society: Singing the Lord's Song in a Strange Land* (Eugene, OR: Wipf & Stock, 2008), p. 64.

[9]Harris Athanasiadis, "In Search of the True Church: Jesus Suspected Bigness and Both Individual and Institutional Success," *Presbyterian Record*, Sept. 2002, http://findarticles.com/p/articles/mi_hb3371/is_/ai_n28947894.

[10]John Calvin, *Commentary on the Book of Psalms*, trans. by James Anderson (Grand Rapids, MI: Baker, 2005), p. 193.

[11]Walter Brueggemann, "Jeremiah—Designed for Conflict," in *Hopeful Imagination*, p. 14.

didn't believe in a sentimental, stained glass window God. He knew that God was the powerful one. Even though Jeremiah had seen his whole world collapse around him, he knew a God who was still ultimately in charge, a God who was still very well able to bring his purposes to pass. Is this not still God's Word to *us* today?

Living in exile, surrounded by what was once Christendom, isn't easy. We have seen churches close, ministries collapse. We live in a society that does not value the unborn, the elderly, the disabled, the unemployed, the underemployed, and the troubled. Sometimes it feels as though we're the only ones left. Sometimes, we are. But wait! Remember who is in charge here, who is sovereign! And it *isn't* us, thank God!

IV. Jeremiah said, "Accept the reality of exile—and 'seek the welfare' (Jer. 29:7, NRSV) of the society where you find yourself." Apparently there were those going about telling the exiles that exile was going to be short lived. Jeremiah said otherwise. "You're going to be there—in Babylon— awhile. Accept that reality. Settle down for the long haul; get on with life, marry, raise families." That's our situation too. There is not going be any kind of return to the center of power—and we never should have been there to begin with, according to Jesus. The reality is exile, being a minority. The past—Christendom—is past. Grieve if you must. But move on. Get used to the new reality.

And in that new situation, you must "seek the welfare" of the place where you are exiled. The Hebrew word here means "wholeness." Jeremiah was telling the exiles to work toward the wholeness, the "shalom" of their place of exile. Doesn't that apply to us too? We are not to huddle together for safety, with no concern for the society around us—to let it go, as it were, to hell in a handbasket. No. We are to work for the wholeness of our society, what Jesus called the Kingdom, God's will realized. We are to do good: feed the hungry, care for the refugee, protect the unborn, heal the sick, care for the environment, protest injustice, and tell others the good news of God's invitation in Jesus. And "God's work" done through us "will be effective . . . for good . . . even [if many] may not realize that God is . . . involved."[12]

---

[12]Terence E. Fretheim, *Jeremiah* (Macon, GA: Smyth & Helwys, 2002), p. 410.

V. **Jeremiah said, "Don't forget who you are."** When Jeremiah writes to the exiles telling them to marry and have children, and not to decrease in number, what he's really saying is, "Don't fall apart, don't disappear, don't forget who you are: God's people, called to follow him."

We are to be followers of God, whom we know best in Jesus Christ. True, everybody else may be sleeping around, engaged in casual sex. Everybody else may cheat. Everybody else may be caught up in the rat race for the bigger car, bigger house, and more exotic vacation. Everybody else may give precious little of their finances to feed the hungry and none to support the work of the Church. Everybody else may measure human value by what people can do, what they can produce. Everybody else may not keep the Lord's day as a day of rest and worship but go to the malls. But that's everybody else. Not us. We *are* different. We are not to be like everybody else. We are not to forget who we are—even in exile.

VI. **Jeremiah said, "Live in hope."** The day will come, wrote Jeremiah, when God "will restore your fortunes . . . and bring you back to the place from which I sent you into exile" (Jer. 29:14, NRSV). And indeed, eventually the exile in Babylon did come to an end. The people were allowed to return home.

The message to we who are exiles today is just the same. We too are promised a homecoming, an end to exile. But in our case, it won't be return to a mere piece of real estate. It will be the ultimate homecoming, the ultimate end of exile. It will be the day that the [whole] "creation itself will be set free" (Rom. 8:21, NRSV).

It will be the day when God, in Jesus Christ, acts finally to end exile, to bring all things to right, when his love and will triumph, the day when Jesus, as promised, will return in triumph. On that day, the promise Jesus made two thousand years ago will finally come to pass. The promise Jesus made standing in the cold morning air before an outraged high priest, who demanded to know "Are you the Messiah?" (Mark 14:61, NRSV), will finally be fulfilled. Jesus said, "I am: and 'you will see the Son of Man seated at the right hand of the Power,' and 'coming with the clouds of heaven'" (14:62, NRSV). Then—and only then—will our exile be over. And we will have come home forever. Thanks be to God! Amen.

THE THIRD SUNDAY IN LENT

Living in Exile–III

TOPIC: It's Not About Us

SCRIPTURE LESSONS: Old Testament Lesson—Ezek. 36:22–32

  Responsorial Psalm—Ps. 145:1–7, 21

  The Epistle—Rev. 7:9–12

  The Gospel—Luke 9:24–27

HYMNS: "Holy, Holy, Holy"

  "O Lord, Throughout These Forty Days"

  "Holy God, We Praise Thy Name"

Exile. That's what we have been giving attention to during Lent. In a very real sense, the Church today in the western world is also in exile. We have moved from a time when Christianity dominated the public square to being a minority, surrounded by those who do not worship Yahweh—whom we know best in Jesus—who do not share our values and beliefs. Exile.

So today we turn to a portion of scripture that was written *in* exile, *about* exile. Ezekiel. According to the book itself, Ezekiel was among those who were deported to Babylon after the fall of Judah and the capture of Jerusalem. We even know where he lived—in his own house, on the Great Canal (see, for example, Ezek. 3:15, 8:1). Do not imagine that conditions in exile were harsh. Apparently not. When eventually the chance came to return to Jerusalem, many chose instead to remain in Babylon. But it was still exile. And it meant trying to figure how to live out faith in a place where doing so made you stand out, an oddity, unusual.

In today's reading we hear God's words spoken through his prophet Ezekiel. God says that he intends to take action. He will return the exiles to their homeland. And in so doing he will put an end to the scoffing of those who think he is only another petty little tribal god, instead of the ruler of the universe and all nations. He will cleanse his people and give them a "new heart" and a "new spirit" (Ezek. 36:26, NRSV). But the key thing, the thing *not* to be missed, is *why* God is going to act, *why* he will do all this, why he will rescue the exiles. Not for the sake of his people or *their* reputation. God will act, as the Old Testament scholar Walter Brueggemann points out, "for the sake of my holy name."[13] *That* is the key thing; the central, key point; the hinge.

Our society says it's all about us. But our faith teaches that it's all about God. And to live out the belief that it is all about God—not us—is to be an exile. You need only check the shelves of your local bookshop or watch an evening's worth of television commercials to discover that our society lives by the creed that it's all about us. We have shelves full of books on self-fulfillment and reaching your potential and getting what you deserve out of life, advertisements urging us to purchase this or that—even if the product is extravagant—because we deserve it. It's about us. But that is *not* what the biblical faith says. It says that it's about God. It's about God in the Church. It's about God in worship. Most of all, it's about God in life.

I. **In the Church: it's not about us—it's about God.** God's ancient people, Judah, had often forgotten that they existed as a people, had been called into existence and created, by God and for God. It is the same for the Church, God's people today. We are not an organization like any other, a service club or fraternal order. We were "founded upon a relationship [we] did not initiate."[14] A relationship with the God we know best in Jesus Christ.

But I wonder if, deep down, we really do believe the Church is about God? Or have we instead accepted the view of our surrounding society? Too often, I fear, we think of the Church in terms of its programs, it activities. It's about us, and whether the Church provides what we want. We go about frantically, with little time for prayer or reflection. We are "busy." And true, there are lots of good and worthy things we should be busy doing. But perhaps, just perhaps, we've forgotten *why* we're busy, on *whose* behalf we are busy. "Having defined the church in terms of *our* involvement and activity [instead of God], we find ourselves . . . on a merciless treadmill of activity. Perhaps this explains why churches find it difficult to win the interest . . . [of those] who *already* have frantically busy lives . . .

---

[13]Walter Brueggemann, " 'For the Sake of My Holy Name' (Ezekiel 36:22–32)," in *Hopeful Imagination*, pp. 69–87.

[14]Douglas John Hall, *Confessing the Faith: Christian Theology in a North American Context* (Minneapolis: Fortress, 1996), p. 46.

the church seems to offer nothing different from what may be found in a thousand other . . . organizations or good causes. The one thing which makes the church different . . . a powerful sense of a relationship with God in Christ—is not very obvious."[15]

II. **In worship: it's not about us—it's about God.** I fear deeply that in many churches the focus has shifted, ever so slowly and subtly from God, to us. "[I]n much contemporary worship. . . . The needs, wants, desires and expectations of the worshiper are to be addressed first. Happiness and fulfillment is the goal."[16] We sing hymns in which the words "I" and "We" and "Our" dominate, which "focus attention not on God, but on the worshiper, and his or her feelings and mindset."[17] This is *not* what I see in scripture. This is not what Ezekiel tells me. In many churches, "Worship becomes a matter of having *my* needs and desires met, rather than . . . honoring and glorifying God, and in so doing discovering my real needs and having them met by God *on his terms*"[18] (emphasis added).

Worship, true worship, worship that is about God, not us, is a radical, deeply countercultural activity, which forms and shapes us as the people of God today. Genuine worship is a "sustained challenge"[19] to the view of things we get every day from our neighbors, the media, and the whole culture.

But if and when worship is no longer about God but us, we have been assimilated by the culture. Like Judah, we are well on our way to forgetting we are God's own people.

III. **In life: it's not about us—it's about God.** The biblical faith is that it's not just church or worship that are about God. It's life, *all* of life. And if you think that doesn't set you apart, make you stand out, make you an exile in our society—just try it for a while!

For God's ancient people in exile, one of the critical questions was whether Yahweh could operate outside the borders of their homeland. Or

---

[15]McKim, *Christian Theology for a Secular Society*, p. 337.
[16]Ibid., p. 359.
[17]Ibid., p. 361.
[18]Ibid.
[19]Leander E. Keck, *The Church Confident* (Nashville: Abingdon Press, 1993), p. 29.

was he just a sort of local, regional god, such that now, living in Babylon, they were outside his jurisdiction? Well, quite plainly he was not. Ezekiel made that quite clear. God promised he was going to restore the exiles to their homes, and by so doing he would make it quite plain that he operated everywhere, in and above *all* the nations. There was nowhere his writ, his jurisdiction did not run.

All of life is about God, every single bit of it. That's part of why we are different, why we are exiles. Because we don't buy what our society tells us—that all this "God stuff" is fine, if he keeps to whatever his assigned place happens to be. Sorry. We're exiles. And we know better than that. God is no more confined to one area of life than he was confined to the national boundaries of ancient Judah.

Twenty-five hundred years after Ezekiel lived in exile in Babylon, Jesus taught the same things. Jesus gave the universal principle that if you want life, real life, you won't get it by grabbing for it and focusing on yourself and us. That's the way to emptiness, loneliness, purposeless existence. That's the way to lose yourself entirely, and in the end to lose your soul. Instead, if you want life, Jesus said, you have to give it up—and focus instead on God and his service. "For those who want to save their life will lose it, and those who lose their life for my sake will find it" (Luke 9:24, NRSV). Glory be to the Father, and to the Son, and to the Holy Ghost. As it was in the beginning, is now, and always will be: world without end. Amen.

THE FOURTH SUNDAY OF LENT

Living in Exile–IV
TOPIC: The Empire *Will* Strike Back
SCRIPTURE LESSONS: Old Testament Lesson—Dan. 3:1, 8–28
  Responsorial Lesson—Ps. 95:1–7
  The Epistle—Rom. 12:1–2
  The Gospel—John 19:1–11b
HYMNS: "Sing Praise to God Who Reigns Above"
  "Dare to Be a Daniel"
  "O Young and Fearless Prophet"
  "The Lord Is King" (F. J. Haydn)

It's strange. Very strange. When people look at the church, what they often see is a bunch of nice, respectable, mainly middle-class folk. Nice. But you know, I don't think that word "nice" even appears in the Bible! But that's what people see, and—let's face it—often that's how we see ourselves: "nice." The ultimate conformists. Often we fit in almost perfectly with our society. Barely a piece of paper could be fit between us and our neighbors who never darken the door of the church. It hardly ever occurs to us that perhaps there are fundamental differences—irreconcilable discrepancies—between what Jesus taught and what we see around us, the way we go about our day-to-day lives.

The setting given for the book of Daniel is of a time when many of God's ancient people, the Jews, were living in exile. No longer did they live in their homeland, where faith was relatively easy. Instead they were surrounded by those who did not accept their convictions and values. There was pressure to assimilate, to "fit in," to be like other nice folk. Regardless of whether these stories were intended as historical records, one thing is obvious. "The stories of Daniel [give] . . . a model for ways to cope in exile."[20] We turn to these stories today because we too are in exile. Not in the sense of having been forcibly deported to a foreign country. But we *have* experienced exile. We have gone from a time when Christianity dominated the public square to being a minority. We are surrounded by those who do not worship Yahweh—whom we know best in Jesus—who do not share our values and beliefs. We feel the social pressure to keep our Christianity to ourselves, to fit in, to conform. So the book of Daniel, as part of God's word, can speak to us, to *our* exile.

The story which was read for us from the book of Daniel this morning is well known. Likely every child who has ever attended Sunday school has heard it. It features not Daniel but rather three of his friends: Shadrach, Meshach, and Abednego. Like Daniel, all three had been forcibly deported from their homeland when their country had been conquered by the Babylonian Empire. They had nevertheless risen to positions of great responsibility in the empire—all the while managing to hold on to their identities as worshippers of Yahweh. Now, however, comes a moment of crisis. The king, Nebuchadnezzar, makes a giant statue. He orders all his officials to worship it on pain of death. Shadrach, Meshach, and Abednego know very well that they are to worship only Yahweh.

---

[20]Sharon Price, *Daniel* (Macon, GA: Smyth & Helwys, 2008), p. 1.

That is the very core of their identity, of their faith. So they refuse to obey. "[W]e will not serve your gods and we will not worship the golden statue that you have set up" (Dan. 3:18d, NRSV). Enraged, the king has them thrown into a blazing furnace. To everyone's amazement, they survive. The astonished king calls them out from the blaze, commends the three for their courage, and promotes them.

I. **The first principle for living in exile is this: you have to live within the empire.** Shadrach, Meshach, and Abednego may have missed the good old days back in Judah when faith was easier. Quite likely they grieved and lamented the loss. But they moved on. They got on with living within the Babylonian Empire, even though it meant living out their faith in a new way.

It is the same for us today. The day when the church dominated the public square is over. The day when public schools demanded everyone pray Christian prayers, when laws enforced explicitly Christian views, is finished. Some may grieve that loss—the good old days, the way things used to be. But just like Shadrach, Meshach, and Abednego, we need to move on. We need to begin to live out our faith in a new way, within the "empire" that surrounds us. We must connect with and engage our society in new ways. No longer because we run things. No longer from a position of influence or control or power. But by the way we live our lives, by reasoned words *matched* by quiet, consistent example. In a greedy and rich society, we are the ones who must speak out for the poor of the world—and then live modestly so we may share the world's resources. Living in western society, an "empire" that rapes and plunders the natural world, we must call for "green" policies, and we must live that out in our own homes by recycling, by driving a fuel-efficient car. In an "empire" where there is spiritual hunger, where people are searching, we must quietly invite—not expect, much less demand—but invite people to journey with us, to come, see, and experience what we have found to be true.

II. **The second principle for living in exile is this: don't accept the empire's definition of reality.** Here are Shadrach, Mechach, Abednego. Surrounded by the power, the splendor of the Babylonian Empire—the superpower of the day. It must have been hard for them to imagine anything else, anything different. This is just the way things are. This is reality. Nothing to be done about it. Whatever the empire says and does is reality. Except they knew a deeper reality, a more real reality. They knew the deepest reality of all. They knew "that what makes life truly valuable and worth living . . . is not . . . political advancement [or even survival] but . . . loyalty . . . to God."[21] The deepest reality, what really mattered, wasn't everything they saw around them, but God.

Martin Luther King Jr. grew up in a culture where it was just reality that black people experienced segregation, discrimination, and violence, could rarely vote, and had to sit at the back of the bus. That was the "empire." That was reality. Few could imagine it any other way. But King knew a deeper reality. He knew of a God who had created all human beings. He knew the reality that simply being created by God gave immense value. So King—and countless others—simply refused to accept the definition of reality all around them. And the world changed: a little piece of God's will accomplished.

Christians in Eastern Europe had spent decades living under governments that told them that what was real, what was important was serving the state, the revolution. Everything they knew pointed to that as reality. Art, television, education, the law—all said that. But they knew a deeper reality. The collapse of the Berlin Wall began when a Lutheran minister, Christian Fuhrer, began organizing prayers for peace in the Nikolai Church in Leipzig. Soon there were thousands and then hundreds of thousands of people gathering to pray, peacefully to march, to refuse anymore the definition of reality they had been told for decades. And that wall came down. And the world changed: a little piece of God's will accomplished. Yes. We must live in western society, as part of it. But we do not have to accept its definition of what is real, of what is important, of what is true, and of what is good.

III. **The third principle for living in exile is this: be prepared for the consequences of refusing to accept the empire's definition of reality.** Shadrach, Meshach, and Abednego refused to worship the golden statue. And they were thrown in the furnace as a result. True, they were miraculously

---

[21]Price, *Daniel*, p. 88.

rescued. But that seems to be the exception to the rule; you may very well not be rescued—at least not immediately.

That even happened to Jesus, standing before Pontus Pilate, who demanded to know who he was and what he was about. "Do you not know that I have the power . . . to crucify you?" (John 19:10, NRSV). And Jesus refused to accept that definition of reality. "You would have no power . . . unless it was given you from above" (19:11, NRSV). You *think* that your power exists apart from God, that you can do as you like. You are wrong. And Jesus was executed. He was not rescued from that.

THE FIFTH SUNDAY IN LENT

Living in Exile–V

TOPIC: Esther's Choice

SCRIPTURE LESSONS: Old Testament Lesson—Esth. 2:5–12, 17, 3:1–2, 5–6, 8–9, 4:1, 5–16

Responsorial Lesson—Ps. 4:1–3, 8, 5:8

The Epistle—1 Pet. 1:17–19

The Gospel—Matt. 8:18–20

HYMNS: "God of Grace and God of Glory"

"I Sing a Song of the Saints"

"Go, Labour On"

She gazed absentmindedly at her own reflection in the pond, by moonlight. And shivered. It was not especially cold even though it was winter, and court resided now at Susa, the winter capital of the great Persian Empire. It was not any outward cold. It was nerves, fear at what she was about to do. There was little doubt why the king had chosen Esther as his queen after Vashti had fallen out of favor. Esther was a very beautiful woman. Out of the king's harem, she had been chosen. For now. But that could change at the king's whim. A woman, even a queen, was expendable.

I. **So much had happened.** How had it come to this? Her people had lived there in Susa for so long, few quite remembered how long it was. But one thing they had not forgotten. They were different. Not like everyone else.

They were Jews. They worshipped Yahweh, Israel's god. Their ancestors had been forcibly deported from Israel by the Babylonians. Then that empire had been taken over by the Persians. But through it all, her people had kept to the old faith and the old ways. Mordecai, her father—well, not her actual father, but the only one she had ever known since her own parents had died—he had taught her the old stories. She smiled as she remembered his telling and retelling the stories. Of how God had chosen Abraham to work with him to accomplish his mysterious purposes. Of how his descendants had eventually formed a nation, Israel. But Israel had become corrupt and had not followed God's ways. So there had been divine judgment, invasion, and exile to Babylon. And then Babylon was overtaken by the Persians. But it was all so very long ago. At times it seemed unreal.

Esther had lived in pleasant obscurity until a few months before. After the queen had been banished, the king became morose. His advisers suggested that all the beautiful virgins in the kingdom should be gathered into his harem, and after he had spent a night with each, he could make one of the women his new queen. It was the way of the world, like it or not. And that was how she, Esther, had ended up as queen. Queen. *I can hardly believe it. Not that it meant much*, she mused. *I come when the king calls—and not otherwise—and do what he says, when he says it. And now this.*

Mordecai had brought it on himself with his stubborn pride. He refused to bow to the new chief minister, Haman. Mordecai never explained why. But bow he wouldn't. And when Mordecai decided on something, that was the end of it. *Just like every other man*, she thought! It hadn't taken Esther long to notice that Haman, the new prime minister, was vain. What she hadn't known until three days ago was just how vain—and how vindictive. His vanity wounded by Mordecai, somehow Haman had persuaded the king to order the mass murder of *all* the Jewish people, completely contrary to usual government practice of leaving conquered peoples alone so long as they remained loyal. There were rumors that the deal involved a large amount of money flowing into the king's treasury. But who knew for sure? There were always rumors at court. What was sure was that a decree *had* gone out in the king's name ordering this massacre.

Mordecai had pleaded with Esther to intercede with the king. But she had not seen the king in over a month. She had not been called. The only way was to enter the throne room unsummoned. But she knew very well that was forbidden, even to her. And if she did enter, it meant death, execution. Unless the king chose to extend his scepter to her. And his moods were unpredictable. Yet she could see no other way if her plan was to have any chance.

She stood up. She had decided. There *was* no other way. She walked quickly, until she came to the curtained entryway. *Lord God*, she prayed quickly, *God of my people—protect me.*

Her knees shook a little. She parted the curtains and walked into the room . . . Sometimes it helps just to imagine for a while what it was like, to picture the scene, the emotions, in our imaginations.

So also with the story of Hadassah, or Esther. The story of Queen Esther contained in the book bearing her name, in our Old Testament, is not without problems. Strangely, there is no explicit reference to God in the entire book. There is also plenty of debate as to whether the story is supposed to be taken as historical or as a sort of tale told to make a point. It also presents us with numerous moral or ethical dilemmas. What are we to make of the fact that although Esther convinces the king to save her people, he does so not by countermanding his order (for once given, his decrees may not be revoked) but instead by allowing the Jews to engage in a "bloody self-defense, which—even worse—is so enjoyable that it is repeated by Esther's request on the following day!"[22]

II. **Esther tells us we must work to retain our identity in exile.** Somehow, though generations had passed, Esther understood she was different. Perhaps it was Mordecai who taught her. It cannot have been easy, surrounded by a culture that had very different priorities and beliefs. Can you imagine how easy it would have been for a young woman, now at the very center of the royal court, to forget slowly, bit by bit?

---

[22]William Sanford LaSor, David Allan Hubbard, and Frederic Wm. Bush, *Old Testament Survey: The Message, Form and Background of the Old Testament* (Grand Rapids, MI: Eerdmans, 1982), p. 624.

We too live in a society that has different priorities and beliefs than our faith teaches us. And it's easy, slowly, to forget. Not to see the vast difference between the teachings of Jesus and what goes on in our society. Slowly to merge the two, almost without noticing it. How often have we all seen it happen? It's so easy. A few Sundays missed from gathering for worship turns into a few months and then a few years. Instead of a day for worship and rest, it becomes a day for shopping and business as usual. Instead of an attitude of compassion for the poor or the refugee, we find ourselves mouthing the hard attitudes of a society that blames the victim for his own troubles and leaves him by the side of the road. We consume more than we really need, because everyone else does. Slowly, slowly, we become part of the culture around us. It isn't easy to maintain our identity surrounded by a foreign culture. It takes work. Hard work.

III. **Esther tells us there is no permanent safety for exiles.** One might think that if anyone was safe in the Persian Empire, surely it would be the queen, at least so long as she continued to please the king. But Esther's position was precarious at best. But even more so as a person of faith. The moment came when Esther had to choose. She could risk everything to save her people—or say nothing and remain secure, for the moment. Few of us will ever face such a dramatic choice as Esther did. But there will be moments when we will have to risk our safety. When the conversation in the lunchroom takes "that" turn, and now—gulp!—there is a perfect opportunity, finally, to say something about Jesus Christ. *But if I do say that I am a Christian, everyone will think I'm a nut. Do I step out of my safe place and risk it, or not? When the boss asks me to do something underhanded, when do I—or do I—say no? Do I step out of my safe place, or not?* There is, for exiles, no permanently safe place—other, of course, than the safety of living within God's own will (Ps. 4:8).

IV. **Esther tells us we need wisdom and courage to live in exile.** Esther found herself facing a difficult situation. From our perspective, it may be easy to criticize her choices. But we *too* live in a complicated world, with complicated lives. It's not always immediately clear what choice is right, which option is the right one, the ethical one. We move, often, amid shades of gray and ambiguity. We need wisdom. But we also need courage. It takes enormous courage to stand alone, or even as part of a small minority.

Living in exile isn't for cowards or the fainthearted. Fortunately, we exiles know where to go or, better worded, *whom* to go to for both things—wisdom and courage.

Centuries after the story of Esther, when God came among us in Jesus Christ, he was approached by a man who claimed he would follow Jesus wherever he went (Matt. 8:19, NRSV).

Jesus responded, saying, "Foxes have holes, and birds of the air have nests; but the Son of Man has nowhere to lay his head" (8:20, NRSV). The immediate meaning was clear enough. This saying did not so much mean that Jesus didn't have any home base, as it were, for "he seems to have made Capernaum and the home of Peter a base of operations, but basically he was on the road . . . an itinerant."[23]

We are to "live in reverent fear," as Peter writes, "During the time of . . . exile" (1 Pet. 1:17). Exile is not an easy place to live. It presents enormous challenges. There is no permanent safe place in exile. We need courage and wisdom to discern complex problems. We must work to retain our identity. But it is that to which we are called. Did we really expect anything else? "It is the way the master went: shall not the servant tread it still?"[24]

PALM SUNDAY

Living in Exile–VI

TOPIC: Alone in a Crowd and Ultimate Exile

SCRIPTURE LESSONS: Old Testament Lesson—Isa. 50:4–9

Responsorial Lesson—Ps. 118:1–2, 19–29

The Epistle—Phil. 2:5–11

The Gospel—Mark 11:1–10

HYMNS: "All Glory, Laud and Honour"

"Hosanna, Loud Hosanna"

"Ride On, Ride On in Majesty"

"O Young and Fearless Prophet"

---

[23]Ben Witherington III, *Matthew* (Macon, GA: Smyth & Helwys, 2006), p. 187.

[24]Horatius Bonar (words), 1843, and William Boyd (music), 1864, "Go, Labour On."

The excited crowd has heard the rumor: Jesus, the strange teacher from Galilee, is coming to the city for the Passover festival. Then they see him coming, riding on a donkey. Perhaps a few of them even remember the old prophecy, written centuries before by Zechariah: "your king comes to you; triumphant and victorious . . . riding on a donkey, on a colt, the foal of a donkey" (Zech. 9:9, NRSV). Many begin to throw their cloaks on the road, for Jesus to ride over; others cut leafy branches and spread them (Mark 11:8).

They begin shouting "Hosanna! Blessed is the one who comes in the name of the Lord!" (11:9, NRSV). We can imagine the disciples of Jesus, not knowing what to make of all this, trying to stay close to him as he rides into Jerusalem, amid the chaos, surrounded by the jostling crowd—alone.

I. **Jesus is alone, in exile, apart from the crowd.** Of course this was hardly the first time there had been crowds around Jesus. It had happened many times before. No doubt the crowds grew as his reputation spread. But very often the crowds came for dubious reasons. They wanted to see Jesus perform. It wasn't much beyond the level of wanting him to do some sort of "magic trick" for them. Others apparently hoped he was going to declare a holy war on the occupying Romans and drive them back into the sea. Few, very few, it seemed, really understood, or cared to understand, what he was about or who he was. There is little reason to think it was much different with this crowd on the day Jesus rode into Jerusalem.

II. **Jesus is alone, in exile, apart from his disciples.** Over and over in the gospels, we find the closest disciples of Jesus just not getting it. Even though they were privileged to go about in his close company over a period of three years, they just don't seem to get it. True, they have moments of rare insight, when we who are reading the story think to ourselves, "Ah, finally! The light bulb has come on!" But then understanding seems to fade once more. And that was certainly the case on this day. John's gospel puts it quite bluntly: "His disciples did not understand these things" (John 12:16a, NRSV).

III. **Jesus is alone, in exile, apart from the leaders of the people.** All through his public ministry, Jesus has been disturbing the status quo, the way things are. A number of those in positions of authority had become increasingly distressed by Jesus. Some of them saw Jesus as a misguided teacher leading people astray with false teaching. Others worried that the turmoil he caused would come to the attention of the Roman authorities, who would do heaven knows what if they even suspected some sort of revolt. No doubt some were concerned for their own cushy positions, which depended on currying favor with the Roman occupiers. Whatever their reasons or motivations, many had concluded that Jesus had to be dealt with; he had to go. In Luke's account, some of the Pharisees, apparently outraged at the crowd's adulation, demand of Jesus that he "order [the] disciples to stop" (Luke 19:39b, NRSV).

Doubtless they were not amused when Jesus refused and told them "I tell you, if these were silent, the stones would shout out" (19:40b, NRSV).

Mark's account of the day puts it darkly and ominously: "And when the chief priests and the scribes heard . . . they kept looking for a way to kill him" (Mark 11:18a, 18b, NRSV).

That is definitely exile, being alone.

IV. **Jesus will soon experience ultimate exile, apartness from God.** While today we focus on the events of Palm Sunday, the triumphant entry into Jerusalem, we cannot and must not forget that a dark cloud hung over those events. Only a few days later, Jesus would be arrested and hustled off in the middle of the night. He would be put through the mockery of two trials, beaten up, sentenced, and finally executed by crucifixion.

And it is clear that he knew what was coming. He knew the old prophets; Isaiah's words of someone being beaten and struck, insulted and spit upon (Isa. 50:6, NRSV) would apply to him. But Jesus *had* "set [his] face like flint" (50:7c, NRSV) determined to see this through to the end, to be "obedient to the point of death" (Phil. 2:8b, NRSV). He warned the disciples. He tried to prepare them. He told them plainly he was going to die in Jerusalem. But they didn't understand, or they couldn't accept that. I suppose that's not too surprising.

On this day that we call Palm Sunday, we reflect on the story. Jesus *surrounded* by the crowd as he rides into Jerusalem. And yet . . . Alone. Alone in the crowd. And soon to become even more alone. Perhaps the message for us is this. Jesus said over and over that we should not expect to receive better treatment than he did. "A disciple is not above the teacher, nor a slave above the master" (Matt. 10:24, NRSV). If even he experienced exile, apartness, then we who are his followers today should expect the same. True, not the ultimate exile he experienced, apartness from God. For by his death he has dealt with that for us. But we should expect every other kind of exile.

We too will have to be alone sometimes. We will have to stand apart from the crowd, swim against the tide. We will have to value all human life, from conception until natural death, when many do not. We will have to insist that *all* people have value, not because of what they can do or produce, but simply because God created them and loves them. We will have to observe the Lord's day, when others flock to the shops and do business as usual. In a culture which talks of hookups and one-night stands, we will have to be different—and often alone. We will have to set our financial priorities so that we can give, and give and give to make the gospel known, to feed the poor, to house the homeless. We will have to endure being called "bleeding hearts" when we advocate for the refugee, and "unrealistic" when we demand real, genuine action by government and business to care for a world that we believe doesn't belong to us but to God. And be very sure: we *will* experience exile. Just as our master Jesus did. But take courage. After the inevitable exile comes inevitable resurrection—and return home. Thanks be to God! Amen.

EASTER SUNDAY

Living in Exile–VII

TOPIC: Freedom from Exile

SCRIPTURE LESSONS: Old Testament Lesson—Gen. 3:1–11, 23–24
    Responsorial Lesson—Ps. 118:1–2, 15–17, 24
    The Epistle—1 Cor. 15:1–8
    The Gospel—John 20:1–18

HYMNS: "Christ the Lord Is Risen Today"
    "Christ Arose"
    "Thine Is the Glory!"
    "Hark the Glad Sound!"

It is an old story—a *very* old story. Two thousand years ago, in an obscure corner of the Roman Empire, from a small, unimportant village, a strange teacher had emerged. One Jesus—a common enough name. Over a three-year period, he had gone about preaching and teaching. Along the way, he had collected about him a group of followers, both men and women. As his reputation had grown, he had attracted large crowds. But he had also attracted enemies. He criticized the religious authorities for hypocrisy, lack of genuine love and compassion, and misunderstanding the Hebrew scriptures. In an occupied country, he no doubt made the political and military authorities wary.

I. **Those paying attention also found that he quite regularly said the most outrageous things about himself.** He told people *he* forgave their sins (Mark 2:1–2, Luke 7:36–50), though most folk believed that only God could do that. In the best known of his sermons that has come down to us, the Sermon on the Mount, he put his own words on the same level as God's (Matt. 5:21–48). He claimed to have sent the old prophets, that everyone else believed God had sent them (Matt. 23:34). He claimed that he had been the lord of Israel's greatest king—David—who had lived a thousand years before, and had known only one superior, God. (See, for example, Matt. 16:13–20, where Jesus claims to be the Messiah, with Mark 2:1–12, where he observes that the Messiah is David's lord.) On one occasion, people in his hometown got so annoyed at him they tried to pitch him off a cliff (Luke 4:14–30)! On another occasion, when a group caught the implication of what he had said to them, claiming to be God, they almost stoned him (John 10:33). Over and over he told people that they should follow him, obey him, prefer him over everything else in life, even friends and family, and to be prepared, if need be, to give it all up in order to follow him (Luke 14:26–27)!

Eventually he ticked off enough people, people with power, people with lots to lose, that he was arrested, beaten up, and executed by crucifixion in the capital city of Jerusalem. And that *should* have been the end of him. He *should* have ended up as barely a footnote in history, known perhaps only to a few scholars who study short-lived popular movements of the ancient Middle East.

Except. Except, of course, that within days of his very public execution, his followers started going about saying that he wasn't dead. He had come back to life. Now the strange thing was that the authorities had been afraid something like this would happen, so they had arranged to have his grave guarded. But still they couldn't scotch the story by just producing the corpse—it had disappeared. Just as his pesky followers said. His followers, who had run for their lives when Jesus was arrested, hiding behind locked doors, why, suddenly they were changed men. Bold, courageous, standing up to the authorities, shouting from the rooftops. Willing to risk trouble. What could possibly have caused that? Unless they really *had* seen him. And even though they lived in a society that devalued and oppressed women, they insisted that it was women, and not even high-ranking women, who had seen him first. At least they should have changed that bit of the story to make it more credible, more likely to be accepted—unless of course they were somehow committed to telling what they knew, regardless. And over and beyond the historical account, the historical evidence, in the centuries since, countless hundreds of millions have claimed that they are convinced, inwardly, by the sixth-sense way of knowing, that he really did rise, and really is alive. But even if it is true, as the evidence suggests, well, it's still a *very* old story. What difference does it make to us now?

II. **To answer that question, I believe we have to go back even further than Jesus' time—much, much further, back to the dim, misty, beginnings of humanity.** In a symbolic way, in allegory, that story is told to us in the Book of Genesis, the book of beginnings (Gen. 1:1–3:24). There we are told that God created everything there is, including humans. He created us to live in intimacy with himself, in harmony with God, ourselves, other people, and the creation. Then came the problem, the disruption of that intended intimacy, harmony, and unity. Humanity decided to do things its own way, instead of God's. Decided we knew better, decided we would miss out on something good if we did it God's way, that he was holding out on us. In the Genesis allegory, the point is made in terms of disobeying God's instruction not to eat fruit from a certain tree (Gen. 3:1–7). But that story, doing it our way, has been repeated down the centuries. And the result? Exile. Just like in that Genesis story.

III. **Exile.** We find ourselves apart, in disharmony, in disunity, away from where we should be, no longer in harmony with God, ourselves, others, or the rest of the creation.

Most important and most tragic, exiled from God. In the story, Adam and Eve are driven from the garden where they had known God so intimately.

And the way back is barred (Gen. 3:24). Apart, exiled from God. The desire to do it their own way has set the pair apart from God. In a cascading list, the exile from God means exile from oneself, from each other, from the garden of creation.

Exiled, apart, from ourselves. In the Genesis story, almost as soon as he finds himself discovered, Adam denies responsibility (3:12). He can't admit it to himself, much less anyone else. He is uncomfortable now, even in his own skin. And is there anyone here who hasn't experienced that? That sense of being, somehow, distant from one's own self? Not understanding who or what one is.

Exiled from one another. What now in the story? Adam blames Eve. It's *her* fault!

The first small step of apartness, separation, exile from one another. And generation upon generation has repeated the story, until families divide, and whole groups and nations are apart from each other. At the extreme, we will kill one another.

Exiled from the wider creation. Only a few lines before, the story was of the wonderful harmony in the garden, of animals, plants, and humans. But now the words are different. Now we hear of "toil," "thorns and thistles," of humanity being driven out of the garden (Gen. 3:17–24, NRSV). Listen to the evening news. Reports of increasing carbon output, ocean dumping and overfishing, indiscriminate cutting down and burning of rain forests. And the results? Rising oceans that drown coastal villages, drought, empty oceans, flash floods. Listen. And then tell me this isn't our thorns and thistles today, our exile from the wider creation . . .

IV. **Exile. That *is* our condition, that is *our experience*, our human story.** And the way back is blocked. Heaven knows we have tried to get back. Across the centuries, how many utopian plans have there been to turn the world into a paradise? How many schemes and programs? How many self-improvement books and courses and gurus? Sometimes we even have been told that we aren't really in exile at all, that everything is or will be fine. But we know, we feel—instinctively—that's not so. We are apart, in exile. And the way back is blocked. That is our real problem.

And that is precisely why I believe that the old story, the story of the Resurrection of Jesus, is *not* just an old story, something that doesn't have anything to do with me, with us. I am convinced it has a great deal to do with me and with us—*now*, today. And if I didn't believe that, I wouldn't be here—in this pulpit, or this church—or *any* church, for that matter.

For according to scripture, the Resurrection is God's loud, trumpeted announcement that there *is* a way back, that the exiles *can* come home! In Jesus Christ, that strange prophet from Nazareth, God chose to come among us. Imagine that! God living as one of the exiles! For that indeed is who Jesus was—as he said so often. And somehow, by his death and Resurrection he opened the way back. It may be an old story, but somehow he pulled down the barrier, to end our exile. Good news! "The gates of brass before Him burst, the iron fetters yield."[25] And now, yes, right now, he invites the exiles to come home.

Just as he invited those long ago, he now invites us to follow him. "Acknowledge me," he says, "as Lord and master, as first concern and priority of your life. Let nothing keep you from this. Not family, not friends, not even the whole world. Follow me—out of exile." *That* is what we celebrate today, on this day of days. Easter Day. The end of exile.

---

[25]Philip Doddridge, "Hark the Glad Sound," 1735.

CHAPTER TWO

The Difficult Sayings of Jesus

Dr. William Powell Tuck

Former Professor of Preaching, Southern Baptist Theological Seminary,
Louisville, Kentucky; Adjunct Professor,
Baptist Theological Seminary of Richmond, Richmond, Virginia

Many find much comfort and assurance in thinking of Jesus as the Good Shepherd, our friend, comforter, and guide. His words "My peace I leave with you" (John 14:27), "I do not call you servants but friends" (John 15:15), "As the Father has loved me, so I have loved you" (John 15:9), "Ask and it will be given you; search, and you will find; knock, and the door will be opened for you" (Matt. 7:7), and many others offer us hope and reassurance. But others of the sayings of Jesus often challenge and disturb our thinking and leave us uncertain how to understand, apply, or discern the meaning intended by Jesus. Some of his more difficult sayings have been used by the enemies of Christianity to throw derision and ridicule on the teachings of Jesus.

Some scholars have suggested that there might be 70 or as many as 150 "hard" or difficult teachings of Jesus. Some believe that many of Jesus' teachings are difficult to comprehend clearly in today's world. F. F. Bruce lists seventy in his book, *The Hard Sayings of Jesus*; William Neil lists sixty-five in his two books titled *The Difficult Sayings of Jesus*. More recent studies have been done by Richard John Neuhaus, Michael Kelly, David Bivin and Roy Blizzard Jr., Ron Rhodes, John Carroll, Lloyd Ogilvie, and others. All these writers note the difficulty in translating the words of Jesus from Aramaic or Hebrew. They believe that much of the difficulty may be in Jesus' use of simile, metaphors, puns, hyperbole, overstatements, irony, and paradox; use of proverbs, riddles, or poetic forms; and use of parallelism.

The kind of difficult sayings of Jesus I am referring to include the following: "Whoever does not hate father and mother cannot be my disciple" (Luke

14:26ff), "You must be perfect as your heavenly father is perfect" (Matt. 5:48), "Love your enemies" (Matt. 5:44), "If your right eye causes you to sin, pluck it out" (Matt. 5:29), Jesus' curse of a fig tree (Mark 11:14), "Go sell what you have" (Mark 10:21), and "Unless you eat the flesh of the Son of Man and drink his blood" (John 6:53). To try to ignore the difficulty of these teachings or simply to act as though they are not puzzling is dishonest. As Christians we need to see if we can grasp their message, especially if we expect to preach on them. Sometimes we have to acknowledge that some of the perplexing teachings of Jesus may be clear enough, but that trying to apply them to our own situation may be more complicated than we thought. At other times the teaching may be clear, such as the command against divorce, but we lack the will or moral determination to follow it.

On other occasions, the hard sayings may challenge our apathy, indecision, callousness about holy things, or our commitment to genuinely following Jesus. Other hard teachings remind us of the difficulty and challenge of walking in the Christlike way. Still others probe deeply into our souls to enlist us to reach for the highest and best within us as followers of the "narrow" way. These teachings may become instruments to enable us to grow spiritually and to discern what it means to "take up our cross and follow" Christ.

I personally believe that the preacher should not try to "explain away" the difficulty and at times the shocking demand that Jesus asserts in these teachings. Without question they cut against the grain of our modern world and our comfortable way of trying to make the teachings of Jesus acceptable and attractive for modern men and women.

Instead, these hard words represent the kind of challenge and expectations Jesus has for those who would follow him. We need to interpret them, understand them, but not short-circuit or lessen their demands. The following six sermons are one preacher's attempt to wrestle with some of the difficult sayings of Jesus.

TOPIC: The Unpardonable Sin
TEXT: Mark 3:28–29

The words from Jesus about a sin that is unpardonable have caused much misery, discomfort, terror, and anguish for many because they have been afraid that they somehow had committed this unpardonable sin. They were afraid that they would be shut out of the presence of God when they died and could not experience forgiveness in this life.

We are startled by these words of Jesus that there can be a sin that is unforgivable, because the heart of the gospel is forgiveness. It was our Lord who declared, "Whosoever will, may come unto me." Jesus taught about God's love through parables about a lost son, a lost sheep, and a lost coin and how all of them symbolized our acceptance by God. The psalmist wrote that the wideness of God's forgiveness removes our sins as far as the east is from the west. Even the dying thief's prayer on the cross to be remembered by Jesus received the generous response from Jesus, "This day you will be with me in Paradise." So we have to be honest and say that these words are upsetting. They seem to contradict God's unconditional love.

I. **The context for this saying.** Notice the setting of this story. The setting for these harsh words from Jesus was Galilee, right after our Lord had healed a man who had been possessed by demons. Some of the Pharisees and scribes had come down from Jerusalem into Galilee where Jesus was teaching and healing, and accused Jesus of healing not by the power of God's Spirit but by the power of Beelzebub. Beelzebub was an old Canaanite word that meant "the prince of demons." The Pharisees accused Jesus of doing his good works by the power of the chief of demons—Satan.

Notice the emphatic response of Jesus to the Pharisees. This phrase has been translated in various ways: "Verily I say unto you" or "Truly I say unto you" or "I tell you this." This phrase is sometimes translated "amen." Jesus himself is described in Revelation as "the Amen"—the faithful witness. Jesus was saying, "Of a truth I am saying something important to you now that you need to hear." Jesus begins by confronting the Pharisees with the absurdity of claiming that the good that he was doing was caused by Satan. Jesus was casting out evil in people. It would not be logical to say this was the result of Satan's action. That would be like Satan trying to destroy himself.

Notice the nature of the sin that Jesus condemned? The word used to describe this sin is called "blasphemy" in some translations and "slander" in others. The word *blaspheme* means to ridicule; to put down in a contemptuous manner; to profane or mock spiritual matters or anything regarded as sacred; to curse, irreverence, or revile God or holy things. Jesus declared that the Pharisees were committing blasphemy because they were ascribing to Satan the good acts that Jesus was doing. They credited the powers of evil to God. They were calling good evil. Because they did not approve of Jesus or agree with his teachings, they were unwilling to acknowledge that the good he was doing came from the work of God's Spirit. Therefore, they called it evil. They were not merely maligning the character of Jesus but slandering the nature of God. Jesus said that whenever a person calls the good work of the Spirit of God evil, then that person is committing the unpardonable sin. Why? Their spiritual and moral blindness has caused them to refuse to acknowledge the obvious good that Jesus was doing and ascribing it to Satan.

II. **The path to committing the unforgivable sin is a lifetime journey.** The unpardonable sin is not some act that an individual commits in an isolated moment or in one single event. It is a path that a person may walk down over a long period of time.

The journey on this pathway begins in "grieving the spirit of God." In Ephesians 4:30, Paul prays this very prayer: "Do not grieve the Holy Spirit of God." God's Spirit seeks to work within our lives to strengthen us whenever temptation comes. God's Spirit whispers in our inner ear or heart to give us guidance and direction. The Holy Spirit is our advocate and helper to enable us to confront whatever difficulties lie before us. The Spirit seeks to empower us to resist temptation and not yield to its power. When you are tempted to sin, whether it is to lie, cheat, steal, or be unfaithful to your spouse, the Holy Spirit's whisper seeks to guide you through this temptation. God always gives us freedom to decide. The choice is up to us. If you do sin, however, then you grieve God's Spirit. The first step down this path, then, is to grieve God's Spirit.

The second step on the pathway to the unforgivable sin is to resist the Spirit of God. The epistle of James reminds us, "Resist the devil and he will flee from you" (James 4:7). Rather than resisting the powers of evil, sometimes persons resist God's Spirit. Instead of following God's leadership, persons turn away from God's guidance. We begin to build up a resistance against the Spirit of God and slowly, ever so slowly, turn away from the

Spirit's guidance. This does not happen in a moment, but is a steady erosion of the influence of the good on our thinking. We don't plan to sin. But slowly we cease to pray, do not worship, ignore our church friends and God's ways. We move down a path of resistance that moves us away from God almost without our knowing it.

The third level is to quench God's Spirit. Paul writes in 1 Thessalonians 5:19, "Quench not the Spirit of God." Our senses become nonresponsive to God's efforts. We shut the door to God and close God out of our lives. Our capacity to respond to God's Spirit has gradually over time grown cold and dead. Our heart has become hardened; our senses are dead, and our capacity to respond is muted.

Because we have not exercised our capacity to respond to God, we have over a period of time lost our ability to respond. Whatever gift or sense we have in our lives, if we do not use it, we will lose it. Our body is certainly an example of this principle. If we do not exercise our muscles, our body will soon become weak and flabby. Many of us lose our physical capacities simply because we do not use them. The same is true with our intellectual or musical capacities. This is also true spiritually. If we do not exercise our spiritual awareness, seek to develop our prayer life and our spirituality depth, then this capacity will begin to shrink, and soon it will be lost.

In our society today, there are many persons who no longer want to acknowledge that anything they do wrong is sin. They may acknowledge what happens as a crime or as something that is the result of heredity, a result of genes or a weak trait, or the result of their environment. The word *sin* seems to be disappearing from the vocabulary in our society, but, unfortunately, sin itself has not disappeared.

Our sinful self can take over the control of our life, and we can lose our sense of sin. But an even sadder fact is that we can get to a point where we, like the Pharisees in this text, call good, evil and evil, good. Some reach the point where they no longer are able to distinguish good and evil. These persons are amoral. Their concept of right and wrong is so confused that they no longer can distinguish good from evil.

III. **Hear this word of comfort.** If you think you have committed the unpardonable sin, this is a sure sign that you haven't. Your remorse or concern indicates that you are still trying to understand God's ways and be responsive to God. Most people who worry about committing the unpardonable sin are never those who have in actuality done it. Hear the good news in this text. "I tell you no sin, no slander is beyond forgiveness" (Matt. 12:31). The slander against the Holy Spirit may never be forgiven. But remember that no sin or slander is beyond God's forgiveness as long as you and I are willing to confess those sins. The problem does not lie with God's unwillingness to pardon us or our sin.

The only sin God cannot forgive is the sin that a person is unwilling to confess or acknowledge. God is always willing to forgive. If you are concerned at all about your sins, be assured that God will forgive you. As Jesus said, "Whosoever will may come." God's grace is abundant. His love is unconditional. If you think you have committed the unpardonable sin, quit worrying. You haven't. Accept God's grace and forgiveness. He wants to love you. Accept his grace and follow him.

TOPIC: How Do I Love My Enemy?
TEXT: Matt. 5:43–44

Jesus' words that we are to love our enemies seem not only difficult but impossible to put into practice. How, for example, are persons who were freed after years of being imprisoned by terrorists to forgive their enemies? How are relatives who stand before the Vietnam Memorial in Washington, D.C., to love the enemies who killed their relatives and friends? How are the millions of Jews who saw their husbands, wives, children, or parents gassed, victimized, and tortured in Nazi concentration camps to forgive them? How are the Japanese who lived in Nagasaki and Hiroshima to forgive us for dropping the bomb on them? How are the relatives of those who were killed in the World Trade Center towers to forgive those who were responsible for the attack?

I. **"Forgive your enemies" sounded difficult in the day when Jesus first uttered it.** He was addressing a people who were at that moment enslaved by the Romans. The tax collectors, their fellow Jews, were working with the Roman government to collect taxes from them. Jewish religious leaders often set up restrictions of the law that were so binding that no person who had any kind of ordinary job could possibly follow their rigid regulations.

In interpreting what he meant by loving your enemies, Jesus gave several examples. If a person smacks you on the right cheek, which would have to be struck with the back of his hand, this would be a double insult. But Jesus said that they were to turn the other cheek as well. If a Roman soldier compelled you to carry his pack one mile as you were walking down a road on matters of your own, don't just go a mile: go two miles. If someone asks for your tunic, give him your cloak also. This would be like giving him not merely your overcoat but your coat or shirt as well. Think how impossible these teachings must have sounded.

His teachings seem to cut against common sense. "If there is anybody you ought to hate," they must have thought, "it is certainly our enemies"—especially the Romans. During war, and especially when a country is occupied by an enemy force, it is easy to arouse feelings of hatred. Hatred was easily stirred up in our country when we were at war with Germany and Japan. Think about your own feelings toward those persons responsible for the 9/11 attacks when you read about their activities in the paper or heard about them on TV.

Who are our enemies? Enemies are easy to define in wartime. Let's put wartime, terrorists, murderers, and rapists aside for a moment and bring our enemies closer to home. Who is our enemy? Our enemy is anybody who hates us or who wishes us harm or injury through word or deed. An enemy comes closer and takes on a familiar face when you see your enemy as someone who may cause you difficulty and turmoil in your job or makes your work miserable. Your enemy may be someone who has caused you to go bankrupt or who smeared your name or hurt your reputation through gossip or slander, or anyone who has told a half-truth about you or sought to cause you harm. Or someone who makes fun of you, puts you down, or ridicules you. An enemy may be someone who has closed the door of communication, or someone who responds differently to you because he or she has misinterpreted something you said or did. All of us feel that we experience some kind of enemy.

II. **The more basic question seems to be, *Why* should I love my enemy?** Why should we try to love somebody who hates us or wants to cause us harm?

If you respond to a person who dislikes you or hates you with the same attitude they are directing toward you, you will soon find that your life is poisoned within. Hatred is a self-destructive attitude. Jesus went so far as to say that the wells of anger and lust within determine our outward behavior.

We need to make a distinction between hating things and hating people. We tend to identify a person with the vicious, destructive, or harmful behavior he or she commits. It is easy to hate a murderer, rapist, or terrorist. Instead let's direct our indignation to the root cause behind the evil and not to the person who is committing the act of evil. We need to love the person and hate the evil. We need to overcome war, prostitution, prejudice, drugs, and other enemies, but not by hating the persons involved in them.

Why should we love our enemy? We love our enemy because love is the only power that can change our enemy. Jesus was not interested in condemning people but in saving them, making them whole. No prostitute was ever changed by treating her as a prostitute. No thief was ever changed by treating him as a thief. An enemy is not changed by treating him as an enemy. Love is the power that can convert an enemy into a friend.

Why do we want to love? Because it is only in forgiving others that we are really forgiven ourselves. This is what Jesus taught us in the Lord's Prayer. "Forgive us our trespasses as we forgive those who have trespassed against us." If you and I refuse to forgive others, we close the door to our own forgiveness by God.

We begin to love our enemy by realizing that we don't always have to *like* our enemy. There are things that our enemies do that we will never like. Who can like somebody who murders and rapes, robs and kills, or somebody who hurts us with words or who victimizes us or who is prejudiced against us? It is difficult to like these people. But we are told not to like them but to love them.

The word *agape* is different from a sentimental concept of love. Agape means that you deliberately direct your will to accomplish what is best for your enemies. This kind of love is not based on emotion or sentiment. When I loved my children by directing my will to recognize and motivate the best within them, there were times that I had to deny them what they wanted. At times I had to discipline them or put restraints on what they wanted to do. I had to correct or try to modify their behavior. I may not have liked what they did, but I continued to love my children. I also continue to love myself when I do some things that I don't like. Real love does not say that it doesn't make any difference what a person does. By an effort of my will—by loving the person—I try to bring about change in his or her life.

III. **Another way to love my enemy is by not identifying the person with his or her sins.** I make a distinction between my *real* self and what I do. I need to do the same for others. I have to see the potential within others. If I refuse, I will never give another a chance to change. Jesus looked at people and saw what they could be through grace and forgiveness. He saw Zacchaeus, a tax collector, who was one of the most despised persons of his day. Yet Jesus saw the difference that could be in Zacchaeus's life if he would follow Jesus and change his life. He saw within the life of Mary Magdalene, a prostitute and an outcast of society, what she could become through transforming love. He saw within Saul, who was persecuting and executing Christians, a pioneering missionary.

This is what God does for us. We can learn to forgive our enemies when we begin to realize how often people do not really understand their own actions. Jesus prayed on the cross, "Father, forgive them for they know not what they do." The influence of friends, relatives, peer groups, community, social or national pressures, gangs, or other pressures cause us to act the way we do. Sometimes we do not really "know what we do." But thank God we can break free from packs and their pressure and experience forgiveness and have the opportunity to start again.

Jesus told his disciples that if they learned to forgive their enemies they would be children of the most high (Luke 6:35). This kind of love reveals that we are like our Father. Even if we are like the prodigal son and go into the farthest country of sin, God will still forgive us when we say, "Father, I have sinned." Out of love, God extends grace that issues in our forgiveness.

This kind of love is not easy. Its claim on our lives and attitude is demanding. The love that Jesus Christ models for us goes beyond anything we can imagine. This love demands the forgiveness of others, the unwillingness to cling to grudges or harbor hatreds, and the goal of being "perfect" like God. Christ calls us to be unselfish, caring, patient, understanding, loving, and sacrificial. Jesus didn't say his way was easy. Loving our enemies is difficult and hard to accept. But it is at the heart of our faith. This teaching makes us realize how far we are from following our Lord's way.

TOPIC: Offensive Words
TEXT: John 6:41–60, 15:12–17

The saying from Jesus that his disciples must eat his flesh and drink his blood is not an easy one to accept. It is offensive to us, and it was offensive to the people who heard it in Jesus' day. This saying was so offensive that many of them turned away and quit following Jesus. The New English Bible translates this phrase, "This is more than we can stomach! Why listen to such talk?" (John 6:60). It was a hard saying, and many could not accept it and would not and did not understand it. Many of us find the words from Jesus that we must "eat his flesh and drink his blood" as among the hardest of his teachings.

I believe that Jesus was affirming that he came to give his followers something greater than the bread Moses gave the children of Israel in the wilderness. Moses was merely the means God used to lead the people to the bread he provided for them. Jesus is saying, "I am the Bread." He was attesting that persons would find the relationship they wanted with the Father, through him. "I am more than just a means to it. I am the way." When you and I attempt to look at that saying and try to understand how it relates to us and our understanding of the Christian faith, it is still not easy. This is especially true when we try to relate it to our own everyday life. We often wonder how we can go about surviving and just living day by day.

Now what is Jesus telling us? Are we literally to feed off his physical body and be nourished? Is that what he is seeking to say? No. It is much more than that, I think. One of the things that he is saying here is that spiritual fellowship with him is one of the deepest mysteries in life. As we gather at the table of Communion, we acknowledge boldly, openly, and emphatically that words are never sufficient to declare the costly grace and love of God. Our words always fail; they are inadequate and insufficient. We cannot express all of our faith. How can one wrap words around the mystery of God's love and say, "I have explained it"? Do not listen to that person. The love of God goes beyond all human explanations. We can only hint at the greatness of God. We have sensed only the edge of God's garment. There is always the element of deep mystery involved in our understanding of God.

I. **What then do we make of these words of Jesus to help us understand the mystery?** You and I must remember that in the day in which Jesus spoke, the people were surrounded with all kinds of religion. They had what was called the mystery religions. Some of the ancient religions of nations around Israel called for meat to be prepared and offered as a sacrifice to their god. They did not destroy all of the meat in their sacrifice. The people themselves would eat part of the meat that had been prepared and offered to their god. They believed that when they ate some of the meat that had been prepared for this god, they literally took this god's presence into their body. By eating the meat, they were sharing in something of the vitality of the life of this god. Later Paul wrote to Christians in the Corinthian church who were very concerned about this very issue. They were asking whether or not they should eat the meat offered to idols. To them, this would be in some way acknowledging that they were taking this false god into their being. You and I can call this attitude whatever we want to—superstition or nonsense. But they believed it to be literally true. Jesus drew on the ancient beliefs that these people understood. But he was not telling them that they were literally to take his flesh and that doing so would make them religiously vital. He was seeking to probe beneath the surface to tell them, and now us, that his presence in our lives has deep inner significance.

In his commentary on John, Raymond Brown tells us that these words probably go back to the primitive preaching tradition and that John has brought them forward here to tell us some truth about the Lord's Supper itself.[1] When we gather at the Communion table, there is here a deeper significance than you and I can ever acknowledge about the presence of Christ in our lives. I have many books on my shelves. One of them is written by Jürgen Moltmann, titled *The Crucified God*. In this book, this German theologian describes what he believes the sacrifice of Christ

---

[1]Raymond E. Brown, *The Gospel According to John* (Garden City: Doubleday & Co., 1966), p. 287.

means. But I can never learn anything from that theologian about the death of Christ if I never read his book and simply leave it on the shelf. To learn from it, I must read it and let it penetrate my mind and thought and become a part of me. No one can ever learn anything from the gospel of John if he or she never reads it or never hears anybody discuss it. We must pick it up and read it and let it penetrate our minds and hearts. At home I have a recording of Handel's *Messiah*. As long as it stays on the shelf, I cannot enjoy that music. But when I play it, it can come into my life and become a part of me. It penetrates me, and I am uplifted by the power of that great music. So Jesus is telling us, "Unless I come into your life and penetrate it, unless you take me into your life and I become a part of you, then I am really not yours, and I do not influence you."

II. **Hear another word: when Christ comes into our lives, we are different because he introduces a new element into our being.** That element is love. This element of love that comes into our lives penetrates us and gives us more than just an instinct for survival. Too often life is depicted as merely surviving. Lucy is standing by the door as Charlie Brown is going to school. She says, "You had better rush. You are going to be late. Here is your lunch." As he walks down the steps to leave, she says, "Survive!" For some of us, that is about all that we do in the world—survive. But Jesus said that he had come that we might have life. He is the living Bread, and when we learn to feast on him, he introduces into our life an element of love that is transforming.

A woman had come to a Communion service. She was a noted prostitute and felt unworthy of taking the elements. A deacon in the church leaned over to her and said, "Take it." She hesitated. "It is for sinners," the deacon continued, "which we all are." The word that we receive from God is that he has first loved us. He has loved us while we were sinners and has drawn us to himself. We come to his Communion table to feed upon him and to experience the transforming love that he has given us. He has first loved us.

Jesus said, "This is my commandment, that you love one another." "But wait a minute now, Jesus," we want to ask, "how can anybody command love? You can't just say, now children, I want you to stand up here and love your parents. I want you to do this. I command it." Do you teach somebody to play the piano by saying, "I command you to sit down and play the piano; if you don't, I'm going to take a hymnbook and beat you across the head until you learn how to play it"? No. You love them into learning how to play by giving them instruction, guidance, care, patience, and understanding. Christ comes into our lives and, through his patience, his care, his understanding, his grace, gives us the ability to learn how to love more lovingly as we are taught by him.

III. **The love that Jesus Christ gives our lives gives us direction in how to live and care.** He tells us that authentic life, when we feed on him, is the loving life. It is not just a life of survival, but it is a loving way, a way filled with meaning and richness because we are daily feasting upon him. Jesus said, "I call you no longer slaves but friends . . . and I lay my life down for you." If Jesus Christ has laid his life down for us, we in turn are called and challenged to lay our lives down in service and ministry for him.

God has never promised us that if we stand up and live or die for him, that we will put an end to all evil, pain, and suffering in the world. But your life and my life, as we love, can help make a difference for a little while. If there are enough of us who are Christlike in our loving, think of the impact it will make in the world.

TOPIC: How Can I Keep from Judging Others?
TEXT: Matt. 7:1–5

Jesus said, "Judge not lest you be judged." If we are honest, this statement from Jesus is troublesome, isn't it? For we do judge all the time, don't we? We make judgments through the kind of clothes we buy, the food we eat, the cars we drive, the houses we live in, the television shows we watch or don't watch, the books we read or don't read, the places we go for vacations, the friends we make, the person we choose for our spouse. We make judgments all the time. We can't avoid them completely. But some of our judgments are based on the color of people's skin, their education level, where they're from, what part of town they live in, the size of their bank account, what college they attended, or the kind of house they live in. We judge people by their southern or Yankee accents. We make judgments of people sometimes harshly, and quickly.

We have committed this sin across the dinner table, over the backyard fence, on the golf course, over the bridge club table, while walking the halls at school or church, or even over the telephone. The character of someone has been assassinated, fingers have been pointed, and we have hurled spears of prejudgment. We have talked about other people and made hasty, uninformed judgments.

I. **Our Lord has commanded us,** "Judge not." But we want to exclaim, "Wait a minute, Jesus. You said that Herod was an 'old fox.' You warned us to beware of the 'leaven of the scribes and Pharisees.' You called them 'whitewashed tombs.' You told us to be careful about persons who dressed in sheep's clothing but were wolves in sheep's skin. You have told us not to be like the persons who seek to have the first seats at a banquet. You instructed us that we would know your disciples 'by their fruits.'"

By his commandment against judgment, did Jesus mean that we are not to have any discrimination at all? Of course not! The Greek word for "judge" is the root for our word "critic." The word *judge* here really means "censure another with unjust criticism." Do not judge someone else quickly, harshly, and without really having thorough knowledge. Do not make hypocritical judgments.

II. **Why are our judgments often so wrong?** In the first place, we need to remember that we are all fallible. None of us is inerrant or infallible in his or her judgments of others. Why? Well, for one thing, we simply never have all the facts. No one can possibly know everything about every situation. We base decisions on inadequate or false information. Someone might ask a question in the office: "Is it true that Mary and Tom are having an affair?" Later when this person is confronted with this accusation, he or she can reply, "Well, I didn't really say they were having an affair. I was just asking a question." But you and I know that the way the person asked the question destroyed the character of two people. "Why does our teacher seem so dull and grim today?" the students asked. They did not know that he had just buried his father.

The old Indian saying is correct: "You should never judge another person until you have walked two moons in his moccasins." If we only knew what was going on in the life of somebody else—what burdens, perplexities, pains, or sorrows—the heavy load she has to handle in life, maybe our judgments of her would be entirely different.

III. **We are also not impartial in our judgments.** Every person has some prejudice. Prejudice may blind us from seeing the another person's gifts. Sometimes we level our criticism and improper judgments on others and then wonder why they behave as they do. Our self-interest and expectation that everyone else has to see things from our perspective keep us from making sound judgments. Remember, our judgments are never infallible.

Judging may have a way of returning to judge us. A lot of the criticism of others is really self-judgment. Psychologists tell us that often the things we most detest in other people may really be a response to the weaknesses we see within ourselves. As the old saying goes, "It takes one to know one." "He's lazy," we say. "She's a good-for-nothing." "He's not mature." We can only say we know about these factors by revealing our own acquaintance with them. "The truth," Theodore H. Robinson notes, "is that no man can pass an opinion on any other person or thing without at the same time recording a judgment on himself. He 'gives himself away' more by his criticism than by any other act or word."[2] Sometimes what we despise in others is a reflection of what we see buried deep within us.

Jesus said, "You must be careful how you judge others, because the standard of judgment that you use to measure other people will be the one by which your own life is measured." It is simply one of the facts of life. Sometimes the persons who are always complaining about someone else gossiping or about another person cheating, or voicing some other matter become individuals who are suspect themselves. People begin to watch these persons to see if they are guilty of the things they accuse other people of doing. If a person always expresses concern about somebody else's honesty, soon others begin to wonder about that person's honesty. If Mr. Smith is always talking about somebody else gossiping, some may begin to listen to what he is saying about other people.

Jesus expressed his concern about hypocritical judging. Here is old "log-eye" who has a huge log sticking out his eye. While this log is protruding out of his eye, he approaches another and complains about the tiny sawdust speck he sees in somebody else's eye. Jesus says, "Old log-eye, you

---

[2]Theodore H. Robinson, *The Gospel of Matthew* (New York: Harper and Brothers, n.d.), p. 60.

quit worrying about somebody else's eye. You get busy taking out the log that is in your own eye." Our primary effort in life is not to be concerned about the faults of others but to look at the faults within ourselves. The way you judge others determines how you will be judged.

IV. **But our religion is ultimately one of grace.** God alone can really judge. Aren't you thankful that God has not passed his judgment on you based entirely on the way you live and act? Salvation is by grace, not by works. Oh, we would all be in real trouble if our salvation were based on our actions. God alone can ultimately judge another rightly.

Try to see with clear eyes. This is one of the significant points in this text. The log or speck is a foreign object in the eye and needs to be removed so a person can see clearly. When some, especially "log-eye," look at another person, all they see is the speck in the other's eye. They can't see the real person for the speck. However, when Jesus looked at persons, he saw not the speck but the potential within them. He looked at Matthew and did not see a tax collector but a faithful disciple. He looked at Thomas and did not see only his doubts but his faithfulness. He looked at Peter and did not see merely his quick temper and anger but courage and faith. He looked at the woman accused of adultery and saw not a harlot but a committed disciple. He looked at Saul and saw not a narrow Pharisee but a missionary to the Gentiles. Jesus looked at a person and saw the real individual when the evil was exorcised from him or her. He did not see the speck but what the person was when made whole.

One day a young daughter, Lisa, had her arms wrapped around her father's neck. She was hugging him tightly, and the father was hugging her back. But the mother, who was standing nearby, noticed that while Lisa was hugging her father, she was sticking out her tongue at her brother, who was standing behind her. "Lisa," her mother said, "you can't hug your father and stick your tongue out at your brother at the same time. Remember, your father loves both of you." Those words are almost a biblical paraphrase, aren't they? If you and I claim we love God, then we will also love others. We will reach out to embrace all persons.

Remember, Jesus said that the judgment you use to judge other people is the means by which you yourself will be judged. Don't be concerned about the tiny speck or fault or weakness that you see in somebody else, but look at the big log—the huge weakness—in your own life. And get busy trying to change your own fault.

TOPIC: Jesus' Teaching on Divorce
TEXT: Mark 10:1–12; Matt. 5:31–32

The gospels of Matthew, Mark, and Luke tell about an experience that Jesus had when he was questioned one day by some lawyers. These Pharisees raised a trick question to him. "Now Moses gave a bill of divorcement. We want to know if you think there are grounds for divorce." There were two schools of thought about divorce among the Jews at that time. The interpretations were based on Deuteronomy 24:1. One school was the Shammai, who taught that there was only one ground for divorce, and that was unchastity or, as sometimes translated, adultery.

The Hillel school held to a more liberal interpretation of Deuteronomy 24:1. Their interpretation of the Hebrew words for "some uncleanness" refer to a number of things a woman might do. The matter might be a trivial thing like putting too much salt in her husband's food or speaking to a man on the street or making disrespectful remarks about her husband's father in his presence. The husband often divorced his wife for very trivial reasons.

The Pharisees raised the question about divorce hoping to entrap Jesus. The Pharisees believed that if they could get Jesus to make an accusatory statement about divorce, they could offend one of the schools of the Pharisees and maybe even get Jesus in trouble with the Roman government.

I. **Note Jesus' teaching regarding divorce.** There is a problem in the biblical texts. Matthew's gospel presents an "except clause." Jesus says that a man should not divorce a woman except for adultery. In Mark's gospel there is no "except clause." Almost all scholars are convinced that Mark's gospel is the older and correct version.

   Let's begin by asserting that Jesus is holding before his listeners *the ideal of marriage*. Jesus' appeal is not to the law but to creation. He reaches behind the law and goes all the way back to the Creation, when God created man and woman. Divorce, he says, is grounded in the law, but marriage is grounded in creation. When God created man and woman, God made them male and female. Jesus stated that Moses gave a bill of divorce because of "your hardness of heart." Hardness of heart means closed-mindedness, stubbornness, or "unteachableness." However you want to translate that passage, Jesus is stating that Moses granted a bill of divorce as a concession to their human weakness.

In this passage, Jesus, like he did on other occasions, championed the cause of women. Women often suffered injustices at the hands of their husbands. Remember, in the Jewish tradition, a woman could not ask for a divorce; only the man had that right. Jesus does not subordinate the woman to the man, but noted that if either man or woman divorces, each has dishonored the permanency of marriage. Jesus declares that a woman, if she gets a divorce, is just as guilty as a man who divorces his wife. The Roman government allowed both men and women the right to get a divorce.

Jesus holds an absolute ideal for all persons, and he finds his reason for this in God's creation. The Jewish word for marriage means consecration. In their covenant together, a man and a woman consecrate themselves completely to each other. Each is exclusively the possession of the other as an offering that is exclusively dedicated to God. Each is so committed to the other that they become one flesh. This union was God's act in creation, and any breaking of this union is the action of men and women, not God.

II. **Divorce is a reality.** These words reflect a sob, a sigh within the heart of Jesus. Although the ideal for marriage is stated here by Jesus, he knows that many fall far short of that ideal and that divorce does take place. Divorce is a reality. The divine intention in marriage, unfortunately, does not always occur. Because of hardness of heart or stubbornness, God's will for marriage is often abated, and divorce, like all sin, rends the heart of God.

Jesus' teaching is not legalism. Some people make Jesus more of a Pharisee than the Pharisees were. These persons try to make this teaching so absolutely binding that they do not believe that a divorce should be granted for any reason other than adultery. These people take the words of Jesus in this passage literally. But they don't take Jesus literally in other places when he said, "Cut off your hand if it offends you" or "Take up your cross and come follow me."

Are there grounds for divorce? What about a husband who habitually abuses his wife, physically or mentally? What does a person do if she or he discovers that the spouse is homosexual? What do you do if your marriage partner has a character or mental disorder or some other kind of problem? Are there then never any grounds for divorce? I think we need to understand that Jesus uncompromisingly placed the indissolubility of marriage as the ideal from God's creation. But Jesus was not trying to set up a more rigid legalism.

Note how Jesus responded to people when they were in trouble. He always held up God's ideal for people. "Seek first the kingdom of God"; "Be ye therefore perfect." But Jesus knows that no one ever seeks God's Kingdom fully. He also knows none of us is perfect. We all fall short of the ideal. Jesus ministered by the priority of love. He did not treat people as they deserved to be treated but according to unconditional grace. When people fall short of this ideal—when they sin—Jesus grants them forgiveness and grace.

III. **The Church's position on divorce and remarriage is difficult for us to understand.** There are times when one person in a marriage is absolutely devastated by the other marriage partner. The ideal is not always realized, even for persons who are Christians. Jesus was not a Pharisee. He fought their narrowness at every corner. What stance then should the Church take regarding divorce and remarriage in the light of Jesus' teachings?

The Church needs to teach and preach clearly the ideal of marriage. We proclaim that from creation God has desired that one man and one woman be bonded in a covenant with one another until death do them part. This is the Christian ideal. We need to remind people that Christ is Lord of our marriage as well as all of life.

When persons fall in their marriages, the Church, rather than rejecting them, heaping guilt and scorn upon them, and increasing their pain, needs to reach out to these persons with love, care, acceptance, and grace. Many want to know if they will be committing adultery if they remarry. A person who is divorced can experience forgiveness and grace from God and the opportunity to begin a new life. The Church has to hold up the Christian ideal of marriage and state that divorce is wrong. But divorce, like any other sin, can be forgiven. Divorced persons, having experienced forgiveness, can now begin to rebuild their lives.

The Church also needs to provide counseling and divorce support groups to help guide and support persons during this difficult period. As a church family, we want to say to persons going through a divorce or already divorced that we still see them as a person, one of God's children, with special needs like all of us that need to be met.

The Church also needs to remind all persons of the inclusive nature of God's love and the Church's acceptance of all persons. No matter who you are, male or female, married or single or divorced, the Church still reaches out its arms to you with a message of Christ's love and invites you to be a part of its fellowship. We are one in Christ.

The Church has to listen more and respond to the needs, hurts, and pain of people who are divorced, in blended families, in the midst of a divorce, struggling as a single parent, or in any other circumstance. Through our teaching and programs, we want divorced persons and children of divorced parents to know we care and want to help them. We present the love and forgiveness of Christ and the opportunity to begin again with their life.

In one hand the Church boldly and unapologetically lifts up the torch of the ideal of marriage where one man and one woman make a commitment to each other until death parts them. This indissoluble union was ordained by God in creation. This is the Christian ideal for marriage. We ought to teach it, guide people in understanding this ideal, counsel them in living up to this standard, and direct them in its path.

Facing the pain of the reality of how many people are divorced, we lift up with the other hand a torch that reaches out to divorced persons to minister, care for, and love them, even as our Lord showed his love to all persons. Looking to our Lord's example of love, may we try to love even as Christ has loved us.

TOPIC: When Jesus Doesn't Bring Peace
TEXT: Matt. 10:34–39, 46–50

The words from our text, "You must not think that I have come to bring peace to the earth. I am not come to bring peace but a sword," are startling to those of us who remember reading the angelic message to the shepherds that the Promised One was heralded that night with the words, "Glory to God in the highest and peace on earth" (Luke 2:14). This text also seems in stark contrast to the words of Jesus when he said, "Blessed are the peacemakers." I believe that these words of Jesus were intended to focus not on the purpose of his coming but on the effect that his coming might have within families and among friends. It is an abuse of this text, I think, to use it as a rallying cry for war.

The view that the Messiah was to bring strife was in conflict with the concept that people in the day of Jesus had of the Messiah. The standard view that people had of the Messiah was that he was to bring peace, not strife. For Jesus to proclaim that any follower of his would have strife seemed to be in contradiction with how people had envisioned the Messiah.

I. **Notice first that our text reminds us that religion often brings conflict.** Jesus was telling his hearers clearly that those who would be his disciples would often find themselves in conflict with others, and sometimes they might be in conflict with those closest to them, those in their own family.

God doesn't always come into our lives to bring peace of mind or to make us feel good. God sometimes comes into our lives to stir us up. Do you think God can possibly be happy with the world the way it is? Our world is filled with wars, murders, rapes, robberies, and continuous conflict. I think God constantly comes into our lives and stirs us up to motivate us toward maturity. Religion often causes conflict in our personal lives or with the established government or with our own family or with other systems of authority around us or with the values of our society. We are challenged to be like God.

When Jesus called us to be his disciples and follow him, he didn't tell us about an easy or comfortable way. Jesus did not hide the sharp "steel flint" in discipleship. Sometimes, he noted, that his disciples would have to turn the other cheek or go the second mile or give somebody else their outer coat. Jesus spoke candidly about taking up one's cross to follow him and being faithful unto death. He made it clear that sometimes his way was going to be hard and difficult. On occasions the disciples would be rejected, not welcomed. Look through the pages of Christian history and you will see again and again that Christians were indeed often rejected, misunderstood, abused, persecuted, and even martyred.

II. **In our text, Jesus states that sometimes the most difficult place to be a Christian may be within one's own home.** Jesus, I think, may have been speaking autobiographically. Other passages of scripture (Mark 3:21; Matt. 12:46–50) state that Jesus' family had come to one of the places where he was teaching because they wanted to take him home. They wanted to restrain him because they thought he was "beside himself" or insane. His own family did not understand him. They were not in agreement with his ministry. They thought that the older son, their elder brother, was demented. Sometimes our problems, like those of our Lord, can be with our own family.

"If you love your father or mother or any family member more than me, then you are not worthy of me," Jesus declared. Jesus Christ demands first place in your allegiance, first place above everyone even your own family. Jesus states that his claim for loyalty overrides all others. I know many ministers who labor for years without any support from their own family. Their families do not understand or lend them any type of encouragement. These ministers spend their lives trying to serve God without any immediate family support.

If we are going to follow Jesus, the answer is not peace at any price. Any person who is a Christian knows how difficult it is to try to talk to one's own family members about Christ. Jesus has not called us to be his disciples at the cost of peace at any price. We have to learn to wage peace. We have got to be willing to stand up for Christ, whether it is in business, at work, or even at home.

III. **Jesus is also challenging his followers to make a choice.** When Jesus Christ confronts you with his presence, you have to decide whether you are for him or against him. You have to decide whether you will follow him or reject him. Not to make a decision is to decide. Jesus says, "If you are not for me, you are against me." You can't be neutral; you must make a choice. You either follow Jesus or reject him. Jesus lifted himself up as the point of response. "I, if I be lifted up, I will draw all men unto me." He is the central point of focus in directing us to God. Matthew uses an interesting image when he observes that Jesus' mother, brothers, and sister were "standing outside" the house where Jesus was teaching (Matt. 12:46–50). Often there are people who stay outside and refuse to come into his presence and follow him. Jesus demands absolute allegiance. Individuals down through the ages who have been willing to give Jesus absolute allegiance have had their lives transformed and have experienced redemption, purpose, and meaning.

When I was in Copenhagen several years ago, I had the opportunity to see a number of statues by the noted Danish sculptor Thorwaldsen. One of Thorwaldsen's famous sculptures is an image of Christ with outstretched arms, positioned at the center of the church. As you walk close to this figure and get right underneath the arms of Christ, you discover that you cannot see the face of Jesus. Then a guide instructs you, "Kneel. Kneel at his feet. When you kneel, look up, and you can see into his face." Jesus Christ is seen by us not merely as an object for study or as someone to read about or sing about or hear preached about. We kneel in adoration at his feet. Then we rise up to follow Christ as Lord of our lives. We are challenged to make a choice.

IV. **Jesus sets forth the paradox of the cross.** "He that loves father or mother more than me is not worthy of me; and he who does not take up his cross and follow me is not worthy of me" (Matt. 10:38–39). Jesus put the primary focus on the cost of discipleship: one is not worthy of Christ if he or she refuses to take up his or her cross and follow him. The people in Jesus' day understood what that image meant. When a person was crucified, that individual often had to bear the crossbeam of his cross on his shoulder to the place where he was to be crucified. He would struggle down the pathway with that heavy crossbeam on his shoulder. Sometimes he would fall; sometimes he was whipped as he walked along the way. When he reached the place of crucifixion, he was stretched out on that crossbeam and lifted up to die on that cross.

Jesus said to his disciples, "You must take up your cross." I do not think Jesus was referring here primarily to a wooden cross that one had to carry someplace. He was speaking about a way of life, a way of self-sacrifice, a way of spending one's life in service. Instead of seeking to save one's life, one was to spend it in ministry. Christ's way was giving instead of receiving, losing one's life in ministry for others instead of trying to hoard things for oneself. This was a call for sacrificing, giving, pouring out one's life in love. The challenge is to take up one's cross and go into the areas of life where there is human need and hurt.

There are many who have walked the sacrificial way: Mother Teresa, Toyohiko Kagawa, Bill Wallace, Tom Dooley, Florence Nightingale, William Booth, Martin Luther King Jr., and a host of others who have served God in a variety of sacrificial ways. But these are not the only individuals who have walked the paradoxical way of Christ. I can point to individuals I have known in churches who served God sacrificially. Some have devoted their lives to Christ through their church. They have served ten, fifteen, twenty, and some even fifty years as Sunday school teachers. Others have gone for years to nursing homes in our city, where they have led services of worship and have given love and care to persons in need. I think of persons who prepared meals and have taken them to shut-ins or to the homeless. There are persons who reach out to the hurting and needy in our community. Some work in our Alzheimer's support group or with another special group in our church or community. These persons have not focused on themselves and what life can do for them, but instead have tried to focus on what they can do to serve God and help others. Many serve God quietly as they follow the way of the cross.

There is no greater joy and peace than following Christ, sensing his impact on your life, and letting his standard guide you. Sometimes this discipleship means that it will be difficult to live with other persons, even your own family, because they may misunderstand or even reject you. Out of love and concern, you will continue to seek to draw them to Christ. You do not do this forcibly or in some artificial way, but gently and lovingly you seek to draw them to Christ.

CHAPTER THREE

Devotions for Advent

Lisa Hill

Lay-leader, First Baptist Church, Arkadelphia, Arkansas

TOPIC: The Hints of Dawn
TEXT: Luke 1:78–79

Some years ago, an ice storm hit our area and left us without power for days. The bone-chilling cold kept me lingering near a crackling fire. The long cloudy days and evenings were spent reading by flashlight. Just as I was dreading another night huddled in a sleeping bag on the hard floor, the electricity came back on. Appliances began humming, and the night-lights glowed. I ran through the house and turned on every light—and cheered aloud as I went. It was a celebration, a new appreciation for the blessing of brightness and warmth.

Zechariah enjoyed a great celebration as he witnessed God's promises coming to fulfillment. As a priest and devout servant of God, Zechariah was a man of prayer and had seen the power of God at work. He believed God's promise of a Messiah. Yet the angel brought him a message he never could have imagined. Zechariah and his wife, Elizabeth, both well advanced in years, knew the pain of childlessness. Perhaps they no longer prayed for a child, assuming it was not possible. The angel's prophecy must have shocked Zechariah. God had chosen them to have a son, and the child would play an important role in preparing the way for the Lord. How could this be?

Because of his doubt, Zechariah could not speak during his wife's pregnancy. In his silence, he must have watched more keenly and understood more clearly. Then he saw the angel's words become true before his eyes. He looked in amazement at his newborn son, and thankfulness overflowed. "His name is John," he wrote on his tablet. "Immediately his mouth was opened and his tongue was loosed, and he began to speak, praising God" (Luke 1:64). Filled with the Holy Spirit, Zechariah spoke boldly of his son and of the one who would come after him, the one who would bring salvation to the people because of God's tender mercy. Uncertainty vanished. The light that would overcome sin's darkness was coming from heaven. A rising Sun would shine on a hurting world. Like a child, Zechariah eagerly awaited the coming dawn. His pathway was clear. He bounded with steps of faith—ready to see the glorious unfolding of God's plan.

We are blessed to know the Messiah. We are blessed to experience the assurance of his continual presence and to learn from his words and his example. The Light of the world guides our journey. As we follow him, we can be assured that "the path of the righteous is like the first gleam of dawn, shining ever brighter till the full light of day" (Prov. 4:18).

Life is best approached with the wonder of a child on Christmas morning. Our days are a precious gift from the Father. Like Zechariah, let us boldly declare the praises of him who has called us out of darkness into his wonderful light (1 Pet. 2:9). And may we walk with a spring in our steps, looking forward to the most glorious light of all: eternity spent with our Savior in a place where "the city does not need the sun or the moon to shine on it, for the glory of God gives it light, and the Lamb is its lamp" (Rev. 21:23).

TOPIC: Keep Watch
TEXT: Matt. 24:42–44

I remember an Advent calendar I enjoyed as a child. It illustrated a manger scene—and I looked forward to opening one of its windows each morning, eager to see what it would reveal. The scene began to take shape as angels, shepherds, wise men, and farm animals took their places in the stable. The illustration was vivid and colorful, and I regarded it with wonder as I thought about Jesus' birth. On Christmas morning, I opened the larger window at the center of the calendar. The picture was complete. There were Mary and Joseph kneeling at the manger, gazing upon the face of the sweet little Jesus boy. His tiny face glowed brightly.

In this Advent season, we have much to celebrate as we think upon God's precious gift to us—his Son, our Lord. In Jesus, we have redemption from sin and abundance of life. In him we have the ultimate example for living. This same Jesus has promised his return. He will take us to our heavenly home, and there we shall live with him forever.

As we enjoy the festivities of Christmas, we look forward to a specific day that is marked on our calendars. We also look forward to a date that is unknown to us, the day of Christ's return. Scripture tells us to keep watch, to be ready for that day which will surely come. While we wait, we can make the most of every opportunity God gives us to point others to Jesus Christ. We marvel that he allows us glimpses into his character and demonstrates his mighty hand at work in our world. We can approach each day with joyous expectancy and readiness for that bright and glorious day when the picture will be complete—when God's promise of eternity will be fulfilled.

TOPIC: People of the First Christmas: Mary
TEXT: Luke 1:26–38

Mary ran her feeble hand along the rocks, steadying herself with her cane as she sat down on the hillside overlooking Nazareth. A smile brightened her face as she reflected over the course her life had taken. It had far surpassed her imagination . . .

She could still recall that day vividly. Busy about her wedding plans, her thoughts had been suddenly interrupted by the voice of the angel Gabriel. His message was perplexing: "You have found favor with God. You will give birth to a son. You are to give him the name Jesus. The holy one to be born will be called the Son of God." A thousand different questions raced through Mary's mind as she considered Gabriel's words. She was a young, poor, ordinary girl. Why had God chosen her? She was a virgin, but what would the people of Nazareth think? What about her family and friends? Would anyone believe her? Most of all, what about Joseph? Would he break off their engagement? What would it be like to bear a child who was the Son of God? Mary had been taught the scriptures, and knew of God's promise of a Messiah who would save his people from their sins. She had never dreamed God would use her as a part of the plan.

Gabriel spoke other words that day to give Mary assurance: "The Lord is with you. Do not be afraid for nothing is impossible with God." Sensing God's peace calming her spirit, Mary offered her response: "I am the Lord's servant. May it be to me as you have said."

Mary's eyes shone as she thought about how her life had changed since that day. God used her, an ordinary girl, to bring glory to himself. God's promise was fulfilled. She bore a son, Jesus, who was the Son of God. She watched him grow up, and was blessed to observe his marvelous ministry. Her heartbreak at his Crucifixion was replaced with great hope as she witnessed his triumphant Resurrection. He no longer walked on earth as a man, yet she knew firsthand the truth of Gabriel's words: "The Lord is with you."

TOPIC: Reason to Sing
TEXT: Zeph. 3:14–20

At Christmastime, my extended family has a tradition of gathering around the piano to sing carols. Our rendition of "The Twelve Days of Christmas" is one of a kind as we sing and act out our assigned solo parts. We join together in fun songs like "Jingle Bells" and "Frosty the Snowman." And we sing beautiful hymns like "Silent Night" and "Joy to the World" that remind us what Christmas is all about. It is a delight to watch the wonder on the children's faces as they express the joy God has placed within their hearts.

In the prophet Zephaniah's day, the people of Judah had become complacent. They were content with the status quo and blind to their need for God. Through Zephaniah, God spoke to the people with a word that both pointed them to the seriousness of their sin and offered a message of hope to those who would repent and turn to God.

God's message spoken through Zephaniah is just as relevant to us today. God calls us away from lukewarmth into a place of wholehearted obedience. He promises wisdom and blessing as we abandon ourselves to his will.

When we surrender our lives to the Father through faith in Jesus Christ, he gives us reason to hope and to sing, reason to be glad and to rejoice with all our hearts:

His provision. He has taken away our punishment and turned back our enemy! Jesus took the punishment for our sins and won the victory over the enemy so that we might live with God eternally.

His presence. We have no need to fear because of his constant presence and the assurance that he is God.

His power. God is mighty to save, and holds our lives in the palm of his hand.

His passion. God takes great delight in us. His love quiets our spirits and fills us with peace. He sings with joy over us!

This year, amid the sights and sounds of Christmas, may we be filled with joy as we meditate on the greatness of God. Let our hearts overflow with thanksgiving for the gift of the Christ child. May we be brought to a place of deeper, more committed service to God, bowing before our Father with humility and with an eagerness to be used for his purposes. This Christmas, and throughout the year, may we be as little children, gazing in wide-eyed wonder at the beauty of our Savior as we unite our voices and our lives in a symphony of praise!

TOPIC: The Good Shepherd
TEXT: Isa. 40:9–11

The prophet Isaiah foretold the Messiah hundreds of years before his coming. How wonderful it must have been to receive such a glimpse into God's great plan for the future. Isaiah 40:9–11 is a passage packed with insight into the Christ child whose coming we celebrate this season: good news to the entire world! Shout the glad tidings from the mountaintop. Here is your God!

Who is this God, this one whose arrival is to be announced with such great joy?

He is sovereign Lord, ruler of the universe, who comes with power. He alone is worthy of our awe and adoration. He is the one who saves us and gives us life.

He is loving, caring, gentle, and faithful. He tends his flock with a gentle hand, loving us, watching over us, caring for our every need. He gathers us tenderly into his arms and carries us close to his heart.

Psalm 23 is a vivid description of our Lord as the Good Shepherd, and of the joys of being his sheep:

> The Lord is my shepherd; I shall not be in want. He makes me to lie down in green pastures, he leads me beside quiet waters, he restores my soul.

He guides me in paths of righteousness for his name's sake. Even though I walk through the valley of the shadow of death, I will fear no evil, for you are with me; your rod and your staff, they comfort me. You prepare a table before me in the presence of my enemies. You anoint my head with oil; my cup overflows. Surely goodness and love will follow me all the days of my life, and I will dwell in the house of the Lord forever. (NIV)

What a privilege to be members of the Lord's flock. How amazing that the sovereign Lord of the universe chooses to care for us so gently and lovingly. As his sheep, we have every reason to be filled with joy. Lift up your voice with a shout, lift it up, do not be afraid . . . here is your God!

A LITTLE
TREASURY
OF SERMON
ILLUSTRATIONS

A good sermon is marked by fidelity to the text, developing design, energy, and contemporary application. It will be a better sermon when punctuated with appropriate illustrations. Like windows that bring light to a magnificent room, illustrations cast light on the sermon. Moods and tempers are often set by illustrations—as are matters of clarity, interest, and memory—that would be missed apart from the illustration. Time spent honing the apt illustration is never wasted.

The best illustrations take time to grow within us. They become a part of us before they become a communication of God's Word to others. The illustrations presented here are not intended to be taken as they are but to be dwelt upon, prayed over, committed to memory, and utilized as one part of the larger proclamation of the gospel. As such they can become part of our devotional life prior to being part of our preaching ministry.

ANGER.   Of the seven deadly sins, anger is possibly the most fun. To lick your wounds, to smack your lips over grievances long past, to roll over your tongue the prospect of bitter confrontations still to come, to savor to the last toothsome morsel both the pain you are given and the pain you are giving back—in many ways it is a feast fit for a king. The chief drawback is that what you are wolfing down is yourself. The skeleton at the feast is you.—Frederick Buechner[1]

ATTENTION.   I recall when I was eight or nine years old, an evangelist came to our church for the annual revival meeting. As he got into his lengthy preaching about the nature of faith and the call to salvation, I'll admit my mind wandered. As an illustration of how we are to receive the gift of salvation, he held up a

---

[1]Frederick Buechner, *Wishful Thinking: A Theological ABC* (New York: HarperCollins, 1973), p. 2.

dollar bill and said, "This is my free gift to you, if you are willing to step out into the aisle, come, and get it." My wandering mind missed most of what he said, and I didn't get the full impact of it until I watched a friend move out from beside me and go to the pulpit and get that dollar bill. It was one of the most exciting things I had ever seen in church—and I was excited for my friend. But then my emotions changed. "That's not fair. The preacher should have given us fair warning about what he was about to do. If he had, that dollar could have been mine." But as I look back, my dismay wasn't justified. He did give us fair warning. I just wasn't paying attention. I wasn't listening to what was being said—at least not with undivided attention. It was a lesson for me.—Lee McGlone

CAUTION.   There was a very cautious man

> Who never laughed or played;
> He never risked, he never tried,
> He never sang or prayed.
> And when he one day passed away
> His insurance was denied;
> For since he never really lived,
> They claimed he never died!
> —Anonymous

CHRISTMAS.   The angel's proclamation is the heart of the Christmas story: good news of great joy *to all people*. It is good news to all people—even to the lowly shepherds. There is no one left out. On the day in Jerusalem some three decades later, when Pentecost came, there were gathered there people from all the world, Partheans, and Medes and Elamites, and dwellers of Mesopotamia. Today God's Spirit is poured out in believers who are Russian, Japanese, Chinese, African, and American, the Negroid, Mongoloid, and Caucasoid, because "Red and Yellow, Black and White, they are precious in his sight." We know this truth. There is only one world—and we are all a part of that one world. There is only one race, the human race, and we are a part of it. Faith in God simply demands such unity. "There is neither Jew nor Gentile, bond nor free, male nor female—we are all one in Christ Jesus." That's the Christmas story.—Lee McGlone

CULTURE.   In his 1983 acceptance speech for the Templeton Prize for Progress in Religion, [Aleksandr Solzhenitsyn] recalled the words he heard as a child, when his elders sought to explain the ruinous upheavals in Russia: "Men have forgotten God; that's why all this has happened." He added, "If I were called upon to identify briefly the principal trait of the entire twentieth century, here too I would be unable to find anything more precise and pithy than to repeat once again: 'men have forgotten God.'"—John Wilson[2]

DEATH.   John Wesley preached his last sermon on February 17, 1791, in Lambeth, on the text "Seek ye the Lord while He may be found, call ye upon Him while He is near" (Isa. 55:6). The following day, a very sick man, he was put to bed in his home on City Road. During the days of his illness, he often repeated the words from one of his brother's hymns: "I the chief of sinners am, But Jesus died for me!" His last words were, "The best of all is, God is with us!" He died March 2, 1791.—Warren W. Wiersbe[3]

DISCIPLINE.   Thou oughtest so to order thyself in all thy thoughts and actions, as if today thou wert about to die. Labor now to live so, that at the hour of death thou mayest rather rejoice than fear.—Thomas à Kempis, *Imitation of Christ*

EASTER.   The German theologian Jürgen Moltmann expresses in a single sentence the great span from Good Friday to Easter. It is, in fact, a summary of human history, past, present, and future: "God weeps with us so that we may someday laugh with him."—Philip Yancey[4]

---

[2]John Wilson, review of Solzhenitsyn and the Modern World, in *Christianity Today*, Feb. 7, 1994, p. 57.
[3]Warren W. Wiersbe, *Wycliffe Handbook of Preaching and Preachers* (Chicago: Moody Press, 1984), p. 245.
[4]Philip Yancey, "God Behind Barbed Wire," *Christianity Today*, Sept. 2005, p. 37.

EMOTIONS.   A man named La Piere sent out letters to the managers of 256 hotels and restaurants across the southern half of the U.S. He told them that he was planning to tour the south with two Chinese companions and he wanted to know ahead of time whether they would be served. Ninety-two percent of the businesses replied that they did not serve Chinese and that La Piere could save himself considerable embarrassment by not showing up with such undesirables. He wasn't surprised. Racial prejudice was a part of southern life in the 1930s, and this was long before a ban was placed on discrimination in interstate commerce. La Piere ignored the managers' advice, however. Accompanied by a Chinese man and his wife, he visited every one of the establishments that said they'd refuse service. Surprise! Ninety-nine percent of the places admitted the oriental couple, and almost all did so without a hassle. The study points out that a person may say he feels one thing and then turn right around and do something completely different.—Em Griffin[5]

EPIPHANY.   "It is better to light a candle than to curse the darkness." So says the Quaker slogan. So also says the Christian Bible. God sent his Son, Jesus, to be the light of the world. God could have condemned the world, but he chose rather to save the world (John 3:16–17). The call of the season of Epiphany is to stand up for something that is eternally good (to light a candle) rather than to crusade against an evil (to curse the darkness). Though it is easier to complain than to commend.—Lee McGlone

EVIL.   If only there were evil people somewhere insidiously committing evil deeds, and it were necessary only to separate them from the rest of us and destroy them. But the line dividing good and evil cuts through the heart of every human being. And who is willing to destroy a piece of his own heart? —Aleksandr Solzhenitsyn[6]

FAITH.   The most pressing question on the problem of faith is whether a man as a civilized being can believe in the divinity of the Son of God, Jesus Christ, for therein rests the whole of our faith.—Dostoevsky

---

[5]Em Griffin, *The Mindchangers* (Carol Stream, IL: Tyndale House, 1976), p. 179.
[6]Aleksandr Solzhenitsyn, *The Gulag Archipelago* (New York: HarperCollins, 2002), p. 121.

FAITH.   The following letter was found in a baking powder can wired to the handle of an old pump that offered the only hope of drinking water on a very long and seldom-used trail across Nevada's Armargosa Desert: "This pump is all right as of June 1932. I put a new sucker washer into it and it ought to last five years. But the washer dries out and the pump has got to be primed. Under the white rock I buried a bottle of water, out of the sun and cork end up. There's enough water in it to prime the pump, but not if you drink some first. Pour about one-fourth and let her soak to wet the leather. Then pour in the rest medium fast and pump like crazy. You'll git water. The well has never run dry. Have faith. When you git watered up, fill the bottle and put it back like you found it for the next feller. (signed) Desert Pete. P.S. Don't go drinking the water first. Prime the pump with it and you'll git all you can hold."—Keith Miller and Bruce Larson[7]

FORGIVENESS.   In the 14th century, Robert Bruce of Scotland was leading his men in a battle to gain independence from England. Near the end of the conflict, the English wanted to capture Bruce to keep him from the Scottish crown. So they put his own bloodhounds on his trail. When the bloodhounds got close, Bruce could hear their baying. His attendant said, "We are done for. They are on your trail, and they will reveal your hiding place." Bruce replied, "It's all right." Then he headed for a stream that flowed through the forest. He plunged in and waded upstream a short distance. When he came out on the other bank, he was in the depths of the forest. Within minutes, the hounds, tracing their master's steps, came to the bank. They went no farther. The English soldiers urged them on, but the trail was broken. The stream had carried the scent away. A short time later, the crown of Scotland rested on the head of Robert Bruce. The memory of our sins, prodded on by Satan, can be like those baying dogs— but a stream flows, red with the blood of God's own Son. By grace through faith we are safe. No sin-hound can touch us. The trail is broken by the precious blood of Christ. "The purpose of the cross," someone observed, "is to repair the irreparable."—Erwin Lutzer[8]

---

[7]Keith Miller and Bruce Larson, *The Edge of Adventure* (Grand Rapids, MI: Revell, 1991), pp. 86–87.
[8]Erwin Lutzer, *Putting Your Past Behind You* (San Bernardino, CA: Here's Life Publishers, 1990), p. 42.

FRIENDSHIP.   It is one of the severest tests of friendship to tell your friend his faults. So to love a man that you cannot bear to see a stain upon him, and to speak painful truth through loving words, that is friendship.—Henry Ward Beecher

GRACE.   A story is told about Fiorello LaGuardia, who, when he was mayor of New York City during the worst days of the Great Depression and all of WWII, was called by adoring New Yorkers "the Little Flower" because he was only five foot four and always wore a carnation in his lapel. He was a colorful character who used to ride the New York City fire trucks, raid speakeasies with the police department, take entire orphanages to baseball games, and whenever the New York newspapers were on strike, he would go on the radio and read the Sunday funnies to the kids. One bitterly cold night in January of 1935, the mayor turned up at a night court that served the poorest ward of the city. LaGuardia dismissed the judge for the evening and took over the bench himself.

Within a few minutes, a tattered old woman was brought before him, charged with stealing a loaf of bread. She told LaGuardia that her daughter's husband had deserted her, her daughter was sick, and her two grandchildren were starving. But the shopkeeper, from whom the bread was stolen, refused to drop the charges. "It's a real bad neighborhood, your Honor," the man told the mayor. "She's got to be punished to teach other people around here a lesson." LaGuardia sighed. He turned to the woman and said "I've got to punish you. The law makes no exceptions—ten dollars or ten days in jail." But even as he pronounced sentence, the mayor was already reaching into his pocket. He extracted a bill and tossed it into his famous sombrero saying: "Here is the ten dollar fine which I now remit; and furthermore I am going to fine everyone in this courtroom fifty cents for living in a town where a person has to steal bread so that her grandchildren can eat. Mr. Baliff, collect the fines and give them to the defendant." So the following day the New York City newspapers reported that $47.50 was turned over to a bewildered old lady who had stolen a loaf of bread to feed her starving grandchildren, fifty cents of that amount being contributed by the red-faced grocery store owner, while some seventy petty criminals, people with traffic violations, and New York City policemen, each of whom had just paid fifty cents for the privilege of doing so, gave the mayor a standing ovation.—Brennan Manning[9]

HELL.   I am the way into the city of woe.
I am the way to a forsaken people.
I am the way to eternal sorrow.
Sacred justice moved my architect.
I was raised here by divine omnipotence,
Primordial love and ultimate intelligence.
Only those elements time cannot wear
Were made before me, and beyond time I stand.
Abandon all hope ye who enter here.
—Dante Alighieri, "The Gate of Hell," *The Inferno*

JUSTICE.   To do injustice is more disgraceful than to suffer it.—Plato

LORD'S SUPPER.   The Lord's Supper is many different things. It is a memory: "As often as you eat this bread and drink this cup, remember me." It is a thanksgiving: "And when he had given thanks, he broke the bread." It is anticipation: "I will not eat this meal with you *until* it is fulfilled in the Kingdom of God." It is a proclamation: "As often as you eat this bread and drink this cup you do *proclaim* the Lord's death until he comes." The Lord's Supper is also a family gathering. What we do here at the table, and in the Church's every intention, we do together. As we share in Communion, we hold things in common. Those who gather around the table share in common a commitment to God. Our designations of each other and of God are family designations. God is our Heavenly Father, Jesus Christ is our elder brother, and to one another we are brothers and sisters in Christ. Families operate with such language.—Lee McGlone

MATURITY.   Human beings grow by striving, working, stretching; and in a sense, human nature needs problems more than solutions. Why are not all prayers

---

[9]Brennan Manning, *The Ragamuffin Gospel* (Sisters, OR: Multnomah, 1990), pp. 91–92.

answered magically and instantly? Why must every convert travel the same tedious path of spiritual discipline? Because persistent prayer, and fasting, and study, and meditation are designed primarily for our sakes, not for God's. Kierkegaard said that Christians reminded him of schoolboys who want to look up the answers to their math problems in the back of the book rather than work them through. . . . We yearn for shortcuts. But shortcuts usually lead away from growth, not toward it. Apply the principle directly to Job: what was the final result of the testing he went through? As Rabbi Abraham Heschel observed, "Faith like Job's cannot be shaken because it is the result of having been shaken."—Philip Yancey[10]

MEANING.   Recall Arthur Miller's famous play *Death of a Salesman*. It's the story of Willy Loman, a salesman who goes through life's ups and downs, never quite measuring up to his own expectations, never quite "making it." In the end, he dies. Standing by his graveside, his son laments that his father lived, died, and really never knew who he was. Notice the play is titled *Death of a Salesman*, not *Death of Willy Loman*. But it's not just the sad story of Willy Loman. It's a clear account of the modern American male focused on our ever-present attempt "to be somebody, to amount to something." All of us, the Willy Lomans of the world, will be encouraged to hear the words of Jesus: "You are the light of the world" (Matt. 5:14)—not because we have accomplished it or deserved it but because it comes with the territory. We are created in the image of God.—Lee McGlone

MISFORTUNE.   Life is thickly sown with thorns, and I know no other remedy than to pass quickly through them. The longer we dwell on our misfortunes, the greater is their power to harm us.—Voltaire

NONVIOLENCE.   Nonviolence is the answer to the crucial political and moral questions of our time: the need for man to overcome oppression and violence without resorting to oppression and violence. Man must evolve for all human conflict a method which rejects revenge, aggression and retaliation. The foundation of such a method is love.—Martin Luther King Jr.[11]

---

[10]Philip Yancey, *Disappointment with God* (Grand Rapids, MI: Zondervan, 1988), pp. 207–208.
[11]Martin Luther King Jr., Nobel Prize acceptance speech, Stockholm, December 11, 1964.

OBEDIENCE.   P. T. Forsythe was right when he said, "The first duty of every soul is to find not its freedom but its Master."—Warren W. Wiersbe[12]

PAIN.   Though thou with clouds of anger do disguise
      Thy face; yet through that mask I know those eyes,
      Which, though they turn away sometimes,
      They never will despise.
      —John Donne, "A Hymn to Christ"

POLITICS.   The penalty that good men pay for not being interested in politics is to be governed by men worse than themselves.—Plato

PRIDE.   Be not proud of race, face, place, or grace.—C. H. Spurgeon

PRIORITIES.   I want the whole Christ for my Savior, the whole Bible for my book, the whole Church for my fellowship, and the whole world for my mission field. —John Wesley

RESURRECTION.   As Vice President, George Bush represented the U.S. at the funeral of former Soviet leader Leonid Brezhnev. Bush was deeply moved by a silent protest carried out by Brezhnev's widow. She stood motionless by the coffin until seconds before it was closed. Then, just as the soldiers touched the lid, Brezhnev's wife performed an act of great courage and hope, a gesture that must surely rank as one of the most profound acts of civil disobedience ever committed: She reached down and made the sign of the cross on her husband's chest. There in the citadel of secular, atheistic power, the wife of the man who had run it all hoped that her husband was wrong. She hoped that there was another life, and that that life was best represented by Jesus who died on the cross, and that the same Jesus might yet have mercy on her husband.—Gary Thomas[13]

---

[12]Warren W. Wiersbe, *The Integrity Crisis* (Nashville: Thomas Nelson, 1991), p. 22.
[13]Gary Thomas, *Christian Times*, Oct. 3, 1994, p. 26.

SALVATION.   The Roman Road to Salvation (Rom. 3:23, 6:23, 5:8, 10:9, 10, 13).—Lee McGlone

SIN.   It comes when we take a perfectly natural desire or longing or ambition and try desperately to fulfill it without God. Not only is it sin, it is a perverse distortion of the image of the Creator in us. All these good things, and all our security, are rightly found only and completely in him.—Augustine, *The Confessions of Saint Augustine*

STEWARDSHIP.   Beware of little expenses; a small leak will sink a great ship. —Benjamin Franklin

THANKSGIVING PROCLAMATION OF 1863.   It is the duty of nations as well as of men to own their dependence upon the overruling power of God; to confess their sins and transgressions in humble sorrow, yet with assured hope that genuine repentance will lead to mercy and pardon; and to recognize the sublime truth, announced in the Holy Scriptures and proven by all history, that those nations are blessed whose God is the Lord.

We know that by His divine law, nations, like individuals, are subjected to punishments and chastisements in this world. May we not justly fear that the awful calamity of civil war which now desolates the land may be a punishment inflicted upon us for our presumptuous sins, to the needful end of our national reformation as a whole people?

We have been the recipients of the choisest bounties of heaven; we have been preserved these many years in peace and prosperity; we have grown in numbers, wealth and power as no other nation has ever grown.

But we have forgotten God. We have forgotten the gracious hand which preserved us in peace and multiplied and enriched and strengthened us, and we have vainly imagined, in the deceitfulness of our hearts, that all these blessings were produced by some superior wisdom and virtue of our own. Intoxicated with unbroken success, we have become too self-sufficient to feel the necessity of redeeming and preserving grace, too proud to pray to the God that made us.

It has seemed to me fit and proper that God should be solemnly, reverently and gratefully acknowledged, as with one heart and one voice, by the whole American people. I do therefore invite my fellow citizens in every part of the United States, and also those who are at sea and those who are sojourning in foreign lands, to set apart and observe the last Thursday of November as a day of Thanksgiving and praise to our beneficent Father Who dwelleth in the heavens.—Abraham Lincoln, October 3, 1863

TIME.   I have so much to do today that I shall spend the first three hours in prayer.—Martin Luther

UNITY.   In one of Charles Schultz's *Peanuts* cartoons, Lucy demanded that Linus change TV channels, threatening him with her fist if he didn't. "What makes you think you can walk right in here and take over?" asks Linus. "These five fingers," says Lucy. "Individually they're nothing but when I curl them together like this into a single unit, they form a weapon that is terrible to behold." "Which channel do you want?" asks Linus. Turning away, he looks at his fingers and says, "Why can't you guys get organized like that?"—Lee McGlone

VISION.   It started like so many evenings. Mom and Dad at home and Jimmy playing after dinner. Mom and Dad were absorbed with jobs and did not notice the time. It was a full moon and some of the light seeped through the windows. Then Mom glanced at the clock. "Jimmy, it's time to go to bed. Go up now and I'll come and settle you later." Unlike usual, Jimmy went straight upstairs to his room. An hour or so later his mother came up to check if all was well, and to her astonishment found that her son was staring quietly out of his window at the moonlit scenery. "What are you doing, Jimmy?" "I'm looking at the moon, Mommy." "Well, it's time to go to bed now." As one reluctant boy settled down, he said, "Mommy, you know one day I'm going to walk on the moon." Who could have known that the boy in whom the dream was planted that night would survive a near fatal motorbike crash which broke almost every bone in his body, and would bring to fruition this dream 32 years later when

James Irwin stepped on the moon's surface, just one of the 12 representatives of the human race to have done so?—Bill Hybels[14]

WILL OF GOD.   Do not hastily ascribe things to God. Do not easily suppose dreams, voices, impressions, visions or revelations to be from God. They may be from Him. They may be from nature. They may be from the Devil.—J. K. Johnston[15]

---

[14]Bill Hybels, *Who You Are When No One's Looking* (Downers Grove, IL: InterVarsity Press, 1987), p. 35.

[15]J. K. Johnston, *Why Christians Sin* (Grand Rapids, MI: Discovery House, 1992), p. 102.

CONTRIBUTORS

Bender, Trudy. Children's ministry and music education; now residing in Sioux Falls, South Dakota

Burnett, Dawn. Co-pastor with her husband, Andrew Burnett, at Prairie Hills Covenant Church, Sioux Falls, South Dakota

Canipe, Sandra. Retired minister for preschoolers and children, First Baptist Church, Greensboro, North Carolina

Crawford, James. Pastor emeritus, The Old South Church, Boston, Massachusetts

Fields, Henry. Pastor, First Baptist Church, Toccoa Falls, Georgia

Fuller, Charlie. Former dean of the School of Fine Arts, Ouachita Baptist University, Arkadelphia, Arkansas; current divinity student at George W. Truett Seminary, Waco, Texas

Hammer, Randy. Author and minister in the United Church of Christ; pastor, United Church of Oak Ridge, Tennessee

Harmon, Sherrie. Youth and family ministry, Evangelical Lutheran Church of America, Greensboro, North Carolina

Hatcher, Karen. Curriculum writer and Bible study instructor, prison fellowship in the James River Correctional Center Re-Entry Program, Virginia

Hewell, Rob. Associate professor of music, Ouachita Baptist University, Arkadelphia, Arkansas

McGlone, Lee. Pastor, First Baptist Church, Arkadelphia, Arkansas

McKim, Mark. Senior minister, First Baptist Church, Regina, Saskatchewan, Canada

Michael, Seth A. Co-pastor, Gateway Covenant Church, Prince Albert, Saskatchewan, Canada

Michael, Stacia. Co-pastor, Gateway Covenant Church, Prince Albert, Saskatchewan, Canada

Mournet, Krista. Ph.D. candidate, Durham University, United Kingdom; worship coordinator, Trinity Baptist Church; and adjunct professor, Sioux Falls Seminary, Sioux Falls, South Dakota

Phillips, E. Lee. Minister and freelance writer, Norcross, Georgia

Pope, Greg. Pastor, Crescent Hill Baptist Church, Louisville, Kentucky

Riddle, Brittany. Student, Baptist Theological Seminary, Richmond, Virginia

Ruffin, Michael. Pastor, First Baptist Church, Fitzgerald, Georgia

Thompson, Marcia. Teacher, Lincoln High School, Sioux Falls, South Dakota; former children's minister, Virginia and Georgia

Tuck, William Powell. Former professor of preaching, Southern Baptist Theological Seminary, Louisville, Kentucky; retired Baptist pastor, Lumberton, North Carolina; adjunct professor, Baptist Theological Seminary, Richmond, Virginia; and now residing in Midlothian, Virginia

Vinson, Richard. Professor of religion, Salem College, Winston-Salem, North Carolina; former dean, Baptist Theological Seminary, Richmond, Virginia

West, Danny. Associate professor of preaching and pastoral studies, M. Christopher White Divinity School, Boiling Springs, North Carolina

Several students from the class "The Worshipping Church" (Spring 2009), Ouachita Baptist University, Arkadelphia, Arkansas, contributed a number of the morning prayers.

Burleson, Tyler
Casey, Sarah
Crecink, Amy
Davis, Jarrett
Dawson, Nick
Howard, Sky
Johnson, Sarah
Konvicka, Jenny
Post, Taylor
Reeves, Ben
Statton, Tim
Summons, Kendall
Williams, Megan

INDEX OF CONTRIBUTORS

SERMON TITLE INDEX

Children's sermons are designated as (cs).

INDEX OF SERMON TEXTS

INDEX OF PRAYERS

INDEX OF MATERIALS USEFUL AS CHILDREN'S STORIES AND SERMONS

INDEX OF MATERIALS USEFUL FOR SMALL GROUPS

TOPICAL INDEX

HOW TO USE THE CD-ROM

SYSTEM REQUIREMENTS
PC with Microsoft Windows 98SE or later
Mac with Apple OS version 8.6 or later

USING THE CD WITH WINDOWS
To view the items located on the CD, follow these steps:

1. Insert the CD into your computer's CD-ROM drive.
2. A window appears with the following options:
   eBook: Allows you to view the electronic version of the book in PDF format.
   Adobe Reader: Adobe Reader software to view PDF files.
   Editor: Displays a page with information about the editor.
   Contact Us: Displays a page with information on contacting the publisher or author.
   Help: Displays a page with information on using the CD.
   Exit: Closes the interface window.

If you do not have autorun enabled, or if the autorun window does not appear, follow these steps to access the CD:

1. Click Start → Run.
2. In the dialog box that appears, type d:\start.exe, where d is the letter of your CD-ROM drive. This brings up the autorun window described in the preceding set of steps.
3. Choose the desired option from the menu. (See Step 2 in the preceding list for a description of these options.)

IN CASE OF TROUBLE

If you experience difficulty using the CD-ROM, please follow these steps:

1. Make sure your hardware and systems configurations conform to the systems requirements noted under "System Requirements" above.
2. Review the installation procedure for your type of hardware and operating system. It is possible to reinstall the software if necessary.

To speak with someone in Product Technical Support, call 800-762-2974 or 317-572-3994 Monday through Friday from 8:30 A.M. to 5:00 P.M. EST. You can also contact Product Technical Support and get support information through our website at www.wiley.com/techsupport.

Before calling or writing, please have the following information available:

*   Type of computer and operating system.
*   Any error messages displayed.
*   Complete description of the problem.

It is best if you are sitting at your computer when making the call.